Regional Human Rights Systems

The Library of Essays on International Human Rights
Series Editor: Stephanie Farrior

Titles in the Series:

The Development of International Human Rights Law
Volume I
David Weissbrodt, Fionnuala D. Ní Aoláin and Mary Rumsey

Equality and Non-Discrimination under International Law
Volume II
Stephanie Farrior

Challenges in International Human Rights Law
Volume III
Menno T. Kamminga

The United Nations System for Protecting Human Rights
Volume IV
Dinah L. Shelton

Regional Human Rights Systems
Volume V
Christina M. Cerna

Regional Human Rights Systems

Volume V

Edited by

Christina M. Cerna

Georgetown University Law Centre, USA

Routledge
Taylor & Francis Group
LONDON AND NEW YORK

First published 2014 by Ashgate Publishing

2 Park Square, Milton Park, Abingdon, Oxfordshire OX14 4RN
711 Third Avenue, New York, NY 10017

Routledge is an imprint of the Taylor & Francis Group, an informa business

First issued in paperback 2018

British Library Cataloguing in Publication Data.
A catalogue record for this book is available from the British Library.

The Library of Congress has cataloged the printed edition as follows: 2013956558

ISBN 13: 978-1-4094-3911-0 (hbk)
ISBN 13: 978-1-138-38402-6 (pbk)

Contents

PART III THE EUROPEAN SYSTEM

PART IV THE AFRICAN SYSTEM

Acknowledgements

Ashgate would like to thank the researchers and the contributing authors who provided copies, along with the following for their permission to reprint copyright material.

American Society of International Law for the essays: Thomas Buergenthal (1975), 'The Revised OAS Charter and the Protection of Human Rights', *American Journal of International Law*, **69**, pp. 828–36; Anna Dolidze (2011), 'African Court on Human and Peoples' Rights – Response to the Situation in Libya', *American Society of International Law: Insights*, **15**, pp. 1–6. Copyright © 2011 by the American Society for International Law, ASIL; Frans Viljoen and Lirette Louw (2007), 'State Compliance with the Recommendations of the African Commission on Human and Peoples' Rights, 1994–2004', *American Journal of International Law*, **101**, pp. 1–34.

Brill for the essay: Christiane Bourloyannis-Vrailas (2012), 'The European Court of Human Rights', in Chaira Giorgetti (ed.), *The Rules, Practice and Jurisprudence of International Courts and Tribunals*, Boston: Martinus Nijhoff, pp. 323–64.

Cambridge University Press for the essays: Jo M. Pasqualucci (2013), 'Introduction' and 'State Compliance with Court-Ordered Reparations', in *The Practice and Procedure of the Inter-American Court of Human Rights*, New York: Cambridge University Press, pp. 1–34; 299–334. Copyright © 2003, 2013 Jo M. Pasqualucci; Francesco Messineo (2012), '"Gentlemen at Home, Hoodlums Elsewhere?": The Extra-Territorial Exercise of Power by British Forces in Iraq and the European Convention on Human Rights', *Cambridge Law Journal*, **71**, pp. 15–18; Obiora Chinedu Okafor (2007), 'Limited Deployment of the African System within African States: Further Evidence and a General Evaluation', in *African Human Rights System, Activist Forces and International Institutions*, New York: Cambridge University Press, pp. 220–72. Copyright © 2007 Obiora Okafor.

Center for Human Rights and Humanitarian Law for the essay: Mónica Pinto (2013), 'The Role of the Inter-American Commission and Court of Human Rights in the Protection of Human Rights: Achievements and Contemporary Challenges', *Human Rights Brief*, **20**, pp. 34–38.

Christina Cerna for the essay: Christina M. Cerna (2004), 'The Inter-American System for the Protection of Human Rights', *Florida Journal of International Law*, **16**, pp. 195–212.

Duke Journal of Comparative and International Law for the essay: Joseph Diab (1992), 'United States Ratification of the American Convention on Human Rights', *Duke Journal of Comparative & International Law*, **2**, pp. 323–43.

Harvard Human Rights Journal for the essay: Mary Ann Glendon (2003), 'The Forgotten Crucible: The Latin American Influence on the Universal Human Rights Idea', *Harvard Human Rights Journal*, **16**, pp. 27–39.

The Johns Hopkins University Press and *Human Rights Quarterly* for the essay: Robert K. Goldman (2009), 'History and Action: The Inter-American Human Rights System and the Role of the Inter-American Commission on Human Rights', *Human Rights Quarterly*, **31**, pp. 856–87. Copyright © 2009 by the Johns Hopkins University Press.

Magnus Killander for the essay: Christof Heyns and Magnus Killander (2006), 'The African Regional Human Rights System', in Felipe Gomez Isa and Koen De Feyter (eds), *International Protection of Human Rights: Achievements and Challenges*, Bilbao: Humanitarian Net, pp. 509–43.

Oxford University Press for the essays: Antônio Augusto Cançado Trindade (1998), 'The Inter-American Human Rights System at the Dawn of the New Century: Recommendations for Improvement of Its Mechanism of Protection', in D.J. Harris and S. Livingstone (eds), *The Inter-American System of Human Rights*, New York: Oxford University Press, pp. 395–420. Copyright © 1998 David Harris and Stephen Livingstone; Anthony Lester (2011), 'The European Court of Human Rights after 50 Years', in Jonas Christoffersen and Mikael Rask Madsen (eds), *The European Court of Human Rights between Law and Politics*, New York: Oxford University Press, pp. 98–115. Copyright © 2011 Jonas Christoffersen and Mikael Rask Madsen; Luzius Wildhaber (2011), 'Rethinking the European Court of Human Rights', in Jonas Christoffersen and Mikael Rask Madsen (eds), *The European Court of Human Rights between Law and Politics*, New York: Oxford University Press, pp. 204–29. Copyright © 2011 Jonas Christoffersen and Mikael Rask Madsen; William Abresch (2005), 'A Human Rights Law of Internal Armed Conflict: The European Court of Human Rights in Chechnya', *European Journal of International Law*, **16**, pp. 741–67. Copyright © 2005 European Journal of International Law. All rights reserved; Helen Keller and Alec Stone Sweet (2008), 'Assessing the Impact of the ECHR on National Legal Systems', in Helen Keller and Alec Stone Sweet (eds), *A Europe of Rights: The Impact of the ECHR on National Legal Systems*, New York: Oxford University Press, pp. 677–712.

Every effort has been made to trace all the copyright holders, but if any have been inadvertently overlooked the publishers will be pleased to make the necessary arrangement at the first opportunity.

Publisher's Note

The material in this volume has been reproduced using the facsimile method. This means we can retain the original pagination to facilitate easy and correct citation of the original essays. It also explains the variety of typefaces, page layouts and numbering.

Series Preface

The *Library of Essays on International Human Rights* provides access, in a single series, to some of the most important and influential journal articles and papers on the subject. Selections include broad overviews of key areas in international human rights law, critical assessments of this law and of human rights institutions and inquiries into areas of contestation. Some are classic works in the field; others are more recent works that provide insight into important developments or debates.

The series comprises five volumes. A volume on the development of international human rights law covers both the historical and philosophical development of human rights law as well as major issues during this development. A volume on challenges of human rights law presents works not only on issues of non-state actors, transitional justice and terrorism, but also articles on a human rights approach to public health, severe poverty as a human rights violation, investment arbitration as a venue of human rights challenges and climate change. The subject of equality and non-discrimination under international law merited its own volume, as the principles of equality and non-discrimination lie at the heart of human rights law. They are the only human rights explicitly included in the UN Charter, and they appear in virtually every major human rights instrument.

The volume on the United Nations system for protecting human rights presents leading articles on the UN bodies specially created to promote and monitor the implementation of human rights, but it also goes beyond those entities to present articles on the human rights work of UN specialized agencies such as the World Health Organization, the International Labour Organization, UNICEF and UNESCO. Finally, the volume on regional systems for protecting human rights provides selections on the regional human rights instruments and on institutions and their jurisprudence, procedures, activities and effectiveness.

Each volume opens with an introductory essay providing an overview of the topic covered and discussing the significance and context of the works selected. It is my hope that this series will serve as a valuable research resource for those already well-versed in the subject as well as those new to the field.

STEPHANIE FARRIOR
Vermont Law School, USA
Series Editor

Introduction

Introduction

The evolution of human rights protection at the international level is a consequence of the failure of the state to afford adequate protection at the national level. The international mechanism provides the victim with a 'last resort', but it is always subsidiary to the state's primary responsibility; the admissibility of any international petition is contingent upon the victim having exhausted all adequate and effective domestic remedies. Over the past 60 plus years the regional human rights systems have surpassed the United Nations human rights bodies in affording protection to the victims of human rights violations. This is largely due to the fact that states have been willing to grant regional human rights courts the power to issue legally binding judgments and reparations for violations of human rights, which they have been unwilling to do at the international level. There is no United Nations human rights court (Kozma *et al.*, 2011). To understand which forum victims prefer, compare the 120,000 pending cases before the European Court of Human Rights to the approximately 550 petitions pending before all the UN human rights treaty bodies.[1]

The essays in this volume examine the structure and functioning of the principal regional human rights systems in the world today: (1) the Inter-American Commission and Court of Human Rights; (2) the European Court of Human Rights; (3) the African Commission and Court of Human and Peoples' Rights; and (4) the ASEAN Intergovernmental Human Rights Commission. Since the Southeast Asian Intergovernmental Human Rights Commission was not established until 2009, it will receive only cursory treatment. As of this writing, there is no comparable regional human rights mechanism in the Middle East.[2] The regional human rights organs selected form part of a regional system or 'regional arrangement', as defined under Chapter VIII of the United Nations Charter; respectively, the Organization of American States (OAS), the Council of Europe, the African Union (AU) and the Association of Southeast Asian Nations (ASEAN) and must be understood in the context of these regional organizations. From an institutional perspective, the inter-American system is the oldest regional system in the world, in continued existence since its establishment in 1890 as 'the International Union of American Republics'.

---

1 According to information provided by the UN Office of the High Commissioner for Human Rights on 18 September 2013, there are 526 petitions pending before Human Rights Committee: HRC (361), Committee Against Torture: CAT (120), Committee on the Elimination of Discrimination Against Women: CEDAW (27), Committee on the Rights of Persons with Disabilities: CRPD (12), Committee on the Elimination of Racial Discrimination: CERD (6). The statistics for the European Court are 119,750 pending applications as of 31 August 2013.

2 Dr Nabil Elaraby, the Secretary-General of the Arab League announced that an Arab Court for Human Rights will be established in Manama, Bahrain, after the Arab League ministerial meeting to be held in September 2014. The proposed Arab Court was the initiative of the King of Bahrain and approved by the Arab League with limited participation of civil society in the elaboration of its statute.

There are difficulties in organizing a volume on regional human rights bodies. First, in all of these regions many interesting commentaries on the work of these systems are published in languages other than English. Second, by the time these essays are published some of the procedures and functions of these systems will have changed. These bodies are dynamic and respond to changing events and the requirements of the stakeholders in the system: the petitioners (in representation of the victims), the states, third parties and the institutional organs of the system, and in a broader sense, the general public.

This year, 2013, is no different. The OAS has been involved in a two-year state-initiated reform process to 'strengthen' the inter-American human rights system; the Council of Europe has been almost constantly in a reform process and the AU is considering the adoption of an additional Protocol to the Statute of the African Court of Justice and Human Rights. Dinah Shelton (1999, p. 398) has termed this dynamic constant reform process the 'promise' of the regional systems in the on-going striving for greater efficiency in the protection of human rights. Since reforms are underway in the three major bodies under consideration, the selection of essays has focused on more recent publications in order to reflect the current reality and present less of an historical narrative.

Central to all four systems is the concept of democracy. The major regional human rights instruments deal primarily with civil and political rights and were written for states with a democratic form of government. They presuppose three branches of government that exert checks and balances on each other; freedom of expression, in particular, the right to criticize the government; the right to vote and to stand for public office; access to justice and fair trials with guarantees of due process. These instruments, however, were not always written by democracies, but despite that fact, democracy has been recognized by all the regional systems as the requisite form of government to guarantee human rights at the national level. The experience of the inter-American system has shown that by chronicling the gross and systematic human rights violations committed by non-democratic governments against their own populations, such states lose legitimacy both within their regional group and at home. African states, which explicitly excluded any reference to 'democracy' when drafting the African Charter, over time, also recognized that a democratic form of government was essential for the realization of human rights.

The essays in this volume describe how all four regional human rights systems were created, the instruments that govern them and the scope of their jurisdiction. The evolution of the systems is also addressed. In addition, we attempt to compare the systems in terms of meeting the very different challenges they are confronted with (Christof Heyns and Magnus Killander).

Why Do We Need Regional Human Rights Organizations?

International protection of human rights by international organizations dates from 1945 and the creation of the United Nations, following the revelation of the shocking atrocities committed before and during World War II. The Pan American Union became the 'Organization of American States' in May 1948, when both the OAS Charter and the American Declaration of the Rights and Duties of Man were adopted; the latter instrument antedated by seven months the United Nations' adoption of the Universal Declaration of Human Rights. As Mary Ann

Glendon describes, in Chapter 2, Latin America was the forgotten crucible of the universal human rights idea (p. 30).

The Council of Europe was created in 1949. Peter Leuprecht, long time head of the Council's Directorate of Human Rights, points out in Chapter 1 that the Council's philosophical and political roots grew out of the fight against Nazism and Fascism. The motto of the Council's founding fathers was 'Never again' (p. 3). The founders were determined to build a new united Europe on solid foundations based on strong, shared values and the principles of pluralist democracy, human rights and the rule of law. Respect for and compliance with these values and principles were to be the chief condition for admission and the continuing obligation of its members. On 5 November 1950, in Rome, 12 member states of the Council of Europe adopted the European Convention on Human Rights, the world's first legally binding human rights treaty. This treaty signified a revolutionary change in international law, which previously was predominantly concerned with relations between and among states. Luzius Wildhaber (Chapter 13), the long time President of the Eurpean Court remarked that the European Convention gave individuals an international remedy against their governments: 'For the first time individuals could challenge the actions of Governments before an international mechanism under a procedure leading to a binding judicial decision' (p. 317). The European Court was to constitute a collective insurance policy against the relapse of democracies into dictatorships. Decades later, Leuprecht noted, since the European Convention has been incorporated into the domestic law of nearly all of its contracting states, any person, in principle, could invoke its provisions directly in applying or appealing to a national court or authority in any of those states.

The European Convention created a European Commission and Court of Human Rights, which were established at the headquarters of the Council of Europe in Strasbourg, France. In 1998, the European Commission and Court were merged and today individuals have direct access to the Court. The European system is generally recognized as the most developed and effective system of human rights protection in the world and until the expansion of the Council of Europe, following the dissolution of the Soviet Union, its strength, according to Leuprecht (Chapter 1), was in the relative homogeneity of the member states and its common shared values. It has been called a 'quasi-constitutional court for the whole of Europe' (p. 6).

The American Declaration on the Rights and Duties of Man (*sic*), like the Universal Declaration and unlike the European Convention, was not designed to be a legally binding instrument. Since its establishment in 1959, however, the Inter-American Commission on Human Rights has applied the American Declaration, the only catalogue of human rights guarantees in the hemisphere (prior to the adoption of the American Convention in 1969), as though it were legally binding. In Chapter 7, Robert K. Goldman notes in his concise history of the Commission that the American states decided not to make the Declaration binding and provided no machinery to promote or protect the rights that they had proclaimed (p. 171). Thomas Buergenthal, in his 1975 seminal essay, presents the rationale for the position that the American Declaration became legally binding by incorporation into the amended OAS Charter (Chapter 4). The Commission has continued to defend the obligatory nature of the Declaration, affirming that it is a 'source of legal obligation for all OAS member states' and 'as a source of legal obligation, states must implement the rights established in the American

Declaration in practice within their jurisdiction'.[3] The obligatory nature of the Declaration is not without controversy as many states, including the US, refuse to accept it as legally binding, but the Declaration serves as the benchmark against which the Commission scrutinizes human rights observance in states that have not yet become parties to the American Convention on Human Rights (Cerna, 2009).

There is a similar debate about the normative status of both the Inter-American Commission's and the former European Commission's decisions under their respective treaties. Since the treaties explicitly state that the respective courts have the power to issue legally binding judgments it is generally considered that Commission decisions are mere recommendations. Dinah Shelton (2012, p. 571) submits that the Inter-American Court 'now consistently reaffirms its insistence on a good faith obligation of compliance with recommendations of the Commission'. But in the final analysis, recommendations remain recommendations. It is worth pointing out, however, that the Inter-American Commission does not consider itself bound by the Inter-American Court's judgments and continues to advocate for its interpretation on points of law that the Court has not yet accepted. Since the Commission effectively controls the Court's case load, this is not a minor matter.

The inter-American system is unique among regional human rights systems because it functions under two basic instruments, the American Declaration and the American Convention on Human Rights. The latter entered into force in 1978, and as a consequence, the Inter-American Court was established in San Jose, Costa Rica, in 1979. Unlike the European system, in which one Commissioner and one Judge were elected for each state party to the European Convention, in the inter-American system seven Commissioners represent 34 OAS member states (Cuba does not participate in the activities of the OAS), not the countries of their nationalities. Similarly, the seven Judges of the Court represent the 23 states parties to the American Convention that elected them. The US is the only founding member of the OAS not to have ratified the American Convention, and, consequently, the US has not participated in the work of the Court since its creation.

Unlike the Commission, which has jurisdiction over all OAS member states, the Court only has jurisdiction over the 20 states party to the American Convention that have also expressly accepted its jurisdiction.[4] Consequently, the Court has evolved as a 'Latin American' and not as an inter-American institution (see Mónica Pinto [Chapter 9], p. 223). Every Spanish-speaking member state of the OAS and Portuguese-speaking Brazil, has become a party to the Convention and accepted the compulsory jurisdiction of the Court, while very few English-speaking countries have done so, resulting in OAS member states undertaking one of three levels of obligations. Venezuela is no longer a state party.[5] This unequal situation provoked the latest reform agenda. We have included Joseph Diab's 1992 essay on the US given the US's failure to ratify the American Convention, the situation has not changed (Chapter 8).

The inter-American system evolved differently from the European system due to very different historical circumstances. The Inter-American Commission was created, in part,

---

3 See, for example, Inter-American Commission on Human Rights: IACHR, Report No. 80/11, Case 12.626, Merits, *Jessica Lenahan (Gonzales) et al.* v. *United States*, 21 July 2011.

4 Three states, Grenada, Jamaica and Dominica are parties to the American Convention but have not accepted the compulsory jurisdiction of the Inter-American Court.

5 Venezuela on 10 September 2012 became the second country to denounce the American Convention (after Trinidad & Tobago, in 1998); its withdrawal became effective on 10 September 2013.

out of the fear that revolutions modelled after the 1959 Cuban revolution would spread throughout the region. As Goldman notes, in Chapter 7, during the Cold War the United States provided counter-insurgency support to numerous authoritarian regimes with questionable human rights practices on the ground that they were bulwarks against communist expansion (p. 180). During the 1960s, 1970s and the early 1980s, many countries in Latin America under military dictatorships faced leftist insurgencies. The governments imposed a form of state terror by means of militarized states of emergency, and engaged in systematic murder, torture, disappearances and widespread arbitrary detentions, censorship of the media and outlawing of political parties, unions and student groups. The inadequacy of the legal machinery at the national level to provide effective judicial remedies rendered a complaint mechanism at the international level ineffective because judicial remedies could not be exhausted and international remedies could not be enforced domestically. Although exhaustion of domestic remedies may be excused for denial of justice reasons, the system is premised on the existence of democratic governments and functioning independent judiciaries. In distinction to the European system, which is limited by the terms of the European Convention to the processing of individual cases, the inter-American system, in the absence of a human rights treaty, was free to invent its own procedures. It began to conduct on-site visits and to chronicle massive human rights violations encountered in the countries visited.

The main criterion for measuring the success of a regional human rights system, Leuprecht (Chapter 1) posits, is whether it effectively helps the people (p. 3). The Inter-American Commission began to receive complaints from victims of human rights violations even though a complaint mechanism was not explicitly provided for, because the very existence of a human rights body will motivate victims to file complaints. The drafters of the European Convention expected the member states of the Council of Europe to respect human rights and the European Commission to serve as the primary human rights body, with victims having only infrequent recourse to the Court. Leuprecht attributes the ability of the human rights organs of the Council of Europe to maintain their high level of compliance to the homogeneity of the membership prior to 1989, however, recourse to the European Court grew more and more frequent over time. The homogeneity of the Council of Europe broke down with the fall of the Berlin Wall and the dissolution of the Soviet Union. As additional countries joined the Council of Europe and redefined the European continent, the European human rights system began to be confronted with the human rights challenges that faced the Americas during the 1960s–1980s.

Cecilia Medina, a Chilean refugee and former Judge of the Inter-American Court, who fled the repression of the Pinochet dictatorship, examined in her doctoral dissertation (Medina, 1988) how the inter-American system confronted gross, systematic violations of human rights in the hemisphere. She reviewed the evolution of the Commission's innovative on-site visits, and described its work on Cuba, Nicaragua and Chile under military dictatorships, at a time when the rule of law was extinguished in the region. Her premise was that violations of human rights can be distinguished between those that constitute a definite pattern and those that could be described as isolated instances of violations. Importantly, she suggests that the international supervisory mechanisms were established to deal almost exclusively with isolated instances and were not very suitable for effectively dealing with gross violations constituting a pattern.

In 2004, the European Court instituted a 'pilot judgment' procedure in an effort to deal with systemic human rights violations that affected large numbers of people; however, these cases deal with massive violations *ex post facto*. In *Broniowski* v. *Poland*, for example, Poland failed to compensate individuals who had lost their land during World War II, a situation that affected as many as 80,000 potential complainants. In deciding *Broniowski*, the Court decided that all similar applications were to be adjourned pending the outcome of this case and the adoption of measures to be taken at the national level (Wildhaber [Chapter 13], p. 328). This development has become the subject of a recent study (Leach *et al.*, 2010).

The African system, similarly, has evolved over time with several additional protocols and the establishment of a court. The Organization of African Unity (OAU), established in 1963, was transformed into the African Union in 2001, and all states in Africa are members, except Morocco which withdrew in 1984, when the OAU recognized Western Sahara (see Heyns and Killander [Chapter 22], pp. 462–63).

The African Charter on Human and Peoples' Rights, also known as the 'Banjul Charter', was adopted in Nairobi, Kenya in June 1981, and entered into force in October 1986. The African Commission on Human and Peoples' Rights was established in 1987 and monitors compliance with the African Charter through state reporting, a complaint mechanism, special rapporteurs and working groups. The Commission has decided 196 cases as of 3 August 2013. Commentators remark that the reporting and complaint mechanisms are not a strength of the African Commission for a host of reasons, but that the Commission has achieved advances via its promotional role through trainings and workshops, involving key players such as police, local government and members of civil society.

A Protocol to establish an African Court on Human and Peoples' Rights was adopted in 1998 and entered into force in January 2004. In January 2006, the first 11 judges were elected to the Court, which was established in Arusha, Tanzania. In July 2008, at an AU summit in Egypt, member states signed a Protocol, which is intended to merge the African Court with a to-be-created African Court of Justice. This Protocol, if ratified by 15 states, will confer upon the to-be-established African Court of Justice and Human Rights the jurisdiction to convict and sentence individuals for international crimes such as genocide, crimes against humanity and war crimes as well as trafficking in hazardous wastes, illegal exploitation of natural resources and corruption. It is generally believed that the proposed international criminal law jurisdiction is the AU's response to the International Criminal Court (ICC)'s prosecution of only African cases. Progress has been slow once again as the political will to establish the African Court of Justice and Human Rights has been lacking and few states have become party to the 2008 Protocol.

The United Nations has been advocating the creation of regional human rights systems throughout the world. Despite the failure to create a pan-Asian mechanism, ASEAN, a sub-regional group created the ASEAN Intergovernmental Human Rights Commission in 2009. The ASEAN Commission or AICHR held its first meeting in Jakarta, Indonesia, from 28 March to 1 April 2010.

Unlike the other regional mechanisms, whose members are not government agents, this Commission is comprised of 10 government representatives whom the governing instrument (known as the 'Terms of Reference') suggests should be appointed following consultation with the appropriate stakeholders. In fact, Indonesia and Thailand used an open and transparent procedure to appoint their representatives as the position was publicly advertised and two independent human rights experts were appointed. Non-governmental organizations (NGOs) and civil society feared that government appointees would not be as independent as experts elected in other regional systems, however, candidates who are elected in the other regional systems are nominated and elected by states, so their 'independence' from states is never absolute. To date, ASEAN has not contemplated the creation of a human rights court. The ASEAN Commission has been criticized by civil society for its secrecy and, in general, unwillingness to consult civil society. In response to the urging of civil society, the ASEAN Commission has launched an official website (www.aichr.org) to share developments in its work with the public. The ASEAN Human Rights Declaration was adopted on 18 November 2012 in Phnom Penh, Cambodia, but AICHR has not yet established a complaint mechanism.

In March 1993, a regional meeting was held in Southeast Asia in preparation for the June 1993 UN Vienna World Conference on Human Rights. This meeting produced Asia's contribution in the form of the 'Bangkok Declaration', which upset the conference by challenging the generally accepted view that human rights are universal. The Asian cultural relativist approach, expressed in this Declaration, suggested that unique regional factors – historical, cultural and economic – determined human rights standards and that this was essentially a domestic matter. The challenge was overcome by the Vienna Declaration's reaffirmation of the universality of human rights.

Starting in 2011, the ASEAN Commission focused on drafting the ASEAN Human Rights Declaration which includes General Principles, Civil and Political Rights, Economic, Social and Cultural Rights, the Right to Development, the Right to Peace and a section on the Cooperation in the Promotion and Protection of Human Rights. The Declaration's General Principles have been harshly criticized, *inter alia*, by Navi Pillay, the UN High Commissioner for Human Rights, as being too reflective of regional and not universal standards. Article 7 of the Declaration states:

> All human rights are universal, indivisible, interdependent and interrelated. All human rights and fundamental freedoms in the Declaration must be treated in a fair and equal manner, on the same footing and with the same emphasis. At the same time, the realization of human rights must be considered in the regional and national context bearing in mind different political, economic, legal, social, cultural, historical and religious backgrounds.

This language echoes the Bangkok Declaration and suggests that the 'Asian Values' debate has not entirely been put to rest.

The Evolution of the Right to Democracy in the Regional Organizations

Europe

The collapse of the Soviet Union has been compared to the fall of the Roman Empire and its impact on Europe cannot be underestimated (see Leuprecht [Chapter 1], p. 16). In 1992, Russia applied for membership in the Council of Europe and was admitted in 1996. Russia's application for membership has been included in the compilation because of the impressive list of human rights commitments undertaken (Chapter 16). On 6 July 1989, Mikhail Gorbachev gave an historic speech at the Council of Europe in which he referred to Europe as 'a Common Home', and which was followed 20 years later by his reflections on the succeeding two decades, which is less well known and for which reason we have included both in this compilation (Chapters 14 and 15).

The Council of Europe grew from 23 member states to 47 and now includes the Russian Federation and many states derived from the former Soviet Union and East and Central Europe. The change has reconfigured the Council of Europe: as of 31 August 2013 five countries dominated two-thirds of the case-load of the European Court – Russia (19.5 per cent), Italy (12.2 per cent), Turkey (11.6 per cent), Ukraine (11.9 per cent) and Serbia (10.2 per cent). Three of these countries were not even members of the Council of Europe in 1989. Pending cases, for example, involving the forced abduction of civilians by members of the military in Chechnya leading to their subsequent disappearance and Russia's failure to conduct an effective investigation echo the forced disappearance cases of the inter-American system.[6] The human rights violations denounced against some of these countries could induce one to call this the 'Latin Americanization' of Europe (Christina M. Cerna [Chapter 6]).

The homogeneity and shared values of the 23 countries that comprised the Council of Europe in 1989 has been compromised by the enlargement of the Council of Europe to 47 members (all European states except Belarus). Leuprecht (Chapter 1) warned that the enlargement of the Council of Europe would entail a dilution of European standards:

> The Convention system seems relatively powerless to address and remedy serious and systematic violations of human rights, a defect which is in striking contrast to the, at times, almost minute attention the Convention bodies devote to comparatively minor matters or 'legal niceties.' This may be seen as part of a wider phenomenon: the inability of international human rights bodies to react speedily and effectively to urgent situations and to gross, systematic human rights violations, including torture, disappearances, summary executions, and arbitrary arrests on a large scale. (p. 7)

Paul Mahoney (2005, p. 3), the former Registrar and now the British judge on the European Court, noted the change in the 'nature of cases', for example, the 'special feature of Turkish cases in the frequency of serious allegations such as destruction of villages, ill-treatment of detainees involving torture or inhuman treatment, prohibition of political parties'.

Leuprecht's lament that the expansion of Europe signified the lowering of standards in the European human rights system warrants renewed consideration of the criterion he posited for assessing the success of a regional human rights organization: does an enlarged Council of Europe effectively help the people? Although the Russian Federation is notorious for not complying with European Court judgments, Russia has not chosen to withdraw from the European Court nor has the Council of Europe taken any steps to expel it, so presumably some benefit must be derived from its continued membership.

In the early 1990s, neither the Council of Europe nor the European Court played a role in the worst European human rights crisis since World War II, simply because Yugoslavia was not a member state of the Council of Europe. But isn't it the point of a regional human rights system to serve as the last resort for the victims of human rights violations when remedies at the national level fail? Given the Council's membership requirement at the time that a state must have achieved a certain threshold of human rights compliance for admission, resulted

---

6 See European Court of Human Rights: ECHR, *Shaipova and Others* v. *Russia*, Application no. 10796/04, Judgment of 6 February 2009, *Saidova* v. *Russia*, Application no. 51432/00, Judgment of 9 December 2013.

in depriving the Yugoslav victims of any recourse before the regional system. The evolution of the European system into a regional body that now includes every state in Europe except one, requiring compulsory acceptance of both the European Convention and the European Court, creates a much more integrated Europe and the triumph of the democratic ideal. As Leuprecht notes, the Council is increasingly assuming the pan-European dimension that was originally intended for it and its 'new task is to play an active role in "democracy building" in the post-communist countries, and to this end important programs have been created and implemented, some of which are conducted jointly with the European Commission' (Leuprecht, p. 16).

That said, Wildhaber (Chapter 12) notes that only a few cases have been so exceptional as to influence the fate of European democracy (p. 308). The *Greek Military Junta* case may qualify, he suggests and also the cases which recognized the existence of a democracy's right to defend itself against its enemies, such as *Rekvényi*, *Refah Partisi*, or *Ždanoka*. In *Refah Partisi*, the Grand Chamber held that *Shari'a* (Islamic law) is incompatible with the fundamental principles of democracy contained in the European Convention.[7]

The Americas

Just as in Europe, by 1991, the political situation in the Americas changed dramatically. In 1991 in Santiago, Chile, the OAS celebrated the fact that the government of every member state, except for Cuba, was democratic and the product of free elections. The end of the military dictatorships in the region produced a kind of 'Europeanization' of Latin America, as the nature of violations presented to the Inter-American Commission now involved issues of due process, access to justice and the rights of indigenous peoples rather than forced disappearances, extrajudicial executions and torture, which had characterized the earlier period (Cerna [Chapter 6]).

As mentioned above, during its first 30 years, the Commission (1959–89) carried out on-site visits and prepared country reports on the situation of human rights in member countries for the OAS's political bodies. The Commission was not given explicit authority to carry out monitoring visits but created that competence by dint of its own initiative. Its Statute, which is approved by the OAS member states, authorized it to hold meetings in any member state and the Commission converted that authorization to displace itself into a mandate to conduct on-site visits and to prepare country reports on the respective human rights situations in the hemisphere. These reports dominated the agenda of the OAS General Assemblies for many years, especially during the long period of military dictatorships in the region, when the Commission critically reviewed the behaviour of these states as regards their failure to respect human rights.

The re-democratization of the hemisphere may be considered, at least in part, a consequence of the work of the inter-American human rights system. The Commission succeeded in de-legitimizing non-democratic governments in the region by setting forth the human rights

---

[7] ECHR, Grand Chamber, *Rekvényi* v. *Hungary*, Application no. 25390/94, Judgment 20 May 1999; *Partisi (The Welfare Party) and Others* v. *Turkey*, Applications nos 41340/98, 41342/98 and 41344/98), Judgment 13 February 2003; ECHR, Grand Chamber, *Ždanoka* v. *Latvia*, Application no. 58278/00, Judgment 16 March 2006.

violations denounced to it in countries where it conducted on-site visits and presented these country reports to the OAS political organs and to the public in general. Argentina, for example, in 1980, felt enough pressure that it threatened to withdraw from the OAS if it were condemned by the General Assembly for the violations set forth in the Commission's report.

The political will to protect from overthrow the democratic governments in the hemisphere evolved from 1991 to September 11, 2001, the date on which it crystallized in the OAS adoption of the Inter-American Democratic Charter, which is the first international instrument to declare 'democracy' a 'human right' of individuals and to ascribe to governments the obligation to promote and defend it. The Democratic Charter calls for collective action on the part of the member states if democracy is interrupted in any OAS state.

Africa

States in Africa resisted including the word 'democracy' in the African Charter on Human and Peoples' Rights and rejected any reference to an African Court of Human Rights. There is no reference to 'representative democracy' in the Preamble to the African Charter, no state of emergency clause and no limitations clauses common to other human rights instruments that restrict the exercise of certain rights as prescribed by law and necessary in a democratic society.

Nonetheless, Africa was not immune from the waves of democratization in the early 1990s epitomized by the elections in Benin in 1991 and by the advent of democracy with the election of Nelson Mandela in South Africa in 1994 (Heyns and Killander [Chapter 22], p. 484)[8] And in 2007, the AU member states adopted the African Charter on Democracy, Elections and Governance, which entered into force on 15 February 2012 and in Article 4 declares 'popular participation through universal suffrage' an 'inalienable right of the people'.

Democracy has also become an underlying principle of the African Union. Article 30 of the AU's Constitutive Act states: 'Governments that come to power through unconstitutional means shall not be allowed to participate in the activities of the Union.' The AU has twice imposed sanctions on Mauritania following an unconstitutional overthrow of government, and sanctions have been imposed after coups in the Central African Republic, Togo, Guinea, Niger, Madagascar and the Ivory Coast.

Southeast Asia

Democracy is also explicitly included in the ASEAN instruments. The ASEAN Charter of 2007 mentions democracy in its Preamble and in its 'Purposes' and 'Principles'. In addition, the ASEAN Human Rights Declaration of 18 November 2012 under 'General Principles' states:

> The human rights and fundamental freedoms of every person shall be exercised with due regard to the human rights and fundamental freedoms of others. The exercise of human rights and fundamental freedoms shall be subject only to such limitations as are determined by law solely for the purpose of securing due recognition for the human rights and fundamental freedoms of others, and to meet the

---

8 Prior thereto (from 1972 to 1990) Benin had been under a Marxist-Leninist government.

just requirements of national security, public order, public health, public safety, public morality, as well as the general welfare of the peoples in a democratic society.

The Parties to the Case and Leading Jurisprudential Trends in the Regional Bodies

The Inter-American System

The second phase of the inter-American system's evolution (1989–present) was dominated by the case system and the growth in influence of the Inter-American Court. The Commission has processed over 17,000 petitions since 1965, when it was authorized to process individual complaints and now receives approximately 1,800 petitions per year and processes as cases only about 180 of them. A number of studies of the Court's early jurisprudence have focused on the first case to be decided by the Court, the *Velasquez Rodriguez* v. *Honduras* (1988) case,[9] in which the Commission found the state responsible for the forced disappearance of an individual, Manfredo Velasquez, by showing that the state engaged in a practice of forced disappearances during 1981–84 and that Velasquez's detention and subsequent disappearance fell within this pattern.

For many years, the Commission assumed two roles in the procedure: first it adjudicated the case pursuant to the proceedings before the Commission and then it appeared as the victim's advocate and a party to the proceedings before the Court vis-à-vis the State (Cerna, 2006, p. 396). The lawyers of the victims were termed 'advisers' to the Commission and understandably, they sought autonomy in litigation before the Court, such as was granted to European applicants by the reform of the European Court's Rules in 1982. In the inter-American system, in 1996, the victims were finally granted independent status to present their own pleadings and evidence as regards reparations. Judge Antônio Cançado Trindade, long-time President of the Inter-American Court and now a judge on the ICJ, advocated repeatedly the importance of granting individual complainants *ius standi* before the Inter-American Court, recognizing that no one better than the victims themselves (or their legal representatives) could defend their rights. We include Judge Cançado's recommendations for improvement of the mechanisms of protection of the inter-American system, which was central to many of his presentations (see Cançado [Chapter 5], pp. 142–45). With the Court's 2009 reforms, the representatives of the victims were finally granted complete autonomy from the Commission and the latter's role was redefined to defending its decision on the case before the Court.

Regional bodies strive to distinguish themselves from other regions by underlining their special attention to group rights, their religion, their treatment of indigenous peoples and the like. As regards jurisprudence, however, it is important to emphasize that there are no regional human rights norms, there are only regional arrangements that supervise compliance with international standards (Cerna, 1994). There are many essays that could be included on the Commission's and Court's cases dealing with the rights of indigenous peoples (Pasqualucci, 2006b, 2009; Anaya, 2009), freedom of expression (Pasqualucci, 2006a), women's rights, amnesty laws (Due Process of Law Foundation, 2007), forced disappearances (Medina, 1988),

---

[9] I/A Court H.R., *Velasquez Rodriguez* v. *Honduras*, Merits. Judgment of July 29, 1988. Series C No. 4.

the death penalty (Tittemore, 2004), the relationship between international human rights law and international humanitarian law (Burgorgue-Larsen and Ubeda de Torres, 2011; Cerna, 2011; Goldman, 2013) and so on, and issues such as provisional measures (Pasqualucci, 1993), reparations (Pasqualucci, 1996; Shelton, 2005) and compliance with Court judgments (Pasqualucci, 2013), but these essays are widely available. We have listed some of them in the bibliography for those seeking further information.

For the jurisprudence of the Court, see its website at http://www.corteidh.or.cr/index-ingles.html and for the jurisprudence of the Commission, see its website: http://www.cidh.oas.org.

The European System

During the European Court's first decade it only decided one case (*Lawless v. Ireland*) and Council of Europe member states initially accepted the right of petition only for a short period of time, and successively renewed it for only a few years at a time (see Anthony Lester, Chapter 11). During the 1960s and 1970s, the main work of the European system was carried out by the now defunct European Commission, which Lester (Chapter 11) suggests it was a mistake to abolish. The right of petition is now obligatory with respect to all Council of Europe member states and given the abolition of the Commission, the individual has direct access to the Court. The Court is structured into five chambers or sections of seven judges, who are assigned 'clone' or repetitive cases, where there is no new question of law presented, whereas the Grand Chamber of 17 judges considers 'new' matters. As mentioned earlier, as of this writing, approximately 120,000 cases are pending before the European Court; cases, not petitions.

The European Court takes very seriously the right of every individual to have his/her petition heard by the Court, but as Wildhaber explains, in Chapter 12, the right of individual application is a right of access to the Court, not a right to have the case decided. Wildhaber states that 96 per cent of the applications are rejected before reaching the admissibility stage, and in 90 per cent of the 4 per cent that are admitted, the Court declares a violation of the European Convention. The vast majority of the decisions taken by the European Court are rejections of the petition for failure to comply with admissibility requirements or for being repetitive 'clone' decisions. Over the decades the European Court has evolved to function somewhat like a factory producing widgets, and Lester presents the situation as follows:

> Strasbourg judges do not manage the cases in any real sense; that key responsibility is left to the Registry staff. It is the staff who manage the cases and make the vital selection as to which cases have priority and which cases are sent to the judges in batches for summary disposal. Lord Woolf noted in his Review that within the 20 divisions in the Registry, arranged primarily according to language and country, 'there is constant pressure to meet targets and increase productivity'. And again, according to Lord Woolf, the lawyers in the Registry 'work to fulfil numerical targets; they have to complete a certain number of cases each year … it is often the more important Chamber cases that get left at the bottom of the pile'. It is a factory system, dominated by the Registry, attempting to achieve high productivity in delivering mass production of mainly negative decisions.
>
> Even cases which have been given priority treatment by the Court – urgent cases involving arbitrary arrest and detention, solitary confinement, inhuman and degrading treatment threatening an applicant's health and life, the coerced sterilization of Romani women, and other gross abuses – may be left in abeyance for years. (p. 282)

Lester suggests that a commission or some other two-tiered system be established to filter the petitions and allow the Grand Chamber to concentrate its efforts on cases involving serious questions of public importance. Wildhaber (Chapter 12), notes that a proposal to create a new Supreme European Court of Human Rights, which would be composed of 15 judges to replace the present Grand Chamber has been made to concentrate and focus the case law and to improve its quality (p. 22). This proposal is different from reconstituting the two-tier system with a purely filtering body below the present Court, but as Wildhaber points out, a 15 member court would exclude many countries and opposition could be expected.

Chapter 10 is an essay published in 2012 by Christiane Bourloyannis-Vrailas to provide a broad-stroked, concise summary of some of the highlights of the Court's jurisprudence. For a systematic analysis of the jurisprudence of the Court until 1996, the cases are digested by Article number in Peter Kempees' (1960–98) *A Systematic Guide to the Case-Law of the European Court of Human Rights*. The full texts of the cases are to be found in European Court of Human Rights, Reports of Judgments and Decisions, Series A, and on the Court's website: http://www.ECtHR.coe.int/Eng/Judgments.htm.

The African System

Regional human rights courts appear to take about a decade before they actually begin to function and decide litigious cases. The African Court on Human and Peoples' Rights, established in 2006, came in under the decade mark with its first judgment on 14 June 2013, in the case of *The Tanganyika Law Society, the Legal and Human Rights Centre & Reverend Christopher Mtikila v. The United Republic of Tanzania*. The case involved the political question of whether a candidate for public office was required to belong to a political party. The African Court held that the candidate was not so required and declared Tanzania's Constitution in violation of Articles 10 and 13 of the African Charter. The respondent, *inter alia*, noted that the Government of Tanzania fully adheres to principles of the rule of law, separation of powers and independence of the judiciary as provided for under the Constitution of the United Republic of Tanzania. In other words, it underlined that the government of Tanzania was a democracy.

In the absence of any substantial jurisprudence of the African Court we have to look at the African Commission on Human and Peoples' Rights. As in the other regional systems, states and individuals may bring complaints to the African Commission alleging violations of rights in the African Charter. Inter-state cases in Africa are rare. The individual bringing the case does not need to be a victim or a relative of the victim, but may be an NGO. NGOs in Africa, unlike the other regional systems, may bring a case in the public interest, a so-called '*actio popularis*', alleging a violation of the African Charter even though the complainant is not a victim of the violation (Heyns and Killander [Chapter 22], p. 14).

The African Commission has received approximately 300 individual complaints in the period 1987–2006 (Heyns and Killander, p. 15). If the Commission finds that a violation of the Charter has been committed by a state it may make recommendations that the violation cease, or specific laws be changed, or that the state 'take all necessary steps to comply with its obligations under the Charter' (Heyns and Killander, p. 16), but there is no formal follow-up or enforcement mechanism.

Article 58 of the African Charter provides that cases involving 'serious or massive violations' of human rights must be referred by the Commission to the Assembly which 'may then request the Commission to undertake an in-depth study of these cases' Although the Commission has referred cases to the Assembly, the Assembly has failed to respond (Heyns and Killander, p. 16). Given the absence of the requisite political will, the dramatic situations of serious and massive violations of human rights in Africa, such as the situation in the Congo, to take one example, have not received the necessary attention of the regional human rights system.

The African Charter does not empower the Commission to take provisional or interim measures requesting state parties to act to prevent serious and irreparable harm. The Commission's Rules of Procedure, however, authorize the Commission to do so and it has issued interim measures in the case of Ken Saro-Wiwa and other Ogoni activits who had been sentenced to death by a military tribunal in Nigeria. In that case, the Nigerian government ignored the Commission's measures and executed them, provoking international condemnation. The Commission determined that the execution in the face of the provisional measures violated Article 1 of the African Charter (Heyns and Killander, p. 16).

Anna Dolidze, in a 26 July 2011 'ASIL Insights', wrote about the provisional measures ordered by the African Court against Libya in the case *African Commission on Human and Peoples' Rights* v. *Great Socialist People's Libyan Arab Jamahiriya* (Chapter 20). The provisional measures required Libya to 'immediately refrain from any action that would result in loss of life or violation of physical integrity of persons, which could be a breach of the provisions of the African Charter ... to which it is a party' (p. 421). The Court ordered Libya to inform it within 15 days of the steps taken to comply with the order, although Libya failed to do so.

Although Libya is a party to the African Court it has not made a declaration under Article 34(6) permitting individuals to file petitions against it. Dolidze notes that three Egyptian NGOs submitted a request for provisional measures to the African Commission. The Commission condemned the actions of the Libyan government and instituted proceedings against Libya in the Court for 'serious and massive violations of human rights' (p. 423). The Commission did not request provisional measures from the Court, but the Court decided to order them *motu proprio*.

The jurisprudence of the African Commission on Human and Peoples' Rights is available on its website: http://www.achpr.org/communications/.

The Southeast Asian System

The ASEAN Commission has received complaints of violations of human rights but, lacking a complaint mechanism, it does not even acknowledge receipt of these complaints or make public how many it has received or regarding which issues or from whom. Informing the public of these complaints on a regular basis could mark the beginning of the creation of a complaint mechanism.

How Regional Human Rights Bodies Deal with Situations of Armed Conflict: The Relationship between International Human Rights Law and International Humanitarian Law

Both the European Court and the Inter-American Court have taken the position that international human rights law is the only law that they are authorized to apply and that international humanitarian law, even though it is the generally recognized *lex specialis* to be applied to situations of armed conflict is not theirs to apply. Instead, the European and the inter-American human rights bodies apply a law enforcement paradigm to situations of armed conflict. According to William Abresch (Chapter 17), the European Court following the Chechen cases will directly apply human rights law to situations of internal armed conflict, not only without reference to humanitarian law but also in a manner that is at odds with humanitarian law (p. 356). Russia, Turkey and the United Kingdom all denied that they faced situations of internal armed conflict and consequently all denied that international humanitarian law applied. Abresch underscores that states are unwilling to apply international humanitarian law because it involves a tacit concession that there is another 'party' wielding power in the putatively sovereign state (p. 364).

Similarly, the Inter-American Court decided in the *Las Palmeras* v. *Colombia* judgment that the Inter-American Commission and Court were only competent to apply international human rights law and not international humanitarian law.[10] This judgment has been subject to assessments as to whether the courts are applying the appropriate law and also to criticism in the literature (Cerna, 2011; Goldman, 2013).

Extraterritorial Jurisdiction – How Far Does a Regional Body Reach?

The *raison d'être* of a regional human rights body is to establish a floor of minimally acceptable conduct within the region; generally, jurisdiction is territorial and the complainant must be within the territorial confines of the region for there to be a case against a member state.

Given US activities outside its borders, and also those of the United Kingdom and the European members of NATO outside their borders, questions have arisen as to the accountability of a member state under regional human rights norms for human rights violations committed outside the territory of the region, especially when exercising military force. We have included Francesco Messineo's short piece on the accountability of the UK for human rights abuses committed in Iraq over persons and territory over which British armed forces exercised control (Chapter 18). Although it seems quite logical that a state should not be permitted to commit abuses abroad that it is not permitted to commit at home, the jurisprudence recognizing this logic is very recent. In the European system, the *Al-Skeini* v. *UK and Al-Jedda* v. *UK* cases,[11] both decided together in 2011, have set this new standard.

In the inter-American system, the jurisprudence has not yet recognized the right of an individual from outside the Americas to bring a case against a member state of the OAS for

---

[10] I/A Court H.R., *Las Palmeras* v. *Colombia*, Preliminary Objections, Judgment of 4 February 2000. Series C. No. 67.

11 ECHR, Grand Chamber, *Al-Jedda* v. *United Kingdom*, App. No. 27021/08, Judgment of 7 July 2011; A*l-Skeini & Others* v. *United Kingdom*, App. No. 55721/07, Judgment of 7 July 2011

a violation of human rights allegedly perpetrated by that member state outside the Americas. For that reason, cases presented by detainees held by the US in Afghanistan or Iraq have not yet been opened, although detainees from these countries held within the region – for example, at the Guantanamo Naval Base in Cuba – are considered within the jurisdiction of the inter-American system. Given the jurisprudential developments in Europe it can be expected that the inter-American system will follow suit.

Lastly, the case of *El Masri* v. *the Former Yugoslav Republic of Macedonia*,[12] decided by the European Court in December 2012, opened the door to litigation in the European system (and probably also the inter-American system) from victims in countries that cooperated with the United States' policy of secret detention and extraordinary rendition.

The Effectiveness of Regional Courts

The Inter-American Court has issued approximately 200 merits judgments since its first merits judgment in *Velasquez Rodriguez* in July 1988. The most important development regarding compliance in the case law of the inter-American system has been the evolution of the 'control of conventionality' doctrine, which the Court has defined as the obligation of the national judiciary to control for the compatibility of its national legislation not only with the American Convention but also with the Court's interpretation thereof.

In Chapter 3, we include Jo Pasqualucci's chapter on 'State Compliance with Court-Ordered Reparations' for a comprehensive look at the Court's reparations history. Also recommended is the Concurring Opinion of Judge *Ad Hoc* Eduardo Ferrer Mac-Gregor Poisot to the Judgment of the Inter-American Court in *Cabrera Garcia and Montiel Flores* v. *Mexico* of 26 November 2010,[13] which sets forth the history of the 'control of conventionality' doctrine. We are not familiar with any law review essays in English on the subject as of yet although a number exist in Spanish.

Since a regional human rights court is empowered to issue legally binding judgments and reparations to the victim, state compliance is of primary importance. The declaration of incompatibility of domestic amnesty laws with a state's obligations under the American Convention has led to the prosecution of approximately 1,000 military officials in Argentina for atrocities committed during the 'dirty war'. Similar prosecutions are occurring in Chile and to a lesser extent, also in Guatemala. The Argentine prosecutions, it should be noted, are in civilian, not military, courts. This is the consequence of a friendly settlement of two cases with the Commission, which led, in 2007, to Argentina abolishing its Code of Military Justice, except for cases of military discipline. Human rights violations are deemed not to fall within the scope of military discipline.

Two recent studies have assessed the impact of the European Convention's jurisprudence on the member states of the Council of Europe. We include an assessment of that impact by Helen Keller and Alec Stone Sweet (Chapter 19), since it is the more recent of the two studies, dating from 2008. Blackburn and Polakiewicz (2001) reviewed the impact of the system on

12 ECHR, Grand Chamber, *El Masri* v. the *Former Yugoslav Republic of Macedonia*, Application no. 38630/09, Judgment of 13 December 2012.

13 I/A Court H.R., *Cabrera García and Montiel Flores* v. *Mexico*. Preliminary Objection, Merits, Reparations and Legal Costs. Judgment of November 26, 2010. Series C. No. 220.

32 states, whereas Keller and Sweet tracked the impact on 18. Notably, they report, Belgium, France, the Netherlands, Switzerland and the UK have incorporated the European Convention as a sort of surrogate Bill of Rights. In Scandinavia, new Bills of Rights have been modelled on the European Convention. In states such as Germany, Ireland, Spain and some Central European states, where Constitutions provide an entrenched Bill of Rights, the European Convention serves as a supplement to the Constitution.

The authors find that the European Court faces two major challenges: an exploding caseload and a large number of applications about very serious human rights violations from a handful of problematic states. In order to increase the effectiveness of the Court, it is again suggested that the Court be enabled to concentrate on cases involving more serious human rights violations and that it be permitted to undertake systemic reform itself to accommodate this task (Keller and Sweet, p. 210).

In assessing the African system, Frans Viljoen and Lirette Louw (Chapter 21) examine compliance with the 44 decisions of the African Charter on Human and Peoples' Rights during 1994–2004 in order to determine whether human rights treaties in fact 'make a difference' (p. 427). The findings of the African Commission, they note, are not legally binding since they are 'recommendations to states parties' rather than orders (p. 428). Furthermore, since the African Commission did not have a follow-up mechanism or policy in order to monitor state compliance it never compiled data on state compliance. The authors found that six of the 44 decisions were fully complied with, 13 were not complied with, 14 were partially complied with and seven had partial or full compliance but due to a change in circumstance rather than governmental response to the recommendations.[14] The violations found in the six cases of compliance involved civil and political rights. They concluded that the most significant factor that might influence compliance is a change in government after years of military dictatorship, as in the death of General Abacha in 1999, ending the dictatorship and initiating a period of democratic governance in Nigeria.

In contrast with the piece by Viljoen and Louw, which assesses compliance with the African Charter by examining compliance with findings of the African Commission, Obiora Chinedu Okafor studies the 'modest' impact the Charter has had on executive and judicial decision-making, legislative action and civil society actors at the national level. Chapter 6 of his book, which we have included in this compilation, draws on a fascinating array of examples of how this impact has been created (Chapter 23). He attributes the catalyst for the impact to 'activist forces' – that is, activist lawyers and judges and civil society associations (NGOs) working in collaboration with the African human rights system. For example, the African Commission's Special Rapporteur on Prisons in Africa was able to conduct on-site inspections in Zimbabwe, Mali, Madagascar and Mozambique, Okafor suggests, because the activist forces were able to influence the decision-makers of the executive branch to consent to the visit. In *Chairperson of the Immigration Selection Board* v. *Frank and another*,[15] the Supreme Court of Namibia held that since the relevant provisions of the African Charter and the ICCPR did not provide special protection for homosexual relationships (both of which influenced the Namibian Constitution), the Court's failure to protect the specific relationship in this case was 'reinforced' by the lack of

---

[14] The authors indicated insufficient information regarding compliance in the remaining four cases.

[15] South African Legal Information Institute: Namibia: Supreme Court, *Chairperson of the Immigration Selection Board v Frank and Another* (SA8/99, SA8/99) [2001] NASC 1 (5 March 2001).

specific protections for homosexuals in the African Charter (Okafor [Chapter 23], pp. 517–18). The point, he emphasized, was that the highest court in Namibia specifically acknowledged the influence of the Charter on its decision, albeit negative.

In the case of Cameroon and Cape Verde, Okafor points out, the African Charter and all duly ratified international agreements override domestic law (p. 525) whereas Judges in other states, like the Congo (Brazzaville) ignore the provisions of the Charter (p. 530). Why, Okafor provocatively asks, does the Charter have a greater impact in Nigeria, under a military government, than in Botswana, known as Africa's most stable liberal democracy, or than in any other country in Africa? (p. 532) Regrettably the question is not answered.

Also highly recommended is the chapter in Okafor's (2007) book on 'Convention Conceptions of the African System for the Promotion and Protection of Human and Peoples' Rights'. That chapter presents a superbly informative overview and evaluation of the works of many leading writers on the African human rights system, including Chidi Odinkalu, Joe Oloka-Onyango, Makau Mutua, Evelyn Ankumah, E.V.O. Dankwah, Rachel Murray and others.

References

Anaya, S. James (2009), *International Human Rights and Indigenous Peoples*, Aspen.

Blackburn, Robert and Polakiewicz, Jörg (eds) (2001), *Fundamental Rights in Europe: The European Convention on Human Rights and its Member States, 1950–2000*, Oxford: OUP.

Burgorgue-Larsen, Laurence and de Torres, Amaya Ubeda (2011), *The Inter-American Court of Human Rights: Case Law and Commentary*, Oxford: OUP.

Cerna, Christina M. (1994), 'Universality of Human Rights and Cultural Diversity: Implementation of Human Rights in Different Socio-Cultural Contexts', *Human Rights Quarterly*, **16**, pp. 740–52.

Cerna, Christina M. (2006), 'Are We Headed in the Right Direction? Reflections on the New (2001) Rules of Procedure of the Inter-American Commission on Human Rights in Light of the Experience of the European System', in Anne F. Bayefsky (ed.), *Human Rights and Refugees, Internally Displaced Persons and Migrant Workers: Essays in Memory of Joan Fitzpatrick and Arthur Helton*, Leiden: Martinus-Nijhoff, pp. 387–441.

Cerna, Christina M. (2009), 'Reflections on the Normative Status of the American Declaration of the Rights and Duties of Man', *University of Pennsylvania Journal of International Law*, **30**, pp. 1211–37.

Cerna, Christina M. (2011), 'The History of the Inter-American System's Jurisprudence as Regards Situations of Armed Conflict', *Journal of Humanitarian Legal Studies*, **2**, pp. 3–52.

Cerna, Christina M. (2013), 'Introductory Note to the ECHR: *El-Masri* v. *The Former Yugoslav Republic of Macedonia* (FYRM)', 13 December 2012, 52 ILM xxx, No. 2.

Due Process of Law Foundation (2007), *Victims Unsilenced: The Inter-American Human Rights System and Transitional Justice in Latin America*, Due Process of Law Foundation.

Goldman, Robert (2013), 'Extraterritorial Application of the Human Rights to Life and Personal Liberty, Including Habeas Corpus, During Situations of Armed Conflict', in Robert Kolb and Gloria Gaggioli (eds), *Research Handbook on Human Rights and Humanitarian Law*, Cheltenham, UK: Edward Elgar, pp. 104–24.

Kempees, Peter (1960–98), *A Systematic Guide to the Case Law of the European Court of Human Rights*, 4 vols, Leiden: Martinus-Nijhoff.

Kozma, J., Nowak, M. and Scheinin, M. (2011), *A World Court of Human Rights – Consolidated Statute and Commentary*, Vienna: Neuer Wissenschaftlicher Verlag.

Leach, Philip, Hardman, Helen, Stephenson, Svetlana and Blitz, Brad (eds) (2010), *Responding to Systemic Human Rights Violations*, Intersentia.

Mahoney, Paul (2005), 'Parting Thoughts of an Outgoing Registrar of the ECHR', *Human Rights Law Journal*, **26**, pp. 345–48.
Medina, Cecilia (1988), *The Battle for Human Rights: Gross, Systematic Violations of Human Rights and the Inter-American System*, Leiden: Martinus-Nijhoff.
Okafor, Obiora Chinedu (2007), 'Convention Conceptions of the African System for the Promotion and Protection of Human and Peoples' Rights', in *African Human Rights System, Activist Forces and International Institutions*, New York: Cambridge University Press, pp. 63–90.
Pasqualucci, Jo (1993), 'Provisional Measures in the Inter-American Human Rights System: An Innovative Development in International Law', *Vanderbilt Journal of Transnational Law*, **26**, p. 803.
Pasqualucci, Jo (1996), 'Victim Reparations in the Inter-American Human Rights System: A Critical Assessment of Current Practice and Procedure', *Michigan Journal of International Law*, **18**, pp. 1–57.
Pasqualucci, Jo (2006a), 'Criminal Defamation and the Evolution of the Doctrine of Freedom of Expression in International Law: Comparative Jurisprudence of the Inter-American Court of Human Rights', *Vanderbilt Journal of International Law*, **39**, pp. 379–433.
Pasqualucci, Jo (2006b), 'The Evolution of International Indigenous Rights in the Inter-American Human Rights System', *Human Rights Law Review*, **6**, pp. 281–322.
Pasqualucci, Jo (2009), 'International Indigenous Land Rights: A Critique of the Jurisprudence of the Inter-American Court of Human Rights in Light of the United Nations Declaration on the Rights of Indigenous Peoples', *Wisconsin International Law Journal*, **27**, pp. 51–98.
Pasqualucci, Jo M. (2013), *The Practice and Procedure of the Inter-American Court of Human Rights*, Cambridge: CUP.
Shelton, Dinah (1999), 'The Promise of Regional Human Rights Systems', in Stephen P. Marks and Burns H. Weston (eds), *The Future of Human Rights*, New York: Transnational Publishers, pp. 351–98.
Shelton, Dinah (2005), *Remedies in International Human Rights Law* (2nd edn), Oxford: OUP.
Shelton, Dinah (2012), 'The Legal Status of Normative Pronouncements of Human Rights Treaty Bodies', in Holger P. Hestermeyer, Doris König, Nele Matz-Lück and Volker Röben (eds), *Coexistence, Cooperation and Solidarity: Liber Amicorum Rüdiger Wolfrum*, Vol. 1, Leiden: Martinus Nijhoff, pp. 553–75.
Tittemore, Brian (2004), 'The Mandatory Death Penalty in the Commonwealth Caribbean and the Inter-American Human Rights System: An Evolution in the Development and Implementation of International Human Rights Protections', *William and Mary Bill of Rights Journal*, **13**, pp. 445–520.

Bibliography

Bibliography of Essays for Further Consultation

General

Henkin, Louis (1995), 'U.S. Ratification of Human Rights Conventions: The Ghost of Senator Bricker', *American Journal of International Law*, **89**, pp. 341–50.

Kozma, J., Nowak, M. and Scheinin, M. (2011), *A World Court of Human Rights – Consolidated Statute and Commentary*, Studienreihe des Ludwig Boltzmann Instituts für Menschenrechte, vol. 22 Vienna: Neuer Wissenschaftlicher Verlag. 114 pages.

Nowak, Manfred (2009), 'Eight Reasons Why We Need a World Court of Human Rights', in Gudmundur Alfredsson, Jonas Grimheden and Bertrand G. Ramcharan (eds), *International Human Rights Monitoring Mechanisms: Essays in Honour of Jakob Moller*, Leiden: Martinus Nijhoff/Brill Academic, pp. 321–32.

Europe

Abdel-Monen, Tariq (2005), 'How Far Do the Lawless Areas of Europe Extend? Extraterritorial Application of the European Convention on Human Rights', *Journal of Transnational Law and Policy*, **14**, pp. 159–215.

Caflisch, Lucius (2006), 'The Reform of the ECHR: Protocol 14 and Beyond', *Human Rights Law Review*, **6**, pp. 403–15.

Cerna, Christina M. (2013), 'Introductory Note to the ECHR: El-Masri v. The Former Yugoslav Republic of Macedonia (FYRM)', 13 December 2012, 52 ILM xxx, No. 2, 558.

De Schutter, Olivier (2006), 'Globalization and Jurisdiction: Lessons from the European Convention on Human Rights', *Baltic Yearbook of International Law*, **6**, pp. 183–245.

Hoffmeister, Frank (2006), 'Germany: Status of European Convention on Human Rights in Domestic Law', *International Journal of Constitutional Law*, **4**, pp. 722–31.

Leach, Philip (2006), 'Access to the ECHR: From a Legal Entitlement to a Lottery?', *Human Rights Law Journal*, **27**, pp. 11–25.

Mahoney, Paul (1999), 'Speculating on the Future of the Reformed European Court of Human Rights', *Human Rights Law Journal*, **20**, pp. 1–4.

Mahoney, Paul (2005), 'Parting Thoughts of an Outgoing Registrar of the ECHR', *Human Rights Law Journal*, **26**, pp. 345–48.

O'Boyle, Michael (2008), 'On Reforming the Operation of the European Court of Human Rights', *EHRLR*, **1**, pp. 1–11.

O'Boyle, Michael (2011), 'The Future of the European Court of Human Rights', *German Law Journal*, **12**, pp. 1862–77.

Ole, Solvang (2008), 'Russia and the European Court of Human Rights: The Price of Non-Cooperation', *Human Rights Brief*, **15**, pp. 14–17.

Pomeranz, William E. (2012), 'Uneasy Partners: Russia and the ECHR', *Human Rights Brief*, **19**, pp. 17–21.

Satterthwaite, Margaret L. (2008), 'The Story of El-Masri v. Tenet: Human Rights and Humanitarian Law in the "War on Terror"', *NYU Public Law and Legal Theory Working Papers*, Paper 109.
Wildhaber, Luzius (2002), 'A Constitutional Future for the ECHR?', *Human Rights Law Journal*, **23**, pp. 161–65.

The Americas

Baluarte, David (2007), 'Strategies for Implementation of the Yean y Bosico v. The Dominican Republic Judgment of the I-A Court', *American University Law Review*, **56**, pp. 1464–68.
Carlos, Ayala (2007), 'Litigating against State Normative Acts within the Inter-American System', *American University Law Review*, **56**, pp. 1413–17.
Cassel, Douglass (2005), 'The Expanding Scope and Impact of Reparation Awarded by the IACtHR', in Koen de Feyter, Stephan Parmentier, Marc Bossuyt and Paul Lemmens (eds), *Out of the Ashes: Reparations for Victims of Gross and Systematic Violations*, Antwerp-Oxford: Intersentia (http://www.intersentia.com).
Cerna, Christina M. (1994), 'Universality of Human Rights and Cultural Diversity: Implementation of Human Rights in Different Socio-Cultural Contexts', *Human Rights Quarterly*, **16**, pp. 740–52.
Cerna, Christina M. (1995), 'Universal Democracy: An International Legal Right or the Pipe Dream of the West?', *NYU Journal of International Law and Politics*, **27**, pp. 289–329.
Cerna, Christina M. (2005), 'How the Inter-American System for the Protection of Human Rights Has Contributed to the Development of International Law', in Delas, Côté, Crépeau and Leuprecht (eds), *Les Jurisdictions Internationales: Complementarite ou Concurrence?*, Bussels: Bruylant, pp. 127–51.
Cerna, Christina M. (2006), 'Are We Headed in the Right Direction? Reflections on the New (2001) Rules of Procedure of the Inter-American Commission on Human Rights in Light of the Experience of the European System', in Anne F. Bayefsky (ed.), *Human Rights and Refugees, Internally Displaced Persons and Migrant Workers: Essays in Memory of Joan Fitzpatrick and Arthur Helton*, Leiden: Martinus-Nijhoff, pp. 387–441.
Cerna, Christina M. (2009), 'Reflections on the Normative Status of the American Declaration of the Rights and Duties of Man', *University of Pennsylvania Journal of International Law*, **30**, pp. 1211–37.
Cerna, Christina M. (2011), 'The History of the Inter-American System's Jurisprudence as Regards Situations of Armed Conflict', *Journal of Humanitarian Legal Studies*, **2**, pp. 3–52.
Cerna, Christina M. (2012), 'The Inter-American Commission on Human Rights and the Inter-American Court of Human Rights', in Chiara Giorgetti (ed.), *The Rules, Practice and Jurisprudence of International Courts and Tribunals*, Leiden: Martinus-Nijhoff, pp. 364–92.
Cerna, Christina M. (2012), 'Comparing the Performance of the Russian Federation and the United States as Regards Human Rights on the Regional and Universal Level', *Baltic Yearbook of International Law*, **12**, pp. 211–27.
Farer, Tom (1997), 'The Rise of the Inter-American Human Rights Regime: No Longer a Unicorn, Not Yet an Ox', *Human Rights Quarterly*, **19**, pp. 510–46.
Goldman, Robert (2013), 'Extraterritorial Application of the Human Rights to Life and Personal Liberty, Including Habeas Corpus, During Situations of Armed Conflict', in Robert Kolb and Gloria Gaggioli (eds), *Research Handbook on Human Rights and Humanitarian Law*, Cheltenham, UK: Edward Elgar, pp. 104–24.
LaRue, Frank (2007), 'Implementation of Decisions of the Inter-American System in Guatemala', *American University Law Review*, **56**, pp. 1459–63.
Medina, Cecilia (1990), 'The Inter-American Commission on Human Rights and the Inter-American Court of Human Rights: Reflections on a Joint Venture', *Human Rights Quarterly*, **12**, pp. 439–64.
Nicola, Fernanda (2007), 'Reparations: A Comparative Perspective', *American University Law Review*, **56**, pp. 1337–81.

Pasqualucci, Jo (1993), 'Provisional Measures in the Inter-American Human Rights System: An Innovative Development in International Law', *Vanderbilt Journal of Transnational Law*, **26**, pp. 803–63.

Pasqualucci, Jo (1996), 'Victim Reparations in the Inter-American Human Rights System: A Critical Assessment of Current Practice and Procedure', *Michigan Journal of International Law*, **18**, pp. 1–57.

Pasqualucci, Jo (2006), 'Criminal Defamation and the Evolution of the Doctrine of Freedom of Expression in International Law: Comparative Jurisprudence of the Inter-American Court of Human Rights', *Vanderbilt Journal of International Law*, **39**, pp. 379–433.

Pasqualucci, Jo (2006), 'The Evolution of International Indigenous Rights in the Inter-American Human Rights System', *Human Rights Law Review*, **6**, pp. 281–322.

Pasqualucci, Jo (2009), 'International Indigenous Land Rights: A Critique of the Jurisprudence of the Inter-American Court of Human Rights in Light of the United Nations Declaration on the Rights of Indigenous Peoples', *Wisconsin International Law Journal*, **27**, pp. 51–98.

Pinto, Monica (2008), 'National and International Courts-Deference or Disdain', *Loyola of Los Angeles International & Comparative Law Review*, **30**, pp. 247–73.

Ramirez, Sergio Garcia (Keynote Speaker) (2007), 'Reparations in the Inter American System: A Comparative Approach Conference', *American University Law Review*, **56**, pp. 1429–35.

Shelton, Dinah (1999), 'The Promise of Regional Human Rights Systems', in Stephen P. Marks and Burns H. Weston (eds), *The Future of Human Rights*, New York: Transnational Publishers, pp. 351–98.

Shelton, Dinah (2010), 'Balancing Rights and Responsibilities: Human Rights Jurisprudence on Regulating the Content of Speech', *GW Law School Public Law and Legal Theory*, Paper No. 2013–49, pp. 211–41.

Shelton, Dinah (2012), 'The Legal Status of Normative Pronouncements of Human Rights Treaty Bodies', in Holger P. Hestermeyer, Doris König, Nele Matz-Lück and Volker Röben (eds), *Coexistence, Cooperation and Solidarity: Liber Amicorum Rüdiger Wolfrum*, Vol. 1, Leiden: Martinus Nijhoff, pp. 553–75.

Tittemore, Brian (2006), 'Ending Impunity in the Americas: The Role of the Inter-American Human Rights System in Advancing Accountability for Serious Crimes under International Law', *Southwestern Journal of Law and Trade in the Americas*, **12**, pp. 429–75.

Tittemore, Brian (2006), 'Guantanamo Bay and the Precautionary Measures of the IACHR', *Human Rights Law Review*, **6**, pp. 378–402.

Africa

Heyns, Christof (2004), 'The African Regional Human Rights System: The African Charter', *Penn State Law Review*, **108**, pp. 679–702.

Ibrahim, Abadir M. (2012), 'Evaluating a Decade of the African Union's Protection of Human Rights and Democracy: A Post-Tahrir Assessment', *African Human Rights Law Journal*, **12**, pp. 30–68.

Killander, Magnus and Abebe, Adam K. (2012), 'Human Rights Developments in the African Union during 2010 and Summary 2011', *African Human Rights Law Journal*, **12**, pp. 199–222.

Matua, M. (1999), 'The African Human Rights Court: A Two Legged Stool?', *Human Rights Quarterly*, **21**, pp. 342–63.

Odinkalu, Chici Anselm (1998), 'The Individual Complaints Procedures of the African Commission on Human and Peoples' Rights: A Preliminary Assessment', *Transnational Law & Contemporary Problems*, **8**, pp. 359–405.

Onoria, H. (2003), 'The AFCHPR and the Exhaustion of Local Remedies under the African Charter', *African Human Rights Law Journal*, **3**, pp. 1–24.

Viljoen, Frans (2007), 'The African Commission: Promotional Mandate', in Frans Viljoen, *International Human Rights in Africa*, Oxford: Oxford University Press, pp. 368–414.

Southeast Asia

Cerna, Christina M. (2009), 'Introductory Note to the Terms of Reference for the Establishment of the ASEAN Intergovernmental Commission on Human Rights (AICHR)', *ILM*, **48**, pp. 1161–64.
Ginbar, Yuval (2010), 'Human Rights in ASEAN – Setting Sail or Treading Water?', *Human Rights Law Review*, **10**, pp. 504–18.
Phan, Hao Duy (2008), 'The Evolution towards an ASEAN Human Rights Body', *Asia-Pacific Journal on Human Rights and the Law*, **1**, pp. 1–12.

Bibliography of Books for Further Consultation

General

Alston, Philip and Goodman, Ryan (2013), *International Human Rights: Texts and Materials*, Oxford: OUP.
Anaya, S. James (2009), *International Human Rights and Indigenous Peoples*, Aspen (www.aspenpublishers.com). 400 pp.
Baluarte, David C. and de Vos, Christian M. (2010), *From Judgment to Justice Implementing International and Regional Human Rights Decisions*, Open Society Foundations, Open Society Justice Initiative (http://www.opensocietyfoundations.org/sites/default/files/from-judgment-to-justice-20101122.pdf). 200 pp.
Coomans, Fons and Kamminga, Menno (2004), *Extraterritorial Application of Human Rights Treaties*, Antwerp-Oxford: Intersentia. (http://www.intersentia.com).
Doswald-Beck, Louise (2011), *Human Rights in Times of Conflict and Terrorism*, Oxford: OUP.
Lessa, Francesca and Payne, Leigh A. (2012), *Amnesty in the Age of Human Rights Accountability: Comparative and International Perspectives*, Cambridge: CUP.
Mahbubani, Kishore (2013), *The Great Convergence: Asia, the West, and the Logic of One World*, New York: Public Affairs.
Orlin, Theodore, Rosas, Allan and Scheinin, Martin (eds), (2000), *The Jurisprudence of Human Rights Law: A Comparative Interpretive Approach*, New York: Syracuse University Press.
Shelton, Dinah (2005), *Remedies in International Human Rights Law* (2nd edn), Oxford: OUP.
Shelton, Dinah L. (2010), *Regional Protection of Human Rights*, Oxford: OUP.
Shelton, Dinah (2012), 'International Law and Domestic Legal Systems: Incorporation, Transformation, and Persuasion', published in Oxford Scholarship Online, January.

Europe

Blackburn, Robert and Polakiewicz, Jörg (eds) (2001), *Fundamental Rights in Europe: The European Convention on Human Rights and its Member States, 1950–2000*, Oxford: OUP.
Casadevall, Myjer, O'Boyle and Austin (eds) (2012), *Freedom of Expression: Essays in Honour of Nicolas Bratza*, Wolf Legal Publishers (www.wolfpublishers.com).
De Salvia, Michele (2003), *Compendium de la Cedh: Les principles directeurs de la jurisprudence relative a la Convention europeenne des droits de l'homme, Vol. 1: Jurisprudence 1960 a 2002*, Engel.

Dutertre, B. and van der Velde, J., *Key Case-Law Extracts: European Court of Human Rights*, Directorate of Human Rights, Council of Europe Publishing, September 1998, Reprinted February 1999, November 1999.

Goldhaber, Michael D. (2007), *A People's History of the European Court of Human Rights*, New Brunswick, NJ: Rutgers University Press.

Gomien, Donna, Harris, David John and Zwaak, Leo (eds) (1996), *Law and Practice of the European Convention on Human Rights and the European Social Charter*, Strasbourg: Council of Europe Publishing.

Harris, D.J., O'Boyle, M. and Warbrick, Colin (eds) (2009), *Law of the European Convention on Human Rights* (2nd edn), Oxford: OUP.

Huber, Denis (1995), *A Decade Which Made History: The Council of Europe 1989–1999*, Strasbourg: Council of Europe Publishing.

Janis, Mark W., Kay, Richard S. and Bradley, Anthony W. (eds) (2008), *European Human Rights Law: Texts and Materials* (3rd edn), Oxford: OUP.

Kempees, Peter (1960–98), *A Systematic Guide to the Case Law of the European Court of Human Rights*, 4 vols, Leiden: Martinus-Nijhoff.

Mowbray, Alistair (2004), *The Development of Positive Obligations under the European Convention on Human Rights by the European Court of Human Rights*, Oxford: Hart.

Pettiti, Louis-Edmond, Decaux, Emmanuel and Imbert, Pierre-Henri (eds) (1995), *La Convention Europeene Des Droits De L'homme: Commentaire article par article*, Paris: Economica.

Sikuta, Jan and Hubalkova, Eva (eds) (2007), *European Court of Human Rights: Case Law of the Grand Chamber 1998–2006*, The Hague: Asser Press.

Van Dijk, Pieter, van Hoof, Fried, van Rijn, Arjen and Zwaak, Leo (eds) (2006), *Theory and Practice of the European Convention on Human Rights* (4th edn), Antwerp-Oxford: Intersentia (http://www.intersentia.com).

The Americas

Burgogue-Larsen, Laurence and de Torres, Amaya Ubeda (2011), *The Inter-American Court of Human Rights: Case Law and Commentary*, Oxford: OUP.

Connell-Smith, Gordon (1966), *The Inter-American System*, Oxford: OUP.

Due Process of Law Foundation (2007), *Victims Unsilenced: The Inter-American Human Rights System and Transitional Justice in Latin America*, Washinton, D.C.: Due Process of Law Foundation.

Harris, David J. and Livingstone, Stephen (eds) (1998), *The Inter-American System of Human Rights*, Oxford: OUP.

Ledesma, Héctor Faúndez (2008), *The Inter-American System for the Protection of Human Rights: Institutional and Procedural Aspects* (3rd edn), San José, Costa Rica: Inter-American Institute of Human Rights.

Medina, Cecilia (1988), *The Battle for Human Rights: Gross, Systematic Violations of Human Rights and the Inter-American System*, Leiden: Martinus-Nijhoff.

Medina, Cecilia (2003), *La Convencion Americana; Teoria y Jurisprudencia*, Chile: University of Chile.

Medina, Cecilia and Rojas, Claudio Nash (2007), *Sistema Interamericano de Derechos Humanos: Introduccion a Sus Mecanismos de Proteccion*, Chile: University of Chile.

Pasqulucci, Jo M. (2013), *The Practice and Procedure of the Inter-American Court of Human Rights* (2nd edn) Cambridge: CUP.

Africa

Banda, Fareda (2005), *Women, Law and Human Rights: An African Perspective*, Oxford: Hart.

Evans, Malcolm and Murray, Rachel (eds) (2008), *The African Charter on Human and Peoples' Rights: The System in Practice 1986–2006* (2nd edn), Cambridge: CUP.

Mbaye, Keba (2002), *Les Droits de l'homme en Afrique* (2nd edn), Paris: Pedone.

Murray, Rachel (2000), *The African Commission on Human and Peoples' Rights and International Law*, Oxford: Hart.

Murray, Rachel (2004), *Human Rights in Africa: From the OAU to the African Union*, Cambridge: CUP.

Murray, Rachel (2007), *The Role of National Human Rights Institutions at the International and Regional Level: The Experience of Africa*, Oxford: Hart.

Murray, Rachel and Evans, Malcolm (2002), *The African Charter on Human and Peoples' Rights: The System at Work*, Cambridge: CUP.

Umozurike, U.O., (1997), *The African Charter on Human and Peoples' Rights*, Leiden: Brill Academic Publishers.

Southeast Asia

Hsien-Li, Tan (2011), *The Asean Intergovernmental Commission on Human Rights: Institutionalizing Human Rights in Southeast Asia*, Cambridge: CUP.

Phan, Hao Duy (2012), *A Selective Approach to Establishing a Human Rights Mechanism in Southeast Asia: The Case for a Southeast Asian Court of Human Rights*, Leiden: Martinus-Nijhoff.

Part I
Overview

[1]

Innovations in the European System of Human Rights Protection: Is Enlargement Compatible with Reinforcement?

*Peter Leuprecht**

I. THE EUROPEAN SYSTEM OF HUMAN RIGHTS PROTECTION

Although various organizations and institutions including the European Community (or European Union) and the Organization for Security and Cooperation in Europe (OSCE) nowadays deal with human rights at the European level, what is commonly referred to as the European system of human rights protection is still the system created within, and operated by, the Council of Europe.

The Council, founded in 1949, was the first European organization to be established after World War II. Its philosophical and political roots go back to the fight and resistance against Nazism and Fascism; the horrors and crimes they had brought about should not be allowed to recur. "Never again" was the motto of the pioneers of post-war European unification and of the founding fathers of the Council of Europe. They were determined to build a new, united Europe on solid foundations, on a set of strong shared values and

* Peter Leuprecht has been an official of the Council of Europe from 1961 to 1997. From 1980 to 1993, he served as Director of Human Rights; in 1993 he was elected Deputy Secretary General. He resigned from this post in 1997 because of disagreement with dilution of Council of Europe standards and values. He has taught at the Universities of Strasbourg and Nancy (France) and at the European Academy of Law in Florence (Italy). He is now Visiting Professor of Law at McGill University and at the Département des Sciences Juridiques de l'Université du Québec à Montréal, and works for the Department of Justice of Canada. He is one of four "wise persons" involved in the preparation of a European Union human rights agenda.

principles, those of pluralist democracy, the rule of law, and human rights, and the Council of Europe was to be the incarnation and the guardian of these fundamental and interconnected values and principles. Under its founding treaty, signed in London on May 5, 1949, respect for, and compliance with, these values and principles was to be both the chief condition for admission of a country to the Council and the main and lasting obligation of all its members.[1]

Over the years, the Council of Europe has set up a system of human rights protection which, in spite of certain weaknesses and shortcomings, can be regarded as the most advanced international human rights structure in the world today. Post-war Europe has gone particularly far in the internationalization of human rights. This worldwide phenomenon, inaugurated by the 1948 Universal Declaration of Human Rights[2], owes a great deal to Europe—not to Europe's virtue, but to its past failure and responsibility, to the monstrous crimes of which it was the theater under totalitarian, Nazi and Fascist regimes, to this explosion of barbarism at the very heart of the European continent, which believed itself so civilized. Bitter experience impressed upon Europeans that the state can fail in its role as the custodian of human rights and become an instrument of oppression, that it can be not only the protector, but also the gravedigger of human rights. In the interest of the defense of these rights, it was felt necessary to give independent international bodies a watching brief over state behavior.

A. The European Convention on Human Rights

The first expression of the new Europe's commitment to the international protection of human rights was the European Convention on Human Rights (ECHR)[3], signed in Rome on November 4, 1950. For the then twelve signatory governments[4], it represented "the first steps for the collective enforcement of

1. *See* Statute of the Council of Europe, May 5, 1949, arts. 1, 3, Europ. T.S. No. 1, *reprinted in* 1 INTERNATIONAL LAW & WORLD ORDER: BASIC DOCUMENTS I.B.4 (Burns H. Weston ed., 5 vols., 1994—) [hereinafter 1 Weston].

2. *See* Universal Declaration of Human Rights, G.A. Res. 217A, U.N. GAOR, 3rd Sess., pt. 1, Resolutions, at 71, U.N. Doc. A/810 (1948) [hereinafter Universal Declaration], *reprinted in* 3 INTERNATIONAL LAW & WORLD ORDER: BASIC DOCUMENTS III.A.1 (Burns H. Weston ed., 5 vols., 1994—) [hereinafter 3 Weston].

3. *See* Convention for the Protection of Human Rights and Fundamental Freedoms, Nov. 4, 1950, Europ. T.S. No. 5 (entered into force Sept. 3, 1953) [hereinafter ECHR], *reprinted in* 3 Weston, *supra* note 2, at III.B.2.

4. *See* Statute of the Council of Europe, *supra* note 1, at Chart of Signatures and Ratifications (showing the original signatories were Belgium, Denmark, France, Germany, Iceland, Ireland, Italy, Luxembourg, Netherlands, Norway, Turkey, United Kingdom).

certain of the rights stated in the Universal Declaration."[5] The ECHR was indeed the first international treaty to translate principles proclaimed in the Universal Declaration into legally binding obligations.

The ECHR, though a regional treaty, is firmly based on the principle of the universality of human rights; it does not guarantee the rights of Europeans, but sets up a European regional system for the protection of universal human rights. In accordance with Article 1, "the High Contracting Parties shall secure to everyone within their jurisdiction the rights and freedoms" enshrined in the Convention. It is significant that a considerable number of individual complaints emanate from persons who are not nationals of the contracting states and who seek, often successfully, the protection of the ECHR and its control machinery.[6]

The wording of the Preamble to the ECHR shows, however, that the ECHR was not seen by its authors to be the last word in the field of human rights protection; a kind of final codification of those rights. The ECHR's catalogue of rights is an open one which, over the years, has been enriched by several additional protocols.[7] In this area, the Council of Europe's approach has been, and must remain, dynamic, in line with Article 1 of its Statute, which refers to the "maintenance and further realization of human rights and fundamental freedoms."[8]

The ECHR guarantees mainly, but not exclusively, civil and political rights. In its famous *Airey* judgment, the European Court of Human Rights stated that there is no "watertight division" separating Convention rights from economic and social rights.[9]

---

5. ECHR, *supra* note 3, at pmbl., para. 5.

6. *See* the statistics published by the European Commission and Court of Human Rights which are available on the web-sites of the Commission <http://www.dhcommhr.coe.fr> and of the Court <http://www.dhcour.coe.fr>.

7. A number of Protocols to the ECHR guarantee additional rights. *See* Protocol No. 1 to the Convention for the Protection of Human Rights and Fundamental Freedoms, Securing Certain Rights and Freedoms Other Than Those Already Included in the Convention, Mar. 20, 1952, Europ. T.S. No. 9 [hereinafter Protocol No. 1], *reprinted in* 3 Weston, *supra* note 2, at III.B.3.; Protocol No. 4 to the European Convention for the Protection of Human Rights and Fundamental Freedoms, Securing Certain Rights and Freedoms Other Than Those Already Included in the Convention and in the First Protocol Thereto, Sept. 16, 1963, Europ. T.S. No. 46 [hereinafter Protocol No. 4], *reprinted in* 3 Weston, *supra* note 2, at III.B.7.; Protocol No. 6 to the European Convention for the Protection of Human Rights and Fundamental Freedoms Concerning the Abolition of the Death Penalty, Apr. 28, 1983, Europ. T.S. No. 114 [hereinafter Protocol No. 6], *reprinted in* 3 Weston, *supra* note 2, at III.B.9.; Protocol No. 7 to the European Convention for the Protection of Human Rights and Fundamental Freedoms, Nov. 22, 1984, Europ. T.S. No. 117 [hereinafter Protocol No. 7], *reprinted in* 3 Weston, *supra* note 2, at III.B.10.

8. Statute of the Council of Europe, *supra* note 1, art. 1(b).

9. Airey v. Ireland, 2 Eur. Ct. H.R. (ser. A) at 316 (A32, para. 26) (1979), *reprinted in* 1 Eur. H.R. Rep. 305.

The importance of the ECHR lies not only in the breadth of the rights it covers, but also, and particularly, in the supranational control machinery it has set up to investigate and remedy alleged violations and ensure compliance with the obligations it imposes. It has been kept under constant review, with the aim of enhancing the protection it affords, by improving the existing procedures.

The Convention and its machinery are, of course, not designed to take the place of national systems for the protection of human rights. Their purpose is, rather, to provide a subsidiary international guarantee, supplementing the right of redress in individual states. Since the ECHR has been incorporated in the domestic law of nearly all of its contracting states, any person can, in principle, invoke its provisions directly in applying or appealing to a national court or authority in any of those states.

In the over forty years since 1953 when it came into force, the ECHR has, in spite of certain weaknesses, matured into probably the strongest and most effective human rights treaty there is today. For many years, much of its effectiveness stemmed from the political determination of its states parties, their relative homogeneity and their common system of values.

The main criterion for measuring the success of a human rights system is whether it effectively helps the people. The ECHR system has certainly done so. It has made it possible not only to put a great number of individual situations straight, but to remedy general situations, laws, and practices which were not in line with the requirements of the Convention. It prevents and remedies human rights violations. It is also revealing to see who turns to the Strasbourg institutions; many of the applicants are poor, destitute, exposed, and vulnerable, and therefore in greatest need of protection of their fundamental rights. The ECHR system is not a luxury for rich people. There are no economic or financial obstacles to access to the Strasbourg bodies; a system of legal aid is provided by the budget of the Council of Europe.

As the European Commission and Court of Human Rights have stated in no uncertain terms, the ECHR has become a constitutional instrument of European public order.[10] In the words of its late President, Rolv Ryssdall, the Court has become "a quasi-constitutional court for the whole of Europe."[11] The Strasbourg case law has had far-reaching and highly positive effects on the legal systems and the social reality in the contracting states. Both the Court and the Commission command a high degree of authority. Although it is in the first place the duty of domestic courts and authorities to apply the ECHR, the Commission and Court have become "'masters' of their treaty"[12]

10. *See* Loizidou v. Turkey, 20 Eur. Ct. H.R. (ser. A) at 134 (1995) (preliminary objections), *reprinted in* 20 Eur. H.R. Rep. 99.

11. Rolv Ryssdall, *The Coming of Age of the European Convention on Human Rights*, 1 EUR. HUM. RTS. L. REV. 22 (1996).

12. Bruno Simma, *From Bilateralism to Community Interest in International Law*, 250 RECUEIL

and are recognized as such. A fruitful dialogue has developed between the Strasbourg institutions and domestic courts whose respective case law mutually support and enrich each other.

Still, though the ECHR "has developed into a regional human rights protection system of unparalleled effectiveness,"[13] there is no room for self-satisfaction or self-congratulation which, together with incantation, hamper rather than advance the cause of human rights. The weaknesses of the ECHR system must not be overlooked. The coming into force of Protocol No. 11 will eliminate two of the most glaring weaknesses—the present length and complexity of proceedings and the insufficiently independent and judicial character of the system.[14] Other weaknesses will not only remain, but may be aggravated, and have an increasingly debilitating effect in the new political environment in which the system will have to operate in the years to come. Four of these may be mentioned:

1) The Convention system seems relatively powerless to address and remedy serious and systematic violations of human rights, a defect which is in striking contrast to the, at times, almost minute attention the Convention bodies devote to comparatively minor matters or "legal niceties." This may be seen as part of a wider phenomenon: the inability of international human rights bodies to react speedily and effectively to urgent situations and to gross, systematic human rights violations, including torture, disappearances, summary executions, and arbitrary arrests on a large scale.

2) The Convention bodies do not, unfortunately, have the power to order binding interim measures to the states parties.[15]

DES COURS 373 (Collected Courses of the Hague Academy of Int'l. Law 1994).

13. Ryssdall, *supra* note 11, at 18.

14. *See* Protocol No. 11 to the European Convention for the Protection of Human Rights and Fundamental Freedoms, Restructuring the Control Machinery Established Thereby, May 11, 1994, Europ. T.S. No. 155 [hereinafter Protocol No. 11], *reprinted in* 3 Weston, *supra* note 2, at III.B.16a.

15. Compare the frequently applied Rule 36 of the Rules of Procedure of the European Commission of Human Rights which reads as follows: 'The Commission, or when it is not in session, the President may indicate to the parties any interim measure the adoption of which seems desirable in the interest of the parties or the proper conduct of the proceedings before it.' R. P. EUR. COMM'N H.R. 36, *reprinted in* LUKE CLEMENTS, EUROPEAN HUMAN RIGHTS: TAKING A CASE UNDER THE CONVENTION 244 (1994). For parallel provisions, see Rule 36 of the Rules of Court 'A' and Rule 38 of the Rules of Court 'B' of the European Court of Human Rights. R. P. EUR. CT. H.R. (ser. A) 36; R. P. EUR. CT. H.R. (ser. B) 38, *reprinted in* LUKE CLEMENTS, EUROPEAN HUMAN RIGHTS: TAKING A CASE UNDER THE CONVENTION 274, 76 (1994). See also the judgment of the European Court of Human Rights in Cruz Varas v. Sweden, 201 Eur. Ct. H.R. (ser. A) (1991), *reprinted in* 14 EUR. HUM. RTS. REP. 1 (1992).

3) It is comparatively easy for the state parties to derogate from the Convention under Article 15 (in time of war or other public emergency) and to maintain these derogations for lengthy periods, until the Convention bodies may have a chance to decide whether they are compatible with the Convention's requirements.

4) The scope of the rights protected is not the same in all the state parties. This is due, first, to the fact that the protocols guaranteeing additional rights are far from having been ratified by all parties to the Convention and, second, to the large number of reservations made by the contracting states.

These shortcomings weaken the "collective enforcement" of human rights called for in the Preamble to the Convention.

B. The European Social Charter

The founders of the Council of Europe had a comprehensive vision of human rights, including both civil and political, and economic, social, and cultural rights. The Council and its member states profess the indivisibility of human rights together with the principle of universality, both of which were strongly reaffirmed by the Vienna Summit Meeting of the Heads of State and Government of Council of Europe member states in October 1993.[16] The truth is, however, that economic, social and cultural rights do not enjoy a similar degree of protection at the European level as civil and political rights. The European Social Charter[17] was not concluded and signed until 1961. It was intended as the ECHR's counterpart; in many respects, however, it actually has been, and still is, its poor relation. In spite of some positive developments in recent years, it must still be said that, to borrow the words of one of the fathers of the ECHR, Pierre-Henri Teitgen, Europe has made far less progress towards "social democracy" than towards "political democracy."[18]

II. INNOVATIONS IN THE EUROPEAN HUMAN RIGHTS SYSTEM

In the last fifteen years, a considerable number of innovations have been introduced into the European human rights system. Some of these predate the enlargement of the Council of Europe towards the East, made possible by

---

16. Vienna Declaration of October 9, 1993, para. 2, [hereinafter Vienna Declaration], *reprinted in* 14 HUM. RTS. L.J. 373 (1993).

17. *See* European Social Charter, Oct. 18, 1961, Europ. T.S. No. 35, *reprinted in* 3 Weston, *supra* note 2, at III.B.4.

18. CONSULT. ASS. DEB. 1st Sess. 210–13 (Aug. 19, 1949).

the collapse of the communist regimes in Central and Eastern Europe. Some have been made even more necessary and urgent or have been provoked or stimulated by this enlargement.

A. The European Convention on Human Rights

Quite spectacular developments have taken place with regard to the ECHR. There has been a considerable effort to extend the scope of rights protected. Protocol No. 6 concerning the abolition of the death penalty[19] was adopted and signed in 1983; this treaty of fundamental importance reflects the evolution of European thinking away from capital punishment.[20] Protocol No. 7,[21] adopted and signed in 1984, guarantees some additional rights; the basic idea was to catch up with the International Covenant on Civil and Political Rights which enshrines certain rights not provided for by the ECHR. Renewed efforts are under way to broaden the scope of the non-discrimination clause found in Article 14 of the ECHR through yet another additional protocol to the Convention.

In addition, the control machinery of the ECHR has been subjected to a radical overhaul, made necessary by the ever-growing number of cases brought before the Strasbourg bodies,[22] their increasing complexity and the rapid expansion of the Council of Europe since 1990. Over the years, the ECHR's supervisory machinery, drawn up for ten or twelve member states, has been running into growing difficulties; it now has to work for forty states with a total population of 800 million people. In the absence of drastic reform, it thus ran a serious risk of becoming a victim of its own success and of collapsing under its own weight.

This reform is enshrined in Protocol No. 11[23] and addresses two of the glaring weaknesses of the original system already mentioned: the length[24]

---

19. *See* Protocol No. 6, *supra* note 7.

20. In the Final Declaration of their Second Summit (Strasbourg, Oct. 10-11, 1997), the Heads of State and Government of the Council of Europe "call[ed] for the universal abolition of the death penalty and insist[ed] on the maintenance, in the meantime, of existing moratoria on executions in Europe." The full text of the proceedings of the Summit and of the Final Declaration and Action Plan adopted by it is available on the Council of Europe's web-site. *See Council of Europe* (visited Oct. 20, 1998) <http://www.coe.fr>.

21. *See* Protocol No. 7, *supra* note 7.

22. Compare the statistics referred to *supra* note 6.

23. *See* Protocol No. 11, *supra* note 14. For an excellent description of the negotiating process and the substance of the Protocol, see generally Andrew Drzemczewski, *A Major Overhaul of the European Human Rights Convention Control Mechanism: Protocol No. 11*, *in* COLLECTED COURSES OF THE ACADEMY OF EUROPEAN LAW 121-244 (vol. VI, bk. 2, 1995).

24. A plaintiff is first required to exhaust domestic remedies. *See* ECHR, *supra* note 3, art. 26. After this potentially lengthy process, it takes on average an additional five to six years for a case to wind its way through the Commission and Court.

and complexity of proceedings, and the insufficiently judicial and independent character of the control machinery. The latter weakness concerns the decision-making power of the Committee of Ministers, a political body, under Article 32 ECHR in cases not referred to the Court, one of the most striking anomalies in the system.

Although the fruit of a difficult political compromise, Protocol No. 11 does mark considerable progress. Its coming into force should strengthen the independent judicial character of the Convention's control machinery. On November 1, 1998, a new single, permanent European Court of Human Rights will come into operation. Its judges will work full-time, proceedings will be streamlined, and the present overlapping of work between the Commission and the Court will be avoided. Additionally, marking a very important step forward, the right of individual petition will be mandatory and the Court will have jurisdiction in all cases, including inter-state cases. The Committee of Ministers will no longer be called upon to decide human rights cases under Article 32 ECHR.

B. The European Social Charter

As far as economic and social rights are concerned, Europe is confronted with two conflicting tendencies. On the one hand, as in most other parts of the world, the pervasive pan-economic ideology is having powerful negative effects regarding human rights.[25] It leads to a singularly constricted view of those rights and indeed of the human being, debased to an economic factor (or, a bit more optimistically, economic actor). In particular, the social and cultural dimension of human rights is being gradually eroded. In the name of fashionable slogans such as flexibility and deregulation, laws, regulations, and rights, particularly social rights, are challenged; they are, it is argued, obstacles and handicaps that stand in the way of a modern labor market, capable of responding to the increasingly competitive world market. On the other hand, there is the pressure of real life: the increase of poverty, even in the more prosperous countries of Europe; the growing social exclusion; and, in most of the post-communist countries of Central and Eastern Europe, the unacceptably high social cost of transition, the dramatic deterioration of the state of health of the populations concerned, and the spectacular decline of the average life expectancy. These alarming phenomena have led to a comeback of social awareness and to a rehabilitation of social rights, clearly demonstrated by the second Council of Europe summit held in Strasbourg in October 1997, at which the Heads of State and Government of member states committed themselves to "promote social standards as embodied in the Social

---

25. *See* Peter Leuprecht, *General Course: Human Rights in the New Europe*, *in* COLLECTED COURSES OF THE ACADEMY OF EUROPEAN LAW 135, 184-189 (vol. V, bk. 2, 1994).

Charter and in other Council of Europe instruments" and called for "the widest possible adherence to these instruments."[26]

In spite of a largely hostile ideological and political environment, considerable efforts have been made since the Ministerial Conference on Human Rights held in Rome in November 1990[27] to give the European Social Charter a fresh impetus. These have led to the adoption of an amending Protocol to improve the Charter's control machinery,[28] an additional Protocol providing for collective complaints[29] and to the revised version of the Charter.[30] The latter strengthens, *inter alia,* the protection of children and young persons, both in employment[31] and in general.[32] It guarantees the right to free primary and secondary education[33] and contains a very important provision concerning special protection for persons who live, or risk living, in social exclusion or poverty.[34]

Additionally, a number of reforms have been carried out to enhance the effectiveness of the Charter's control machinery, which is based on periodic reports by the contracting states. Positive results have been obtained through the anticipated implementation of most provisions of the amending Protocol which is not formally in force. Since 1993, the Committee of Ministers has at last brought itself to adopting individual recommendations addressed to specific contracting states. The entry into force on July 1, 1998, of the Protocol providing for a system of collective complaints is expected to reinforce the control mechanism further through increased participation on the part of management and labor and NGOs. In spite of these positive developments, however, it must be admitted that the Charter's supervisory machinery remains considerably less stringent and effective than that of the ECHR.

---

26. *Council of Europe, supra* note 20.

27. *See 40 Years of Human Rights Protection by the Council of Europe: Achievements, Prospects and Pan-European Vocation and 40th Anniversary of the Signing of the European Convention of Human Rights,* Celebration, Palazzo Barberini, Rome November 5, 1990 (Council of Europe 1994).

28. *See* Protocol Amending the European Social Charter, Oct. 21, 1991, Europ. T.S. No. 142 (not in force as of Apr. 1, 1998), *reprinted in* 3 Weston, *supra* note 2, at III.B.15.

29. *See* Additional Protocol to the European Social Charter Providing for a System of Collective Complaints, Nov. 9, 1995, Europ. T.S. No. 158 [hereinafter Additional Protocol to the European Social Charter], *reprinted in* 3 Weston, *supra* note 2, at III.B.16c.

30. *See* Revised European Social Charter, May 3, 1996, Europ. T.S. No. 163 (not in force as of Apr. 1, 1998) [hereinafter Revised European Social Charter], *reprinted in* 3 Weston, *supra* note 2, at III.B.16d.

31. *See id.* art. 7, paras. 2, 4, 7.

32. *See id.* art. 17.

33. *See id.* art. 17, para. 2.

34. *See id.* art. 30; *see also id.* art. 31 (the right to housing).

C. The European Convention for the Prevention of Torture and Inhuman or Degrading Treatment or Punishment

This Convention[35] can be regarded as one of the most positive innovations in the field of international human rights protection. Its originality lies in the use of inspection as a means of preventing human rights violations, and its non-judicial, preventive machinery complements the ECHR's judicial system both usefully and effectively.

The Convention has set up a very far-reaching monitoring mechanism, the European Committee for the Prevention of Torture and Inhuman or Degrading Treatment or Punishment (CPT). Composed of independent and impartial personalities, the CPT is authorized to visit any place where persons are deprived of their liberty. The CPT has extensive powers. It visits not only prisons and police establishments, but also psychiatric institutions, detention areas in military barracks, holding centers for foreigners, correctional establishments for young persons, and the like. Two kinds of visits are provided for by the Convention: periodic and ad hoc. Periodic visits are carried out to all parties to the Convention on a regular basis; ad hoc visits, targeted at particular situations or places of detention, are conducted where they appear to the CPT "to be required in the circumstances." To date, the CPT has carried out some fifty periodic and over twenty ad hoc visits to over thirty Council of Europe member states.[36]

The effectiveness of the CPT's work is enhanced by two fundamental and inter-related principles: cooperation and confidentiality. Its primary objective is not to publicly criticize or condemn states, but to assist them in finding ways to eradicate torture and ill-treatment, and its visits and subsequent reports are surrounded by confidentiality. The Convention does, however, provide for two forms of publicity.

First, under Article 11(2), a report may be published, with any comments by the state concerned, at that state's request; in practice, reports are, rather, published with the state's agreement. Publication has in fact become the rule and non-publication the exception, with well over forty CPT visit reports having been made public. As a result of the strength of precedents, governments are now under considerable pressure to agree to publication.

Second, the Convention provides for another form of publicity that is more in the nature of a sanction. In accordance with Article 10 (2), the CPT may decide to make a public statement "if the Party fails to co-operate or refuses to improve the situation in the light of the Committee's

---

35. *See* European Convention for the Prevention of Torture and Inhuman or Degrading Treatment or Punishment, Nov. 26, 1987, Europ. T.S. No. 126, *reprinted in* 3 Weston, *supra* note 2, at III.K.4.

36. *See generally, European Committee for the Prevention of Torture and Inhuman or Degrading Treatment or Punishment* (visited Oct. 22, 1998) <http://www.cpt.coe.fr> (providing information on the Committee's activities as well as its published reports).

recommendations." So far, two such public statements have been made regarding the practice of torture and other forms of severe ill-treatment in Turkey.[37]

The Convention for the Prevention of Torture has considerably enriched and completed the European system of human rights protection. At the same time, the CPT's findings have confirmed that torture and inhuman or degrading treatment have not been eradicated in Council of Europe member states, that people in police custody run a serious risk of ill-treatment, and that there remains much room for improvement in conditions of detention.

D. Minority Rights

Protecting minority rights has become one of the most serious and pressing issues in today's Europe and within the enlarged Council of Europe. The Council seeks to contribute to the peaceful solution of these problems by the elaboration and implementation of legal instruments, by cooperation and assistance programs and by a program of "confidence-building measures in civil society."

In 1994, the Framework Convention for the Protection of National Minorities was adopted.[38] Entered into force on February 1, 1998, it is the first ever legally binding multilateral instrument devoted to the protection of national minorities in general. Article 1 stipulates that "the protection of national minorities and of the rights and freedoms of persons belonging to those minorities forms an integral part of the international protection of human rights . . . ." The Convention sets out principles to be respected as well as goals to be achieved by the contracting parties to ensure the protection of persons belonging to national minorities.

The Framework Convention also establishes a system of monitoring based on reports from the contracting states. These reports will be examined first by an Advisory Committee of independent experts. The Advisory Committee is to prepare an opinion for transmittal to the Committee of Ministers which, in turn, will adopt final decisions ("conclusions") and, where appropriate, recommendations.

---

37. *Id.* (statements issued on December 15, 1992 and December 6, 1996).

38. *See* Framework Convention for the Protection of National Minorities, Feb. 1, 1995, Europ. T.S. No. 157, *reprinted in* 3 Weston, *supra* note 2, at III.I.7.

The purpose of the European Charter for Regional or Minority Languages,[39] which was adopted in 1992 and entered into force on March 1, 1998, is to protect and promote the various regional and minority languages spoken in different European countries. It thus is contributing to the preservation of Europe's cultural wealth.

Since both of these important and complementary legal instruments entered into force very recently, it is too early to assess their practical effectiveness. It is, however, to be hoped that they will provide a strong legal protection for minorities and regional and minority languages.

Some of the Council of Europe's cooperation and assistance programs for Central and East European countries as well as certain joint programs, co-financed by the Council of Europe and the European Commission's Phare and Tacis programs, relate to the protection of minorities.[40] The Council's program of "confidence-building measures in civil society" aims, through concrete projects at the grass roots level, at defusing tensions and promoting a climate of mutual understanding, tolerance, and respect for different cultures.

Aware of the fact that human dignity and human rights are not only threatened by state power, but also increasingly by non-state actors and phenomena, the Council of Europe has recently become involved in new areas, two of which are mentioned briefly below.

E. Combating Racism, Xenophobia, Anti-Semitism and Intolerance

In response to the alarming resurgence of racism, xenophobia, anti-semitism and other forms of intolerance, all of which are an affront to human rights and human dignity, the October 1993 Vienna Summit of Heads of State and Government of the Council of Europe member states adopted a Declaration and Plan of Action to combat these phenomena.[41] One element of this Plan was the establishment of a new body, the European Commission against Racism and Intolerance (ECRI), which issues country-specific reports and addresses general policy recommendations to the member governments. Reports on all forty member states of the Council of Europe will be nearing completion by the end of 1998. Those published so far identify problems such as intolerance towards foreigners, ill-treatment of members of minority groups by police, and discrimination in the workplace; they analyze the

39. *See* European Charter for Regional or Minority Languages, Nov. 5, 1992, Europ. T.S. No. 148.

40. *See 11th Quadripartile Mtg. Council of Europe/European Union, Apr. 1998* (visited Oct. 24, 1998) <http:www.coe.fr/cp/98/226a(98).htm> (discussing Phare which is a program of the European Commission for the post-communist countries of Central and Eastern Europe and Tacis, a Commission program for the countries of the former Soviet-Union).

41. *See* Vienna Declaration, *supra* note 16.

causes of these problems and offer advice and solutions. In parallel with its country-by-country studies, ECRI has thus far issued four general policy recommendations to governments, which include guidelines for the development of comprehensive national policies to prevent racism and discrimination and to combat intolerance against Roma/Gypsies.[42]

F. Bioethics

The Convention for the Protection of Human Rights and Dignity of the Human Being with Regard to the Application of Biology and Medicine: Convention on Human Rights and Biomedicine,[43] another innovation, was signed in Oviedo, Spain, on April 4, 1997. It is to be completed by a series of additional protocols dealing with specific issues. The first of these concerns the prohibition of cloning human beings,[44] which was elaborated following a decision of the October 1997 Strasbourg Summit. The Convention is the first binding legal instrument ever drafted on an international scale with a view to safeguarding human dignity and fundamental rights against any improper applications of medicine and biology. It exerts an influence far beyond Europe's boundaries.

III. THE COUNCIL OF EUROPE'S ENLARGEMENT: OPPORTUNITIES AND THREATS

A. 1989 - An Historical Turning Point and its Consequences

Europe and the world have undergone dramatic changes in the last few years. Human rights have been a decisive factor in those changes, but have also been, and will continue to be, affected by them. We may still be too close to the event or too short-sighted to measure the full significance of what occurred in 1989, but it certainly is no exaggeration to say that, with the fall of communism and the ending of the cold war, 1989 marked an historical turning point. Vaclav Havel, whose personal itinerary from dissident to President of the Czech Republic symbolizes the magnitude of the change, has expressed the view that the collapse of the communist empire is an event

---

42. *See generally European Commission against Racism and Intolerance* (visited Oct. 22, 1998) <http://www.ecri.coe.fr>.

43. *See* European Convention for the Protection of Human Rights and Dignity of the Human Being with Regard to the Application of Biology and Medicine: Convention on Human Rights and Biomedicine, Apr. 4, 1997, Europ. T.S. No. 164 (not in force as of Apr. 1, 1998), *reprinted in* 3 Weston, *supra* note 2, at III.K.6.

44. *See* Additional Protocol to the European Convention for the Protection of Human Rights and Dignity with Regard to the Application of Biology and Medicine on the Prohibition of Cloning Human Beings, Sept. 22-26, 1997, Europ. T.S. No. 168 (not in force as of Apr. 1, 1998).

comparable in scale to the fall of the Roman empire. However, this historic transformation is not, as some people have argued, the "end of history" or the "final victory" of the "Western system," liberalism, capitalism, or whatever. Talking about the end of history and final victories reveals an unhistorical or anti-historical way of looking at the world.

From a value–oriented perspective, the 1989 upheavals in Central and Eastern Europe seem to have signified a decisive comeback of the free and responsible human being, belonging to a democratic society and possessed of inalienable rights and dignity, a stinging rejoinder to those who, in East and West alike, in the name of different totalitarian doctrines, had celebrated the death of the individual and human rights. The aspiration to pluralist democracy, the rule of law, justice, freedom, and human rights made powerful, surging headway in Central and Eastern Europe and swept away old totalitarian regimes. But the situation of post-1989 Europe gives rise to fear as well as hope; this is a period not only of tremendous opportunity, but also of formidable threat and challenge. Europe now has a historic opportunity to overcome its anti-cultural and anti-historical division and to reconcile its geography with its history.

As far as the Council of Europe is concerned, Sir Winston Churchill's vision of the 1940's, according to which the Council should one day embrace all the nations of Europe, is becoming a reality. The Council is increasingly assuming the pan-European dimension that was originally intended for it, but for forty years prevented by Europe's post-World War II ideological division; it now has the chance to promote its basic values and principles in the "other Europe" which, until recently, had been deprived of their enjoyment.

Since 1989, the Council of Europe has undergone spectacular enlargement. A reunited Germany is part of the organization, whose membership has soared from twenty-three states in 1989 to forty as of this writing. Sixteen new members from the former Soviet bloc have joined the Council, including Russia, and others are knocking at its door. One of the questions now is where Europe ends. This enlargement reflects, of course, a highly positive development and remarkable progress for the cause which is the Council's *raison d'être*. At the same time, it brings with it new challenges. The Council's role is no longer limited to the defense of pluralist democracy, the rule of law, and human rights. Its new task is to play an active role in "democracy-building" in the post-communist countries, and to this end important programs have been created and implemented, some of which are conducted jointly with the European Commission.

In any event, the experience of the last few years proves that the transition from totalitarian to democratic societies is an extremely difficult and demanding process. History shows that a country can rapidly slide from democracy into totalitarianism. Going the opposite way, as Karl Popper rightly recalled in 1990,[45] seems much more difficult and requires an enormous effort. Some of the countries concerned, especially Hungary, the Czech Republic, Poland and Slovenia, have managed this difficult transition remarkably well and the Council of Europe has undoubtedly made an important contribution to this development. Other countries, particularly those of the former Soviet Union, still have a long way to go on the road to democracy, the rule of law, and respect for human rights.

B. Enlargement without Dilution?

The Council of Europe's Statute lays down precise and strict conditions for the admission of members.[46] At the 1993 Vienna Summit, the Heads of State and Government, after having affirmed that the Council is "the pre-eminent European political institution capable of welcoming, on an equal footing and in permanent structures, the democracies of Europe freed from communist oppression," elaborated on the statutory requirements for accession to the Council:

> Such accession presupposes that the applicant country has brought its institutions and legal system into line with the basic principles of democracy, the rule of law and respect for human rights. The people's representatives must have been chosen by means of free and fair elections based on universal suffrage. Guaranteed freedom of expression and notably of the media, protection of national minorities and observance of the principles of international law must remain, in our view, decisive criteria for assessing any applications for membership. An undertaking to sign the European Convention on Human Rights and accept the Convention's supervisory machinery in its entirety within a short period is also fundamental. We are resolved to ensure full compliance with the commitments accepted by all member states within the Council of Europe.[47]

The full acceptance of the ECHR has become a political condition for admission to the Council. The practice is that new members sign the ECHR on the day they formally join the organization and then proceed rapidly to ratify it. All forty member states of the Council are now parties to the ECHR.[48]

---

45. Interview published in MOSCOW NEWS WEEKLY No. 46, 1990.

46. *See* Statute of the Council of Europe, *supra* note 1, arts. 3, 4.

47. Vienna Declaration, *supra* note 16.

48. These forty states are: Albania, Andorra, Austria, Belgium, Bulgaria, Croatia, Cyprus, Czech Republic, Denmark, Estonia, Finland, France, Germany, Greece, Hungary, Iceland, Ireland, Italy, Latvia, Liechtenstein, Lithuania, Luxembourg, Malta, Moldova, Netherlands, Norway,

Under Article 4 of the Statute of the Council of Europe, the Committee of Ministers is empowered to invite "any European state which is deemed to be able and willing to fulfill the provisions of Article 3" to join the Council.[49] Before doing so, however, it must consult the Parliamentary Assembly, and while the power of decision lies with the Committee of Ministers, it is politically unthinkable that it would proceed without the Assembly's approval. In fact, the Assembly and its committees and rapporteurs play the main role in scrutinizing applications for membership. In addition, it has become the Assembly's practice to involve "eminent lawyers" in the examination of applications for membership. These "eminent lawyers" are members of the European Commission and Court of Human Rights, acting in a personal capacity.

In the time between a country's applying for membership and actually joining the Council of Europe, there is a "give and take" period of negotiation with the Assembly's rapporteurs and committees, which may last several years. Experience has shown that it is at the pre-accession stage that the Council's representatives have the most leverage and can press for the reforms needed to bring the applicant country into line with the Council's standards.

Strictly speaking, admission to the Council implies that its supreme political bodies, the Parliamentary Assembly and the Committee of Ministers, consider the applicant country "willing and able" to comply with the Council's basic standards and the essential requirements of pluralist democracy, the rule of law, and respect for human rights. The idea implied in both Article 4 of the Council's Statute and in the passage of the Vienna Declaration quoted above is that a country must have put its house in order *before* being admitted to the Council.[50] In reality, of course, transition from a totalitarian to a democratic regime is a long and arduous undertaking; pluralist democracy, the rule of law, and respect for human rights are not achieved overnight. It therefore may be difficult to judge whether the process of transition is sufficiently advanced and whether and when admission to the Council can be justified. This said, intellectual honesty requires acknowledging that some of the countries admitted in recent years clearly did not comply with the statutory requirements at the time of accession. This is demonstrated by the fact that, to be admitted, they had to undertake specific

---

Poland, Portugal, Romania, Russia, San Marino, Slovakia, Slovenia, Spain, Sweden, Switzerland, the "former Yugoslav Republick of Macedonia," Turkey, Ukraine, United Kingdom. *See* 3 Weston, *supra* note 2, app. I, at 5.

49. Statute of the Council of Europe, *supra* note 1, art. 4. Article 3 of the Statute stipulates: "Every Member of the Council of Europe must accept the principles of the rule of law and of the enjoyment by all persons within its jurisdiction of human rights and fundamental freedoms, and collaborate sincerely and effectively in the realisation of the aim of the Council...." *Id.* art. 3.

50. *Compare* Statute of the Council of Europe, *supra* note 1, art. 4, *with* Vienna Declaration, *supra* note 16.

and, in certain cases, numerous and far-reaching commitments,[51] referred to explicitly in the Assembly's Opinions on the accession of new members, and often referred to by the Committee of Ministers in its Resolutions inviting states to join the Council. It is not without significance that, in its Opinion on Russia's request for membership,[52] the Parliamentary Assembly, while referring to Article 4 of the Statute, actually departs from its wording by using the future tense: "the Assembly believes that Russia—in the sense of Article 4 of the Statute—is clearly willing and *will* be able in the near future to fulfill the provisions for membership . . . ."

It thus is indisputable that the Council of Europe has lowered its standards for admission in recent years. This critical development probably began with the accession of Romania in October 1993, which at the time was far from fulfilling the statutory conditions (although it must be admitted that, since then, the situation in Romania has improved considerably). After the adhesion of Romania, there developed a kind of "domino effect:" following the admission of country X, it was argued that, although country Y did not comply with the statutory requirements, the situation in country Y was not really worse than in country X and that therefore, as a matter of fairness and justice, country Y should be admitted also. The two most recent admissions are telling examples of the opportunistic and unprincipled "Realpolitik" pursued by the political bodies of the Council of Europe

The Russian Federation formally applied for membership in the Council on May 7, 1992. The competent Committees of the Parliamentary Assembly gave serious consideration to the application. "Eminent lawyers" produced a detailed "Report on the conformity of the legal order of the Russian Federation with Council of Europe standards"[53] with very clear conclusions. The report said that Russia was on the road to democracy, but that it still had a long way to go, that there was no rule of law there, and that, despite considerable progress, Russia did not (yet) comply with the principle "of the enjoyment by all persons within its jurisdiction of human rights and fundamental freedoms." The overall conclusion of the "eminent lawyers" was that Russia's legal order did not, for the time being, comply with the norms of the Council of Europe as provided for by the Statute and developed by the organs of the ECHR.

On February 2, 1995, the Parliamentary Assembly, referring to the conflict in Chechnya, condemned "the indiscriminate and disproportionate use of force by the Russian military, in particular against the civil population,

51. See, for example, the commitments referred to in Parliamentary Assembly Opinions No. 175 (1993) on the application by Slovakia for membership of the Council of Europe, No. 176 (1993) on Romania and No. 190 (1995) on Ukraine.

52. *See* Opinion No. 193 (1996).

53. *Report Prepared by MM. Bernhardt, Trechsel, Weitzel and Ermacora, Oct. 1994*, Council of Europe Doc. AS/Bur/Russia (Oct. 7, 1994).

which is in violation of the 1949 Geneva Conventions and their 1977 Second Protocol as well as of the OSCE Code of Conduct on Politico-Military Aspects of Security, accepted by Russia as recently as December 1994."[54] The Assembly stated that "these actions also constitute a grave violation of the Council of Europe's most elementary human rights principles, which Russia, by requesting membership of the Organisation, pledged to uphold."[55] Considering these factors, the Assembly decided "to suspend the procedure concerning its statutory opinion on Russia's request for membership."

A year later, on January 15, 1996, notwithstanding that the war in Chechnya continued with increased intensity and atrocity, the Parliamentary Assembly recommended that the Committee of Ministers invite the Russian Federation to become a member of the Council of Europe.[56] How does one explain this "U-turn?" The numerous "commitments and understandings" listed in the Assembly's Opinion certainly do not suffice to explain it. What factors led the Assembly to change its attitude? Before its vote, several governments, particularly of major West European countries, actively lobbied parliamentarians to obtain a favorable decision. Germany's Chancellor Kohl threw his whole weight in for the same purpose, and other West European leaders obviously did not want to be perceived as being less enthusiastic than him. One underlying motive certainly was to help President Yeltsin in his then forthcoming presidential election; and he did, of course, not fail to celebrate Russia's admission to the Council as a major success of his policies. The Russian leadership itself gave to understand that Russian accession would occur "now or never," a move of blackmail or poker that ultimately produced the desired effect.

The way in which Russia has honored its numerous commitments leaves much to be desired. One of these was "to sign within one year and ratify within three years from the time of accession Protocol No. 6 to the European Convention on Human Rights on the abolition of the death penalty. . ., and to put into place a moratorium on executions with effect from the day of accession." A year after Russia's accession, the Assembly was led to "condemn Russia for having violated her commitment to put into place a moratorium on executions" and to deplore the executions that had taken place. The Assembly had received reliable information that 53 executions had been carried out in Russia in the first half of 1996.[57] It appears that, since then, a moratorium on executions has been put into place in the country.

54. Parliamentary Assembly, 1995 Sess., Res. No. 1055 (Jan.-Feb. 1995).

55. *Id.*

56. *See* Opinion No. 193 (1996).

57. *See* Res. No. 1111 (1997) on the honouring of the commitment entered into by Russia upon accession to the Council of Europe to put into place a moratorium on executions, adopted on January 29, 1997.

The last country to have joined the Council of Europe as of this writing is Croatia. It applied for membership on December 10, 1992. After lengthy debates, the Assembly recommended, on April 24, 1996, on the basis of numerous commitments undertaken by Croatia, that the Committee of Ministers invite the country to join.[58] On July 2, 1996, the Committee of Ministers took an unprecedented decision, namely, to invite Croatia to become a member of the Council

> subject to the possibility for the Committee of Ministers, at a meeting . . . during the second fortnight of September 1996, to reconsider this decision in the light of the manner in which, according to information they may receive from all relevant sources, Croatia:
>
> – has respected its obligations deriving from the Peace Agreement for Bosnia and Herzegovina, and in particular has contributed to the proper conduct of the elections in Bosnia and Herzegovina;
>
> – has demonstrated its willingness to honour all its commitments and to respond to the priority expectations of the Council of Europe . . ., as well as its ability to comply with the other conditions required by the Statute; and
>
> – co-operates with the Council of Europe, *inter alia,* in applying the Constitutional Law on Human Rights and Freedoms and the Rights of National and Ethnic Communities or Minorities in the Republic of Croatia.[59]

As indicated, one of the concerns of member governments of the Council was that Croatia should not impede the conduct of elections in Bosnia and Herzegovina. But once these elections were over, the Committee of Ministers did not take the trouble to check whether the other conditions it had fixed had been met. Some countries, particularly Germany and Austria, clearly wanted to push Croatia into the Council of Europe as quickly as possible. The accession ceremony, on November 6, 1996, gave rise to a "premiere," namely, a demonstration by the international media representatives against the limitations of freedom of expression and information in the new member state.

The politicians and diplomats responsible for this policy of enlargement (incoherent and unprincipled, in my judgment) are, of course, trying to justify it. One of the official arguments is that the Council pursues a policy of "enlargement without dilution, without any lowering of its standards"—an argument which clearly does not withstand scrutiny. According to another argument (in my view extremely simplistic), "it is better to include than to

58. *See* Opinion No. 195 (1996) on Croatia's request for membership of the Council of Europe.

59. Committee of Ministers Resolution (96) 31.

exclude." To include into what? Into an amorphous arrangement without principles and values? This is not what the Council of Europe was supposed to be, and it is not what Europe needs. It also is argued that by admitting countries, even if they are far from meeting the statutory requirements, one helps to promote the cause of democracy, the rule of law, and human rights in the countries concerned. With a certain irony, I have called this the policy of "therapeutic" admission.[60] The idea of therapy cannot be lightly dismissed. Some of the countries concerned suffer from serious evils and will have to go through a long healing process, but success in therapy presupposes the consent of the "patient." Unfortunately, some of the leaders of the countries involved do not appear really willing to push through the necessary reforms and to honor their commitments.

The Council of Europe should by no means be indifferent or inactive with regard to the countries in transition; on the contrary, it has a moral duty to help them. The question is: how can it most effectively contribute to the building not of a façade or Potemkin village of democracy, but of a genuinely democratic regime and society? Much greater efforts should have been made before the accession of certain countries, when the Council could still hold out the "carrot," *i.e.*, the certificate of democracy which membership in the organization used to confer and which the post-communist countries were so eager to obtain, not only and not principally because of its intrinsic value, but because it is regarded as a key that opens other doors, particularly those of the European Union. Unfortunately, this certificate has been devalued by its over-generous distribution.

In the new circumstances, the need for monitoring compliance with commitments undertaken has been increasingly felt—that is to say, political monitoring, in addition to the numerous supervisory mechanisms provided for by different Council of Europe conventions. Such monitoring is conducted by the two main political bodies of the Council, the Committee of Ministers[61] and the Parliamentary Assembly. The former conducts its monitoring behind closed doors; as a rule, "offenders" do not run the risk of publicity.[62] This is one of the major drawbacks of the system. Monitoring by the Assembly seems to have more "teeth," the system having developed over the years.[63] In April

60. Leuprecht, *supra* note 25, at 174-176.

61. *See Declaration on Compliance with Commitments Accepted by Member States of the Council of Europe*, adopted by the Committee of Ministers, 95th sess. (Nov. 10, 1994).

62. A rare exception is the not very informative press release issued on March 11, 1998, according to which the Ministers' Deputies, meeting on March 10, 1998, had "expressed their extreme concern at recent declarations made at the highest level by the Croatian authorities and at certain negative developments in Eastern Slavonia since the transfer of sovereignty to the Croatian government. They stressed that they were very anxious to see Croatia respect all its obligations to the international community - and especially the Council of Europe." *See Croatia Asked to Honour its Commitments*, COUNCIL OF EUROPE (press release), Mar. 11, 1998 (visited Oct. 28, 1998) <http://www.coe.fr/cp/98/157a(98).htm>.

63. *See* Parliamentary Assembly: Order 488, 1993 Sess. (June 29, 1993); *Resolution 1031 [1993]:*

1997, the Assembly created a special Committee on the Honouring of Obligations and Commitments by Member States (Monitoring Committee),[64] and its results seem relatively promising.[65] In any event, serious monitoring is essential if the basic values and standards of the Council of Europe are not to be further diluted.

C. What Future for the European Human Rights System?

The highly sophisticated European human rights system will be able to function properly only in a political environment that is genuinely "human rights friendly." A growing number of European states is adhering to the Council of Europe's human rights treaties and becoming "subjected" to their supervisory mechanisms. All forty member states of the Council are now parties to the ECHR. Without doubt, this is a highly positive development. However, it must not be overlooked that, in many cases, there is a glaring gap between what certain governments and parliaments have accepted on paper and the real situation in the countries concerned, between the "*pays légal*" and the "*pays réel.*" Very often reality is far removed from the promises contained in the treaties and conventions ratified. As far as the ECHR is concerned, some of the new member states have rushed into ratification without bringing domestic law and reality into line with its requirements. The serious way in which Hungary prepared for the ECHR's ratification and adapted its domestic law is an exception rather than the rule.

With the new single European Court of Human Rights, the ECHR's control machinery will move into unchartered waters. The new Court bears a heavy responsibility. It is to be hoped that it will face up to the challenge and that it will command at least the authority that, over the years, the present Commission and Court have acquired, thanks to their indisputable independence and integrity. The new Court will have to demonstrate the same qualities; it will not only have to *be* independent, but to be *seen* to be independent. The independence and integrity of many of the judges elected to the new Court is beyond doubt. Some of them have previously demonstrated the same essential qualities as members of the old Commission or Court. Others will have to demonstrate them.

On the Honouring of Commitments Entered into by Member States When Joining the Council of Europe, Parliamentary Assembly, 1994 Sess., Res. 1031 (Apr. 14, 1994); *Order 508 [1995]: On the Honouring of Obligations and Commitments by Member States of the Council of Europe*, Parliamentary Assembly, 1995 Sess., Order 508 (Apr. 26, 1995).

64. *See Resolution 1115 [1997]: On the Setting Up of an Assembly Committee on the Honouring of Obligations and Commitments by Member States of the Council of Europe (Monitoring Committee)*, Parliamentary Assembly, 1997 Sess., Res. 1115 (Jan. 29, 1997).

65. *See The Report on the Progress of the Assembly's Monitoring Procedures (April 1997 - April 1998)*, Parliamentary Assembly, 1998 Sess., Doc. 8057 (April 2, 1998).

A number of other questions arise. The ECHR must be implemented, in the first place, at the domestic level. How will this be done in some of the new member states? Are their institutions, particularly the judiciary, strong enough and sufficiently equipped to play the role that is expected from them? One can imagine that in some countries it will be extremely difficult for potential applicants to exhaust domestic remedies. And will all contracting states loyally execute the Court's judgments? The Committee of Ministers which, also under the new control machinery, has the duty to supervise the execution of the Court's judgments, may be required to adopt a firm attitude in this respect. Will it do so? In the new European context, the new Court will have to handle some of the concepts developed in the old Commission's and Court's case law—*e.g.* the "margin of appreciation"[66] and the "European consensus"[67]—with extreme care if the substance of the rights guaranteed is not to be diluted. The common denominator of the contracting states relative to pluralist democracy, the rule of law, and human rights has been considerably lowered.

Ratification of the European Social Charter is not considered an essential requirement for new member states. This is regrettable, but can hardly be otherwise as long as some of the old member states have not become parties to the Charter. It is, however, interesting to note that post-communist countries are showing a growing interest in the Charter. For some time there was, in certain quarters of the countries concerned, a rejection of the very concept of economic and social rights, going hand in hand with a rejection of the old regime, which officially promoted economic and social rights at the expense of civil and political rights. Under the pressure of the dramatically deteriorating social situation, many in these countries seem to have rediscovered economic and social rights and to have become aware of their literally vital importance.[68]

---

66. *See* D.J. HARRIS, M.O'BOYLE, AND C. WARBRICK, LAW OF THE EUROPEAN CONVENTION ON HUMAN RIGHTS 12-15 (1995) (reference the abundant literature referred to therein).

67. *Id.* at 9-11.

68. 22 member states have ratified the European Social Charter. European Social Charter, The Council of Europe (Dec. 16, 1966),<http://www.dhdirhr.coe.fr/SocialCharter/English/CG/governme.htm>. Among the "West European" member states, 4 (Andorra, Liechtenstein, San Marino and Switzerland) have not ratified. *Id.* So far, the only post-communist countries that ratified are Poland and Slovakia; others are preparing ratification. *Id. See also* COUNCIL OF EUROPE, THE SOCIAL CHARTER OF THE 21ST CENTURY (1997) (proceedings of a colloquy held in Strasbourg in May, 1997, discussing the future prospects for the European Social Charter).

With only one exception, all Council of Europe member states are now parties to the European Convention against Torture.[69] This is a welcome development. At the same time, it confronts the CPT with a daunting task. Enormous improvements are called for relative to the conditions of detention in numerous European countries.

D. Relations with the European Union

In the years to come, one of the key issues for the Council of Europe will be the definition of its relationship with the European Union. Different scenarios can be imagined. One is that the Council will be increasingly marginalized with what might be left of its human rights system whereas the "serious" political and economic matters will be dealt with by the Union. Another possible scenario is that the Union will play an increasing role in the field of human rights[70] and possibly even set up its own system of human rights protection;[71] here again, the Council of Europe probably would be reduced to "second fiddle." A third scenario, in my view the most appealing, would be that the two institutions join their efforts to protect and promote human rights within Europe and in Europe's relations with the outside world. Recently, the Parliamentary Assembly of the Council of Europe again advocated the accession of the European Community (or Union) to the ECHR.[72] It is indeed a striking anomaly that the Community should be the only power in Europe not formally subject to the ECHR. This certainly is not what its founders had in mind. Unfortunately, however, the prospects for Community (or Union) accession seem rather more remote than a few years ago. Nevertheless, in the interest of a coherent and effective European approach to human rights, the objective of Community (or Union) accession to the ECHR as well as to the European Social Charter should be further pursued.

---

69. The only exception is Lithuania which has signed, but not yet ratified. *See* European Social Charter, *supra* note 68.

70. *See* the provisions of the Treaty of Amsterdam. *See also* Leading by Example: A Human Rights Agenda for the European Union for the year 2000, Agenda of the Comité des Sages and Final Project Report. European University Institute, Florence 1998 (visited Oct. 29, 1998) <http://www.iue.it/AEL/>.

71. *See* Frédéric Sudre, *La Communauté européenne et les droits fondamentaux après le traité d'Amsterdam: Vers un nouveau système européen de protection des droits de l'homme?*, LA SEMAINE ÉURIDIQUE, ÉDITION GÉNÉRALE, Jan. 7, 1998, No. 1 - 2, at 9-16.

72. *See Relations with the European Union (follow-up to the European Union's Amsterdam Summit), Report of the Political Affairs Committee*, Parliamentary Assembly, 1998 Sess., Doc. No. 8051 (April 1, 1998).

IV. CONCLUSION

In the years before and during its enlargement to the East, the Council of Europe was successful in completing and strengthening its legal instruments and control mechanisms for the protection of human rights. The political environment in which these legal instruments and mechanisms will have to operate in the future, however, has clearly become more complex and difficult. It has lost a lot of its earlier homogeneity.

The creation and gradual development of the European human rights system has undoubtedly been one of the most positive features of Europe's post-war history. Since 1989, Europe has been experiencing a new post-war period. Like the period after 1945, the post-cold-war period is one of great uncertainty, of threats and dangers, and also of tremendous opportunities. Pluralist democracy, the rule of law, and human rights now have a chance of becoming a living reality in the whole of Europe. A superficial reading of the official political discourse could lead one to believe that this goal has been achieved already. Indeed, as has been strikingly demonstrated by the October 1997 Council of Europe Summit, the political leaders of the forty member states now all recite the same credo praising pluralist democracy, the rule of law, and human rights. This does not mean that all of them genuinely share these values, nor that all are determined to abide by them and to translate them into reality. Double-talk and double-think as described by George Orwell are still a widespread practice. The cause of human rights in Europe will not be helped if the ideological confrontation of the past is replaced by a hollow, deceptive consensus. It would be disastrous if the attention given the values and principles of pluralist democracy, the rule of law, and human rights were mere lip-service, an institutional ritual with no real significance.

Europe will need enormous strength and determination to meet the challenges and to resist the dangers that the cause of human rights is facing. It is to be hoped that the Council of Europe will retain or recover that strength and determination. It must spare no effort to get closer to the realization of that great and challenging objective: to implement human rights in their universality and indivisibility, to guarantee all human rights and human rights for all. At the 1997 Strasbourg Summit, Vaclav Havel called the Council of Europe "an anchor of values - unique and irreplaceable." Europe would be poorer, less human and less humane without it.

Part II
The Inter-American System

[2]

The Forgotten Crucible: The Latin American Influence on the Universal Human Rights Idea

Mary Ann Glendon*

With the passage of time and the deaths of all the main participants, the origins of the post–World War II international human rights project have been obscured by forgetfulness and myth. The polestar of that movement, the 1948 Universal Declaration of Human Rights ("UDHR"), is widely regarded as nothing more than a compendium of classical Western political and civil liberties. Its provisions relating to the family and to social and economic justice are routinely ignored, even by major human rights organizations. Yet those provisions, based in large part on Latin American models, played a key role in helping the UDHR to gain wide acceptance among diverse cultures. Indeed, Latin American diplomats, documents, and traditions had such a profound influence upon both the decision to include human rights protection among the purposes of the UN, and the content of the Universal Declaration, that it is fair to refer to Latin America as the forgotten crucible of the universal human rights idea.

I. Latin American Influences on the UN Charter

In April 1945, when delegates from fifty countries gathered in San Francisco to put the finishing touches on a proposed charter for the United Nations, representatives of Latin American and Caribbean nations arrived with a plan to work for the inclusion of an international bill of rights. That idea was far from the minds of the Allied leaders who called the conference. Their draft proposal for the new organization had been negotiated in a much more exclusive meeting a few months earlier at Dumbarton Oaks. It was only after Churchill, Roosevelt, and Stalin had settled everything that was most important to them that they announced a meeting where the rest of the Allies could have a say. The "Big Three" leaders do not seem to have contem-

---

* Learned Hand Professor of Law, Harvard Law School. The author gratefully acknowledges the research assistance of Sarah Glendon, and comments and suggestions from: John Hobbins, Associate Director of Libraries, McGill University; Professor Paolo Carozza, Notre Dame Law School; colleagues at Harvard Law School, where this Article was presented at a faculty workshop; and colleagues at the Athenaeum Regina Apostolorum in Rome, who commented on an earlier version presented as a public lecture.

plated that the San Francisco conference might produce major changes in their design. As Churchill had put it to Roosevelt and Stalin at Yalta, when discussing the extent to which "smaller powers" should participate in the peace process: "The eagle should permit the small birds to sing and care not wherefore they sang."[1] What Churchill, Roosevelt, and Stalin wanted was a collective security arrangement for the postwar period. Human rights ranked so low among the priorities of the major powers that they mentioned it only once, briefly, in their draft charter.

Among the delegates who came to the UN founding conference, however, were several who had a more expansive vision of the new organization: a vision that included protection of human rights. The twenty-nation Latin American contingent, as the single largest bloc, was in a position to press the human rights agenda.[2] The delegates were well-suited for that role by experience as well as numbers, for they had been engaged for some time in thinking about human rights at the supranational level. As early as 1938, with war impending, the Inter-American Conference (the predecessor of the Organization of American States) adopted a "Declaration in Defense of Human Rights" at its eighth international meeting in Lima, Peru. That Declaration stated that when "recourse is had to war in any other region of the world, respect [should] be given to those human rights not necessarily involved in the conflict, to humanitarian sentiments, and to the spiritual and material inheritance of civilization."[3] At the same conference, three forward-looking resolutions were adopted: one condemning racial and religious persecution,[4] one in favor of women's rights,[5] and one on freedom of association for workers.[6] In addition, in 1945, just before the San Francisco gathering, the Inter-American Conference held a meeting in Mexico City where they resolved to seek inclusion of a transnational declaration of rights in the UN Charter.[7]

That surge of regional interest in supranational human rights had grown out of several Latin American countries' efforts to establish constitutional democracies where rights of citizens would be legally protected. According to Hector Gros Espiell, vice-president of the Inter-American Court of Human Rights, the 1940s were "a moment of idealistic optimism and demo-

1. Charles E. Bohlen, Witness to History, 1929–1969, at 181 (1973). Churchill was recalling lines from Shakespeare's *Titus Andronicus*: "The eagle suffers little birds to sing/And is not careful what they mean thereby." William Shakespeare, Titus Andronicus, 4.4.84–.85 (Russ McDonald ed., Penguin Books 2000) (1594).

2. The countries represented were Argentina, Bolivia, Brazil, Chile, Colombia, Costa Rica, Cuba, the Dominican Republic, Ecuador, El Salvador, Guatemala, Haiti, Honduras, Mexico, Nicaragua, Panama, Paraguay, Peru, Uruguay, and Venezuela.

3. Carnegie Endowment for International Peace, International Conferences of American States, First Supplement, 1933–1940, at 246 (1943).

4. *Id.* at 260.

5. *Id.* at 250.

6. *Id.* at 238.

7. Mary Ann Glendon, A World Made New: Eleanor Roosevelt and the Universal Declaration of Human Rights 15 (2001).

cratic euphoria."[8] As Johannes Morsink puts it, "In their joint reaction to the Great Depression and to the absolutism of both right and left, they all (or almost all) hit a democratic stretch at the same time."[9] Cuba, for example, adopted a democratic constitution in 1940 and voted out its corrupt leader, Fulgencio Batista, in 1944. Within eight years, Batista would return to power with the aid of the military and would suspend all constitutional guarantees; the Batista regime, in turn, would be overthrown by Fidel Castro in 1959. But in 1945, Cuba was enjoying a brief interlude of political hope and promise. The nation sent an eloquent young democrat, thirty-year-old Guy Pérez Cisneros, to be its representative at the San Francisco meeting.

As soon as the San Francisco proceedings got underway, Panama submitted a draft declaration of human rights (complete with rights to education,[10] work,[11] health care,[12] and social security[13]). Delegates from Chile, Cuba, and Mexico joined Panama in waging an unsuccessful fight to have that declaration incorporated into the UN Charter. In a more productive effort, the Latin coalition joined forces with delegates from newly independent countries like the Philippines and Lebanon, and with observers from Catholic, Protestant, and Jewish religious groups, civic associations, and labor organizations, to try to make sure the Charter would at least proclaim a serious commitment to the protection of human rights.[14]

The reaction of the major powers to those human rights initiatives ranged from coolness on the part of the United States to outright hostility on the part of the Soviet Union and colonial nations like France and Britain. But in May 1945, two developments gave a decisive boost to the movement for raising the profile of human rights in the Charter. First, the conference members were shocked by the photographs that began to arrive from the newly liberated concentration camps in Europe. Second, and no doubt related to those revelations, the United States dropped its opposition to the idea of creating a UN Human Rights Commission.[15] By the time the conference ended in June 1945, principles of human rights had been inserted

8. Hector Gros Espiell, *La Declaración Americana: Raíces Conceptuales y Políticas en la Historia, la Filosofía y el Derecho Americano*, Número Especial, REVISTA INSTITUTO INTERAMERICANO DE DERECHOS HUMANOS 41, 44 (1989).

9. JOHANNES MORSINK, THE UNIVERSAL DECLARATION OF HUMAN RIGHTS: ORIGINS, DRAFTING, AND INTENT 130 (2000).

10. *Id.* at 6. The draft was the product of cross-national collaboration conducted under the auspices of the American Law Institute. AMERICAN LAW INSTITUTE, *Statement of Essential Rights*, *in* AMERICAN LAW INSTITUTE, SEVENTY-FIFTH ANNIVERSARY 1923–1998, at 272 (1998).

11. AMERICAN LAW INSTITUTE, *supra* note 10, at 283.

12. *Id.* at 286.

13. *Id.* at 285.

14. For an account of the initiative, see GLENDON, A WORLD MADE NEW, *supra* note 7, at 15–18.

15. M. Glen Johnson, *The Contributions of Eleanor and Franklin Roosevelt to the Development of International Protection for Human Rights*, 9 HUM. RTS. Q. 19, 26 (1987).

into the UN Charter in seven places, including a provision establishing a commission on human rights.[16]

II. Latin American Influences on the Drafting of the Universal Declaration of Human Rights

Latin American delegates remained active on the human rights front once the UN was up and running. One of the first tasks the new organization assigned to its Human Rights Commission (chaired by Eleanor Roosevelt) was the preparation of what was then referred to as an "international bill of rights."[17] The Commission was to produce a set of common standards that would serve as a kind of yardstick by which all countries could measure their own and each others' progress toward making human rights a reality. The eighteen-member Commission, constituted with a view toward cultural and political diversity, was reasonably well-suited for that assignment. Three of the eighteen seats were given to Latin American countries: one to Chile, one to Uruguay, and one to Panama. The other seats were held by Australia, Belgium, China, Egypt, France, India, Iran, Lebanon, the Philippines, the United Kingdom, the United States, and four Eastern bloc members: Byelorussia, the Soviet Union, the Ukraine, and Yugoslavia.[18]

That very heterogeneity, however, posed daunting challenges. Not least of these was that no one really knew whether there were any rights with a plausible claim to acceptance in all the cultures of the world, or, if so, what they might be.[19] As an initial step, the Human Rights Commissioners asked the Director of the UN's Human Rights Division, the Canadian international lawyer John Humphrey, to prepare a first draft.[20] Humphrey began by having his staff conduct a complete survey of the world's existing rights documents, together with all the proposals that had been submitted to the UN. Following up on their initiative at San Francisco, the first three governments to submit proposed bills of rights were Panama, Chile, and Cuba.[21] After studying the material he had received and collected—over four hundred

---

16. U.N. Charter, pmbl. and arts. 1, 13, 55, 62, 68, 76.

17. Morsink, *supra* note 9, at 13. For detailed histories, *see id.* and Glendon, A World Made New, *supra* note 7.

18. U.N., Yearbook on Human Rights for 1947 at 422, U.N. Sales No. 1949.XIV.I (1949).

19. To examine those questions, UNESCO appointed a committee of philosophers, including some, such as Jacques Maritain and Benedetto Croce, who were prominent in the West, and others who belonged to Confucian, Hindu, and Muslim traditions. The philosophers in turn sent a questionnaire to other leading thinkers all over the world—from Mahatma Gandhi to Teilhard de Chardin. In due course, the Committee reported that, somewhat to their surprise, the responses they received indicated that there were a number of principles of basic decency that were widely shared—though not always formulated in the language of rights. Gandhi, for example, recommended framing a bill of duties. The Committee's report, the questionnaire, and several responses are collected in Human Rights: Comments and Interpretations (United Nations Educational, Scientific and Cultural Organization ed., 1949).

20. A. J. Hobbins, *René Cassin and the Daughter of Time: The First Draft of the Universal Declaration of Human Rights*, 2 Fontanus 7, 10 (1989).

21. Morsink, *supra* note 9, at 131.

pages—Humphrey took as his principal models the Panamanian and Chilean submissions.[22]

The Panamanian-sponsored document was the same proposal that Latin American delegations had unsuccessfully put forward at San Francisco.[23] It was the product of a cross-national study conducted in 1942 and 1943 under the auspices of the American Law Institute ("ALI"), an organization of U.S. judges, practitioners, and academics dedicated to the improvement of the law. With assistance from the ALI, a multinational committee had consulted experts from "Arabic, British, Canadian, Chinese, French, pre-Nazi German, Italian, Indian, Latin American, Polish, Soviet Russian and Spanish"[24] countries and cultures in order to ascertain to what extent there could be worldwide agreement respecting rights.[25] In 1944, reporting that it had "found a very large measure of agreement which, in view of its multinational makeup, was most encouraging," the committee had produced a "Statement of Essential Human Rights" that they believed to have a claim to acceptance "by men of good will in all nations."[26] In their preface, the drafters took pains to emphasize: "This is not a statement made by the American Law Institute, which is composed exclusively of United States citizens. It is a statement by a committee representing many different nations."[27] It was this Statement that Panama's Foreign Minister, Ricardo Alfaro, a member of the drafting group, had proposed for inclusion in the UN Charter.

The Chilean draft was a preliminary version of the American Declaration of the Rights and Duties of Man, commissioned by the Mexico City Inter-American Conference in 1945.[28] Its authors, too, had consulted a wide variety of sources, including an early version of the Statement of the ALI group.[29] Dated December 31, 1945, the draft was signed by a four-person committee that included Felix Nieto del Río, who represented Chile at the first meeting of the UN Human Rights Commission.[30] The American Declaration, often known as the Bogotá Declaration, became the world's first international human rights declaration when it was adopted on April 30, 1948, at Bogotá, Colombia.[31]

---

22. JOHN P. HUMPHREY, HUMAN RIGHTS AND THE UNITED NATIONS: A GREAT ADVENTURE 31–32 (1984).

23. MORSINK, *supra* note 9, at 6. For the actual draft, see UNITED NATIONS, GENERAL ASSEMBLY, STATEMENT OF ESSENTIAL HUMAN RIGHTS, STATEMENT SUBMITTED BY THE DELEGATION OF PANAMA, U.N. Doc. A/148 (1946).

24. *Statement of Essential Rights*, *supra* note 10, at 269.

25. *Id.* at 267.

26. *Id.*

27. *Id.*

28. MORSINK, *supra* note 9, at 131. For the actual draft, see UNITED NATIONS, ECONOMIC AND SOCIAL COUNCIL, DRAFT DECLARATION OF THE INTERNATIONAL RIGHTS AND DUTIES OF MAN, DRAFT SUBMITTED BY THE INTER-AMERICAN JURIDICAL COMMITTEE, U.N. Doc. E/CN.4/2 (1947).

29. Gros Espiell, *supra* note 8, at 48.

30. The other signers were Francisco Campos, Charles Fenwick, and Antonio Gómez Robledo. *Id.* at 45.

31. *American Declaration of the Rights and Duties of Man*, *in* BASIC DOCUMENTS ON HUMAN RIGHTS

Morsink's line-by-line comparison of the Panamanian- and Chilean-sponsored drafts with the first draft of the Universal Declaration led him to conclude that "Humphrey took much of the wording and almost all of the ideas for the social, economic, and cultural rights of his first draft" from those two proposals.[32]

What made the Latin American-sponsored drafts such important sources for Humphrey and the Human Rights Commission was their compatibility with the broad range of cultures and philosophies represented in the United Nations. No small part of that wide appeal was due to the fact that several elements of Latin American legal traditions resonated with non-Western traditions. As I have described elsewhere, the modern language of rights, from the outset, developed two main branches.[33] The differences were ones of degree, but their spirit had penetrated every corner of the societies affected. One branch, influenced by the rhetoric of the American revolution and by early modern Anglo-American thinkers, placed greater emphasis on individual liberty and property than on equality and fraternity (or, as we would say today, solidarity). This dialect was infused with a good deal of mistrust of government. The other dialect was more influenced by the continental European branch of the Enlightenment, where the break with classical, biblical, feudal, and Roman-law thinking about man and government had been less complete. Continental rights documents had more room for equality and fraternity along with liberty; they often explicitly tempered rights with duties and limits; and they generally presented government in a positive light as a guarantor of rights and protections for the needy.

When Latin American nations gained independence in the nineteenth century, those two strains converged, and merged with an older, more universalist, natural law tradition. The result was a distinctively Latin American form of rights discourse. Paolo Carozza traces the roots of that discourse to a distinctive application, and extension, of Thomistic moral philosophy to the injustices of Spanish conquests in the New World.[34] The key figure in that development seems to have been Bartolomé de Las Casas, a sixteenth-century Spanish bishop who condemned slavery and championed the cause of Indians on the basis of a natural right to liberty grounded in their membership in a single common humanity.[35] "All the peoples of the world are

---

488 (Ian Brownlie ed., 3d ed., 1992). The Bogotá conference where the Declaration was adopted was the scene of a violent far-left demonstration (known as the Bogotazo) in which 5000 persons lost their lives. Among the participants in the Bogotazo was the young Fidel Castro. CLAUDIO F. BENEDI, HUMAN RIGHTS: THE THEME OF OUR TIMES 38–39 (1997).

32. MORSINK, *supra* note 9, at 131.

33. *See* MARY ANN GLENDON, RIGHTS TALK: THE IMPOVERISHMENT OF POLITICAL DISCOURSE 20–46 (1991); MARY ANN GLENDON, ABORTION AND DIVORCE IN WESTERN LAW: AMERICAN FAILURES, EUROPEAN CHALLENGES 112–34 (1987).

34. *See generally* Paolo G. Carozza, *From Conquest to Constitutions: Retrieving a Latin American Tradition of the Idea of Human Rights*, 24 HUM. RTS. Q. (forthcoming 2002) (on file with author).

35. BRIAN TIERNEY, THE IDEA OF NATURAL RIGHTS: STUDIES ON NATURAL RIGHTS, NATURAL LAW AND CHURCH LAW 1150–1625, at 272–74 (1997).

humans," Las Casas wrote, and "all the races of humankind are one."[36] According to Brian Tierney, Las Casas and other Spanish Dominican philosophers laid the groundwork for a doctrine of natural rights that was independent of religious revelation "by drawing on a juridical tradition that derived natural rights and natural law from human rationality and free will, and by appealing to Aristotelian philosophy."[37] Carozza builds on Tierney's work to show how an identifiably Latin American understanding of human rights emerged from the fusion of the teachings of Dominican opponents of slavery and conquest with French revolutionary ideas, United States constitutionalism, and the Pan-American vision of the Liberator, Símon Bolivár.

Upon independence, most of the new nations in South and Central America retained their European-style legal systems based on civil codes but adopted constitutions inspired by the U.S. founding documents, the rhetoric of the French Revolution, and a natural law tradition to which the idea of the common humanity of all persons was central. These constitutions were less libertarian than the U.S. model and bore no trace of the anti-clericalism that characterized the French constitutions of the revolutionary period. Later, in the first half of the twentieth century, many Latin American countries supplemented their constitutions with protections for workers and the poor. Though conventional history treats Latin American constitutionalism as merely derivative of American and European models, it is more accurately regarded as representing a distinctive fusion of moral and political traditions. The insistence on the correlation between human rights and duties, for example, has been a characteristic feature of Latin American political philosophy and constitutional law since the beginning of the nineteenth century.[38] The universalizing, internationalist dimension of this heritage was furthered by the Inter-American Conference, established in 1890.

In view of that background, it is not surprising that Humphrey found the Panamanian- and Chilean-sponsored drafts especially useful resources for a UN declaration that aspired to be universally applicable. In the first place, by emphasizing the importance of the family and the idea that rights are subject to duties and limitations,[39] both drafts resonated with several non-Western as well as continental European traditions. Secondly, they were both based on extensive cross-national research with the aim of finding acceptance from a large group of countries that are far from homogeneous. And thirdly, they were prime examples of the modern constitutional trend to combine

36. *Id.* at 273.

37. *Id.* at 287. Tierney says that Las Casas's "essential achievement, on a theoretical level, was to graft, quite consciously, a juridical doctrine of natural rights onto Aquinas's teaching on natural law." *Id.* at 276.

38. Gros Espiell, *supra* note 8, at 53.

39. "The fulfillment of duty by each individual is a prerequisite to the rights of all. Rights and duties are interrelated in every social and political activity of man. While rights exalt individual liberty, duties express the dignity of that liberty." *American Declaration of the Rights and Duties of Man*, *supra* note 31, at 489.

"first generation" political and civil liberties with "second generation" rights relating to social justice. Though many other cultures contributed to the Universal Declaration of Human Rights, the UN document bears unmistakable marks of the strong influence of the same ideas and sources that helped to shape the 1948 American Declaration of the Rights and Duties of Man ("ADRDM").[40]

40. An emphasis on human dignity, for example, is pervasive in both documents, and both begin by sounding the theme of liberty, equality, and fraternity (solidarity):

> UDHR, Article 1: All human beings are born free and equal in dignity and rights. They are endowed with reason and conscience and should act towards one another in a spirit of brotherhood.
>
> ADRDM, Preamble: All men are born free and equal, in dignity and in rights, and, being endowed by nature with reason and conscience, they should conduct themselves as brothers one to another.

Both documents also recognize the importance of the family:

> UDHR, Article 16 (3): The family is the natural and fundamental group unit of society and is entitled to protection by society and the State.
>
> ADRDM, Article 6: Every person has the right to establish a family, the basic element of society, and to receive protection therefor.

Both recognize a right to social security:

> UDHR, Article 22: Everyone, as a member of society, has the right to social security and is entitled to realization, through national effort and international cooperation and in accordance with the organization and resources of each State, of the economic, social and cultural rights indispensable for his dignity and the free development of his personality.
>
> ADRDM, Article 16: Every person has the right to social security which will protect him from the consequences of unemployment, old age, and any disabilities arising from causes beyond his control that make it physically or mentally impossible for him to earn a living.

Both recognize a worker's right to remuneration that assures a decent existence for the worker and the worker's family:

> UDHR, Article 23 (3): Everyone who works has the right to just and favorable remuneration ensuring for himself and his family an existence worthy of human dignity, and supplemented, if necessary, by other means of social protection.
>
> ADRDM, Article 14 (2): Every person who works has the right to receive such remuneration as will, in proportion to his capacity and skill, assure him of a standard of living suitable for himself and for his family.

Both accord special protection to motherhood and childhood:

> UDHR, Article 25 (2): Motherhood and childhood are entitled to special care and assistance.
>
> ADRDM, Article 7: All women, during pregnancy and the nursing period, and all children have the right to special protection, care and aid.

Both expressly state that people have duties as well as rights:

> UDHR, Article 29 (1): Everyone has duties to the community in which alone the free and full development of his personality is possible.
>
> ADRDM, Preamble: The fulfillment of duty by each individual is a prerequisite to the rights of all. Rights and duties are interrelated in every social and political activity of man. While rights exalt individual liberty, duties express the dignity of that liberty.

Both expressly state that rights have limits:

> UDHR, Article 29 (2): In the exercise of his rights and freedoms, everyone shall be subject only to such limitations as are determined by law solely for the purpose of securing due recognition and respect for the rights and freedoms of others and of meeting the just requirements of morality, public order and the general welfare in a democratic society.
>
> ADRDM, Article 28: The rights of man are limited by the rights of others, by the security of all, and by the just demands of the general welfare and the advancement of democracy.

The texts of the Universal Declaration and the American Declaration can be found in BASIC DOCUMENTS ON HUMAN RIGHTS, *supra* note 31, at 21–27 and 489–94.

When Humphrey finished the initial draft of the UDHR, he turned it over to the Human Rights Commission ("HRC"), which appointed an eight-member drafting committee to continue the work. A key member of that subcommittee was Hernán Santa Cruz, who succeeded Nieto del Río as Chile's representative on the HRC after the first meeting. Contrary to what many suppose today, it was Santa Cruz, far more than any Soviet bloc representative, who was the Commission's most zealous promoter of social and economic rights. Indeed, in his study of the origins of the Declaration, Morsink has concluded that the social and economic rights in the Declaration are mainly derived from the traditions of Latin American socialism.[41]

That the rights in question owe much to Latin American models is clear, but whether those models are best described as socialist depends on what one means by "socialist." By the 1940s, social and economic rights had found their way into the constitutions of many Latin American and continental European countries via the programs of socialist, social democratic, labor, Christian democratic, and Christian social parties.[42] Except in Mexico, which adopted a socialist constitution in 1917, the particular formulations of rights in Latin America—with their emphasis on the family, religion, and the dignity of the person—are significantly at odds with Marxist anthropology and with state socialism.

One feature that set most twentieth-century Latin American rights documents apart from Marxist models was their resemblance to two influential papal encyclicals that grounded social justice in respect for human dignity: the 1891 encyclical *Rerum Novarum*, and *Quadragesimo Anno*, published on the fortieth anniversary of *Rerum Novarum*. As Michael Novak has observed:

> [U]nless one understands the Catholic intellectual traditions of southern Europe and Latin America, one cannot really enter the horizon of Latin American intellectual discourse. Many Latin Americans do not think of themselves as Catholic at all, and many may be quite irreligious. But even the irreligious have become used to expressing themselves within the horizon of Latin Catholic history.[43]

In *Rerum Novarum*, Pope Leo XIII deplored a state of affairs in which "working men have been surrendered, isolated and helpless, to the hard-heartedness of employers and the greed of unchecked competition,"[44] and

41. *See* MORSINK, *supra* note 9, at 130.

42. At least ten Latin American countries rewrote their constitutions in the 1940s, five others did so in the 1930s, and two had done so in the first quarter of the twentieth century. *Id. See* Mary Ann Glendon, *Rights in Twentieth Century Constitutions*, 59 U. CHI. L. REV. 519 (1992) on the constitutional incorporation of social and economic rights.

43. MICHAEL NOVAK, THIS HEMISPHERE OF LIBERTY: A PHILOSOPHY OF THE AMERICAS, at 1 (1992).

44. POPE LEO XIII, Rerum Novarum (May 15, 1891), *reprinted in* 2 THE PAPAL ENCYCLICALS, 1878–

gave a ringing endorsement to workers' rights on the basis of human dignity.[45] At the same time, he vigorously rejected state socialism as a remedy for grave social ills.[46] Forty years later, Pius XI observed that his predecessor's dignitarian approach to rights had played a role—via Christian political parties, labor organizations, and social action groups—in shaping social legislation enacted after the Great War.[47] He noted that "[a] new branch of law, wholly unknown to the earlier time, has arisen from this continuous and unwearied labor to protect vigorously the sacred rights of the workers that flow from their dignity as men,"[48] and he reaffirmed the duty to provide for the needy,[49] the right to form and join unions,[50] the right to an adequate wage for the worker and his family,[51] and the need to avoid the "twin rocks of shipwreck" of extreme individualism and collectivism.[52]

The contributions to the UDHR of Hernán Santa Cruz, the principal advocate of social and economic rights on the Human Rights Commission, were in keeping with that tradition. Santa Cruz was an aristocratic man of the left, a member of the Chilean Popular Front, and a close friend from boyhood of the ill-fated Salvador Allende, but he was seldom aligned with the socialist bloc in the UN. His vision of human rights—melding freedom, dignity, and social justice—is well-captured in the following amendment proposed by Chile to the UDHR's article on the right to life:

> Unborn children and incurables, mentally defectives and lunatics, shall have the right to life.
>
> All persons shall have the right to the enjoyment of conditions of life enabling them to live in dignity and to develop their personality adequately.
>
> Persons unable to maintain themselves by their own efforts shall be entitled to maintenance and assistance.[53]

Santa Cruz was unsuccessful in his efforts to have unborn children recognized in the Declaration as members of the human family, but no one played a greater role than he in securing recognition for the rights of persons who cannot provide for their own needs.

1903, at 241, ¶ 3 (Claudia Carlen ed., 1981), *available at* http://www.vatican.va/holy_father/leo_xiii/encyclicals/documents/hf_l-xiii_enc_15051891_rerum-novarum_en.html.

45. *Id.* at ¶ 20, 34, 36, 42, 45, 49.

46. *Id.* at ¶ 4, 5, 6, 15.

47. Pope Pius XI, Quadragesimo Anno (May 15, 1931), *reprinted in* 3 The Papal Encyclicals, 1903–1939, at 415, ¶ 12, 21, 22, 27 (Claudia Carlen ed., 1981), *available at* http://www.vatican.va/holy_father/pius_xi/encyclicals/documents/hf_p-xi_enc_19310515_quadragesimo-anno_en.html.

48. *Id.* at ¶ 28.

49. *Id.* at ¶ 25, 50.

50. *Id.* at ¶ 29, 30, 87.

51. *Id.* at ¶ 71.

52. Pope Pius XI, *supra* note 47, at ¶ 46. *See also* ¶ 10, 14, 110.

53. Glendon, A World Made New, *supra* note 7, app. 3, at 282.

III. Latin Americans in the Debates Leading to Approval of the UDHR by the General Assembly

In the autumn of 1948, the Human Rights Commission presented its draft declaration to the UN's Committee on Social, Humanitarian, and Cultural Affairs, a large body composed of representatives from each of the fifty-eight member nations, for review. Approval by that group was a necessary step before the Declaration could be presented for a final vote in the General Assembly. The Latin American countries were still the largest single group in the UN, and their delegates were eager to bring the experience gained in preparing the Bogotá Declaration to bear on the UN's human rights project. So proud were they of the newly minted American Declaration, that many backed a movement spearheaded by Cuba to send the draft UN Declaration to a committee to be compared line by line with the American one.[54] When that idea was rejected, several Latin American delegates began offering amendments aimed at conforming the UN draft to the Bogotá Declaration.[55]

This activity, though it produced a number of important last-minute changes to the UDHR, produced alarm among many of the Declaration's supporters, for it unwittingly aided Soviet efforts to delay the proceedings. Among those who feared that the Declaration's chance of approval would be dead forever if it were not adopted at the 1948 session was John Humphrey. In his memoir, referring to the Latin American initiatives as "the Bogotá Menace," Humphrey recalled his feelings of frustration as the "[h]ighly intelligent, Pérez Cisneros used every procedural device to reach his end. His speeches were laced with Roman Catholic social philosophy, and it seemed at times that the chief protagonists in the conference room were the Roman Catholics and the communists, with the latter a poor second."[56] In Humphrey's private diaries, published after his death, he describes Pérez Cisneros as a man who "combines demagogy with Roman Catholic social philosophy," remarking that the Cuban "should burn in hell, but he will probably go down in history as a great defender of freedom."[57]

Fortunately, Hernán Santa Cruz, who sympathized both with Humphrey's sense of urgency and with the aims of his fellow Latin Americans, was in a position to intervene effectively. As a member of the drafting committee, he was able to point out to delegates who were seeing the UDHR for the first time how much of the document had in fact been based on the preparatory work for the Bogotá Declaration.[58]

54. Carozza, *supra* note 34, at 7–8.

55. *Id.* at 8.

56. Humphrey, *supra* note 22, at 65–66.

57. Diary of John Humphrey (Dec. 4, 1948), *in* On the Edge of Greatness: The Diaries of John Humphrey 87 (A. J. Hobbins ed., 1994).

58. Santa Cruz's account can be found in his memoir, Hernán Santa Cruz, Cooperar o Perecer: El Dilema de la Comunidad Mundial 184–93 (1984). *See also* Glendon, A World Made New, *supra* note 7, at 140–41.

The persistence of the Latin American delegates did result, however, in significant additions to the UDHR in the course of debates that stretched out over October and November 1948. On the motion of Minerva Bernardino of the Dominican Republic, the preamble was amended to emphasize that the Declaration's rights belong to women as well as men.[59] At the instance of Pérez Cisneros, the reference to the needs of families was inserted into what would become Article 23(3) on the right to just remuneration.[60] On the motion of Ecuador, what would become Article 9 was amended to include protection against arbitrary exile.[61] And at Mexico's behest, a new article (which would become Article 8) was added adopting the Latin American institution known as the *amparo* (the right to an effective remedy for acts in violation of fundamental rights).[62]

The importance of the Latin American contributions was officially recognized on December 9, 1948, when Charles Malik, as Rapporteur of the UN's Human Rights Commission, presented the draft Universal Declaration of Human Rights to the General Assembly for its vote.[63] Malik began by describing the document as a landmark in history: a synthesis of all existing rights traditions.[64] After noting that a great number of proposals for an international bill of rights had been submitted from all over the world, he singled out the Panamanian, Chilean, and Cuban drafts for special mention.[65] He recognized Hernán Santa Cruz for having "kept alive in our mind the great humane outlook of his Latin American world";[66] "Mr. Cisneros of Cuba and Mr. Carrera de Andrade of Ecuador [who] have contributed from the great fund of their erudition and high idealism";[67] "the keen legal logic of Mr. De Aréchaga of Uruguay";[68] and noted that "credit must go to Miss Minerva Bernardino of the Dominican Republic" for the mention of the equal rights of men and women in the Preamble.[69] He then proceeded to point the member States to places in the Declaration where they could either find their own contributions or the influence of the cultures to which they belonged.[70]

On the following day, the Universal Declaration was adopted by the UN General Assembly without any dissenting votes (although the Soviet bloc, Saudi Arabia, and South Africa recorded abstentions). As Malik had noted,

59. Charles Malik, Speech of Thursday 9 December 1948, *in* THE CHALLENGE OF HUMAN RIGHTS: CHARLES MALIK AND THE UNIVERSAL DECLARATION 124 (Habib C. Malik ed., 2000).
60. *Id.*
61. *Id.*
62. *Id.*
63. *Id.* at 117.
64. Charles Malik, *supra* note 59, at 117–18.
65. *Id.* at 118.
66. *Id.* at 121.
67. *Id.* at 123.
68. *Id.*
69. *Id.* at 124.
70. Charles Malik, *supra* note 59, at 124.

many nations contributed to that impressively, if imperfectly, multicultural document. The Latin American contributions, however, were among the major factors that helped it to avoid extremes of individualism or collectivism and to become the principal model for the majority of rights instruments in the world today. Neither a U.S.- nor a Soviet-style document could have commanded a consensus from a United Nations that included representatives from so many different cultures.

IV. Conclusion

As this brief survey demonstrates, the efforts of Latin Americans were instrumental in securing a place for human rights in the UN Charter, in providing models for the Human Rights Commission in its drafting process, and in endowing the UDHR with broad cross-cultural appeal. It is desirable to retrieve what Latin Americans brought to the human rights project, not only for the sake of giving credit where credit is due, but also because the expansive vision that inspired so many post–World War II rights instruments is currently at risk of being displaced by narrowly individualistic and libertarian interpretations.[71] I need to emphasize, however, that I have only excavated the top layer of a story that needs to be more fully explored. My hope is that Latin American thinkers and statespersons will soon recover this part of their heritage in its fullness, not only for the sake of their own democratic experiments, but for the sake of the human rights movement. In 1948, they helped to prevent the Universal Declaration from falling into the excesses of individualism or collectivism. Now that the UDHR has become the single most important reference point for discussions of human rights in international settings today, Latin America may once again help the human rights movement to realize the full promise of the Declaration's vision of human dignity.

71. *See* Glendon, Rights Talk, *supra* note 33.

[3]

Introduction*

Jo M. Pasqualucci

The status of individuals under international law is no longer in doubt: individuals are subjects of international law and as such are accorded rights. Yet rights are illusory without the procedural capability to enforce them. They are no more than high-minded principles if individuals whose rights have been violated have no avenue for complaint and relief. International courts and commissions are often empowered to enforce human rights and to attribute responsibility to States that violate their obligations. These enforcement bodies must employ equitable procedures that balance victims' rights and States' treaty obligations. The practice and procedures of these bodies can ensure or impede an individual victim's access to justice.

The Inter-American Court of Human Rights is the sole judicial organ in the Inter-American human rights system. As such, it is the final arbiter of human rights in those States of the Western hemisphere that have ratified the American Convention on Human Rights and accepted the Court's jurisdiction. The Court has substantially revised its Rules of Procedure several times to more effectively address issues of timeliness and victim representation before the Court. The latest major change in its Rules became effective on January 1, 2010. In addition, the increasing number of decisions issued by the Inter-American Court in recent years has presented the Court with diverse procedural issues, resulting in the establishment of consistent practices in applying its procedures. Cases involving multiple victims – sometimes hundreds of victims in the case of massacres – have contributed to the evolution of victim-centered and community-based reparations. This book analyzes the practice and procedures of the Inter-American Court and critiques its effectiveness in developing procedures and practices that protect the rights of individual applicants. It covers the period from the Court's inception in 1979 through May, 2012.

* Introduction to *The Practice and Procedure of the Inter-American Court of Human Rights*, 2nd edn, CUP (2013).

THE INTER-AMERICAN HUMAN RIGHTS SYSTEM

A brief background of the Inter-American human rights system is necessary for a thorough understanding of the practice and procedure of the Inter-American Court. Human rights protection in the Americas is overseen by the Organization of American States (OAS), an international organization comprising the thirty-five independent States of the Western hemisphere.[1] Formerly, Cuba was suspended from participating in the OAS because it adopted a Marxist-Leninist form of government. On June 3, 2009, the OAS General Assembly voted by acclimation to revoke the 1962 OAS resolution that suspended Cuba. The OAS set certain conditions for Cuba's reinstatement: first, Cuba must request readmission to the OAS, and second, it must take part in negotiations. As of July 1, 2012, Cuba had not complied with these conditions. Should Cuba decide to again participate in the OAS, it is hoped that it will also play a more active role in the Inter-American human rights system by ratifying human rights treaties, nominating members to the Commission and judges to the Court, and accepting the Court's jurisdiction.

OAS Member States have worked together to structure a regional system to promote and protect human rights in the Americas. The organization has promulgated a series of instruments governing human rights in the region. These instruments include the Charter of the OAS,[2] which is the constitutive treaty forming the alliance between the American States. Although the OAS Charter is not solely concerned with human rights, it established the Inter-American Commission on Human Rights as an organ of the OAS.[3] Over time the Charter has been amended to incorporate other provisions on human rights. Other OAS documents and treaties specifically dedicated to human rights include the American Declaration of the Rights and Duties of Man;[4] the American Convention on Human Rights;[5] two Protocols to the American Convention (the Protocol on Economic, Social and Cultural Rights,

[1] OAS website, www.oas.org. OAS member States include Antigua and Barbuda, Argentina, The Bahamas, Barbados, Belize, Bolivia, Brazil, Canada, Chile, Colombia, Costa Rica, Cuba (currently inactive), Dominica, Dominican Republic, Ecuador, El Salvador, Grenada, Guatemala, Guyana, Haiti, Honduras, Jamaica, Mexico, Nicaragua, Panama, Paraguay, Peru, Saint Kitts and Nevis, Saint Lucia, Saint Vincent and the Grenadines, Suriname, Trinidad and Tobago, United States, Uruguay, and Venezuela.

[2] Charter of the Organization of American States (as amended), 30 April 1948, entered into force on 13 December 1951, 2 UST 2394, TIAS No. 2361; amended effective 1970, 21 UST 607, TIAS No. 6847.

[3] *Ibid.*, Art. 51.

[4] Adopted in 1948 by the OAS General Assembly, reprinted in 2010 Basic Documents, at 13.

[5] American Convention on Human Rights, 22 November 1969, 9 ILM 673, OEA/Ser.K/XVI/I.1, doc. 65 rev. 1 corr. 1 (1970), reprinted in 2010 Basic Documents at 19. The American Convention and other Inter-American human rights documents can be viewed on the website of the OAS, http://www.oas.org, or on the website of the Inter-American Court of Human Rights, http://www.corteidh.or.cr; An excellent source of information on the Inter-American Court is Ruiz-Chiriboga, Oswaldo R., CORTE IDH BLOG, http://corteidhblog.blogspot.com

known as the "Protocol of San Salvador,"[6] and the Protocol to Abolish the Death Penalty[7]); the Inter-American Convention to Prevent and Punish Torture;[8] the Inter-American Convention on the Forced Disappearance of Persons;[9] the Inter-American Convention on the Prevention, Punishment and Eradication of Violence Against Women;[10] and the Inter-American Convention on the Elimination of All Forms of Discrimination Against Persons with Disabilities.[11] The OAS also promulgated the Inter-American Democratic Charter, which provides that "[d]emocracy is indispensable for the effective exercise of fundamental freedoms and human rights."[12] The OAS relied on the Inter-American Democratic Charter in 2009 when the OAS General Assembly adopted a resolution immediately suspending Honduras from OAS participation as a result of a coup d'état that deposed the constitutionally elected president. Honduras was readmitted to the OAS in June 2011.

The American Convention on Human Rights, also known as the "Pact of San José," is the principal human rights treaty in the system. The American Convention empowers two bodies – the already established Inter-American Commission on Human Rights and the Inter-American Court of Human Rights – to ensure State compliance with the human rights set forth in the instrument.[13] The American Convention protects some two dozen rights, many more than the number protected initially by the European Convention on Human Rights and Fundamental Freedoms. The rights protected by the American Convention include, inter alia, the rights to life, a name, nationality, property, privacy, humane treatment, personal liberty, a

6 Additional Protocol to the American Convention on Human Rights in the Area of Economic, Social and Cultural Rights ("Protocol of San Salvador"), signed at San Salvador, El Salvador, on 17 November 1988 at the eighteenth regular session of the General Assembly, and entered into force on 16 November 1999, reprinted in 2010 Basic Documents, at 63.

7 Protocol to the American Convention on Human Rights to Abolish the Death Penalty, Approved at Asunción, Paraguay, on 8 June 1990, at the twentieth regular session of the General Assembly of the OAS, entered into force on 28 August 1991, reprinted in 2010 Basic Documents, at 75. This Convention was most recently ratified by Honduras and the Dominican Republic in 2011.

8 Signed at Cartagena de Indias, Colombia, on 9 December 1985 at the fifteenth regular session of the General Assembly of the OAS, entered into force on 28 February 1987, reprinted in 2010 Basic Documents, at 55.

9 Resolution Adopted at Belem do Pará, Brazil, 9 June 1994 at the twenty-fourth regular session of the General Assembly of the OAS, entered into force on 28 March 1996, reprinted in 2010 Basic Documents, at 89.

10 Adopted in Belem do Pará, Brazil, on 9 June 1994 during the twenty-fourth regular session of the General Assembly of the OAS, entered into force on 5 March 1995, reprinted in 2010 Basic Documents, at 79.

11 Inter-American Convention on the Elimination of All Forms of Discrimination Against Persons with Disabilities, adopted at Guatemala City, Guatemala, at the twenty-ninth regular session of the General Assembly of the OAS, 7 June 1999, entered into force on 14 September 2001, reprinted in 2010 Basic Documents, at 97.

12 Inter-American Democratic Charter, adopted by the OAS General Assembly at its special session held in Lima, Peru held on 11 Sept, 2001, 40 ILM 1289, Art. 7.

13 American Convention, Art. 33.

fair trial, assembly, and compensation when there has been a miscarriage of justice. It also provides for rights of the family and the child and for freedom of religion, thought, expression, movement, and residence. The Convention received the necessary eleven ratifications and entered into force in 1978. As of July 1, 2012, twenty-four of the thirty-five Member States of the OAS are States Parties to the American Convention. These States are Argentina, Barbados, Bolivia, Brazil, Chile, Colombia, Costa Rica, Dominica, Dominican Republic, Ecuador, El Salvador, Grenada, Guatemala, Haiti, Honduras, Jamaica, Mexico, Nicaragua, Panama, Paraguay, Peru, Suriname, Uruguay, and Venezuela.[14] Trinidad and Tobago, which had been a State Party, denounced the American Convention on May 26, 1998, effective May 26, 1999.

Although the American Convention is modeled on UN human rights instruments and on the European Convention for the Protection of Human Rights and Fundamental Freedoms, its drafters refused to simply replicate those treaties. Rather, the delegates to the drafting conference argued that "it was appropriate to introduce any modifications that were desirable in the light of circumstances prevailing in the American Republics."[15] The circumstances and social reality of the developed States – of which the European human rights system was then composed – differed greatly from those of the many underdeveloped States in the Inter-American system. Extremes of poverty and wealth contributed to political instability in the Inter-American system. Misery, injustice, and exploitation were endemic. Not surprisingly, social and economic oppression gave rise to political oppression and to human rights violations. The distinctions between the European and American systems were also manifest in the types of human rights violations confronted by the two systems. For many years the principal cases in the Inter-American system involved forced disappearances and extrajudicial executions resulting from intentional governmental policies. The Inter-American system benefited immeasurably from the European experience, but it had to forge its own practice and procedures. As Buergenthal stated, "For better or for worse, the problems of our Hemisphere are more unique to the Americas than they are universal or European. They can only be solved within the framework of our own legal, cultural, political, and social traditions."[16] Regional human rights organs, such as the Inter-American Court and Commission, have an understanding of the cultural, historical, and legal background

[14] The States Parties are listed in 2010 Basic Documents, at 41. See Appendix 1, p. 360. The only American States that have not ratified the American Convention are Antigua and Barbuda, Bahamas, Belize, Canada, Cuba, the United States, St. Kitts and Nevis, St. Lucia, and St. Vincent and the Grenadines. Trinidad and Tobago ratified the American Convention but subsequently denounced it.

[15] Council of Europe, *Report on the Inter-American Specialized Conference on Human Rights* (Strasbourg, 22 December 1969), reprinted in *Human Rights: The Inter-American System*, Booklet 15 vol. 3, at 67, 71 (Thomas B. Buergenthal and Robert E. Norris eds., 1982).

[16] Thomas Buergenthal, "The American and European Conventions on Human Rights: Similarities and Differences," 30 *American University Law Review*, 155, 156 (1980–1).

of the States in the system and thus can better evaluate human rights claims and craft relevant reparations.[17]

Traditionally, only States had automatic standing to file petitions or complaints against other States in international law. Individuals did not have standing, even when their own rights were violated. This was also true in international human rights law, which had been created to protect individuals. When injured by the action of a State, an individual's only recourse was to convince his or her government to file a complaint. If that government were the violator, the victim had no recourse. When human rights abuses became endemic, only rarely did one State complain or take action against another, and these actions were often politically motivated. Even when a State is concerned about human rights violations, political reality often inhibits it from making accusations about another for fear of jeopardizing its economic interests or of having its own practices evaluated. The drafters of the American Convention had the foresight to give individuals the right to petition.

Standing to file an individual petition with the Commission is not limited to the individual victim or family members of the victim. Any person, group of persons, or nongovernmental entity that is legally recognized in a Member State of the OAS may file a petition alleging that an individual's rights have been violated.[18] This provision has proved to be especially important in the Inter-American system, where victims or their family members may be too intimidated or indigent to submit a petition. A nongovernmental organization (NGO) often has more resources than the individuals involved and is less susceptible to threats of retaliation.

The Convention delineates the procedures that the Commission and the Court are to apply in processing individual complaints of human rights abuse. These procedures specify that an individual who alleges that a State Party to the American Convention has violated his or her rights must first file a complaint directly with the Inter-American Commission, located in Washington, DC.[19] The Commission received 1,658 complaints in 2011.[20] It is composed of seven commissioners, who are chosen from the Member States of the OAS.[21] The Commission's Secretariat – comprising a full-time staff of lawyers, an Executive Secretary, and a Deputy Executive Secretary – performs the routine work of the Commission, including the initial review of petitions. The Commission solicits information from the parties, makes a decision as to the admissibility of the petition, engages in fact-finding procedures, and attempts to bring about a friendly settlement between the parties. If the Commission attributes the human rights violation to the State, the Commission may

17 Gerald L. Neuman, "Import, Export, and Regional Consent in the Inter-American Court of Human Rights," 19 *European Journal of International Law*, 101, 106 (2008).

18 American Convention, Art. 44.

19 *Ibid.*

20 2011 Annual Report, IACHR, at 54. Available at http://www.cidh.oas.org/annualrep/2011eng/TOC.htm.

21 American Convention, Art. 34.

make recommendations to the State.[22] A State Party to the Convention that decides to challenge the Commission's attribution of responsibility may submit the case to the Inter-American Court.[23] The Commission may submit a case to the Court only if the State has accepted the Court's jurisdiction.[24] The Court then conducts contentious proceedings to determine whether the State is responsible for the human rights violation. If the Court holds the State accountable, the Court may order the State to make reparations. The State is legally bound to comply with the judgment of the Court.[25]

A CONCISE HISTORY OF THE INTER-AMERICAN COURT

The Inter-American Court of Human Rights was established in 1979.[26] During its early years, the Court's prospects for improving the human rights of the people of the Americas appeared uninspiring. Dictatorships in the Western hemisphere perpetrated gross and systematic violations of human rights.[27] State-sponsored forced disappearances, extrajudicial killings, and torture were commonplace. Few observers expected the Court to have a significant impact, and initially, the skeptics were right. The Commission did not forward contentious cases to the Court until 1986, seven years after the Court's inception. Although Costa Rica attempted to bypass the Commission in one instance by referring a case directly, the Court determined that the Convention-mandated procedures could not be circumvented.[28] The Court, therefore, refused to consider the case and sent it to the Commission.[29] The Court's principal vehicle for contributing to international law during that period was through its advisory opinions.

When the Commission began to refer contentious cases to the Court, the governments of newly emerging democracies were shocked to be charged with human rights violations. These States equated the need for human rights enforcement with dictatorships. As a result, it was initially feared that States would refuse to participate in proceedings before the Court, a recurring problem for the International Court of Justice at that time. This did not happen. States responded to applications filed against them by designating agents, filing memoranda, and appearing and arguing at public hearings. To be sure, States often filed preliminary objections, many of

22 *Ibid.*, Art. 50(3).

23 *Ibid.*, Art. 61.

24 *Ibid.*, Art. 62(3).

25 *Ibid.*, Art. 68(1).

26 The first judges were elected to the Court on 22 May 1979 during the Seventh Special session of the OAS General Assembly. http://www.corteidh.or.cr/historia.cfm.

27 See Cecilia Medina Quiroga, *The Battle of Human Rights: Gross Systematic Violations and the Inter-American System*, 2 (Kluwer, 1988).

28 *Matter of Viviana Gallardo et al.* (Costa Rica), IACtHR, Decision of 13 November 1981, No. G101/81, para. 28. Available at http://www.corteidh.or.cr/opiniones.cfm.

29 *Ibid.*, Resolutions 3 and 4.

which were frivolous, arguing that the Court did not have jurisdiction or the case was not admissible; however, if the Court rejected those objections, the States fully participated in the case.

The reputation of the Inter-American Court has been strengthened as a result of the quality of its jurisprudence. Its status may be reflected in the caliber of State witnesses who have appeared before it to defend State actions. For example, in the *Baena Ricardo Case*, in which 270 former Panamanian State employees alleged that they were illegally dismissed from their jobs as a result of an ex post facto law, Guillermo Endara, the former president of Panama, and his vice president testified before the Court.[30] Many States currently accept full or partial responsibility for human rights violations, acknowledging their liability once they are before the Court. State acceptance of international responsibility is an indirect acknowledgment on the part of the State that an Inter-American Court judgment attributing responsibility to a State for human rights violations is taken seriously domestically and internationally.

State compliance with Court-ordered reparations has similarly evolved. Because the Court has no effective mechanism to enforce its judgments, it was initially feared that States would simply ignore them and refuse to make Court-ordered reparations to the victims. Honduras, under the presidency of Carlos Roberto Reina, a former Inter-American Court judge, paid the compensation ordered in the *Honduran Disappearance Cases*, the first contentious cases decided by the Court. Since that time, States have paid the financial compensation ordered by the Court in more than 80 percent of the cases.[31] Compensation, however, is not the only form of reparation ordered by the Inter-American Court. The Court may also order the State to take action or to desist from particular acts. When Peru complied with the Court's order to release from prison María Elena Loayza Tamayo, a college professor,[32] a new level of State compliance was reached. Subsequently, in certain cases when the Court has declared a domestic law or judgment to be in violation of the American Convention, States have amended the law,[33] domestic courts have declared the law in question to be unconstitutional,[34] or domestic court judgments have been annulled.[35] States have complied with Court orders to apologize to victims, provide them with health care or educational training, and return the body of the victim to the family. The Court also orders the State to make community-based reparations, such as reallocating resources to housing, education, health care, or employment in a community

[30] *Baena Ricardo et al.* v. *Panama* (Merits, Reparations, and Costs), IACtHR, 2 February 2001, Ser. C, No. 72. paras. 65(h) and (i).

[31] 2010 Annual Report IACtHR, at 12. Available at http://www.corteidh.or.cr/docs/informes/2010_eng.pdf.

[32] See *Loayza Tamayo* v. *Peru* (Merits), IACtHR, 17 September 1997, Ser. C, No. 33, para. 84, operative para. 5.

[33] *Cantoral Benavides* v. *Peru* (Reparations and Costs), IACtHR, 3 December 2001, Ser. C, No. 88, para. 76.

[34] *Suárez Rosero* v. *Ecuador* (Reparations and Costs), IACtHR, 20 January 1999, Ser. C, No. 44, paras. 81–83.

[35] *Cesti Hurtado* v. *Peru* (Reparations and Costs), IACtHR, 31 May 2001, Ser. C, No. 78, para. 15.

that suffered massive human rights violations. Many of these reparations were unprecedented in human rights law.

There is, however, another level of State compliance with Court-ordered reparations that is not yet commonly observed in the Inter-American system. In almost every case, the Court orders the State to investigate, prosecute, and punish the individuals responsible for the human rights violations; however, these orders are seldom fulfilled. In most States impunity reigns, and the State power structure lacks the means or the will to bring the perpetrators of human rights violations to justice. Domestic statutes of limitations or laws on double jeopardy may bar investigations and trials. When Court orders to prosecute and punish the violators are consistently fulfilled, the Court will have contributed substantially to limit impunity and to the specific and general deterrence of human rights violations.

The initial fear that States would withdraw their acceptance of the Court's jurisdiction or denounce the American Convention has not been warranted. Only one State, Trinidad and Tobago, has denounced the Convention and the Court's jurisdiction.[36] Peru, which had announced its intention to withdraw its recognition of the Court's jurisdiction, has since reaffirmed its acceptance of the Court's jurisdiction.[37] Moreover, additional States have ratified the Convention and accepted the Court's jurisdiction.

COMPOSITION OF THE COURT

The Court is composed of seven judges, who must be "jurists of the highest moral authority" recognized for their competence in human rights law.[38] The judges must also "possess the qualifications required for the exercise of the highest judicial functions in conformity with the law of the State of which they are nationals or of the State that proposes them as candidates."[39] Judges are independent; they do not represent States. Although judges must be nationals of OAS Member States,[40] they need not be nationals of States that have ratified the American Convention or accepted the jurisdiction of the Court. Judges are elected by a vote of the States Parties to the Convention.[41] A State Party may propose up to three candidates for judge, provided that at least one of the three is a national of another Member State.[42] The judges are elected for six years and may serve no more than two terms.[43]

36 See 2010 Basic Documents, at 52.

37 See Peruvian Legislative Resolution No. 271532 in the Inter-American Court of Human Rights Press Release CP2/01 on the Court's website at http://corteidh.or.cr.

38 American Convention, Art. 52(1).

39 *Ibid.*

40 *Ibid.* The judges must be nationals of different States. *Ibid.*, Art. 52(2).

41 American Convention, Art. 53(1).

42 *Ibid.*, Art. 53(2).

43 *Ibid.*, Art. 54.

The judge serving as President of the Court serves on a permanent basis.[44] The other judges serve on a part-time basis, although the increased number of cases and requests for provisional measures warrant a full-time Court.[45]

When a sitting judge is a national of a State Party to a contentious case, the judge must recuse himelf or herself from consideration of the case.[46] States Parties in contentious cases no longer have the right to name a judge ad hoc for that case, if a sitting judge is not a national of that State.[47] If a judge on the Court is a national of one of the States Parties to the case, only with interstate complaints may the other State Party designate a judge ad hoc.[48]

The Court has a full-time Secretariat that is based at the seat of the Court in San José, Costa Rica. The Secretariat, like the Commission's Secretariat, is composed of the Secretary, Deputy Secretary, and staff attorneys and assistants. The Court may convene at its seat,[49] but increasingly it is meeting in other States Parties. In recent years the Court has held special sessions in Argentina, Barbados, Bolivia, Brazil, Chile, Colombia, the Dominican Republic, Ecuador, El Salvador, Guatemala, Honduras, Mexico, Paraguay, Peru, and Uruguay. By holding its sessions in OAS Member States the Court increases public awareness of the workings of the Inter-American system and develops a more collaborative and cooperative working relationship with the judiciary and governments in those countries. While in the host countries, the Court holds public hearings, deliberates on cases, and conducts court business. In addition, the judges and Court attorneys often meet with government officials and civil society and hold training seminars to foster a better understanding of the Inter-American human rights system. In this way, the Court brings the system and its work of protecting human rights to the attention of domestic courts, prosecutors, attorneys, law students, other government officials, and the public. This exposure should enhance compliance with Inter-American Court judgments.

44 Statute of the Inter-American Court of Human Rights, adopted by the General Assembly of the OAS at its ninth regular session, held in La Paz, Bolivia, October 1979 (Resolution No. 448), Art. 16(2), reprinted in 2010 Basic Documents, at 209.

45 Evaluation of the Workings of the Inter-American System for the Protection and Promotion of Human Rights with a View to its Improvement and Strengthening, Resolution 1(e), AG/RES. 1828 (XXXI-O/01), Resolution adopted at the third plenary session, held on 5 June 2001 in which the OAS General Assembly suggested that the possibility of a permanent Court and Commission be examined. Available on the OAS website at http://www.oas.org.

46 Rules of Procedure of the Inter-American Court of Human Rights, entered into force 1 January 2010, Art. 19, approved by the Court during its LXXXV Regular Period of Sessions, held from November 16 to November 28, 2009, reprinted in Basic Documents Pertaining to Human Rights in the Inter-American System (updated to June 1010), OEA/Ser.L/V/I.4 rev. 13, 30 June 2010, at 185. Available at http://www.corteidh.or.cr/reglamento.cfm [hereinafter "IACtHR Rules of Procedure"].

47 American Convention, Art. 55(2).

48 *Ibid.*

49 *Ibid.*, Art. 58(1).

10 The Practice and Procedure of the Inter-American Court of Human Rights

OVERVIEW OF JURISDICTION

Under its contentious jurisdiction, the Inter-American Court rules on whether a State has violated an individual's human rights. The Inter-American Court is not a criminal court and does not determine whether individuals are guilty of human rights violations; rather, it determines State liability.[50] State domestic courts have the competence to determine individual criminal liability. The Inter-American Court has clarified that

> [t]he international protection of human rights should not be confused with criminal justice. When States appear before the Court, they do so not as defendants in a criminal proceeding, since the Court does not impose punishment on those responsible for violating human rights. Its function is to protect the victims and to determine the reparation of the damages caused by the States responsible for such actions.[51]

The Court must assess the truth of the applicant's allegations and determine whether the facts as proved constitute a violation of the Convention imputable to the State. The Court can exercise contentious jurisdiction only over States Parties to the Convention that have accepted its jurisdiction as binding ipso facto or on an ad hoc basis by special agreement for a particular case.[52] A State Party to the American Convention accepts the Court's jurisdiction as binding ipso facto when it files a special declaration to that effect.[53] As of May 1, 2012, twenty-one States Parties to the American Convention had accepted the compulsory jurisdiction of the Inter-American Court. The States subject to the Court's jurisdiction are Argentina, Barbados, Bolivia, Brazil, Chile, Colombia, Costa Rica, Dominican Republic, Ecuador, El Salvador, Guatemala, Haiti, Honduras, Mexico, Nicaragua, Panama, Paraguay, Peru, Suriname, Uruguay, and Venezuela.[54] In denouncing the American Convention, Trinidad and Tobago also denounced the Court's jurisdiction.

The Court's early contentious cases dealt with disappearances or extrajudicial executions. In later years, a broader range of alleged violations have been submitted for the Court's consideration. For instance, in *"The Last Temptation of Christ" Case*, the Court held that Chile's prior censorship of a movie was a violation of freedom

50 *La Cantuta* v. *Peru* (Merits, Reparations, and Costs), IACtHR, 29 November 2006, Ser. C, No 162, para. 156.

51 *Constitutional Court* v. *Peru* (Merits, Reparations, and Costs), IACtHR, 31 January 2001, Ser. C, No. 71, para. 47; see also *Cantoral Benavides* v. *Peru* (Merits), IACtHR, 18 August 2000, Ser. C. No. 69, para. 46.

52 American Convention, Art. 62. See Restrictions to the Death Penalty (Arts. 4(2) and 4(4) of the American Convention on Human Rights), IACtHR, Advisory Opinion OC-3/83 of 8 September 1983, Ser. A, No. 3, para. 21.

53 American Convention, Art. 62.

54 See 2010 Basic Documents, at 41.

of expression as guaranteed by the American Convention.[55] In the *Constitutional Court Case*, the Court ruled on the dismissal of three Peruvian Constitutional Court justices, who argued that they were impeached because they refused to hold constitutional a law that would allow President Fujimori to run for an additional term in office.[56] The Court also has ruled on several cases in which communities have been massacred or indigenous communities have demanded the return of their ancestral lands and title to those lands. The increasing breadth of rights litigated is important for the evolution of the Inter-American human rights system in that the Court's caseload is coming to reflect the spectrum of rights protected by the Convention.

The Inter-American Court also has advisory jurisdiction that can be exercised without the express consent of States. Even OAS Member States that have not ratified the American Convention may request an advisory opinion or find their actions subject to the Court's advisory jurisdiction.[57] There are no "parties" to an advisory procedure, and there is no case to be settled by the Court.[58] The Court's advisory jurisdiction enables it "to perform a service for all of the members of the Inter-American system and is designed to assist them in fulfilling their international human rights obligations."[59] Through its advisory opinions, the Court fosters uniform legal standards throughout the Americas. Although an advisory opinion is not binding (unlike the Court's judgment in a contentious case), it does have undeniable legal and moral effects on both national and international law.[60]

The Court is also empowered to act quickly in "cases of extreme gravity and urgency" by ordering a State to protect persons who are in danger.[61] Whether the case is already being considered by the Court or is submitted to the Court by the Commission only for the purpose of requesting provisional measures, the Court may order a State to take measures to protect persons from irreparable harm.[62] The Court's provisional measures orders are binding on the State.[63] Requests for provisional measures have proliferated, putting a burden on the Court to oversee their implementation. The danger of irreparable harm and the corresponding duty

55 *"The Last Temptation of Christ" (Olmedo Bustos et al.)* v. *Chile* (Merits, Reparations, and Costs), IACtHR, 5 February 2001, Ser. C, No. 73, operative para. 1.

56 *Constitutional Court* v. *Peru* (Competence), IACtHR, 24 September 1999, Ser. C, No. 55, para. 2.

57 Advisory Opinion OC-3/83, para. 43.

58 Reports of the Inter-American Commission on Human Rights (Art. 51 of the American Convention on Human Rights), IACtHR, Advisory Opinion OC-15/97 of 14 November 1997, Ser. A, No. 15, para. 25.

59 *"Other Treaties" Subject to the Consultative Jurisdiction of the Court* (Art. 64 of the American Convention on Human Rights), IACtHR, Advisory Opinion OC-1/82 of 24 September 1982, Ser. A, No. 1, para. 39; *The Right to Information on Consular Assistance within the Framework of the Guarantees of Legal Due Process*, IACtHR, Advisory Opinion OC-16/99 of 1 October 1999, Ser. A. No. 16, para. 64.

60 Advisory Opinion OC-15/97, para. 26.

61 American Convention, Art. 63(2).

62 *Ibid.*

63 *Constitutional Court* (Peru), Provisional Measures, IACtHR, 14 August 2000, para. 14.

of oversight often continue for years. Nonetheless, provisional measures have proved effective in protecting victims who are in imminent danger.

THE COURT'S INTERPRETATION OF THE AMERICAN CONVENTION

When interpreting the American Convention on Human Rights, the Inter-American Court applies the Vienna Convention on the Law of Treaties, which specifies that "a treaty shall be interpreted in good faith, in accordance with the ordinary meaning to be given to the terms of the treaty in their context and in the light of its object and purpose."[64] The object and purpose of the American Convention "is the protection of the basic rights of individual human beings irrespective of their nationality, both against the State of their nationality and all other contracting States."[65] In accordance with that objective, the Court has stated that it must interpret the Convention so "as to give full effect to the system of human rights protection."[66]

The Court applies the *pro homine* principle and interprets the Convention and State declarations "in accordance with the canons and practice of International Law in general, and with International Human Rights Law specifically, and [in a manner] which awards the greatest degree of protection to the human beings under its guardianship."[67] The Court has stated that the American Convention must "be interpreted in favor of the individual, who is the object of international protection, as long as such an interpretation does not result in a modification of the system."[68] Under the *pro homine* principle, the dignity of the individual is of primary concern when interpreting the rights specified in international human rights law and in the American Convention, in particular. Human dignity can only be attained if the rights protected by the American Convention are "interpreted and enforced so that its guarantees are truly practical and effective (*effet utile*)."[69] Moreover, the domestic law of States Parties must also be interpreted so as to comply with the American Convention and the interpretations of the Inter-American Court if it is to satisfy the principle of *effet utile*.[70]

The Inter-American Court, like the European Court of Human Rights, holds that "human rights treaties are living instruments whose interpretation must consider

64 Vienna Convention on the Law of Treaties, UN Doc. A/CONF.39/27, 23 May 1969, Art. 31, entered into force 27 January 1988.

65 Advisory Opinion OC-2/82, para. 29.

66 Advisory Opinion OC-15/97, para. 29.

67 *Benjamin et al.* v. *Trinidad and Tobago* (Preliminary Objections), IACtHR, 1 September 2001, Ser. C, No. 81, para. 70.

68 *Matter of Viviana Gallardo*, 13 November 1981, Ser. 101, para. 16.

69 *Vargas Areco* v. *Paraguay* (Merits, Reparations, and Costs), IACtHR, 26 September 2006, Ser. C, No. 155, para. 85.

70 *Lori Berenson Mejía* v. *Peru* (Merits, Reparations, and Costs), IACtHR, 25 November 2004, Ser. C, No. 119, para. 220.

the changes over time and present-day conditions."[71] The Court does not take a strict constructionist position in its interpretation of the Convention. In this regard, the Court has stated that it may not ignore the important developments in the last fifty years that have enriched human rights law.[72] Therefore, it interprets the Convention "within the framework of the entire legal system prevailing at the time of the interpretation."[73] The Inter-American Court engages in an "evolutive interpretation" of the American Convention on Human Rights and of international human rights law in general.[74] It does not impose a static interpretation of human rights on the American Convention. Rather, the concept of the basic rights owing to individuals has expanded over time. The Convention does not purport to grant human rights; it merely recognizes them and codifies them.[75]

When interpreting the rights protected by the American Convention, the Inter-American Court references the *corpus juris* of international human rights law.[76] This *corpus juris* comprises treaties, conventions, resolutions, and declarations.[77] The Court regularly supplements its interpretation of the provisions of the American Convention with references to other treaties, its own case law, and that of other international tribunals and bodies. The Inter-American Court effectively contributes to the harmonization of international law and principles by influencing and being influenced by other sources of international law.[78] This expansive interpretation of rights comports with the American Convention's requirement that the norms protected by the Convention cannot be interpreted so as to preclude other rights that are "inherent in the human personality."[79]

Moreover, the American Convention does not permit the interpretation of its provisions to restrict "the enjoyment or exercise of any right or freedom recognized by virtue of the laws of any State Party."[80] The Inter-American Court relies on domestic laws and constitutional provisions when interpreting rights under the American Convention. Doing so is especially persuasive when the rights at issue are domestically politically sensitive, such as the property right to social security in

71 *Right to Information on Consular Assistance Within the Framework of the Guarantees of Legal Due Process*, IACtHR, Advisory Opinion OC-16/99 of 1 October 1999, Ser. A, No. 16, para. 114.
72 *Ibid.*, para. 113.
73 *Ibid.*
74 *Ibid.*, para. 114.
75 Cecilia Medina Quiroga, *La Convención Americana: Teoría y Jurisprudencia: Vida, Integridad Personal, Libertad Personal, Debido Proceso, y Recurso Judicial*, Ch. I, para. 5 (Universidad de Chile, 2003).
76 Advisory Opinion OC-16/99, para. 114.
77 *Ibid.*, para. 114–15.
78 Cecilia Medina Quiroga, *La Convención Americana: Teoría y Jurisprudencia*, para. 4 (Universidad de Chile, 2003).
79 American Convention, Art. 29(c).
80 *Ibid.*, Art. 29(b).

Peru,[81] or the rights of indigenous groups to regain their ancestral lands in Paraguay,[82] where the Paraguayan Constitution provides that indigenous peoples have the right to their ancestral land.[83]

AN ILLUSTRATIVE CONTENTIOUS CASE

The facts and procedures of an actual contentious case may help the reader better understand the subject matter of this book. The Inter-American Court decided the *Kawas Fernández* v. *Honduras Case* on April 3, 2009.[84] The case is representative in that it involves the extrajudicial execution of an environmental activist. Human rights defenders, including environmental activists, have been targeted for their activities. The case includes all procedural phases before the Commission and the Court. The only difference from recent cases is that in 2009, both the victim's representatives and the Commission were representing the alleged victims, whereas currently the Commission no longer represents the alleged victims.

Facts

The Court found the following facts to be proved. Blanca Jeannette Kawas Fernández was a Honduran environmental activist and the president of a foundation to protect and preserve the environment. Through the foundation, she reported cases of illegal logging and damage to the nearby national park and other protected areas. She was also openly opposed to economic development projects in the area. Kawas Fernández was murdered in her home in 1995 by two armed men. The police took witnesses statements, and a 16-year-old boy confessed to the murder. He subsequently recanted his testimony, claiming that he had been coerced. A year later, the Honduran General Bureau of Criminal Investigations filed reports indicating that public officials participated in the planning of the murder and in the obstruction of the investigation. The report also stated that certain witnesses were in danger of death.

Nothing more was done on the case in Honduras until the complaint was filed with the Inter-American Commission eight years later in 2003. Subsequently, the Honduran Attorney General's office issued a report stating that Kawas Fernández's

81 *Acevedo Buendía et al. ("Discharged and Retired Employees of the Comptroller") v. Peru* (Preliminary Objection, Merits, Reparations, and Costs), IACtHR, 1 July 2009, Ser. C, No. 198, para. 86.

82 *Yakye Axa Indigenous Community* v. *Paraguay* (Merits, Reparations, and Costs), IACtHR, 17 June 2005, Ser. C, No. 125, para. 64; *Mayagna (Sumo) Awas Tingni Community* v. *Nicaragua* (Merits, Reparations, and Costs), IACtHR, 31 August 2001, Ser. C, No. 79, para. 148.

83 *Yakye Axa Indigenous Community* v. *Paraguay* (No. 125, 2005), para. 138, quoting the Paraguayan Constitution at Article 64. See Lucas Lixinski, "Treaty Interpretation by the Inter-American Court of Human Rights: Expansionism at the Service of the Unity of International Law," 21 *European Journal of International Law*, 585, 600 (2010).

84 *Kawas Fernández v. Honduras* (Merits, Reparations, and Costs), 3 April 2009, No. 196.

murder was the result of her environmental activities and that State agents were allegedly involved in planning her murder and obstructing the investigation. Investigations revealed that the young man who had incriminated himself died violently in 2008. At the time of the Court's judgment, sixteen years after the death of Kawas Fernández, the domestic criminal proceedings were still in the preliminary stage.

During the decade that followed the death of Blanca Jeannette Kawas Fernández, there were several reports of threats and executions of environmental activists in Honduras. At least five environmental activists were murdered during that time period.

Procedures before the Commission

The petition was lodged with the Commission in 2003 by two nongovernmental organizations (NGOs): the Center for Justice and International Law (CEJIL) and the Equipo de Reflexión, Investigación and Comunicación de la Compañía de Jesús (ERIC). The Commission found the petition to be admissible in 2005 and adopted its report on the merits in 2006 in which it made recommendations to the State. When Honduras did not make progress in following the recommendations, the Commission referred the case to the Inter-American Court.

Jurisdiction of the Court

The Commission submitted the case against Honduras to the Court on March 7, 2008. Honduras had ratified the American Convention on Human Rights in 1977, and accepted the compulsory jurisdiction of the Court in 1981. Therefore, because Ms. Kawas Fernández was murdered in 1995, the Inter-American Court had contentious jurisdiction to rule on her extrajudicial execution and the State's failure to conduct an adequate investigation into her death.

Initial Procedures before the Court

The Commission's submission of the case to the Court included its reasons for submitting the case, a copy of the entire case file, and the evidence that was received in the proceedings before the Commission. The Court notified Honduras and the alleged victims' representatives as soon as the case was filed. The alleged victims' representatives then filed their brief containing pleadings, motions, and evidence. In the State's answer to both the Commission's submission and the alleged victims' brief, the State was required either to accept each fact or claim or to contradict it. The State also had to submit its evidence in an organized form, identify the declarants and expert witnesses that it proposed to have testify orally or in writing, and present its legal arguments. The State did not interpose preliminary objections to the admissibility of the case or to the jurisdiction of the Court. The President of the Court determined which alleged victims, declarants, and expert witnesses would submit their testimony through sworn affidavits and which would testify in court.

Provisional Measures

At the request of the victims' representatives, the Court ordered Honduras to take provisional measures to protect the life and personal integrity of an eyewitness to the murder.

Partial Acceptance of International Responsibility

Honduras accepted international responsibility for violations of the right to a fair trial and the right to judicial protection to the detriment of the deceased's next of kin. The State denied that it had violated the deceased's right to life, her right to freedom of association, and her next of kin's right to humane treatment. The State repeated its acknowledgment of responsibility during the public hearing and in its final written arguments.

Proceedings on the Merits

A public hearing was held in Mexico City where the Court was holding a special session. The Court received seven affidavits from victims, witnesses, and expert witnesses. The parties were given the opportunity to respond to the affidavits. At the public hearing, the Court heard the testimony of three witnesses: the brother of the deceased, the former director of the foundation for which the deceased worked, and the former Honduran Special Prosecutor for the Environment who testified in her capacity as an expert witness. The State did not present witnesses at the hearing. The Court accepted documentary evidence from the expert witness and newspaper articles that referred to well-known public facts or declarations of State officials. At the conclusion of the oral testimony and questions, the parties gave their final oral arguments on the merits, reparations, and costs. The judges asked the State and the representatives to submit complementary information with their final written arguments. The Environmental Defense Law Center filed an amicus curiae brief with the Court, which the Court then distributed to the State and the victims' representatives.

Decision on the Merits

The Court held that Honduras had violated the right to life and freedom of association of Blanca Jeannette Kawas Fernández. It also held the State liable for the violation of the right to humane treatment of the direct relations of the deceased, as well as the violation of the rights to a fair trial and judicial protection of the deceased and her direct relations.

Reparations

The injured parties in the case were the deceased as well as her parents, children, and siblings. The Court ordered monetary compensation for the deceased's loss of earnings, consequential damages, and the pain and suffering of her next of kin, as well as for the costs and expenses in bringing the case domestically and before the organs of the Inter-American system.

The Court also ordered Honduras to make equitable reparations by publishing the relevant parts of the Inter-American Court judgment, holding a public ceremony, constructing a monument in Kawas Fernández's memory, placing plaques in the national park named in her honor, and providing free psychological care to members of her family. Honduras was also ordered to acknowledge responsibility and publicly apologize to the family of Ms. Kawas Fernández and also to the families of all the environmentalists who were murdered subsequent to her death. Further, the Court ordered the State to institute criminal proceedings and investigate, prosecute, and punish all persons involved in planning and executing her murder and obstructing justice. In addition, Honduras was ordered to carry out a national awareness and sensitivity campaign regarding the importance of the work performed by environmentalists in Honduras and their contribution to the defense of human rights.

State Compliance

As of February 27, 2012, Honduras had paid the financial compensation and costs and expenses ordered by the Court, published the relevant paragraphs of the Court's judgment in two sources, and held a public ceremony in which it accepted international responsibility for the violations. Honduras had not complied with its obligations to initiate or continue criminal proceedings for the assassination of the environmental advocate and obstruction of justice, erect a monument in her honor, or conduct a national campaign to raise national awareness about the work of environmental activists and their defense of human rights. Neither the State nor the family offered information on whether the State had provided the family with health and psychiatric care or whether the family had requested it.[85]

PAST PROCEDURAL ADVANCES MADE BY THE COURT AND THE COMMISSION

Since the initial contentious cases, the Court and the Commission have refined their procedures to enhance the role of the individual and to expedite the processing of cases. The Convention authorizes the Court and the Commission to draw up their

[85] *Kawas Fernández* v. *Honduras* (Monitoring Compliance), IACtHR, 27 February 2012, declares paras. 1 – 2.

Rules of Procedure,[86] and many of the advances have resulted from amendments to their Rules. The Court has revised its Rules of Procedure several times, with a substantial revision entering into force on January 1, 2010.[87] The Commission also made major changes to its Rules of Procedure in the same period.[88]

One of the most pervasive criticisms of the Inter-American system had concerned the inadequacy of the role of the victim. Although petitioners have always been able to bring and present cases before the Commission, initially they had no recourse if the Commission chose not to forward the case to the Inter-American Court, and no role before the Court if the Commission did submit the case. The Convention makes no provision for the victim or petitioner to seize the Court. The right of an individual to bring a case before a human rights court is a logical step in the evolution of human rights law. As explained with respect to the European system, "[t]he situation whereby the individual is granted rights but not given the possibility to exploit fully the control machinery provided for enforcing them, could today be regarded as inconsistent with the spirit of the Convention, not to mention incompatible with domestic law procedures in States parties."[89]

To circumvent this limitation, when the State involved has accepted the Court's jurisdiction, the Commission now refers the case to the Court "unless there is a reasoned decision by an absolute majority of the members of the Commission to the contrary."[90] A primary criterion in the Commission's decision is the petitioner's position as to whether the case should be referred to the Court.[91] If the petitioner is in favor of carrying the case forward, there is a strong possibility that the Commission will do so. However, without a protocol to the American Convention, the Commission's Rules of Procedure cannot address all limitations upon the individual's right to submit a case to the Court. Most fundamentally, the Commission, not the individual, still makes the ultimate decision as required by the American Convention.

Throughout the years, the Court and Commission have also streamlined their procedures to shorten the time between the filing of a petition and a final judgment. Lengthy proceedings do not serve the needs of any victim, particularly those who may be facing torture or death. As explained by a former member of the Commission, "[l]ong before all of these procedures have been completed, however, the patience of the complainant, although not his injury, may have come to an end, and in many

86 American Convention, Arts. 39, 60.

87 IACtHR Rules of Procedure, Art. 66.

88 Rules of Procedure of the Inter-American Commission on Human Rights, entered into force 31 December, 2009, approved by the Commission at its 137th regular period of sessions held from October 28 to November 13, 2009, and modified on September 2nd, 2011. Available at the website of the Inter-American Commission on Human Rights, http://www.cidh.oas.org.

89 Explanatory Report to Protocol No. 9 to the Convention for the Protection of Human Rights and Fundamental Freedoms, reprinted in 12 *Human Rights Law Journal*, 51, at 52 (1991).

90 IACHR Rules of Procedure, Art. 45(1).

91 *Ibid.*, Art. 45(2)(a).

cases it may be the end of the endurance or the life of the person tortured."[92] To minimize the length of proceedings, the Commission curtailed the time period for response to communications and limited the possibility of extensions. States still complain about the Commission's failure to deal expeditiously with petitions when they are initially filed. The Commission, however, does not have the financing to employ an adequate number of staff attorneys necessary to promptly process all the petitions that it receives.

In addition, the Commission introduced practices that would enhance the transparency of its procedures. It registers petitions, issues a formal report on the admissibility of new cases, offers to mediate a friendly settlement between the parties, and ensures confidentiality.

MORE RECENT PROCEDURAL CHANGES

As a result of the participatory and transparent communication process among all system participants, including Inter-American Court judges, Commissioners, States, and civil society, in November 2009 the Inter-American Commission and the Inter-American Court made important changes in their procedures to strengthen the Inter-American human rights system. The revised procedures make the Inter-American human rights system more efficient and transparent and further enhance the role of the victim within the parameters set forth in the American Convention.

In brief, the procedural changes before the Commission deal primarily with the processing of petitions and precautionary measures, referral of cases to the Inter-American Court, and hearings on human rights situations in OAS Member States.[93] A primary focus of the amendments to the Rules of Procedure of the Commission has been to increase its procedural efficiency and economy. Although the amendments to the Commission's rules have increased time limits for the State and petitioners to respond, other changes should minimize the average time of processing.[94]

States, when proposing amendments to the Commission's rules, recommended that the Commission archive cases when petitioners did not follow through on their complaints. Ecuador stated in this regard that "[t]here are cases that have not advanced for nearly 10 years, in which even the petitioners have not continued to take steps to move forward with the matter before the Commission."[95] The Commission's rules now explicitly provide for the archiving of petitions and cases.

92 Fernando Volio, "The Inter-American Commission on Human Rights," 30 *American University Law Review*, 65, at 76–77 (1980).

93 CIDH, Press Release No. 84/09, CIDH Publishes its New Rules of Procedure.

94 IACHR Rules of Procedure, Art. 37.

95 Ecuador, Presentations by States at the Dialogue on the Workings of the Inter-American Human Rights System among Member States, Members of the Inter-American Commission on Human Rights, and the Judges of the Inter-American Court of Human Rights on April 4, 2008, OEA/Ser.G, CP/CAJP-2615/08 add.3, 12 May 2008.

Whenever the basis of the petition does not exist, has ceased, or the necessary information is unavailable, thereby impeding a Commission decision, at any time during the proceedings the Commission may request that the petitioners submit the required information by a certain date.[96] If the petitioners do not comply, the Commission is likely to close the case.

The Court's reforms primarily alter the role of the Inter-American Commission in proceedings before the Court; eliminate ad hoc judges in cases brought originally through an individual petition (rather than an interstate petition); introduce the use of public defenders and legal assistance for victims; provide rules on common legal representation to present the case before the Court when there is more than one victim who has separate representation; condone electronic means of expediting cases; and attempt to increase protection for all persons appearing before the Court, including the victims' legal advisors.[97]

The most significant changes in the Court's procedures concern the role of the Commission in individual contentious cases before the Court. These changes have effectively minimized the Commission's role in contentious cases. Before they were implemented, both the Commission and the alleged victims' representative represented the position of the alleged victims in proceedings before the Court. As a result, the role of the Commission as a litigant carried the potential to undercut its position as a mediator in friendly settlement negotiations in other cases involving the same State or in gaining the State's cooperation in other matters.[98] Moreover, States argued that they were prejudiced by a procedural imbalance, because in effect the State faced two procedural parties, as both the Commission and the representatives of the alleged victims presented evidence and arguments separately against the State.[99]

Under the procedural changes, the Commission no longer serves as an advocate for the victim once the case is before the Court. The revised function of the Commission is to represent and defend the "Inter-American public order of human rights."[100] As such, the Commission serves as an objective and impartial participant. This is akin to the role of the former European Commission on Human Rights before the European Court, which served more as an advisory body that offered independent and impartial positions on questions of fact and law. The separation of roles is important for the Inter-American system because the victim's objective in pursuing the case may differ from that of the Inter-American Commission. The role of the victim is to protect his or her individual interests, whereas that of the Commission

96 IACHR, Rules of Procedure, Art. 42.

97 IACtHR, Statement of Motives for the Reform of the Rules of Procedure. Available at http://www.corteidh.or.cr/regla_eng.pdf. The Court adopted two sets of rules changes in 2009.

98 Dinah Shelton, "The Participation of Nongovernmental Organizations in International Judicial Proceedings," 88 *American Journal of International Law*, 611, 615 (1994).

99 Ecuador, Presentations by States at the Dialogue on the Workings of the Inter-American Human Rights System among Member States.

100 IACtHR Rules of Procedure, Arts. 35(1)(f), 52(3).

is broader than the consideration of individual petitions. The Commission's main function is "to promote respect for and defense of human rights," and to do so, it requires the general cooperation of States.[101]

Yet the transformed role of the Commission, wherein it no longer represents the alleged victims, does not leave victims unrepresented. Once the case is submitted to the Court by either the Commission or the State, alleged victims are represented by private attorneys or public interest NGOs, or, if they cannot afford an attorney, the Court may appoint, on its own motion, an Inter-American public defender to represent the victim.[102] The Inter-American Court and the Inter-American Association of Public Defenders (Asociación Interamericana de Defensorías Públicas [AIDEF]) signed an Agreement of Understanding to provide free legal assistance to alleged victims of human rights violations who lack the financial means to bring a case before the Inter-American Court.[103] The Court provides training courses for Inter-American public defenders in person and by means of distance learning.[104]

When initiating a case before the Court, the Commission no longer submits an application: rather it submits its Article 50 report on the merits of the case, thus avoiding duplicative and sometimes contradictory paperwork.[105] The Commission's report is generally referred to as its "Article 50 Report" because it is mandated by Article 50 of the American Convention on Human Rights. The Commission specifies its reasons for submitting the case to the Court and its observations on the State's response to the Commission's recommendations.[106] The Commission also more specifically indicates to the Court which of the facts contained in the Article 50 report it is submitting to the Court for its consideration.[107] The State, in turn, must accept or contradict each fact and claim at issue.[108] If the State does not expressly deny a fact or expressly controvert a claim, the Court may consider it to be accepted.[109] These procedural changes allow the Court to focus its attention solely on matters that are contested and eliminate needless repetition.

The Commission, in its role representing the Inter-American public order before the Court, does not generally call or question witnesses. If there is a hearing, the Commission begins it by stating the grounds of its report and its presentation of the case to the Court. At that time it sets out any matter that it considers to be relevant

[101] American Convention, Art. 41.
[102] IACtHR, Rules of Procedure, Art. 37.
[103] Rules of Procedure for the Operation of the Legal Assistance Fund of the Inter-American Human Rights System, CP/RES. 963 (1728/09), OEA/Ser.G, CP/RES. 963 (1728/09), 11 November 2009. Available at http://www.oas.org/CONSEJO/resolutions/res963.asp; IACtHR 2011 Annual Report, at 64–65.
[104] IACtHR 2011 Annual Report, at 76.
[105] IACtHR, Rules of Procedure, Art. 35(1).
[106] *Ibid.*, Art. 35(1)(c)
[107] *Ibid.*, Art. 35(3).
[108] *Ibid.*, Art. 41(1)(a).
[109] *Ibid.*, Art. 41(3).

to the resolution of the case.[110] When, however, the Commission perceives that the case affects the "Inter-American public order of human rights in a significant manner," the Commission may name and call expert witnesses.[111] The Commission will likely do so when it perceives that jurisprudence is lacking in a particular human rights area that is affected by the facts of the case. It may then attempt, through the case, to influence the Court to develop jurisprudence in that area. At the conclusion of the oral proceedings, the Commission presents its final observations.[112]

The Court has the authority under its rules to limit the number of victims' legal representatives arguing before it in any given case. It has adjudicated several cases in which there have been multiple – sometimes hundreds – of alleged victims. In some cases, there were several attorneys representing various groups of plaintiffs. The Court's former rules required that the victims decide on one representative, called a common intervener, who was then the only authorized person to present motions, pleadings, and evidence in the public hearings or during any phase of the proceedings.[113] Under the new rules, if multiple alleged victims cannot decide on a common intervener, the Court may allow up to three representatives to act as common interveners.[114] If the disagreement continues, the Court will make the determination as to who will serve as interveners in the proceedings before the Court.[115]

The Court finally has a means to provide financial legal assistance to impoverished victims. A regional human rights system is of little value to petitioners who do not have the financial resources necessary to pursue justice and remedies before the enforcement organs. The reimbursement of costs and expenses directly influences the individual victim's access to justice. If the petitioner is not reimbursed for the financial outlays and commitments incurred in human rights adjudication, the Convention's mandate that reparations be awarded to remedy the consequences of the violation will not be fulfilled.[116]

Therefore the Inter-American system has created a Victims' Legal Assistance Fund "to facilitate access to the Inter-American human rights system by persons who currently lack the resources needed to bring their cases before the system."[117] The Legal Assistance Fund, which is maintained primarily through voluntary contributions and is replenished by States that are held liable for violations, was created to facilitate

[110] *Ibid.*, Art. 51(1).
[111] *Ibid.*, Art. 35(1)(f)
[112] *Ibid.*, Art. 51(8).
[113] *Ibid.*, Art. 25(2).
[114] *Ibid.*
[115] *Ibid.*
[116] See *Garrido and Baigorria* v. *Argentina* (Reparations and Costs), IACtHR, 27 August 1998, Ser. C, No. 39, para. 79.
[117] AG/RES. 2426 (XXXVIII-O/08), Resolution adopted by the OAS General Assembly during the celebration of its XXXVIII Ordinary Period of Sessions of the OAS, celebrated 3 June, 2008.

access of all victims to the Inter-American human rights organs.[118] In their initial brief to the Court, victims may request financing from the fund to cover their expenditures of producing evidence.[119] In doing so, they must provide the Court with a sworn affidavit and any other relevant evidence that shows that they lack the finances necessary to pay the costs of litigation before the Court.[120] They must also specify exactly the use to which the funds will be applied, such as witness transportation to the Court or document production.[121] The President of the Court then evaluates each request and specifies which costs are to be covered by the Fund.[122] When the Court has appointed a public defender to provide free legal assistance to the victim, the attorney's expenses also are compensated from the Legal Assistance Fund.[123]

The Court is further expediting its proceedings. From 2006 to 2010, the average duration of the proceedings for a contentious case before the Court was 17.4 months from the date the case was submitted to the Court until it issued its judgment on reparations.[124] In 2011, the Court reduced the duration of cases to 16.4 months.[125] One channel authorized by the Court to accelerate its decisions is the increased use of electronic means to facilitate communications between those involved in a case.[126] The Court can transmit all communications, orders, judgments, and advisory opinions by electronic means, provided that it has adequate guarantees of security.[127] The Court noted the importance of an international human rights tribunal's use of modern electronic means to facilitate rapid communications with the parties.[128] Expeditious means of communication are particularly important in the Inter-American human rights system, because the Commission is seated in Washington, DC; the Court is located in San José, Costa Rica; and the judges are located in seven different States. The alleged victims, witnesses, and expert witnesses may now provide their statements through electronic audiovisual means.[129] In 2011, for the first time an alleged victim testified before the Court by audiovisual means allowing direct participation in the Court proceedings.[130] One advantage

[118] *Ibid.*; Rules of Procedure for the Operation of the Victims' Legal Assistance Fund of the Inter-American Court of Human Rights, Art. 5, OEA/Ser.G, CP/RES. 963 (1728/09), 11 November 2009. Available at http://www.corteidh.or.cr/docs/libros/eng_docs2011.pdf at 231.

[119] Rules for the Operation of the Victims' Legal Assistance Fund of the Inter-American Court of Human Rights, Art. 2.

[120] *Ibid.*

[121] *Ibid.*

[122] *Ibid.*

[123] *Ibid.*; IACtHR, 2010 Annual Report, at 16.

[124] IACtHR 2011 Annual Report, at 8.

[125] *Ibid.*

[126] IACtHR Rules of Procedure, Arts. 28, 44, and 51.

[127] *Ibid.*, Art. 33.

[128] *Paniagua Morales et al.* v. *Guatemala* (Preliminary Objections), IACtHR, 25 January 1996, Ser. C, No. 23, para, 35.

[129] IACtHR Rules of Procedure, Art. 51(11).

[130] IACtHR, 2011 Annual Report at 3, *citing Diaz Peña v* Venezuela.

of using electronic means to receive testimony is a reduction in expenses. It is the responsibility of the party who offers a declarant to ensure the declarant's appearance before the Court, submit his or her affidavit, and bear the costs of producing the witness.[131] In the past, the Commission and the State generally bore this burden. However, because the Commission no longer proposes testimonial witnesses, that share of the burden will likely fall on the petitioner in the future.

Finally, the Court has been publicizing its cases more effectively. It makes a video of the public hearings, which can be live-streamed or watched subsequently on the Court's website.[132] This use of electronic technology makes the hearings accessible to a larger interested audience, which is especially important in the country where the human rights violations allegedly took place. The Court also posts all its decisions, opinions, and orders on its website and sends out press releases when there are new developments.

LIMITATIONS INFLUENCING THE EFFECTIVENESS OF THE INTER-AMERICAN SYSTEM

Limitations on the Inter-American human rights system have an adverse impact on its effectiveness. The ultimate success or failure of this system rests on the financial, political, and moral support of the OAS Member States. State action or inaction influences the effectiveness of the Inter-American Court and Commission. The system today is confronted by limitations that include inadequate funding, lack of universality, necessity of domestic implementation, failure of the OAS political organs to carry out the role assigned to them by the American Convention, and absence of a control mechanism to review the qualifications of nominees to the Commission and the Court.

Inadequate Funding of the Court and the Commission

Although the promotion and protection of human rights in the Americas are a priority, the OAS does not adequately fund the Court and the Commission. Lack of funding means a shortage of staff attorneys. The size of the legal staffs of the secretariats of the Commission and Court has not kept pace with their expanding caseloads. States continue to demand that the Commission process cases more rapidly and set deadlines for its decisions,[133] but the Commission is seriously hampered by its limited legal staff. With the increase in Court cases, the Court is in a similar position.

[131] *Ibid.*, Arts. 50(4), 60.

[132] Court hearings can be viewed at http://vimeo.com/corteidh.

[133] Consejo Permanente de la Organizacíon de los Estados Americanos, Grupo de Trabajo Especial de Reflexi6n sobre el Funcionamiento de la CIDH para el Fortalecimiento del SIDH, OEA/Ser.G CT/SIDH/INF.17/11 rev. 1, 7 Noviembre 2011, Compilaci6n de las Presentaciones de los Estados Miembros sobre los Temas del Grupo de Trabajo, see Presentacion of Brazil.

Limited funding also translates into fewer Court sessions. Hearings require the presence of the judges and corresponding expenditures. Since its inception the Court has functioned on a part-time basis. Judges are at the disposal of the Court and thus are expected to travel to sessions as needed.[134] Most judges have full-time positions in their countries of residence. The requirement that judges be readily available reflects the urgent nature of many cases within the Court's competency. In the years immediately following the Court's inception, the infrequent meetings may have been adequate, but they are not sufficient to deal efficiently with the ever-increasing caseload of the Court. Only twelve advisory opinions were issued and three joined contentious cases were decided in the Court's first ten years of existence.[135] The number of cases, provisional measures requests, and monitoring judgment sessions has increased steadily since that time. The caseload of the Court has increased substantially since the Commission began to refer every case against a State that has accepted the Court's jurisdiction to the Court "unless there is a reasoned decision by an absolute majority of the members of the Commission to the contrary."[136] In 2011, twenty-three contentious cases were submitted to the Inter-American Court.[137] That number is expected to increase in future years.

The Court's draft Statute originally envisioned a permanent court with full-time judges. The OAS General Assembly found this proposal unjustified until such time as the Court had a substantial caseload.[138] In 2011, the OAS General Assembly in a resolution on strengthening the Inter-American system again resolved to examine the possibility of the Inter-American Court and Commission operating on a permanent basis.[139]

A permanent Court or even an increase in the number of Court sessions requires a corresponding increase in financing. Unfortunately, the OAS experiences almost continual financial shortfalls that show no sign of improvement.[140] The Court budget approved by the OAS General Assembly for 2011 represented 51.7% of the Court's income.[141] The remaining 47.3% was made up of voluntary contributions from States and organizations.[142] Nikken argued convincingly that organizations that make

[134] IACtHR Statute, Art. 16.

[135] Note that the Court did not accept the contentious case of the Government of Costa Rica. *Matter of Viviana Gallardo*, para. 28.

[136] IACHR Rules of Procedure, Art. 45(1).

[137] IACtHR, 2011 Annual Report at 8.

[138] Thomas Buergenthal, "The Inter-American Court of Human Rights," 76 *American Journal of International Law*, 231, 232–33, nn. 11 and 17 (1982) (citing the draft Statute, OEA/Ser.P/AG/doc.1112/79 [10 October 1979], Arts. 20 and 22).

[139] OAS AG/RES. 2675 (XLI-O/11) Strengthening of the Inter-American Human Rights System Pursuant to the Mandates Arising from the Summits of the Americas (Adopted at the Fourth Plenary Session, held on 7 June 2011), resolution 1(e).

[140] OAS Quarterly Resource Management Report, September 2011 http://scm.oas.org/pdfs/2011/CP27616E.ppt.

[141] 2011 IACtHR Annual Report, at 68.

[142] *Ibid.*

voluntary contributions regulate their use, requiring that their contributions fund predetermined special projects and not salaries and ordinary expenses.[143] If the OAS cannot obtain additional voluntary funding for the Court and Commission, then the OAS will need to reevaluate its priorities and eliminate all but the most essential spending. A top priority in the Inter-American system must be the promotion and protection of human rights, because the violation of human rights is one of the gravest problems facing the Americas. This priority is not reflected in the budget of the OAS.

Lack of Universality

The proper functioning of the Inter-American human rights system requires universality of State ratification or accession to the American Convention and the other OAS human rights treaties, as well as State acceptance of the jurisdiction of the Court. Twenty-four of the thirty-five Member States of the OAS are currently parties to the American Convention.[144] The States that have not yet ratified the Convention are the United States and Canada, as well as Belize, Guyana, and several Caribbean nations. Twenty-one of the States Parties to the American Convention, including all Latin American States, have accepted the compulsory jurisdiction of the Inter-American Court.[145]

Lack of universality complicates the functioning of the Inter-American Commission, which must apply somewhat different criteria depending on whether a State is or is not a party to the American Convention. The OAS Charter authorizes the Commission "to promote the observance and protection of human rights" in all Member States.[146] Under its Statute, the Commission must apply the human rights provisions of the American Declaration of the Rights and Duties of Man – and not those of the American Convention – to those OAS Member States that are not parties to the American Convention.[147] To further complicate matters, not all States Parties to the Convention have accepted the compulsory jurisdiction of the Court. The Commission may refer cases to the Court only where the State concerned has

[143] Pedro Nikken, "Observaciones Sobre el Fortalecimiento del Sistema Interamericano de Derechos Humanos en Visperas de la Asamblea General de la OEA," 13 *Revista Inter-Americano Instituto de Derechos Humanos*, 38 (2001, special edition).

[144] The States Parties to the American Convention are Argentina, Barbados, Bolivia, Brazil, Chile, Colombia, Costa Rica, Dominica, Dominican Republic, Ecuador, El Salvador, Grenada, Guatemala, Haiti, Honduras, Jamaica, Mexico, Nicaragua, Panama, Paraguay, Peru, Suriname, Uruguay, and Venezuela.

[145] The only three States Parties to the American Convention that have not also accepted the jurisdiction of the Inter-American Court are Dominica, Granada, and Jamaica.

[146] OAS Charter, Art. 106.

[147] Statute of the Inter-American Commission on Human Rights, Art. 1(1), approved by General Assembly Resolution 447 at its ninth regular session, held in La Paz, Bolivia, Arts. 19 and 20(a), October 1979, reprinted in 2010 Basic Documents, at 171.

accepted the Court's jurisdiction.[148] Finally, States may make reservations to rights protected by the Convention, thereby altering the rights applied to the reserving State from those of the other States Parties to the Convention.

States that have not ratified the American Convention and accepted the jurisdiction of the Court are at a disadvantage, as are the persons who live in those States. Politically, those States that have not ratified the Convention, such as the United States and Canada, have less credibility and influence in the human rights sphere when they attempt to encourage other countries to observe human rights.[149] Moreover, persons whose rights were violated in States that have not ratified the American Convention and accepted the jurisdiction of the Court are handicapped because their cases cannot be heard by the Court.[150] All persons in the Americas should have the same rights and equal access to the Inter-American Court. Every year the OAS General Assembly calls on the American States to ratify or accede to the American Convention and to the other OAS human rights treaties.[151]

Domestic Implementation

The universality of the system is irrelevant if States do not domestically implement the rights protected by the Convention, the judgments of the Court, and the recommendations of the Commission. The American Convention mandates that States give domestic legal effect to the rights it delineates.[152] All States Parties are to "undertake to adopt, in accordance with their constitutional processes and the provisions of this Convention, such legislative or other measures as may be necessary to give effect to those rights or freedoms."[153] Thus, States Parties must take steps to internalize the international human rights norms that they committed themselves to ensure and protect when they ratified the Convention. When States fulfill their duties to ensure and protect rights on the domestic plane, the burden on the international enforcement organs will be lightened.

States Parties must take legal measures to promptly execute the judgments of the Court.[154] The observance of the human rights obligations enshrined in the American Convention and their national enforcement require changes to those domestic laws that contravene Convention provisions.[155] States Parties to the American Convention

[148] American Convention, Art. 62.

[149] Robert K. Goldman, "History and Action: The Inter-American Human Rights System and the Role of the Inter-American Commission on Human Rights," 31 *Human Rights Quarterly*, 856, 887 (2009).

[150] *Ibid.*

[151] OAS General Assembly Resolution Evaluating the Workings of the Inter-American System, para. 3(a).

[152] American Convention, Art. 2.

[153] *Ibid.*

[154] See *Loayza Tamayo* v. *Peru* (Monitoring Compliance), IACtHR, 17 November 1999, decision 1; *Durand and Ugarte* v. *Peru* (Monitoring Compliance), IACtHR, 27 November 2002, resolution 1.

[155] American Convention, Art. 2.

must pass legislation to that effect, and domestic courts must follow the Inter-American Court's interpretation of the protected human rights.[156] Only in this way will human rights be harmonized in the Western hemisphere.

Failure of the Political Organs to Exert Political Pressure on States

The OAS political organs have not fulfilled their intended role of providing formal support to the Commission and the Court. Their failure to exert the political pressure on States Parties that had been foreseen by the drafters of the American Convention has been a notably unsuccessful aspect of the functioning of the Inter-American system. The Convention does not provide for formal enforcement of judgments. It provides only that the Court shall present its annual report to the OAS General Assembly.[157] The Court's report should individually denote cases in which States have not complied with Court judgments.[158] The General Assembly may then discuss the State's noncompliance and, if appropriate, adopt political measures against the delinquent State. This provision was introduced to correlate in some degree to the role of the Committee of Ministers in the European human rights system, which supervises the execution of judgments. Commenting on the Inter-American Convention provision, the European system's observer to the American drafting conference expressed the expectation that "the reporting of a state for non-compliance to the General Assembly, which will be attended by several hundred delegates and widely publicized, is undoubtedly a procedure which most governments would prefer to avoid."[159]

Yet political pressure to comply with the Inter-American Court's judgments has not materialized. The Court's annual reports are not directly reviewed by the OAS General Assembly and receive only perfunctory recognition each year. The General Assembly has never issued a comment on State noncompliance with Court judgments. No urging by the Court has been effective in encouraging the General Assembly to take action against recalcitrant States. Scholars of the Inter-American human rights system, such as Faúndez Ledesma, have voiced regret

> that the inter-American system does not have a more effective mechanism to ensure compliance with the judgments of the Court, and that the OAS General Assembly has not assumed an active role in this area by applying very costly political sanctions that would allow achieving the desired effect. [160]

[156] *Almonacid Arellano et al .v. Chile* (Preliminary Objections, Merits, Reparations, and Costs), IACtHR, 26 September 2006, Ser. C, No. 154, para. 124.

[157] American Convention, Art. 65.

[158] *Ibid.*; IACtHR Statute, Art. 30.

[159] Council of Europe, *Report on the Inter-American Specialized Conference on Human Rights* (Strasbourg, 22 December 1969), reprinted in Buergenthal and Norris (eds.), *Human Rights: The Inter-American System*, booklet 15, vol. 3, at 67.

[160] Héctor Faúndez Ledesma, *The Inter-American System for the Protection of Human Rights: Institutional and Procedural Aspects*, 940 (IIHR, 3rd ed.)

Even in egregious situations, the General Assembly has failed to recognize, much less act, against State noncompliance. For example, when Trinidad and Tobago denounced the Convention, the General Assembly remained silent on the withdrawal. Subsequently, when Trinidad and Tobago rejected the provisional measures ordered by the Court in death penalty cases, the OAS ignored requests to include the matter on the General Assembly's agenda.[161] Theoretically, the General Assembly's censure of States in this context could have a positive influence on State compliance.

In other contexts, political pressure by the OAS General Assembly has proved effective. For example, after the OAS Meeting of Consultation of Ministers of Foreign Affairs passed a resolution condemning the Somoza government's treatment of the Nicaraguan people, Somoza finally resigned. In doing so, he stated, "What role do I play when I have the OAS down my neck?"[162] Also, at the OAS General Assembly in 2000 in Windsor, Canada, when the Inter-American Commission released a special report on Peru documenting the Fujimori government's violations of the rule of law, the OAS General Assembly took collective action.[163] It required the Fujimori government to take certain measures that are said to have influenced Fujimori's decision to resign.[164] One would expect that a State's concern that it could be censured by the OAS for failing to comply with the judgments of the Inter-American Court would improve implementation.

Fear of adverse international publicity has often been a powerful tool in discouraging human rights violations. It has proven most effective when regional or international organs, such as the OAS General Assembly or the UN General Assembly, condemn the violator. Optimally, widespread publicity would accompany the Court's annual report. The General Assembly would debate the contents of the report and single out States that had not complied with judgments. The General Assembly would then call on those States to fulfill their duties under the Convention. Not surprisingly, most States are sensitive about their international reputations and world image. As explained by a former member of the UN Commission on Human Rights, "[d]espite the harsh realities of power politics, world opinion is a force to be reckoned with. Governments do devote much time and energy, both in and out of the UN, to defending and embellishing their own human-rights image and demeaning that of others."[165] When Argentine government agents caused thousands of people to disappear during the "Dirty War," Argentina hired

[161] See Douglass Cassel, "Peru Withdraws from the Court: Will the Inter-American Human Rights System Meet the Challenge?", 20 *Human Rights Law Journal*, 167, 173 (1999), citing letters signed by the Inter-American Court judges to the President of the OAS Permanent Council, dated 14 and 25 May 1999, and to the OAS Secretary General, dated 27 May 1999.

[162] See Christina Cerna, "Human Rights in Conflict with the Principle of Non-Intervention: The Case of Nicaragua Before the Seventeenth Meeting of Consultation of Ministers of Foreign Affairs," in *Derechos Humanos, Direitos Humanos, Human Rights en Las Americas, Homage to the Memory of Carlos A. Dunshee de Abranches* (1984).

[163] Goldman, "History and Action," at 878

[164] *Ibid.*

[165] Morris B. Abram, "The UN and Human Rights," 47 *Foreign Affairs*, 363, 371 (1969).

a high-powered public relations firm in New York to improve its international image.[166]

The threat of embarrassment or shame is a principal tool currently in use to prevent human rights abuses.[167] The likelihood of negative publicity often persuades governments to comply with their international human rights obligations. It would, therefore, be beneficial for the OAS political organs to play their intended role in the Inter-American human rights system. However, it appears that until participation in the Inter-American system is universal – or at least includes the United States and Canada – the OAS General Assembly may not be willing to chastise those States that have ratified the Convention and accepted the jurisdiction of the Court.

A recurring suggestion is that the OAS political organs become involved in the oversight of State compliance with the judgments of the Inter-American Court. The OAS General Assembly and the Permanent Council have the authority to attempt to enforce State compliance with a Court judgment.[168] The OAS could establish a permanent working group, perhaps as part of the Committee on Juridical and Political Affairs, to monitor and promote State compliance. Alternatively the Permanent Council could sponsor an annual conference on State implementation, commending those States that have complied, soliciting their insight as to how they were able to comply with the various types of reparations, and discussing problems encountered by States in complying with specific types of remedies.[169]

Quality Control of Judges Elected to the Court

The judges elected to the Inter-American Court must be of the

> highest moral authority and of recognized competence in the field of human rights, who possess the qualifications required for the exercise of the highest judicial functions in conformity with the law of the state of which they are nationals or of the state that proposes them as candidates. [170]

[166] David Weissbrodt and Maria L. Bartolomei, "The Effectiveness of International Human Rights Pressures: The Case of Argentina, 1976–1983," 75 *Minnesota Law Review*, 1009, 1030 (1991).

[167] David Weissbrodt and Teresa O'Toole, "The Development of International Human Rights Law," in *The Universal Declaration of Human Rights 1948–1988: Human Rights, the United Nations and Amnesty International*, 17, 25 (AIUSA Legal Support Network, New York, 1988).

[168] American Convention, Art. 65; see Thomas Buergenthal, "Implementation of the Judgments of the Court," 185, 186 in *El Sistema Interamericano de Protección de los Derechos Humanos en el Umbral del Siglo XXI*.

[169] See Open Society Justice Initiative, *From Judgment to Justice: Implementing International and Regional Human Rights Decisions*, Executive Summary at 22 (2010). Available at http://www.soros.org/initiatives/justice/articles_publications/publications/from-judment-to-justice20101122/from-judgment-to-justice-20101122.pdf.

[170] American Convention, Art. 52.

Judges are elected in "their individual capacity," not as representatives of the States that nominate them.[171] Consequently, the election process, both at the national level and in the OAS, must be such as will ensure that well-qualified and experienced individuals are elected to the Court.

Several excellent human rights jurists and scholars have graced the bench of the Inter-American Court. Their judicial opinions and decisions reflect a depth of understanding of public international law in general and international human rights law in particular. The contributions of judges who are well grounded in law and concerned about the protection of human rights enhance the standing of the Court. The first judges to be elected to the Court were among the most impressive figures in human rights law in the Western hemisphere. Moreover, the members of the original Court themselves had firsthand experience in human rights – four of the Court's initial judges had been jailed for political reasons at different times.[172] Since that time, two Inter-American Court judges, Thomas Buergenthal and Antônio Augusto Cançado Trindade, have been elected to the International Court of Justice.

Subsequent nominations to the Court have not been of uniformly commanding quality. Despite the Convention's requirements, governments may intentionally or unintentionally undermine the Court by electing judges who lack the required expertise.[173] With only seven judges[174] as compared to more than forty judges on the European Court of Human Rights, the Inter-American Court must be ever vigilant as to the qualifications of its judges.

There is a two-stage process for electing judges to the Court. During the domestic phase, each State Party to the American Convention can identify and propose candidates. The process by which States choose the candidates they will nominate should be transparent and should include the participation of civil society.[175] Mexico currently has such a system, but most other American States do not. In most States, the executive makes the decision without other input. As a result, some nominations have reflected cronyism rather than qualifications.[176]

Once the candidates have been nominated, the OAS should provide for less politicized election procedures to ensure the quality of judges. Politics has sometimes influenced the elections, with certain States reportedly voting in a bloc to elect a candidate even if the candidate has weak credentials.[177] The only step required by

[171] *Ibid.*

[172] Carlos Roberto Reina, Rodolfo Piza Escalante, Maximo Cisneros, and Thomas Buergenthal.

[173] See Douglass Cassel Jr., "Somoza's Revenge: A New Judge for the Inter-American Court of Human Rights," 13 *Human Rights Law Journal*, 137, 139 (1992).

[174] American Convention, Art. 52(1).

[175] See CEJIL, Aportes para el proceso de selección de miembros de la Comisión y la Corte Interamericanas de Derechos Humanos. Available at http://www.cejil.org/documentos/Separata%208%205x11.pdf.

[176] Martin Anderson, "Human Rights Nominee Has Clouded Past," *Miami Herald*, 7 April 1994, A11.

[177] See Thomas Buergenthal and Douglass Cassel, "The Future of the Inter-American Human Rights System," in *El Futuro del Sistema Interamericano de los Derechos Humanos*, 544–45 (Méndez and Cox,

the OAS General Assembly is the inclusion of the curriculum vita of each judicial candidate on the OAS website.[178] One means of ensuring greater transparency would be to publish the names of proposed candidates and to invite comments from domestic bar associations, institutions, and civil society.[179] In the European system, a committee of the Parliamentary Assembly of the Council of Europe reviews the curriculum vitae and interviews all judicial candidates.[180] In addition, the European Committee of Ministers has an informal procedure to "weed out (off-the-record) any unacceptable or totally unmeritorious candidatures."[181] This examination of candidates takes place before the list is formally submitted to the Parliamentary Assembly.[182] A similar practice in the OAS could derail nominations of unqualified judges or those who might have a conflict of interest.

CONTINUING PROPOSALS TO ALTER THE INTER-AMERICAN SYSTEM

Less than a year after the Inter-American Commission and the Court made significant changes in their functioning, States again lobbied the OAS political organs to "strengthen" the Inter-American system.[183] The proposals, although cloaked in positive language, often appear to be thinly veiled attempts to weaken the Inter-American human rights system by States that have been held liable for human rights violations. Challenges to the system have been ongoing for several years. At one stage, it was proposed that the American Convention be reformed. Nikken challenged the States underlying reasons for the proposals. He argued that it was no more necessary to reform the American Convention to improve the Inter-American human rights system than it would be to tear down a cathedral to kill a mouse that was living in it, unless the real desire was to tear down the cathedral and the mouse was only a pretext to do it.[184]

eds., Inter-American Institute of Human Rights, 1998); Cassel, "A New Judge for the Inter-American Court," at 139.

178 OAS AG/RES. 2166 (XXXVI-O/06), Public Presentation of Candidates for Membership on the Inter-American Commission on Human Rights and the Inter-American Court of Human Rights (Adopted at the fourth plenary session, held on June 6, 2006), res. 3.

179 Buergenthal and Cassel, "The Future of the Inter-American Human Rights System," at 545.

180 See Andrew Drzemczewski, "The European Human Rights Convention: Protocol No. 11 Entry into Force and First Year of Application," in *El Sistema Interamericano de Protección de los Derechos Humanos en el Umbral del Siglo XXI*, 357, 367 (2001).

181 *Ibid.*, at 367.

182 *Ibid.*

183 See Consejo Permanente de la Organizacíon de los Estados Americanos, Grupo de Trabajo Especial de Reflexión sobre el Funcionamiento de la CIDH para el Fortalecimiento del SIDH, OEA/Ser.G GT/SIDH/INF.17/11 rev. 1, 7 Noviembre 2011, Compilación de las Presentaciones de los Estados Miembros sobre los Temas del Grupo de Trabajo.

184 Pedro Nikken, "Observaciones Sobre el Fortalecimiento del Sistema Interamericano de Derechos Humanos en Visperas de la Asamblea General de la OEA," at 13 *Revista Inter-Americano Instituto de Derechos Humanos*, 38 (2001, special edition).

One complaint is that the Inter-American Commission on Human Rights is too slow in processing individual petitions. States propose instituting deadlines for each stage of the proceedings.[185] Although this complaint is justified, it is also inevitable considering the lack of adequate financing to allow for a full-time Commission and a larger legal team. The complaining States offer no means of attaining the finances needed to pay for additional staff attorneys to do the work.

Periodically States have also threatened to withdraw from the Inter-American human rights system or from some aspect of the system. Trinidad and Tobago denounced the American Convention and the contentious jurisdiction of the Inter-American Court in 1998. Peru under Fujimori attempted to withdraw from the contentious jurisdiction of the Inter-American Court without withdrawing from the American Convention or the OAS. However, the subsequent Peruvian government announced that Peru considered itself bound by the Court's jurisdiction.[186] Venezuela has threatened to withdraw from the Inter-American Court and Commission. However, there is no way to withdraw from the Commission without withdrawing from the OAS. Under the OAS Charter, the Commission has the authority to oversee the human rights obligations of all OAS Member States. Thus, just by virtue of the Member State's ratification of the OAS Charter, the Inter-American Commission has competence to consider individual petitions concerning alleged human rights violations that occur in the jurisdiction of any OAS Member State.[187] Ecuador has suggested creating a human rights commission as an alternative to the the Inter-American Commission on Human Rights and independent of the OAS.

There is a proposal to alter the Statute of the Inter-American Commission, which must be approved by the OAS General Assembly.[188] These changes could compromise the autonomy of the Commission. Statutory changes would likely eliminate or curtail the Commission's authority to issue precautionary measures to order States to protect persons that are in extreme gravity and ugency of irreparable harm. The Commission's Statute as originally drafted did not refer to precautionary measures. Its authority to issue them arises from its self-drafted Rules of Procedure.[189] Other changes to the Commission's Statute could also be likely.

185 Informe del Grupo de Trabajo Especial de Reflexión Sobre el Funcionamiento de la Comisíon Interamericana de Derechos Humanos para el Fortalecimiento del Sistema Interamericano de Derechos Humanos para la Consideración del Consejo Permanente, OEA/Ser.G Cp/doc.4675/12, 25 enero 2112.

186 See Chapter 4, Jurisdiction *ratione temporis* over States That Attempt to Withdraw Acceptance of the Jurisdiction of the Court at notes 221–28.

187 See Chapter 3, text at notes 1–2.

188 Informe del Secretario General sobre las Recomendaciones del Grupo de Trabajo de Reflexión del Consejo Permanente sobre el Funcionamiento de la Comisión Interamericana de Derechos Humanos para el Fortalecimiento del Sistema Interamericano de Derechos Humanos y del Comité Juridíco Interamericano, OEA/Ser.G Cp/doc.4711/12

189 IACHR Rules of Procedure, Art. 25.

CONCLUSION

This book analyzes and critiques the practice and procedure of the Inter-American Court of Human Rights. It examines the Court's advisory jurisdiction, its contentious jurisdiction, and its authority to order provisional measures. Where relevant, it compares the practice and procedure of the Inter-American Court with those of the European Court of Human Rights, the International Court of Justice, the Permanent Court of International Justice, and the United Nations Human Rights Committee. It does not treat the substantive rights protected by the American Convention except when those rights are relevant to the evaluation and discussion of the Court's procedures. The treatise details the Court's contribution to the emergence and conceptual evolution of international human rights law.

The Inter-American Court's practice and procedures are of theoretical and practical importance on national and international levels. An understanding of the Court's practices and procedures will better inform other international human rights bodies in the United Nations system, as well as the developing African and expanding European human rights systems. In the Western hemisphere, it will help educate attorneys on how to represent victims and States. On a theoretical level, it will serve as a resource for scholarship on the system.

State Compliance with Court-Ordered Reparations

States Parties must comply promptly and completely with all Inter-American Court judgments to which they are a party.[1] Under the principle of *pacta sunt servanda*, States have an obligation to comply with their treaty obligations, including the rulings of international tribunals.[2] All authorities of the State – executive, legislative, and judicial – are bound by the Court's judgments,[3] and the domestic authorities must use all necessary means to ensure the implementation of the Court's decisions so as to redress the rights violated.[4] The executive branch of State governments generally comply with Inter-American Court orders. There is a lower level of State compliance when national legislatures are called on to amend, pass, or repeal legislation and when State judicial authorities must investigate, prosecute, and punish alleged human rights violators or comply with an Inter-American Court order to retry or release defendants whose human rights were violated.[5]

The Inter-American Court has asserted repeatedly in its case law that

> States Parties to the Convention must guarantee compliance with its provisions and its effects (*effet utile*) within their own domestic laws. This principle is applicable not only with regard to the substantive provisions of human rights treaties (*i.e.* those dealing with the protected rights) but also with regard to procedural rules, such as those concerning compliance with the decisions of the Court. These obligations are to be interpreted and enforced in a manner such that the protected guarantee

[1] American Convention on Human Rights, 22 November 1969, 9 ILM 673, OEA/Ser.K/XVI/I.1, doc. 65 rev. 1 corr. 1 (1970), Art. 68.

[2] *Castillo Páez* v. *Peru* (Monitoring Compliance), IACtHR, 3 April 2009, "considering" para. 5.

[3] *Baena Ricardo et al.* v. *Panama* (Competence), IACtHR, 28 November 2003, Ser C, No. 104, para. 60.

[4] IACtHR 2010 Annual Report IACtHR, at 9.

[5] See Alexandra Huneeus, "Courts Resisting Courts: Lessons from the Inter-American Court's Struggle to Enforce Human Rights," 44 *Cornell International Law Journal*, 493, 494–95 (2011).

is truly practical and effective, bearing in mind the special nature of human rights treaties.[6]

Full implementation of a court's reparations orders is an integral aspect of the right of access to justice.[7]

CONVENTIONALITY CONTROL

In some Latin American States the human rights protections of the American Convention are automatically incorporated into domestic law. The Constitutions of these States provide that international human rights treaties have a status at the same level or higher than the State's Constitutions. The Constitutions of Colombia, Guatemala, and Honduras, for example, give human rights treaties that have been ratified by the State a "supraconstitutional" rank, which permits the States' highest courts to directly apply the American Convention and other international human rights treaties when deciding cases.[8] In 2011, Mexico amended its Constitution to elevate the human rights protected in the international treaties ratified by Mexico to the rank of constitutional law.[9] Thus, the Constitutional or Supreme Courts in these States can enforce the rights set forth in the American Convention even though the State's Constitution does not provide directly for the rights.[10] In other States, such as Argentina, the Constitution specifically enumerates the international human rights treaties that have the same rank as the Constitution.[11] The American Convention on Human Rights is one of the treaties listed in the Argentine Constitution. Consequently, when a domestic statute conflicts with a provision of the American Convention, the Argentine Supreme Court should uphold the Convention provision and declare the statute to be unconstitutional and therefore invalid.[12] This authority of the courts is called the "control of conventionality" or "conventionality control." It is akin to the oversight or control that courts generally exercise to ensure that laws do not violate the constitution. If the law is unconstitutional, it is invalid and cannot be enforced. In the case of treaties, also called "conventions," that have the status of constitutions, courts exercise oversight to ensure that domestic

6 *Cesti Hurtado* v. *Peru* (Monitoring Compliance), IACtHR, 4 February 2010, "considering" para. 6, citing *Ivcher Bronstein* v. *Peru* (Competence), IACtHR, 24 September 1999, Ser. C, No. 54, para. 37; *"Five Pensioners"* v. *Peru* (Monitoring Compliance), IACtHR, 24 November 2009, "considering" para. 7.

7 *Baena Ricardo et al.* v. *Panama* (No. 104, 2003), para. 72.

8 Allan R. Brewer-Carías, *Constitutional Protection of Human Rights in Latin America: A Comparative Study of Amparo Proceedings*, at 32 (Cambridge, 2009).

9 Diario Oficial de la Federacion, Organo Oficial del Gobierno Constitucional de los Estados Unidos Mexicanos. Available at http://www.aida-americas.org/sites/default/files/Reforma%20DHs%20junio%202011.pdf

10 Brewer-Carías, *Constitutional and Protection of Human Rights in Latin America*, at 33.

11 *Ibid.*, at 38.

12 *Ibid.*, at 38–39.

statutes do not conflict with the provisions of the treaty. If they do, the statute is invalid. In other States, treaties have the same rank as statutes.[13]

The Inter-American Court takes the position that the American Convention on Human Rights should be inherently self-executing and, therefore, automatically incorporated into the domestic law of States Parties to the Convention.[14] If a domestic law conflicts with the State's international treaty obligations, the State is in violation of its international obligations, and the Inter-American Court may order the State to amend or repeal the law so as to comply with the treaty provisions. The Inter-American Court may also order that the domestic law that violates a right protected by the American Convention have no legal effect. Many domestic courts and legislatures are complying with these judgments and advisory opinions. The principle of effectiveness provides that, unless international law is given priority over State domestic law, international law cannot be applied in a harmonized, reasonable, and useful way.[15] This reasoning is even more applicable when the subject matter of the laws in question is the protection of individual human rights.

Several Latin American Constitutional and Supreme Courts have recognized the constitutional status and binding nature of the Inter-American Court's interpretation of the American Convention and its determination as to the compatibility of domestic laws with the rights set forth in the Convention. The Argentine Supreme Court of Justice holds that Inter-American Court decisions are binding on Argentina, and therefore, in principle, the Argentine Supreme Court's decisions must be subordinated to the decisions of the Inter-American Court.[16] In fact, the Argentine Supreme Court has directly applied the provisions of the American Convention, thereby "modifying, wherever necessary, the scope of the domestic laws."[17]

The Colombian Constitution provides that constitutional rights must be interpreted "according to the international human rights treaties ratified by Colombia."[18] Therefore, the Constitutional Court of Colombia has determined that the case law

[13] *Ibid.*, at 50–53, citing Mexico, Uruguay, and the Dominican Republic.

[14] *Cabrera García and Montiel Flores* v. *Mexico* (Preliminary Objections, Merits, Reparations, and Costs), IACtHR, 26 November 2010, Ser. C, No. 220, para. 225 (translation corrected by author), citing *Almonacid Arellano et al.* v. *Chile* (Preliminary Objections, Merits, Reparations, and costs), IACtHR, 26 September 2006, Ser. C, No. 154, para. 124; see also Christina Binder, "The Prohibition of Amnesties by The Inter-American Court Of Human Rights," 12 *German Law Journal*, 1203, 1204 (2011).

[15] *Proposed Amendments to the Naturalization Provisions of the Constitution of Costa Rica*, IACtHR, Advisory Opinion OC-4/84, 19 January 1984, Ser. A, No. 4, para. 56.

[16] *Cabrera García and Montiel Flores* v. *Mexico* (No. 220, 2010), para. 231, quoting Judgment of 23 December 2004, Supreme Court of Justice, Republic of Argentina (Case file 224. XXXIX), "*Esposito, Miguel Angel s/* motion of statute of limitations of the criminal proceeding brought by his defense," considering clause 6.

[17] *Cantos* v. *Argentina* (Merits, Reparations and Costs), IACtHR, 28 November 2002, Ser. C, No. 97, para. 62, citing *Ekmedjian, Miguel Angel c/Sofovich, Gerardo y otros*, Supreme Court of Argentina, Case No. E.64.XXIII, Judgment of 7 July 1992.

[18] *Cabrera García And Montiel Flores* v. *Mexico* (No. 220, 2010), para. 232, quoting Judgment C-010/00 Constitutional Court of Colombia, issued 19 January 2000, para. 6.

of international tribunals that have the authority to interpret the treaties to which Colombia is a party "constitutes a relevant interpretative criterion to establish the meaning of the constitutional rules on fundamental rights."[19] The Constitutional Chamber of the Supreme Court of Justice of Costa Rica has held that the Inter-American Court is the organ empowered to interpret the American Convention on Human Rights and that its decisions on the compatibility of domestic laws, whether emanating from contentious cases or advisory opinions, have the same force as the Convention provision interpreted.[20] The Bolivian Constitutional Court held that "following a 'systemic' criterion of constitutional interpretation," the American Convention and "its decisions, also form part of this collection of constitutional rules."[21] The Bolivian Court based its reasoning on the jurisdiction of the Inter-American Court and the "application of the '*effet util*' doctrine to judgments concerning Human Rights."[22] The Supreme Court of Justice of the Dominican Republic holds that both the norms of the American Convention and the "interpretations made by the competent organs," including the Inter-American Commission and the Inter-American Court, are binding on the Dominican State and its judiciary.[23]

The Constitutional Court of Peru has referred to the Inter-American Court as the "ultimate guardian of rights in the region."[24] The Peruvian Constitutional Court asserts that the Inter-American Court's judgments and interpretations of the Convention's provisions in those proceedings are binding on the national government of Peru, including on the Constitutional Court, even when Peru is not a party to the case.[25] The Peruvian Tribunal holds that the binding nature of Inter-American Court judgments also extends to the Court's rationale (*ratio decidendi*) for its decision.[26] It has stated that there are restorative and preventive aspects arising from the relationship between the Inter-American Court and the Peruvian Constitutional Tribunal.[27] On the one hand, once the Inter-American Court has found that a human right has

[19] *Cabrera García and Montiel Flores* v. *Mexico* (No. 220, 2010), para. 232.

[20] *Ibid.*, para. 226, citing Constitutional Chamber of the Supreme Court of Justice of Costa Rica. Constitutional motion, Opinion 2313–95 (Case File 0421-S-90), Judgment of May 9, 1995, considering clause VII.

[21] *Cabrera García and Montiel Flores* v. *Mexico* (No. 220, 2010), para. 227, quoting Judgment of May 10, 2010, Constitutional Tribunal of Bolivia (Case file N° 2006–13381-27-RAC), chapter III.3 on "The Inter-American System of Human Rights: Grounds and Effects of the Judgments Issued by the Inter-American Court of Human Rights."

[22] *Ibid.*

[23] *Cabrera García and Montiel Flores* v. *Mexico* (No. 220, 2010), para. 228, citing Resolution N° 1920–2003 issued November 13, 2003, Supreme Court of Justice of the Dominican Republic.

[24] Cartegena Vargas, No. 218–02-HC/TC, Tribunal Constitucional de Peru, 17 April 2002, "Fundamentos," para. 2.

[25] *Cabrera García and Montiel Flores* v. *Mexico* (No. 220, 2010), para. 229, citing Judgment of July 21, 2006, Constitutional Tribunal of Peru (case file N° 2730–2006-PA/TC), Ground 12.

[26] Colegio de Abogados del Callao c. Congreso de la República, No. 00007–2007-PI/TC, Tribunal Constitucional de Peru, Pleno Jurisdiccional, 19 June 2007.

[27] *Ibid.*

been violated, it can be adequately and effectively protected.[28] On the other hand, the preventive aspect allows the State to avoid an Inter-American Court judgment against the State.[29]

Not all States Parties to the American Convention that have voluntarily accepted the jurisdiction of the Inter-American Court agree with the principle of conventionality control. Although the Venezuelan Constitution gives human rights treaties a supranational status, in recent years the Venezuelan Supreme Court has not chosen to interpret them as such.[30] The Venezuelan Court, in which many of the justices were chosen by President Chávez, stated that

> the Inter-American Court of Human Rights persists in diverting the philosophy of the American Convention and the Court's own jurisdiction, remitting direct orders to organs of the public power of Venezuela (the National Assembly and the National Electoral Council), usurping functions as if it were a colonial power, and trying to impose on a sovereign and independent nation, political judgments and ideologies that are absolutely incompatible with its constitutional system.[31]

MONITORING STATE COMPLIANCE WITH JUDGMENTS

The Inter-American Court monitors State compliance with the reparations it orders until they have been completely fulfilled. The Court asserts that monitoring State compliance with its judgments is an inherent attribute of its jurisdiction.[32] The effectiveness of the Inter-American Court's judgments and reparations orders is dependent on their execution and implementation by the State. If its decisions are not implemented in State domestic systems, the protections of the Inter-American human rights system are merely illusory and more akin to declaratory judgments. Thus, the Court maintains contentious cases on its docket until full reparations are made.

The Court's Rules set forth the procedures the Court follows when monitoring State compliance with its judgments. Generally, the Court's judgments require that the State submit a report on the steps it has taken to comply. This obligation is fundamental if the Court is to assess the status of State compliance with its judgments.[33] The report must specify in what way and to what extent the State is complying with each measure of reparations ordered in the Court's judgment,

[28] *Ibid.*

[29] *Ibid.*

[30] Brewer-Carías, *Constitutional Protection of Human Rights in Latin America*, at 34–35.

[31] Corte IDH Blog: Tribunal Supremo Venezolano Declara "Inejecutable" la Sentencia de la Corte IDH dictada en el caso López Mendoza. (translation by author). Available at http://corteidhblog.blogspot.com/

[32] *Acevedo Buendía et al. ("Discharged and Retired Employees of the Comptroller")* v. *Peru* (Monitoring Compliance), IACtHR, 1 July 2011, "considering" para. 1; *Baena Ricardo et al.* v. *Panama* (No. 104, 2003), para. 72.

[33] *Suárez Rosero* v. *Ecuador* (Monitoring Compliance), IACtHR, 10 July 2007, "considering" para. 5.

and it must be accompanied by documentation, so that the Court can verify State compliance. For instance, if the State asserts that it has complied with the legislative reform ordered by the Court, the State must append the new law to the report. The Court has stated that the State has the dual obligation to formally present the documentation within the time frame set forth by the Court and to accompany the documentation with "specific, true, current and detailed information on the issues to which this obligation refers."[34] The victim or the victim's legal representative then submits observations on the State report, and the Commission presents observations on both the State and victim's submissions.[35] The Court also can request expert opinions or information from other sources to evaluate State compliance.[36]

Since 2007, the Court has convened the State, victim's representatives, and Commission to public or private hearings to monitor State compliance.[37] These hearings usually last approximately two hours. The Court has reduced its workload somewhat by holding one hearing on multiple cases from the same State that involve at least one similar measure of reparation pending compliance.[38] The State often sends high-level authorities to the hearings to represent the State's position, which allows for compromise between the parties. The State takes the lead in the hearings by describing its progress in complying with the reparations ordered by the Court. The victims' representatives and the Inter-American Commission then present information on whether and to what extent the State has complied with each reparations measure. The face-to-face meetings of the parties under the Court's oversight may result in good will and a cooperative spirit between the parties.[39] The Court attempts to facilitate compliance by promoting compromises between the parties, suggesting alternatives, and setting timetables.[40] The Court can then assess the level of compliance and issue binding orders on how the State should fulfill the reparations ordered.[41] In 2011, the Court held four private hearings and one public hearing to monitor State compliance. The information garnered from these proceedings allowed the Court to provide guidance to the State and to report to the OAS General Assembly on State compliance. The General Assembly has recognized that the private hearings are important and constructive and that they have yielded positive results.[42]

34 *Ibid.*

35 Rules of Procedure of the Inter-American Court of Human Rights, entered into force 1 January 2010, Art. 69(1), approved by the Court during its LXXXV Regular Period of Sessions, held from November 16 to November 28, 2009.

36 *Ibid.*, Art. 69(2).

37 *Ibid.*, Art. 69(3).

38 IACtHR 2011 Annual Report, at 14. See Order of the President of the Inter-American Court, 8 February 2010, Monitoring Compliance with Reparations Measures Regarding Medical and Psychological Attention in Nine Colombian Cases, Summons to a Private Hearing.

39 *Zambrano Vélez et al.* v. *Ecuador* (Merits, Reparations, and Costs), IACtHR, 4 July 2007, Ser. C, No. 166, para. 73.

40 IACtHR 2011 Annual Report, at 30.

41 IACtHR Rules of Procedure, Art. 69(4).

42 AG/RES. 2652 (XLI-O/11), Observations and Recommendations on the Annual Report of the Inter-American Court of Human Rights, (Adopted at the fourth plenary session, held on June 7, 2011).

The Court reasons that only by monitoring State compliance can it fulfill its Article 65 Convention obligation to report yearly to the OAS General Assembly on the "cases in which a State has not complied with its judgments."[43] The American Convention's mandate that the Court note the specific instances of State noncompliance in its annual report has not been effective in increasing compliance.[44] The General Assembly does not take action to influence those States that have not complied, but it has passed a resolution informing States Parties that they must deliver the information on compliance to the Court in a timely manner for the Court to comply with its obligation to inform the General Assembly of State compliance with its judgments.[45]

At the conclusion of 2011, the Court was monitoring compliance with judgments in 124 contentious cases.[46] In that year it issued thirty-two orders, which detail with which measures States have or have not complied. The orders are posted on the Court's website. The Court's 2011 caseload can be compared with the Court's caseload at the end of 2002 when it was monitoring compliance with its judgments in only twenty-seven contentious cases.[47] The Court will not close a case until the State has fully complied with its judgment. Thus far it has closed only a small percentage of cases.[48]

The high number of cases in which the Court is monitoring compliance should not lead to the assumption that States are not complying with Court judgments. States are fulfilling many types of reparations, but in general, they have not been successful in fulfilling all reparations ordered by the Court in each case. There is a high level of State compliance with Court orders to pay compensation, publish the Court's judgment, and perform an act of recognition of State responsibility.[49] There is a medium level of State compliance with orders to provide education or to undertake symbolic measures, such as building a monument in honor of the victims. States have a low level of compliance with locating the whereabouts of the disappeared; providing

43 *Baena Ricardo et al.* v. *Panama* (No. 104, 2003), para. 101; American Convention, Art. 65; Statute of the IACtHR, adopted 1979, Art. 30.

44 American Convention, Art. 65.

45 AG/RES. 2292 (XXXVII-0/07) approved in the fourth regular session, held on June 5, 2007, titled "Observations and Recommendations to the Annual Report of the Inter-American Court of Human Rights."

46 IACtHR 2011 Annual Report, at 14.

47 See IACtHR 2002 Annual Report.

48 More recent cases closed by the Court include *Herrera Ulloa* v. *Costa Rica* (Monitoring Compliance) IACtHR, 22 November 2010, Res. 1; *Mayagna (Sumo) Awas Tingni Community* v. *Nicaragua* (Monitoring Compliance), IACtHR, 3 April 2009, decides para. 2; *Tristán Donoso* v. *Panama* (Monitoring Compliance), IACtHR, 1 September 2010, decides paras. 1 and 2; *"The Last Temptation of Christ"* v. *Chile* (Olmedo Bustos et al.) (Monitoring Compliance), IACtHR, 28 November 2003, decides para. 2; *Claude Reyes et al.* v. *Chile* (Monitoring Compliance), IACtHR, 24 November, 2008, decides para. 1; *Ricardo Canese* v. *Paraguay* (Monitoring Compliance), IACtHR, 6 August 2008, decides para. 1; *Acosta Calderón* v. *Ecuador* (Monitoring Compliance), IACtHR, 7 February 2008, "order" para. 1.

49 Carlos Martin Beristain, 1 *Diálogos sobre la reparación: Experiencias en el sistema interamericano de derechos humanos*, 548 (IIDH, 2008).

medical or psychological care to victims; investigating, prosecuting, and punishing the violations; and providing other guarantees of nonrepetition, including legislative reform.[50] Some States have complied more regularly with Court-ordered reparations, and others, such as Venezuela in recent years, have been recalcitrant. State compliance also may be cyclical in that, after a change in government, the State may be more or less willing to fulfill Court-ordered reparations. The Court continues monitoring State compliance with a judgment until all the Court-ordered reparations have been fulfilled. As stated in the Court's Annual Report, "[m]onitoring compliance with its judgments has become one of the most demanding activities of the Court."[51]

STATE ACCEPTANCE OF INTERNATIONAL RESPONSIBILITY

Some States are now accepting partial or total responsibility before the Inter-American Court for human rights violations. For example, in the *Tiu Tojín Case*, Guatemala accepted responsibility for the forced disappearances of María Tiu Tojín and her daughter, and for the denial of justice resulting from the State's failure to investigate their disappearances.[52] In *Abrill Alosilla et al.*, Peru acknowledged international responsibility for the retroactive application of a law that affected the salaries of 233 members of the Union of Lima Water and Sewer Service Functionaries, Professionals, and Technicians.[53] Colombia accepted partial responsibility for the extrajudicial execution of Senator Manuel Cepeda Vargas and the resulting violation of his rights and those of his family.[54]

The Commission and the Court find that State acceptance of international responsibility reflects progress.[55] The Court has stated that a State's "acknowledgment of responsibility constitutes a positive contribution to this proceeding and to the application of the principles that inspire the American Convention."[56] Cavallaro and Brewer, however, warn that State acknowledgment of responsibility in some instances may merely represent the State's attempt to "play the system."[57] States may accept responsibility and apologize to save face and as "a forum to proclaim

50 *Ibid.*
51 IACtHR 2011 Annual Report, at 19.
52 *Tiu Tojín v. Guatemala* (Merits, Reparations, and Costs), IACtHR, 26 November 2008, Ser. C No 190.
53 *Abrill Alosilla et al.* v. *Peru* (Merits, Reparations, and Costs), IACtHR, 4 March 2011, Ser. C, No. 223, para. 5.
54 *Manuel Cepeda Vargas* v. *Colombia* (Preliminary Objections, Merits, and Reparations), IACtHR 26 May 2010, Ser C, No. 213, paras. 13–14.
55 See Manuel Ventura Robles, "The Discontinuance and Acceptance of Claims in the Jurisprudence of the Inter-American Court of Human Rights," 5 *International Law Students Association Journal of International and Comparative Law*, 603, 619 (1999).
56 *Kawas Fernández* v. *Honduras* (Merits, Reparations, and Costs), IACtHR, 3 April 2009, Ser. C, No. 196, paras. 32, 202.
57 James L. Cavallaro and Stephanie Erin Brewer, "Reevaluating Regional Human Rights Litigation in the Twenty-First Century: The Case of the Inter-American Court," 102 *American Journal of International Law*, 768, 808–16 (2008).

their commitment to human rights."[58] No statistics are as yet available on whether States that have accepted international responsibility for human rights violations have higher rates of compliance with Court-ordered reparations.

Voluntary Apology and Dissemination of the Truth

Some States have voluntarily apologized to victims or to their next of kin even without a Court order to do so. It is a sign of the true advancement of human rights when States accept international responsibility and, as an act of grace, voluntarily and publicly apologize to the victim or the family of deceased and disappeared victims. At times they do so voluntarily during the public hearings before the Court or when they accept international responsibility for the human rights violations. At the public hearing in the *Catia Detention Center Case*, for instance, Venezuela asked for a moment of silence in memory of the victims and expressed its deepest regrets for all the pain they had endured.[59] Bolivia voluntarily accepted international responsibility for the disappearance of the victim in the *Trujillo Oroza Case* and informed the Court in the public hearing that it had sent a written apology to the victim's family.[60] Likewise, Peru volunteered to publicly apologize to the victims in the *Durand and Ugarte*[61] and the *Barrios Altos Cases*.[62] State apologies are often eloquent. In the public hearing before the Court, Guatemala expressed "its profound condolences for the acts lived and suffered by the community of Plan de Sánchez . . . [and asked] the pardon of the victims, the survivors, and the family members, as a first sign of respect, reparation and the guarantee of non-repetition."[63] The Government of Colombia, during a public hearing before the Court, expressed "its deep respect and sympathy for the victims of the acts that took place in Mapiripán in July 1997, and it evoke[d] their memory to state its regret and to apologize to their next of kin and to Colombian society."[64] An apology is no longer considered to be a blemish on the honor of the State; it is instead a mark of integrity for the State to disavow abusive acts and express its regret that those acts were perpetrated in its jurisdiction.

Some States have also voluntarily disseminated the truth and cleared the victim's reputation. Victims have often been maligned by the State and accused of being

[58] *Ibid.*, at 810.
[59] *Montero Aranguren et al. (Detention Center of Catia)* v. *Venezuela* (Preliminary Objection, Merits, Reparations, and Costs), IACtHR, 5 July 2006, Ser. C, No. 150, para. 42.
[60] *Trujillo Oroza* v. *Bolivia* (Merits), IACtHR, 26 January 2000, Ser. C, No. 64, para. 37.
[61] *Durand and Ugarte* v. *Peru* (Reparations and Costs), IACtHR, 3 December 2001, Ser. C, No. 89, para. 39(b).
[62] *Barrios Altos* v. *Peru* (Reparations and Costs), IACtHR, 30 November 2001, Ser. C. No. 87, para. 44(e).
[63] *Plan de Sánchez Massacre* v. *Guatemala* (Merits), IACtHR, 29 April 2004, Ser. C, No. 105, para. 38.
[64] *"Mapiripán Massacre"* v. *Colombia* (Merits, Reparations, and Costs), IACtHR, 15 September 2005, Ser. C, No. 134, para. 314.

criminals or terrorists. In the *Benavides Cevallos Case*, Ecuador's agent before the Court said at the public hearing,

> I wish to state for the record that my country accepts and acknowledges its responsibility in the disappearance and death of Professor Consuelo Benavides Cevallos . . . [and that] the name of Professor Benavides has also been cleared in all the spoken and written media in [Ecuador], as the struggle that her family has waged for so many years to bring the truth to light has been publicized at all levels.[65]

Rehabilitation of the victim's reputation is another positive step in the State's recognition of victim's rights.

Anticipatory Remedial State Action

The jurisprudence of the Inter-American Court is now sufficiently well-defined that States can anticipate the type of reparations the Court is likely to order. Consequently, in a gesture of goodwill or as a result of a prior agreement with the victims, the State may perform some anticipated reparations or suggest its willingness to perform certain reparations in advance of an Inter-American Court decision. For example, in *De la Cruz Flores* v. *Peru*, the State released the victim shortly before the public hearing before the Inter-American Court.[66] Likewise, before the public hearing in *Ximenes Lopes* v. *Brazil*, the State undertook measures to improve conditions in certain mental health centers.[67] In the case of *Valle Jaramillo*, which involved the extrajudicial execution of a Colombian human rights defender, the State proposed as part of a settlement to establish a two-year "Jesús María Valle Jaramillo" grant to the Human Rights Defenders Unit of the Inter-American Commission on Human Rights.[68] Colombia also offered to establish a "Human Rights Defenders Policy," in an attempt to curtail the violence and threats against human rights defenders.[69]

In at least two instances, the State voluntarily reinstituted victims to their former positions while the case was pending before the Court. Although the State had maintained the legality of terminating their employment throughout the proceedings before the Commission and during much of the processing of the case before the Court, the State reinstated the victims before the Court issued a judgment. This occurred in *Mejía Idrovo* v. *Ecuador*, when the Ecuadoran Constitutional Court ordered the victim's reinstatement to his position as army colonel.[70] He was reinstated

[65] *Benavides Cevallos* v. *Ecuador* (Merits), IACtHR, 19 June 1998, Ser. C, No. 38, para. 35.

[66] *De la Cruz Flores* v. *Peru* (Merits, Reparations, and Costs), IACtHR, 18 November 2004, Ser. C, No. 115, para. 73(48).

[67] *Ximenes Lopes* v. *Brazil* (Merits, Reparations, and Costs), IACtHR, 4 July 2006, Ser. C, No. 149.

[68] *Valle Jaramillo et al.* v. *Colombia* (Merits, Reparations, and Costs), IACtHR, 27 November 2008, Ser. C. No. 192, para. 227(c).

[69] *Ibid.*, para. 230.

[70] *Mejía Idrovo* v. *Ecuador* (Preliminary Objections, Merits, Reparations, and Costs), IACtHR, 5 July 2011, Ser. C, No. 228, paras. 137–38.

before the Inter-American Court issued the judgment in the case.[71] Likewise, in the *Constitutional Court Case* in which three Constitutional Court justices had been unconstitutionally dismissed from the Court, Peru reinstated them while their case was before the Inter-American Court.[72] There is no definitive way to know if the reinstatements were related to the cases before the Court, but the timing of the State's actions indicates that there was a connection to the regional court proceedings.

Although the Court has not ordered a State to ratify relevant international conventions, States have voluntarily offered to do so as one means of reparation. In the *Benavides Cevallos Case*, Ecuador stated that, in the interest of deterrence, it welcomed the Commission's recommendation that it ratify the Inter-American Convention on Forced Disappearance of Persons.[73] Likewise, in the voluntary agreement reached between the victims' representatives and the State in the *Barrios Altos Case*, Peru agreed to promote ratification of the International Convention on the Non-Applicability of Statutory Limitations to War Crimes and Crimes Against Humanity.[74]

IMPLEMENTATION OF INTER-AMERICAN COURT ORDERS TO PAY COMPENSATORY DAMAGES

States have been most consistent in paying financial compensation to victims. The Court reports that States have paid Court-ordered compensation in 80% of cases.[75] State payment of compensation is sometimes late, and then States must add interest for the overdue amount. This may be problematic for States in that they sometimes have difficulty in obtaining authorization for the additional funds.[76]

Not all victims have been willing to accept Court-ordered compensation. In the *Radilla Pacheco Case*, two of the victim's next of kin refused to accept their compensation because there had been no advancement in the investigations into what happened to their father, and they refused to apply for his death certificate because there was no proof that he was dead.[77] States could provide a certificate of disappearance or certificate verifying "inability to locate" in order to avoid this sensitive issue for the relatives of the disappeared.

It is not sufficient, however, that States pay compensation if they neglect to comply with other Court-ordered reparations that are meant to deter future violations. States should not be perceived to be allowed to pay for their human rights violations.

[71] *Ibid.*

[72] *Constitutional Court* v. *Peru* (Merits, Reparations, and Costs), IACtHR, 31 January 2001, Ser. C, No. 71, para. 56(30).

[73] *Benavides Cevallos* v. *Ecuador* (No 38, 1998), para. 52.

[74] *Barrios Altos* v. *Peru* (No. 87, 2001), para. 44(c).

[75] IACtHR 2010 Annual Report, at 12.

[76] *Zambrano Vélez et al.* v. *Ecuador* (No. 166, 2007), paras. 28–31.

[77] *Radilla Pacheco* v. *Mexico*, (Monitoring Compliance), IACtHR, 19 May 2011, "considering" paras. 51, 55.

Prior Payment Authorized by States

Some States have already paid out reparations to victims of human rights violations before the Court issues a judgment. The Court honors State domestic reparations that compensate victims of human rights violations when the State payments satisfy the Court's criteria of "objectivity, reasonableness and effectiveness."[78] Domestically established reparations procedures, provided that they are adequate and fair, benefit those victims whose cases are heard by the Inter-American Court because they are compensated much sooner, as well as the vast majority of victims who do not receive international awards. Moreover, when States remedy human rights violations domestically, it lessens the burdens on international courts.

The Court's case law appears to have developed to allow States more autonomy to employ criteria that are somewhat different from those used by the Inter-American Court in determining reparations but that are objectively fair. In *Manuel Cepeda Vargas* v. *Colombia*, for instance, the Court refused to supplement the damages for lost earnings already paid by the State, even though the State applied criteria and calculation methods that differed from those generally applied by the Inter-American Court.[79] Instead, the Court honored the domestic determination, finding that it was based on "objective and reasonable criteria" and that the calculation was reasonable in light of the Court's case law.[80] The Court did not accept the argument that it should order additional payment because State proceedings paid all lost earnings of the victim to his common-law wife and none to his adult children, although the Court usually includes children in its awards for lost earnings.[81]

If the amount is reasonable in terms of the Court's jurisprudence, the Court will accept the domestic reparations, even though the State law does not specify which aspect of the compensation is for pecuniary and which is for nonpecuniary damages.[82] In *Gomes Lund et al. (Guerrilha do Araguaia)*, the Brazilian government had passed a law that authorized the next of kin of the deceased and disappeared persons to request reparations from the government.[83] Fifty-eight individuals had already received compensation, and only four families had not claimed compensation at the time of the Court's judgment.[84] The Court accepted the State's decisions on the amount of reparations it had paid, and it instructed the State to make the domestic processes available to those who had not yet requested compensation.[85]

78 *Manuel Cepeda Vargas* v. *Colombia* (Preliminary Objections, Merits, and Reparations), IACtHR, 26 May 2010, Ser. C, No. 213, para. 246

79 *Ibid.*, paras. 243–46.

80 *Ibid.*, para. 246.

81 *Ibid.*

82 *Gomes Lund et al. (Guerrilha do Araguaia)* v. *Brazil* (Preliminary Objections, Merits, Reparations, and Costs), IACtHR, November 24, 2010, Ser. C, No. 219, para, 303.

83 *Ibid.*, para. 301.

84 *Ibid.*, para. 302.

85 *Ibid.*, para. 303.

The Court may, however, order additional reparations to compensate the next of kin of the victims for other expenses, such as those incurred in searching for their loved ones.[86]

When the State has paid pecuniary or nonpecuniary damages pursuant to an agreement between the State and the victims or a friendly settlement agreement monitored by the Inter-American Commission, the Court will not scrutinize the agreement or order further damages for the type of injury compensated and the beneficiaries included in the agreement.[87] This holding encourages States and victims to negotiate a friendly settlement that may result in the termination of the case before it reaches the Court. Furthermore, States are more likely to pay reparations to which they have freely agreed.

The Inter-American Court has not always been consistent in its decisions as to whether to honor domestic lost earnings awards or to reassess the amount of lost earnings using the Court's established criteria.[88] As recently as 2007, when the domestic proceedings used criteria distinct from that used by the Inter-American Court, the Court recalculated the amount and ordered the State to pay the difference.[89] The Court did not address the reasonableness of the domestic criteria used to make the determination. A complicating factor in that case may have been that some victims had not applied for or received any reparations in domestic proceedings. If the Inter-American Court had applied its traditional criteria only to those victims and not to the victims who had already received a domestic award for lost wages, those to whom the Inter-American Court applied its own criteria would have received more than those who had been awarded domestic reparations.[90] The Court could have employed the requirement that it later used in *Gomes Lund et al. (Guerrilha do Araguaia)* v. *Brazil*, by ordering the State to reopen its reparations procedures and make reparations available to the other victims.[91]

IMPLEMENTATION OF MEASURES OF RESTITUTION

Measures of restitution include releasing from prison a person who has been convicted of a crime in violation of his or her rights, returning illegally seized property, protecting displaced persons so they can return to their homes, reinstating employment, expunging criminal records, and returning ancestral lands to indigenous peoples. States have at times encountered difficulties in complying with

86 *Ibid.*, para. 304; see *La Rochela Massacre* v. *Colombia*, (No. 163, 2007), paras. 271–72.

87 *"Las Dos Erres" Massacre* v. *Guatemala* (Preliminary Objection, Merits, Reparations, and Costs), IACtHR, 24 November 2009, Ser. C, No. 211, para. 281; *Valle Jaramillo et al.* v. *Colombia* (No. 192, 2008), para. 209.

88 See *La Rochela Massacre* v. *Colombia*, (No. 163, 2007), para. 246.

89 *Ibid.*

90 *Ibid.*

91 *Gomes Lund et al. (Guerrilha do Araguaia)* v. *Brazil* (Preliminary Objections, Merits, Reparations, and Costs), IACtHR, November 24, 2010, Ser. C, No. 219, para. 303.

Court-ordered measures of restitution when they require legislative reform or infringe on the rights of third parties.

The Inter-American Court has ordered the State to release only one person from prison, and the State complied with that order. In the *Loayza Tamayo Case*, the victim was released pursuant to an executive pardon.[92] Executive pardons, however, are not reliable, in that they depend on the will of a government official. A pardon also fails to clear the name of an innocent person. A better avenue to fulfill this form of reparations would entail minor domestic legislative reform. Most domestic criminal statutes permit the reopening of a criminal conviction for specific reasons, such as error, newly discovered facts, or fraudulent evidence. States could reform their Codes of Criminal Procedure to include as an additional ground for reopening a criminal proceeding that the Inter-American Court has determined that the person was tried in violation of the rights protected by the American Convention.[93] The Committee of Ministers of the Council of Europe recommended that the Contracting States of the European Convention revise their national laws to provide that a case be reexamined or judicial proceedings be reopened when the European Court of Human Rights has determined that the State has violated the European Convention.[94] Luxemburg, Bulgaria, Austria, Turkey, Greece, and other States have provisions in their Codes permitting the reopening of cases based on a judgment of the European Court of Human Rights.[95] A similar suggestion made by the OAS political organs to the States Parties to the American Convention could be beneficial.

Victims who are illegally convicted of crimes are returned to the status quo ante only if their criminal record is totally expunged. States have, in general, complied with Court orders to expunge public records when the Inter-American Court has ordered that a domestic conviction be vacated due to human rights violations.[96] States have also waived fines and canceled debts that resulted from the convictions.[97]

92 *Loayza Tamayo* v. *Peru*, Letter from the State of Peru dated 20 October 1997 concerning compliance with the Judgment of the Court, reprinted in IACtHR 1997 Annual Report, at 245.

93 See Viviana Krsticevic, "Reflexiones Sobre la Ejecución de las Decisiones del Sistema Interamericano de Protección de Derechos Humanos," at 47 in *Implementatión de las Decisiones del Sistema Interamericano de Derechos Humanos: Jurisprudencia, Normativa y Experiencias Nacionales* (CEJIL, 2007). Available at http://cejil.org/sites/default/files/implementacion_de_las_decisiones_del_sidh_0.pdf.

94 *Ibid.*

95 *Ibid.*, at 47–50.

96 *Loayza Tamayo* v. *Peru* (Monitoring Compliance), IACtHR, 1 July 2011, "considering" paras. 20–23; *Acosta Calderón* v. *Ecuador* (Monitoring Compliance), IACtHR, 7 February 2008, declaration 1; *Herrera Ulloa* v. *Costa Rica* (Monitoring Compliance), IACtHR, 22 November 2010, declaration 1; But see *Kimel* v. *Argentina* (Monitoring Compliance), IACtHR, 15 November, 2010, paras. 7–13 (wherein the State had not yet nullified the criminal judgment or expunged the records).

97 *Berenson Mejía* v. *Peru* (Monitoring Compliance), IACtHR, 22 September 2006; *Cantos* v. *Argentina* (Monitoring Compliance), IACtHR, 6 July 2009; *Suárez-Rosero* v. *Ecuador* (Monitoring Compliance), IACtHR, Order of President, 20 March 2009.

A possible problem with restitutionary measures that require the return of illegally seized property or the return of ancestral territory to indigenous peoples is that third parties may be affected by the order. The property may have been transferred to innocent parties who will be injured by State action to recover the property for the victim. Before ordering restitution, the Inter-American Court often attempts to educate itself on the effects of the measures on the rights of third parties by considering information provided by the State, victims, civil society, and experts.[98] To date, however, the Court has not been willing to consider information provided directly to the Court by the third parties who may be affected.[99]

State compliance with Court-ordered return of ancestral lands to indigenous communities has not been uniform. The Inter-American Court has ordered Nicaragua, Paraguay, and Suriname to return, demarcate, and title land to the indigenous and tribal people who regard the lands as their ancestral territory. Nicaragua was the only one of the three States that fully complied with the Court's judgment. The State established the boundaries and conveyed title of ownership to 73,394 hectares of their communal ancestral lands to the Awas Tingni People as a result of the Court's reparations order in the *Mayagna (Sumo) Awas Tingni Community Case*.[100] The Awas Tingni were living on their land when they brought the case before the Inter-American system, which may partly account for why they were successful. In Paraguay, conversely, the indigenous peoples who brought their cases to the Inter-American system did not have access to their ancestral lands. Paraguay has not complied with the Inter-American Court's orders to return at least a part of the ancestral lands to the Yakye Axa, Sawhoyamaxa, and Xákmok Kásek indigenous peoples.[101] In 2009, Paraguayan lawmakers voted against the expropriation of ancestral lands, rejecting the 2005 decision by the Inter-American Court.[102] The State has instead attempted to buy the land from the current owners or to find alternative land for the indigenous communities. Suriname formed a National Commission on Land Rights to study the demarcation of the ancestral lands in the *Moiwana Case*, but it has not made significant progress.[103]

One of the least successful forms of restitution has been State measures allowing human rights victims to return to their homes. In general, States have not been successful in assuring displaced persons that they will be protected if they wish to return to areas of the country that are still in conflict. People are especially afraid

98 Krsticevic, "Reflexiones," at 67.

99 See *Ibid.*, at 63.

100 *Mayagna (Sumo) Awas Tingni Community* v. *Nicaragua* (Monitoring Compliance), IACtHR, 3 April 2009, "considering" para. 11.

101 *Yakye Axa Indigenous Community* v. *Paraguay*, (Merits, Reparations, and Costs), IACtHR, 17 June 2005, Ser. C, No. 125, para. 242.

102 See Amnesty International at http://www.amnesty.org/en/news-and-updates/news/paraguayan-congress-risks-lives-of-90-indigenous-families-20090628.

103 *Moiwana Community* v. *Suriname* (Monitoring Compliance), IACtHR, 22 November 2010, "considering" para. 28.

to return to areas of Colombia where entire villages have been displaced and where the conflict continues.[104] In *Moiwana Community* v. *Suriname*, the State's only assurance that it will protect community members who chose to return is that it is renovating police departments in the area.[105] The continued impunity of those who had raided their village leaves the villagers too fearful to return.[106]

IMPLEMENTATION OF MEASURES OF REHABILITATION

In general, States have seldom fully implemented Court-ordered reparations to provide ongoing health and psychological care and medications through the national health services.[107] Future medical expenses are so uncertain that utilizing the State health care system to provide ongoing medical and psychological treatment to victims would appear to be the preferable alternative to ordering the payment of a set amount of compensation. The executive branch of the government is normally responsible for arranging for these rehabilitation measures. Perhaps the need to coordinate the services of the national ministry of health and the local bureaucrats who run the local health centers contributes to the low implementation rate.

The Inter-American Court had mandated medical and psychological treatment through national institutions twenty-eight times as of the end of 2010, and yet States have seldom fully complied.[108] Some States have made concerted efforts to implement Court-ordered rehabilitation, although their efforts have not been completely successful. In the *Vargas Areco Case*, Paraguay enrolled the family of the deceased victim in the regular health care plan provided for families of deceased soldiers, but the hospital that was to treat them was 570 kilometers from their home.[109] Peru also encountered problems, despite its effort to comply in the *Cantoral Benavides Case*.[110] Although Peru registered the victim in the State's health system, the local health center required that she effectively reregister and wait several hours each time she sought treatment.[111] Moreover, it did not stock the medications she required.[112]

104 *"Mapiripán Massacre"* v. *Colombia* (Monitoring Compliance), IACtHR, 8 July 2009, "considering" para. 56.

105 *Moiwana Community* v. *Suriname* (Monitoring Compliance), IACtHR, 22 November 2010, "considering" paras. 29–30.

106 *Ibid.*

107 See *"Las Dos Erres" Massacre* v. *Guatemala* (Monitoring Compliance), IACtHR, 6 July 2011, "considering" para. 43; *Serrano Cruz Sisters* v. *El Salvador* (Monitoring Compliance), IACtHR, 3 February 2010, "considering" paras. 32–37.

108 See Thomas M. Antkowiak, "An Emerging Mandate for International Courts: Victim-Centered Remedies and Restorative Justice," 47 *Stanford Journal of International Law*, 279, 296 (2011).

109 *Vargas Areco* v. *Paraguay* (Monitoring Compliance), IACtHR, 24 November 2010, "considering" para. 19.

110 *Cantoral Benavides* v. *Peru* (Monitoring Compliance), IACtHR, 14 November 2010, "considering" para. 14.

111 *Ibid.*

112 *Ibid.*

Following the judgment in the "*Juvenile Reeducation Institute*" *Case*, in which the Court ordered Paraguay to provide psychological treatment to all former inmates who had been in the Institute at some point during a five-year period, as well as medical and psychological treatment for former inmates who had been injured in fires in the Institute, Paraguay delivered medical identification cards to those beneficiaries it could locate.[113] Forty-three of the victims were registered to receive medical attention, but this was only a small percentage of the thousands of possible beneficiaries.[114] Several victims were too distrustful of State authorities to take advantage of the program.[115] Also, Colombia failed to implement Court orders to provide medical and psychological treatment free of charge through the Colombian national health services to victims in nine cases.[116] The Court and the State are attempting to remedy the overall problem.[117]

IMPLEMENTATION OF MEASURES OF SATISFACTION

States often comply with the Court's order to undertake a symbolic public act, such as participating in a public ceremony.[118] After the Court's judgment in the *Myrna Mack Chang Case*, in which a prominent Guatemalan anthropologist and social activist was murdered, Guatemala held a ceremony at the presidential palace, and the Guatemalan President asked forgiveness of the family and the Guatemalan people.[119] In *Kimel* v. *Argentina*, even though the State had not nullified the victim's judgment, the President of Argentina led a ceremony in which there was an acknowledgment of responsibility that was attended by the Minister of Foreign Affairs, International Trade, and Worship; the Minister of Justice, Security, and Human Rights; the Secretary of Human Rights; the family of the victim; and the press.[120]

Although the public act is to be performed within six months of the notification of the Court's judgments, some States delay doing so. In its 2005 judgment

[113] "*Juvenile Reeducation Institute*" v. *Paraguay* (Monitoring Compliance), IACtHR, 19 November 2009, "considering" paras. 18–19.

[114] *Ibid.*, paras. 19, 24.

[115] *Ibid.*, para. 19.

[116] See Order of the President of the Inter-American Court, 8 February 2010, Monitoring Compliance with Reparations Measures Regarding Medical and Psychological Attention in Nine Colombian Cases, Summons to a Private Hearing.

[117] *Ibid.*, para. 6.

[118] *Serrano Cruz Sisters* v. *El Salvador* (Monitoring Compliance), IACtHR, 3 February 2010, "considering" para. 11; *Moiwana Community* v. *Suriname* (Monitoring Compliance), IACtHR, 21 November 2007, declaration 1; *Zambrano Vélez et al.* v. *Ecuador* (Monitoring Compliance), IACtHR, 21 September 2009, "considering" para. 24; *Vargas Areco* v. *Paraguay* (Monitoring Compliance), IACtHR, 24 November 2010, "considering" para. 16.

[119] Los Angeles Times, "The World: Guatemala Officials Apologize for Killing," 23 April 2004.

[120] *Kimel* v. *Argentina* (Monitoring Compliance), IACtHR, 15 November, 2010, "considering" paras. 14–17.

in the *Girls Yean and Bosico Case*, the Inter-American Court ordered the Dominican Republic to undertake a public act recognizing international responsibility for the human rights violations and apologizing to the victims.[121] As of October 2011, the State had still not complied with this form of reparations, although it had paid the compensation owed the victims.[122] Likewise, in the *Carpio Nicolle Case* in which the Inter-American Court handed down its judgment in November 2004, the State had not yet held the public act as of July 1, 2009, when the Inter-American Court issued an order monitoring judgment in the case.[123]

States are generally willing to comply with the Court's order to make a public apology to the victims. The Ecuadoran Minister of Justice and Human Rights publicly apologized on national Ecuadoran television to all the persons whom the Inter-American Court had found to be victims of human rights violations by Ecuador.[124] Also in accordance with the Court's order in the *Tibi Case*, in which the victim was a French national, Ecuador publicly apologized in a French newspaper.[125] As stated by Judge Cançado Trindade, "[n]o one would have forecast, some years ago, that respondent States would publicly apologize to victims of human rights violations, or their relatives, as a satisfaction owed to them as a result of sentences of the Inter-American Court of Human Rights."[126]

States also have a high level of compliance with Court orders to publish the pertinent parts of the judgment in newspapers and on the State's website.[127] In *Radilla Racheco* v. *Mexico*, eighteen months after the judgment, the only reparation with which Mexico had complied was that it had published the judgment as ordered.[128] Subsequently, in November 2011, the State held a public ceremony attended by high-level State functionaries and put up a plaque commemorating the victim.[129]

States have willingly complied with Court-ordered reparations to name schools after child victims and to name streets and put up plaques in public places to

[121] *Girls Yean and Bosico* v. *Dominican Republic* (Preliminary Objections, Merits, Reparations, and Costs), IACtHR, 8 September 2005, Ser. C, No. 130, para. 235.

[122] *Girls Yean and Bosico* v. *Dominican Republic* (Monitoring Compliance), IACtHR, 10 October 2011, "considering" para. 11.

[123] *Carpio Nicolle* v. *Guatemala* (Monitoring Compliance), IACtHR, 1 July 2009, "considering" para. 30.

[124] *Tibi* v. *Ecuador* (Monitoring Compliance), IACtHR, 3 March 2011, "considering" para. 10.

[125] *Ibid.*

[126] Antônio Augusto Cançado Trindade, "The Human Person and International Justice," 47 *Columbia Journal of Transnational Law*, 16, 21–22 (2008).

[127] *Acosta Calderón* v. *Ecuador* (Monitoring Compliance), IACtHR, 7 February 2008, declaration 1; *Girls Yean and Bosico* v. *Dominican Republic* (Monitoring Compliance), IACtHR, 10 October 2011, having seen para. 4; *"Las Dos Erres" Massacre* v. *Guatemala* (Monitoring Compliance), IACtHR, 6 July 2011, "considering" para. 31.

[128] *Radilla Pacheco* v. *Mexico* (Monitoring Compliance), IACtHR, 19 May 2011, declaration 1.

[129] *Radilla Pacheco* v. *Mexico* (Monitoring Compliance), IACtHR, 1 December 2011, "considering" para. 8.

commemorate victims,[130] but erecting monuments has proved problematic. Guatemala has not built a monument on the site of the Dos Erres Massacre, claiming that the property is owned privately and that it had to get the permission of the owner.[131] The once tiny village is now reportedly a ranch owned by a powerful Guatemalan drug-dealing family, and relatives of the victims must beg permission to mourn at the site.[132]

There has been some backlash against certain monuments that the Court ordered to be built. As a result of the Court's ruling in the *Cotton Field* case, Mexico built a memorial costing more than a million dollars dedicated to the young women who had been murdered and their bodies dumped in a cotton field.[133] Relatives of other missing women interrupted the unveiling ceremony, saying that the monument was a waste of money.[134] The father of a fourteen-year-old girl who was still missing objected, saying, "After ten years you come to inaugurate a mausoleum that will become a tourist center for the rest of the world's morbid fascination."[135] One representative of the victims said that the monument had been a low-ranking priority.

The backlash was stronger in Peru, when the Court ordered that the names of the victims of the *Miguel Castro Castro Prison Case*, some of whom were considered to be terrorists, be included in the monument, El Ojo Que Llora (The Eye That Cries), which was dedicated to the victims of the internal conflict in Peru.[136] Although it had been the State that had suggested this specific form of reparations,[137] when the public reacted negatively to the inscription of the names of persons who were labeled "terrorists," the Peruvian President called the reparations "outrageous" and condemned the Court's judgment.[138] In its interpretation of the judgment in the case, the Court allowed the State to substitute another remedial measure, such as a park.[139] It might be better if the Court were to recommend the placement of

[130] *Trujillo Oroza* v. *Bolivia* (Monitoring Compliance), IACtHR, 12 September 2005, declaration 1(a); *Gómez Paquiyauri Brothers* v. *Peru* (Monitoring Compliance), IACtHR, 3 May 2008, "considering" para. 14; *Myrna Mack Chang* v. *Guatemala* (Monitoring Compliance), IACtHR, 26 November 2007, "having seen" para. 3.

[131] *"Las Dos Erres" Massacre* v. *Guatemala* (Monitoring Compliance), IACtHR, 6 July 2011, "considering" para. 36.

[132] Lomi Kriel, Seeking Justice for Guatemalan Village Where Hundreds Were Raped, Tortured, Killed, Houston Chronicale, May 26, 2012.

[133] El Paso Times, "Memorial for Murdered, Missing Women Unveiled in Juarez," 8 November 2011.

[134] *Ibid.*

[135] *Ibid.*

[136] *Miguel Castro Castro Prison* v. *Peru* (Merits, Reparations, and Costs), IACtHR, 25 November 2006, Ser. C, No. 160, para. 454; see also *La Cantuta* v. *Peru* (Monitoring Compliance), IACtHR, 20 November, 2009, "considering" paras. 19–21.

[137] *Miguel Castro Castro Prison* v. *Peru* (No. 160, 2006), para. 453.

[138] Cavallaro and Brewer, "Reevaluating Regional Human Rights Litigation in the Twenty-First Century," at 825.

[139] *Miguel Castro Castro Prison* v. *Peru* (Interpretation of Judgment on Merits, Reparations, and Costs), IACtHR, 2 August 2008, Ser. C, No. 181, para. 57.

an engraved plaque, rather than the expense of a monument, except perhaps to commemorate the scene of a massacre.

A successful form of satisfaction to date, in a limited number of cases, has been State compliance with Inter-American Court orders to annul the death penalty. Guatemala twice complied with such orders from the Inter-American Court. In the *Raxcacó Reyes Case*, the Court ordered Guatemala to annul the death sentence that had been handed down for kidnapping and to order a new punishment without the necessity of a new trial.[140] The State complied and the defendant was sentenced to forty years in prison.[141] In the *Fermín Ramírez Case*, Guatemala retried the defendant in accordance with the Inter-American Court's order.[142] The State then also sentenced him to forty years in prison.[143] In ordering the new trial, the Guatemalan Supreme Court of Justice stated that "since the State of Guatemala is subject to the compulsory jurisdiction of the Inter-American Court of Human Rights, the judgments that the latter delivers concerning the interpretation and application of the American Convention on Human Rights are final and are unappealable."[144] Trinidad and Tobago commuted the death penalty to life in prison for most of those who were represented in the *Hilaire, Constantine, and Benjamin et al. Case*, although that may have resulted more from the ruling of the Privy Council.[145]

Perhaps surprisingly, a measure of satisfaction with which States have encountered difficulties is in providing the educational grants and scholarships required by the Court.[146] Peru did provide funding for Mr. Cantoral Benavides to pursue his university studies in Brazil.[147] The Ministry of Education processed and made the payment in accordance with the estimates that were budgeted by the Ministry of Economy and Finance.[148] Despite the State's willingness to pay for the victim's education, the parties disagreed on the amount to be paid in his final years of study, and the Court was required to resolve the issue.[149] An alternative reparations approach that could possibly be taken by the Court would be to order that the State either provide a full

140 *Raxcacó Reyes* v. *Guatemala* (Merits, Reparations, and Costs), IACtHR, 15 September 2005, Ser. C, No. 133, para. 133.

141 *Raxcacó Reyes* v. *Guatemala* (Monitoring Compliance), IACtHR, 9 May 2008, "considering" paras. 16–19.

142 *Fermín Ramírez* v. *Guatemala* (Monitoring Compliance), IACtHR, 9 May 2008, declares para. 1.

143 *Ibid.*

144 *Fermín Ramírez* v. *Guatemala* (Monitoring Compliance), IACtHR, 22 September 2006, "considering" para. 9.

145 Hands Off Cain report available at http://www.handsoffcain.info/bancadati/schedastato.php?idstato=15000098&idcontinente=24 .

146 *Gómez Palomino* v. *Peru* (Monitoring Compliance), IACtHR, 5 July 2011, "considering" paras. 28–32, declaration 3(d).

147 *Cantoral Benavides* v. *Peru* (Monitoring Compliance), IACtHR, 14 November 2010, "considering" para. 12.

148 *Ibid.*

149 *Ibid.*, "considering" paras. 8–12.

scholarship to the victim or, if bureaucratically that proved difficult, provide him or her with an amount of money set by the Court to be used for educational purposes.

In general, States have not successfully implemented Court orders to determine the whereabouts of disappeared victims and return their remains to the family for burial. This remedy was reportedly ordered in at least twenty-four cases, but the State has fully complied in only a few of those cases.[150] Peru was able to partially comply with its obligation in the *La Cantuta Case* by identifying and returning the remains of some of the victims.[151] Also, the Guatemalan Foundation of Forensic Anthropology has exhumed the bodies from the site of the Dos Erres Massacre and is attempting to extract sufficient DNA to match them with the next of kin, so as to return the remains of the victims to their families for burial.[152]

Often the victims have been missing for decades. They may have been buried in mass graves, or their bodies may have been destroyed. In Argentina, it has been reported that persons who had been held in clandestine prisons were drugged and dropped into the ocean or the Rio Plata.[153] These remains cannot be recovered. When bodies are located, forensic specialists are needed to identify them. In searching for the remains of the victim in the *Trujillo Oroza Case*, Bolivia excavated an area and found forty-four bone fragments, but the State did not analyze them.[154] In some instances, the remains have deteriorated to the point where DNA cannot be extracted so as to identify the person.[155] Despite excavating in areas likely to contain human remains, States seldom are able to comply with this type of reparations. Moreover, States have at times appeared to raise unnecessary difficulties, claiming that they do not have the financial resources to continue excavations or to pay forensic specialists.[156] They have also questioned the credentials of specialists recommended

150 Antkowiak, "An Emerging Mandate for International Courts," at 293–94, citing full compliance in *Juan Humberto Sánchez* v. *Honduras* (Monitoring Compliance), IACtHR, 21 November 2007; *Las Palmeras* v. *Colombia* (Monitoring Compliance), IACtHR, 3 February 2010; *Paniagua Morales et al.* v. *Guatemala* (Monitoring Compliance), IACtHR, 27 November 2007; and *"Street Children" (Villagrán Morales et al.)* v. *Guatemala* (Monitoring Compliance), IACtHR, 27 January 2009.

151 *La Cantuta* v. *Peru* (Monitoring Compliance), IACtHR, 20 November, 2009, "considering" paras. 11–12.

152 *"Las Dos Erres" Massacre* v. *Guatemala* (Monitoring Compliance), IACtHR, 6 July 2011, "considering" para. 19.

153 Kurt Fernández, Alleged Death Flight Pilot Fights Charges with Legal Tools Denied to Victims of Argentina"s Dirty War, Pulse, available at http://pulsemedia.org/2010/05/22/alleged-death-flight-pilot-fights-charges-with-legal-tools-denied-to-victims-of-argentinas-dirty-war/.

154 *Trujillo Oroza* v. *Bolivia* (Monitoring Compliance), IACtHR, 16 November 2009, "considering" para. 9.

155 *"Las Dos Erres" Massacre* v. *Guatemala* (Monitoring Compliance), IACtHR, 6 July 2011, "considering" para. 19.

156 *Radilla Pacheco* v. *Mexico* (Monitoring Compliance), IACtHR, 19 May 2011, "considering" paras. 13–16.

by the families.[157] Yet, the next of kin will not have closure until they know what happened to their loved ones and can bury them.

As an alternative to this form of reparations, the Court could order the State to form a governmental department staffed with personnel experienced in forensic anthropology that would search for and attempt to identify the remains of all persons who were forcibly disappeared in the State. The department should have the necessary political and financial support of the State and the authority to search and excavate any private or public area where remains may be buried. It should also have the authority to gather information from public records and from persons who have knowledge of the situation. The department should provide genetic testing of relatives of the disappeared and maintain a database with the results. If the State can show that this governmental department is making progress and is locating and identifying remains, that aspect of reparations should be satisfied, even though individual victims may not yet have been located.

IMPLEMENTATION OF MEASURES OF NONREPETITION

Capacitation Programs

Many States have complied with Court-ordered capacitation programs to train public officials in human rights obligations. Ecuador reported that, in accordance with an Inter-American Court ruling, it had held training programs for more than 2,500 police officers in fourteen cities, and it was training police officers to lead the programs.[158] Despite Ecuador's efforts, the Court did not close the *Tibi Case* because the State had not yet trained medical and psychiatric personnel as required by the Court's judgment.[159] Likewise in the *La Cantuta Case*, Peru had instituted human rights training programs, but the Court did not consider them sufficient to address every aspect of the Court's order.[160] Colombia entered into a cooperation agreement with the United Nations High Commissioner on Human Rights and hired three international consultants to conduct a study to develop a training program in human rights and humanitarian law for its armed forces.[161] The Colombian Ministry of Defense designed a "Comprehensive Human Rights and International Humanitarian Law Policy" based on the study to institute the training. A human

[157] *Ibid.*, "considering" para. 13.

[158] *Tibi* v. *Ecuador* (Monitoring Compliance), IACtHR, 3 March 2011, "considering" paras. 14–15; see also *Zambrano Vélez et al.* v. *Ecuador* (Monitoring Compliance), IACtHR, 21 September 2009, "considering" paras. 50–62.

[159] *Tibi* v. *Ecuador* (Monitoring Compliance), IACtHR, 3 March 2011, "considering" paras. 14–15.

[160] *La Cantuta* v. *Peru* (Monitoring Compliance), IACtHR, 20 November 2009, "considering" para. 35.

[161] *"Mapiripán Massacre"* v. *Colombia* (Monitoring Compliance), IACtHR, 8 July 2009, "considering" para. 62.

rights office was created within the army to internalize the policy, and Colombia entered into a cooperation agreement with the Inter-American Institute of Human Rights to oversee progress.[162] It would be useful and effective if States would share with other States their models for human rights capacitation programs.

Capacitating trainers to continue leading the courses is especially important for long-term results. Short-term training programs that are meant to do no more than comply with Court-ordered reparations are not sufficient to bring about structural changes. These programs need to be made permanent if they are to have a lasting influence. The Court's more recent orders require that the State institute permanent capacitation programs.

Legislative Reform

Legislative reform requires both political will to overcome entrenched interests and agreement between the political parties needed to pass the legislation. It also requires coordination between the branches of government and time to make the changes within the applicable domestic procedures. Inter-American Court reparations orders to reform domestic legislation so that it will comply with the American Convention are still pending in several judgments.[163]

Nonetheless, it is noteworthy that in many instances States have successfully changed their laws and even their constitutions to comply with judgments of the Inter-American Court. For instance, by adopting the Law on Transparency in Public Office and Access to Information on State Administration, Chile complied with the Inter-American Court's order to adopt the necessary measures to ensure the right of access to State-held information.[164] The law "guarantees to all persons the right to request and receive information from any entity of the State Administration."[165] At the public hearing held to monitor State compliance in the case, the State emphasized that the Court's judgment made an "extraordinary contribution to the access to public information and the strengthening of the freedom of expression" and that the comprehensive language of the law was a result of the impact of the Court's judgment.[166] Chile also complied with the Court's judgment in *"The Last Temptation of Christ" Case*, in which Chilean authorities had refused to allow a movie to be shown in Chile. The Court ordered Chile to modify a constitutional provision to eliminate prior censorship that was incompatible with the American

[162] *Ibid.*

[163] *"Las Dos Erres" Massacre* v. *Guatemala* (Monitoring Compliance), IACtHR, 6 July 2011, "considering" para. 18, declares para. 3(c).

[164] *Claude Reyes et al.* v. *Chile* (Monitoring Compliance), IACtHR, 24 November 2008, "considering" para. 8.

[165] *Ibid.*

[166] *Ibid.*, "considering" para. 10.

Convention's provision on freedom of thought and expression.[167] In response, the Chilean Congress amended the Chilean Constitution to guarantee artistic freedom.[168]

Other States have also reformed their laws in response to Inter-American Court orders. Peru amended its antiterrorism and treason laws to conform to the American Convention, after the Inter-American Court's judgments in the *Loayza Tamayo* and *Castillo Petruzzi Cases*.[169] The Inter-American Court ordered Ecuador to adapt its domestic legislation and administrative provisions on states of emergency and suspension of guarantees, in particular certain provisions of its National Security Law, to comply with the American Convention.[170] Subsequently, the Ecuadoran Constitutional Court declared those provisions of the National Security Law that allowed military courts to try civilians during states of emergency to be unconstitutional.[171] The Inter-American Court held that the decision of the Constitutional Court and the additional measures taken by Ecuador to amend or repeal domestic laws satisfied the Court-ordered reparations in that area.[172] Ecuador also complied with Court-ordered legislative reform in the *Chaparro Álvarez and Lapo Íñiguez Case* by adapting its domestic laws and regulations so as to eliminate charges for the handling and storage of assets seized and confiscated from persons who ultimately were not convicted of drug offenses.[173] Costa Rica complied with the Court's order in the *Herrera Ulloa Case* by amending its Code of Criminal Procedure to reform its procedures for case review and add the right to appeal criminal judgments.[174] Following the *Kimel Case*, Argentine modified its criminal code to eliminate the possibility that opinions on issues of public interest could result in a criminal charge of slander.[175]

Beginning with its decision in *Barrios Altos* v. *Peru*, the Inter-American Court ruled in several cases that amnesty laws that bar the prosecution and punishment of individuals who committed crimes against humanity and other serious human rights

[167] *"The Last Temptation of Christ"(Olmedo-Bustios et al.)* v. *Chile* (Merits, Reparations, and Costs), IACtHR, 5 February 2001, Ser. C, No. 73, operative para. 4; See also *Caesar* v. *Trinidad and Tobago* (Merits, Reparations, and Costs), IACtHR, 11 March 2005, Ser. C, No. 123, operative para. 3 (ordering the State to abrogate the Corporal Punishment Act).

[168] Santiago Times, Monday, May 10, 2004, News Briefs.

[169] *Loayza Tamayo* v. *Peru* (Reparations and Costs), IACtHR, 27 November 1998, Ser. C, No. 42, operative para. 5; *Castillo Petruzzi et al.* v. *Peru* (Merits), IACtHR, 30 May 1999, Ser. C, No. 52, operative para. 14.

[170] *Zambrano Vélez et al.* v. *Ecuador* (No. 166, 2007), operative para. 9.

[171] *Zambrano Vélez et al.* v. *Ecuador* (Monitoring Compliance), IACtHR, 21 September 2009, "considering" paras. 33, 42.

[172] *Ibid.*, "considering" para. 49.

[173] *Chaparro Álvarez and Lapo Íñiguez* v. *Ecuador* (Monitoring Compliance), IACtHR, 19 May 2010, "considering" paras. 18, 21–22.

[174] *Herrera Ulloa* v. *Costa Rica* (Monitoring Compliance), IACtHR, 22 November 2010, "considering" para. 11

[175] *Fontevecchia and D'Amico* v. *Argentina* (Merits, Reparations, and Costs), IACtHR, 29 November 2011, Ser. C, No. 238, para. 95.

violations are incompatible with the American Convention and, thus, are without legal effect.[176] The Court's ruling applies to all amnesty laws that preclude the investigation and punishment of serious human rights violations.[177] It is not limited to self-amnesties that were passed by the government that was responsible for the violations.[178] One after another, State amnesty laws have been repealed as a result of the Court's rulings.[179] The Argentine Supreme Court, in divesting its amnesty laws of all legal effects, stated in the *Simón Case* that it must apply "the findings of the Inter-American Court in '*Barrios Altos*' if the decisions of the Inter-American Court are to be "interpreted in good faith as jurisprudential guidelines."[180] The Chilean Supreme Court annulled a not guilty verdict and invalidated the application of the Chilean amnesty law in the domestic case of *Lecaros Carrasco*.[181] The Constitutional Court of Peru stated in the domestic *Santiago Martín Rivas Case* that it considered the amnesty laws referred to in the case to be null and void and to lack legal effect.[182] The Supreme Court of Uruguay held that the amnesty passed by national referendum was unconstitutional.[183] Subsequent to the Inter-American Court's holding in the *Gelman* v. *Uruguay Case*, Uruguay enacted Law No. 18.831, which specifies that the crimes committed during the dictatorship are not covered by statutes of limitation and "reestablishes the full exercise of the State's punitive powers" for crimes covered by the State's amnesty law.[184] Moreover, the Constitutional Courts and Supreme Courts of Honduras, El Salvador, and Colombia made similar rulings.[185] Brazil is the final holdout, but it has created a truth commission.[186] As stated by Jose Miguel Vivanco of Human Rights Watch, "no matter how many years go by, laws that block justice for gross abuses of human rights remain a thorn in the side of democratic

[176] *Barrios Altos* v. *Peru* (Merits), IACtHR, 14 March 2001, Ser. C, No. 75, operative para. 4; *Almonacid Arellano et al.* v. *Chile* (Preliminary Objections, Merits, Reparations, and costs), IACtHR, 26 September 2006, Ser. C, No. 154, para. 119; *Gomes Lund et al. (Guerrilha do Araguaia)* v. *Brazil* (No. 219, 2010), para. 174; *Gelman* v. *Uruguay* (Merits and Reparations), IACtHR, 24 February 2011, Ser. C. No. 221, paras. 196, 229.

[177] *Gelman* v. *Uruguay* (No. 221, 2011), para 229.

[178] *Ibid.*

[179] See Diego García-Sayán, "The Inter-American Court and Constitutionalism in Latin America," 89 *Texas Law Review*, 1836, 1941–47 (2011).

[180] *Gelman* v. *Uruguay* (No. 221, 2011), para. 215, quoting Supreme Court of Justice of the Nation of Argentina. *Case of Simón, Julio Héctor et al. s/illegal deprivation of liberty*, June 14, 2005 "considering" clause 31.

[181] Supreme Court of Justice of Chile, *Case of Claudio Abdón Lecaros Carrasco*, Rol No. 47.205, Remedy No. 3302/2009, Resolution 16698, Appeals Judgment, and Resolution 16699, Replacement Judgment, of May 18, 2010, quoted in *Gelman* v. *Uruguay* (No. 221, 2011), para. 217.

[182] Constitutional Tribunal of Peru, *Case of Santiago Martín Rivas*, Constitutional tort remedy, Case file No. 679–2005-PA/TC, Judgment of March 2, 2007, para. 60.

[183] Supreme Court of Justice of Uruguay, *Case of Nibia Sabalsagaray Curutchet*, considering clause III.8, paras. 11, 15, quoted in *Gelman* v. *Uruguay* (No. 221, 2010), para. 219.

[184] IACHR, Press Release 117/11, IACHR Brings its 143rd Session to a Close.

[185] *Gelman* v. *Uruguay* (No. 221, 2011), paras. 220–23.

[186] Andres Gaudin, Uruguay, Brazil Tackles Impunity Laws, NotiSur South American Political and Economic Affairs, 18 November 2011.

governments."[187] Although States are not always amenable to altering their laws, when States comply, society benefits and human rights are advanced because future violations likely are prevented.

The Court has not been as successful in convincing States to reform their military codes. Six years after the Inter-American Court ruling in *Palamara Iribarne*, Chile still had not repealed laws in its Military Code of Justice criminalizing defamation.[188] The Inter-American Court has often ordered States to try military personnel who commit human rights abuses in civilian courts rather than in military courts.[189] In this regard, the Inter-American Court held that Article 57 of Mexico's Military Code of Justice (Código de Justicia Militar), which ensures that military personnel could be tried only in military courts, was in violation of international human rights codes.[190] The Mexican Supreme Court subsequently held, in accordance with the Inter-American Court, that cases against members of the military charged with human rights abuse should be removed from military jurisdiction.[191] To date, however, no action has been taken by the military authorities. Consequently, cases alleging similar violations are likely to be brought before the organs of the Inter-American human rights system. As pointed out by Ruiz-Chiriboga, when States do not comply with Inter-American Court orders to reform or repeal legislation that violates the Inter-American Convention, this noncompliance results in additional victims of the offending law, more State-paid compensation, and an increased caseload for the Inter-American Commission and Court.[192]

A State has even reformed its legislation in a negative respect to counteract an order of the Inter-American Court. In *Girls Yean and Bosico* v. *Dominican Republic*, in which the State refused to issue birth certificates to children who had been born in the Dominican Republic to Haitian parents, the Inter-American Court held that the State "should adopt within its domestic laws, the legislative, administrative and

[187] Human Rights Watch, Argentina: Amnesty Laws Struck Down: Supreme Court's Long-Awaited Ruling Allows Prosecution of "Dirty War" Crimes, June 14, 2005. Available at http://www.hrw.org/news/2005/06/14/argentina-amnesty-laws-struck-down.

[188] *Palamara Iribarne* v. *Chile* (Monitoring Compliance), IACtHR, 1 July 2011, "considering" para. 12.

[189] *Cabrera García and Montiel Flores* v. *Mexico* (No. 220, 2010), para. 256: *Radilla Pacheco* v. *Mexico*, (Preliminary Objections, Merits, Reparations, and Costs), IACtHR, 23 November 2009, Ser. C, No. 209, paras. 341–42; *Rosendo Cantú et al.* v. *Mexico* (Preliminary Objections, Merits, Reparations, and Costs), IACtHR, 31 August 2010, No. 216, paras. 221–22; *Fernández Ortega et al.* v. *Mexico* (Preliminary Objections, Merits, Reparations, and Costs), IACtHR, 30 August 2010, Ser. C, No. 215, paras. 238–39.

[190] *Cabrera García and Montiel Flores* v. *Mexico* (No. 220, 2010), paras. 205–07, order 15.

[191] Mexican Supreme Court, decision of 12 July 2011, reported in Supreme Court Rules That Military Human Rights Violations Now Under Civilian Jurisidiction, Justice in Mexico Project. Available at http://justiceinmexico.org/2011/07/15/supreme-court-rules-that-military-human-rights-violations-now-under-civilian-jurisidiction/.

[192] Oswaldo Ruiz-Chiriboga, "The Conventionality Control: Examples of (Un)Successful Experiences in Latin America," in *Inter-American and European Human Rights Journal/ Revista Interamericana y Europea de Derechos Humanos*, 200, 209 (2010).

any other measures needed to regulate the procedure and requirements for acquiring Dominican nationality by late declaration of birth."[193] Instead, the Dominican Republic amended its Constitution so as to deny citizenship to children born in the country to parents who were in the country illegally, which could exacerbate the problem that had been before the Court.[194]

Annul or Execute Domestic Court Rulings

States have not been consistent in complying with Inter-American Court orders to annul domestic judicial decisions. Panama did comply with the Inter-American Court order to reverse the conviction and acquit the victim of the charge of false accusations in the *Tristán Donoso Case*.[195] In doing so, the Panamanian Supreme Court of Justice stated that "the Republic of Panama, as a member of the international community, recognizes, respects, and complies with the decisions of the Inter-American Court of Human Rights."[196] Peru complied with the Court's order to adopt the necessary measures to annul the victim's conviction in the *Cantoral Benavides Case*.[197] Also, in the *Cesti Hurtado Case*, Peru executed the domestic habeas corpus decision in accordance with the Inter-American Court order, resulting in Cesti Hurtado's release from prison.[198] Conversely, Peru has not complied with the Inter-American Court order to observe the rulings of its Peruvian Constitutional Court to pay the compensation owed to 273 workers.[199]

IMPLEMENTATION OF ORDERS TO INVESTIGATE, PROSECUTE, AND PUNISH

Although the Inter-American Court holds that the State has a duty to investigate, prosecute, and punish those responsible for human rights violations, most States have not complied with this form of reparations.[200] Even States that have willingly fulfilled other measures of reparations have seldom satisfied this order. In

[193] *Girls Yean and Bosico* v. *Dominican Republic* (No. 130, 2005), para. 239.

[194] Dominican Constitution Reform Threatens to Increase Number of Stateless Persons, Robert F. Kennedy Center, 5 February 2010. available at http://www.rfkcenter.org/node/426.

[195] *Tristán Donoso* v. *Panama* (Monitoring Compliance), IACtHR, 1 September 2010, "considering" para. 12.

[196] *Ibid.*

[197] *Cantoral Benavides* v. *Peru* (Monitoring Compliance), IACtHR, 17 November 2004, declarations 1(d) and (e).

[198] *Cesti Hurtado* v. *Peru* (Request for Interpretation of Judgment on the Merits), IACtHR, 19 November 1999, Ser. C, No. 62, para. 6.

[199] *Acevedo Buendía et al. ("Discharged and Retired Employees of the Comptroller")* v. *Peru* (Monitoring Compliance), IACtHR, 1 July 2011, declaration 2

[200] See *Gómez Palomino* v. *Peru* (Monitoring Compliance), IACtHR, 5 July 2011, declaration 3; *Tiu Tojín* v. *Guatemala* (Monitoring Compliance), IACtHR, 16 May 2011, "considering" para. 9; *Serrano-Cruz Sisters* v. *El Salvador* (Monitoring Compliance), IACtHR, 3 February 2010, "considering" paras. 13–19.

some cases, governments lack the power to bring to justice influential persons or those who have the backing of persons in power. Alternately, government officials may be complicit or fear that they could be charged with violations in the future. In some instances when domestic remedies have been exhausted in a national court, judges may resent a regional Court essentially overturning their former judgments.

States have complied with their duty to investigate, prosecute, and punish in only a few cases. Peru tried sixteen officers of the National Police Force for the disappearance of Ernesto Castillo Páez.[201] Four of the defendants were convicted and received prison sentences.[202] Following the Inter-American Court judgment in the *Myrna Mack Chang Case*, a member of the Guatemalan Presidential Guard was sentenced to thirty years in prison for ordering her murder.[203] However, the Appeals Court freed him, and by the time the Guatemalan Supreme Court overturned the Appeals Court ruling, he could not be located.[204] Another Guard Member is serving a twenty-five-year sentence for her murder.[205] Guatemala has also convicted five soldiers for their roles in the Dos Erres massacre in which more than 250 villagers were murdered.[206] Moreover, a Guatemalan judge has held that General Rios Montt, the dictator in power during the massacre of several villages, including the Dos Erres massacre, could be tried for genocide.[207]The Constitutional Court of Colombia has ordered investigations into deaths and disappearances, stating that "[t]hose affected have the right to know what has happened to their next of kin, as the Inter-American Court of Human Rights has established."[208]

Three types of domestic laws or legal principles have deterred States from trying persons accused of committing human rights violations: amnesty laws, statutes of limitations, and the guarantee against double jeopardy or *res judicata*. These laws should not, in fact, bar domestic investigations and prosecutions in the case of serious human rights violations. The Vienna Convention on the Law of Treaties provides that no domestic law may prevent a State from fulfilling its international

[201] *Castillo Páez* v. *Peru* (Monitoring Compliance), IACtHR, 3 April 2009, "considering" para. 8.

[202] *Ibid.*

[203] Los Angeles Times, "The World: Guatemala Officials Apologize for Killing," 23 April 2004; *Myrna Mack Chang v. Guatemala* (Monitoring Compliance), IACtHR, 16 November 2009, "considering" paras. 7–8.

[204] *Ibid.*

[205] *Ibid.*

[206] Amnesty International, Fifth former soldier convicted over role in Dos Erres massacre, March 14, 2012. Available at http://www.amnesty.org/en/news/guatemala-fifth-former-soldier-convicted-over-role-dos-erres-massacre-2012-03-14

[207] Lomi Kriel, Houston Chronicle, Seeking justice for Guatemalan village where hundreds were raped, tortured, killed, May 26, 2012. Available at http://www.chron.com/news/houston-texas/article/Seeking-justice-for-Guatemalan-village-where-3587668.php

[208] Constitutional Court of Colombia, Sala Plena, Sentence T-275/94, 15 June 1994, cited in García-Sayán, "The Inter-American Court and Constitutionalism in Latin America," 1847.

obligations.[209] The Inter-American Court holds that in no case may the State "apply amnesty laws or argue prescription [statute of limitations], non-retroactivity of the criminal law, *res judicata*, the principle of *ne bis in idem* [double jeopardy], or any other similar mechanism that excludes responsibility" for conducting an investigation and punishing the perpetrators of the abuse.[210]

Domestic amnesty laws attempt to bar the prosecution of certain crimes that occurred during a specific period of time in a State. The Court holds that amnesty laws, in cases of serious human rights violations, are incompatible with both the letter and spirit of the American Convention in that they prevent investigation and punishment and, consequently, preclude the next of kin's access to the truth.[211] As stated, following the Inter-American Court's ruling in *Barrios Altos* and subsequent cases, these laws have fallen in most Latin American States, except Brazil.[212]

The statute of limitations, also called the law of prescription, restricts the period of time within which a lawsuit may be brought. Thus, for human rights violations that took place years earlier, some domestic judicial systems have held that the statute of limitations has run, and thus, the defendant cannot be tried for the crimes.[213] For instance, following the Inter-American Court's judgment in *Bueno Alves* v. *Argentina*, in which the victim had been tortured, the Argentine Supreme Court held that the statute of limitations had run, and therefore the authorities could not investigate, prosecute, and punish the torturers.[214] In November 2011, however, the Argentine Supreme Court revoked its earlier judgment and reopened the case.[215]

Certain crimes, such as murder, are never subject to a statute of limitations. Likewise, under international law, there is no prescription for crimes against humanity, which include forced disappearances, extrajudicial executions, and torture.[216] Several American States have ratified the Convention on the Non-Applicability of Statutory Limitations to War Crimes and Crimes Against Humanity.[217] Those States

[209] Vienna Convention on the Law of Treaties, UN Doc. A/CONF.39/27, 23 May 1969, entered into force 27 January 1988, Art. 27; *Vargas Areco v. Paraguay* (Merits, Reparations, and Costs), IACtHR, 26 September 2006, Ser. C, No. 155, para. 156.

[210] *Manuel Cepeda Vargas* v. *Colombia* (No. 213, 2010), para. 216(d); *Almonacid Arellano et al.* v. *Chile* (No. 154, 2006), paras. 154–55; *Barrios Altos* v. *Peru* (No. 75, 2001), para. 41, operative para. 4.

[211] *Gelman* v. *Uruguay* (No. 221, 2011), para. 226.

[212] *Barrios Altos* v. *Peru* (No. 75, 2001), para. 41.

[213] See *Trujillo Oroza* v. *Bolivia* (Monitoring Compliance), IACtHR, 12 September 2005, "considering" para. 4(e).

[214] *Bueno Alves* v. *Argentina* (Monitoring Compliance), IACtHR, 5 July 2011, "considering" paras. 21–23.

[215] Corte Suprema de Argentina reabre el caso Bueno Alves, Corte IDH Blog, 2 December 2011, citing the Argentine newspaper Diario La Nación.

[216] Convention on the Non-Applicability of Statutory Limitations to War Crimes and Crimes Against Humanity, UN General Assembly Resolution 2391 (XXIII), entered into force 11 November 1970.

[217] The following OAS member States have ratified the Convention on the Non-Applicability of Statutory Limitations to War Crimes and Crimes Against Humanity: Argentina, Bolivia, Costa Rica, Cuba,

that have not done so could ratify the treaty or pass domestic legislation barring the application of the statute of limitations to crimes against humanity.

The principle of *non bis in idem*, also known as double jeopardy, prohibits the prosecution of a person for the same crime more than once. Those persons to whom amnesty laws previously applied may attempt to claim the benefit of this right against double jeopardy. However, it should not be applicable because these individuals have never been tried for the offenses.[218] The guarantee of *non bis in idem* assumes that there has been a final, unappealable judgment. Moreover, those who were tried in military courts or in sham civilian trials in which an investigation was not seriously conducted should not have the benefit of this principle. The Inter-American Court has stated that the principle of *non bis in idem* is not applicable when

> the actions of the court that heard the case, and decided to dismiss it or absolve the person responsible for a violation of human rights or of international law, intended to shield the accused from his/her criminal liability; the procedure was not conducted independently or impartially in accordance with the guarantee of due process, or there was no real intention to bring the responsible to justice.[219]

In the *Carpio Nicolle Case*, the Inter-American Court found that the domestic trial had been contaminated by defects.[220] It, therefore, held that the State could not "invoke the judgment delivered in proceedings that did not comply with the standards of the American Convention, in order to exempt it from its obligation to investigate and punish."[221]

States should pass the necessary legislation to overcome these legal obstacles. Until impunity is eradicated and States willingly arrest and try the perpetrators of human rights abuse, the Court's docket will continue to be overburdened by its need to monitor State compliance with many of its judgments.

ALTERNATIVE FORMS OF REPARATIONS

In exceptional circumstances, the Inter-American Court may agree to alter its reparations orders when a remedy it specified cannot be fulfilled, especially when the State and victims are in agreement. Reparations that appear feasible at the time the Court issues a judgment may not be viable in practice. At such times, the State may request that the Court allow it to fulfill its obligation by an alternative means. For

Honduras, Mexico, Nicaragua, Panama, Paraguay, Peru, St. Vincent and the Grenadines, and Uruguay. Available at http://treaties.un.org/

218 See *La Cantuta* v. *Peru* (Merits, Reparations, and Costs), IACtHR 29 November 2006, Ser. C, No. 162, para. 180.

219 *Ibid.*, para. 153; *Ivcher Bronstein* v. *Peru* (Monitoring Compliance), IACtHR, 27 August 2010, "considering" para. 14.

220 *Carpio Nicolle* et al. v. *Guatemala* (Merits, Reparations, and Costs), IACtHR, 22 November 2004, Ser. C, No. 117, para. 132.

221 *Ibid.*

example, when there was strong negative public sentiment against including the names of the victims of the *Miguel Castro Castro Prison Case*, some of whom were considered to be terrorists, on a monument dedicated to the victims of the internal conflict in Peru,[222] the Court agreed that the State could substitute another measure, such as naming a park after the victims.[223]

Occasionally, despite the willingness of the State to comply with the measures ordered, the situation results in the victim's inability to benefit from a specific form of reparations. In such circumstances, there is precedent that the State and the victim, with the Court's consent, may agree to substitute an alternative remedy that will be more appropriate to the victim's circumstances. For instance, while monitoring compliance in the *Valle Jaramillo Case*, the Court granted a joint request made by the victims' representatives and the State to alter a measure of reparations.[224] The Court had ordered the State to provide scholarships to the adult victims to pursue professional training.[225] The victims' representatives, however, explained that one of the victims was not in a physical or emotional condition to undertake academic studies. The State expressed its willingness to comply with the reparation and alleviate in some measure the suffering and needs of the beneficiary by granting the scholarship to her son, who was a university student. The Court found that the request from both the State and the victim was based on their good faith agreement, and it consequently approved the change.[226]

Although the Court has ordered States to provide protection to allow victims to return to their homes and ordered States to return ancestral lands to indigenous peoples, the parties may agree to be relocated to an alternative location if their former location is still dangerous or the lands are unavailable. In *"Mapiripán Massacre" v. Colombia*, the victims were afraid to return to the municipality of Mapiripán, where paramilitary groups were still engaging in criminal activities.[227] Colombia and the victims attempted to work together to relocate the victims to a safer región.[228] Similarly, in Paraguay, where the government unsuccessfully attempted to buy the ancestral lands of indigenous communities, the State may purchase alternative lands to comply with the Inter-American Court order to return lands to the indigenous communities.

If the State does not comply with a Court-ordered measure, the Court may modify the remedy on its own. In the *Gómez Paquiyauri Brothers Case*, Peru had

[222] *Miguel Castro Castro Prison* v. *Peru* (No. 160, 2006), para. 454; see also *La Cantuta* v. *Peru* (Monitoring Compliance), IACtHR. 20 November, 2009, "considering" paras. 19–21.

[223] *Miguel Castro Castro Prison* v. *Peru* (Interpretation of Judgment on Merits, Reparations, and Costs), IACtHR 2 August 2008, Ser. C, No. 181, para. 57.

[224] *Valle Jaramillo et al.* v. *Colombia* (Monitoring Compliance), IACtHR, 15 May 2011, "considering" para. 8.

[225] *Valle Jaramillo et al.* v. *Colombia* (No. 192, 2008), operative para. 19.

[226] *Valle Jaramillo et al.* v. *Colombia* (Monitoring Compliance), IACtHR, 15 May 2011, "considering" para. 8.

[227] *"Mapiripán Massacre" v. Colombia* (Monitoring Compliance), IACtHR, 8 July 2009, para. 56.

[228] *Ibid.*

been ordered to pay for the schooling of the victim's child up to the university level. When the State had not fulfilled this measure of reparation three years after the Court's time limit for doing so, the Court extended the scholarship to include the child's university studies.[229]

EFFORTS TO IMPROVE COMPLIANCE WITH COURT ORDERS

There are various reasons for States' failure to fulfill certain forms of reparations other than the lack of political will to do so. Most Inter-American States do not have laws or policies that establish procedures or assign competencies to the branch of government that is responsible for fulfilling international reparations orders.[230] Thus, there may be confusion as to which branch or branches bear the responsibility to fulfill aspects of the judgment. Although the executive branch of the domestic government has interacted with the Court throughout the case and may be more inclined to comply with Inter-American Court orders, domestic judicial courts and prosecutors, who are called on to fulfill many injunctive rulings, may be "only dimly aware of the Inter-American Court" and do not feel a legal obligation to act in accordance with the Inter-American Court-ordered reparations.[231] Moreover, State norms on *res judicata*, prescription, and amnesties could inhibit compliance with orders of the Inter-American Court to investigate, prosecute, and punish human rights offenders.[232] A lack of resources may likewise delay the fulfillment of Inter-American Court reparations orders,[233] or the reparations order may not be sufficiently specific.

Some States, such as Venezuela, may question or deny the authority of the organs of the Inter-American system to review domestic judgments, or they may require that an international judgment be verified or accepted by national courts.[234] The Venezuelan Supreme Court, for example, refused to implement the judgment of the Inter-American Court in *López Mendoza* v. *Venezuela*, holding that it would not comply with Inter-American Court rulings that violated Venezuela's Constitution or sovereignty.[235] Trinidad and Tobago went further and denounced the American Convention in 1998 in response to a Commission order that the State suspend the

[229] *Gómez Paquiyauri Brothers* v. *Peru* (Monitoring Compliance), IACtHR, 3 May 2008, "considering" paras. 15–18.

[230] Oswaldo R. Ruiz-Chiriboga, "Current Challenges of the Inter-American Court of Human Rights, and in Particular the Challenges of the Implementation of Sentences," presentation to the EU Parliament, Sub-Commission of Human Rights (25 January 2012).

[231] Huneeus, "Courts Resisting Courts: Lessons from the Inter-American Court's Struggle to Enforce Human Rights," at 495.

[232] See infra Chapter 8, Investigate, Prosecute, and Punish.

[233] Ruiz-Chiriboga, "Current Challenges of the Inter-American Court of Human Rights, and in Particular the Challenges of the Implementation of Sentences."

[234] *Ibid.*

[235] Human Rights Watch, "Venezuela Supreme Court Disregards Rights in Election Case", October 18, 2011. Available at http://www.hrw.org/news/2011/10/18/venezuela-supreme-court-disregards-rights-election-case. Corte IDH Blog: Tribunal Supremo Venezolano Declara

execution of prisoners on death row while their cases were being reviewed in the Inter-American system.[236]

The level of State compliance with all forms of Court-ordered reparations must be improved. Noncompliance not only affects the victims but it also undermines the authority of the Inter-American Court and the Inter-American human rights system as a whole.

National laws and procedures must be established in States' domestic jurisdictions to facilitate the implementation of Inter-American Court judgments and orders. The execution of the judgments of the Inter-American Court does not depend solely on the political will of the State. It also depends on the State's institutional, administrative, and legal structures as well as judicial precedents in its domestic courts.[237]

The Court must continue forging relationships with all branches of domestic governments and members of civil society. Holding Court sessions in various States puts the Court in closer contact with its constituents. Moreover, Inter-American Court judges are taking those opportunities to meet with their local judicial counterparts as well as legislators and members of the executive and public ministry. While in a State for a Court session, Inter-American Court staff attorneys and judges also hold seminars on the Inter-American system to better inform the government and the public of the functioning and goals of the Inter-American human rights system.[238] The Court is also forming Agreements of Institutional Cooperation with universities throughout the region and with several governmental and nongovernmental national bodies, such as the Colombian Ministry of Foreign Relations, the Constitutional Court of Peru, public defenders throughout the region, the Peruvian Diplomatic Academy, and the Ibero-American Federation of Ombudsmen.[239]

The special working group of the OAS Permanent Council to strengthen the Inter-American human rights system recommended that Member States meet to exchange information on successful practices in complying with the reparations ordered by the Commission and the Court.[240] The working group also recommended that a guide or reference document be published that illustrates effective national, institutional, and legislative practices in implementing the recommendations of the Inter-American Commission and the decisions of the Inter-American Court.[241] Costa Rica iterated

"Inejecutable" la Sentencia de la Corte IDH dictada en el caso López Mendoza. Available at http://corteidhblog.blogspot.com/.

[236] Reprinted in 2010 Basic Documents, at 52.

[237] Viviana Krsticevic, "Reflexiones Sobre la Ejecución de las Decisiones del Sistema Interamericano de Protección de Derechos Humanos," at 15, 16. Available at http://cejil.org/sites/default/files/implementacion_de_las_decisiones_del_sidh_0.pdf.

[238] IACtHR 2010 Annual Report, at 21–25.

[239] *Ibid.*, at 21–22.

[240] The Special Working Group of the OAS Permanent Council Reflecting on the Functioning of the Inter-American Commission for the Strengthening of the Inter-American Human Rights System, at 10.

[241] *Ibid.*

that the guide should set forth institutional means that could be incorporated into States' domestic law to aid them in complying with Inter-American Commission recommendations and Inter-American Court judgments.[242] The model could rely in part on laws and initiatives that are already functioning well in other States Parties to the American Convention.

These laws and initiatives have enhanced State compliance and could do so in other States if they were put into practice. Peru and Colombia have such legislation in effect.[243] The Open Society Justice Initiative reports that Peru's legislation sets forth specific steps to implement the judgments of supranational courts that order pecuniary damages or declaratory relief.[244] Colombia has also passed national legislation that outlines the process to be followed in paying compensation ordered by international human rights bodies.[245] Implementation legislation is also reportedly being considered in Argentina and Brazil.[246] The legislation, however, primarily appears to deal with State payment of compensation and does not include State compliance with other forms of reparations. Legislation that encompasses full compliance with Inter-American Court-ordered reparations would be even more beneficial.

States also could establish commissions to deal overall with reparations ordered by international bodies. Costa Rica created the Inter-Institutional Commission for the Monitoring and Implementation of International Human Rights Obligations.[247] The Commission's duties include compiling, analyzing, and supervising recommendations made by international and regional human rights organs and establishing procedures for their domestic implementation.[248] Paraguay has established the Inter-Institutional Commission on Compliance with International Judgments (CISI) to serve in this role.[249] A consortium of NGOs recommended that every OAS Member State establish a similar commission composed of high-ranking State authorities

242 See Consejo Permanente de la Organizacíon de los Estados Americanos, Grupo de Trabajo Especial de Reflexión sobre el Funcionamiento de la CIDH para el Fortalecimiento del SIDH, OEA/Ser.G GT/SIDH/INF.17/11 rev. 1, 7 Noviembre 2011, Compilación de las Presentaciones de los Estados Miembros sobre los Temas del Grupo de Trabajo, Presentacion of Costa Rica citing Colombian Law No. 288 of 1996 and Peruvian Law No. 27.775 of 2002.

243 *Ibid.*

244 Open Society Justice Initiative, From Judgment to Justice: Implementing International and Regional Human Rights Decisions, Executive Summary at 65 (2010). Available at http://www.soros.org/initiatives/justice/articles_publications/publications/from-judment-to-justice20101122/from-judgment-to-justice-20101122.pdf.

245 *Ibid.*

246 *Ibid.*, at 22.

247 Costa Rican Decreto Ejecutivo 36776-RE, published in the Diario Oficial La Gaceta, 30 September 2011.

248 Consejo Permanente de la Organizacíon de los Estados Americanos, Grupo de Trabajo Especial de Reflexión sobre el Funcionamiento de la CIDH para el Fortalecimiento del SIDH, OEA/Ser.G GT/SIDH/INF.17/11 rev. 1, 7 Noviembre 2011, Compilación de las Presentaciones de los Estados Miembros sobre los Temas del Grupo de Trabajo, Presentacion de Costa Rica.

249 *Sawhoyamaxa Indigenous Community* v. *Paraguay* (Monitoring Compliance), IACtHR, 20 May 2009, "having seen" para. 6.

from the Public Ministry and any other governmental unit that should be involved in complying with the reparations ordered.[250]

When States do not have a body in place to implement international orders, the Inter-American Court could mandate that the State establish a high-ranking commission to oversee State compliance with aspects of the reparations ordered in a particular case. For instance, following the Inter-American Court's order in *Tibi* v. *Ecuador* to establish an inter-institutional committee to oversee the establishment of training programs,[251] Ecuador created the Ministry of Justice and Human Rights to coordinate capacitation programs with other government departments.[252] Suriname formed the Commission on the Implementation of the Moiwana judgment in accordance with the Court's order.[253] Likewise, in the "*Mapiripán Massacre*" *Case*, the Court ordered Colombia to establish a special mechanism that included the participation of the next of kin to monitor compliance with the reparations ordered.[254] Victims subsequently reported that the national monitoring mechanism, called "M.O.S. Mapiripán," was useful and would be extended past the two years required by the Court.[255] The State bodies established to ensure the implementation of Court reparations orders could serve as the liaison to manage actions that must be undertaken by the executive, judicial, and legislative bodies to fulfill all reparations ordered.

After receiving a judgment in their favor, victims may struggle to get State bureaucracies to comply with specific measures of reparations, such as providing educational scholarships, medical care, or locating the remains of their loved ones. Bureaucracies or individual bureaucrats are not always receptive to their efforts, and some victims have expressed the feeling that they are treated as if they are requesting a favor rather than asking to have their legal rights fulfilled.[256] Also, victims have expressed frustration that, once the judgment is rendered, they receive no information from the State until the time for compliance is reached or has passed.[257] This also raises their level of anxiety. One member of the State implementation body could be assigned to communicate with victims and their representatives and

250 Consejo Permanente de la Organizacíon de los Estados Americanos, Grupo de Trabajo Especial de Reflexión sobre el Funcionamiento de la CIDH para el Fortalecimiento del SIDH, Compilación de las Recomendaciones de las Organizaciones de la Sociedad Civil en respuesta a la convocatoría abierta con plazo 31 de 2011 y las presentaciones realizadas ante el Grupo de Trabajo en su reunion con las Organizaciones de la Sociedad Civil del 28 de octubre de 2011, at 4–5.

251 *Tibi* v. *Ecuador* (Preliminary Objections, Merits, Reparations, and Costs), IACtHR, 7 September 2004, No. 114, Ser. C, operative para. 13.

252 *Tibi* v. *Ecuador* (Monitoring Compliance), IACtHR 3 March 2011, "considering" para. 14.

253 *Moiwana Community* v. *Suriname* (Monitoring Compliance), IACtHR, 22 November 2010, "considering" para. 40.

254 "*Mapiripán Massacre*" v. *Colombia* (No. 134, 2005), para. 311.

255 "*Mapiripán Massacre*" v. *Colombia* (Monitoring Compliance), IACtHR, 8 July 2009, "considering" paras. 14–16.

256 Open Society Justice Initiative, From Judgment to Justice, at 539.

257 Beristain, 1 Diálogos sobre la reparación, at 538.

update them about progress made in executing the Court's reparations orders. The Court could also specify that one person be assigned to oversee particular reparations, as it did when suggesting that Colombia appoint a special prosecutor to be exclusively in charge of the investigation into those responsible for the Mapiripán Massacre.[258]

CONCLUSION

The Inter-American human rights system has made significant advances in the protection of human rights in the region. Many of these advances are directly attributable to the evolution of the practice and procedures of the Inter-American Court of Human Rights. The new autonomy granted to the victim before the Court and the expedited procedures of both the Commission and the Court bring justice within the reach of individuals. Through its liberalized procedures the Court has also paved the way for NGOs that espouse the position of civil society to express their views before the Court. Much still needs to be done. As explained by Buergenthal, however, "[e]ven some success in the international human rights field, however small, will make this world a little better place to live in. And that, after all, is what law is all about."[259] The Inter-American Court is having greater success than many would have expected.

258 Mapiripan "considering" para. 36.

259 Remarks by Thomas Buergenthal, American Society of International Law, Annual Meeting, 24 April 1981, Proceedings.

[4]

THE REVISED OAS CHARTER AND THE PROTECTION OF HUMAN RIGHTS

By Thomas Buergenthal *

I.

INTRODUCTION

The "Protocol of Buenos Aires," which revised the Charter of the Organization of American States, entered into force in 1970.[1] It changed the legal status of the Inter-American Commission on Human Rights in a number of important respects and strengthened the normative character of the American Declaration of the Rights and Duties of Man. These are most significant developments, and yet they have gone largely unnoticed in the literature.

The purpose of this note is to analyze the transformation that the inter-American system for the protection of human rights has undergone as a result of the revision of the OAS Charter. To understand what changes have been effected, it is necessary to describe the evolution of that system. We shall deal with this subject first.

II.

HUMAN RIGHTS AND THE 1948 OAS CHARTER

The 1948 Charter of the Organization of American States [2] contained a number of general human rights provisions. Most important of these was Article 5(j), which declared that "the American States proclaim the fundamental rights of the individual without distinction as to race, nationality, creed or sex." [3] But the Charter neither defined the rights mentioned in Article 5(j) nor did it establish any procedures to ensure their implementation.

* Of the Board of Editors.

[1] The "Protocol of Buenos Aires" was signed at that city on February 27, 1967. The amended OAS Charter entered into force on February 27, 1970. 21 UST 607, TIAS No. 6847, 64 AJIL 996 (1970). *See generally* Sepúlveda, *The Reform of the Charter of the Organization of American States*, 137 HAGUE REC. DES COURS 83 (1972); Dreier, *New Wine and Old Bottles: The Changing Inter-American System*, 22 INT. ORG. 477 (1968); Robertson, *Revision of the Charter of the Organisation of American States*, 17 INT. & COMP. L. Q. 346 (1968).

[2] The original Charter of the Organization of American States [hereinafter [1948] OAS Charter] was signed at Bogotá, Colombia, on April 30, 1948, and entered into force on December 13, 1951, [1951] 2 UST 2394, TIAS No. 2361, 119 UNTS 48, 46 AJIL SUPP. 43 (1952).

[3] *See also* [1948] OAS Charter, Article 13, which declared that "each State has the right to develop its cultural, political and economic life freely and naturally. In this free development, the State shall respect the rights of the individual and the principles of universal morality." Both Articles 5(j) and 13 have been retained in the amended Charter as Articles 3(j) and 16, respectively.

The same conference that produced the OAS Charter—the Ninth International Conference of American States which met in Bogotá, Colombia, in 1948—also proclaimed the American Declaration on the Rights and Duties of Man.[4] This instrument was adopted in the form of a simple resolution which declared that "the international protection of the rights of man should be the principal guide of an evolving American law." But whatever the legal effect in the inter-American system of conference resolutions embodying statements of legal principle—this is a subject of considerable controversy[5]—the Bogotá conference went on record with an understanding that Article 5(j) of the OAS Charter did not, through incorporation by reference, transform the provisions of the American Declaration into "contractual" obligations.[6] A year later the Inter-American Juridical Committee ruled that "it is obvious that the Declaration of Bogotá does not create a legal contractual obligation"[7] and that, consequently, it lacked the status of "positive substantive law."[8]

Efforts to establish an institutional framework for the promotion of human rights within the inter-American system proved unsuccessful for many years.[9] Finally, in 1959, the Fifth Meeting of Consultation of Ministers of Foreign Affairs adopted a resolution[10] creating "an Inter-American Commission on Human Rights, composed of seven members elected, as individuals, by the [OAS] Council." It further stipulated that "the Commission, which shall be organized by the Council . . . and have the specific functions that the Council assigns to it, shall be charged with furthering respect for [human] rights." The OAS Council complied with this man-

[4] Res. XXX, *Final Act of the Ninth International Conference of American States, Bogotá, Colombia, March 30–May 2, 1948*, at 38 (PAU 1948); INTER-AMERICAN COMMISSION ON HUMAN RIGHTS, HANDBOOK OF EXISTING RULES PERTAINING TO HUMAN RIGHTS [hereinafter cited as I-ACHR, HANDBOOK], OAS OFF. REC., OEA/Ser.L/V/II.23, Doc. 21 (English) Rev. 2, at 15 (1975).

[5] *See generally* C. FENWICK, THE ORGANIZATION OF AMERICAN STATES 155–57 (1963); M. BALL, THE OAS IN TRANSITION 119–20 (1969).

[6] DEPT. OF STATE, REPORT OF THE DELEGATION OF THE UNITED STATES OF AMERICA TO THE NINTH INTERNATIONAL CONFERENCE OF AMERICAN STATES, BOGOTÁ, COLOMBIA, MARCH 30–MAY 2, 1948, at 35–36 (Publ. No. 3263, 1948). For a useful discussion of the legislative history of the interrelationship between the human rights provisions of the [1948] OAS Charter and the American Declaration, *see* A. SCHREIBER, THE INTER-AMERICAN COMMISSION ON HUMAN RIGHTS 16–22 (1970). *See also* PAN AMERICAN UNION, HUMAN RIGHTS IN THE AMERICAN STATES 115–16 (Prelim. ed. 1960).

[7] Inter-American Juridical Committee, Report to the Inter-American Council of Jurists Concerning Resolution XXXI of the Bogotá Conference, September 26, 1949, reprinted in PAN AMERICAN UNION, HUMAN RIGHTS IN THE AMERICAN STATES 163, at 164 (Prelim. ed., 1960).

[8] *Id.* at 165.

[9] For a review of developments between 1948 and 1959, *see* I-ACHR, THE ORGANIZATION OF AMERICAN STATES AND HUMAN RIGHTS: ACTIVITIES OF THE INTER-AMERICAN COMMISSION ON HUMAN RIGHTS 1960–1967, at 3–9 (1972); M. Ball, *Issues for the Americas: Non-Intervention v. Human Rights and the Preservation of Democratic Institutions*, 15 INT. ORG. 21, 25–26 (1961).

[10] Res. VIII, *Fifth Meeting of Consultation of Ministers of Foreign Affairs, Santiago, Chile, August 12–18, 1959, Final Act*, OAS OFF. REC. OEA/Ser.C/II.5 (English), at 10–11 (1960).

date in 1960 when it promulgated the Statute of the Commission,[11] its constitutive instrument, and elected the seven individuals who shortly thereafter were sworn in as the first members of the Commission.[12]

The Statute described the newly created Commission as "an autonomous entity" of the OAS the function of which was "to promote respect for human rights." [13] Significantly, it declared that "for the purpose of this Statute, human rights are understood to be those set forth in the American Declaration of the Rights and Duties of Man." [14] The principles proclaimed in the American Declaration thus became the standards to be applied by the Commission in exercising its functions.

The powers of the Commission were set out in Article 9 of its Statute, which reads as follows:

> In carrying out its assignment of promoting respect for human rights, the Commission shall have the following functions and powers:
>
> (a) To develop an awareness of human rights among the peoples of America;
>
> (b) To make recommendations to the governments of the member states in general, if it considers such action advisable, for the adoption of progressive measures in favor of human rights within the framework of their domestic legislation and, in accordance with their constitutional precepts, appropriate measures to further the faithful observance of those rights;
>
> (c) To prepare such studies or reports as it considers advisable in the performance of its duties;
>
> (d) To urge the governments of the member states to supply it with information on the measures adopted by them in matters of human rights;
>
> (e) To serve the Organization of American States as an advisory body in respect of human rights.

Shortly after assuming office, the Commission formally interpreted Article 9(b) of its Statute to empower it "to make general recommendations to each individual member state, as well as to all of them." [15] Relying on this interpretation, the Commission asserted the authority to study the so-called "situation relating to human rights" in various American Repub-

[11] The text of the 1960 Statute of the Commission is reproduced in I-ACHR, BASIC DOCUMENTS, OAS OFF. REC. OEA/Ser.L/V/I.4 Rev. (English), at 9 (1963). The amended Statute now in effect is reproduced in I-ACHR, HANDBOOK, *supra* note 4, at 23.

[12] [1960] *Annual Report of the Secretary General,* OFF. REC. OEA/Ser.D/III.12 (English), at 19–20 (1961).

[13] Statute of the Inter-American Commission on Human Rights [hereinafter cited as Statute], Art. 1.

[14] Statute, Art. 2.

[15] I-ACHR, *Report on the Work Accomplished During its First Session, October 3–28, 1960,* OAS OFF. REC. OEA/Ser.L/V/II.1, Doc. 32 (English), at 10 (1961). *See* Sandifer, *Human Rights in the Inter-American System,* 11 How. L. J. 508, 517–18 (1965); Scheman, *The Inter-American Commission on Human Rights,* 59 AJIL 335, 337–39 (1965).

lics; to address recommendations to governments that engaged in large-scale violations of human rights; and to publish reports documenting violations of human rights in various countries, among them Cuba, Haiti, and the Dominican Republic.[16] In carrying out these and subsequent country studies, the Commission examined complaints, heard witnesses, and in some cases undertook on-the-spot investigations.[17]

With regard to individual complaints, the Commission formally ruled in 1960 that its Statute did not empower it "to make any individual decision regarding the written communications . . . it receives involving the violation of human rights in the American states, although, for the most effective fulfillment of its functions, the Commission shall take cognizance of them by way of information."[18] Repeated attempts by the Commission to obtain authorization to act on individual communications remained unsuccessful until 1965.[19] In that year the Second Special Inter-American Conference enlarged the powers of the Commission in a number of significant respects.[20] The Conference requested the Commission "to conduct a continuing survey of the observance of fundamental human rights in each of the [OAS] member states," and "to give particular attention in this survey to [the] observance of the human rights referred to in Articles I, II, III, IV, XVIII, XXV, and XXVI of the American Declaration of the Rights and Duties of Man."[21] To enable it to carry out these functions, the Conference authorized the Commission to examine communications from individuals charging violations of the aforementioned rights;[22] to "address to the government of any American state a request for information deemed pertinent by the Commission;" and to make recommendations

[16] For a review of this practice, *see* Thomas & Thomas, *The Inter-American Commission on Human Rights,* 20 Sw. L. J. 282, 287–305 (1966); K. Vasak, La Commission Interaméricaine des Droits de l'Homme 124–38 (1968). Some of the "country reports" are reproduced in I-ACHR, The Organization of American States and Human Rights: Activities of the Commission on Human Rights 1960–1967, pt. III (1972); L. Sohn & T. Buergenthal, International Protection of Human Rights 1293–340 (1973).

[17] *See, e.g.,* A. Schreiber & P. Schreiber, *The Inter-American Commission on Human Rights in the Dominican Crisis,* 22 Int. Org. 508, 510–19 (1968); Inter-American Institute of International Legal Studies, The Inter-American System: Its Development and Strengthening 45–55 (1966).

[18] I-ACHR, *Report on the Work Accomplished During its First Session, October 3 to 28, 1960,* OAS Off. Rec., OEA/Ser.L/V/II.1, Doc. 32 (English), at 13 (1961).

[19] *See, e.g.,* I-ACHR, *Report on the Work Accomplished During its Third Session, October 2–November 4, 1961,* OAS Off. Rec. OEA/Ser.L/V/II.3, Doc. 32 (English), at 16–17 (1962). *See also* Ball, *supra* note 5, at 375–77.

[20] Res. XXII, *Second Special Inter-American Conference, Rio de Janeiro, Brazil, November 17–30, 1965, Final Act,* OAS Off. Rec., OEA/Ser.C/I.13 (English) at 32–34 (1965).

[21] These provisions deal with the right to life, liberty, and personal security (Art. I); equality before the law (Art. II); freedom of religion (Art. III); freedom of expression (Art. IV); right to a fair trial (Art. XVIII); freedom from arbitrary arrest (Art. XXV); and due process of law (Art. XXVI).

[22] The Commission's power to deal with these communications was conditioned on its preliminary determination that applicable domestic remedies were exhausted. Res. XXII, para. 5, *supra* note 20.

"with the objective of bringing about more effective observance of fundamental human rights." The Commission was also requested to submit an annual report to the OAS General Assembly [23] containing, *inter alia,* "such observations as the Commission may deem appropriate on matters covered in the communications submitted to it."

The additional powers which the Commission acquired in 1965 were incorporated into the Statute by an amendment designated as Article 9 (*bis*).[24] Using its combined authority under Articles 9 and 9 (*bis*), the Commission has since 1966 dealt with communications and investigated charges alleging violations of human rights directed against most American Republics.[25] Among its most important recent activities are a very thorough study documenting large-scale violations of human rights by Brazil [26] and an on-the-spot investigation carried out in 1974 by the Commission in Chile.[27]

[23] Prior to the amendment of the OAS Charter this report was to be submitted either to the Inter-American Conference or to the Meeting of Consultation of Ministers of Foreign Affairs. It now goes to the OAS General Assembly. OAS Charter, Art. 52(f).

[24] Res. XXII, para. 8, *supra* note 20, authorized the amendment of the Commission's Statute to give effect to the provisions of the resolution. The relevant amendments—two other provisions (Articles 7 (*bis*) and 14 (*bis*)) in addition to Article 9 (*bis*)—were adopted by the Commission in 1966. I-ACHR, *Report on the Work Accomplished During its Thirteenth Session, April 18–28, 1966,* OAS Off. Rec. OEA/Ser.L/V/II.14, Doc. 35 (English), at 22–24 (1966). Article 9 (*bis*) reads as follows:

> The Commission shall have the following additional functions and powers:
> a) To give particular attention to observance of the human rights referred to in Articles I, II, III, IV, XVIII, XXV, and XXVI of the American Declaration of the Rights and Duties of Man;
> b) To examine communications submitted to it and any other available information; to address the government of any American state for information deemed pertinent by the Commission; and to make recommendations, when it deems this appropriate, with the objective of bringing about more effective observance of fundamental human rights;
> c) To submit a report annually to the Inter-American Conference or to the Meeting of Consultation of Ministers of Foreign Affairs, which should include: (i) a statement of progress achieved in realization of the goals set forth in the American Declaration; (ii) a statement of areas in which further steps are needed to give effect to the human rights set forth in the American Declaration; and (iii) such observations as the Commission may deem appropriate on matters covered in the communications submitted to it and in other information available to the Commission;
> d) To verify, as a condition precedent to the exercise of the powers set forth in paragraphs b) and c) of the present article, whether the internal legal procedures and remedies of each member state have been duly applied and exhausted.

[25] *See, e.g.,* I-ACHR, *Activities of the Inter-American Commission on Human Rights (1965–1969),* OAS Off. Rec., OEA/Ser.L/V/II.23, Doc. 11 (English) Rev., at 7–25 (1971); *Annual Report of the Inter-American Commission on Human Rights for the Year 1973,* OAS Off. Rec., OEA Ser.P/AG/Doc. 409/74 (English), at 38–100 and 106–49 (1974).

[26] *Annual Report of the Inter-American Commission on Human Rights for the Year 1973, supra* note 25, at 38–81.

[27] I-ACHR, *Report on the Status of Human Rights in Chile: Findings of "On-the-Spot" Observations in the Republic of Chile, July 22–August 2, 1974,* OAS Off. Rec., OEA/Ser.L/II.34, Doc. 21 (English) Corr. 1 (1974); *Observations by the Government of Chile on the "Report on the Status of Human Rights in Chile" Prepared by the Inter-American Commission on Human Rights,* OAS Off. Rec., OEA/Ser.G/CP/Doc. 385/74 (English).

III.

The Revised OAS Charter and the Protection of Human Rights

The pre-1970 practice and achievements of the Commission gain in significance once it is remembered that prior to the revision of the Charter the inter-American human rights system, described in the preceding section, owed its existence not to a treaty or other legally binding instrument but to OAS resolutions and pronouncements of uncertain authority. The entire system lacked a solid constitutional basis and seemed to be shrouded in legal and institutional ambiguities. The Commission was designated an "autonomous entity" of the OAS, no doubt because this was as good a name as any for a body which was not provided for in the OAS Charter or any other treaty, was established by a simple conference resolution, and qualified neither as an organ of the OAS Council nor as a so-called "specialized organization" of the OAS.[28] Moreover, the human rights the promotion and observance of which the Commission was to ensure were proclaimed in the American Declaration of the Rights and Duties of Man,[29] an instrument not deemed to create binding legal obligations for OAS member states.[30] Consequently, an aura of make-believe attached to the inter-American human rights system, denying it the political authority that flows from constitutional legitimacy.

This unsatisfactory state of affairs has been dramatically altered by the revised OAS Charter. Article 51 of that instrument designates the "Inter-American Commission on Human Rights" as a principal organ of the Organization. Its functions are spelled out in Article 112 of the Charter, which reads as follows:

> There shall be an Inter-American Commission on Human Rights, whose principal function shall be to promote the observance and protection of human rights and to serve as a consultative organ of the organization in these matters.

28 For a careful analysis of the institutional status of the Commission, *see* Vasak, *supra* note 16, at 41–44. The [1948] OAS Charter, Art. 57, established only three organs of the OAS Council (the Inter-American Economic and Social Council, Council of Jurists, and Cultural Council) and did not provide for the creation of additional ones. *See generally* Inter-American Institute of International Legal Studies, *supra* note 17, at 12–14 and 16–24. The Commission did not qualify as an "Inter-American Specialized Organization" because it was not an "intergovernmental organization established by multilateral agreement" as required by Article 95 of the [1948] OAS Charter. The Commission was established by a resolution of the Fifth Meeting of Consultation of Ministers of Foreign Affairs, which was implemented by the OAS Council when it adopted the Commission's Statute. *See* discussion on pp. 829–30, *supra*. But even assuming that the Ministers' resolution could be regarded as a "multilateral agreement" within the meaning of Article 95, the fact remains that the steps necessary to confer that status on the Commission were never taken. *See* [1948] OAS Charter, Ch. XV. *See also* Inter-American Institute of International Legal Studies, *supra* note 17, at 349.

29 Statute, Art. 2.

30 See discussion on p. 829, *supra*.

> An inter-American convention on human rights shall determine the structure, competence, and procedure of this Commission, as well as those of other organs responsible for these matters.

Although an "American Convention on Human Rights" was adopted and opened for signature in 1969, it has not as yet entered into force,[31] having to date been ratified by only two of the required eleven states.[32] Anticipating this possibility, Article 150 of the revised OAS Charter provides that "until the inter-American Convention on human rights, referred to in Chapter XVIII [Article 112], enters into force, the *present* Inter-American Commission on Human Rights shall keep vigilance over the observance of human rights." (Emphasis added.)

What is the legal effect of the foregoing amendments? Read together, Articles 51, 112, and 150 of the revised OAS Charter indicate that today the Inter-American Commission on Human Rights is a principal organ of the OAS having two major functions: it is to promote the observance and protection of human rights, and it serves as a consultative organ of the Organization in human rights matters. How the Commission is to discharge these functions depends upon whether or not the American Convention on Human Rights has entered into force. If it has, the provisions of the Convention will "determine the structure, competence, and procedure" to be followed by the Commission.[33] But as long as the Convention has not entered into force, "the present Inter-American Commission on Human Rights shall keep vigilance over the observance of human rights." [34] In view of the fact that the Charter speaks of the "present Commission" without otherwise indicating what its "structure, competence, and procedure" shall be, and since these matters are regulated by the Statute of the Commission which predates the adoption in 1967 and the entry into force in 1970 of the revised OAS Charter, it is reasonable to assume that the reference to "present Commission" embraces the Statute and thus incorporates it by reference. In other words, by assigning certain functions to the "present Commission" without providing how these functions are to be exercised, the revised Charter must have intended the Commission to act as it is empowered to act under its Statute.[35] It follows that

[31] The American Convention on Human Rights was opened for signature at the Inter-American Specialized Conference on Human Rights, San José, Costa Rica, on November 22, 1969. The text of the Convention is reproduced in I-ACHR, HANDBOOK, *supra* note 4, at 44. For an analysis of the Convention, *see* Fox, *The American Convention on Human Rights and Prospects for United States Ratification*, 3 HUMAN RIGHTS 243 (1973); Thomas & Thomas, *Human Rights and the Organization of American States*, 12 SANTA CLARA LAW. 319, 349–74 (1972); Buergenthal, *The American Convention on Human Rights: Illusions and Hopes*, 21 BUFFALO L. REV. 121 (1971). *See also* SOHN & BUERGENTHAL, *supra* note 16, at 1356–74.

[32] The Convention was ratified by Costa Rica in 1970 and by Colombia in 1973.

[33] OAS Charter, Art. 112.

[34] OAS Charter, Art. 150.

[35] This conclusion finds some support in the extremely sparse *travaux préparatoires* relating to the human rights provisions found in the revised OAS Charter. *See Acta de la Decima Sesion de la Comision "B," Third Special Inter-American Conference, Buenos Aires, Argentina, February 15–27, 1967*, OAS OFF. REC., OEA/Ser.E/XIV.1, Doc. 63, at 32–37 (1967). *See also*, INTER-AMERICAN INSTITUTE OF INTERNATIONAL LEGAL STUDIES, *supra* note 17, at 317.

all provisions of the Statute not in conflict with the Charter have become for the time being an integral part of the Charter.[36]

A number of specific legal consequences can be deduced from the revision of the OAS Charter and the conclusion that it incorporates the Statute of the Commission by reference. First, Article 51 of the Charter supersedes Article 1 of the Statute and transforms the Commission from an "autonomous entity" of the OAS into one of its principal organs. Second, the Commission now derives its existence as well as its powers from a duly ratified multilateral treaty. It cannot consequently be abolished nor divested of its powers without an amendment of the OAS Charter. Since the powers of the Commission, particularly those set out in Articles 9 and 9 (*bis*) of its Statute, now have a treaty basis, they need no longer to be legitimated by reference to controversial theories regarding the legal effect of OAS conference resolutions. Finally, by transforming the legal status of the Commission and its Statute, the revised OAS Charter has also significantly strengthened the normative character of the American Declaration of the Rights and Duties of Man.

In analyzing the changed status of the American Declaration, it should be recalled that Article 2 of the Statute provides that "for purposes of this Statute, human rights are understood to be those set forth" in the American Declaration. This provision must be read together with Article 150 of the OAS Charter which requires the Commission to "keep vigilance over the observance of human rights." The OAS Charter does not, however, define "human rights." Therefore, since Article 150 incorporates the provisions of the Statute by reference, "human rights" within the meaning of Article 150 are those "set forth" in the American Declaration. The human rights provisions of the American Declaration can today consequently be deemed to derive their normative character from the OAS Charter itself. This means, at the very least, that until the American Convention enters into force, the Commission is empowered by the OAS Charter to judge the conduct of its member states by holding them to the standards articulated in the American Declaration.[37]

[36] Although this subject seems never to have been systematically analyzed or formally acted upon by the Inter-American Commission on Human Rights, some of its members have expressed views similar to those advanced herein. *See* Carlos A. Dunshee de Abranches, *Work of the Inter-American Commission on Human Rights in Accordance with the Protocol of Buenos Aires*, OAS OFF. REC. OEA/Ser.L/V/II.23, Doc. 25 (English) Rev. 1 (1970); I-ACHR, *Report on the Work Accomplished During its Twenty-Fourth Session, October 13–22, 1970*, OAS OFF. REC. OEA/Ser.L/V/II.24, Doc. 32 (English) Rev. Corr., at 37–40 (1971); I-ACHR, *Report on the Work Accomplished During its Twenty-Sixth Session, October 27–November 4, 1971*, OAS OFF. REC., OEA/Ser.L/V/II.26, Doc. 37 (English) Rev. 1, at 42–44 (1972).

[37] *Cf.* I-ACHR, *Report on the Status of Human Rights in Chile*, *supra* note 27, where the Commission, after finding that the Government of Chile has violated various provisions of the American Declaration, looks to Article 27 of the American Convention on Human Rights to support its conclusion that even a national emergency does not permit a state to violate some of these rights. Interestingly enough, the Commission justifies its reliance on the "derogation clause" of the unratified American Convention (the American Declaration does not have a comparable clause) by noting that "with respect to American international law—which is the normative system that the Com-

IV.

Conclusion

The revised OAS Charter has established a treaty-based inter-American system for the promotion and protection of human rights. Today the Inter-American Commission on Human Rights derives its powers directly from the Charter. As an organ of the OAS, the Commission has acquired incontrovertible institutional legitimacy in the inter-American system, a status it lacked before the amendment of the Charter. Most importantly, the Commission now has a solid constitutional basis for the exercise of its powers and for applying the American Declaration of the Rights and Duties of Man. These developments have greatly strengthened the legal authority of the decisions of the Commission and no doubt also enhance their political significance.

The Commission has not thus far thoroughly assessed the legal and political significance of its changed status. Such an assessment is urgently needed, if only because it is not widely known within the inter-American system that the "Protocol of Buenos Aires" has effected a fundamental constitutional transformation of inter-American human rights law and institutions. The sooner the Commission itself fully understands these changes and begins to educate the OAS community to them, the faster it will be able to make some progress in bringing about the implementation of human rights in the Americas.

---

mission must take primarily into account—it must be understood that, in the absence of conventional standards in force in this area, the 'most accepted doctrine' is that which is set forth in the American Convention. . . ." *Id.* at 2–3. This theory applies with even greater force to the American Declaration and the Commission's reliance on it in cases like those involving the Government of Chile.

[5]

The Inter-American Human Rights System at the Dawn of the New Century: Recommendations for Improvement of its Mechanism of Protection

ANTÔNIO AUGUSTO CANÇADO TRINDADE

EVOLUTION AND PRESENT STATE OF THE SYSTEM

The idea of a general revision of the inter-American system of human rights protection seems to have lately been gathering momentum in the American continent, aiming at the improvement of its mechanism of protection. A Seminar of Experts to that effect was held by the Inter-American Commission on Human Rights on 2–3 December 1996 at the headquarters of the Organization of American States in Washington DC. This Seminar was preceded by another event, the Conference of Experts on the Future of International Human Rights, co-sponsored by the Inter-American Institute of Human Rights and the International Rule of Law Institute of George Washington University,[1] which was held in Washington DC, 20–22 May 1996, and which also dwelt upon the subject of the perspectives of the inter-American system of protection in particular. Other related initiatives are likely to follow, and discussions are bound to develop in the forthcoming months; as this takes place, any projection as to the future of the inter-American system of human rights protection cannot but take into account the experience accumulated in this domain over the last decades.

A reassessment of this regional human rights system requires a clear understanding of its formation and development which, in turn, leads, in our view, to the identification of five stages in its evolution, namely: that of the origins of the system; that of the formation of the system (with the gradual expansion of the powers of the Inter-American Commission on Human Rights); that of the conventional institutionalization of the system

[1] This Conference was coordinated, on behalf of the two institutions, by Professors Thomas Buergenthal, Antônio A. Cançado Trindade and Michael Singer. The Conference Report was published in December 1996.

(as from the entry into force of the American Convention on Human Rights); that of the consolidation of the system (with the development of the case-law of the Inter-American Court of Human Rights and the adoption of the two Protocols to the American Convention and of other 'sectorial' inter-American Conventions); and that of the improvement of the system, a stage that has recently commenced. The first part of this Chapter will survey these stages of evolution, and the present state of the system. This will be followed by the presentation of recommendations *de lege ferenda* for the improvement of the system and its perspectives at the dawn of the new century.

Origins

The 1948 American Declaration on the Rights and Duties of Man, accompanied by the 1948 Inter-American Charter of Social Guarantees,[2] represent the starting point of the process of generalization of human rights protection in the American continent. The American Declaration, like the Universal Declaration of Human Rights of the same year, comprised a wide range of human rights (civil, political, economic, social and cultural), aiming at the protection of human beings not only under certain circumstances or in circumscribed sectors as in the past, but in all circumstances and in all areas of human activity. The following may be considered to have been, in historical perspective, the major contributions of the 1948 American Declaration to the development of the inter-American system of protection: a) the conception of human rights as inherent to the human person; b) the integral conception of human rights (encompassing civil, political, economic, social and cultural rights); c) the normative basis of protection vis-à-vis States not Parties to the (subsequent) American Convention on Human Rights; and d) the correlation between rights and duties.[3]

[2] Ninth International Conference of American States, *Final Act* , Resolution XXIX, 29.

[3] In recent years, the 1948 American Declaration has been referred to, on distinct occasions, by the Inter-American Court of Human Rights, e.g.: a) in the first Advisory Opinion (of 1982), for the integration between the universal and regional systems of protection; b) in the sixth Advisory Opinion (of 1986), in relation to the concept of the common good (Article 32(2) of the American Convention); c) in the tenth Advisory Opinion (of 1989), as to the interpretative interaction between the Declaration and the American Convention. On the American Declaration, cf., generally: Buergenthal, 'La Relación Conceptual y Normativa entre la Declaración Americana y la Convención Americana sobre Derechos Humanos', *Revista del Instituto Interamericano de Derechos Humanos*—special issue [May 1989] 111–19; A. A. Cançado Trindade, 'El Sistema Interamericano de Protección de los Derechos Humanos (1948–1995): Evolución, Estado Actual y Perspectivas', *Derecho Internacional y Derechos Humanos/Droit international et droits de l'homme* (D. Bardonnet and A.A. Cançado Trindade (eds.), San José de Costa Rica/La Haye, Académie de Droit International de La Haye/Instituto Interamericano de Derechos Humanos, 1996, 47–95; A. A. Cançado Trindade, 'Reflexiones sobre las Declaraciones Universal y Americana de Derechos Humanos de 1948 con Ocasión de

In this first stage, the 1948 Declaration and Charter of Social Guarantees were preceded or accompanied by other instruments of varying content and legal effects, generally oriented to certain situations or categories of rights.[4] Some were binding, others purely recommendatory, instruments (treaties and resolutions respectively). They formed a complex normative corpus, disclosing a diversity of ambits of application (for example, as to its beneficiaries) and paving the way to the devising of distinct means of implementation. This was to mark the operation of the future inter-American system of human rights protection in the years to follow.

Formation

One decade after the adoption of the American Declaration, the Inter-American Commission on Human Rights was created in 1959 by a resolution[5] (and not a treaty), with a mandate originally limited to the promotion of human rights, and enjoying a *sui generis* position within the regional system. Soon it endeavoured to enlarge its own competence, as an organ of *in loco* investigation of situations of human rights and of examination of petitions alleging violations of human rights. Its enlarged attributions and powers were also to comprise the reporting system (reports of distinct kinds, such as session and annual reports, and reports on specific countries). With the 1967 Protocol of Reform of the OAS Charter (which entered into force in 1970) the Commission was at last established as one of the main organs of the OAS and thus endowed with a conventional basis. With the entry into force of the American Convention on Human Rights, the Commission has had a duality of functions, exercising jurisdiction over States Parties to the American Convention as well as States not Parties to the Convention (as to these latter, on the basis of the OAS Charter and the 1948 American Declaration).

The Inter-American Commission on Human Rights has developed its vast practice through the application of the three methods of implementation, namely, the petitioning system (examination of complaints or petitions), the reporting system (elaboration of country reports on the human

Su Cuadragésimo Aniversario', *Revista del Instituto Interamericano de Derechos Humanos*—special issue [May 1989] 121–9; H. Gros Espiell, 'La Declaración Americana: Raíces Conceptuales y Políticas en la Historia—Filosofía y el Derecho Americano', *Revista del Instituto Interamericano de Derechos Humanos*—special issue [May 1989], 41–64; D. Uribe Vargas, *Los Derechos Humanos y el Sistema Interamericano*, (Madrid, 1972).

[4] These were the conventions on the rights of aliens and naturalized citizens (1902, 1906 and 1928), on asylum (1928), on the rights of women (1948); resolutions adopted at inter-American Conferences on various aspects of human rights protection (1938 and 1945); and declarations of inter-American Conferences referring to the subject (1945 and 1948).

[5] Resolution VIII, of the Vth Meeting of Consultation of Ministers of External Relations (Santiago, 1959).

rights situations in particular countries in the region), and the fact-finding system (undertaking of missions of observation *in loco* in various countries).[6] On several occasions the Commission has called upon OAS member States to incorporate certain rights into the texts of their Constitutions and to harmonize their national legislation with the provisions contained in human rights treaties. In its Annual Reports, particularly in recent years, the Commission has related the question of the protection of human rights to its concern about the political organization itself of OAS member-States and the effective exercise of representative democracy as a principle enshrined in the OAS Charter.

The observations *in loco* have been undertaken by the Commission either in the course of the examination of petitions (so as to determine or prove the facts denounced) or else in the investigation of general situations of human rights in given States. Some of those missions became particularly important at different times in the Commission's history, such as those in the case of the Dominican Republic (1965–1966), in the armed conflict between Honduras and El Salvador (1969), in the case of Chile (starting in 1973) and in the enforced or involuntary disappearances in Argentina (report of 1979). By the end of the seventies, the Commission had undertaken eleven such missions, a total which had doubled by the end of the eighties. The Commission is certainly one of the human rights international supervisory organs which has made most use of missions of *in loco* observation.

As for individual petitions, while by the late seventies the Commission

[6] On the work of the Commission in general, cf., e.g.: Comisión Interamericana de Derechos Humanos, *Diez Años de Actividades—1971–1981*, (Washington DC, 1982; K. Vasak, *La Commission Interaméricaine des Droits de l'Homme*, (Paris, 1968); A. Schreiber, *The Inter-American Commission on Human Rights*, (Leyden, 1970); Cançado Trindade, 'The Evolution of the OAS System of Human Rights Protection: An Appraisal', 25 *German Yearbook of International Law* (1982), 498–514; C. Grossman, 'Proposals to Strengthen the Inter-American System of Protection of Human Rights', 32 *German Yearbook of International Law* (1989), 264–75. On the methods of operation of the Commission in general, cf., e.g.: A. Aguilar, 'Procedimiento que Debe Aplicar la Comisión Interamericana de Derechos Humanos en el Examen de las Peticiones o Comunicaciones Individuales sobre Presuntas Violaciones de Derechos Humanos', *Derechos Humanos en las Américas—Homenaje a la Memoria de C.A. Dunshee de Abranches,* (Washington DC,1984), 199–216; B. Santoscoy, *La Commission interaméricaine des droits de l'homme et le développement de sa compétence par le système des pétitions individuelles* (Paris, 1995); M. Pinto, *La Denuncia ante la Comisión Interamericana de Derechos Humanos* (Buenos Aires, 1993); Goldman, 'Uruguay: Amnesty Law in Violation of Human Rights Convention', 49 *Review of the International Commission of Jurists* (1992), 37–45; C. Sepúlveda, 'El Procedimiento de Solución Amistosa ante la Comisión Interamericana de Derechos Humanos', *Derechos Humanos en las Américas—Homenaje a la Memoria de C.A. Dunshee de Abranches*, (Washington DC, 1984), 242–52; E. Vargas Carreño, 'Las Observaciones *In Loco* Practicadas por La Comisión Interamericana de Derechos Humanos', *Derechos Humanos en las Américas—Homenaje a la Memoria de C.A. Dunshee de Abranches*, (Washington DC,1984), 290–305; E. Márquez Rodríguez, 'Visitas de Observación *In Loco* de la Comisión Interamericana de Derechos Humanos y Sus Informes', in Cançado Trindade, G. Elizondo and J. Ordóñez (eds.), *Estudios Básicos de Derechos Humanos, Vol. III* (San José, 1995), 135–44.

had examined more than three thousand cases, by the early nineties that total had surpassed ten thousand communications. In its vast practice on the matter, the Commission has adopted resolutions that vary in content according to the facts of the cases. In these resolutions, the Commission has, for example, declared that the alleged acts constitute *prima facie* violations of human rights, or recommended a full investigation of what appeared to constitute violations of human rights, or decided to adjourn consideration of the cases until the results of ongoing investigations are known, or else declared that the alleged violations of human rights have not been proved.

In its decisions on individual cases, or in its *in loco* observations, or else in its country reports on human rights situations, the Commission has dwelt upon such topics as the right to minimal conditions in prisons, the prevalence of judicial guarantees and the due process of law, the characterization of arbitrary detention, the restrictions on death penalty, the requisites of states of emergency and control of suspension of guarantees, the rights to personal freedom and political participation, the presumption of innocence and the absolute condemnation of torture, among others. The Commission has recently indicated that it would be prepared also to survey economic, social and cultural rights. To the concrete results obtained in numerous cases, one may add the preventive function exercised by the Commission. By virtue of its general recommendations addressed to some governments or formulated in its reports, changes have been introduced in national laws or other provisions which violated human rights and domestic remedies and procedures have been set up or perfected so as to ensure the observance of and respect for human rights in the countries of the region.

Conventional Institutionalization

The entry into force in mid-1978 of the 1969 American Convention on Human Rights[7] represented the conventional institutionalization of the regional inter-American system of protection, bringing about the placing of the competence of the Commission (and the newly established Court) on a firm treaty basis as well as legal effects in the domestic law of States Parties. The Convention was largely devoted, like its European counterpart, to the protection of civil and political rights. The Convention contains only one general provision (Article 26) on the 'progressive development' of economic, social and cultural rights. The historical normative gap vis-à-vis economic, social and cultural rights was to be filled and remedied only

[7] On the preparatory work of this latter (not always as illuminating as it might be), see Organización de los Estados Americanos (OAS), *Conferencia Especializada Interamericana sobre Derechos Humanos—Actas y Documentos* (San José de Costa Rica), OEA doc. OEA/Ser.K/XVI/1.2 (1969).

later, with the adoption of the 1988 San Salvador Protocol, which has not yet entered into force. A second Protocol, on the abolition of the death penalty, was adopted in 1990. The two Protocols expand in a significant way the scope of the rights protected in the American Convention system (cf. below).

The Convention provides for a general obligation to 'respect' the protected rights and to 'ensure' their full exercise (Article 1(1)). The scope of this general obligation has been the object of jurisprudential interpretation, notably in the judgments of the Inter-American Court of Human Rights in the *Honduran cases* (merits, 1988–1989).[8]

It cannot pass unnoticed that the draftsmen of the Convention took trouble to include a provision (Article 29) which contains clear norms of interpretation: they expressly rejected an interpretation of the provisions of the Convention which would involve suppressing or limiting the enjoyment and exercise of the protected rights under the Convention by reference to the domestic law of States Parties, or to other international instruments on human rights. The essentially objective character of the obligations entered into by States Parties as to the protection of human rights is beyond question.

The extent of obligations under the American Convention[9] can be measured by its legal effects in the domestic law of States Parties. It is acknowledged today, for example, that Article 2 of the Convention contains an obligation to harmonize national legislation with the provisions of the Convention, a duty which is added to the general obligation under Article 1 of the Convention. Article 2 is certainly not meant to deny the self-executing character of the provisions of the Convention, but, on the contrary, it is intended to single out the general duty of States Parties to harmonize their domestic law with the Convention, or to incorporate the provisions of this latter into their domestic law, in addition to the specific duties that states parties have in relation to each of the protected rights. Moreover, the Convention recognizes the right of everyone to an effective

[8] *Velásquez Rodríguez* case, I/A Court H.R. Series C No.4 (1988), 9 *HRLJ* 212; *Godínez Cruz* case, I/A Court H.R. Series C No.5 (1989).

[9] Cf., in general, e.g.: T. Buergenthal, R. Norris and D. Shelton, *Protecting Human Rights in the Americas—Selected Problems*, 3rd. rev. ed.(Kehl/Strasbourg, 1990); A. A. Cançado Trindade, 'Formación, Consolidación y Perfeccionamiento del Sistema Interamericano de Protección de los Derechos Humanos', *XVII Curso de Derecho Internacional Organizado por Comité Jurídico Interamericano (1990)*, (Washington DC, 1991), 9–47; H. Gros Espiell, 'Le Système Interaméricain comme Régime Régional de Protection Internationale des Droits de l'Homme', *Recueil des Cours de l'Académie de Droit International* II (1975), 7–11; E. Vargas Carreño, 'Algunos Problemas que Presentan la Aplicación y la Interpretación de la Convención Americana sobre Derechos Humanos', *La Convención Americana sobre Derechos Humanos,* Washington DC, CIDH/OAS General Secretariat, 1980, 149–69; C. Medina, 'The Inter-American Commission on Human Rights and the Inter-American Court of Human Rights: Reflections on a Joint Venture', 12 *Human Rights Quarterly,* 439–64 (1990).

remedy before national courts to protect the rights guaranteed by the Convention or by the Constitution or domestic laws (Article 25, and Article 8 on the right to a fair trial).

As the American Convention entered into force, the Inter-American Commission, as already indicated, was endowed with a duality of functions, vis-à-vis States Parties (on the basis of the Convention itself) as well as non-Parties which were OAS members (on the basis of the OAS Charter and the 1948 American Declaration). The Commission has undertaken its work by making use of the above-mentioned methods of examination of individual petitions, preparation of reports (of distinct kinds) and conduct of *in loco* observations (fact-finding). The American Convention also provides for 'friendly settlement' on the basis of respect for human rights (Articles 48–50), a possibility which has been resorted to in some cases.

The American Convention confers the right of individual petition in an expansive and unqualified way, to any person (Article 44), without the petitioner having to claim to be himself/herself a victim of a violation of the Convention. This simplified formula has enabled a greater number of persons to lodge complaints with the Inter-American Commission than is the case under some comparable international petition procedures. The Commission has, in turn, applied the conditions of admissibility of petitions with particular sympathy for the need to protect human rights. For example, in the application of the local remedies rule, the Commission has adopted a diversity of solutions (such as requests for further information or the postponement of the examination or the taking of a decision in a case), instead of an early rejection of a complaint and the subsequent re-opening of the case. In the so-called 'general cases' the Commission has dispensed with the exhaustion rule and has applied presumptions (for example, the non-existence or ineffectiveness of local remedies) in favour of the alleged victims.[10] This practice demonstrates that the exhaustion of domestic remedies rule does not have an absolute character, and may be applied with flexibility in the present context of human rights protection.

In its turn, the Inter-American Court has likewise dwelt upon the extent of the exceptions to the local remedies rule, going beyond the generally recognized exceptions of undue delays and denial of justice (for example, by allowing exceptions in cases of indigence and of generalized fear in the legal community to represent victims), as well as upon the issues of the shifting of the burden of proof with regard to exhaustion and the express or tacit waiver of the local remedies rule. The Court has, furthermore, applied the criterion of the reasonable probability of success in the utilization of a remedy, and has insisted on the need for effectiveness of local remedies. It

[10] The 'general cases' are ones in which the local situation is such that it can be assumed that adequate and effective remedies are generally not available. See Cerna, 87, above

has rightly pointed out, for example, that in cases of disappearances of persons as a 'state practice' or of negligence or tolerance on the part of public authorities there must be a presumption in favour of the victim, and that there is no point in insisting on the application of the exhaustion rule (as there are in effect no remedies to exhaust). More recently, the Court has rightly ruled[11] that, if the respondent government has failed to invoke the preliminary objection of non-exhaustion in the admissibility proceedings before the Commission, it may not raise it subsequently before the Court (estoppel).

The contribution of the Commission and the Court on this matter point in the right direction, paving the way for developing the application of the local remedies rule so as to pay special attention to the overriding need to protect human rights and the particularities of the context of international implementation of human rights. That contribution shows that the incidence of the local remedies rule in human rights protection is certainly distinct from its application in the practice of diplomatic protection of nationals abroad (in customary international law), and that the rule is far from being an immutable or sacrosanct principle of international law. We are here in a domain of protection which is fundamentally victim-oriented, concerned with the rights of individual human beings rather than of States. Generally recognized rules of international law (to which the formulation of the local remedies rule in human rights treaties refers), besides following an evolution of their own in the distinct contexts in which they apply, necessarily suffer, when inserted in human rights treaties, a certain degree of adjustment or adaptation, dictated by the special character of the object and purpose of those treaties and by the widely recognized specificity of the international protection of human rights.[12]

In recent years, attention has been given to the issue of the relationship of the inter-American human rights system with other systems of protection,[13] be it in order to avoid the conflict of competences, the undue

[11] Cases *Castillo Páez* and *Loayza Tamayo* (1996).

[12] See A. A. Cançado Trindade, *The Application of the Rule of Exhaustion of Local Remedies in International Law*, (Cambridge, 1983), 1–443; A. A. Cançado Trindade, *El Agotamiento de los Recursos Internos en el Sistema Interamericano de Protección de los Derechos Humanos* (San José, 1991); A. A. Cançado Trindade, *O Esgotamento de Recursos Internos no Direito Internacional*, (Brasilia, 1984), 19–285. And, on the role of domestic remedies, cf., e.g. : H. Fix-Zamudio, 'La Protección Judicial de los Derechos Humanos en Latinoamérica y en el Sistema Interamericano', 8 *Revista del Instituto Interamericano de Derechos Humanos* (1988), 7–64; H. Fix-Zamudio, 'El Derecho Internacional de los Derechos Humanos en las Constituciones Latinoamericanas y en la Corte Interamericana de Derechos Humanos', in Cançado Trindade (ed.), *The Modern World of Human Rights—Essays in Honour of Thomas Buergenthal* (San José, 1996), 159–207; E. Jiménez de Aréchaga, 'La Convención Interamericana de Derechos Humanos como Derecho Interno', 69/71 *Boletim da Sociedade Brasileira de Direito Internacional (1987/1989)*, 35–55.

[13] On the question of their co-ordination, cf., e.g.: A. A. Cançado Trindade, 'Co-existence and Co-ordination of Mechanisms of International Protection of Human Rights (At

duplication of proceedings and the diverging interpretation of corresponding provisions of co-existing international instruments on the part of the supervisory organs (petitioning system), or to achieve uniform guidelines concerning the form and contents and the standardization of reports (reporting system), or to obtain the regular exchange of information and reciprocal consultations between the supervisory organs (fact-finding system). In so far as the petitioning system is concerned, the early practice of the Inter-American Commission on Human Rights, prior to adoption of the American Convention on Human Rights, disclosed considerable flexibility on the question of the relationship with other procedures, as well as complying with the test of the freedom of choice of procedures on the part of the complainants.

With the entry into force of the American Convention, the relevant provisions of this Convention (Articles 46(1)(c) and 47(d)) are complemented by the guidelines on 'duplicity of procedures' found in the Commission's Regulations (Article 39). The criteria indicated in the Regulations are the following: the Commission will not refrain from taking up and examining a complaint when another international procedure is 'limited to an examination of the general situation on human rights in the State in question and there has been no decision on specific facts that are the subject of the petition submitted to the Commission, or is one that will not lead to an effective settlement of the violation denounced'; and the Commission will not refrain from taking up a complaint when 'the petitioner before the Commission or a family member is the alleged victim of the violation denounced' and the petitioner in the other procedure 'is a third party or a nongovernmental entity having no mandate from the former'.

These are precise guidelines, which, in so far as the petitioning system is concerned, allow the Commission to proceed with the examination of the case, to the benefit of the alleged victims. As for the system of fact-finding or observations *in loco*, there are examples of the concomitant application of two or more mechanisms of protection. Thus, the situation of human rights in El Salvador was the object of examination on the part of a Special Representative of the UN Commission on Human Rights as well as of the

Global and Regional Levels)', 202 *Recueil des Cours de l'Académie de Droit International de La Haye* (1987), 21–435; C. A. Dunshee de Abranches, 'Comparative Study of the United Nations Covenants on Civil and Political Rights and on Economic, Social and Cultural Rights and of the Draft Inter-American Convention on Human Rights', *Inter-American Yearbook on Human Rights* (1968), 169–213; H. Gros Espiell, 'La Convention Américaine et la Convention Européenne des Droits de l'Homme—Analyse Comparative', 218 *Recueil de Cours de l'Académie de Droit International* (1989), 175–411; R. Piza, 'Co-ordination of the Mechanisms for the Protection of Human Rights in the American Convention with Those Established by the United Nations', 30 *American University Law Review* (1980), 167–87; A. H. Robertson, 'The American Convention on Human Rights and the European Convention: A Comparative Study', 29 *Annuaire européen/European Yearbook* (1981), 50–76.

Inter-American Commission on Human Rights (period 1982–1985). Likewise, the situation of human rights in Bolivia was investigated both by a Special Envoy of the UN Commission on Human Rights and by the Inter-American Commission on Human Rights (period 1981–1983). The case of enforced or involuntary disappearances in Argentina was the object of observations *in loco* on the part of the Inter-American Commission as well as the Working Group of the United Nations on the subject (period 1979–1984). The Chilean case was likewise examined at global and regional levels by the Ad Hoc Working Group and the Special Rapporteur on Chile of the United Nations, the ILO Committee on Freedom of Association, and the Inter-American Commission on Human Rights (observations *in loco* in the period 1974–1979).

In sum, the mechanisms of human rights protection at global and regional levels are essentially complementary, and the inter-American system of protection has been no exception to that.

Consolidation

The consolidation of the inter-American system of human rights protection can be taken to have occurred with the development of the case-law of the Inter-American Court, as well as the adoption of the two Protocols to the American Convention and of other 'sectorial' inter-American Conventions. The Inter-American Court, it may be recalled, exercises, under the American Convention, two types of jurisdiction:[14] contentious (Article 62) as well as advisory (Article 64), this latter being particularly wide in scope (cf. below).

[14] See, e.g., T. Buergenthal, 'The Advisory Practice of the Inter-American Human Rights Court', 79 *American Journal of International Law* (1985), 1–27; M. Cisneros, 'Algunos Aspectos de la Jurisdicción Consultiva de la Corte Interamericana de Derechos Humanos', *La Corte Interamericana de Derechos Humanos—Estudios y Documentos*, (San José de Costa Rica, 1985), 53–66; H. Gros Espiell, 'Contentious Proceedings before the Inter-American Court of Human Rights', 1 *Emory J. Int. Dispute Res.* (1987), 175–218; A. A. Cançado Trindade, 'El Sistema Interamericano de Protección de los Derechos Humanos (1948–1995): Evolución, Estado Actual y Perspectivas', in Bardonnet and Cançado Trindade (eds.), *Derecho Internacional y Derechos Humanos / Droit international et droits de l'homme* (San José de Costa Rica/La Haye, 1996), 47–95. On other aspects of the Court's faculties, cf., e.g.: C. M. Cerna, 'The Structure and Functioning of the Inter-American Court of Human Rights (1979–1992)', *British Year Book of International Law* (1992), 135–229; A. A. Cançado Trindade, 'Formación, Consolidación y Perfeccionamiento del Sistema Interamericano de Protección de los Derechos Humanos', *XVII Curso de Derecho Internacional Organizado por el Comité Jurídico Interamericano (1990)* (Washington DC, 1991), 9–47; T. Buergenthal, 'Judicial Fact-Finding: Inter-American Human Rights Court', in R. Lillich (ed.), *Fact-Finding before International Tribunals*, (Ardsley-on-Hudson; N.Y.,1990), 261–74; J. E. Méndez and J. M. Vivanco, 'Disappearances and the Inter-American Court: Reflections on a Litigation Experience', 13 *Hamline L Rev.* (1990), 507–77; F. O. Salvioli, 'Algunas Reflexiones sobre la Indemnización en las Sentencias de la Corte Interamericana de Derechos Humanos', in Cançado Trindade, Elizondo and Ordóñez (eds.), *Estudios Básicos de Derechos Humanos Vol. III*, (San José of Costa Rica, 1995), 145–64.

In its fourteen Advisory Opinions delivered to date, the Court has been called upon to pronounce upon a wide range of legal issues that are of the utmost importance to the operation of the inter-American system for the protection of human rights. An account of the Court's opinions is given in Chapter 5 above.

In the exercise of its contentious jurisdiction, the Court has on a number of occasions found violations of certain guaranteed rights under the American Convention, in particular the rights to life, to personal freedom and to personal integrity.[15] On three occasions the respondent States recognized their international responsibility for violation of guaranteed rights under the American Convention.[16] There has been one case of friendly settlement to date.[17] And there have been judgments on reparations in five cases so far.[18] In addition, the Court has very recently been seized of some other new cases.

Thus, in the mid-nineties, after more than a decade of exercising mainly its advisory jurisdiction, contentious proceedings now take place on a regular basis before the Inter-American Court. After more than fifteen years of continuous functioning of the Court, the number of contentious cases sent to it by the Commission is now at last clearly and steadily growing. In relation to the Court's case-law in such cases to date, the contribution of three of its judgments may be singled out as being particularly significant: the two judgments as to the merits in the cases of *Velásquez Rodríguez* and *Godínez Cruz*, and the judgment on reparations in the *Aloeboetoe* case.

In the first two, the contribution of the Court consisted in pointing out the threefold duty of States to prevent, investigate and punish the violations of protected rights, as well as to provide redress, and in linking the substantive provisions on violated rights to the general obligation under Article 1(1) to *respect* and to *ensure* the exercise of the rights provided for in the Convention. Ever since, this link has been invoked systematically in other cases by both the Court and the Commission. The next step forward would appear to be a similar exercise in combining the substantive provisions on violated rights with the general obligation under Article 2 to harmonize domestic law with the American Convention. In the third judgment above-mentioned, in the *Aloeboetoe* case, the contribution of the Court consisted in placing reparations for the violations of the protected rights within the social context to which they apply, taking sensibly

[15] See the account of the Court's jurisprudence in contentious cases in Chap. 5, above.

[16] Cases *Aloeboetoe* (1991, concerning Suriname), *Garrido and Baigorria* (1996, concerning Argentina), and *El Amparo* (1995, concerning Venezuela).

[17] Case *Maqueda* (1995, concerning Argentina).

[18] Namely, cases *Velásquez Rodríguez* and *Godínez Cruz* (1989–90), *Aloeboetoe* (1993), *Neira Alegría* (1996), and *El Amparo* (1996).

into account the cultural practices in the community of the saramacas (maroons) in Suriname.

Besides the exercise of its advisory and contentious jurisdictions (above), the Court has ordered (under Article 63(2) of the American Convention) provisional or interim measures of protection in cases of extreme gravity and urgency and in order to avoid irreparable damages to the persons.[19] Those measures have been ordered in situations implying an imminent threat to life or of serious physical or mental harm. The granting of provisional measures of protection is assuming an increasingly great importance in the practice of the Court, given their eminently preventive function.

Two Additional Protocols to the American Convention have been adopted to date, namely, the Protocol on Economic, Social and Cultural Rights (of 1988), and the Protocol on the Abolition of Death Penalty (of 1990). As to the former, the old dichotomy between civil and political rights and economic, social and cultural rights (which found expression in the two UN Covenants on Human Rights) had left its traces also in the inter-American system of protection of human rights. The 1969 American Convention on Human Rights was to cover only civil and political rights, and to contain but one provision (Article 26) on the 'progressive realization' of economic, social and cultural rights. If in the course of the preparatory work of the American Convention the projects submitted by Chile and Uruguay in 1965, and by the Inter-American Council of Jurists six years later, had been adopted, economic, social and cultural rights would have been included in the American Convention. Thus, in spite of the existence of the 1948 Inter-American Charter of Social Guarantees, there remained a historical gap in the inter-American system of protection with regard to economic, social and cultural rights.

The gradual overcoming of the old dichotomy, inaugurated by the reassessment of the matter by the 1968 Teheran Proclamation followed by the landmark UN General Assembly resolution 32/130, of 1977, advocating the interrelatedness or indivisibility of all human rights, led quickly to developments on the American continent. The Inter-American Commission on Human Rights, which had taken account of the situation of some economic, social and cultural rights in some Latin American countries (for example, reports on El Salvador, 1978, and Haiti, 1979), acknowledged, in its Annual Report of 1979–1980, the 'organic relationship' between civil and political rights, and economic, social and cultural rights. The field was open for the next step, that is, the preparation of an international instrument for the protection of the latter. Such work, initiated in 1982, culminated in the adoption in 1988 of the Additional Protocol to the American

[19] See the account of the Court's jurisprudence on provisional measures in Chap. 5. above.

Convention on Human Rights in the Area of Economic, Social and Cultural Rights ('Protocol of San Salvador').

The 1988 Protocol opens new courses of action: it contemplates (Article 19(6)), for example, the application of the system of individual petitions or communications (regulated by Articles 44–51 and 61–69 of the American Convention) to the right of association and trade union freedom (Article 8(1)(a)) and the right to education (Article 13). Furthermore, it provides for the formulation, by the Inter-American Commission, of such observations and recommendations as it may deem pertinent concerning the situation of economic, social and cultural rights enshrined in the Protocol (Article 19(7)).[20] Such measures disclose a new perspective for the protection of those rights.

It so happens, however, that the San Salvador Protocol has not yet obtained the number of ratifications sufficient for its entry into force; the probability that this may happen in the near future is uncertain. In spite of that, Article 42 of the American Convention opens a possibility of future action while the San Salvador Protocol does not enter into force: it provides that States Parties to the Convention are to transmit to the Inter-American Commission a copy of each of the reports and studies that they submit annually to the Executive Committees of the Inter-American Economic and Social Council (CIES) and the Inter-American Council for Education, Science and Culture (CIECC), so as to enable the Commission to watch over the promotion of the rights ensuing from the economic, social, educational, scientific and cultural norms or provisions of the amended OAS Charter. In fact, the Commission's Annual Report of 1991, for example, contains indications to the effect that the Commission will from now on be devoting closer attention to the situation of economic, social and cultural rights in the American States.

The second Protocol to the American Convention, pertaining to the abolition of the death penalty, adopted in 1990, constitutes a step forward in relation to the provisions of Article 4(2) to (6) of the American Convention. Article 1 of the Protocol determines that the States Parties will not apply the death penalty in their territory to any person subject to their jurisdiction. The Protocol gives a new impetus to the tendency towards the abolition of the death penalty, expressly acknowledged in its preamble. The Protocol does not admit reservations, and makes exception only for the pertinent provisions of domestic law applicable in wartime—

[20] For a study of the San Salvador Protocol of 1988, cf., e.g.: A. A. Cançado Trindade, *La Questión de la Protección Internacional de los Derechos Económicos, Sociales y Culturales: Evolución y Tendencias Actuales* (San José of Costa Rica, 1992); A.A. Cançado Trindade, 'La question de la protection internationale des droits économiques, sociaux et culturels: évolution et tendances actuelles', 94 *Revue générale de Droit international public* (1990), 913–46.

thus paving the way for the largest possible number of ratifications by States of the region.

The contemporary inter-American system of human rights protection does not exhaust itself in the American Convention on Human Rights and its two Protocols adopted to date. To them the three new Inter-American Conventions are to be added, concerned with the protection in particular of human rights of certain persons or in given situations, which could thereby be called 'sectorial'. The Inter-American Convention to Prevent and Punish Torture (adopted one year after the UN Convention, and two years before the European Convention, on this matter),[21] establishes individual responsibility for the crime of torture (Article 3) and establishes obligations on the part of States Parties to prevent and punish torture within their jurisdiction (Articles 6–8 and 11–14). To these latter obligations, it adds the duty to pay suitable compensation for victims of torture (Article 9). Its mechanism of international supervision (Article 17) consists in the submission by States Parties to the Inter-American Commission of Human Rights of information on legislative, judicial, administrative, or other measures they adopt in application of the Convention. The Commission, in its turn, will 'endeavour' to analyse the existing situation in its Annual Reports. It is the weakest mechanism of the three existing Conventions against torture.

The Inter-American Convention on Forced Disappearance of Persons, adopted in 1994, had its preparatory work[22] marked by the prolonged debate as to whether the forced disappearance of persons should be considered a crime against humanity or whether such denomination should correspond only to its systematic practice;[23] the latter was the view that prevailed. The Convention provides for the principle of individual respons-

[21] For a comparative study, cf. e.g., H. Gros Espiell, 'Las Convenciones sobre Tortura delas Naciones Unidas y dela Organización de los Estados Americanos', *XIV Curso de Derecho Internacional Organizado por el Comité Jurídico Interamericano (1987)* (Washington DC, 1988), 221–42.

[22] See, e.g., Organización de los Estados Americanos (OAS)/Consejo Permanente, *Informe del Presidente del Grupo de Trabajo Encargado de Analizar el Proyecto de Convención Interamericana sobre Desaparición Forzada de Personas*, doc. OEA/Ser.G/CP/ CAJP/925/93/rev.1, of 25 Jan. 1994, 1–49; OAS, *Informe de la Comisión de Asuntos Jurídicos y Políticos acerca del Proyecto de Convención Interamericana sobre Desaparición Forzada de Personas*, doc. OEA/ Ser.G/CP/doc.2458/94, of 22 Feb. 1994, 1-65; OAS, *Report of the Permanent Council on the Draft Inter-American Convention on Forced Disappearance of Persons*, doc. OEA/Ser.P/ AG/ doc.3072/94, of 29 Apr. 1994, 1–56, and doc. OEA/Ser.P/AG/doc.2821/92, of 22 Apr. 1992, 1–22.

[23] On gross violations of human rights and the inter-American system of human rights protection, cf., in general, e.g., C. Medina Quiroga, *The Battle of Human Rights—Gross, Systematic Violations and the Inter-American System* (Dordrecht, 1988); and cf. G. Peytrignet, 'Acción Humanitaria Convencional y Extraconvencional del CICR en América Latina: Evaluación y Proyecciones', in Irigoin (ed.), *Nuevas Dimensiones en la Protección del Individuo* (Santiago, 1991), 143–50; H. Hey, *Gross Human Rights Violations: A Search for Causes*, (Dordrecht,1995).

ibility in the crime of forced disappearance (as do the Inter-American Convention against Torture, the 1948 Convention against Genocide, and the 1973 Convention against Apartheid). Besides the individual responsibility of the perpetrators and the international responsibility of the State, the new Convention sets forth the following other legal consequences of its characterisation of the crime of forced disappearance of persons[24] as an international crime (Article II): universal jurisdiction and the obligation to extradite or judge those responsible for the crime; the obligation not to grant political asylum to those responsible for the crime; the imprescriptibility of the action; the obligation of the States to investigate and punish those responsible for the crime; the inadmissibility of the excuse of obedience to superior orders; the inadmissibilility of benefiting from the condition of being a member of the Executive or Legislative power from which impunity may result from acts constitutive of forced disappearance of persons. As to its international supervision, the Convention refers to the procedures of the Inter-American Commission and Court of Human Rights (Articles XIII-XIV).

The Inter-American Convention on the Prevention, Punishment and Eradication of Violence against Women (Convention of Belém do Pará), also adopted in 1994, covers the subject in both public as well as private ambits (Articles 1 and 3), from an integral outlook encompassing civil, political, economic, social and cultural rights (Articles 4, 5 and 6). To the obligations of States Parties (Articles 7–8), bearing especially in mind the 'situation of vulnerability to violence' which women may suffer (Article 9), it adds a mechanism for international supervision, with provision for a system of reports to the Inter-American Commission on Women (Article 10), and referral to the procedures of the Inter-American Commission and Court of Human Rights (Articles 11–12).

The Inter-American Commission has recently appointed a special rapporteur for the above subject. The mandate of this latter covers an evaluation, in the light of the inter-American norms on the human rights of women, of national legislation and discriminatory practices in the countries of the region. The Inter-American Commission is now concluding the [Inter-American] Declaration of the Rights of Indigenous Peoples (the adoption of which has been postponed in the last four years); its preparatory work has taken into account the endeavours of codification in this area within the United Nations and the International Labour Organization (ILO). Another subject which has recently attracted attention is that of the independence and integrity of members of the Judiciary,[25] resulting in the

[24] See, recently, Inter-American Court of Human Rights, *Blake* case (concerning Guatemala), Judgment of 2 July 1996 (Preliminary Objections), and Separate Opinion of Judge A. A. Cançado Trindade.

[25] See Commission Annual Report 1992–3, 207–15.

conclusion that there are deficiencies in the administration of justice in several countries of the American continent.

As to the major question of the preservation and strengthening of representative democracy in the American continent, the OAS Charter itself, it may be recalled, refers to democracy as one of its pillars (preamble and Articles 2(b) and 3(d)). But it was above all by means of Resolution 1080 of the OAS General Assembly of 1991, in combination with the so-called Compromise of Santiago (of the same year), that was intended to instrumentalize the inter-American system so as to promote and enhance representative democracy in the region. The monitoring procedure created has since been applied in the cases of Haiti (1991), Peru (1992) and Guatemala (1993).[26] The subject has been the object of attention also in the Declaration of Nassau (adopted by the 1992 OAS General Assembly) and the 1992 Protocol of Washington of Reform of the OAS Charter.

Under the American Convention on Human Rights, the Inter-American Commission on Human Rights itself has affirmed its competence to examine such matters. For example, in its decision of 1990 in the case of the Mexican elections of 1985–1986, in spite of not having pronounced on the merits, the Commission pointed out that representative democracy presupposes the 'observance of other basic human rights'. In its Annual Reports of 1985–1986 and 1990–1991, the Commission again underlined the direct relationship between representative democracy and the guarantee of the observance of human rights.

RECOMMENDATIONS *DE LEGE FERENDA* FOR THE IMPROVEMENT OF THE SYSTEM

A new stage in the evolution of the inter-American system of protection is now under way: that of its improvement. To this end, we shall present our thoughts and personal recommendations *de lege ferenda*, in a constructive spirit. There is, in our view, room for improvement in several respects in the contemporary operation of the mechanism of the American Convention on Human Rights.

To begin with, in so far as the composition of the two supervisory organs

[26] For a study of the matter, see, e.g.: A. A. Cançado Trindade, 'Democracia y Derechos Humanos: Desarrollos Recientes, con Atención Especial al Continente Americano', *Federico Mayor Amicorum Liber—Solidarité, Égalité, Liberté; Livre d'hommage, vol. I*, (Bruxelles, 1995), 371–90; D. Shelton, 'Representative Democracy and Human Rights in the Western Hemisphere', 12 *Human Rights L J* (1991), 356–8; W. M. Reisman, 'Humanitarian Intervention and Fledging Democracies', 18 *Fordham Int. L J* (1995), 794–805; J. Crawford, 'Democracy in International Law' (Inaugural Lecture, 5 Mar. 1993), Cambridge, Cambridge University Press, 1994, 1–43; C. M. Cerna, 'Universal Democracy: An International Legal Right or the Pipe Dream of the West?', 27 *N Y U J Int'l. L and Pol.* (1995), 289–329.

is concerned, besides the strict observance of the requisites set forth in the American Convention, there is need to establish clear rules of incompatibility of function (for example, avoiding undue accumulation of jobs or professional activities), expressly defined, for the members of both organs (the Commission and Court), as an additional safeguard of the total independence and impartiality of those organs. As to their conditions of work, which are at present precarious, it is essential that considerably more resources (human and material) are attributed to the Commission and the Court, so that they may fully exercise their functions and satisfy the increasingly varied demands placed upon them to protect human rights.

As to the procedures under the American Convention, they can be improved at virtually all stages. First of all, the opening of cases should be prompt, avoiding all unnecessary delay, and uniform vis-à-vis all States Parties to the Convention (non-selectivity). To the extent that one achieves the 'universal ratification' of human rights treaties by all of the states of the American continent to which the inter-American system is intended to apply, the much-needed and desirable 'jurisdictionalisation'[27] of the mechanisms of human rights protection, and their consequent and equally necessary and desirable depolitization, are bound to accelerate. With the integral ratification by all States[28]—without reservations or interpretative declarations and comprising optional instruments and clauses—of all human rights treaties, the universality of human rights will find expression not only in theory but also in practice, entailing the application of the same norms and criteria to all countries (bearing in mind that the supervisory organs are endowed with clear mandates). The 'jurisdictionalisation' of the procedures of protection constitutes a guarantee for all, against the temptations of selectivity, discretion and casuism. It secures the primacy of the rule of law in the endeavours to realize justice.

With regard to the decisions of the Inter-American Commission as to the admissibility of communications or petitions, these ought to be pronounced *in limite litis*, and not postponed. The decision of admissibility falls, of course, within the exclusive competence of the members of the Commission; the secretariat cannot but assist them. Such decisions ought to be very well founded, as they should not be susceptible of reopening or revision. To allow decisions of admissibility of the Commission to be later reopened and questioned before the Court by the respondent governments generates an unbalance between the parties, in favour of governments (even more so as individuals currently do not even have direct access to the Inter-American Court). If admissibility decisions

[27] By this is meant that the supervisory organs (the Commission and the Court) should emphasise and operate on the basis of the functions and procedures specifically attributed to them by the American Convention.

[28] See Appendix VIII for a list of those states which have ratified the Convention.

continue, as now, to be capable of being reopened by governments before the Court, decisions of inadmissibility of the Commission should also be capable of being reopened by the alleged victims and submitted to the Court. Either all the decisions of the Commission—whether declaring a petition admissible or inadmissible—are reopened before the Court, or they are all kept within the exclusive domain of the Commission.

Once the examination of a case on the merits is concluded by the Commission, if the case is not referred to the Court by the Commission, there is a need for a follow-up procedure for verification and monitoring of the degree of compliance by the State concerned with the decisions of the Commission. If, however, the Commission decides to submit the case to the Court, the dossier must then be very well prepared and founded, so as, for example, to avoid the Court having most of its time consumed with a repetition of the process of fact-finding, and to enable the Court to concentrate on the task of developing its case-law, especially now that new and successive contentious cases begin to be regularly submitted to it by the Commission.

Moreover, clear criteria need to be devised for the referral of cases by the Commission to the Court, so that the present situation of uncertainty on the matter no longer persists. The following elements could be taken into consideration for the formation of such criteria: a) whether fundamental rights (for example, non-derogable rights) are at stake; b) whether there exist questions which could generate a jurisprudential contribution to the interpretation and application of the American Convention; c) whether the questions at issue are susceptible of adequate judicial settlement (for example, 'individualized' cases that are justiciable); d) whether the questions at issue disclose new aspects requiring, or deserving of, judicial determination; e) non-selectivity as between the States Parties to the American Convention which have recognized the compulsory jurisdiction of the Court.

There is also a pressing need to search for a greater balance between the parties at distinct procedural stages. Such balance, for example, should encompass the notification to *both* parties of all and any information on the handling of the case, at all stages, it being incumbent upon the parties to comply with the conventional requisites (including those as to confidentiality). In order to attain that balance, one needs to reconsider more critically the question of re-opening the examination of preliminary objections as to admissibility before the Court which have already been decided by the Commission.[29] Likewise, the joinder of those objections to the merits

[29] See I/A Court H.R., *Castillo Páez* case (Preliminary Objections), Judgment of 30 Jan. 1996, Separate Opinion of Judge A. A. Cançado Trindade; I/A Court of H.R., *Loayza Tamayo* case (Preliminary Objections), Judgment of 31 Jan. 1996, Separate Opinion of Judge A. A. Cançado Trindade.

should be avoided, except in very exceptional situations, and on good legal grounds.[30]

The Court should further seek to avoid the situation in which the parties (complainant or respondent), by lack of care or for other reasons, make procedural errors—for example, by the 'withdrawal' of the case—especially when this may render the alleged victims wholly defenceless.[31] Once seized of a case, the Court is master of its own jurisdiction; faced with procedural 'incidents' which may render the alleged victims defenceless, the Court can and ought to retain jurisdiction over the case,[32] even more so because there exist superior interests—of international *ordre public*—at stake.

Last but not least, a point of capital importance ought to be made, one that is closely linked to the doctrinal issue of the procedural capacity of the individual in international law and, more particularly, before international tribunals. In so far as the two existing international courts of human rights—the European and the Inter-American Courts of Human Rights—are concerned, the developments on the matter within the European Court of Human Rights are instructive. As the result of a process beginning in the very first case before the European Court and culminating in the 1980s, the individual is now treated in effect as a party to proceedings before the Court. He may 'request the adoption of interim measures or measures for obtaining evidence, file written pleadings, appear at oral hearings, claim just satisfaction under Article 50 and negotiate friendly settlements'.[33] In addition, by virtue of the Ninth Protocol,[34] which entered into force in 1994, the applicant may, in a case brought against a state party to the Protocol, refer his or her case to the Court after the Commission has reported on the merits; he or she does not have to depend upon the European Commission on Human Rights doing so. In so far as the inter-American system of protection is concerned, the participation of non-

[30] See I/A Court H.R., *Genie Lacayo* case, Order of 18 May 1995, 17 *HRLJ* 24, 3 IHRR 397 (1996) Dissenting Opinion of Judge A. A. Cançado Trindade.

[31] See *Cayara* case (Preliminary Objections), I/A Court H.R. Series C No.14, 14 *HRLJ* 159, 1 IHRR Vol 1 175 (1994).

[32] See Art. 43(3) of the 1991 Rules of Procedure of the Court.

[33] D. Harris, M. O'Boyle and C. Warbrick, *The Law of the European Convention on Human Rights* (London, 1995), 661. What the applicant can still not do before the Court is lodge preliminary objections and file a request for revision or interpretation of a judgment.

[34] ETS 140. 18 parties. For comment, see Council of Europe, *Protocol n. 9 to the Convention for the Protection of Human Rights and Fundamental Freedoms—Explanatory Report*, Strasbourg, C.E., 1992, 8–9, and cf. 3–18. For other comments, cf. J.-F. Flauss, 'Le droit de recours individuel devant la Cour européenne des droits de l'homme—Le Protocole n. 9 à la Convention Européenne des Droits de l'Homme', 36 *Annuaire français de droit international* (1990), 507–19; M.-A. Eissen, *El Tribunal Europeo de Derechos Humanos* (Madrid, 1985), 26–43; G. Janssen-Pevtschin, 'Le Protocole Additionnel n. 9 à la Convention Européenne des Droits de l'Homme', 2 *Revue trimestrielle des droits de l'homme* (1991), n. 6, 199–202; M. de Salvia, 'Il Nono Protocollo alla Convenzione Europea dei Diritti dell'Uomo: Punto di Arrivo o Punto di Partenza?', 3 *Rivista Internazionale dei Diritti dell'Uomo* (1990), 474–82.

governmental organizations and other *amici curiae* in the proceedings for Advisory Opinions before the Inter-American Court is well known. The question which can today be raised is in relation to the procedure for contentious cases: can or should the alleged victims (or their legal representatives) have *locus standi in judicio* before the Inter-American Court?

The Court's concern to secure an equitable and fair procedure ought necessarily to lead it to seek to ensure that some form of *locus standi* is granted to the alleged victims (or their legal representatives) before the Court in cases which have already been referred to it by the Commission. This can be achieved pursuant to criteria and rules clearly and previously defined, and with the necessary adaptations to the present procedures and practices (for example, foreseeing ex officio legal assistance on the part of the Commission whenever the victims or other petitioners are unable to provide their own legal representative). This requires the reform of the pertinent provisions of the Statute and Rules of Procedure of the Court. The consequence would be to remedy some distortions brought about by the present system, which inadequately considers, as 'parties' before the Court, the Commission—instead of the victims themselves, as should be the case—and the respondent State (cf. below).

No one better than the victims themselves (or their legal representatives) can defend their rights before the Court, pursuant to previously and clearly defined criteria. No one better than the victims themselves are well motivated to avoid and overcome procedural 'incidents' which may render them defenceless. The *locus standi* of the victims (or their legal representatives) is the logical consequence, at procedural level, of a system of protection providing for individual rights at international level. It is not reasonable to conceive of rights without the procedural capacity to vindicate them. The insufficiencies and deficiencies of the paternalistic mechanism of intermediation by the Commission between the individual and the Court has already been clearly demonstrated in practice. This mechanism was fed by considerations developed in another epoch under the spectrum of State sovereignty, in order to avoid the direct access of the individual to the international legal organs.

It is a mechanism which belongs to the past, as shown by the experience of the European Court of Human Rights and the Ninth Protocol thereto. Once the Eleventh Protocol (of 1994) to the European Convention, on the reform of the mechanism of the European Convention on Human Rights and the establishment of a new European Court as the sole jurisdictional organ of supervision of the European Convention, enters into force, the Ninth Protocol will cease to apply and will become only of historic interest in Europe.[35] However, the Ninth Protocol retains great utility as a model

[35] Under the Eleventh Protocol, all states accept an automatic right of individual petition against them upon becoming ECHR parties, with cases being processed by the new single Court

during the current consideration of an eventual revision of the inter-American system of protection, given that the two regional systems are at different stages of development.

Endeavours to improve the inter-American system of protection in this respect would do well to take into consideration the experience of the European Convention, with necessary adaptions to allow for the realities of the operation of our system. Such evolution should take place *pari passu* with the gradual judicialisation of the mechanism of protection: it can hardly be denied that judicial protection is the most advanced form of safeguard of human rights, and the one which best abides by the imperatives of law and justice.

In practice, those who currently act in fact as the lawyers of the victims before the Inter-American Court are euphemistically designated 'assistants' to the Inter-American Commission, and are incorporated as such in the delegation of the Commission appearing before the Court. This pragmatic solution was, so to speak, 'endorsed' by a joint meeting of the Inter-American Commission and the Court (held in Miami) on 24–25 January 1994. Rather than solving the problem, this expedient has created ambiguities, which have lasted ever since. This is not surprising, bearing in mind that the roles of the Commission (as guardian of the Convention assisting the Court) and of the individuals (as the true complainant party) are clearly different.

In the last joint meeting of the Inter-American Court and the Commission (held in Washington DC) on 12 April 1995, support was voiced—although not conclusive—for granting individual complainants *locus standi* before the Court, in cases already referred to it by the Commission. An initial step in this direction has in fact just been taken by the Inter-American Court, in its XXXIV ordinary session, in adopting its new Rules of Procedure on 16 September 1996. The new Rules of Court contain, for the first time, in addition to the provisions on the representation of the respondent States (Article 21) and of the Commission (Article 22) before the Court, a specific provision on the 'representation of the victims or of their relatives' (Article 23), which reads as follows:—'At the stage of reparations the representatives of the victims or of their relatives may present their own arguments and evidence in an autonomous way'.[36]

This is a significant first step, but it is only the first. This provision paves the way for further developments in the same direction. In cases of proven or substantiated violations of human rights, it is the victims themselves—

to the point of a final legally binding decision by it in all admitted cases, with there being no need for individual applicants or others (the European Commission will disappear) to refer cases to the Court for a final decision. Individual applicants will continue to have their now established rights as parties to their case before the Court at all stages in the proceedings.

[36] Unofficial translation from the original Spanish.

the true complainant party before the Court—(or their relatives or heirs) who receive, or are entitled to receive, the reparations and indemnities. As the individual victims are present at the *beginning* (before the Commission) as well as at the *end* of the process, there is no sense in denying their presence (before the Court) *during* the process. Coherency is here necessary: the right of access to international justice is to be accompanied by the guarantee of equality of arms in the proceedings before the Court, which is essential to any judicial system of international protection of human rights. The opposition of individual victims of human rights violations to respondent governments—the adversarial element in the arguments of the parties —is of the essence of contentious cases involving the international protection of human rights.

To the acknowledgment of rights, at national as well as international levels, corresponds the capacity to vindicate or exercise them. Without such capacity, any system of protection is ineluctably flawed; in those circumstances, the parties are in flagrant unbalance, and the procedure is partly devoid of an essential element in the search for truth and justice. The 'jurisdictionalisation' of the procedure greatly facilitates the process of remedying this situation and putting an end to those insufficiencies and deficiencies, which can no longer find any justification at the present time.

The full participation of the alleged victims in the procedure before the Court contributes, furthermore, to the more effective presentation of evidence relevant to the case, as no one better than they (or their legal representatives) know how to defend their interests. The exercise of the right of freedom of expression, which the human rights treaties determine to be respected at the level of the domestic law of the States Parties, finds application also at the international level. The precepts of due process of law, which the human rights treaties require to be observed within the legal systems of the States Parties, find application equally at international level. The equity and transparency of the procedure, which are equally applicable to the international supervisory organs, are beneficial to all, including the complainants and the respondent governments.

As if these considerations of principle were not sufficient, there are others, of a more practical nature, that equally militate in favour of the direct access of individuals to the Court, in cases already submitted to it by the Commission. Such advance, on the basis of previously and clearly defined criteria and rules, is convenient not only to the alleged victims but to all concerned: to the governments, to the extent that it contributes to the 'jurisdictionalisation' of the mechanism of protection; to the Court, to enable it to count on more precise and complete information on the facts; and to the Commission, to put an end to the current ambiguity of its role and to enable it to concentrate on its proper function of guardian of the correct and just application of the American Convention (and no longer with the additional function of 'intermediary' between the individual petitioner and the Court).

An advance in this direction is, in the present stage of evolution of the inter-American system of protection, ultimately the *joint* responsibility of both the Court and the Commission. The latter ought always to be prepared to express its point of view before the Court, even if it is not entirely coincident with that of the representatives of the victims; and the Court ought to be prepared to receive, examine and evaluate the arguments of the delegates of the Commission and of the representatives of the victims, even if they are diverging. As the roles of those delegates and representatives are distinct (above), differences in their arguments in the hearings before the Court are normally bound to happen, and are to some extent inevitable.

Finally, only through the *locus standi in judicio* of the alleged victims before the international courts of human rights (in the regional systems of protection) will human beings attain full international procedural capacity to vindicate their rights, when the national organs are incapable of securing the realization of justice. In the improvement of the mechanism of protection under the American Convention, the emphasis ought to fall upon the 'jurisdictionalisation' of that mechanism, particularly in so far as the operation of the method of petitions or complaints is concerned, without prejudice to the continued use by the Inter-American Commission of the methods of reporting and fact-finding. The improvement of the mechanism of the inter-American system of protection ought to be the object of considerations of an essentially juridico-humanitarian character, even as an additional guarantee to the parties in contentious cases of human rights. Every international lawyer, faithful to the historical origins of his/her discipline, will surely contribute to rescue the position of the human being in the law of nations, and sustain the recognition and crystallization of the international personality and full legal capacity of the human being.

The much-needed recognition of the *locus standi* of the alleged victims (or their legal representatives) before the Inter-American Court constitutes an important step forward, but not necessarily the final stage of improvement of the inter-American system of protection. From the *locus standi in judicio* of the individuals before the Inter-American Court one ought to evolve towards the recognition in the foreseeable future of the right of the individuals to lodge a case directly with the [future] Inter-American Court, as the sole organ of protection of the inter-American system of tomorrow. To this end, we wait for the day when, in the parallel regional European system, the Eleventh Protocol to the European Convention on Human Rights enters into force, showing the way to the recognition of the full international legal capacity of the human being to vindicate his/her own rights.

PERSPECTIVES OF THE SYSTEM AT THE DAWN OF THE NEW CENTURY

Despite the undeniable advances of the inter-American system of protection of human rights, from 1948 to 1996, there still remains a long way to go. Until the early eighties, attention was turned mainly to gross and massive violations of human rights (for example, practice of torture, enforced or involuntary disappearances of persons, inhuman or degrading treatment or punishment, illegal or arbitrary detentions) committed by oppressive regimes. Nowadays, there appears to be a diversification in the sources of violations of human rights (for example, those perpetrated by clandestine or assassination groups, or those perpetrated in inter-individual relations, or those resulting from corruption and impunity). To this phenomenon—which stresses in particular the relevance of the preventive dimension of human rights protection—one ought to add the problems of human rights which result not necessarily from political confrontation or repression, but appear rather as endemic or chronic problems of the social milieu of Latin American countries, aggravated by the iniquities of concentration of income and the growing socio-economic disparities. It is necessary to equip the inter-American system of protection, within its possibilities and the parameters of its mandate, so as to be able to face these new or aggravated situations of denial or violation of human rights.

The work of international protection of human rights in the American continent has been transformed in the sense that, after confronting violations of human rights in authoritarian regimes in the recent past, it ought today to focus on violations in the context of the so-called democratic 'transition' or 'consolidation'. This requires a systemic or global outlook of human rights, encompassing the protection of the person in all domains of human activity (civil, political, economic, social and cultural). If one looks towards the future, one ought also to reckon that special emphasis is needed, within States, upon the role of public organs, and in particular of the judiciary, in the protection of human rights. In this respect additional resources are needed so that such national organs may fully exert the functions (for example, the duty of investigation) conferred upon them by human rights treaties such as the American Convention (for example, the guarantee of access to justice and the right to an effective local remedy before national tribunals).

The incorporation of the international norms of human rights protection into the domestic law of the States of the region is of paramount importance today. The contemporary Constitutions of Latin American countries, in growing number, contain in fact express references (in the form of a *renvoi*) to the rights protected under treaties and conventions on human rights protection to which the State concerned is a Party.[37] It is necessary to give practical expression to the present-day coincidence of purpose of international law and internal public law as to the protection of the human being; the consequences of this reassuring coincidence of purpose between international law and municipal law still remain legally unexplored to date.

One ought to keep in mind that each of the three regional systems of human rights protection in operation (that is, the inter-American, the European and the African) is at a distinct stage in its historical development. In Africa, the possible creation of an African Court of Human Rights to complement the work of the African Commission on Human and Peoples' Rights is being discussed. In the ambit of the inter-American system, ways and means of achieving a closer coordination between the Inter-American Commission and Court of Human Rights are being contemplated. And in the European system, the Eleventh Protocol to the European Convention foresees the merging of the European Commission and Court of Human Rights towards the establishment of a sole—judicial—supervisory organ, which would in fact come to function as a true European Constitutional Court.

Each regional system of protection has evolved and operates at its own pace, and lives its own historical moment. But all current efforts point to the gradual strengthening of each system. The existing regional systems have lately been followed by the 1994 Arab Charter on Human Rights. The perspectives of the regional systems of protection ought to be considered necessarily within the framework of the universality of human rights. Universality does not amount to uniformity; on the contrary, it is enriched by regional particularities. Universality prevails at both normative and operational (non-selectivity) levels.

The lessons and results of the Second World Conference on Human Rights (Vienna, 1993) are valid also for the inter-American system as well as for other regional systems of protection of human rights. They are marked, above all, by the integrated and global outlook of all human rights; by the special attention to those in greater need of protection (the weaker and more vulnerable); by the temporal dimension (with measures of prevention and follow-up) of protection; and by the omnipresence of human rights. This last consideration finds expression in the recognition that human rights entail obligations *erga omnes* (binding on States, as well as international organizations, private groups and individuals), everywhere and at all times.

[37] Cf., e.g., in South America: Constitution of Brazil of 1988, Art. 5(2); Constitution of Chile (after the reform of 1989), Art. 5(II); Constitution of Colombia of 1991, Art. 93; Constitution of Argentina (after the reform of 1994), Art. 75(22); Constitution of Peru of 1978, Art. 105, followed by the Constitution of 1993, 4th. final and transitory provision; and, in Central America: Constitution of Guatemala of 1985, Art. 46; Constitution of Nicaragua of 1987, Art. 46.

Human rights violations continue to occur virtually everywhere, but the prompt responses to them are indeed much stronger today than they used to be in the past. We have reached a stage of evolution characterized today by the recognition of the legitimacy of the concern of the whole international community with the promotion and protection of human rights by everyone and everywhere. This corresponds to a new ethos, universally acknowledged, bringing about, as already pointed out, obligations *erga omnes*. We are, ultimately, in the course of a process of construction of a universal culture of observance of human rights. In the pursuance of this goal, a significant role is reserved, in the American continent, to the inter-American system of protection of human rights in general, and to its international supervisory organs in particular.

[6]

THE INTER-AMERICAN SYSTEM FOR THE PROTECTION OF HUMAN RIGHTS

Christina M. Cerna[*]

I. INTRODUCTION

I would like to deal with four issues in my Article. First, what is the inter-American system for the protection of human rights? Second, what have we learned from looking at the history of the system? Third, what can we say about state compliance and state noncompliance with the recommendations of the Inter-American Commission on Human Rights and the judgments of the courts? And lastly, what recommendations can we make to this conference?

---

* Principal Specialist at the General Secretariat of the Organization of American States' Secretariat for the Inter-American Commission on Human Rights. The opinions expressed in this Article are in the author's personal capacity and are not to be attributed to the Inter-American Commission on Human Rights, the General Secretariat of the Organization of American States, or to the Organization of American States.

II. WHAT IS THE INTER-AMERICAN SYSTEM FOR THE PROTECTION OF HUMAN RIGHTS?

To understand the inter-American system for the protection of human rights it is useful to place it in its historical context. International concern for human rights dates from the end of World War II. It evolved as a consequence of the international community's expressed vow to never again let such events occur, events characterized by the shock and horror at the photographs of the prisoners who emerged from the Nazi concentration camps. In order to prevent such atrocities from ever occurring again, the international community resolved to define human rights norms and to adopt the measures to protect them.

Although natural law and concepts of rights are not new to this century, the modern human rights movement was born with the adoption of the grandfather instrument of them all, the Universal Declaration of Human Rights, approved by the U.N. General Assembly on December 10, 1948, which is commemorated annually as Human Rights Day throughout the world. Six months prior to the adoption of the Universal Declaration, the American Declaration of the Rights and Duties of Man was approved by the member states of the Organization of American States (OAS) at the renewal of the inter-American system. The inter-American system was established in 1890 as the Union of American Republics, and was renamed the Pan American Union in 1910. Following the creation of the United Nations, in 1948 it was renamed the OAS in Bogotá, Colombia, to fit into the architecture of the postwar new world order. The American Declaration was adopted virtually simultaneously with the OAS Charter, its constitutive instrument, and the relationship of the Declaration to the Charter can be compared to the Bill of Rights to the U.S. Constitution.

The American Declaration is what its name suggests it to be. It is simply a declaration, in spite of the fact that the human rights organs of the inter-American system have interpreted it to be legally binding. The OAS member states that are subject to the jurisdiction of the Inter-American Commission on Human Rights, however, refuse to accept that the American Declaration has any binding force. This group includes, notably, the United States, Canada, and many of the countries of the English-speaking Caribbean.

Following the adoption of the Universal Declaration, the Council of Europe was the first regional organization to adopt a legally binding human rights instrument. In 1950, it adopted the Convention for the Protection of Human Rights and Fundamental Freedoms, more commonly known as the European Convention on Human Rights. This Convention entered into force in 1953 and created both a European Commission and European Court of Human Rights. This was the model for the eventual American Convention on Human Rights.

In the interim, as a reaction to the Cuban Revolution in 1959, the Inter-American Commission on Human Rights was created, not by a treaty, but by a political resolution of the OAS, with the very limited function of observing and studying the human rights situation in the Americas. It was authorized by the OAS political bodies to make general recommendations to the member states, but it was not until 1965 that the Inter-American Commission was granted the authority to receive, examine, and make decisions on individual complaints from inhabitants of the countries of the hemisphere. The worldwide decolonization movement increased the original OAS membership of 21 states to the current number of 35. The English-speaking Caribbean countries now comprise about a third of the OAS membership, and more recent members include Canada, which finally joined the Organization in 1990, and Belize and Guyana, which became members in 1991.

It was only after 1966 and the adoption of the two U.N. human rights covenants, the primary international human rights instruments in the world, that the inter-American system acknowledged the necessity of adopting a legally binding human rights treaty in the Americas. In 1969 the American Convention was adopted, but it did not enter into force until 1978, and the institutions created by the Convention were not in place until 1979. These institutions include a re-creation of the Inter-American Commission on Human Rights and the establishment of an Inter-American Court of Human Rights. The Inter-American Commission is located at the headquarters of the OAS, in Washington, D.C., whereas the Inter-American Court has its seat in San Jose, Costa Rica.

The Inter-American Commission on Human Rights currently holds two regular meetings of three-week duration per year, one in the spring and one in the fall, with an occasional one or two extraordinary meetings that can be as short as one day or as long as a week. The second week of each session is devoted exclusively to hearings between the parties on pending contentious cases. The Inter-American Court of Human Rights, for its part, holds four regular meetings of two weeks each per year, and has been advocating its eventual transformation into a full-time institution to deal with the ever-increasing workload. The Inter-American Commission effectively determines the workload of the Inter-American Court since only the Commission and state parties to the American Convention are authorized to present cases to the Inter-American Court, and a state has yet to present a case. To be presented to the Inter-American Court, a case must have been processed by the Inter-American Commission and a decision taken. The literature in this field indicates that the Inter-American Commission is not to be understood as a court of first instance, and that the two organs are to be equal in competence. However, in practice, the Commission is becoming just such a court.

Each of the Inter-American human rights bodies has seven members, unlike the European system, which had a commissioner and judge for each state party to the European Convention. All thirty-four active member states of the OAS participate in the nomination of candidates to the Inter-American Commission on Human Rights and in their election.[1] Only the twenty-four state parties to the American Convention, however, are authorized to participate in the nomination of candidates to the Inter-American Court of Human Rights and in their election. Currently, the Inter-American Commission has five male commissioners and two female commissioners, and the Inter-American Court has seven male judges. The seven commissioners serve four-year terms and may be re-elected only once. The seven judges serve six-year terms and also may be re-elected only once. In early June 2003, elections were held for four members of the Inter-American Commission and four judges of the Inter-American Court at the recent OAS General Assembly in Santiago, Chile. At the General Assembly, four new judges were elected to the Inter-American Commission, whereas one judge of the Inter-American Court was re-elected and three new judges elected for the first time. The new composition of the Inter-American Commission as of January 1, 2004, will be six male commissioners and one female commissioner, and the Inter-American Court, similarly, will have six male judges and one female judge. As a result of the elections, these bodies tend to reinvent themselves with each new configuration.

Currently, the Inter-American Commission on Human Rights has a professional staff of seventeen lawyers, of which I am one, and carries out basically two functions. The first is the examination and preparation of draft decisions of individual petitions, and the second is the performance of on-site visits and the preparation of draft country reports on the situation of human rights in the member states of the hemisphere. During approximately the first thirty years of the Inter-American Commission's history, from 1959 to 1989, that second function was really its primary function. The Inter-American Commission's reputation was built on the

1. The 35th member state of the OAS, Cuba, is still considered to be a member state of the Organization since the OAS Charter does not provide for the expulsion of any member state. The government of Fidel Castro, however, is considered to have voluntarily separated itself from the principles and purposes set forth in the OAS Charter, by adopting Marxism/Leninism, and since 1962 it has been excluded from participation in OAS activities.

importance of its on-site visits and the seriousness of the approximately two or three hundred page country studies that analyzed the human rights situations in these member states.

Since the entry into force of the American Convention and the creation of the Inter-American Court of Human Rights, the Inter-American Commission's functions regarding individual petitions have increased in importance as its on-site visits and country reports have faded. Since 1965, the Inter-American Commission has opened approximately 12,500 cases, whereas the Inter-American Court has taken decisions in approximately 45 cases since its first judgments were issued in 1987. The Inter-American Court has two principal functions: first, issuing legally binding decisions on contentious cases, and second, issuing advisory opinions. It has issued 17 advisory opinions to date.

The Inter-American Commission on Human Rights was not given explicit authority to carry out on-site visits; it created that competence by dint of its own initiative. The Inter-American Commission's Statute, which is prepared by the member states of the OAS, authorized it to hold meetings in any state in the hemisphere, and the Commission converted that authorization into a mandate to conduct monitoring and the preparation of a report on the human rights situation in the country visited. These reports dominated the agenda of the OAS General Assemblies for many years, especially during the long period of military dictatorships in the region, when the Inter-American Commission critically reviewed the behavior of these states as regards their failure to respect human rights norms.

After the initial period of on-site visits and country reports (1959-1989), the period from 1989 to the present, which can be called the second period, has been characterized by the creation of the Inter-American Court of Human Rights. The Inter-American Court was created in 1979, but did not issue its first decisions on the merits in contentious cases until 1988-1989. This second period has been dominated by the processing of individual petitions. As a result of the re-democratization of the Americas, the barrier to the presentation of petitions, which is the exhaustion of domestic remedies, has been easier to overcome since there are now domestic remedies to exhaust. States tend to answer complaints that the Inter-American Commission sends them, which for years they did not do, or did so erratically. The Inter-American Court took approximately ten years to begin to function properly. From 1979–1986, it received no contentious cases. But since 1986, the Inter-American Commission has been presenting cases regularly to the Inter-American Court.

Any individual may present a petition to the Inter-American Commission on Human Rights, alleging the violation of a right set forth either in the American Convention, for state parties thereto, or in the American Declaration, for those OAS member states that are not parties to the Convention. The violation must be attributable to agents of the state, or the failure of the state to act, for example, as in the investigation of a crime, or in the execution of a judicial sentence. Before the Inter-American Commission will consider a petition, the alleged victims must have exhausted domestic remedies at the national level. This requirement is crucial and underlines the general principle of international law that the international system plays a subsidiary role and is triggered by the failure of national law to function properly. If every member state had a functioning and effective Bill of Rights as part of its Constitution that included all the rights adopted at the international level, then the inter-American machinery would be redundant. It is the failure to observe human rights at the national level that has created the necessity for the adoption of international standards and mechanisms. If there has been a manifest denial of justice, then the exhaustion requirement is waived. A manifest denial of justice occurs: 1) if the state fails to act or provide a remedy for the alleged violations; 2) if the judicial system does not function, and there has been an unwarranted delay in reaching a decision in the national courts; or 3) if the alleged victims have been denied access to the remedy.

As with the newly created International Criminal Court, if a state demonstrates good will and seeks to resolve the issue at the national level, then there is no reason for the Inter-American Commission on Human Rights to initiate processing of the complaint. Obviously, reality is more complicated, and many issues cannot be solved easily or quickly. National judicial systems may get bogged down by overuse, creating due process violations, which in many cases are also violations of domestic law. These problems, in turn, are not solved at the national level because of the inability of the national system to cope with the large number of pending cases.

On balance, today there are twenty-four state parties to the American Convention on Human Rights, which includes all of Spanish-speaking Latin America and Brazil. Of those twenty-four state parties, twenty-one have accepted the contentious jurisdiction of the Inter-American Court of Human Rights, including all the Spanish-speaking countries, as well as Brazil, Suriname, and Haiti. Grenada and Jamaica have ratified the American Convention but have not accepted the Inter-American Court's jurisdiction. Barbados and Trinidad and Tobago have ratified the Convention and accepted the Inter-American Court's contentious jurisdiction, but Trinidad and Tobago denounced the Convention on May 26, 1998, over the issue of the death penalty — the first country to do so.

That denunciation went into effect one year later, and, consequently, there are now twenty-four (rather than twenty-five) state parties to the American Convention and twenty-one (rather than twenty-two) states that currently accept the Inter-American Court's contentious jurisdiction. As mentioned earlier, neither the United States nor Canada has ratified the American Convention.

III. WHAT HAVE WE LEARNED FROM LOOKING AT THE HISTORY OF THE SYSTEM?

The Inter-American Commission's greatest contribution to the inter-American system has been in de-legitimizing nondemocratic governments by means of the monitoring conducted during its on-site visits, and as a result of the presentation of its country reports to the OAS political organs and to hemispheric public opinion in general. These country reports are presented to the political organs and have dominated the agendas of the OAS General Assemblies for many years. The documentation presented by an intergovernmental organization of human rights violations committed by states against their own populations has a credibility not achieved by reports issued by nongovernmental organizations, and every state will fight not to be censured by its peers. In 1980, Argentina, for example, threatened to pull out of the OAS fearing censure because of the Inter-American Commission's report on human rights violations in that country, which focused, *inter alia*, on the military regime's policy of "forced disappearances."

Also, it has been one of the first acts of governments that have made the transition from dictatorship to democracy to ratify the American Convention on Human Rights, as was the case with Nicaragua, Argentina, and Chile. In the past two decades, we have also seen a dramatic increase in the number of states accepting the contentious jurisdiction of the Inter-American Court of Human Rights, with ten states accepting its jurisdiction in the 1980s, and another eleven in the 1990s. Barbados is the first to accept the Inter-American Court's jurisdiction in this decade (June 4, 2000) which we hope is an auspicious sign suggesting increased participation by the English-speaking states in the system.

The democratization of the hemisphere is the central political advance in the region during the twentieth century, and the Inter-American Commission's role in this political development has been crucial. In 1991, the OAS General Assembly adopted Resolution 1080, which has now evolved into a treaty, the Inter-American Democratic Charter, which attempts to guarantee democracy in the Americas. The obligations incumbent upon member states under this Charter require the convocation of a meeting to discuss collective action in the case of any interruption of the democratic process in any member state in the region.

The fact that the region now attempts to guarantee democracy has also brought about a change in the nature of the violations presented to the Inter-American Commission on Human Rights. Whereas the earlier period (1959-1989) of the Inter-American Commission's history was replete with petitions concerning forced disappearances, extrajudicial executions and torture, petitions presented in recent years concern problems common to most democratic states, such as violations of due process, delays in judicial proceedings, disputes over property rights, and status questions (e.g. loss of employment, decrease in pension, and the like). One might even characterize this change as the Europeanization of the inter-American system. At the same time, the European system, (which, since Protocol 11 now comprises only a single organ, the European Court of Human Rights, with the European Commission having been fused into the new European Court), also is dealing with different violations due to the composition of the newly democratic governments of the new member states of the Council of Europe. The membership of the Council of Europe now, in July 2003, comprises forty-five member states, and the conflicts occurring in these states, such as the conflict in Russia with Chechen rebels, and the incidents of torture in Turkey, might justify characterizing this development as the Latin-Americanization of the European system.

But there are many things that the inter-American system can still learn from the European model. The inter-American system is on the road set by the Europeans and if it continues to function as it is at present, it can be assumed that there will also be an eventual fusion of the Inter-American Commission on Human Rights and the Inter-American Court of Human Rights. The President of the Inter-American Court, the distinguished Brazilian jurist, Antonio Cancado Trindade, in his public appearances during the past few years, has called for a Protocol 11 for the inter-American system and direct access for alleged victims to the Inter-American Court. I do not see this happening tomorrow, but I see it clearly on the horizon.

What have we learned? We have learned that, in general, the member states of the Organization, the state parties to the American Convention, have accepted this system of monitoring and supervision. They have accepted the judgments of the Inter-American Court of Human Rights and, this is surprising, because the decisions of the Commission still generally remain unobserved in comparison.

I was glad to hear Jorge Santistevan expand on Dennis Jett's comments regarding the lack of confidence in the judicial system in the Americas.

But there is a greater problem, which is the total degradation of democratic institutions in the hemisphere. That is what I understood him to say and that is also what our Inter-American Commission on Human Rights has said in its most recent Annual Report.

The most remarkable development in the evolution of the inter-American human rights system, and I cannot emphasize this enough, is that it has become accepted. All of the Latin countries in the hemisphere have ratified the American Convention. I can recall approximately twenty-two years ago, Cesar Sepulveda, a distinguished Mexican jurist and member of the Commission, telling me, "Christina, this system was not made for supervising the human rights performance of our countries," meaning Mexico and the United States. In his view, the inter-American system was designed to monitor small countries that are considered insignificant on the world stage, but not big countries such as Mexico, Brazil, and the United States; that view has now been totally superseded. Brazil and Mexico are state parties to the American Convention and have accepted the contentious jurisdiction of the Inter-American Court, whereas the United States, although it signed the Convention during the Carter Administration, still has not ratified it. The struggle for legitimacy of the inter-American human rights system has been largely won in Latin America but has yet to be won in the English-speaking states in the region.

IV. What Can We Say About State Compliance and State Noncompliance with the Recommendations of the Inter-American Commission on Human Rights and the Judgments of the Inter-American Court of Human Rights?

The American Convention provides that the judgments of the Inter-American Court of Human Rights are legally binding. A court judgment generally consists of two parts: 1) the reparations, which includes both material and moral damages, and costs and expenses, and 2) the obligation to investigate, try, and punish those responsible for the violation. Given that Latin America has now demonstrated ownership of the system, and approximately forty-five cases have been decided by the Inter-American Court, some preliminary critical observations are in order. In most cases, the state is prepared to pay the pecuniary reparations ordered by the Inter-American Court, but only in the rarest case is it willing to investigate, try and punish the perpetrators, and in those rare cases where it does punish them, they tend to be released from prison after short periods, or never serve prison terms at all.

This climate of impunity characterizes the Americas, and amnesty laws have proliferated throughout the region. The Inter-American Commission on Human Rights, in 1992, was the first international human rights body to declare in two cases, dealing with victims in Argentina and in Uruguay, that amnesty laws were incompatible with the obligations of a state in the inter-American system.[2] These were, perhaps, the Inter-American Commission's most important decisions, and their effects are still being felt. The Inter-American Commission also took the issue to the Inter-American Court of Human Rights in the context of the Peruvian amnesty laws in *Barrios Altos*, and in a judgment issued on March 14, 2001, accepted the Commission's arguments that the amnesty laws were incompatible with the state's obligations under the American Convention.

The Commission amended its Rules of Procedure in 2001 in order to give greater normative value to their decisions which, according to the American Convention, are not explicitly defined as legally binding. The most important amendment has been in Rule 44, which provides that if the state has not complied with the Inter-American Commission's recommendations as set forth in the merits report on the case, the case shall be sent to the Inter-American Court of Human Rights, unless four members of the Commission take a reasoned decision that it should not be sent. This change in the Rules will undoubtedly lead to a greater number of cases being sent to the Inter-American Court. In this year alone, ten cases had already been sent as of July, whereas in all of last year only seven cases were sent to the Inter-American Court.

The Inter-American Court of Human Rights also amended its Rules of Procedure, and the most significant amendment was to Rule 23, which grants autonomy to the representatives of the victims. Whereas previously the alleged victims could only speak before the Inter-American Court through the Inter-American Commission on Human Rights, except for the reparations stage of the proceedings, now they are autonomous throughout the entire proceedings. Unlinking the alleged victims from the Inter-American Commission will doubtless also result in a change in the role of the Commission before the Inter-American Court. Until now, the Inter-American Commission's role was that of a quasi-judicial organ when the

2. Report No. 28/92, Cases 10.147, 10.181, 10.240, 10.262, 10.309 and 10.311 (Argentina), Oct. 2, 1992 and Report No. 29/92, Cases 10.029, 10.036, 10.145, 10.305, 10.372, 10.373, 10.374 and 10.375 (Uruguay), Oct. 2, 1992 in OEA/Ser.L/V/III.27, doc. 10, IACHR, ANNUAL REPORT 1992. The Annual Reports of the Commission are accessible on the Commission's web site, *available at* http://www.cidh.oas.org (last visited Aug. 22, 2003).

case was pending before it; when it decided the case, it was transformed into the advocate of alleged victims before the Inter-American Court. The representatives of alleged victims, in many ways the true party to the case, were euphemistically known as the assistants of the Inter-American Commission's delegates. Now, the courtroom will be reconfigured and alleged victims and the state will have their respective seats before the Inter-American Court as the parties to an individual case, whereas the Inter-American Commission is a party only in the procedural sense, and will modify its role, foreseeably, to that of defender of the best interests of the system.

As regards the larger issue of state compliance with decisions of the system, having been very much involved with the cases presented by the Inter-American Commission on Human Rights to the Inter-American Court of Human Rights against the government of Peru during the 1990s, I will take my examples from that period.

In April 1992, President Fujimori abolished the Peruvian Congress and Supreme Court, and was accused of having perpetrated a coup against his own government, a so-called autogolpe. In an act of political brinkmanship, President Fujimori appeared a month later at the OAS General Assembly, held in the Bahamas, normally a political gathering of foreign ministers of the region, which is generally only attended by one head of state, that of the host country. President Fujimori came to the OAS General Assembly in order to make a plea to the foreign ministers of the region to accompany him in a democratization process which would culminate in the election of a more representative Congress. The OAS, which was actively involved in monitoring democratic transitions in the hemisphere and observing electoral processes, could not refuse to provide the assistance requested by the Peruvian head of state. With OAS assistance, elections were held and a new Congress was elected. Soon thereafter, a new constitution, the Peruvian Constitution of 1993, was adopted. The 1979 Peruvian Constitution did not permit the re-election of the President, but the 1993 Constitution allowed one re-election. As a consequence, President Fujimori was re-elected in 1995. He sought re-election again five years later, although the 1993 Constitution only allowed one consecutive re-election.

In order to deal with the problem of one consecutive re-election, President Fujimori's lawyers argued that since the 1993 Constitution came into force in 1993, that period should be considered as his first term under the new Constitution, although in reality it was his second term. The new Congress, which was controlled by President Fujimori's political party, adopted a law to allow the President to run for re-election. Three judges of Peru's Constitutional Tribunal, however, decided that this law, facilitating the President's unprecedented re-election, was unconstitutional. In reprisal, the government-party-dominated Congress impeached the three judges of the Constitutional Tribunal. These three judges, in turn, presented a petition to the Inter-American Commission on Human Rights, alleging violation of their rights, stating that their impeachment had been driven by political motives and without the requisite guarantees of due process. The case was a quintessential political case, presented to the Inter-American Commission by Lourdes Flores, a lawyer and politician, who, before the Inter-American Court of Human Rights, was considered the assistant to the Delegates of the Commission.

The processing of *Constitutional Tribunal* was complicated by the fact that on July 9, 1999, the government of Peru withdrew its acceptance of the Inter-American Court's contentious jurisdiction under Article 62(2) of the American Convention.

In May 1999, the Inter-American Court of Human Rights had issued its judgment in *Castillo Petruzzi*, which involved four Chilean civilian nationals who were convicted of terrorism by a military court in a judicial proceeding that was held to be devoid of due process. The Inter-American Court, in its judgment, called for the Chileans to be retried in a civilian court and to be provided with due process guarantees. In an earlier case, however, *Maria Elena Loayza,* the Inter-American Court, in a judgment dated September 19, 1997, ordered the release of a Peruvian wrongfully imprisoned on charges of terrorism. Loayza, a civilian, had been tried twice, first by a military court and then by a civilian court, on the same facts and for the same crime, in violation of the principle *non bis in idem* (double jeopardy) set forth in the American Convention. The government of Peru, to everyone's surprise, within a month of the decision, released Loayza in compliance with this judgment, but two years later, in 1999, in the context of the *Castillo Petruzzi* judgment, it announced that it would not release the four Chileans. President Fujimori accused the Inter-American Court of calling for the release of all three thousand terrorist prisoners in Peruvian prisons.

Ostensibly, in order to prevent being ordered to release all the convicted terrorists, President Fujimori announced that Peru would withdraw from the Inter-American Court of Human Rights, and on July 9, 1999, it presented its declaration of withdrawal from the Inter-American Court's contentious jurisdiction to the OAS Secretary General. A week earlier, on July 2, 1999, the Inter-American Commission on Human Rights had filed its Application on behalf of the three impeached judges in *Constitutional Tribunal* with the Inter-American Court. The Inter-American Court had to determine whether it still had the competence to examine the case.

Article 78 of the American Convention allows a state to denounce the American Convention at the expiration of a five-year period from the date of its entry into force and by means of notice given one year in advance. Peru, however, did not attempt to denounce the American Convention, but rather expressed its intent to remain a state party, while withdrawing its unilateral acceptance of the Inter-American Court's contentious jurisdiction, effective immediately. It argued that since several states had ratified the American Convention without accepting the jurisdiction of the Inter-American Court of Human Rights (e.g., Grenada and Jamaica), that a state that had accepted the contentious jurisdiction could subsequently withdraw that acceptance, if it chose to do so. It would simply be placed in that earlier position which Grenada and Jamaica found themselves in at the time.

The Commission, for its part, argued that the Convention did not provide for the withdrawal of acceptance of the Inter-American Court's jurisdiction once it was accepted and, therefore, it was not possible for Peru to do so. The only possibility for the state to remove itself from the Inter-American Court's jurisdiction was by means of a complete denunciation of the American Convention, under Article 78, and that denunciation would not take effect immediately, but only following the expiration of a one year period.

The Inter-American Court of Human Rights, in its decision on the issue of competence raised in this case, accepted the Commission's argument, and held that it was competent to decide this case and also a second pending case that was filed on behalf of Baruch Ivcher Bronstein, the majority owner of a television station that broadcast investigative reports critical of the government. Ivcher, a Peruvian-Israeli dual national, was stripped of his Peruvian nationality in a procedure devoid of due process guarantees in order to remove the television station from his control, since under Peruvian law telecommunications could only be in the hands of Peruvian nationals.

Consequently, in both of these cases, *Constitutional Tribunal* and *Baruch Ivcher Bronstein*, the government of Peru, despite having participated in the litigation of the case before the Commission and initially before the Inter-American Court on the issue of competence, refused to participate in the actual litigation of the merits. Given the high profile of these cases and the scandal surrounding Peru's withdrawal from the Inter-American Court of Human Rights, the existence of these cases before the human rights organs of the inter-American system without the participation of the Peruvian state contributed to the undermining of the integrity of the Fujimori government. Since the Inter-American Court held Peru's purported withdrawal to be "inadmissible" since it did not conform to Article 78 of the Convention, it proceeded to hear the case on the merits, but without the presence of the governmental representatives. In fact, the first day of the public hearing on the merits of *Baruch Ivcher Bronstein* before the Inter-American Court took place on Monday, November 20, 2000, the same day on which President Fujimori, from Japan, presented his letter of renunciation of the Presidency to the Peruvian Congress.

Following the renunciation of President Fujimori, the Inter-American Commission on Human Rights encountered completely changed circumstances in dealing with the transitional government of President Paniagua, a highly regarded constitutional lawyer. The Peruvian government did not participate in the litigation of *Constitutional Tribunal* and *Baruch Ivcher Bronstein* before the Inter-American Court of Human Rights, and the Inter-American Court found for the Inter-American Commission/petitioners. On February 9, 2001, the Minister of Justice of Peru, Diego Garcia Sayan traveled to Costa Rica and presented the Inter-American Court with a note reaffirming Peru's acceptance of the contentious jurisdiction, without interruption, since its original declaration was deposited with the OAS on January 21, 1981, thereby disavowing former President Fujimori's attempt to withdraw in 1999. Under the transitional government, the three magistrates were reinstated in their former positions as magistrates of the Constitutional Tribunal and Baruch Ivcher regained control over his television station.

Another politically important case by the Inter-American Commission on Human Rights presented to the Inter-American Court against the government of Peru was *Barrios Altos*, which involved the Peruvian amnesty laws. This case involved the mistaken killing, in 1991, of some fifteen individuals and the injury of four others at a private block party in an apartment as a result of a raid carried out by a paramilitary commando team. The Peruvian security forces had targeted suspected members of the terrorist organization, Sendero Luminoso, but their information was incorrect and instead innocent civilians were killed and injured. This case was being investigated when, in order to halt the investigation, the Peruvian Congress passed an amnesty law to prevent the investigation from continuing and the prosecution of those responsible. Judge Saquicuray, who presided over the judicial proceedings in this case, took the position that the amnesty law did not affect the case that she was trying. In response, the Peruvian Congress passed a second amnesty law, which specifically prohibited any judicial review of the first amnesty law. On February 19, 2001, the transitional government of President Paniagua acknowledged Peru's international responsibility in the case. Subsequently, on March 14, 2001, the Inter-American Court delivered its judgment on the merits and as a result the Peruvian amnesty laws were rendered ineffectual.

It is also worth mentioning some cases in which the member states of the OAS have not complied with the decisions of the human rights organs of the inter-American system. One prominent case of noncompliance involves the United States and the detention of over three hundred persons at the U.S. Naval Base at Guantanamo Bay, Cuba. These persons were detained in early 2002 in Afghanistan, Pakistan, Bosnia, Algeria, and other locations and brought to Cuba; they represent approximately forty nationalities, including those of U.S. allies, such as Great Britain and Australia. They are being indefinitely held without charges, without access to lawyers, in conditions described as humiliating, and are being deprived of any information regarding their status or their future.

On November 13, 2001, President Bush issued a Military Order that stated that no U.S., foreign, or international court has jurisdiction over suspected terrorists. As early as January 2002, U.S. lawyers filed for habeas relief on behalf of the Guantanamo detainees in the U.S. District Court in the Central District of California. The district court dismissed the suit for lack of standing since none of the lawyers had contact with any of the detainees, and did not even know any of their names. Shortly thereafter, in February 2002, a second habeas suit was filed on behalf of several British, Australian, and Kuwaiti detainees who had been identified, since delegations from the International Committee of the Red Cross and from these friendly governments had been allowed to visit their nationals at Guantanamo and to facilitate correspondence with family members, who were thereby notified of their whereabouts. Yet, once again, the district court, this time in the D.C. Circuit, threw out the request for habeas relief on the grounds of lack of jurisdiction, basing its decision on the precedent set forth in an old Supreme Court case, *Johnson v. Eisentrager*.

The petitioners in both cases appealed to the respective courts of appeal. Both the Ninth Circuit and the D.C. Circuit Courts of Appeal threw out the appeals, for lack of standing and for lack of jurisdiction, respectively.

In March 2002, having exhausted their domestic remedies, the petitioners came to the Inter-American Commission on Human Rights and requested precautionary measures, arguing the seriousness of the violations and the urgency of their situation, since these individuals had been arbitrarily detained for over a year, and were in danger of irreparable harm.[3] The Inter-American Commission granted the request for precautionary measures and requested that the United States clarify the status of these persons who were under its jurisdiction and control.

The United States rejected the Inter-American Commission's precautionary measures and responded that there was no doubt as to the status of the detainees, that they were enemy combatants and that only international humanitarian law was applicable to their situation, not international human rights law. Further, the United States had never consented to the Inter-American Commission applying norms of international humanitarian law to OAS member states.

Another important example of noncompliance involves the mandatory application of the death penalty in certain states in the Caribbean. The Inter-American Commission on Human Rights has held in a number of cases that the mandatory application of the death penalty for murder violates the American Convention for failure to give individual consideration in the sentencing phase. In a case involving the United States, it held that the execution of juvenile offenders who commit capital crimes also violates the American Declaration, even though the Declaration does not specifically address the issue of juvenile offenders who commit capital crimes, in contrast to the American Convention. The Inter-American Commission, however, uses the American Convention to interpret the Declaration, since the two instruments must be seen as complementary, and as interpreting the same rights in the same way. This has led to criticism, however, that the Inter-American Commission is holding states that have not yet ratified the Convention to the same standard of compliance as those that have, despite the difference in the instruments.

Article 4 of the American Convention specifically prohibits the imposition of the death penalty on persons who committed capital crimes under the age of 18. In addition, the member states of the OAS have adopted an Additional Protocol to the American Convention, calling for the abolition of the death penalty. The tendency of international human rights law is toward the abolition of the death penalty, although the death penalty, per se, is not yet illegal. In this recent decision of the Inter-American Commission on Human Rights, involving the imposition of the death penalty in the United States, the Commission held that the international human rights law prohibition on the execution of minors had

3. The filings in this request for precautionary measures are on the petitioners' web site. *See* Center for Constitutional Rights web site, *available at* http://www.ccr-ny.org (last visited Aug. 22, 2003).

evolved into a norm of *jus cogens*.[4] As with the Guantanamo detainees case, the United States has ignored this decision.

V. WHAT RECOMMENDATIONS CAN WE MAKE TO THIS CONFERENCE?

Since this conference deals with the issue of the rule of law I would recommend that the University of Florida's law school teach the OAS system. Currently, only one law school in the United States seriously teaches the inter-American system for the protection of human rights. The Washington College of Law at American University has sponsored for a number of years an annual Moot Court competition on the inter-American system, and approximately two hundred law schools throughout the hemisphere now participate in this annual event. It is an excellent way for students to learn the jurisprudence of the inter-American system for the protection of human rights. Furthermore, American University's law school, with the assistance of donors in the Netherlands, has established a case law digest of inter-American jurisprudence, which is available on the University's web site. It also has a clinic where students learn how to present cases to the Inter-American Commission on Human Rights, and since they are located in Washington, students attend hearings while the Commission is in session. Lastly, American University's law school sponsors a Summer Human Rights Academy, where students study the inter-American and European systems, as well as the United Nations system for the protection of human rights and international humanitarian law and other subjects.

There is no reason why the Washington College of Law at American University should be the only U.S. law school engaged in teaching the inter-American system as a separate course and not simply as part of international humanitarian law or international law generally. The University of Florida could create a legal aid clinic, for example, to assist petitioners in bringing cases to the Inter-American Commission on Human Rights. It could send students to work as fellows and interns at the Inter-American Commission and the Inter-American Court of Human Rights in an arrangement such as the one we have with Notre Dame's law school, where the University pays half of the student's maintenance expenses and the Commission pays the other half. The Inter-American Commission and Inter-American Court are seriously understaffed and would be pleased to take on more students as junior lawyers.

4. Report No. 62/02, Michael Domingues, Case 12.285 (United States), Oct. 22, 2002. OEA/Ser.L/V/II.117, Doc. 5, rev. 1, Mar. 7, 2003, IACHR, ANNUAL REPORT 2002, vol. 2.

Further, the law school could hold training seminars for judges and lawyers on the obligations of state parties to the American Convention. There are model laws, such as Law 288 in Colombia, which could be used as examples for other countries to follow in reforming their own legislation to achieve compliance with the judgments of the Inter-American Court of Human Rights.

Also, the University of Florida's law school, in conjunction with other law schools, could advocate and propose to the government suitable candidates for membership on the Inter-American Commission on Human Rights and the Inter-American Court of Human Rights. Each body has seven members, who pursuant to their respective statutes, are persons of recognized competence in the field of human rights. As states seek candidates for these posts, law schools and bar associations could play a significant role in promoting distinguished individuals in order to prevent the process deteriorating into a political patronage system.

Lastly, the Inter-American Commission on Human Rights has established Rapporteurships in a number of areas, such as freedom of expression, women's rights, children's rights, indigenous people's rights, etc. The University of Florida's law school could advocate the creation of new Rapporteurships and could assist the Inter-American Commission's Rapporteurs by presenting their own studies in these areas and identifying new directions of study. Further, members of the University of Florida's law school faculty could write articles about the work of the Inter-American Commission and the Inter-American Court, studying and analyzing its growing jurisprudence, and educating the public at large about U.S. obligations in the field of international law. Recently, in *Lawrence v. Texas*, the U.S. Supreme Court for the first time recognized the existence of the jurisprudence of the European Court. While the United States is not in Europe, it is in the Americas, and common sense would suggest that U.S courts will soon look to the jurisprudence of the Inter-American Court as well. The academic community could play a greater role in assisting and analyzing the work of the inter-American system, and thereby improving it. More importantly, scholars can help the system achieve legitimacy as an important vehicle for upholding the rule of law in this country, as well as in this hemisphere.

[7]

History and Action: The Inter-American Human Rights System and the Role of the Inter-American Commission on Human Rights

*Robert K. Goldman**

ABSTRACT

This article examines the historical origins of the Inter-American human rights system and key achievements of the Inter-American Commission on Human Rights over the past fifty years. It explores the Commission's use of on sight visits and country reports to expose human rights violations of military governments during the 1970s and its increased use of the case system since the restoration of democratic rule in the 1990s. The article also notes how shifts in US foreign policy toward the region impacted the Commission's work. It concludes by noting certain obstacles and challenges currently faced by the Commission.

I. INTRODUCTION

The year 2009 marked the fiftieth anniversary of the creation of the Inter-American Commission on Human Rights (Commission) and the thirty-first anniversary of the entry into force of the American Convention on Human Rights (American Convention) and the creation of the Inter-American Court of Human Rights (Court). Although the Commission is neither as old, nor as

---

* *Robert K. Goldman* is Professor of Law & Louis C. James Scholar and Co-Director, Center for Human Rights & Humanitarian Law, American University Washington College of Law. He was a member of the Inter-American Commission on Human Rights from 1996 to 2004 and its President from February 1999 to March 2000.

I am greatly indebted to Diego H. Alcala Laboy, Esq. and Matias Hernandez, Esq., my former Dean's Fellows, for their considerable assistance in the preparation of this article.

well known for its accomplishments as the European Court of Human Rights or the former European Human Rights Commission, no regional human rights body has continuously had to cope with more crises and endemic problems in more countries than has the Commission and, to some extent, the Court. Indeed, if the saving of lives and the securing of broad reparations to victims are appropriate measurements of the effectiveness of any such supervisory bodies, then arguably no other system has been more successful than the Inter-American system.

This article traces the historical origins of the Inter-American human rights system and identifies some of the conflicting policies that helped shape it. The article also focuses on various notable activities and achievements of the Commission during three discreet periods between 1960 and 2004. In addition, it briefly notes key themes and shifts in US foreign policy toward the region and how they impacted the Commission's work. The article concludes by examining certain obstacles faced by the Commission in discharging it mandate.

II. ORIGINS OF THE INTER-AMERICAN HUMAN RIGHTS SYSTEM

The persistent intervention of the United States into the domestic affairs of its Latin American neighbors in the early part of the twentieth century stimulated Latin American efforts to establish a regional public order system based on the principles of non-intervention and the sovereign equality of states. Early efforts in support of human rights were directed primarily toward this goal. One commentator has noted that "[t]he apparent readiness to overlook the inherent contradiction between the international protection of human rights and the regional doctrine of non-intervention has been a familiar and notable characteristic of Inter-American conferences and of the work product of regional juridical bodies. When the contradiction was perceived at all, it was some time resolved in favor of the doctrine of non-intervention."[1]

Expressions of commitment to the protection of human rights were common in the early Inter-American conferences and occasionally were embodied in agreements concerning civil and political rights. For example, the Third Pan American Conference of 1906 approved the Convention Establishing the Status of Naturalized Citizens who Again Take up Their Residence in the Country of Their Origin. The Sixth International Conference of American

1. José Cabranes, *The Protection of Human Rights by the Organization of American States*, 62 Am. J. Int'l L. 889, 892-93 (1968). *See also* Thomas Buergenthal & Dinah Shelton, Protecting Human Rights in the Americas: Cases and Materials (4th rev. ed. 1995); Scott Davidson, The Inter-American Human Rights System (1997); The Inter-American System of Human Rights (David J. Harris & Stephen Livingstone eds., 1998).

States, held in Havana in 1928, approved the Convention on the Status of Aliens and the Convention on the Right to Asylum.

The Good Neighbor Policy, proclaimed by President Franklin D. Roosevelt in his inaugural address of 1933 put Latin America on notice that unilateral intervention would no longer be the operative principle of US diplomacy in the region. At the Seventh International Conference of American States held later that year, the United States and the Latin American republics ratified the Convention on the Rights and Duties of States, which declares: "No state has the right to intervene in internal or external affairs of another."[2] The Conference also approved conventions on Political Asylum and on Extradition. In 1936, at the Inter-American Conference for the Maintenance of Peace, the American states again affirmed their collective commitment to the principle of non-intervention by adopting a protocol declaring the inadmissibility of any form of intervention, regardless of the reason.[3] The Conference also approved a resolution on the Duties and Rights of Women with Respect to Problems of Peace. In 1938, the American states convened in Lima and adopted two significant resolutions concerning Freedom of Association and Freedom of Expression for Workers and Defense of Human Rights. It was not until the end of World War II, however, that concern for human rights became the subject of regional as well as worldwide attention.

The American states began shaping an incipient regional program for the protection of human rights at the Inter-American Conference on Problems of War and Peace, the so-called Chapultepec Conference, convened in 1945 to consider the postwar directions of the Inter-American system. The participants adopted a resolution on the International Protection of the Essential Rights of Man that stated in part:

> International protection of essential rights of man would eliminate the misuse of diplomatic protection of citizens abroad, the exercise of which has more than once led to the violation of the principles of non-intervention and of equality between nationals and aliens, with respect to the essential rights of man.[4]

The language of the resolution highlights the intent of the states to strengthen the doctrine of absolute non-intervention.

The Conference assigned the Inter-American Juridical Committee (IAJC) the task of drafting a convention on the International Rights and Duties of Man for submission to an International Conference of American Jurists.

---

2. Convention on Rights and Duties of States, Seventh International Conference of American States, *signed* 26 Dec.1933, 49 Stat. 3097, T.S. No. 881, in The International Conferences of American States 121-23 (1st Supp. 1940).
3. Additional Protocol Relative to Non-Intervention, Inter-American Conference for the Maintenance of Peace, *signed* 23 Dec.1936, 51 Stat. 41, T.S. No. 922, in The International Conferences of American States 129 (1st Supp. 1940).
4. Resolution XL, in *Report of the Delegation of the United States of America to the Inter-American Conference on Problems of War and Peace* 108 (1946).

The goal of the Latin American republics to establish non-intervention as an authoritative principle of the region's public order was finally realized by the signing of the Charter of the Organization of American States[5] at the Ninth International Conference of American States held in Bogotá in 1948. Articles 19 and 21 of the Charter restate the 1933 and 1936 declarations in the following language:

> Art. 19: No State or group of States has the right to intervene, directly or indirectly, for any reason whatever, in the internal or external affairs of any other State. The foregoing principle prohibits not only armed force but also any other form of interference or attempted threat against its political, economic, and cultural elements.
>
> Art. 21: The territory of a State is inviolable; it may not be the object, even temporarily, of military occupation or of other measures of force taken by another State, directly or indirectly, on any grounds whatever. No territorial acquisitions or special advantages obtained either by force or by other means of coercion shall be recognized.[6]

Another essential tenet of the new Inter-American system was expressed in the preamble of the Charter: "[T]he true significance of American solidarity and good neighborliness can only mean the consolidation on the continent, within the framework of democratic institutions, of a system of individual liberty and social justice based on respect for the essential rights of man."[7]

III. THE AMERICAN DECLARATION OF THE RIGHTS AND DUTIES OF MAN

Consistent with the preamble of the Charter and the declarations of the Chapultepec Conference, the American States signed on 2 May 1948, the world's first major international document on human rights, the American Declaration of the Rights and Duties of Man (American Declaration),[8] which preceded the UN Universal Declaration of Human Rights by seven months.

Reflecting natural law theory, the American Declaration asserts that the fundamental rights of man "are not derived from the fact that he is a national

---

5. Charter of the Organization of American States, *adopted* 30 Apr.1948, 2 U.S.T. 2394, 199 U.N.T.S. 3 (*entered into force* 13 Dec. 1951).
6. *Id.*
7. *Id.*
8. American Declaration on the Rights and Duties of Man, O.A.S. Res. XXX, *adopted* 2 May 1948, *reprinted* in Basic Documents Pertaining to Human Rights in the Inter-American System, O.A.S. Doc. OEA/Ser.L.V//II.82, doc.6 rev.1, at 17 (1992).

of a certain state, but are based upon attributes of his human personality."[9] The international protection of these rights "should be the principal guide of an evolving American law" and strengthened "as conditions become more favorable."[10]

The document enumerates civil and political as well as economic and social rights. The civil and political rights largely restate those already guaranteed in the constitutions of most American states. Among these are the rights to equality before the law, to due process of law, of petition and assembly, to religious freedom and worship, to protection from arbitrary arrest, and to the inviolability of the home. In contrast, the economic and social rights proclaimed therein had not been the objects of legislative prescription or judicial protection in many of the American republics. The most significant of these rights are: right to the preservation of health and to well-being; to the benefits of culture; to work and to a fair remuneration for work; to leisure time, to wholesome recreation, cultural, and physical benefit. The American Declaration also proclaims affirmative duties or standards of conduct which are meant to guide individuals in their societal relations. Among these are: the duty to receive instruction; to vote; to obey the law; to serve the community and the nation; to work; and to pay taxes.

Despite their noble statement, the American states chose not to make the American Declaration binding on its signatories, nor did they create any machinery to promote, much less protect, the rights they had just proclaimed. The Conference instead passed a resolution recognizing the need for an Inter-American Court to protect these rights and requested the IAJC to draft a statute for such organ. The IAJC politely declined the invitation on the ground that it was premature to do so and that it "would involve a radical transformation of the constitutional systems in all the American countries"[11] and also advised the Inter-American Council of Jurists that the preparation of a binding agreement on human rights should precede the statute of the proposed court.

Consideration of the statute was postponed until 1953 when the Council of Jurists asked the Council of the Organization of American States (OAS) if it would be appropriate to place the matter of the statute on the agenda of the Tenth Conference. The OAS Council, reflecting the views of the IAJC, felt that the time was not yet ripe to discuss the proposed statute. In the meantime, further development on human rights were still ongoing as evidenced by the approval of new resolutions on Improvement of the Social, Economic,

9. *Id.*
10. *Id.*
11. Appendix III, Inter-American Juridical Committee, *Report to the Inter-American Council of Jurists concerning Resolution XXXI of the Bogotá Conference*, in Pan American Union, Human Rights in the American States, at 166 (1960).

and Cultural Levels of the Peoples of the Americas and The Strengthening and Effective Exercise of Democracy by the Ministers of Foreign Affairs at the Fourth Meeting of Consultation in 1951.

The Tenth Inter-American Conference, held in Caracas in 1954, did nothing to implement the American Declaration but discussed measures tending to promote human rights, without detriment to national sovereignty and the principle of non-intervention. The American states approved resolutions on Racial Discrimination, Universal Suffrage, and The Strengthening of the System for the Protection of Human Rights. Reaffirming the American states' commitment to the rights enunciated in the American Declaration, the Conference urged its constituency to "adopt progressively measures to adjust their domestic legislation to the Declaration" and to take appropriate measures "to ensure the faithful observance of these rights."[12] The Conference asked the Council of the OAS to continue studying the juridical aspects of regional protection of human rights and the feasibility of creating an Inter-American Court to protect them. The Council delegated the matter to its Juridical Committee and its Subcommittee on Human Rights, where no further action was taken until political events propelled the matter to the forefront.

In 1959 the Fifth Meeting of Consultation of Foreign Ministers was convened in Santiago, Chile to consider the political unrest in the Caribbean, followed by the Sixth Meeting of Ministers of Foreign Affairs which met in 1960 to hear Venezuela's charge that the Dominican Republic's dictator, Rafael Trujillo, had attempted to have Venezuela's president assassinated.

It was at these Conferences that the American states shed their apathy toward human rights problems and began to shape a regional program for their protection. José Cabranes noted that

> [t]he alleged external terrorist activities of the Trujillo regime began to turn the O.A.S. toward the view that violations of human rights and denials of democratic freedoms within member states might affect the peace of the Americas and might thus become a proper concern of the Organization. It is important to stress, however, that it was the Dominican regime's alleged violation of the non-intervention doctrine itself that first prompted the O.A.S. to examine its role in promoting respect for human rights.[13]

Taking note of the wholesale disregard of fundamental liberties in Trujillo's country, the 1959 Conference stressed the interrelationship between the deprivation of human rights and the existence of anti-democratic regimes. The Foreign Ministers proclaimed this concern in the Declaration of Santiago

12. *Id.* Appendix IV, Resolution XXVII, Strengthening of the System for the Protection of Human Rights, at 170.
13. José Cabranes, *Human Rights and Non-Intervention in the Inter-American System*, 65 Mich. L. Rev. 1147, 1164 (1967).

which states that "the harmony among the American Republics only can be effective as long as respect of human rights and fundamental freedoms and the exercise of representative democracy are a reality in the internal workings of each of them."[14] The Ministers, thereupon, passed a two-part resolution entitled Human Rights. Part I entrusted the Inter-American Court of Justice (IACJ) with the task of drafting a convention(s) establishing a regional court and other machinery to protect these rights, while Part II called for the creation of an Inter-American Commission on Human Rights having "the specific functions that the Council [of the OAS] assigns to it" and "charged with furthering respect of such rights."[15]

In May-June 1960, the Council of the OAS approved the statute of the Inter-American Commission on Human Rights. Under the statute, the Commission is "an autonomous entity"[16] of the OAS whose function is to promote respect for human rights as set forth in the Declaration of the Rights and Duties of Man. The Commission was assigned the following functions and powers in Article 9 of its Statute:

(a) To develop an awareness of human rights among the peoples of America;

(b) To make recommendations to the governments of the member states general, if it considers such action advisable, for the adoption of progressive measures in favor of human rights within the framework of their domestic legislation and, in accordance with their constitutional precepts, appropriate measures to further the faithful observance of those rights;

(c) To prepare such studies or reports as it considers advisable in the performance of its duties;

(d) To urge the governments of the member states to supply it with information on the measures of human rights;

(e) To serve the O.A.S. as an advisory body in respect of human rights.[17]

The Commission would consist of seven members, all nationals of OAS member states, "of high moral character and recognized competence in the field of human rights."[18] Its members are elected for four-year terms by the governments of the member states and may be re-elected for one additional term.

14. Final Act, Fifth Meeting of Consultation of Ministers of Foreign Affairs, Santiago, Chile, Inter-Am. C.H.R., O.A.S. Doc. OEA/Ser. C/11.5, at 3 (1960).
15. *Id.* at 10-11.
16. Statute of the Inter-American Commission on Human Rights, *adopted* 25 May 1960, O.A.S. Doc. OEA/Ser.L/V/I.1 (1960).
17. *Id.* art. 9.
18. *Id.*

IV. THE BACKGROUND OF THE AMERICAN CONVENTION ON HUMAN RIGHTS

As previously mentioned, the American Declaration was merely a non-binding statement of moral obligations. In view of the widespread denial of fundamental liberties in many American states, the OAS realized that moral obligations are best observed when translated into binding legal obligations. As discussed in 1959, the Foreign Ministers at the Fifth Meeting of Consultation assigned the IACJ to draft a binding convention on human rights including the instrumentalities for their protection. However, compared with the rapid development of the Inter-American Commission, the elaboration of the American Convention proceeded slowly.[19]

The IACJ undertook the assignment and approved at its Fourth Meeting in Santiago on 8 September 1959, a draft convention on human rights for adoption at the Eleventh Inter-American Conference. Its draft enumerated substantive economic, social, and cultural rights as well as civil and political rights. Because of the Bay of Pigs fiasco, the Inter-American Conference was not held in 1961, and consideration of the draft convention was postponed until the Second Special Inter-American Conference that met in November 1965 in Rio de Janeiro. There it was decided to send the draft convention and alternative drafts submitted by Chile and Uruguay to the Council of the OAS. The Council was instructed to receive the views of the Commission and other interested bodies on the draft and prepare a final draft by 1966 for submission to a specialized conference on human rights in March 1967.

After reviewing the IACJ draft, the Commission suggested to the OAS Council that the economic, cultural, and social rights, except those rights concerning labor unions, be deleted. It also recommended the deletion of provisions on permanent sovereignty over natural resources and self-determination. The Commission stated that it was inappropriate to reaffirm and include such rights and principles in a convention on human rights. Instead, it suggested the inclusion of general provisions calling upon member nations to adopt domestic means to implement and further these rights.

Consideration of the new draft convention was postponed in 1967, once again, by a new development. The General Assembly of the United Nations, on 16 December 1966, approved the International Covenant on Economic, Social, and Cultural Rights, the International Covenant on Civil and Political Rights, and an Optional Protocol to the latter covenant. By the end of September 1967, the first covenant was signed by Costa Rica, Colombia, Honduras, El Salvador, and Uruguay, and the second, by the same countries

19. American Convention on Human Rights, *signed* 22 Nov. 1969, O.A.S.T.S. No. 36, 1144 U.N.T.S. 123, O.A.S. Doc. OEA/Ser.L/V/II.23, doc. 21, rev. 6 (1979) (*entered into force* 18 July 1978).

and Ecuador. (By the end of 1970, however, only Costa Rica, Colombia, Ecuador, and Uruguay had ratified the covenants.) Noting this action by member states and the similar substantive rights proposed in the IACJ draft and the UN covenants, but different institutional machinery to protect these rights, in May 1967, the OAS Committee on Legal and Political Affairs alerted the OAS Council of the possibility of conflict between the worldwide and regional programs aimed to protect human rights. Accordingly, it suggested, and the Council concurred, that further consideration of the IACJ draft be deferred until member states were consulted. The Council then submitted the following two questions to member states:

> 1. Whether the governments of the American states, in approving, at the Twenty-first Session of the General Assembly of the United Nations, Resolutions A, B, and C, concerning the international covenants on human rights, wished to establish a single universal system of regulation of human rights; or whether on the contrary they contemplated the possibility of the coexistence and co-ordination of the worldwide and regional conventions on the same rights.
>
> 2. Whether, in the latter case, those governments consider that the Inter-American Convention on Human Rights provided for in Article 112 of the Protocol of Amendment to the Charter of the Organization of American States should be limited to establishing an inter-American institutional and procedural system for the protection of those rights that would include the Inter-American Commission on Human Rights and, eventually, an Inter-American Court of Human Rights.[20]

Of the twelve states replying to the first question, ten—including Bolivia, Chile, Colombia, Costa Rica, Ecuador, Guatemala, Mexico, the United States, Uruguay, and Venezuela—expressed their opinion in favor of "the coexistence and coordination" of the UN covenants and an Inter-American convention. Only two countries, Argentina and Brazil, deemed it inadvisable to continue drafting a regional convention in light of the UN actions. In response to the second question, however, only five states—Ecuador, Guatemala, Venezuela, Colombia, and Costa Rica—advocated that the proposed convention should include procedural rules as well as substantive principles. Chile and Uruguay, on the other hand, stated that the Convention should provide only for the creation of an institutional and procedural system. Chile took the position that to avoid conflict between the two systems, the Inter-American machinery should apply only substantive law approved by the United Nations. The United States and Mexico took no definitive position on this question. The United States equivocated in its response, stating that the American

---

20. Permanent Council, *Report on a Consultation with the Member States Regarding the Draft Convention on Human Rights,* submitted by the Committee on Juridical and Political Affairs, Inter-Am. C.H.R., O.A.S. Doc. OEA/Ser.G/IV Rev. 3, 4 (1967).

Convention should not necessarily be limited to institutional and procedural articles, although this might be a satisfactory approach.[21] In view of the possible conflict between the UN covenants and the IACJ draft, the United States indicated that it could make an informed judgment on the matter if a study comparing the substantive provisions of the UN covenants and the various Inter-American conventions were made available to member states. The Secretariat of the Commission undertook these studies and concluded that both systems could coexist.[22] Specifically, it stated:

> The need for, and the desirability of, a regional convention for the Americas are based on the existence of a body of American international law built up in accordance with the specific requirements of the countries of this hemisphere. That need and desirability also follow from the close relationship that exists between human rights and regional economic development and integration, in accordance with the statements of the Chiefs of State made at the meeting in Punta del Este.
>
> Consequently the Inter-American Convention on the Protection of Human Rights should be autonomous rather than complementary to the United Nations covenants, although it should indeed be coordinated with those covenants.[23]

Despite the failure of many American states to respond to either question and the obvious reluctance of many of those responding to support a separate regional system to protect substantive rights, in 1968 the OAS Council asked the IACJ to prepare a final text of the draft convention for submission to member states and adoption at a Special Inter-American Conference to be held in San Jose, Costa Rica during November 1969. The Special Conference finally approved the American Convention on Human Rights, also called the Pact of San Jose, that November.[24] The American Convention entered into force in 1978 after eleven states ratified it.

V. THE AMERICAN CONVENTION ON HUMAN RIGHTS

The American Convention with its substantive guarantees and institutional machinery is perhaps the most ambitious and far-reaching instrument of

---

21. *Comparative Study of the United Nations Covenants on Civil and Political Rights and on Economic, Social and Cultural Rights and of the Draft*, Inter-Am. C.H.R., O.A.S. Doc. OEA/Ser.L/V/II.19, doc. 18, at 10 (1968).
22. *Id. See also Comparative Study of the United Nations Covenants on Civil and Political Rights and on Economic, Social and Cultural Rights and the Draft*, Inter-Am. C.H.R., O.A.S. Doc. OEA/Ser.L/II.19, doc. 26 (1968).
23. *Comparative Study of the United Nations Covenants on Civil and Political Rights and on Economic, Social and Cultural Rights and the Draft*, Inter-Am. C.H.R., O.A.S. Doc. OEA/Ser.L/II.19, doc. 26, at 3 (1968).
24. American Convention on Human Rights, *supra* note 19.

its kind ever developed by an international body.[25] It considerably widens the scope and content of the 1948 American Declaration by the inclusion of more elaborate and specific civil and political rights. The organs for the protection of these rights in the American Convention parallel, in large measure, the institutional machinery of the European Convention. The American Convention provides for a Commission, which replicates the existing body and a purely jurisdictional organ, the Court. Unlike its European and UN counterparts, the American Convention incorporates both the rights guaranteed and their means of protection.

The entry into force of the American Convention effectively created a dual system for protecting human rights throughout the hemisphere. The American Convention became the primary source of the human rights obligations of state parties thereto, while the American Declaration and the OAS Charter continued to define the human rights obligations of those states not parties to the American Convention. The Commission, under its Statute and Regulations, is empowered to receive petitions and decide cases lodged against both kinds of states. However, it can only refer cases to the Court that are directed against states that have ratified the American Convention and have expressly accepted the Court's jurisdiction.

It is from its far-reaching nature that the American Convention derives both its strengths and weaknesses. The creation of a regional machinery to supervise domestic implementation of American Convention based rights seemed to suggest at the time that the doctrine of non-intervention was waning in the human rights area. Recognition of the right of individuals to make claims regarding violations of human rights certainly constituted a step toward the goal of vesting individuals with juridical personality under international law. Additionally, the existence of such agreements helped to promote regional and global awareness of efforts undertaken for the protection of human rights and thereby strengthened the efforts of domestic proponents supporting such measures.

It is clear, however, that at the time of its drafting, the American Convention guaranteed many civil and political rights which, although enshrined in domestic law, were largely ignored by the governments of many hemispheric countries. In this sense the American Convention essentially prescribed maximum, not minimum, human rights. Moreover, the framers of the American Convention largely transposed or projected a whole set of values and attitudes toward the law that were not widely entrenched in Latin America. The American Convention, as conceived and propounded, was surely more readily adoptable to nations with well developed, stable legal institutions and a political culture that cherished and upheld the rule of law. For example, the states that drafted and approved the European Conven-

25. *Id.*

tion were mostly genuine liberal democracies with strong and independent judiciaries. Their purpose in elaborating that convention was to strengthen and preserve existing rights, rather than to create new rights. The experience of Latin America stands in stark contrast.

Despite their nominal commitment to constitutional democracy, many Latin American states had histories of vacillating between authoritarianism and rather unsuccessful experiments in democracy. Professors Henry Steiner and Philip Alston have observed:

> The development of the inter-American system followed a different path from that of its European counterpart. Although the institutional structure is superficially very similar and the normative provisions are in most respects very similar, the conditions under which the two systems developed were radically different. Within the Council of Europe, military and other authoritarian governments have been rare and short-lived, while in Latin America they were close to being the norm until the changes that started in the 1980s.
>
> The major challenges confronting the European system are epitomized by issues such as the length of pre-trial detention and the implications of the right to privacy. Cases involving states of emergency have been relatively few. The European Commission and Court have rarely had to deal with completely unresponsive or even antagonistic governments or national legal systems, or with deep structural problems that led to systematic and serious human rights violations. . . . By contrast, states of emergency have been common in Latin America, the domestic judiciary has often been extremely weak or corrupt, and large-scale practices involving torture, disappearances and executions have not been uncommon. Many of the governments with which the Inter-American Commission and Court have had to work have been ambivalent towards those institutions at best and hostile at worst.[26]

VI. THE CREATION OF THE INTER-AMERICAN COMMISSION ON HUMAN RIGHTS: ITS PRINCIPAL ACTIVITIES BETWEEN 1960 AND 1973

Even in its formative years, the Commission attempted rather vigorously to promote and protect human rights in the Americas by examining individual complaints, making recommendations, and preparing reports concerning flagrant violations of these rights. As the late Professor Durward V. Sandifer, an early member of the Commission, observed: "With no other sanction than publicity, the Commission has effectively established its role of guard-

26. Henry Steiner & Philip Alston, International Human Rights in Context: Law, Politics, Morals 869 (2d ed. 2000). *See also* Thomas Buergenthal, *The American and European Conventions on Human Rights: Similarities and Differences*, 30 Am.U. L. Rev. 155 (1980).

ian and critic, a substantial gloss on the jealously guarded doctrine of non-intervention."[27]

For example, at its first session in 1960, the Commission broadly interpreted its authority under its statute as permitting it to make general recommendations to each, as well as to all member states concerning the adoption of progressive human rights measures within the framework of their domestic legislation.[28] In a related matter, the Commission determined that it was not empowered to rule on petitions filed with it by individuals or groups alleging human rights violations by member states. Nevertheless, it determined that it could take cognizance of such petitions by way of information. However, the uncertainty surrounding this interpretation of its competence prompted the Commission to request the OAS Council to make explicit those powers it had implicitly carved out for itself.

In 1965 the OAS passed Resolution XXII, which called for expanding the Commission's functions and powers. Accordingly, the Commission's statute was amended in 1966 to include Article 9(bis) which formally empowered it

> [t]o examine communications submitted to it and other available information; to address the government of any American state for information deemed pertinent by the Commission; and to make recommendations, when it deems this appropriate, with the objective of bringing about more effective observance of fundamental human rights.

The revised statute, Article 9(bis)(a), also requested the Commission to pay "particular attention" to observing the following human rights referred to in the American Declaration of 1948: right to life, liberty, and personal security; equality before the law; religious freedom; freedom of investigation, opinion, expression and dissemination; right to fair trial; protection from arbitrary arrest; and to due process of the law. In addition, Article 9 (bis)(c) requested the Commission

> [t]o submit a report annually to the Inter-American Conference or to the Meeting of Consultation of Ministers of Foreign Affairs, which should include: (i) a statement of progress achieved in realization of the goals set forth in the American Declaration; (ii) a statement of areas in which further steps are needed to give effect to the human rights set forth in the American Declaration; and (iii) such observations as the Commission may deem appropriate on matters covered in the communications submitted to it and in other information available to the Commission.

---

27. Durward V. Sandifer, *Human Rights in the Inter-American System,* 11 How. L.J. 508, 521-22 (1965).
28. *Report on the Work Accomplished During its First Session,* Inter-Am. C.H.R., O.A.S. Doc. OEA/Ser.L/V/III.1, doc. 32, art. 9-10 (1961).

Certainly, some of the Commission's early priorities and activities were shaped in part by the realities of the Cold War and by the agenda that the United States was pushing within the political organs of the OAS, which the United States effectively dominated at the time. With the advent of the Cold War, US Latin American policy underwent significant transformation. The Roosevelt administration's Good Neighbor Policy was replaced in the 1950s by a policy that sought to contain the spread of communism in the hemisphere. Accordingly, the United States began providing a variety of support to numerous authoritarian regimes with questionable human rights practices on the ground that they were bulwarks against communist expansion. Thus, despite its formal espousal of non-intervention and support for human rights, the United States began to intervene, militarily and otherwise, in the domestic affairs of those Latin American states it deemed sympathetic to communist ideologies.

For example, in 1954 the CIA engineered the overthrow of Jacobo Árbenz Guzmán, Guatemala's left leaning President, and succeeded in replacing him with a pro-American, rightist regime. In 1962, after the Bay of Pigs, the Eighth Meeting of Consultation, at the urging of the United States and its supporters, declared that the principles of Marxist-Leninism were incompatible with the Inter-American system and that "the alignment of . . . a government with the communist bloc breaks the unity and solidarity of the Hemisphere."[29] Shortly thereafter, Castro's government was expelled from the OAS. In 1965, President Johnson dispatched US forces without prior consultation with the OAS to the Dominican Republic with the ostensible purpose of rescuing US nationals endangered by civil strife. He subsequently clarified that the real goal of the US intervention was to help prevent the establishment of another communist government in the hemisphere.[30]

It is not surprising, therefore, that the condition of human rights in Cuba was an early priority of the Commission and has remained the object of the Commission's scrutiny since 1961. At that time, the Commission began receiving numerous petitions denouncing the inhuman treatment accorded to political prisoners by Cuban authorities. In 1962, the Commission requested the government's permission to visit and to supply relevant information concerning these denunciations. The Cuban government did not respond to either request. Thereafter, the Commission detailed human rights violations in Cuba in three reports published in 1962, 1963, and 1967.[31]

---

29. Part One, Resolution II of the Eighth Meeting of Consultation of Ministers of Foreign Affiars, (22-31 Jan. 1962), Inter-Am. C.H.R., O.A.S. Doc. *available at* http://avalon.law.yale.edu/20th_century/intam17.asp.
30. *Statement by President Johnson*, 52 Dep't St. Bull. 740, 747 (1962).
31. *Informe sobre la Situación de Derechos Humanos en la República de Cuba*, Inter-Am.C.H.R., O.A.S. Doc. OEA/Ser.L/V/II.4, doc. 2 (1962); *Informe sobre la Situación de los Presos Políticos y su Familiares en Cuba*, Inter-Am. C.H.R., O.A.S. Doc. OEA/Ser.L/V

The Commission also published two reports in 1963 and 1969, regarding charges of repeated human rights violations in Haiti.[32] In 1962 and 1964, it addressed communications to the Haitian government asking for information concerning these charges and requested permission to hold sessions in that country. The government refused to cooperate with the Commission, denouncing its requests for information as intervention in its domestic affairs. During this period, the Commission investigated and published reports concerning human rights violations in Guatemala, the Dominican Republic, Paraguay, and Nicaragua, for its own use.[33] Undoubtedly, the Commission's most notable success in this period occurred during its extraordinary mission to the Dominican Republic in 1965.[34]

Following the US intervention in the Dominican civil strife of 1965, the Foreign Ministers of the American states decided to create and send an Inter-American Peace Force whose purpose was to restore normal conditions and to uphold the human rights of the people in the Dominican Republic. Shortly thereafter, the Secretary General of the OAS asked the Commission to visit Santo Domingo to investigate numerous charges of human rights violations lodged by rival factions contending for power. From the time it arrived, the Commission played an active and important role in the peacekeeping operations. It helped protect the lives of innocent bystanders, negotiated mutual prisoner releases, and secured the release and safe-passage from the country of various political leaders. The Commission, at the invitation of the Provisional Government of the Dominican Republic, remained in the country to observe and report on the presidential election held in June of 1966. This historic mission marked the genesis of the *in loco* visit by the Commission to OAS member states.

In recognition of these efforts and others designed to protect human rights, the American states at the Third Special Inter-American Conference, held in Buenos Aires in 1967, made the Commission "a principal organ" of the OAS by signing a Protocol of Amendment to the Organization's Charter.[35] Two years later, the Commission once again became actively engaged in protecting human rights under difficult circumstances.

II.7, doc. 4 (1963); *Informe sobre la Situación de Derechos Humanos en la República de Cuba*, Inter-Am. C.H.R., O.A.S. Doc. OEA/Ser.L/V/II.17, doc. 4 (1967).

32. *Informe sobre la Situación de Derechos Humanos en Haití*, Inter-Am. C.H.R., O.A.S. Doc. OEA/Ser.L/V/II.8, doc. 5 (1963); *Informe sobre la Situación de Derechos Humanos en Haití*, Inter-Am. C.H.R., O.A.S. Doc. OEA/Ser.L/V/II.21, doc. 6 rev. (1969).
33. *See* Organization of American States, Country Reports, Inter-Am. C.H.R., O.A.S. Doc. *available at* http://www.cidh.org/pais.eng.htm.
34. *Report on the Activities of the Inter-American Commission on Human Rights in the Dominican Republic*, Inter-Am. C.H.R., O.A.S. Doc. OEA/Ser.L/V/II.13, doc.14 rev. (1965).
35. Tom Farer, *The Rise of the Inter-American Human Rights Regime: No Longer a Unicorn, Not Yet an Ox*, 19 Hum. Rts. Q. 510, 515 (1997).

Prior to the outbreak of hostilities between Honduras and El Salvador in July 1969, each state had requested that the Commission send a mission to its territory to investigate charges of atrocities committed against its nationals within the borders of the other state. The Commission immediately appointed a subcommittee to visit both countries to investigate the acts denounced. From 4-10 July 1969, the Subcommittee interviewed officials and private parties and received complaints from both governments. When hostilities erupted between the two countries on 14 July the Commission, at the request of El Salvador and other American states, sent the Preliminary Report of its Subcommittee to the Thirteenth Meeting of Consultation of Ministers of Foreign Affairs, which had convened to consider the crisis. The Commission continued to study the situations in both countries and recommended that both governments adopt appropriate procedures to ensure effective remedies to those injured and to protect against future human rights violations.[36]

In the early 1970s, the Commission began expressing concern over increasing and destabilizing acts of violence frequently perpetrated by non-state actors. Specifically, in its 1971 Annual Report, the Commission denounced terrorist acts within member states as "a massive crime that tends to create a climate of insecurity and anxiety, on the pretext of bringing about a greater degree of social justice for less-favored classes."[37]

The Commission also began urging member states to streamline judicial proceedings so that accused persons could be tried without undue delay. In addition, it stressed that penal systems should be improved so that prisons would fulfill their purpose of rehabilitation and that prisoners not endure inhuman and degrading treatment. The Commission similarly called for states to ensure that everyone have access to education, noting that illiteracy had actually increased throughout the Americas in recent years.

Most importantly, the Commission began to stress the link between the effective exercise of democracy and respect for human rights—a theme that it has continuously reiterated to this day. Taking note of the political instability in the Americas in the early 1970s, it warned rather presciently, that unless countries began to address and solve the root causes of this problem, efforts to protect human rights would be largely ineffective.

VII. COMMISSION ACTIVITIES FROM 1973 TO THE EARLY 1990S

It is worth recalling that when the American Convention was being negotiated in the mid 1960s, most OAS member states, despite their pronounced

36. *Informe sobre la situación de Derechos Humanos en El Salvador y Honduras,* Inter-Am. C.H.R., O.A.S. Doc. OEA/Ser.L/V/II.23, doc. 9 rev. (1970).
37. *Annual Report of the Inter-American Commission on Human Rights 1971,* Inter-Am. C.H.R., O.A.S. Doc. OEA/Ser.L/V/II.27, doc. 11 rev. (1972).

institutional weaknesses, did have nominally democratic and freely elected governments. However, by the time the American Convention entered into force in 1978, Argentina, Brazil, Bolivia, Chile, Peru, and Uruguay, as well as several Central American states, were ruled either by coupist military regimes or weak civilian governments under military tutelage. Many of these regimes, facing leftist insurgents or other violent groups, instituted policies that violated the most basic human rights and norms of international humanitarian law. Systematic murder, torture, and disappearances; proscription of political parties, unions, and student groups; and the censorship of the media, were among their most common emblematic practices. Furthermore, many of these regimes, particularly in South America, were particularly zealous advocates of the doctrine of national security and justified their actions, which amounted to state sponsored terrorism, as necessary to win the so called "Third World War" against international communism at home and abroad.

These regimes consistently labeled local and foreign based NGOs that denounced their excesses to the Commission as apologists for subversion. Human rights advocacy in the1970s through the late 1980s thus became identified by many elites throughout the Americas as a kind of leftist ideology which, in turn, had the unfortunate effect of tainting and politicizing the subject. Indeed, many of these governments regarded the Commission's inquiries into and eventual exposure of their illicit practices as providing aid and comfort to their internal enemies.

For its part, during the 1970s and 1980s, the United States, with the notable exception of the Carter administration, pursued policies throughout the hemisphere that further helped to politicize the effort to promote respect for human rights. This was especially the case during the Reagan administration. By largely viewing human rights through the prism of the Cold War, Reagan's government supported many of the worst human rights violators in the hemisphere based on their avowedly anti-communist credentials. In furtherance of its policy to confront and "bleed" the Soviet Union and its putative proxies throughout the world, it armed, financed and/or backed the counter-insurgency efforts of the governments of El Salvador, Guatemala, and Honduras, as well as the Nicaraguan insurgents, despite their abysmal human rights practices. It is little wonder that many in the hemisphere came to identify human rights not as a body of protective legal rules and procedures, but rather as a tool of US foreign policy that was perceived as being selectively and often inconsistently applied. At the same time, while more states in the region edged toward ratifying the American Convention, the United States declined to do so. These realities need to be understood in order to appreciate the complex environment in which the Commission operated during this period.

Perhaps the Commission's foremost achievement during this difficult period of authoritarian rule was its preparation and publication of country reports that evaluated the human rights practices of governments throughout the region, especially in Southern Cone countries.[38] Particularly noteworthy in this regard were its 1974, 1976, and 1977 reports on Chile;[39] its 1978 reports on Paraguay and Uruguay;[40] and its 1980 report on Argentina.[41] Several of these reports were the result of *in loco* visits by the Commission, while others were written at the Commission's own initiative because the states denied it permission to visit. Tom J. Farer, a member of the Commission during this period, aptly described the Commission's role thusly: "it converted itself into an accusatory agency, a kind of "Hemispheric Grand Jury," storming around Latin America to vacuum up evidence of high crimes and misdemeanors and marshalling it into bills of indictment in the form of country reports for delivery to the political organs of the OAS and the court of public opinion."[42] These reports and *in loco* visits significantly enhanced the Commission's credibility, visibility, and prestige throughout the region.

Undoubtedly, the Commission's visit to Argentina in 1979 was its most successful in terms of results.[43] Arriving in Buenos Aires at the height of the *de facto* regime's "dirty war," the Commission received the testimonies of thousands of persons, including relatives of the disappeared and other victims of the regime's excesses. The Commission's 1980 report chronicled and exposed the systematic nature of the human rights violations being perpetrated by that country's military government.[44] The report's publication has been widely credited in Argentina as having helped decrease the number of reported disappearances. Outside the hemisphere, the report was relied upon by governments and intergovernmental bodies in Europe in shaping their policies toward Argentina.

During this period, the individual petition system was not widely known outside of the Southern Cone and, hence, not that frequently used by victims

---

38. See Farer, *supra* note 35 for an insightful discussion of the Commission's activities during the late 1970s and early 1980s by a former president of that body. *See also* CECILIA MEDINA, THE BATTLE FOR HUMAN RIGHTS: GROSS, SYSTEMATIC VIOLATIONS OF HUMAN RIGHTS AND THE INTER-AMERICAN SYSTEM (1988).
39. *Report on the Status of Human Rights in Chile*, Inter-Am. C.H.R., O.A.S. Doc. OEA/Ser.L/V/II.34, doc. 21 corr. 1 (1974); *Second Report on the Situation of Human Rights in Chile*, Inter-Am. C.H.R., O.A.S. Doc. OEA/Ser.L/V/II.37, doc. 19 corr. 1 (1976); *Third Report on the Situation of Human Rights in Chile*, Inter-Am. C.H.R., O.A.S. Doc. OEA/Ser.L/V/II.40, doc. 10 (1977).
40. *Report on the Situation of Human Rights in Paraguay*, Inter-Am. C.H.R. O.A.S., Doc. OEA/Ser.L/V/II.43, doc. 13 corr. 1 (1978); *Report on the Situation of Human Rights in Uruguay*, Inter-Am. C.H.R., O.A.S. Doc. OEA/Ser.L/V/II.43, doc. 19 corr. 1 (1978).
41. *Report on the Situation of Human Rights in Argentina*, Inter-Am. C.H.R., O.A.S. Doc. OEA/Ser.L/V/II.49, doc. 19 corr. 1 (1980).
42. Farer, *supra* note 35, at 512.
43. *Report on the Situation on Argentina*, *supra* note 41.
44. *Id.*

of human rights violations from other parts of the hemisphere. Moreover, when the Commission did open cases, many governments either disputed the facts or simply refused to cooperate with the Commission by ignoring its requests for information.[45] Consequently, decisions finding violations of rights under the American Declaration or the American Convention did not constitute a significant part of the Commission's work until the 1990s. This does not mean, however, that the Commission did not render some very important and innovative merits decisions. For example, its decisions that found the amnesty measures in Argentina and Uruguay violative of the American Convention were truly ground breaking and gave impetus to the global movement against impunity.[46] In addition, in early 1986 the Commission, fortunately, broke with its past practice and began submitting cases to the Inter-American Court.

VIII. COMMISSION ACTIVITIES FROM THE EARLY 1990S TO THE PRESENT

The late 1980s marked the end of most authoritarian regimes throughout the region. By the early 1990s all OAS member states had freely elected governments except for Cuba. The collapse of the Soviet Union, the end of the Cold War and the armed conflicts in Central America, and the emergence and strengthening of civil society institutions throughout the hemisphere seemed to bode well for enhancing respect for human rights at the national and regional levels. At the same time, the Clinton administration maintained a less ideological and more multilateralist approach in its policies toward the region than had the two previous administrations. Although it continued

---

45. Farer, *supra* note 35, at 528. "[W]hile European cases almost always presented issues of law, in Inter-American ones it was almost invariably the facts which were disputed. No government claimed that torture and summary execution were permissible even in states of emergency; they simply denied torturing and killing." "Occasionally, certain governments absolutely failed to respond [to the commission's request for information regarding petitioner's claimed violations] no matter how often prodded and were finally subjected to the time limit and the presumption of truth set by the Commission's Regulations." Tom Farer, *The Rise of the Inter-American Human Rights Regime: No Longer a Unicorn, Not Yet an Ox, in* The Inter-American System of Human Rights 31, 48 (David J. Harris & Stephen Livingstone eds., 1998).

    Indeed, because many governments, particularly *de facto* military regimes, compromised the already fragile independence of the civilian judiciary by the wholesale purge of judges and/or transferring jurisdiction from civilian to military courts to try suspected "subversives," the Commission excused petitioners from exhausting domestic remedies and in effect became a court of first instance where petitioners could press their human rights claims against the offending state.

46. Consuelo v. Argentina, Cases 10.147, 10.181, 10.240, 10.262, 10.309, 10.31, Inter-Am. C.H.R., Report No. 28/92, OEA/Ser.L/V/II.83, doc. 14, corr.1 (1992-93); Mendoza v. Uruguay, Cases 10.029, 10.036, 10.145, 10.305, 10.372, 10.373, 10.374, 10.375, Inter-Am. C.H.R., Report No. 29/92, OEA/Ser.L/V/II.83, doc. 14, corr. 1 (1992-93).

supporting past policies to isolate Castro and to eradicate coca production in the Andean region, it undertook new initiatives to improve the rule of law and democratic institutions in Latin America by promoting judicial reform and anti-corruption measures. It also took a far more aggressive approach in pursuing US economic interests throughout the region, insisting on market liberalization as a condition of external financial assistance. In addition, it strongly supported the work of the Commission and the Court within the political organs of the OAS.

Within the region, a number of states emerging from years of authoritarian rule took certain symbolic and important steps to break from the past. Truth Commissions were established in Argentina, Chile, El Salvador, and eventually Guatemala. Moreover, among the first acts of the newly elected governments of Argentina, Chile, and Uruguay were to ratify the American Convention and accept the Court's contentious jurisdiction. By the mid 1990s, the governments of Mexico and Brazil for the first time invited the Commission to carry out on site visits to evaluate the human rights situation in both countries, and, in 1998, they both accepted the jurisdiction of the Court. During this period, several states, including Argentina, Brazil, Colombia, and Mexico, also began to design national human rights plans, which were in part shaped by the jurisprudence of the Commission and the Court.

Another rather immediate consequence of the new political conditions throughout the region was a substantial increase in the number of petitions filed with the Commission seeking redress for past violations under authoritarian rule. Although the newly elected governments in the region no longer violated human rights as a matter of state policy, it soon became apparent from the nature of other complaints received that many countries had deep seated structural deficiencies and/or endemic problems, such as police violence, racial and other forms of discrimination, exclusion of vulnerable groups from meaningful political participation, and inefficient, corrupt, or weak judiciaries. Moreover, and disturbingly, a significant number of these new complaints, echoing the past, detailed violations of fundamental rights, such as the right to life and freedom from torture.

Realizing that these problems and deficiencies, unless remedied, could undermine democratic institutions and respect for human rights, the Commission, in the early 1990s, began to closely monitor those countries with the most fragile democratic institutions and/or which were still experiencing political violence. The situations in Guatemala and Haiti were particularly worrisome in this regard. Apart from periodic visits to both countries, the Commission published four reports on the human rights situation in Haiti between 1990 and 1995[47] and three reports on Guatemala between 1993

47. *Report on the Situation of Human Rights in Haiti,* Inter-Am. C.H.R., O.A.S. Doc. OEA/Ser.L/V/II.77, doc. 18 rev.1 (1990); *Report on the Situation of Human Rights in Haiti,* Inter-Am. C.H.R., O.A.S. Doc. OEA/Ser.L/V/II.83, doc. 18 rev. 1 (1993); *Report on the*

and 2001.[48] Colombia and Peru, which were, at the time, the only countries in the hemisphere with ongoing internal armed conflicts, also received special attention, albeit for different reasons.[49]

Despite protracted internal hostilities and failed negotiations with dissident armed groups that have controlled at times large portions of national territory, Colombia has had relatively strong democratic institutions, regular elections, a free press, and governments that have largely cooperated with and sought advice from the Commission and other inter-governmental bodies. Since the late 1990s, the Commission's concerns in Colombia have primarily focused on the close links between the country's security forces and various paramilitary groups, extreme violence both within and outside of the context of the armed conflict, the plight of millions of internally displaced persons, the use of military courts to shield members of the security forces from responsibility for serious human rights violations, attacks against human rights defenders, and a pervasive culture of impunity reflecting the inability of law enforcement authorities and the civilian judiciary to investigate and punish virtually all kinds of criminal conduct.

In light of the country's endemic violence and civil strife, the Commission's top priority during this period was to try to save the lives of as many persons as possible who were under serious threat of harm from state agents, their proxies, and other violent actors. To this end, the Commission issued numerous precautionary measures requiring the government to take concrete actions to protect hundreds of human rights defenders, labor union leaders, and reporters, as well as members of indigenous and Afro-descendant communities and large groups of internally displaced persons. While not always effective, these measures, which Colombia's Constitutional Court has declared binding on the state, unquestionably have helped save the lives of innumerable persons. More recently, the Commission has closely monitored the legal measures and process that have lead to the demobilization of some of the country's most notorious paramilitary groups. The

Situation of Human Rights in Haiti, Inter-Am. C.H.R., O.A.S. Doc. OEA/Ser.L/V/II.85, doc. 9 rev. 1 (1994); *Report on the Situation of Human Rights in Haiti,* Inter-Am. C.H.R., O.A.S. Doc. OEA/Ser.L/V/II.88, doc. 10 rev. (1995).

48. *Fourth Report on the Situation of Human Rights in Guatemala,* Inter-Am. C.H.R., O.A.S. Doc. OEA/Ser.L/V/II.83, doc. 16 rev. (1993); *Special Report on the Human Rights Situation in the so-called "Communities of Peoples in Resistance" in Guatemala,* Inter-Am. C.H.R., O.A.S. Doc. OEA/Ser.L/V/II.86, doc. 5 rev. 1 (1994); *Fifth Report on the Situation of Human Rights in Guatemala,* Inter-Am. C.H.R., O.A.S. Doc. OEA/Ser.L/V/II.111, doc. 21 rev. (2001).

49. *Report on the Situation of Human Rights in Peru,* Inter-Am. C.H.R., O.A.S. Doc. OEA/Ser.L/V/II.83, doc. 31 (1993); *Second Report on the Situation of Human Rights in Peru,* Inter-Am. C.H.R., O.A.S. Doc. OEA/Ser.L/V/II.106, doc. 59 rev. (2000); *Second Report on the Situation of Human Rights in Colombia,* Inter-Am. C.H.R., O.A.S. Doc. OEA/Ser.L/V/II.84, doc. 39 rev. (1993); *Third Report on the Situation of Human Rights in Colombia,* Inter-Am. C.H.R., O.A.S. Doc. OEA/Ser.L/V/II.102, doc. 9 rev. 1 (1999).

Commission has also regularly visited Colombia. For example, it undertook on-site visits in 1990, 1992, and 1997. Based on the information gathered during its 1997 visit, the Commission published in 1999 a major report on the human rights situation in Colombia in which for the first time it used international humanitarian law, i.e., the law of armed conflict, to identify the legal regime governing the ongoing internal armed conflict and to detail emblematic violations of international humanitarian law attributable to state security forces, paramilitary groups, and dissident armed groups alike.[50] Furthermore, it is worth noting that Colombia in the 1990s enacted legislation that streamlined procedures for its compliance with Commission recommendations regarding the payment of monetary compensation to victims of human rights violations. In addition, the country's Constitutional Court, the most progressive in the hemisphere, has issued numerous innovative opinions and orders that have protected the effective exercise of basic rights enshrined in the American Convention.

The nature and tenor of the Commission's relations with the Fujimori government in Peru were quite different. After his "self-coup" in April 1992, which shut down the legislature and effectively purged judicial personnel involved in every aspect of the administration of justice, President Fujimori made various commitments to the OAS concerning the prompt restoration of democracy. Unfortunately, the political organs of the OAS did little to hold him to those undertakings. The Commission soon began receiving a flood of complaints detailing violations of fair trial guarantees in connection with the application of Peru's anti-terrorist legislation. Other petitions tended to reveal systematic violations of the right to life, including disappearances, the right to humane treatment, the right to personal liberty, and freedom of expression.

Because the government refused to settle cases or adopt the Commission's recommendations where it had found violations, the Commission began referring to the Inter-American Court cases that were most emblematic of the Fujimori government's illicit practices. In response, Peru spearheaded—unsuccessfully—several initiatives within the political organs of the OAS supposedly to "strengthen" the region's human rights system, but whose real purpose was to dramatically curb, if not gut, the supervisory powers of the Commission. Furthermore, in 1999, Peru attempted to withdraw its declaration of acceptance of the Court's jurisdiction to avoid litigating several high profile cases. Although the Court found Peru's putative withdrawal to be without effect and thereafter proceeded to decide these cases[51] and

50. *Third Report on the Situation of Human Rights in Colombia*, *supra* note 49.

51. *See Second Report on the Situation of Human Rights in Colombia*, *supra* note 49; Bronstein v. Peru, Case 11.762, Inter-Am. C.H.R., Report No. 20/98, OEA/Ser.L/V/II.98, doc. 6 rev. (1997); Constitutional Court v. Peru, 1999 Inter-Am. Ct. H.R. (ser. C) No. 55 (24 Sept. 1999).

other cases against Peru, Fujimori's government continued to defy the Court by ignoring its orders and decisions. In the face of that defiance, the OAS remained largely passive despite its role as the ultimate guarantor of the integrity of the human rights system.

In 1998, the Commission effectively maneuvered Fujimori into inviting it to conduct an on-site visit to Peru, and, based on that visit and other material, it prepared a comprehensive report on the human rights situation. Although the report was completed in early 2000, the Commission decided not to release it until 4 June 2000 on the eve of the OAS General Assembly meeting in Windsor, Canada in order to have maximum media exposure and impact on the organization.[52]

The strategic release proved successful as the report's findings dominated the discussions during the General Assembly. The report meticulously detailed the progressive destruction of the rule of law and democracy during Fujimori's tenure and contained a challenge to the OAS to act by pointedly stating that the recent presidential election, whereby Fujimori was elected to a third term, was "an irregular interruption of the democratic process." This time, the political organs of the OAS rose to the occasion by requiring the Fujimori government to take a series of measures that most certainly influenced Fujimori's decision to resign the presidency in disgrace several months after the publication of the report.

The Commission's overall work on Peru during the Fujimori era showed it at its best. Not since its visit to and reporting on Argentina in the late 1970s had the Commission been so effective in its efforts to expose rank lawlessness in an OAS member state. By utilizing all the tools at its disposal, including exercising its "diplomatic/political" role within the OAS, the Commission, together with the Court, was not only able to mete out justice in individual cases, but also through its public reporting to act as an "early warning" mechanism which kept the region as a whole informed of things that were going terribly wrong in an important hemispheric state.

Another country which merits special mention is Argentina. Since the restoration of democracy in 1983, Argentina has done more than any other hemispheric state to squarely confront and break with the legacy of its authoritarian past. Specifically, it annulled the military's self-amnesty law, created the National Commission on the Disappeared (CONADEP), prosecuted members of the military juntas, and enacted a broad reparations scheme for victims of the military regime's human rights violations. In addition, apart from ratifying the American Convention, Argentina in 1994, as part of its constitutional reform, accorded constitutional rank to that treaty. This, in turn, has resulted in Argentine judges at all levels regularly applying the

---

52. *Second Report on the Situation of Human Rights in Peru, supra* note 49.

Court's and the Commission's jurisprudence in assessing the compatibility of national laws with the American Convention.

This period also marked the beginning of a rather unique pattern of cooperation between successive Argentine governments and litigants with the Commission in the use of the friendly settlement mechanism established in the American Convention. Indeed, in 1993 Argentina pioneered the use of this mechanism for resolving litigation before the Commission in the case of *Guillermo Birt, et al.*[53] Thereafter, every Argentine government has entered into at least two such settlements with the assistance of the Commission. Many of these settlements were quite innovative in that they recognized a new right under domestic law, for example, the right to the truth concerning the disappeared in the *Lapaco* case[54] or required the state to change its domestic law by eliminating the crime of contempt from the criminal code in the *Verbitsky* case.[55] Additionally, many other Argentine cases, which were not so settled, presented sophisticated questions of first impression whose resolution contributed greatly to the development of the Commission's jurisprudence, especially on due process and related issues. Moreover, Argentina has been in the forefront of those OAS member states that have consistently opposed periodic attempts to curb the Commission's powers, and thereby weaken the region's human rights system.

During this same period, human rights NGOs, which were flourishing and proliferating throughout the region, began filing numerous petitions posing new and novel legal claims involving, women's rights, freedom of expression, indigenous people's rights, environmental rights, labor rights, HIV/AIDS, and other economic, social, and cultural rights. Their efforts were certainly spurred on by the entry into force of the Inter-American Convention on the Prevention, Punishment, and Eradication of Violence Against Women (Convention of Belem Do Para)[56] and the Additional Protocol to the American Convention on Human Rights in the Area of Economic, Social and Cultural Rights (Protocol of San Salvador)[57] in 1995 and 1999, respectively.

---

53. Report on the Friendly Settlement Procedure in Cases 10.288, 10.310, 10.436, 10.496, 10.631, and 10. 771, Inter-Am. C.H.R., Report No. 1/93, OEA/Ser.L/V/II.83, doc. 14, corr. 1 (1992-93).
54. Augiar de Lapacó v. Argentina, Case 12.059, Inter-Am. C.H.R., Report No. 21/00, OEA/Ser.L/V/II.106, doc. 6 rev. (1999).
55. Verbitsky v. Argentina, Case 11.012, Inter-Am. C.H.R., Report No. 22/94, OEA/Ser.L/V.88, doc. 9 rev. 1 (1994).
56. Inter-American Convention on the Prevention, Punishment, and Eradication of Violence Against Women ("Convention of Belem Do Para"), *adopted* 9 June 1994, 24th Sess., O.A.S. Doc. OEA/Ser.L/V/II.92 doc. 31 rev. 3 (1994) (*entered into force* 5 Mar. 1995), *reprinted in* 33 I.L.M. 1534 (1994).
57. Additional Protocol to the American Convention on Human Rights in the Area of Economic, Social and Cultural Rights ("Protocol of San Salvador"), *adopted* 7 Nov. 1988, O.A.S.T.S. No. 69 (*entered into force* 16 Nov. 1999), *reprinted in* Basic Documents Pertaining to Human Rights in the Inter-American System, OAS Doc. OEA/Ser.L.V/II.82 doc.6 rev.1 at 67 (1992).

By the mid-1990s, despite holding regular elections and the existence of freer and more open societies, many states, most particularly in South America, began experiencing severe economic problems and a sharp deterioration in the functioning of democratic institutions, which helped spark attempted coups and other means to achieve regime change. If such attacks on the constitutional order were not yet entirely a thing of the past, the OAS at least began to take action to repudiate them. Resolution 1080,[58] excluding coupist regimes from the OAS, and the 2001 Inter-American Democratic Charter[59] make clear that coups are no longer acceptable to the Organization and its member states. Consistent with these positive developments, the Commission began playing close attention to the conflictive political situation in Venezuela, especially since the attempted coup against President Chavez in April 2002. In March 2003, the Commission published a comprehensive report on Venezuela that analyzed the reasons for the highly polarized political climate in that country and its negative impact on human rights protections.[60] It has also closely followed the situations in Bolivia, Ecuador, Guatemala, and Haiti.

The region's human rights system suffered something of a setback in 1998 when Trinidad and Tobago formally denounced the American Convention. This unprecedented action was largely taken in response to the Commission's examination of numerous petitions alleging that Trinidad and Tobago's imposition of the mandatory death penalty in all capital cases violated numerous provisions of the American Convention. The Commission's preliminary reports in 1999[61] and the Court's 2002[62] judgment confirmed these violations. In 1999, the Trinidadian government also executed several persons in direct contravention of binding orders issued by the Court. However, the OAS's political organs did nothing. Although the Commission has rendered comparable decisions on the use of the mandatory death penalty by other Caribbean states, none of these states has followed Trinidad and Tobago's example. Hopefully, Trinidad will decide to re-accede to the American Convention in due course.

As a result of the increased number of petitions received, the Commission made resolution of cases its top priority during this period. Many of the Commission's decisions since the mid 1990s consolidated existing juris-

58. *Represenative Democracy, adopted* 5 June 1991, AG/RES. 1080 (XXI-O/91), 21st Sess., O.A.S. Doc. OEA/Ser.P/XXI.O.2 (1991).
59. *Resolution of San Jose, Costa Rica Inter-American Democratic Charter, adopted* 5 June 2001, AG/RES. 1838 (XXXI-O/01), 31st Sess., O.A.S. Doc. OEA/Ser.P/XXXI-O.2 (2001).
60. *Report on the Situation of Human Rights in Venezuela*, Inter-Am. C.H.R., O.A.S. Doc. OEA/Ser.L/V/II.118, doc. 4 rev. 2 (2003).
61. *See, e.g.*, Hilaire v. Trin. & Tobago, Case 11.816, Inter-Am. C.H.R., Report No. 43/98, OEA/Ser.L/V/II.102, doc. 6 rev. (1998).
62. Hilaire v. Trin. & Tobago, 2002 Inter-Am Ct. H.R. (ser. C) No. 94 (21 June 2002).

prudence or broke new ground in such diverse areas as amnesty laws, the death penalty, military justice, anti-terrorism measures, fair trial guarantees, indigenous peoples' rights, rights of disabled persons, and labor rights. In addition, the number of friendly settlements brokered by the Commission in recent years has increased dramatically. These settlements, which the Commission routinely offers to litigants generally after declaring a petition admissible and opening a case, offer an attractive alternative to protracted litigation before the Commission and the Court. As previously noted, they frequently have resulted in highly creative and generous reparation measures for broad categories of victims of human rights abuses. As such, they have become a significant, albeit very time consuming, activity of the Commission.

This new emphasis on cases has not been to the detriment of *in loco* visits and the preparation of country reports. These continue to be an important part of the Commission's work, particularly with respect to those countries experiencing armed conflict or serious institutional problems, such as Colombia, Guatemala, Haiti, and Venezuela. However, "working" visits in recent years by the Commissioner and staff member responsible for the country have supplanted to some degree the more cumbersome and expensive on-site visit by the entire Commission. It can be expected that future country visits and ensuing reports, instead of examining the "global" human rights situation in the country concerned, will be far more focused by addressing and formulating recommendations concerning very specific human rights practices. The Commission's recent country report on Haiti[63] published in April 2007 and the various thematic reports on access to justice[64] are indicative of this trend.[65]

During the 1990s, the Commission considerably expanded the number of its Special Thematic Rapporteurships either at its own initiative or in response to requests from NGOs and the political organs of the OAS. These rapporteurships have not only spotlighted public attention on the plight of certain vulnerable groups or obstacles to the free exercise of certain key rights, but also have lead to new standard setting in the field. The work of these mechanisms also has enriched and reinforced the Commission's more general monitoring of human rights practices in the countries visited.

63. *Observations of the Inter-American Commission on Human Rights upon Conclusions of its April 2007 Visit to Haiti*, Inter-Am. C.H.R., O.A.S. Doc. OEA/Serv.L/V/II.131, doc. 36 (2008).

64. *Access to Justice as a Guarantee to Economic, Social, and Cultural Rights: A Review of the Standards Adopted by the Inter-American System of Human Rights*, Inter-Am. C.H.R. OEA/Ser.L/V/II.129, doc. 4 (2007); *Report on the Implementation of Justice and Peace Law: Initial Stages of the Demobilization of the AUC and First Judicial Proceedings*, Inter-Am. C.H.R., O.A.S. Doc. OEA/Ser.L/V/II.129, doc. 6 (2007).

65. *Justicia e Inclusión Social: Los Desafíos de la Democracia en Guatemala, 2003*, Inter-Am. C.H.R., O.A.S. Doc. OEA/Ser.L/V/II.118, doc. 5 rev. 1 (2003); *Report on the Situation of Human Rights in Venezuela*, *supra* note 60.

As of 2009, the Commission had Special Rapporteurs for the rights of the child, women, indigenous peoples, internally displaced persons, migrant workers, prison conditions, Afro-descendents and against racism, and freedom of expression. Reflecting its concern about the growing number of attacks on human rights workers in the region, in 2001 the Commission established within its Executive Secretariat the Human Rights Defenders Functional Unit. This unit regularly evaluates the situations of at risk human rights workers and organizations and recommends to the Commission the issuance of precautionary measures to protect these persons and groups from irreparable harm. Many of these thematic mechanisms are supported by voluntary financial contributions from OAS member states, the Inter-American Development Bank, or various European aid agencies. Assuming an infusion of additional resources to support these rapporteurships, it is most likely that working visits by these thematic mechanisms to member states will increase dramatically.

By the close of the 1990s, the so-called decade of transition to democracy in the region had ended. It is clear that initial hopes for consolidating democratic institutions and the rule of law, which are indispensable for protecting human rights at the local level, fell well short of expectations in many nations. Progress, however, has been made in certain areas. The people of the region are now far more knowledgeable of their entitlement to basic human rights and how to seek legal redress from the Commission. Moreover, they have shown themselves to be far less tolerant of official corruption and generally expect far more transparency and accountability from their elected representatives than they had in the past. In addition, various governments, most notably in Argentina, Chile, and Mexico, have recently taken new steps to fight impunity and come to grips with the divisive legacies of the past.

As previously indicated, changes in governments and their policies, as well as changing political and economic conditions in the region, have presented new challenges to the Commission over the years. In this regard, there are certain challenges and obstacles facing the Commission and the Court that merit special attention and are discussed below.

IX. CHALLENGES AND OBSTACLES

Without question, the single greatest obstacle to the effective functioning of the Commission and the Court is the lack of adequate human and financial resources. Simply put, the system of petitions and cases is in imminent danger of collapse. The Commission's thirty staff lawyers, who are presently handling nearly 1,250 open cases, cannot keep pace with the annual increase in the number of petitions and thus cannot meet the reasonable expectations of states and victims for their prompt resolution. The annual average number of petitions received between 1997 and 2001 was 609.[66] The Commission received 1,456 new complaints in 2007, an approximate 70 percent increase in a ten-year period.[67]

The situation of the Court is even more precarious. As a result of the Commission's reform of its regulations in 2001, whereby presumptively all cases are now referred to the Court, that body's thirteen staff lawyers cannot be expected to deal with the fifty-plus current cases and over sixty provisional measures on its docket, much less with the anticipated referral of fifteen to twenty new cases a year from the Commission.

Although the Commission is the OAS's principal organ in the area of human rights, its budget represents less than 4.6 percent of the organization's total budget. It is important to understand that the commissioners and the judges of these organs are not salaried employees of the organization. Instead, they receive an honoraria and a per diem when they are in session or engaged in other official activities. Approximately two-thirds of the Commission's total budget goes to staff salaries and benefits. The remainder is barely adequate to cover the costs of two regular sessions, publication of the annual and special reports, and the costs of performance contracts. This means that the budget contains no money for a single *in loco* visit or for litigating a single case before the Court. In order to carry out these and other mandated activities, the Commission has had to rely on the voluntary contributions from the United States and various European countries. For its part, the Court has received funds from the European Union to help cover the costs of its publications. It is clear that without additional resources, neither organ will be able to continue carrying out many of the tasks entrusted to them. As the OAS is an organization in perpetual financial crisis, the prospects of increased funding are quite bleak.

The failure of most state parties to the American Convention to adequately implement that instrument's rights and guarantees under domestic law or to fully comply with orders and decisions of the Commission and Court have also adversely affected the functioning and integrity of the system. It is a frequently overlooked fact that the primary responsibility for implementing the American Convention rests with the states parties themselves. Under the American Convention, states parties not only pledge to secure to all persons subject to their jurisdiction the free exercise of the rights and freedoms recognized in that instrument, but also undertake to accord domestic legal effect to, as well as harmonize their interpretations of domestic rules with

66. *Annual Report of the Inter-American Commission on Human Rights 2002,* Inter-Am. C.H.R., O.A.S. Doc. OEA/Ser.L/V/II.117, doc. 1 rev. 1 (2003), at Ch. III.B.

67. *Annual Report of the Inter-American Commission on Human Rights 2007,* Inter-Am. C.H.R., O.A.S. Doc. OEA/Ser.L/V/II.130, doc. 22 rev. 1 (2007), at Ch. IIIB.

those rights and freedoms. As a corollary, they may have to modify and perhaps even derogate any domestic legal norm that is incompatible with their obligations under the American Convention. States parties are similarly required to provide effective judicial remedies to all persons claiming violations of these rights and freedoms.

It is therefore quite troubling that the Commission has routinely encountered many instances where states parties have not made Convention based rights operative under domestic law or where judges have applied norms of domestic law in contravention of their state's engagements under the American Convention. Clearly, if such rights are not recognized under domestic law, there can be no effective domestic remedies to redress their violation. Fortunately, various states have taken certain measures to remedy this situation. For example, some states, such as Argentina and Peru, directly incorporate provisions of the American Convention into domestic law, while others, such as Colombia, Costa Rica, and Guatemala have constitutions which accord supremacy to the American Convention and other human rights treaties over domestic law.

It is worth noting that the record of state party compliance with Commission and Court decisions relating to the payment of monetary compensation to victims of human rights violations has improved when compared to the period of authoritarian rule. However, no state has yet put in place internal legal mechanisms and procedures that mandate *full* compliance with the decisions and orders of the Commission and the Court. The great majority of states parties regularly plead *res judicata* or prescription under domestic law as excuses for their failure to comply with orders and decisions requiring them to identify, prosecute, and punish state agents responsible for human rights violations. As a consequence, impunity for such violations continues to be the norm throughout the region. This in turn undermines the credibility and efficacy of the system.

If the region's human rights system is to be fully effective, then member states of the OAS must take seriously their role as the collective and ultimate guarantors of the system's integrity. It is quite revealing that the political organs of the OAS generally showed greater willingness to take initiatives supporting Commission decisions when dictatorships held sway in the region than they have in the last decade under freely elected governments. As noted previously, these organs did absolutely nothing when the governments of Peru and Trinidad and Tobago were openly defying the Commission and the Court. It was only after the fall of Fujimori in 2002 that several member states began presenting various proposals to establish an annual review procedure by the General Assembly and Permanent Council of the OAS to assess compliance with Commission and Court decisions. However, despite ongoing debate, the OAS has not yet created any kind of mechanism for this purpose. Consequently, when it revised its regulations in 2000, the Commission included a new provision whereby it can adopt the follow-up measures it deems appropriate, such as requesting information from litigants and holding hearings, in order to verify compliance with its decisions. Further, it introduced in its 2001 Annual Report a new chapter that depicts the status of compliance with its recommendations in cases decided and published during the previous two years.[68] It is worth noting that within the Council of Europe, noncompliance with decisions of the European Court of Human Rights is subject to sanctions, including exclusion from the regional system.

Another challenge for the Commission is the need to develop a coherent strategy for dealing with economic, social, and cultural rights. Although the Protocol of San Salvador entered into force in 1999 and the Commission has dealt with these rights in its country reports and various cases, it has not yet fully articulated its views concerning the justiciability of these rights under the American Declaration and the American Convention.[69] Backsliding throughout the region in the protection of basic civil and political rights, which has required very time consuming scrutiny and action by the Commission, largely accounts for this. However, substantial cutbacks in social spending in many countries, combined with increased awareness of economic, social, and cultural rights, have generated new and difficult cases that the Commission will have to address in a more comprehensive manner than it has in the past.

Terrorism has been a rather commonplace feature in Latin America and has presented significant challenges to the Commission over the past fifty years. Consequently, the Commission has acquired considerable expertise in dealing with the subject. For example, in the 1970s and 1980s the Commission's reports analyzed and exposed state sponsored terrorism being perpetrated by the military regimes in the Southern Cone. In the 1980s and 1990s anti-terrorist legislation and related counter-insurgency measures in Guatemala and Peru were priority concerns of the Commission. Since the 1990s, it has closely scrutinized comparable laws and practices in Colombia. Although states are the primary focus of its mandate and activities, the Commission has repeatedly condemned terrorist acts perpetrated by private persons or dissident armed groups. In recognition of the threat that terrorism poses to democracy and the protection of human rights, the Commission has consistently affirmed the right and duty of states to protect their citizens from terrorist violence. At the same time, it has recognized that the people of the region must be protected against disproportionate state responses to such violence.

---

68. *See Annual Report of the Inter-American Commission on Human Rights 2001*, Inter-Am. C.H.R., O.A.S. Doc. OEA/Ser./L/V/II.114, doc. 5 rev. (2002), at Ch. III.
69. Additional Protocol to the American Convention on Human Rights in the Area of Economic, Social and Cultural Rights, *supra* note 57.

As a result of the Bush administration's legislative and other initiatives in the wake of the 11 September 2001 terrorist attacks, the Commission realized that it had to provide guidance to OAS member states on how to craft anti-terrorism and related measures so that they do not run afoul of their international legal obligations. Accordingly, in late 2002, the Commission published its comprehensive Report on Terrorism and Human Rights.[70] This several hundred page report was the result of twelve months of intensive study and deliberations within the Commission and drew in part upon the views of internationally recognized experts on human rights law and terrorism, as well as the written observations of member states and various NGOs. As part of its methodology, the report recognizes that terrorist violence may occur in times of peace, in states of emergency, and in situations of armed conflict, and therefore examines member states' obligations under both international human rights and international humanitarian law. The report considers standards of protection under these legal regimes in six main areas: the right to life; the right to humane treatment; the right to personal liberty and security; the right to a fair trial; freedom of expression; the right to judicial protection and non-discrimination; and the protection of migrants, refugees, asylum seekers, and other non-nationals.

The report makes clear that, in taking measures to prevent, punish, and eradicate terrorist violence, states remain bound by their human rights obligations in all circumstances, subject only to suspensions and restrictions expressly authorized by applicable instruments. The Commission emphasized that the terrorist attacks of 11 September, although unprecedented in their magnitude, have not changed this basic precept. The Commission also made clear that the report would guide it in assessing the anti-terrorism practices of all OAS member states. In this connection the Commission, while preparing this report, felt it necessary to adopt precautionary measures requesting that United States take urgent measures to have the legal status of the detainees at Guantánamo Bay, Cuba determined by a competent tribunal.

The Commission's report was well received by the OAS and has been widely disseminated and cited within the United Nations and the Council of Europe. In light of the continuing threat of terrorist violence and the proliferation of anti-terrorism measures within the region, it is clear that the the subject of terrorism will continue to figure prominently on the Commission's agenda.

Finally, ratification of the American Convention by all OAS member states remains an elusive goal and challenge for the system. By virtue of the distinctive nature of the region's human rights arrangements, member states are not obliged to ratify the American Convention or other human

70. *Report on Terrorism and Human Rights,* Inter-Am. C.H.R., O.A.S. Doc. OEA/Ser.L/V/II.116, doc. 5 rev. 1 corr. (2002).

rights treaties elaborated by the Organization. The United States, Canada, and various Caribbean island states are currently the only members that have not yet ratified this instrument. This means that the system established under the American Convention, including supervision by the Court, applies by and large only to Latin American states.

This situation is hardly ideal for various reasons. From a human rights standpoint, it creates a disadvantage for the inhabitants of non-ratifying countries by effectively denying them access to the Court in claims against their respective states. From a political standpoint, it also has negative consequences, particularly for non-signers. By remaining outside of the Convention structure the United States and Canada have increasingly found their clout and credibility challenged in the Organization's political bodies when they have pressed various Latin American states to live up to their human rights obligations under the American Convention. This was abundantly clear when, during discussions in 1999 concerning possible reform of the American Convention, various Latin American governments, led by Brazil, Mexico, and Peru, initially sought to exclude the United States and Canada from participating in the deliberations because they were not states parties to that treaty.

Moreover, from a policy perspective, it is highly desirable for a region that is moving increasingly toward integration in other areas to have all its states be bound by the same legal obligations and their peoples have the same rights, as well as equal access to the protections offered by both of the American Convention's supervisory organs. In this regard, it is worth noting that although the prospects of ratification by Canada in the near future have improved, the same, unfortunately, cannot be said in the case of the United States, unless the Obama administration seriously pushes for the treaty's ratification.

[8]

UNITED STATES RATIFICATION OF THE AMERICAN CONVENTION ON HUMAN RIGHTS*

Joseph Diab

I. INTRODUCTION

On June 26, 1945, a delegation from the United States Department of State met in San Francisco with representatives from fifty countries to sign the Charter of the United Nations.[1] Affirming "faith in fundamental human rights"[2] and pledging to promote "universal respect for, and observance of . . . fundamental freedoms for all,"[3] the members of the United Nations elevated individual rights to the level of international concern, and the United States formalized its commitment to the protection of human rights worldwide.

The human rights provisions in the U.N. Charter were largely a result of efforts by the United States[4] toward "the day when all worthy human beings may be permitted to live decently as free people."[5] This effort soon led to the Universal Declaration of Human Rights,[6] a cornerstone of contemporary human rights law and the first part of an international bill of rights modeled after the U.S. Constitution.

> Americans were prominent among the architects and builders of international human rights, and American constitutionalism was a principal inspiration and model for them. As a result, most of the Universal Declaration of Human Rights, and later the International Covenant on Civil and Political Rights, are in their essence American constitutional rights projected around the world.[7]

---

* This work has benefited from the generous advice and contributions of Professor Benedict Kingsbury, Exeter College, Oxford; Christina Cerna, Inter-American Commission on Human Rights; Professor Tom Farer, American University School of Law; Pat Rengel, Chief Counsel, Amnesty International, U.S.A.; Lynn Boyer, Legislative Counsel to Senator Jesse Helms; Dr. Robert Friedlander, Chief Legislative Counsel to Minority Members, United States Senate Foreign Relations Committee; Melisandre Hodges, Perkins Library, Duke University.

1. For a discussion of events surrounding the signing of the Charter, see John H. Crider, *Truman Closes U.N. Conference with Plea to Translate Charter into Deeds*, N.Y. TIMES, June 27, 1945, at A1.

2. U.N. CHARTER, pmbl., para. 2.

3. *Id.* art. 55, para. c.

4. Louis Sohn, *A Short History of United Nations Documents on Human Rights*, *in* COMMISSION TO STUDY THE ORGANIZATION OF PEACE, THE UNITED NATIONS AND HUMAN RIGHTS 39, 43-56 (1968).

5. Harry S. Truman, Address to the Closing Session of the United Nations Conference, San Francisco, Program Closing Plenary Session, June 26, 1945, 1 U.N.C.I.O. Docs. 687, 717 (1945).

6. G.A. Res. 217A (III) U.N. GAOR, 3d Sess. at 71-77, U.N. Doc. A/810 (1948) [hereinafter Universal Declaration].

7. Louis Henkin, *Rights: American and Human*, 79 COLUM. L. REV. 405, 415 (1979). *See generally* Richard B. Lillich, *The United States Constitution and International Human Rights Law*, 3 HARV. HUM. RTS. J. 53 (1990) (arguing United States constitutionalism contributed significantly to the development of international human rights law).

During the drafting of the U.N. Charter and the Universal Declaration, the United States took the lead in shaping international human rights programs and policies.[8] It was among the most diligent nations in promoting U.N. efforts toward human rights protection throughout the late 1940s.[9] In fact, it was an American, Eleanor Roosevelt, who was the driving force behind the Universal Declaration of Human Rights.[10]

The momentum to formalize international human rights protection soon carried into regional organizations which created their own instruments to safeguard human rights. The European nations were the first to undertake legally binding obligations by adopting the European Convention for the Protection of Human Rights and Fundamental Freedoms (European Convention).[11] Likewise, the Organization of American States (OAS) formalized a regional system of protection in the Americas with a similar instrument, the American Convention on Human Rights (American Convention).[12]

While the European Convention enjoys support among all the principal European nations,[13] the American Convention lacks the support of one of the most influential nations of the Americas — the United States. With twenty-three American nations already parties to the American Convention,[14] the United States has yet to ratify it. Although the Convention was signed by President Carter in 1978, it has yet to attain a two-thirds vote in the Senate as required for ratification

8. *Hearings Before the Subcommittee on International Organizations and Movements of the House Committee on Foreign Affairs*, 93d Cong., 1st Sess. 188 (1973) (testimony of Professor Thomas Buergenthal).

9. J. GREEN, THE UNITED NATIONS AND HUMAN RIGHTS 28-29, 37 n.20 (1956).

10. For an account of Mrs. Roosevelt's participation in drafting the Universal Declaration of Human Rights, see Richard Gardner, *Eleanor Roosevelt's Legacy: Human Rights*, N.Y. TIMES, Dec. 10, 1988, at 27.

11. Convention for the Protection of Human Rights and Fundamental Freedoms, *opened for signature* Nov. 4, 1950, 213 U.N.T.S. 221 [hereinafter European Convention]. For a discussion of the development of regional systems, see Thomas Buergenthal, *International Human Rights Law and Institutions: Accomplishments and Prospects*, 63 WASH. L. REV. 1 (1988).

12. American Convention on Human Rights, *opened for signature* Nov. 22, 1969, 9 I.L.M. 101 (1970) (OAS Doc. OEA/SER. K/XVI/1.1 Doc. 65 (1970)) [hereinafter American Convention]. For a discussion of the evolution of the American system for human rights protection and the American Convention, see Thomas Buergenthal, *Introduction to the Inter-American System*, *in* PROTECTING HUMAN RIGHTS IN THE AMERICAS: SELECTED PROBLEMS 1-22 (Thomas Buergenthal et al. eds., 3d ed. 1990).

13. Jean-Bernard Mairie, *International Instruments Relating to Human Rights: Classification and Chart Showing Ratifications as of 1 January 1990*, 11 HUM. RTS. L.J. 175, 184 (1990). Signatories include Austria, Belgium, Cyprus, Denmark, France, Germany/Fed. Rep., Greece, Iceland, Ireland, Italy, Liechtenstein, Luxembourg, Malta, the Netherlands, Norway, Portugal, San Marino, Spain, Sweden, Switzerland, Turkey, and the United Kingdom. *Id.*

14. The following states are parties to the American Convention as of January 1, 1990: Argentina, Barbados, Bolivia, Colombia, Costa Rica, Dominican Republic, Ecuador, El Salvador, Grenada, Guatemala, Haiti, Honduras, Jamaica, Mexico, Nicaragua, Panama, Paraguay, Peru, Suriname, Uruguay, and Venezuela. *Id.* at 186.

by Article VI of the United States Constitution.[15] While the Senate held hearings to discuss the issues surrounding ratification in 1979,[16] it has not taken action on the Convention for the past thirteen years.[17]

Senate action on the American Convention requires more than a willingness to endorse a general declaration of human rights. It mandates a commitment to accept the human rights norms in the Convention as legally binding obligations; a commitment which raises diplomatic, political, and legal concerns that have forestalled ratification.[18]

This Note advocates ratification of the American Convention. Through an examination of legal issues surrounding ratification, it demonstrates that there are no significant legal barriers blocking the United States from becoming a party, and that participation in this international treaty would best serve the interests of the United States.

II. THE AMERICAN CONVENTION

Negotiated at San José, Costa Rica in 1969, with the active participation of the United States,[19] the American Convention is an international agreement that operates within the framework of the OAS. The Convention catalogs human rights to be protected in the region and provides for international monitoring and enforcement of those rights.[20] The current Inter-American human rights system is based on three legal sources: the OAS Charter (Charter),[21] the American Declaration of Human Rights (Declaration),[22] and the American Convention. The

15. U.S. CONST. art. VI.

16. *International Human Rights Treaties: Hearings Before the Comm. on Foreign Relations*, 96th Cong., 1st Sess. 1 (1979) [hereinafter *Human Rights Hearings*].

17. In addition to the American Convention, President Carter signed three other human rights conventions that were also sent to the Senate for their advice and consent. *See* President's Message to the Senate on Human Rights Treaties, PUB. PAPERS 395-96 (1978). The other conventions are the following: *The International Covenant on Economic, Social, and Cultural Rights*, G.A. Res. 2200 (XXI), U.N. GAOR, 21st Sess., Supp. No. 16, at 49, U.N. Doc. A/6316 (1967); *The International Covenant on Civil and Political Rights*, G.A. Res. 2200 (XXII), U.N. GAOR, 21st Sess., Supp. No. 16, at 52, U.N. Doc. A/6316 (1966); *The International Convention on the Elimination of All Forms of Racial Discrimination*, G.A. Res. 2106A (XX), U.N. GAOR, 20th Sess., Supp. No. 14, at 47, U.N. Doc. A/6014 (1965). Although the United States Senate recently gave its advice and consent to the International Covenant on Civil and Political Rights, the United States has yet to ratify any of these conventions. 138 CONG. REC. S4781 (daily ed. Apr. 2, 1992).

18. For a discussion of diplomatic, political, and legal concerns regarding U.S. ratification of human rights treaties, see Bruno Bitker, *U.S. Policy on Ratification of Human Rights Covenants*, 11 HUM. RTS. J. 653 (1969). *See also* David Weissbrodt, *United States Ratification of the Human Rights Covenants*, 63 MINN. L. REV. 35 (1978) (discussing the background of human rights covenants and reasons why U.S. citizens should be interested in their ratification).

19. For drafting history, see Buergenthal, *supra* note 12, at 4-6.

20. American Convention, *supra* note 12, art. 41, 9 I.L.M. at 112.

21. Charter of the Organization of American States, Apr. 30, 1948, 2 U.S.T. 2394, 119 U.N.T.S. 3.

22. American Declaration on the Rights and Duties of Man, Res. XXX of the Ninth

Charter serves as the constitution of the OAS and includes a legally binding obligation on the part of member states to "respect the rights of the individual and the principles of universal morality."[23] This phrase, however, is vague, and neither individual rights nor principles of morality are defined in the Charter. The Declaration, originally drafted as a nonbinding conference resolution,[24] has come to serve as the authoritative interpretation of the "fundamental rights of the individual" included in the Charter.[25]

The American Convention creates legally binding obligations for OAS member states that have signed and ratified it. The Convention specifies the basic civil and political rights to be protected throughout the western hemisphere.[26] It protects many of the same basic liberties guaranteed by the United States Bill of Rights,[27] including freedom of religion, speech, assembly,[28] the right to a fair trial,[29] the right to property,[30] freedom from slavery,[31] and equal protection of the law.[32] The American Convention also establishes an Inter-American Court[33]

International Conference of American States, OEA/Ser. L/V/II.50 doc. 6, rev. 1, (1953), *reprinted in* HANDBOOK OF EXISTING RULES PERTAINING TO HUMAN RIGHTS 237 (1953).

23. OAS CHARTER art. 13.

24. Thomas Buergenthal, *The Revised OAS Charter and the Protection of Human Rights*, 69 AM. J. INT'L L. 828, 829 (1975).

25. Buergenthal, *supra* note 11, at 16.

> Although the American Declaration, not unlike the Universal Declaration, was not deemed to be legally binding at the time it was proclaimed in 1948, it has now been accepted as a normative instrument of the Inter-American System that contains the authoritative catalogue of the Human Rights which all State Parties to the OAS Charter are required to promote.

Id.

26. American Convention, *supra* note 12, 9 I.L.M. at 101.

27. Although the wording of the provisions of the American Convention differs from that of the U.S. Constitution, the United States Department of Justice has determined that with the appropriate reservations, the provisions of the Convention accord with U.S. Constitutional law. *U.S. Dept. of State, Letter to President Carter, Dec. 17, 1977, in* RICHARD B. LILLICH, U.S. RATIFICATION OF THE HUMAN RIGHTS TREATIES: WITH OR WITHOUT RESERVATIONS? 105 (1981) [hereinafter *Letter to President Carter*]. *See also Human Rights Hearings*, *supra* note 16, at 7 (statement of Warren Christopher) ("In essence, the [pending human rights] treaties create an international commitment to the same basic human rights that already are guaranteed to citizens of the United States by our own laws and constitution.").

28. *Compare* U.S. CONST. amend. I *with* American Convention, *supra* note 12, arts. 12-13, 15, 9 I.L.M. at 105-06 (granting rights to freedom of religion, expression, and assembly).

29. *Compare* U.S. CONST. amends. V-VI *with* American Convention, *supra* note 12, arts. 7-8, 9 I.L.M. at 103-04 (granting freedom from arbitrary arrest and the right to fair trial).

30. *Compare* U.S. CONST. amend. XIV *with* American Convention, *supra* note 12, art. 21, 9 I.L.M. at 107 (granting right to property).

31. *Compare* U.S. CONST. amend. XII *with* American Convention, *supra* note 12, art. 6, 9 I.L.M. at 103 (granting freedom from slavery).

32. *Compare* U.S. CONST. amend. XIV *with* American Convention, *supra* note 12, art. 24, 9 I.L.M. at 108 (granting right to equal protection).

33. The Inter-American Court of Human Rights (Court) was established by Article 33 of

and expands the authority of the Inter-American Commission (Commission)[34] to serve as the enforcement mechanism for the rights provided by the Convention. The effectiveness of this human rights protection system depends upon the participation of all American countries.[35]

The American Convention reflects an effort by its drafters to provide a minimum standard of decency among American countries in their treatment of individuals. In many ways this effort resembles that of the drafters of the Universal Declaration, in which the United States played a significant role.[36] The crucial difference, however, is that the

---

the Convention to oversee the application and interpretation of the Convention. American Convention, *supra* note 12, art. 33, 9 I.L.M. at 111. It consists of seven judges elected from the OAS member states. Only state parties to the Convention have *locus standi* before the Court; however, complaints brought by individuals may be forwarded to the Court through the Inter-American Commission on Human Rights. *See id.* art. 61, para. 1, 9 I.L.M. at 117. The Court has advisory jurisdiction to interpret the provisions of any OAS treaty concerning human rights. It also has jurisdiction to render judgment against states in breach of the Convention provided that those states have recognized the Court's jurisdiction through declaration or agreement. *Id.* art. 63, 9 I.L.M. at 118. It may determine the rights to be accorded an injured party and the amount of damages due. It may also grant temporary injunctions. Decisions by the Court are final and are not subject to appeal. *See* Thomas Buergenthal, *The Inter-American Court of Human Rights*, 76 AM. J. INT'L L. 231 *passim* (1982).

34. The Inter-American Commission on Human Rights consists of seven members elected by the OAS General Assembly from a list of candidates submitted by the governments of member states. It was established under the Convention as a body to receive complaints from private individuals concerning human rights violations by OAS member states. American Convention, *supra* note 12, arts. 34, 41, 9 I.L.M. at 111-12. Its authority has expanded under the Convention and it now serves as a body to: develop an awareness of human rights issues in the Americas; make recommendations to governments for the progressive adoption of human rights measures; conduct studies and prepare regular reports; request information from member states regarding the measures they have taken to further human rights; and take action on complaints brought under the Convention. Complaints (communications) may be brought before the Commission either by a state against another state or by an individual or non-governmental organization against a state. When presented with a communication from an individual or member state alleging a violation of the Convention, the Commission will forward relevant portions of the communication to the government of the member state involved and request a response, usually within sixty days. The Commission then establishes the facts involved in the case and seeks a friendly settlement. If no settlement is reached, it may send the case to the Inter-American Court of Human Rights for a decision, or it may set forth its own conclusions and opinions, making recommendations and setting a time limit for state compliance. If a state fails to comply, the Commission may choose to publish a report on the situation. *See generally* Robert Norris, *The New Statute of the Inter-American Commission on Human Rights*, 1 HUM. RTS. L.J. 379 (1980) (discussing the background and content of the statute establishing the Inter-American Commission on Human Rights).

35. Thomas Buergenthal, *The American Convention on Human Rights*, *in* U.S. RATIFICATION OF HUMAN RIGHTS TREATIES, *supra* note 27, at 47, 51 ("[I] doubt very much that without full U.S. participation the Inter-American system will realize its full potential, and that would be a great pity indeed.").

36. *See supra* note 27 and accompanying text. *See also* Bruno Bitker, *The United States and International Codification of Human Rights: A Case of Split Personality*, *in* NATALIE KAUFMAN HEVENER, THE DYNAMICS OF HUMAN RIGHTS 77, 77 (1981) (stating that the history of United States policy on human rights treaties reflects a classic case of split personality; although

standards set out in the Universal Declaration were intended to be nonbinding, whereas the American Convention carries with it legal obligations that the United States is reluctant to assume.

The principal reason for this reluctance is fear that international obligations created by the Convention will interfere with the domestic affairs of the United States. These obligations would place the supervision and control of human rights in the hands of an international body over which the United States does not have exclusive control.[37] The most common arguments against ratification can be divided into three categories.

The first of these categories is comprised of federalist arguments which assert that ratification by the United States would legitimize federal interference in areas that are within the exclusive jurisdiction of the states.[38] The second category of objections are sovereignty arguments. This debate centers around the idea that human rights are exclusively a domestic issue and therefore beyond the jurisdiction of an international organization.[39] Finally, the third type of argument consists of objections to the "right-to-life" provision in Article 4 of the Convention, since this Article raises questions about the legality of the death penalty and abortion.[40]

III. FEDERALIST CONCERNS: THE ISSUE OF STATES' RIGHTS

One of the most prevalent arguments against ratification of the American Convention is based on the belief that it would interfere with the federalist system to allow the President to enter into an international agreement that would legally bind the states. Because Article VI of the United States Constitution establishes that treaties become the "supreme law of the land,"[41] certain provisions of the Convention potentially could interfere with state legislation or force the states to rearrange their current criminal codes.[42]

---

leading multinational crusades for human rights in the 1940s, the U.S. has ratified only one human rights treaty since then).

37. Arthur Rovine, *Defense of Declarations, Reservations, and Understandings*, *in* U.S. RATIFICATION OF THE HUMAN RIGHTS TREATIES, *supra* note 27, at 55, 61. *See also* Natalie Hevener Kaufman & David Whiteman, *Opposition to Human Rights Treaties in the United States Senate: The Legacy of the Bricker Amendment*, 10 HUM. RTS. Q. 309 (1988) (discussing Cold War fears that led to the Bricker Amendment).

38. *See* discussion *infra* part III.B.

39. *See* discussion *infra* part IV.

40. *See* discussion *infra* part V.A.

41. U.S. CONST. art. VI.

42. *See* American Bar Association, *Report of the Standing Committee on Peace and Law Through United Nations Human Rights Conventions and Recommendations*, 1 INT'L LAW. 600, 616

The United States traditionally has been reluctant to change domestic laws through international treaties.[43] Rather than welcome international human rights treaties as potential improvements of domestic law, it has taken measures to weaken the domestic effect of ratified international human rights instruments in general, and of this Convention in particular.

A. Self-Executing Treaties

A primary means used by the United States to undercut the domestic effect of human rights treaties has been to classify these treaties as not self-executing. The judicial doctrine of self-executing treaties first became a standard part of United States treaty interpretation in *Foster & Elam v. Neilson.*[44] In *Foster,* the Supreme Court considered the domestic effect of an 1819 treaty conveying West Florida from Spain to the United States. Chief Justice Marshall stated that,

> [A treaty is] to be regarded in Courts of justice as equivalent to an act of the legislature, whenever it operates of itself without the aid of any legislative provision. But when the terms of the stipulation import a contract, when either of the parties engages to perform a particular act, the treaty addresses itself to the political, not the judicial department; and the legislature must execute the contract before it can become a rule for the Court.[45]

Thus, a self-executing treaty automatically gains domestic force once it is ratified. In contrast, an agreement which is not self-executing requires legislative enactments by Congress in order to gain domestic application in the United States.

Deciding whether a treaty is self-executing is largely a matter within the interpretive discretion of the judiciary.[46] In its analysis, the court will look to the wording of the treaty for any language which expressly calls for implementing legislation.[47] Courts will consider the intent of

---

(1967) (The federal government, being a government of limited powers, is still precluded from regulating large areas of intrastate matters. It is unnecessary and unsound to cut down this area of intrastate jurisdiction over human rights through the medium of international agreements). *See also* Rovine, *supra* note 37, at 60 (comparing genocide to murder, which is a matter of domestic jurisdiction and not international law).

43. LOUIS HENKIN, FOREIGN AFFAIRS AND THE CONSTITUTION 151-56 (1972).

44. Foster & Elam v. Neilson, 27 U.S. (2 Pet.) 253 (1829).

45. *Id.* at 314.

46. United States v. Postal, 589 F.2d 862, 876 (5th Cir.), *cert. denied,* 444 U.S. 832 (1979). *See also* Whitney v. Robertson, 124 U.S. 190 (1888) (holding that a treaty must stipulate that it is self-executing).

47. Aerovias Interamericanas de Panama, S.A. v. Bd. of County Comm's, 197 F. Supp. 230 (S.D. Fla. 1961), *rev'd on other grounds sub nom.* Bd. of County Comm's v. Aerolineas Peruanasa, S.A., 307 F.2d 802 (5th Cir. 1962), *cert. denied,* 371 U.S. 961 (1963).

the drafters to determine what the parties intended the domestic effect of their agreement to be.[48] Treaty drafters are usually able to structure the language of a treaty so that the executing nature of the treaty is predetermined. In fact, a major issue in the United States of many, if not most, international treaties is whether the document will be self-executing. The general position that the United States maintains on the nature of human rights treaties is that they are not self-executing and do not supersede state law in the absence of implementing legislation by Congress.[49]

While many countries do not make this distinction,[50] the United States has used this judicial doctrine as a method to prevent human rights treaties from creating domestic legal obligations in the absence of Congressional legislation. Without such legislation, no individual may sue in a United States court to enforce the provisions of the Convention.

The plain language of the American Convention, however, strongly supports an interpretation that it is self-executing. Article 2 specifically addresses the means by which the American Convention is to be incorporated into the domestic law of state parties:

> Where the exercise of any of the rights or freedoms referred to in Article 1 is not already ensured by legislative or other provisions, the

---

> Where a treaty is incomplete either because it expressly calls for implementing legislation or because it calls for the performance of a particular affirmative act by the contracting sovereigns, which act or acts can only be performed through a legislative act, such a treaty is for obvious reasons not self-executing and subsequent legislation must be enacted before such treaty is enforceable by the courts. . . . On the other hand, where a treaty is full and complete, it is generally considered to be self-executing by the courts.

Aerovias Interamericanas, 197 F. Supp. at 245-46.

48. *Postal*, 589 F.2d at 876 ("As in the case of all matters of interpretation, the courts attempt to discern the intent of the parties to the agreement so as to carry out their manifest purpose.").

49. HENKIN, *supra* note 43, at 159-60. For an example of the United States position towards human rights treaties, see Sei Fujii v. State, 217 P.2d 481 (Cal. Dist. Ct. App. 1950) *rev'd* 242 P.2d 617 (1950). The California Court of Appeals held California's Alien Land Law unenforceable since it was discriminatory towards Asians in violation of the human rights provisions of the U.N. Charter. The Court reasoned that the Charter, as a treaty of the United States, was equal in rank to federal statutes and was "supreme law of the land" thus superseding any inconsistent state legislation. *Id.* at 486-88. Senator John Bricker of Ohio was one of the most vocal opponents of this interpretation of the domestic effect of the U.N. Charter. 98 CONG. REC. 911 (1952) ("If the Fujii case (Court of Appeals ruling) should eventually be affirmed by the United States Supreme Court, or if the principle announced therein should be sustained, literally thousands of federal and state laws will automatically become invalid.").

Fujii was overturned. The California Supreme Court determined that the human rights provisions of the U.N. Charter were not self-executing, that is, they could not supersede state laws unless they were implemented by Congressional legislation. *Sei Fujii*, 242 P.2d at 617.

50. HENKIN, *supra* note 43, at 156 (stating that the distinction between self-executing and not self- executing treaties is characteristic of Western parliamentary systems).

> State Parties undertake to adopt, in accordance with their constitutional processes and the provisions of this Convention, such legislative or other measures as may be necessary to give effect to those rights or freedoms.[51]

This language does not call for implementing legislation before the rights and freedoms of the American Convention are applicable domestically. It states, unambiguously, that if the enumerated rights are not already ensured by domestic legislation, states are required to take legislative action to give effect to those rights.[52] The United States, however, has interpreted this Article to mean that the Treaty is not self-executing, thus barring domestic application until the legislature takes action to translate its provisions into domestic law. According to the United States:

> The article is sufficiently flexible so that each country can best implement the treaty consistent with its domestic practices. . . . Some countries may choose to make the articles of the treaty directly effective as domestic law and this article would permit them to do so. In the U.S. we would interpret this article as authorizing . . . us to refer, where appropriate, to our Constitution, to our domestic legislation already in existence, to our court decisions and to our administrative practice as carrying out the obligations of the Convention. In other words, it is not the intention of the U.S. to interpret the articles of the treaty in Part I as being self-executing.[53]

Nothing in the language of the Treaty or the intent of the drafters indicates that a state may, at its leisure, refer to its domestic legislation, its court decisions, or its administrative law and practice before determining which rights of the American Convention to implement, how to incorporate them into domestic law, and when to make them domestically applicable. Both the plain language of the Treaty and the intent of its drafters indicate that once a state becomes a party, the provisions of the Convention become binding and the state is required to provide its citizens with the rights and freedoms enumerated therein.[54]

---

51. American Convention, *supra* note 12, art. 2, 9 I.L.M. at 102.

52. *Id.*

53. *Conferencia Especializada Interamericana Sobre Derechos Humanos, San Jose, Costa Rica, 7-22 de Noviembre 1969, Actas y Documentos,* 146-47, OEA/SER. K/XVI/1.2 (1973) [hereinafter *Conferencia Especializada Interamericana*] (United States delegation statement). *See also* Donald T. Fox, *The American Convention on Human Rights and Prospects for United States Ratification,* 3 HUM. RTS. 243, 259-60 (1973) (saying the United States delegation explained that United States law would not consider the Convention self-executing).

54. American Convention, *supra* note 12, art. 1, para. 1, 9 I.L.M. at 101 ("The State Parties to this Convention undertake to respect the rights and freedoms recognized herein and to ensure to all persons subject to their jurisdiction, the free exercise of these rights and

B. Federal Clause

Interpreting the treaty as not self-executing, however, is only one method pursued by the United States to weaken the potential domestic effect of the Convention. The United States has also relied on a "federal clause" in the treaty to lessen the federal government's responsibility for compliance by the individual states.[55] At the insistence of the United States delegation, a clause was included in the American Convention which limits the obligations of a national government in a federal system to assure compliance with the treaty by the local governments of its constituent units.[56]

In an effort to protect the legislative power of its fifty states, the United States interprets the federal clause to relieve the federal government of the duty to prevent violations of the American Convention by state governments and from interfering in affairs which are within the exclusive jurisdiction of the states.[57]

This interpretation allows the states to retain their existing laws, adopt changes on their own terms, and does not require the United States government to exercise its jurisdiction "over subject matter over which it would not exercise authority in the absence of the Convention. The United States is merely obligated to take suitable measures to the end that state and local authorities may adopt provisions for the fulfillment of this Convention."[58]

---

freedoms.").

For the drafters' intent that the treaty be self-executing, see Thomas Buergenthal, *The Self-Executing Character of the Convention*, *in* PROTECTING HUMAN RIGHTS IN THE AMERICAS: SELECTED PROBLEMS, *supra* note 12, at 51, 52-53.

55. Fox, *supra* note 53, at 250-54.

56. Thomas Buergenthal, *The Federal Clause of the American Convention*, *in* PROTECTING HUMAN RIGHTS IN THE AMERICAS: SELECTED PROBLEMS, *supra* note 12, at 49, 49-51. The Convention states:

> 1. Where a State Party is constituted as a federal state, the national government of such State Party shall implement all the provisions of the Convention over whose subject matter it exercises legislative and judicial jurisdiction.
>
> 2. With respect to the provisions over whose subject matter the constituent units of the federal state have jurisdiction, the national government shall immediately take suitable measures, in accordance with its constitution and its laws, to the end that the competent authorities of the constituent units may adopt appropriate provisions for the fulfillment of this Convention.

American Convention, *supra* note 12, art. 28, 9 I.L.M. at 109.

57. *United States: Report of the Delegation to the Inter-American Specialized Conference on Human Rights (April 22, 1970)*, 9 I.L.M. 710, 733 (1970).

58. *Id.* at 733 (citation omitted). "Suitable measures could consist of recommendations to the states, for example. The determination of what measures are suitable is a matter for internal decision. The Convention does not require enactment of legislation bringing new subject matter within the federal ambit." *Id.*

The United States interpretation, however, reduces the effectiveness of the American Convention by relieving the federal government of responsibility for the action of its states. The language of the treaty's federal clause requires a federal government to "take suitable measures" to bring the laws of the constituent units into compliance with the provisions of the Convention. Nowhere does the language imply that a federal government is relieved of responsibility for violations by the individual states. Nowhere does the language of the federal clause assert that a state party may be in compliance with the Convention while its constituent units fail to adhere to its provisions. Theoretically, under the United States interpretation, individual state governments could maintain legislation inconsistent with the American Convention's requirements without risking treaty violations by the national government. States which fail to comply with Convention requirements may, under this interpretation of the federal clause, be advised or persuaded, but not forced to change their laws by the federal government. Thus, noncompliance by an individual state would not hold the United States in violation of the Convention.[59]

C. Declarations, Reservations, and Understandings

The United States Department of Justice has suggested a number of reservations, declarations, and understandings to the Convention which would further weaken the treaty's effect.[60] For example, to assure that the treaty will not be self-executing, the Justice Department suggests a declaration to accompany ratification stating that "the United States declares that the provisions of Articles 1 through 32 of this Convention are not self-executing."[61] To insure that the federal government need not interfere with state regulation of the death penalty, another reservation is suggested: "United States adherence to Article 4 is subject to the Constitution and other laws of the United States."[62] These are only two examples of the thirteen reservations or declarations suggested by the Justice Department to accompany United States ratification of the American Convention.[63] While such provisions address any fears that United States' participation could minimize state sovereignty, they also weaken the effectiveness of the Convention. Declarations that render the treaty not self-executing prevent individuals from bringing claims in domestic courts for violations of the treaty. They also deprive the Inter-

59. For example, "individual states within the United States with laws that provide for the death penalty could retain them by virtue of Article 28 [Federal Clause] without the United States being in violation of the Convention." *Id.* at 717.

60. *Letter to President Carter, supra* note 27, at 104-13.

61. *Id.* at 105.

62. *Id.*

63. *Id.* at 104.

American Court and Commission of the benefit of United States court decisions that interpret the Convention, preventing interaction between domestic courts in the United States and the Inter-American Court.[64] A treaty crippled by reservations designed to make the treaty fully consistent with United States law is not a legal obligation at all. The treaty's effectiveness as an incentive for domestic legal reform or improvement is weakened by this attitude. United States ratification of a less forceful version of the Convention will reflect a lack of good faith on the part of the United States to enter into legal obligations that other members of the Convention have already agreed upon.[65]

IV. SOVEREIGNTY CONCERNS: DOMESTIC JURISDICTION OVER HUMAN RIGHTS

> The American people want to make certain that no treaty or executive agreement will be effective to deny or abridge their fundamental rights. Also, they do not want their basic human rights to be supervised or controlled by international agencies over which they have no control.[66]

These are the concerns of Senator John Bricker which contributed to his proposed Constitutional amendment in 1953 (Bricker Amendment). The Bricker Amendment was designed to restrict the President's treaty making authority and to impose limits on a treaty's content.[67] Although the amendment was narrowly defeated in the Senate,[68] it led

---

64. Buergenthal, *supra* note 35, at 51-52.

65. *Human Rights Hearings, supra* note 16 (statement of Charles Yost, former U.S. Ambassador to the United Nations).

> Our refusal to join in the international implementation of the principles we so loudly and frequently proclaim cannot help but give the impression that we do not practice what we preach . . . we seriously undermine our own case when we resist joining in the international endeavor to enforce these rights, which we ourselves had so much to do with launching.

Id.

66. *Hearings on S.J. Res. 1 and S.J. Res. 43 Before Subcomm. on the Judiciary of the United States Senate*, 83d Cong., 1st Sess. 3 (1953) [hereinafter *Hearings on S.J. Res. 1 and S.J. Res. 43*] (statement of Hon. John W. Bricker, Ohio).

67. Thomas Buergenthal, *International Human Rights: U.S. Policy and Priorities*, 14 VA. J. INT'L L. 611, 612 (1974). The Bricker Amendment had three basic aims: 1) to establish that all international agreements require implementing legislation and are thus not self-executing, 2) to reverse the Supreme Court's ruling in *Missouri v. Holland*, 252 U.S. 416 (1920), that the Tenth Amendment does not apply to treaty implementing legislation since the power to make treaties rests with the federal government, and 3) to establish that treaties are subject to the same constitutional constraints which limit the power of the federal government. *Id.* at 612.

68. *Bricker Treaty Amendment Debate, Report on Defeat of Bricker Amendment, 83rd Congress 2nd Session, in* CONGRESSIONAL QUARTERLY ALMANAC X, 254-62 (1954). *See also* Symposium,

to a statement by former Secretary of State John Foster Dulles that the United States Department of State would not seek ratification of any human rights treaties,[69] and created a legacy which is still reflected in current Senate deliberations over human rights treaties.[70] The ideology behind the Bricker Amendment and Secretary of State Dulles' declaration have left a lasting mark on human rights policy in the United States.[71]

Arguments against passage of human rights treaties have not changed substantially since the 1950s.[72] These arguments reflect the attitude that human rights are a matter to be left exclusively to the domestic legislation of a sovereign state. They are not to be controlled through international agreement or monitored by international tribunals.[73] Many Senators feel that "there are severe limits to the extent that a nation can and should shape its domestic, social, economic, and political order by making a treaty. These matters are for local communities, towns, cities, and states."[74] From this perspective, human rights and civil liberties are exclusively within the domestic jurisdiction of the United States and are not the proper subject of an international agreement.[75] This isolationist perspective, however, is marked by residual fears lingering from the days of the Bricker Amendment which are unfounded and create unnecessary obstacles to ratification of human rights treaties in the United States.[76]

The United States Constitution imposes no limitations on the subject matter of international agreements in which the government may participate. The Constitution refers to treaties and agreements with foreign powers,[77] but does not define such agreements or limit their subject matter. There is no constitutional requirement that treaties exclusively address matters of "international concern."[78] In fact, the Supreme Court has upheld treaties on matters that were exclusively

---

Should the Constitution Be Amended to Limit the Treaty Making Power?, 26 S. CAL. L. REV. 346 (1953) (expressing arguments both for and against the Bricker Amendment).

69. *Hearings on S.J. Res. 1 and S.J. Res. 43*, *supra* note 66, at 825 (statement of Hon. John Foster Dulles, Secretary of State of the United States).

70. Hevener Kaufman & Whiteman, *supra* note 37, at 310.

71. *Id.*

72. *Id.* at 334.

73. Henkin, *supra* note 7, at 422.

74. Rovine, *supra* note 37, at 60.

75. *Report of the Standing Committee on Peace and Law Through United Nations, Human Rights Conventions and Recommendations*, *supra* note 42, at 601. *See also* John M. Raymond, *Don't Ratify the Human Rights Conventions*, 54 A.B.A. J. 141 (1968) (arguing that the treaties will be ineffective against oppressive governments and would meddle in domestic affairs).

76. Bitker, *supra* note 36, at 90.

77. U.S. CONST. art. I, § 10, art. II, § 2, art. VI.

78. RESTATEMENT (THIRD) OF THE FOREIGN RELATIONS LAW OF THE UNITED STATES § 302 cmt. c (1986) [hereinafter RESTATEMENT (THIRD) OF FOREIGN RELATIONS].

domestic in nature and generally regarded to be within state, rather than federal, authority.[79] The Court, in defining the scope of the President's treaty making power has never held a treaty invalid because it dealt with an "improper" subject, nor has the President or Senate ever rejected a treaty because the subject matter was not constitutionally "proper."[80]

Furthermore, international law imposes no limitations on the purpose or subject matter of international agreements other than that they may not conflict with a peremptory norm of international law.[81] While the principle of "non-interference in domestic affairs" as defined by Article 2(7) of the U.N. Charter does limit the jurisdictional authority of the U.N. over matters of domestic concern,[82] human rights have been carved out as a specific exception.[83]

In addition, the Vienna Convention on the Law of Treaties recognizes the "ever-increasing importance of treaties" as a means of assuring "universal respect for, and observance of human rights and fundamental freedoms."[84] In light of the wording of the Vienna Convention, it is clear that human rights are a proper subject of international agreements.

By becoming parties to human rights treaties, states have acknowledged that their treatment of individuals is not solely a matter of domestic concern.[85] The principle of noninterference in domestic affairs does not shield states from scrutiny or censure should they torture, murder, or arbitrarily imprison their citizens.[86] The modern development of an international body of human rights law, the existence of universal and regional structures to monitor human rights protection and the increasing influence of nongovernmental human rights organizations in the international community grow out of the ideology

---

79. Missouri v. Holland, 252 U.S. 416 (1920) (protection of migratory waterfowl); De Geofrey v. Riggs, 133 U.S. 258 (1890) (rights of inheritance in land).

80. Louis Henkin, *The Constitution, Treaties and International Human Rights*, 116 U. PA. L. REV. 1012, 1020 (1968).

81. RESTATEMENT (THIRD) OF FOREIGN RELATIONS, *supra* note 78, § 302 cmt. c. *See also* LASSA OPPENHEIM, 1 INTERNATIONAL LAW § 21 (Hersch Lauterpacht ed., 8th ed. 1955) (stating both international and domestic law regulate the same individual conduct; international law, however, attributes this individual conduct to the state).

82. U.N. CHARTER art. 2, para. 7 ("Nothing contained in the present Charter shall authorize the United Nations to intervene in matters which are essentially within the domestic jurisdiction of any state.").

83. *See generally* Michael Reisman, *Sovereignty and Human Rights in Contemporary International Law*, 84 AM. J. INT'L L. 866 (1990) (arguing that no serious scholar maintains that human rights are a purely domestic concern).

84. Vienna Convention on the Law of Treaties, Apr. 24, 1970, pmbl., 8 I.L.M. 679, 680 (1969) (sent to the Senate Nov. 22, 1971).

85. "Today, human rights are of deep 'international concern;' they have an important place in the foreign relations of the United States. Human rights in other countries have become, ineluctably, this country's business." Henkin, *supra* note 80, at 1030.

86. *Id.* (human rights in a given nation have become ineluctably the business of other nations).

that fundamental human rights are of universal concern.[87] International agreements which protect individual rights, therefore, have a primary place in international law.[88]

V. Specific Objections

A. Abortion

Specific provisions of the American Convention have caused concerns in the United States over the potential effect on legal abortions and the death penalty. The American Convention describes the right-to-life in the following terms: "Every person has the right to have his life respected. This right shall be protected by law and, in general, from the moment of conception. No one shall be arbitrarily deprived of his life."[89]

The unique wording of Article 4 differs from the right-to-life provisions in either the Universal Declaration, the U.N. Covenant on Civil and Political Rights, or the European Convention.[90] Undertaking the protection of life "from the moment of conception" has caused concern that ratification could result in a prohibition of legal abortions in the United States.

Some have argued[91] that the United States has failed to protect life "from the moment of conception" by permitting abortions in accordance with the Supreme Court ruling in *Roe v. Wade*.[92] Ratification of the Convention, therefore, may expose the United States to an international lawsuit and potentially unfavorable ruling by the Inter-American Court or Commission.

In fact, because of its participation in the American Declaration, the United States already has faced such a challenge before the Inter-

87. *Id.* at 1012.

88. "For decades now, 'in the ordinary intercourse of nations,' human rights have 'been made subjects of negotiation and treaty.' Surely, the Constitution does not prohibit the United States from negotiating and adhering to such treaties." *Id.* at 1031.

89. American Convention, *supra* note 12, art. 4, para. 1, 9 I.L.M. at 102.

90. Marco Gerardo Monroy Cabra, *Rights and Duties Established by the American Convention on Human Rights*, 30 AM. U. L. REV. 21, 26 (1981) (discussing differences between the wording of the Convention and the International Covenant on Civil and Political Rights).

91. On January 19, 1977, the group "Catholics for Political Action" filed a petition with the Commission against the United States and the Commonwealth of Massachusetts for permitting legal abortions in violation of the American Declaration's "right to life provision." Case 2141, Inter-Am. C.H.R. 25, OEA/Ser.L/V/II.54, doc. 9, rev. 1, para. 1 (1981) (*White, Potter v. United States*, commonly known as the *Baby Boy Case*). The Inter-American Commission rejected this argument and suggested that neither the Declaration's nor the Convention's right to life provisions prohibited abortion. *Id.* para. 19(e)-(h). For a discussion of the *Baby Boy Case*, see Dinah Shelton, *Abortion and the Right to Life in the Inter-American System: The Case of Baby Boy*, 2 HUM. RTS. L.J. 309 (1979).

92. Roe v. Wade, 410 U.S. 113 (1973).

American Commission on Human Rights. In the case of *White & Potter v. United States*,[93] United States' laws permitting abortion were challenged as a violation of the right-to-life provision of Article I of the Declaration. Based upon legislative history, the Commission found that the obligations incurred under the American Declaration of Human Rights did not include a prohibition of abortion.[94] The legislative history of the Declaration reveals that a right-to-life "from the moment of conception" was deliberately excluded by the drafters of the Declaration because such a provision was incompatible with the laws governing the death penalty and abortion in the majority of the American states.[95]

A similar examination of the legislative history of the American Convention reveals the same sensitivity on the part of the drafters toward domestic laws of member states allowing abortion. The original draft of the Convention, submitted to the Commission by the Inter-American Council of Jurists, provided a right-to-life "protected by law from the moment of conception."[96] Recognizing that this could be interpreted as a prohibition of abortion, the words "in general" were added as a qualification to Article 4. Thus, the phrase, "in general, from the moment of conception," was intended by the drafters to refer to a right-to-life which did not interfere with the status of legal abortions in American countries at the time the Convention was drafted. Accordingly, the legal implications of the terminology "in general from the moment of conception" are substantially different from the shorter phrase "from the moment of conception."[97]

The legislative history behind the Declaration and the Convention indicate that neither document was intended to require member states with laws permitting abortions to alter their domestic legislation. Both the United States and Brazil made statements on the record at the San José Conference affirming this interpretation of the Convention. Both countries interpret the language of paragraph 1 of Article 4 as "preserving to State Parties discretion with respect to the content of

---

93. *Case 2141*, Inter-Am. C.H.R. 25.

94. *Id.* paras. 19(e)-(h).

95. *Id.*

96. *Opinion Prepared by the Inter-American Commission on Human Rights on the Draft Convention on Human Rights Approved by the Inter-American Council of Jurists at Its Fourth Meeting (Santiago Chile, 1959)*, OEA/Ser.L/V/II.15, doc. 26 at 3-4 (1966) (giving preference to a draft of the Convention submitted by Uruguay but suggesting that the words "in general" be added to the protection of life "from the moment of conception"). *See also IACHR Annotations on the Draft Inter-American Convention on Protection of Human Rights*, OEA/Ser.L/V/11.19, doc. 53 at 10 (1969).

97. *Case 2141*, Inter-Am. C.H.R. 25, para. 30 ("In the light of this history, it is clear that the . . . addition of the phrase 'in general, from the moment of conception' does not mean that the drafters of the Convention intended to modify the concept of the right to life that prevailed in Bogota, when they approved the American Declaration.").

legislation in the light of their own social development, experience and similar factors."[98] The government of Mexico made a similar interpretive declaration at the time of ratification, stating its belief that the right-to-life language of the Convention would not require Mexico to outlaw abortions.[99] The legislative history of the American Convention and declarations made by the U.S. at the time of drafting indicate that the wording of Article 4 should not prohibit legal abortions in the United States.

B. The Death Penalty

Another example of the potential for interference with state legislation created by the American Convention is found in Article 4's prohibition of the death penalty for persons under 18 or over 70.[100] Since several states in the United States currently permit the death penalty for persons under the age of 18,[101] supporters of current death penalty statutes oppose ratification claiming it would interfere with the legislative discretion of states by compelling the federal government to regulate use of the death penalty among the states.[102]

Despite concerns over the right-to-life language in the American Convention, it is important to note that it does not prohibit the death penalty. Rather, the Convention limits use of the death penalty to only the most serious crimes and explicitly prohibits a sentence of death for political offenders, persons under the age of 18 or over 70, and pregnant women.[103] It also insures the right of appeal and prohibits the re-establishment of the death penalty in countries where it has been abolished.[104] These restrictions would only affect states that have already abolished the death penalty or that allow execution of juveniles under the age of 18. Opposition to the Convention on the basis that states may have to change their death penalty laws is unwarranted. The changes required under the American Convention are no different than

98. *United States: Report of the Delegation of the Inter-American Specialized Conference on Human Rights*, *supra* note 57, at 717.

99. *Basic Documents Pertaining to Human Rights in the Inter-American System*, OEA/Ser.L./V/II.71, doc. 6 rev. 1 at 62 (1987) ("[T]he Government of Mexico considers that the expression 'in general' does not constitute an obligation to adopt, or keep in force, legislation to protect life 'from the moment of conception,' since this matter falls within the domain reserved to the States.").

100. American Convention, *supra* note 12, art. 4, para. 5, 9 I.L.M. at 102.

101. Amnesty International, *The Truth About the Death Penalty in the United States Is Real News*, Briefing Paper, Amnesty International, U.S.A., N.Y. Office, June 1990.

102. Joan Hartman, *"Unusual" Punishment: The Domestic Effects of International Norms Restricting the Application of the Death Penalty*, 52 U. CIN. L. REV. 655, 687 (1983) (discussing United States reluctance to adopt international norms which invalidate inconsistent state legislation).

103. American Convention, *supra* note 12, art. 4, paras. 2-6, 9 I.L.M. at 102.

104. *Id.* art. 4, paras. 1-4, 9 I.L.M. at 102.

those already required under the American Declaration.[105] While the Convention would force the federal government to limit state laws governing application of the death penalty in certain cases, the Declaration has already imposed such obligations on the federal government.[106] The United States is currently in violation of the international human rights obligations it has undertaken in the Declaration for failure to assure uniform, nonarbitrary application of the death penalty nationwide.[107] Accordingly, adoption of the Convention would not impose any greater requirement on the federal government than has already been imposed by United States participation in the Declaration, and would be a means of approaching a uniform standard regulating the use of the death penalty throughout the nation.

VI. REASONS FOR RATIFICATION

Promotion of any human rights treaty in this country requires two steps. First, proponents of ratification must overcome the legacy of the Bricker Amendment and the Cold War era when human rights treaties were immediately suspect in the United States.[108] The foregoing analysis of objections to the Convention has attempted to address these fears by demonstrating that the Convention poses no threat to the domestic legal order of the United States.[109]

Overcoming the legal objections to ratification is, however, only part of the process. The central problem behind ratification is a political one.[110] Legal barriers to ratification can be overcome if the political

---

105. The Inter-American Commission on Human Rights has ruled the U.S. is currently in violation of its duties under the American Declaration because of its failure to regulate the laws of those states which allow for execution of juveniles.

> For the federal government of the United States to leave the issue of the application of the death penalty to juveniles to the discretion of State officials results in a patchwork scheme of legislation which makes the severity of punishment dependent, not, primarily, on the nature of the crime committed, but on the location where it was committed. . . . The failure of the federal government to preempt the states as regards this most fundamental right—the right to life—results in a pattern of arbitrary deprivation of life and inequality before the law, contrary to Articles I and II of the American Declaration of the Rights and Duties of Man, respectively.

Case 9647, Inter-Am. C.H.R. 30, OEA/Ser. L./V./II.71, doc. 9 rev.1, para. 63 (1987).

106. Donald Fox, *Current Development: Inter-American Commission on Human Rights Finds United States in Violation*, 82 AM. J. INT'L L. 601 (1988).

107. *Id.*

108. Hevener Kaufman & Whiteman, *supra* note 37, at 310.

109. The United States Department of Justice has expressed the opinion that, with the appropriate reservations and declarations, there are no Constitutional or legal objections to ratification of the Convention. *Letter to President Carter, supra* note 27.

110. Richard Falk, *Ideological Patterns in the United States Human Rights Debate, in* THE DYNAMICS OF HUMAN RIGHTS, supra note 36, at 29. In order for a human rights policy to be

will exists to move this treaty through the Senate. Unfortunately, there is an almost universal perception in the Senate that human rights treaties are controversial, politically costly, and lack tangible rewards.[111] Ratification will depend largely upon how successfully supporters of the Convention can demonstrate the political, diplomatic, economic, and social advantages of participation in the American Convention.

Senate reluctance to act on the Convention can be overcome through popular support for human rights treaties and a growing awareness of human rights issues in the United States. In 1977, the year when President Carter sent the Convention to the Senate for approval, one of the world's foremost human rights organizations, Amnesty International, had 10,000 members in the United States.[112] Today that number has grown to 386,000.[113] Recognizing the increasing popular concern with international human rights, the United States administration has found it politically expedient to take an increasingly moralistic stand in its dealings with other countries in this hemisphere. "Operation Just Cause" in Panama,[114] the United States "rescue mission" in Grenada,[115] and "Operation Desert Storm"[116] demonstrate the tendency to couch strategic operations in the language of moral justification to elicit popular support and approval. In addition, the United States has also been quick to criticize many Central American countries for widespread and persistent abuses of human rights[117] and regularly conditions its foreign assistance funds on human rights

---

politically successful in the United States it must be supported by a "right-leaning centrist coalition" and political leaders must reconcile human rights initiatives with the "short and long-term geopolitical interests of the United States." *Id.* at 46.

111. Hevener Kaufman & Whiteman, *supra* note 37, at 332-33.

112. Figures as of July 1, 1991. Telephone conversation with Amnesty International U.S.A., National Membership Office, New York, N.Y. (July 1, 1991).

113. *Id.*

114. Michael R. Gordon, *U.S. Troops Move in Panama*, N.Y. TIMES, Dec. 20, 1989, at A1 (presidential spokesman Marlin Fitzwater saying that the operation was designed to restore democracy in Panama and to bring Noriega to the United States to face drug trafficking charges).

115. Ed Magnuson, *D-Day in Grenada*, TIME, Nov. 7, 1983, at 22 (saying the invasion was intended to protect and rescue 1,000 Americans trapped on the island after a bloody Marxist coup).

116. Ann Reilly Dowd, *How Bush Decided*, TIME, Feb. 11, 1991, at 45.

> As the U.N. deadline approached, the President grappled one last time with the morality of going to war. At the Christmas Holidays, he pored over every one of the 82 pages of Amnesty International's agonizing report of arrests, rape and torture in Kuwait. In the first staff meeting after his 12-day respite at Camp David, he told them his conscience was clear. Recalls one who was there: "He said, 'it's black and white, good vs. evil. The man has to be stopped!'"

Id.

117. *See generally* U.S. DEPT. OF STATE, COUNTRY REPORTS ON HUMAN RIGHTS PRACTICES FOR 1990, 486-800 (1991) (publishing lengthy analysis of abuses in each Latin American country).

criteria.[118] While dictating standards of behavior to other nations and enforcing those standards financially and militarily, the United States refuses to adhere to the basic instrument which represents the generally recognized standard of human rights protection among American nations. The United States threatens the integrity of its posture before the nations of this hemisphere when it fails to bind itself to standards to which it holds others and on which it justifies military intervention or the denial of foreign financial assistance.[119] Thus, the United States appears hypocritical in holding the rest of this hemisphere to a standard to which it refuses to adhere.[120] Recent world events indicate that in this era, if the United States wishes to increase its influence among the nations of this hemisphere, multilateral, rather than unilateral, action must prevail.[121] The Organization of American States is an effective framework for such multilateral action and enables the United States to cooperate with its American allies for mutual gain.

In addition, the long-term economic interests of the United States are best promoted by a foreign policy that assures the continued stability and growth of smaller nations in this hemisphere with which it intends to do business.[122] Assuring protection of human rights is a means of promoting social and economic progress particularly in countries frequently torn by social injustice and civil disorders.[123] Those nations which ratify and adhere to the American Convention will safeguard social and economic progress and create a better climate for business, cultural, and political relations.[124] More effective human rights protection in many South and Central American countries would help to forestall the possibility of uprising and civil disorders that disturb peace and world security. As U.S. Senator William Proxmire stated: "[W]here human rights are secure, peace is attendant. When the human rights of any people are threatened, peace itself is threatened."[125]

---

118. *See* David Weissbrodt, *Human Rights and the United States Foreign Policy*, 7 GA. J. INT'L & COMP. L. 231, 232 (1977). *See also* Foreign Assistance Act of 1961, 22 U.S.C. § 2151n (1990) ("No assistance may be provided to the government of any country which engages in a consistent pattern of gross violations of internationally recognized human rights.").

119. Nigel Rodley, *On the Necessity of United States Ratification of the International Human Rights Conventions*, *in* U.S. RATIFICATION OF THE HUMAN RIGHTS TREATIES, *supra* note 27, at 3, 3-19.

120. Buergenthal, *supra* note 35, at 49 ("[I]f the United States does not ratify the Convention, our political involvement in the American Convention system will, of necessity, decrease, as will our influence."). *See also Human Rights Hearings*, *supra* note 16, at 4 (statement of Hon. Charles Yost, former United States Ambassador to the United Nations).

121. Louis B. Sohn, *International Consequences of United States Human Rights Policy*, *in* THE DYNAMICS OF HUMAN RIGHTS, *supra* note 36, at 63.

122. Richard N. Gardner, *A Costly Anachronism*, 53 A.B.A. J. 907, 908 (1967) (arguing that peace, economic and social development, and human rights form a triangle of interdependence).

123. Donald Fraser, *Freedom and Foreign Policy*, 25 FOREIGN POL'Y 140 (1977).

124. *Id.*

125. 113 CONG. REC. 30,902, 30,903 (1967) (speech of Sen. Proxmire on the subject of the

VII. CONCLUSION

Promotion and support of human rights treaties is in the best interest of the United States. As the drafters of the Restatement of Foreign Relations Law recognized:

> Although such conventions generally specify standards already observed in the United States, it has an interest in seeing that they are observed by as many states as possible, not merely to protect its own standards, but to promote conditions abroad that will foster economic development and democratic institutions that are conducive to prosperity in the United States and achievement of its foreign policy objectives. It cannot effectively urge other states to adhere to such conventions without doing so itself.[126]

In order to increase its credibility as a nation committed to human rights around the world, to enhance the level of its cooperation with other nations in this hemisphere, and to promote an environment of social and economic progress in this hemisphere, the United States should ratify the American Convention.

Supplementary Slavery Convention).

126. RESTATEMENT (SECOND) OF THE FOREIGN RELATIONS LAW OF THE UNITED STATES § 118 (1965).

[9]

The Role of the Inter-American Commission and Court of Human Rights in the Protection of Human Rights: Achievements and Contemporary Challenges

*Remarks of Mónica Pinto**

The Inter-American Commission on Human Rights (IACHR) and the Inter-American Court of Human Rights (IACtHR) have been route companions for many, many years. The Commission was created by a political decision of the Consultation Meeting of Ministers of Foreign Affairs, in Santiago, Chile, in 1959 in order to further the respect for the human rights mentioned in the Organization of American States (OAS) Charter and embodied in the American Declaration, "to promote the observance and defense of human rights." The Statute charges the Commission with developing an awareness of human rights among the peoples of the Americas, which is more far-reaching than the mere handling of cases or drafting of reports.[1] It clearly has a political scope, which includes the task of making human rights a cultural value.

The idea of having an organ dedicated to human rights was part of the region's very essence. In fact, the American Declaration states that "the American peoples have acknowledged the dignity of the individual, and their national constitutions recognize that juridical and political institutions, which regulate life in human society, have as their principal aim the protection of the essential rights of man and the creation of circumstances that will permit him to achieve spiritual and material progress and attain happiness" and that "the international protection of the rights of man should be the principal guide of an evolving American law."[2] This means that, in contrast to the universal process in which human rights had to be listed and defined for a huge part of the world, in the Americas, because of the effect of European colonialism, individual rights and civil liberties were already in our constitutions and the regional process had the purpose of providing them with an international framework. The Declaration is a typical example of the listing of rights and duties of republican states.

The idea of having an organ dedicated to human rights was part of the region's very essence.

In the 1960s, when several democracies in the region were overthrown, the IACHR was authorized to deal with communications lodged by any individual against any Member State alleging a violation of the human rights protected in the American Declaration.

It was in this capacity that the Commission started its *in loco* visits to many countries, including my own, Argentina, where it had to deal with the perverse enforced disappearance of many thousands, as well as with the criminal behavior of the military. Today, its report remains a masterpiece of how the clandestine world of the military junta was built up and how it was able to breach all and every human right.[3]

In the 1970s, the Commission started to serve as a consultative organ of the OAS in this field. As such, the IACHR is one of the main organs of the OAS, and therefore, a political organ too.

When the American Convention entered into force, the Court was established in Costa Rica. It spent almost eight years delivering advisory opinions. Its jurisdiction was first recognized by Costa Rica in 1980; by Venezuela, Peru, and Honduras in 1981; by Ecuador and Argentina in 1984; by Colombia and Uruguay in 1986 (when the Court issued its judgment on the preliminary exceptions in the Honduran cases); and by Suriname and Guatemala in 1987.[4] It is true then that the IACHR perhaps was not used to sharing its power with the newcomer court, but it is also true that the court's constituency was not very broad at that time.

In 1988, the Inter-American Court of Human Rights produced its first judgment, the *Velásquez-Rodríguez* case,[5] a manual of international human rights law, where the first chapter deals with the theoretical legal problems posed by the System and the following one applies the law to the given case. Still today, *Velásquez-Rodríguez* continues to be the leading case in the hemisphere for State obligations in human rights. The Court's citation of its own jurisprudence has become lengthy; however, the vast majority of the citations refer to the founding paragraphs of *Velásquez-Rodríguez*. Furthermore, the wisdom of

* *Mónica Pinto is Professor of International Law and Human Rights Law at the University of Buenos Aires Law School, where she currently serves as Dean. She held mandates from the UN for the examination of the human rights situation in Guatemala (1993–97) and Chad (2004–05), and advised on technical cooperation in the matter of human rights (2006–11). She is a member of the Assembly of the Inter-American Institute of Human Rights. She sits on the international boards of the Association for the Prevention of Torture and the International Commission of Jurists. She has appeared before several human rights bodies and tribunals, and before arbitral tribunals both as an attorney and as an expert. This piece is a summary of her remarks at the American University Washington College of Law Conference on the Future of the Inter-American System for the Protection and Promotion of Human Rights (October 15, 2012).*

the definition of enforced disappearance (it was the first time that a court dealt with such a crime) as "a multiple and continuous violation of protected rights," is such that even today it has continued to remain valid, even through the 1994 and 2006 Conventions dealing with enforced disappearance at the regional and at the universal level.[6]

The Court has now, as per the entering into force of the 2000 Rules of both the Commission and the Court,[7] a good docket of cases. Its judgments are important and deal with fundamental aspects of the rights protected by the Inter-American System of Human Rights (IASHR).

The IASHR's Achievements

The System has been able to strengthen human rights with few tools when authoritarian governments were the rule in the region, but it became stronger when democracies returned.

The System set standards in many areas:

1. In 1992, the IACHR adopted two reports, 28 and 29/92,[8] in the cases of the so-called "pardon laws" adopted by Argentina and Uruguay. In both cases, and notwithstanding the differences between them, both countries were in breach of their duties according to the American Declaration and the American Convention on Human Rights. Those reports gave birth to a regional rule according to which States are under the duty to prosecute and punish those responsible for gross human rights violations, to which the statute of limitations is not applicable, and to provide reparation to the victims of these violations.
2. A bunch of Argentinean cases the year before allowed the first friendly settlement dealing with reparations. The Court decided the cases on massacres, both in Colombia and in Guatemala, through friendly settlement as well. The duty to prosecute for gross violations of human rights and the inapplicability of amnesties, self-amnesties, any pardon laws or measures, and the statute of limitations were the object of the Court's judgment in the case of *Barrios Altos* in 2001.[9] The *Lapaco* case in 1999 gave room to the right to truth.[10]
3. The Commission has its own leading case on the compatibility between the Inter-American System of Human Rights and domestic laws — the *Marzioni* case on the "fourth instance formula" in 1996.[11]
4. The System has established many landmarks on freedom of expression. It has not only created a rapporteurship that works independently, the head of which is currently Catalina Botero of Colombia, but in 1996, the Commission also decided that the *desacato,*[12] a crime included in various criminal codes, breached freedom of expression and equality, and it drafted a report stating that crimes relating to freedom of expression should be abolished from criminal legislation. The Court's ruling on *The Last Temptation of Christ*[13] and the *Kimel*[14] cases sets standards that are universally recognized. Access to information is the theme of *Claude Reyes.*[15]
5. Women's rights are dealt with in many relevant cases. Violence against women has a leading case with *Maria da Penha.*[16] Rape as torture is considered in the case of *Raquel Mejía.*[17] The lack of adequate legislation and the need to introduce amendments to the laws in force are considered in the cases of *María Eugenia Morales de Sierra*[18] and *Maria Teresa Morini.*[19] Gender identity and the rights derived from this are the object of the Court's judgment in *Atala Riffo.*[20] Last but not least, the reports on the *Ciudad Juárez*[21] cases brought the international responsibility of the State by omission to the table.
6. The rights of the child are wisely dealt with in the *Street Children*[22] case, which also proposes an interesting cross-fertilization with the universal system and the respective Convention on the Rights of the Child.
7. The right to a free and fair trial is involved in the vast majority of cases lodged against Peru when the Fujimori administration introduced the use of "faceless judges." That is when it formalized the anonymity of judges allegedly to protect their integrity but, at the same time, inhibiting the prosecuted to know who was judging them and *de facto* inhibiting the possibility of challenging the judges.
8. The rights of indigenous peoples are considered in the *Awas Tigny* case.[23]
9. The overlapping of international human rights law and international humanitarian law, namely Common Article 3 of the Geneva Conventions, is dealt with in the Commission's report on the attack to the *La Tablada* barrack.[24]
10. Limits to military jurisdiction are considered in many cases by both the Commission and the Court.

All of these cases and many others gave room for a fluid dialogue with domestic laws, and because of that, have exerted a crucial influence on human rights as enjoyed and exercised by men, women, and children in this region.

We arrived to this point because our states adopted and ratified the conventions and accepted the customary rules. When I say states, I mean states with democratic governments. Neither Videla nor Pinochet, the dictators in Argentina and Chile in the 1970s, ratified the American Convention. We had to wait for elected presidents Alfonsín and Alwyn to express the consent of our communities to be bound by those conventions.

However, the System is not universal. Only 24 out of the 35 OAS Member States have actually ratified the American Convention and have it in force and only 21 of those 24 have accepted the Court's jurisdiction.[25] It should also be mentioned that seven Caribbean countries — Antigua & Barbuda, the Bahamas, Belize, Guyana, St. Kitts & Nevis, St. Lucia, and St. Vincent & the Grenadines — have only ratified the Convention of *Belém do Pará.*[26] This is a typical attitude of many countries that view the rights of women and children as "soft" and, as a result, become bound by those treaties but actually never enforce them. Two other Caribbean countries — Dominica and Grenada — are States Parties to the American Convention and to *Belém do Pará*. Finally, the United States and Canada are outside any conventional link, and last but not least, Cuba has not made up its mind yet on the possibility of returning to the OAS.

In the 21st century, the System became more institutionalized; when the Commission's Article 50 report is not observed by the given government, the case is sent to the Court. The role of the victim is increased in the procedure.

Nowadays, the Inter-American System on Human Rights applies to 500 million individuals. However, it is more Latin American than Inter-American. There is a strong demand for the U.S. and Canada to become States Parties to the Inter-American treaties. The traditional position of the English-speaking Caribbean States of remaining outside the System should also be the object of debate.

What are we talking about when we talk about democracy? Only periodical free and fair elections? Democracy is also a system in which each individual should be in a position to enjoy and exercise his or her human rights.

Ariel Dulitzky, former Deputy Executive Secretary of the Commission and currently Clinical Professor of Law and Director of the Human Rights Clinic, and Director of the Latin America Initiative at the University of Texas Law School, summarized the present situation of the IACHR by stating that there are actually three levels of protection (Commission & Court, Convention, Declaration), and the number of complaints lodged with the Commission is increasing, the procedure is slower than desired, there is a low level of observance of the recommendations, and the trend is to send to the Court the non-observed reports. However, the System has the capacity of producing an important positive impact on actual human rights in the region.

It is said that the IASHR is facing a crisis and that it needs a reform. This is not the first time in which the System faces a situation considered as critical. Beyond the threats, there have been at least three situations in which the IASHR turned into a more sensitive environment. In each of those situations, some states played on the side of the System and a few others on a different one.

When Fujimori decided to withdraw Peru's acceptance of the Court's jurisdiction, the System reacted by drafting a democratic clause that was later included in the OAS Charter and both the Commission and the Court expressed a position. The OAS sided with the human rights system and this helped a lot. Afterwards, on different grounds, an international commission composed of very well-known jurists, including former Inter-American Commissioner and Professor Robert K. Goldman and former Minister of Justice of Argentina León Carlos Arslanian, visited Peru and went public with a critical report. We all know that Fujimori left the government through the back door and that Valentín Paniagua's government came back home.[27]

When Trinidad and Tobago denounced the American Convention because of the enforcement of the Privy Council's ruling in *Re Pratt and Morgan v. the Attorney General for Jamaica*[28] on the human rights of death row inmates, many states made known in the General Assembly that the government could not be released from the observance of a great number of obligations that had already entered into the "property" of each individual.

Now we have the decision of the Bolivarian Republic of Venezuela of September 6, 2012, to denounce the Convention.[29] This is along with the criticism from Brazil because of the precautionary measures granted by the Commission for the members of indigenous communities in the basin in which the Belo Monte hydroelectric power plant is being constructed; the loud criticism of President Correa of Ecuador because of the freedom of expression standards applicable to the dispute he has with *El Universo* (this was the object of a press release by the Special Rapporteur on Freedom of Expression of the IACHR and of the UN);[30] the uncomfortable situation of Peru that came with the Commission's decision to bring to the Court the case on the recovery of the Japanese diplomatic mission in Lima on the grounds that the Government did not conduct an exhaustive investigation on the *Operation Chavin de Huántar*, especially on the extrajudicial execution of three members of MRTA; and the inexplicable silence of Argentina.[31]

How close or how far from the System are these governments? Venezuela was the land of asylum when our southern countries were under military rule; it was the friend who opened the door to a safer life.

All of these heads of state propose reforming the System to be more functional to the popular democracies that rule the majority of the countries in the region. The IACHR decided to take the lead in that sense and started a consultation on what could or should be the object of a reform. The Court — which lacks jurisdiction on Trinidad and Tobago and will experience the same with respect to Venezuela next year — observes this process. The IACHR — which maintains its capacity to handle complaints against those states on the grounds of the rights protected by the American Declaration — is viewed as the main protagonist at this time.

Victims and rights are absent from this debate. Instead, democracy is the main issue. The point is: What are we talking about when we talk about democracy? Only periodical free and fair elections? Democracy is also a system in which each individual should be in a position to enjoy and exercise his or her human rights. Democracy comes into the human rights picture as a context element; it is the better-known system for human rights to be respected. Through the protection of human rights, democracy is strengthened.

Some years ago, writing on the future of the Inter-American System on Human Rights, Juan Méndez, former Inter-American Commissioner and Special Rapporteur of the United Nations on Torture, stated that it must be noted that the OAS instruments refer to "representative democracy" and not simply to democracy. This expression seems to be different from "participatory democracy" and is meant to convey an emphasis on the legitimacy of the representation of those who have been elected to posts and who for that reason are supposed to know what is best for all concerned.

Present criticism does not include any consideration on the financing of the System, which today depends mainly on foreign sources. It does not include any proposal for new recruitments in order to cope with the great number of complaints more efficiently and in less time. It does not underline any of the obstacles that the System — mainly the Commission — faces as a victim of its own success. The number of complaints lodged every year with the IACHR reaches 1,500, a figure that expresses the confidence of individuals and NGOs in the Commission as an independent body to monitor human rights. Its autonomy is the System's greatest asset, an autonomy that can be dramatically killed or hurt, but also that can be undermined through details, which is an important threat. Facts brought to this process are not the expression of new patterns. The Commission's decision in the Peruvian case of the Japanese Embassy (in which President Fujimori entered the Embassy to assure that no one would survive) is consistent with its previous report on the *La Tablada* case in 1997 (in which President Alfonsín entered the barrack to assure that all those alive would survive).[32]

We are here because we need this Inter-American System of Human Rights to be there — amended or not — composed by the best, protecting human beings, elevating the level of protection, enlarging the scope of existing human rights, and increasing the protected rights.

Unfortunately, there is no room to believe that governments' approach to the IASHR is fair. It seems like a process that is after the softening of the States' duties towards the System. As explained above, all of the governments mentioned have *parti pris* against the System. All of them are popular democracies, which seem to believe that as such they should not be the object of any human rights monitoring. It should be recalled that being an effective democracy is a condition to be an active member of the Council of Europe, a status that includes the binding nature of the European Convention on Human Rights and of its organs' decisions. There are no alternatives to this system because it is an expert system and others are mainly political, be it the UNASUR, ALBA, or CELAC,[33] where political necessity plays a central role and where chiefs of state and of government are in command.

Human rights emerged after the Second World War and became the great feature of the legal and political order that was established then. Its "western" origin was nuanced by the political action of the decolonization process and the third world positions, as well as by the strong interpretations provided by treaty bodies and fed by NGOs and civil society. In this field, the IASHR has achieved important goals that impose themselves as regional rules and look broader than the reading in force in the United States, Canada, and even the European System.

Lots of technicalities may be amended or even introduced in this process. In fact, an academic community to study and construct a critical analysis of the decisions and judgments should be established. A formal statute for civil society expressed by NGOs should be considered. New and clearer rules should be adopted relating to precautionary measures, to rights protected, and to the integration and the role of rapporteurships in the protection system. But it is not because of their absence that we are here now. We are here because we need this Inter-American System of Human Rights to be there — amended or not — composed by the best, protecting human beings, elevating the level of protection, enlarging the scope of existing human rights, and increasing the protected rights. We, the community of individuals living in the countries covered by the Inter-American System do need the System; we do thank the expert and independent advice of the experts. Our governments should adopt a decisive policy in favor of the strengthening of the System; they should speak loudly because they are bound to this System.

It is our hope that the end of this transition will leave us with a better, stronger Inter-American System to further advance the actual enjoyment of human rights in the region.

Endnotes

1 Statute of the Inter-American Commission on Human Rights, art.18(a), Oct. 1, 1979, O.A.S. Res. 447 (IX-0/79), OEA/Ser.P/IX.0.2/80.

2 American Declaration of the Rights and Duties of Man, O.A.S. Official Rec., OEA/Ser. L./V./II.23, doc. 21 rev. 6 (1948) (reprinted in Basic Documents Pertaining to Human Rights in the Inter-American System, OEA/Ser. L.V/II.82, doc. 6 rev. 1, at _ (1992)).

3 Report on the Situation of Human Rights in Argentina, OEA/Ser.L/V/II.49, doc. 19 corr.1 (April 11, 1980).

4 Organization of American States, American Convention on Human Rights, Nov. 22, 1969, O.A.S.T.S. No. 36, 1144 U.N.T.S. 123, *available at* http://www.oas.org/en/iachr/mandate/Basics/4.RATIFICATIONS%20AMERICAN% 20CONVENTION.pdf.

5 Velásquez-Rodríguez v. Honduras, Merits, Judgment, Inter-Am. Ct. H.R. (ser. C) No.4 (July 29, 1988).

6 Convention Against Torture and Other Cruel, Inhuman or Degrading Treatment or Punishment, 10 December 10, 1984, 1465 U.N.T.S. 85; Inter-American Convention to Prevent and Punish Torture, O.A.S. Treaty Series No. 67, *entered into force* Feb. 28, 1987, *reprinted in* Basic Documents Pertaining to Human Rights in the Inter-American System, OEA/Ser.L.V/II.82 doc. 6 rev.1 at 83, 25 I.L.M. 519 (1992).

7 Basic Documents Pertaining to Human Rights in the Inter-American System, OEA/Ser. L.V/II.82 doc.6 rev.1 at 17 (1992), *available at* http://www.corteidh.or.cr/docs/libros/Basingl01.pdf.

8 Report Nº 28/92, Inter-Am. Comm'n H.R. (Oct. 2, 1992) (concerning cases 10.147, 10.181, 10.240, 10.262, 10.309 and 10.311 re Argentina), *available at* http://www.cidh.oas.org/annualrep/92eng/Argentina10.147.htm;

Report N° 29/92, Inter-Am. Comm'n H.R. (Oct. 2, 1992) (concerning cases 10.029, 10.036, 10.145, 10.305, 10.372, 10.373, 10.374 and 10.375 re Uruguay), *available at* http://www.cidh.oas.org/annualrep/92eng/Uruguay10.029.htm.

[9] Barrios Altos v. Peru, Merits, Judgment, Inter-Am. Ct. H.R. (ser. C) No. 75 (Mar. 14, 2001).

[10] Report N° 70/99, Inter-Am. Comm'n H.R. (May 4, 1999) concerning Case No. 12.059, Carmen Aguiar De LaPaco v. Argentina), *available at* http://www.cidh.oas.org/annualrep/99eng/Admissible/Argentina12059.htm.

[11] Where it states that "in democratic societies, where the courts function according to a system of powers established by the Constitution and domestic legislation, it is for those courts to review the matters brought before them. Where it is clear that there has been a violation of one of the rights protected by the Convention, then the Commission is competent to review." Report N° 39/96, Inter-Am. Comm'n H.R., ¶ 60 (Oct. 15, 1996) (concerning case No. 11.673 re. Argentina), *available at* http://www.cidh.oas.org/annualrep/96eng/Argentina11673.htm.

[12] *Desacato* laws criminalize expression which offends, insults, or threatens a public official in the performance of his or her official duties. *See* Report on the Compatibility of "Desacato" Laws with the American Convention on Human Rights, Inter-Am. Comm'n H.R., OEA/Ser. L/V/II.88, doc. 9 rev., 212 (1995).

[13] "The Last Temptation of Christ" (Olmedo-Bustos et al.) v. Chile, Merits, Reparations and Costs, Judgment, Inter-Am. Ct. H.R. (ser. C) No. 73 (Feb. 5, 2001).

[14] Kimel v. Argentina, Merits, Reparations and Costs, Judgment, Inter-Am. Ct. H.R. (ser. C) No. 177 (May 2, 2008).

[15] Claude-Reyes et al. v. Chile, Merits, Reparations and Costs, Judgment, Inter-Am. Ct. H.R. (ser. C) No. 151 (Sept. 19, 2006).

[16] Report N° 54/01, Inter-Am. Comm'n H.R. (April 16, 2001) (concerning Case No. 12.051: Maria Da Penha Maia Fernandes & Brazil), *available at* http://www.cidh.oas.org/women/Brazil12.051.htm.

[17] Report N° 5/96, Inter-Am. Comm'n H.R. (March 1, 1996) (concerning Case No. 10.970: Peru) *available at* http://www.cidh.oas.org/women/Peru10970.eng.htm.

[18] Sierra v. Guatemala, Case 11.625, Inter-Am. Comm'n H.R., Report No. 4/01, OEA/Ser./L/V/II.111, doc. 20 rev. (2001).

[19] Morini v. Argentina, Case 11.307, Inter-Am, Comm'n H.R., Report No. 102/99. OEA/Ser.L/V/II.106 doc. 3 rev. (1999).

[20] Atala Riffo and daughters v. Chile, Merits, Reparations, and Costs, Judgment, Inter-Am. Ct. H.R. (ser. C) No. 239 (Feb. 24, 2012).

[21] González et al. ("Cotton Field") v. Mexico, Preliminary Objections, Merits, Reparations and Costs, Judgment, Inter-Am. Ct. H.R. (ser. C) No. 205 (Nov. 16, 2009).

[22] Street Children v. Guatemala, Merits, Judgment, Inter-Am. Ct. H.R. (ser. C) No. 63 (Nov. 19, 1999).

[23] Awas Tingni Community v. Nicaragua, Merits, Reparations and Costs, Judgment, Inter-Am. Ct. H.R. (ser. C) No. 79 (Aug. 31, 2001).

[24] Abella v. Argentina, Case 11.137, Inter-Am. Comm'n H.R., Report 55/97, OEA/Ser.L/V/II.98, doc. 6 rev. (1998).

[25] States bound by the American Convention are Argentina, Barbados, Bolivia, Brazil, Chile, Colombia, Costa Rica, Dominica, Dominican Republic, Ecuador, El Salvador, Grenada, Guatemala, Haiti, Honduras, Jamaica, Mexico, Nicaragua, Panama, Paraguay, Peru, Suriname, Uruguay and Venezuela. All of them with the exception of Dominica, Grenada, and Jamaica have accepted the Court's jurisdiction. Trinidad and Tobago denounced the Convention in 1999 and Venezuela announced its denunciation in 2012. *See* American Convention on Human Rights, *supra* note 5.

[26] Inter-American Convention on the Prevention, Punishment and Eradication of Violence Against Women, OAS Treaty Series A- June 9, 1994, 33 I.L.M. 1534 (entered into force on March 5, 1995).

[27] Alberto Fujimori was a democratically elected President of Perú. On April 5, 1992 he dissolved the Parliament and started governing *de facto*. In May 1999, he decided to unrecognize the jurisdiction of the Inter-American Court of Human Rights. Valentín Paniagua took office as President of Perú when Fujimori was removed from office through the impeachment process by the National Congress in 2000.

[28] Pratt and Morgan v. Jamaica, Commc'n No. 210/1986, U.N. Doc. CCPPR/C/35/D/210/1986 (1989). In its decision, the Privy Council considered that inmates on death row for more than five years were suffering cruel treatment and were being punished twice for a crime, thus, in breach of the *non bis in idem* principle.

[29] The Bolivarian Republic of Venezuela denounced the American Convention on the grounds of the unequal standards applied by the Inter-American Commission of Human Rights.

[30] Press Release R72/11: Office of the Special Rapporteur Expresses Profound Concern Regarding Conviction of Journalist, Directors and Media Outlet in Ecuador, ORGANIZATION OF AMERICAN STATES (July 21, 2011), *available at* http://www.oas.org/en/iachr/expression/showarticle.asp?artID=857&lID=1.

[31] IACHR Takes Case Involving Peru to Inter-American Court, Press Release No. 137/11 (Dec. 30, 2011).

[32] Cruz Sanchez v. Peru, Petition 136/03, Inter-Am. Comm'n H.R., Report No. 13/04 (2004); Abella v. Argentina, Inter-Am. Comm'n H.R., *supra* note 24.

[33] Union of South American Nations, Bolivarian Alliance for Peoples of Our America, Community of Latin American and Caribbean States.

Part III
The European System

[10]

The European Court of Human Rights

Christiane Bourloyannis-Vrailas

> *The European Court of Human Rights is surely one of the busiest and most exemplary of international judicial bodies. It exerts a profound influence on the laws and social realities of its Member States and has become the paradigm for other regional human rights courts, not to mention other international judicial bodies in general.*
>
> Dame Rosalyn Higgins, on the occasion of the Court's 50th anniversary[1]

A. *Overview: The Mechanism of the European Court of Human Rights*

1. *Brief History*

The drafters of the 1950 European Convention on Human Rights[2] could hardly have predicted its impact over the years on the lives of the people covered by its protective provisions, as well as on the development of international human rights law more generally. This progress resulted in no small measure from the visionary decision of the Council of Europe (CoE) Member States, to build, from the very start, the foundations of what would become a remarkable enforcement mechanism.

---

[1] Speech by the President of the International Court of Justice, Jan. 30, 2009: "The International Court of Justice and the European Court of Human Rights: Partners for the Protection of Human Rights," p. 9, *available at* http://www.ECHR.coe.int/NR/rdonlyres/38D1E6A5-DE24-42BD-BC3D-45CCCC8A7F8A/0/30012009PresidentHigginsHearing_eng_.pdf.

[2] Convention for the Protection of Human Rights and Fundamental Freedoms, Nov. 4, 1950, 213 U.N.T.S. 222, Eur. T.S. No. 5 (hereinafter: "Convention").

The original system involved three institutions. The now defunct European Commission of Human Rights would decide on the admissibility of a complaint and offer a non-binding opinion on the merits. The matter could then be referred to the European Court of Human Rights (ECtHR) for a binding decision either by the State concerned or the Commission – individuals did not have direct access to the Court. Otherwise, the case was decided by the CoE Committee of Ministers. Acceptance by a State Party of the right of individual petition was optional at the time.

The idea of merging the Commission and the Court – and doing away with the quasi-judicial role of the Council of Ministers – began to take hold in the late eighties, but it was not until 1994 that the decision to reform the system was taken. As resort to the Convention's enforcement machinery developed into a familiar procedure for Europeans and State acceptance of the right of individual complaint became the standard, the backlog of cases submitted to the lengthy and complex procedure increased steadily. The situation was only going to worsen with the surge in the number of Parties to the Convention after the end of the Cold War.[3] Protocol No. 11 to the Convention[4] was thus adopted, vesting competence to consider alleged violations of the Convention in a single organ – a full-time Court – and rendering acceptance of the right of individual petition mandatory for all States Parties.

This development, coupled with the expansion of the Court's jurisdiction over a population of more than 800 million, resulted in a monumental increase in its activity: more than 90% of the judgments in the Court's first fifty years were delivered between 1998 (the year when Protocol No. 11 entered into force) and 2009. The 10,000th judgment mark was hit on September 18, 2008.[5]

It quickly became apparent that the system was not sustainable in the long term, with the number of new applications – inadmissible for the most part – growing annually in the tens of thousands, resulting in an unmanageable backlog. Only two years after the entry into force of Protocol No. 11, a

[3] *See, e.g.*, V. Miller, "Protocol 11 and the New European Court of Human Rights," *House of Commons Library Research Papers*, No. 98/109 (1998), pp. 7–10.

[4] Protocol No. 11 to the Convention for the Protection of Human Rights and Fundamental Freedoms, restructuring the control machinery established thereby, May 11, 1994, Eur. T.S. No. 155.

[5] *50 Years of Activity: The European Court of Human Rights – Some Facts and Figures* (ECtHR Pub., 2010), pp. 3, 5. By Dec. 31, 2010, the full-time ECtHR had delivered over 12,500 judgments (*Annual Report 2010 of the European Court of Human Rights* (CoE Pub., 2011), p. 14). All CoE/ECtHR documents and publications on the Court referred to in this Chapter are *available at* http://www.ECHR.coe.int/ECHR/homepage_EN. Judgments and decisions are *available at* http://ECHR.coe.int/ECHR/en/hudoc).

process for further reform was initiated, culminating in the adoption on May 12, 2004, of Protocol No. 14.[6] After an unduly long time, that instrument entered into force on June 1, 2010.[7] The description of the Court in sections 2–5 below is thus based on the provisions of the Convention as amended by both Protocols Nos. 11 and 14 (read together with the Rules of Court).[8]

With the number of pending applications already close to 120,000 by the start of 2010,[9] the CoE adopted a ten-year Action Plan outlining a series of practical measures to address the continuing challenges facing the Court[10] and calling for consideration of further reform proposals, including enhancement of the filtering of applications. The situation will be reviewed after five years and again by the end of 2019, when, if necessary, "more profound changes" will be envisaged.[11]

2. *Organization*

a. *Seat*

Since it became operational, in 1959, the ECtHR has had its seat in the French city of Strasbourg – the Headquarters of the CoE. It moved into the "Human Rights Building," one of the city's architectural landmarks, in 1995.

[6] Protocol No. 14 to the Convention for the Protection of Human Rights and Fundamental Freedoms, amending the control system of the Convention, Eur. T.S. No. 194. For an analysis, *see, e.g.*, P. Lemmens, & W. Vandenhole, eds., *Protocol No. 14 and the Reform of the European Court of Human Rights* (Antwerpen: Intersentia, 2005).

[7] Entry into force was contingent on ratification by *all* 47 Member States of the CoE. Russia refused to do so for many years, essentially because of a perception of bias by the Court against it, rather than opposition to the reform process as such (*see, e.g.*, B. Bowring, "The Russian Federation, Protocol No. 14 (and 14*bis*), and the Battle for the Soul of the ECHR," 2 *Goettingen J. Int'l. L.* 589 (2010), pp. 605 *et seq*). This delay prompted the other Member States to conclude an interim arrangement to cope with the situation: Protocol No. 14*bis*, which allowed, after only three ratifications, immediate operationalization of some reforms envisaged in Protocol No. 14 to increase the efficiency of the Court (Protocol No. 14 *bis* to the Convention for the Protection of Human Rights and Fundamental Freedoms, May 27, 2009, Eur. T.S. No. 204). Protocol No. 14*bis* was in force from Oct. 1, 2009, until the entry into force of Protocol No. 14.

[8] The latest version of the Rules of Court, brought in line with the provisions of Protocol No. 14, is dated June 1, 2010.

[9] *Annual Report 2009 of the European Court of Human Rights* (CoE Pub., 2010), p. 139.

[10] The number of pending applications by Dec. 31, 2010 has risen to 139,650. Of these, 63.2% concern only 5 out of the 47 States Parties (Russia leading with 28.9%, followed by Turkey, Romania, Ukraine and Italy (*Annual Report 2010, supra* note 5, pp. 145, 147)).

[11] *High-level conference on The Future of the European Court of Human Rights*, Interlaken Declaration, Feb. 19, 2010, "Implementation," ¶ 6. For a more detailed discussion, *see, e.g.*, A. Mowbray, "The Interlaken Declaration – The Beginning of a New Era for the European Court of Human Rights?," 10 *Hum. Rts. L. Rev.* 519 (2010), pp. 519–528.

b. *Composition*

The Court is composed of the same number of judges as there are States Parties to the Convention on Human Rights, i.e. forty-seven.[12] The judges are elected by majority by the CoE Parliamentary Assembly from lists of three candidates proposed by each State Party.

Article 21(1) of the Convention requires judges to be "of high moral character" and "either possess the qualifications required for appointment to high judicial office or be jurisconsults of recognized competence," but leaves the national selection procedure up to each State. The Parliamentary Assembly has taken its electoral task seriously, given that the Court's authority "is contingent on the stature of judges and the quality and coherence of the Court's case law."[13] It has repeatedly called on States to ensure that national procedures are consistent, fair and transparent; it wants to be presented with a real choice. The Assembly has also taken steps to improve its own procedure for examining the candidates, including by conducting interviews. It has further introduced linguistic requirements and adopted a policy aimed at achieving gender balance within the Court.[14]

Judges serve for a non-renewable term of nine years[15] (but there is an age-limit at seventy). They sit on the Court in their individual capacity. During their tenure, they cannot engage in any activity incompatible with their independence or impartiality.

A judge takes part in proceedings against the State in respect of which he or she has been elected[16] before a Chamber or Grand Chamber, but only

---

12 These are also the members of the CoE: Albania, Andorra, Armenia, Austria, Azerbaijan, Belgium, Bosnia and Herzegovina, Bulgaria, Croatia, Cyprus, Czech Republic, Denmark, Estonia, Finland, France, Georgia, Germany, Greece, Hungary, Iceland, Ireland, Italy, Latvia, Liechtenstein, Lithuania, Luxembourg, Malta, Moldova, Monaco, Montenegro, Netherlands, Norway, Poland, Portugal, Romania, Russian Federation, San Marino, Serbia, Slovakia, Slovenia, Spain, Sweden, Switzerland, the former Yugoslav Republic of Macedonia, Turkey, Ukraine, United Kingdom.

13 Parliamentary Assembly Resolution 1726 (2010) entitled "Effective Implementation of the European Convention on Human Rights: the Interlaken Process," ¶ 7.

14 In the same vein, the Committee of Ministers established in Nov. 2010 a Panel of Experts to advise States on the suitability of candidates (Resolution CM/Res(2010)26). For a more detailed discussion of the selection process by the Assembly, *see, e.g.*, A. Drzemczewski, "Election of Judges to the Strasbourg Court: An Overview," *Eur. Hum. Rts. L. Rev.* 377 (2010), pp. 377–83.

15 Prior to the entry into force of Protocol No. 14, judges were elected for a renewable six-year period. The reform was introduced to enhance the independence and impartiality of the Court.

16 This formulation is used as a judge need not be of the same nationality as the State that has submitted his or her candidature. For the sake of simplicity, that person will be referred to hereinafter as "national judge."

exceptionally before committees. Any judge must withdraw from a case where his or her impartiality or independence may be called into doubt. When the national judge withdraws or is otherwise unable to hear a case, the President appoints an *ad-hoc judge* from a reserve list previously submitted by the State concerned.

c. *Structure*

Every judge is assigned to one of the five Sections of the Court for a three year-period. Each Section has a President and a Vice-President. It has to be geographically and gender balanced and reflect the different legal systems among the Parties to the Convention. The Court sits in the formations below.

i. Plenary

The Plenary performs a number of organizational functions, such as electing its President, two Vice-Presidents and the Presidents of the Sections for a three-year renewable term,[17] setting up Chambers, as well as adopting the Rules of the Court. The Plenary also elects the Registrar and Deputy-Registrar(s) for a renewable five-year term.

ii. Single-Judge Formation

Single judges are appointed, by rotation, for a twelve-month period by the President of the Court and are assigned in advance to consider applications with respect to particular States, excluding the State in respect of which they have been elected. A single judge considers, with assistance from a rapporteur of the Registry, manifestly ill-founded individual applications and can declare them inadmissible or strike them from the list. In case of doubt, the case is referred to a committee or a Chamber.[18]

iii. Committees of Three Judges

Committees are constituted within each Section for a twelve-month period. They can, unanimously, declare individual applications inadmissible where such decision can be taken "without further examination." They can also declare such applications admissible and render simultaneously a judgment

[17] Each Vice-President of the Court is also President of a Section.

[18] Establishment of the single-judge formation is one of the major innovations of Protocol No. 14 – previously, such filtering had to be performed by a committee of three judges. About 90% of applications are clearly inadmissible or ill-founded (*Annual Report 2010, supra* note 5, p. 17).

on the merits, if the underlying question is already the "subject of well-established case-law of the Court."[19]

iv. Chambers

Chambers of seven judges are constituted within each Section to decide on the admissibility and merits of both individual and inter-State applications. For each case, the Chamber includes the President of the Section and the national judge(s). The other members are designated by the Section's President in rotation from among the judges of that Section.

v. Grand Chamber

The Grand Chamber is composed of seventeen judges, including the President and Vice-Presidents of the Court and the Presidents of the Sections, as well as the national judge(s). It has the following competences:

1) to hear a case relinquished by a Chamber either because it raises a "serious question" affecting the interpretation of the Convention or its Protocols or because there is a risk that the outcome may be inconsistent with a previous judgment, if none of the parties objects;[20]
2) to hear a case referred by one of the parties within three months following a Chamber judgment. The request for referral is accepted only if the case raises a "serious question" affecting the interpretation or application of the Convention or its Protocols or "a serious issue of general importance";[21]

---

[19] This new competence under Protocol No. 14 constitutes a significant development, since around 50% of admissible applications concern so-called "repetitive" or "clone" cases (*see, e.g.*, Committee of Ministers Doc. CM(2009)181, Dec. 2, 2009, ¶ 6). As indicated in the *Explanatory Report* on Protocol No. 14, " '[w]ell-established case-law' normally means case-law which has been consistently applied by a Chamber. Exceptionally, however, it is conceivable that a single judgment on a question of principle may constitute 'well-established case-law', particularly when the Grand Chamber has rendered it" (¶ 68, *available at* http://conventions.coe.int/Treaty/EN/Reports/Html/194.htm).

[20] In such instance, the members of the Chamber which relinquished jurisdiction also sit in the Grand Chamber. Such relinquishment occurs rather infrequently. Examples include a recent case concerning the legality of national measures implementing Security Council sanctions against persons associated with the Taliban and al-Qaeda (*Nada v. Switzerland*, App. No. 10593/08), *see* Eur. Ct. H.R. Press Release No. 769 (Oct. 20, 2010).

[21] Only a small proportion of such requests for referral under Article 43 of the Convention are accepted: *e.g.* in 2010, only 11 out of 264 (*Annual Report 2010, supra* note 5, p. 141). In that event, none of the judges associated with the case sit in the Grand Chamber except the President of the relevant Chamber and the national judge.

3) to give advisory opinions, at the request of the CoE Committee of Ministers, on legal questions concerning the interpretation of the Convention and its Protocols, as long they do not relate to any issue (such as the scope of protected rights and freedoms) which could give rise to an individual or State application;[22] and
4) to consider a referral by the Committee of Ministers for non-compliance with a judgment.[23]

d. *Registry*
The Registry provides legal and administrative support to the ECtHR in the exercise of its judicial functions. It receives and processes the applications lodged with the Court. Each Section is assisted by the Section Registrar and Deputy Registrar.[24]

3. *Jurisdiction*

The ECtHR has the power to decide on the scope of its own jurisdiction.

a. *Jurisdiction Ratione Materiae*
The Court's jurisdiction extends to "all matters concerning the interpretation and application of the Convention and the Protocols thereto."[25] It has thus

[22] So far the Court has only issued two advisory opinions under Article 47 of the Convention, both regarding the lists of candidates submitted with a view to the election of judges (the first on Feb. 12, 2008, the second on Jan. 22, 2010; another request was found inadmissible).

[23] This is a new competence under Protocol No. 14, aimed at bringing additional means of pressure on a State to abide by the Court's judgments – especially when the underlying issue is a structural one, giving rise to a considerable number of repetitive applications. *See Explanatory Report, supra* note 19, ¶¶ 98–100. In such case, the judges rendering the original judgment sit in the Grand Chamber.

[24] By the end of 2010, the Registry had about 630 staff members (*Annual Report 2010, supra* note 5, p. 16). The budget of the Court and Registry (financed out of the CoE budget, to which all Member States contribute based on population and GDP) was €58.48 million for 2010 (*id.*, pp. 20–21).

[25] Article 32(1). In addition to those Protocols amending procedural articles of the original 1950 Convention, there are several that enlarge the scope of protected rights: Protocol (No. 1) to the Convention for the Protection of Human Rights and Fundamental Freedoms, Mar. 20, 1953, Eur. T.S. No. 9; Protocol No. 4 to the Convention for the Protection of Human Rights and Fundamental Freedoms, securing certain rights and freedoms other than those already included in the Convention and in the first Protocol thereto, Sep. 16, 1963, Eur. T.S. No. 46; Protocol No. 6 to the Convention for the Protection of Human Rights and Fundamental Freedoms concerning the Abolition of the Death Penalty, Apr. 28, 1983, Eur. T.S. No. 114; Protocol No. 7 to the Convention for the Protection of Human Rights and Fundamental Freedoms, Nov. 22, 1984, Eur. T.S. No. 117; Protocol No. 12 to

been called upon to determine the scope of the rights protected by these instruments when examining the admissibility of applications. In interpreting the meaning of terms and notions in the Convention and the Protocols, the Court takes into account other elements of international law and their interpretation by competent organs, as well as the "practice of European States reflecting their common values."[26]

b. *Jurisdiction Ratione Personae*

The Court has jurisdiction to examine complaints against a State Party for violations of the Convention or its Protocols. These can be referred to it by two types of applicants: 1) another State Party or 2) a person, a non-governmental organization or group of individuals – the overwhelming majority of cases. Applicants in the second category must claim to be victims of a violation of their rights: the Court does not accept individual applications *in abstracto* or as *actio popularis*.[27]

Article 1 of the Convention provides that States Parties must secure to "everyone within their jurisdiction" the rights and freedoms enshrined therein.[28] In accordance with ECtHR jurisprudence, in exceptional circumstances, acts of States Parties performed or producing effects outside their territory may amount to exercise of State jurisdiction within the meaning of this provision and thus fall within the Court's competence. This is the case, in particular, where a State Party exercises "effective control" over an area or has, at the very least, "a decisive influence" over it.[29] State X may also be held accountable for the violation of rights and freedoms of persons present in the territory of State Y who are found to be under the authority and control of State X through its agents operating – whether lawfully or unlawfully – in State Y.[30]

---

the Convention for the Protection of Human Rights and Fundamental Freedoms, Nov. 11, 2000, Eur. T.S. No. 177 and Protocol No. 13 to the Convention for the Protection of Human Rights and Fundamental Freedoms, concerning the Abolition of the Death Penalty in All Circumstances, May 3, 2002, Eur. T.S. No. 187.

26 *See, e.g., Demir and Baykara v. Turkey* (GC), App. No. 34503/97 (Eur. Ct. H.R. Nov. 12, 2008), ¶ 85.

27 Nevertheless, the Court has interpreted the notion of "victim" in a broad sense. *See, e.g., Practical Guide on Admissibility Criteria* (ECtHR Pub., 2009), pp. 12–15.

28 Objections to the Court's jurisdiction in this context may also be raised as objections *ratione loci*, but they are generally considered in terms of the personal jurisdiction of the Court.

29 *See, e.g., Loizidou v. Turkey* (GC), Eur. Ct. H.R. 1996-VI, ¶ 52 or *Ilaşcu and Others v. Moldova and Russia* (GC), Eur. Ct. H.R. 2004-VII, ¶¶ 314, 392.

30 *See, e.g., Issa and Others v. Turkey*, App. No. 31821/96 (Eur. Ct. H.R. Nov. 16, 2004), ¶ 71.

The terms "within their jurisdiction" have also been interpreted restrictively. Thus, in the controversial *Banković* decision, the Court held that extra-territorial acts such as bombing operations conducted by State Parties in the territory of a non-Party could not engage the formers' responsibility under the Convention, given the lack of jurisdictional link with the victims under the circumstances.[31] The ECtHR has also rejected as inadmissible *ratione materiae* applications where the impugned acts were carried out by States Parties on behalf of an international organization, as scrutinizing such acts would amount to interference with the latter's mission.[32]

c. *Jurisdiction Ratione Temporis*

The critical date for purposes of determining whether the ECtHR has temporal jurisdiction over an application is the date of the entry into force of the Convention – and, where relevant, one or more of its Protocols – in respect of the Respondent State.[33] In each specific case, the Court must therefore identify the exact time of the alleged interference with an applicant's right. In so doing, it "must take into account both the facts of which the applicant complains and the scope of the Convention right alleged to have been violated."[34]

Where an alleged violation is based on facts that occurred prior to the entry into force of the Convention for the Respondent State but persists after that date, i.e. situations involving a continuing violation, the case has been considered to fall within the Court's temporal jurisdiction.[35]

The ECtHR has held that the procedural obligation under Article 2 on the right to life[36] to carry out an effective investigation into a death constitutes a "detachable obligation" binding on a State, even when such death occurred before the critical date. The Court's temporal jurisdiction may thus cover

[31] *Banković and Others v. Belgium and 16 Other Contracting States* (GC) (dec.), Eur. Ct. H.R. 2001-XII, ¶ 82.

[32] *Behrami and Behrami v. France and Saramati v. France, Germany and Norway* (GC) (dec.), Joined App. Nos. 71412/01 and 78166/01 (Eur. Ct. H.R. May 2, 2007), ¶¶ 146–152. For additional jurisprudence regarding the meaning of "jurisdiction" under Article 1 of the Convention, *see, e.g., Practical Guide on Admissibility Criteria, supra* note 27, pp. 39–46.

[33] For States Parties to the Convention prior to the adoption of Protocol No. 11, the date and content of their optional declaration of acceptance of the Court's jurisdiction is also relevant to determine the critical date.

[34] *See, e.g., Blečić v. Croatia* (GC), App. No. 59532/00 (Eur. Ct. H.R. Mar. 8, 2006), ¶ 82.

[35] For a survey of relevant ECtHR jurisprudence *see, e.g.*, A. Van Pachtenbeke & Y. Haeck, "From De Becker to Varnava: The State of Continuing Situations in the Strasbourg Case Law," *Eur. Hum. Rts. L. Rev.* 47 (2010), pp. 47–58.

[36] *See* section B.1.e. below.

procedural acts and/or omissions occurring after that date, subject to certain conditions.[37]

4. *Procedure Before the Court*

a. *Initial Stages of the Proceedings*

Applications are submitted to the Registry in one of the official languages of the Court, i.e. English or French; as regards individual complaints, the original submission may also be in one of the official languages of a State Party.[38] States must be represented by agents from the very beginning of the procedure, whereas individuals can also lodge a complaint directly. However, once the procedure has started, legal representation of the applicant is required.[39]

The application is assigned to a Section by the President of the Court and, except for manifestly ill-founded complaints, the Respondent State is notified and requested to submit written observations (including, as the case may be, preliminary objections on admissibility). The applicant is then invited to submit observations in reply. Parties may also be invited to a further round of written submissions. All such documentation is normally accessible to the public.[40]

b. *Admissibility Criteria*

To be declared admissible, applications must meet the jurisdictional requirements set out in section 3 above. But an individual complaint must also fulfill a number of procedural criteria, in accordance with Article 35 of the Convention. It must:

1) comply with the rule of exhaustion of local remedies. However, the Court has demonstrated some degree of flexibility and has taken into account, in particular, the effectiveness and availability of such remedies;[41]

---

[37] *Šilih v. Slovenia* (GC), App. No. 71463/01 (Eur. Ct. H.R. Apr. 9, 2009), ¶¶ 159–163. There must exist a "genuine connection" between the death and the entry into force of the Convention in respect of the Respondent State, such as the fact that a significant proportion of the procedural steps required under Article 2 have (or should have) been carried out after the critical date.

[38] For more details, see Rule 34 of the Rules of Court.

[39] Such representative can be any lawyer qualified to practice in one of the States Parties to the Convention, or any person so authorized by the President of the Chamber. The Court can also grant free legal aid to an applicant under certain conditions (*see* Rules 100–105).

[40] Public access may be restricted in exceptional cases in the interests of morals, public order or national security, in the interests of juveniles or as required for the protection of private life or where publicity would prejudice the interests of justice (Rule 33, ¶ 2).

[41] *See, e.g., Khashiyev and Akayeva v. Russia*, App. Nos. 57942/00 and 57945/00 (Eur. Ct. H.R. Feb. 24, 2005), ¶¶ 116–117.

2) respect a six-months time-limit from the date of the final national decision;
3) not be anonymous;
4) not be redundant (not "substantially the same" as a matter already examined by the Court);
5) not have been submitted to another international judicial or quasi-judicial body; and
6) not constitute an abuse of the right of individual application.

Moreover, the Court will declare inadmissible applications which are "manifestly ill-founded" on any of the following grounds: they are unsubstantiated, confused, or far-fetched, result from a misapprehension as to the Court's role or do not disclose any appearance of a violation.[42] In yet another effort to address the Court's caseload, Protocol No. 14 has added the *de minimis* principle as an admissibility criterion: thus, the applicant must have suffered a "significant disadvantage."[43]

c. *Third-Party Intervention*

Article 36 of the Convention allows for third-party intervention before a Chamber or the Grand Chamber – both written submissions and participation in hearings. This right is automatic for an applicant's State of nationality and the CoE Commissioner for Human Rights. Other States Parties or "any person concerned" may also be so invited or authorized by the President. NGOs often avail themselves of this opportunity.

d. *Interim Measures*

Rule 39 of the Rules of Court provides for the possibility of indication of interim measures. In practice, the ECtHR has done so only in situations of "imminent risk of irreparable damage" – usually involving the right to life, the right not to be subjected to torture or inhuman treatment, and, exceptionally, other rights such as the right to respect for private and family life. The vast majority of interim measures indicated by the Court have involved the suspension of a deportation or extradition order.[44] Failure to comply with

---

[42] *Practical Guide on Admissibility Criteria, supra* note 27, pp. 83–91.

[43] This new condition, however, comes with two safeguard clauses: it does not apply where respect for human rights requires an examination of the application on the merits and if the case has not been duly considered by a domestic tribunal (Article 35(3)(b) of the Convention).

[44] *See Mamatkulov and Askarov v. Turkey* (GC), App. Nos. 46827/99 and 46951/99 (Eur. Ct. H.R. Feb. 4, 2005), ¶ 104. The Court is being flooded with requests for interim measures, which increased by 4,000% between 2006 and 2010 (4,786 were received in 2010 alone). This is adding to the heavy workload of the Court and does not allow it to give appropriate

interim measures has been considered to undermine the effective exercise of the right to individual application under Article 34 of the Convention.[45]

e. *Consideration of the Case and Judgment*

The entire procedure before the ECtHR is normally written, but the Court may decide to hold a hearing which is in principle public.[46] Exceptionally, an on-site investigation may be carried out. With respect to inter-State applications, admissibility and merits are normally considered in two stages. A Chamber to which an individual application has been referred may decide to jointly examine admissibility and merits.

At any stage of the proceedings, a friendly settlement may be negotiated between the parties through the Registrar. The Court, having ascertained that the settlement terms are based on respect for human rights, strikes out the case by means of a decision, the execution of which is subject to supervision by the Committee of Ministers.[47]

A Chamber decides by majority vote. The judgment must be reasoned and concurring or dissenting opinions may be appended to it. It becomes final after three months, unless a request for referral to the Grand Chamber has been granted, or earlier if the parties indicate that they will not seek such referral, or when the request has been refused. Judgments of the Grand Chamber, also adopted by majority, are final.

5. *Execution of Judgments*

All final judgments are binding on the Respondent State. Where the Court has found a violation, this may entail two types of obligations. Firstly, vis-à-vis the applicant: (1) payment of just satisfaction that may be awarded,[48]

---

priority to cases where applicants are indeed at serious risk. On Feb. 11, 2011, the President urged both Governments and applicants to improve cooperation with the Court in this regard, reminding them that the latter is not an immigration appeals tribunal (Press Release No. 127).

[45] *Mamatkulov, ibid.*, ¶¶ 108–128. Interestingly, this judgment departed from previous case-law regarding the legal consequences of interim measures. The Court took into account the recent jurisprudence of other international bodies to reach its conclusion (*see* text at note 26 *supra*). *See also* C. Harby, "The Changing Nature of Interim Measures Before the European Court of Human Rights," *Eur. Hum. Rts. L. Rev.* 73 (2010), pp. 73–84.

[46] Similar restrictions as in the case of written documentation may apply (Rule 63, ¶ 2). Hearings are broadcast on the website of the Court.

[47] For an analysis of the practice, *see* H. Keller, M. Forowicz & L. Engi, *Friendly Settlements before the European Court of Human Rights: Theory and Practice* (Oxford: Oxford University Press, 2010).

[48] Although common, an award of just satisfaction in terms of a specific monetary amount is not automatic. Article 41 of the Convention, provides that the Court shall do so "if the

covering, as appropriate, pecuniary and non-pecuniary damage and/or costs and expenses;[49] (2) where necessary, individual measures to put an end to the violation and redress, as far as possible, its effects, such as re-opening domestic proceedings or revoking a deportation order. Secondly, adoption of general measures to prevent similar violations, for instance introducing or amending legislation. Disseminating judgments at the national level and ensuring their direct effect in domestic law are particularly important in this respect, given their potential multi-dimensional impact.

In principle, States have a large degree of discretion as regards the means to execute a judgment. But in the last few years, the Court has more frequently indicated specific individual measures where these clearly represent the best – or only – option for redress.[50] It has further developed the "pilot-judgment procedure": where a significant number of applications result from the same root cause (i.e. repetitive cases), the Court selects one or more for a pilot-judgment in which it will identify the underlying systemic or structural problems and provide a clear indication to the Respondent State as to how to address them.[51]

The execution of the Court's judgment is very closely monitored by the CoE Committee of Ministers – a political body.[52] Until the Committee is satisfied that the Respondent State has taken the necessary measures, the case remains on its agenda. "Interim resolutions" are often adopted, noting non-compliance, acknowledging progress, setting time-tables for reforms or suggesting possible measures of compliance (after contact with national authorities). The Committee relies primarily on persuasion to achieve its

---

internal law of the High Contracting Party concerned allows only partial reparation to be made" and "if necessary." The Court rules on a claim of just satisfaction either in the context of the judgment on the merits or at a later stage.

49 If no violation is found, the individual will not be requested to bear the legal costs of the Respondent State.

50 *E.g.* the release of a person arbitrarily detained (*Assanidze v. Georgia* (GC), Eur. Ct. H.R. 2004-II, ¶ 203) or the re-inclusion of property in a land register *(Fener Rum Patrikliği (Ecumenical Patriarchate) v. Turkey*, App. No. 14340/05 (Eur. Ct. H.R. June 15, 2010), ¶ 35).

51 The Court may adjourn consideration of all related applications for a period of time, to allow the adoption of the required domestic measures and the consequent settlement of these cases at national level. *See, e.g.*, Philip Leach, Helen Hardman, Svetlana Stephenson & Brad Blitz, *Responding to Systemic Human Rights Violations: An Analysis of 'Pilot Judgments' of the European Court of Human Rights and Their Impact at National Level* (Antwerpen: Intersentia, 2010).

52 For a detailed analysis, *see, e.g.*, E. Lambert-Abdelgawad, *The Execution of Judgments of the European Court of Human Rights* (Strasbourg: CoE Pub., Human Rights Files No. 19, 2d ed., 2008 (not available at website)).

goals, but it can, exceptionally, resort to more serious political pressure[53] or bring infringement proceedings to the Grand Chamber.[54]

B. *Review of Case Law*

Given the richness, both in quality and quantity of ECtHR judgments, any brief overview of jurisprudence can only be incomplete and subjective. Volumes of analysis can – and have been – written about the case law on each particular provision scrutinized by the Court. The following is merely intended as a basic introduction to its interpretation of certain rights and freedoms under the Convention and the Protocols.

As the ECtHR itself has said, its judgments have an impact beyond the particular case, as they serve, "more generally, to elucidate, safeguard and develop the rules instituted by the Convention, thereby contributing to the observance by the States of the engagements undertaken by them as Contracting Parties."[55] This is of particular significance given the Convention's special character as "an instrument of European public order (*ordre public*) for the protection of individual human beings."[56] Among other principles of interpretation, it is important to mention here that the ECtHR views the Convention as "a living instrument which must be interpreted in light of present-day conditions"; it is further "intended to guarantee not rights that are theoretical or illusory but rights that are practical and effective."[57] On certain issues, the Court allows States a "margin of appreciation," i.e. a measure of discretion in the manner they implement the standards of the Convention, taking into account their national particular circumstances. A balance is thus struck between uniform application and the need to defer to the diverse social, political, cultural and legal traditions of States Parties.[58]

---

[53] *Id.*, pp. 41 *et seq.* Technically, a State could have its voting rights suspended or be expulsed from the CoE, but this extreme (and counter-productive) measure has not been used by the Committee.

[54] This is a new option under Protocol No. 14. The Committee now may also refer a judgment for interpretation to the Court, where this could facilitate execution.

[55] *Ireland v. the United Kingdom*, 25 Eur. Ct. H.R. (ser. A) (1978), ¶ 154.

[56] *Cyprus v. Turkey* (GC), Eur. Ct. H.R. 2001-IV, ¶ 78.

[57] For a survey of jurisprudence on both these principles, *see* A. Mowbray, "The Creativity of the European Court of Human Rights," 5 *Hum. Rts. L. Rev.* 57 (2005), pp. 57–79.

[58] For a comprehensive analysis, *see* H. C. Yourow, *The Margin of Appreciation Doctrine in the Dynamics of European Human Rights Jurisprudence* (Dordrecht: Martinus Nijhoff Publishers, 1996). The leading case is *Handyside v. the United Kingdom* (24 Eur. Ct. H.R. (ser.A) (1976)).

1. *Right to Life*

As repeatedly underlined by the ECtHR,[59] the right to life in Article 2 of the Convention is a fundamental right, enshrining one of the basic values of the democratic societies making up the CoE. It is a non-derogable right.[60] This is why the Court has interpreted this provision both restrictively as concerns the exceptions allowed thereunder and broadly as regards the obligations it imposes on States.[61]

a. *Scope*

i. Applicability with Respect to a Fetus

Although the Court has been confronted with cases relating to abortion, it has not so far taken a definite stand as to whether the unborn child falls or not within the scope of Article 2. In fact, since the issue of when the right to life begins remains controversial both within most State Parties and at European level, the Court has held that the matter comes within the margin of appreciation afforded to States. It has not excluded, however, that there could be exceptional circumstances under which certain safeguards could be extended to a fetus.[62]

ii. Assisted Suicide

In *Pretty v. the United Kingdom*, a case that gained wide publicity, the ECtHR rejected the argument of the applicant that the right to life under Article 2 encompassed the right to chose to die: "no right to die, whether at the hands of a third person or with the assistance of a public authority, can be derived from Article 2 of the Convention."[63] At the same time, the Court did not *a priori* exclude the possibility that a national law permitting assisted suicide

---

[59] *See, e.g., Al-Saadoon and Mufdhi v. the United Kingdom*, App. No 61498/08 (Eur. Ct. H.R. Mar. 2, 2010), ¶ 118.

[60] Except as regards deaths resulting from lawful acts of war (Article 15(2) of the Convention).

[61] For a comprehensive analysis of relevant ECtHR case-law, *see, e.g.* D. Korff, *The Right to Life: A Guide to the Implementation of Article 2 of the European Convention on Human Rights* (Strasbourg: CoE Pub., Human Rights Handbooks Series No. 8, 2006); *INTERIGHTS Manual for Lawyers - The Right to Life under the European Convention on Human Rights (Article 2)* (London: Interights, 2008).

[62] *See Vo v. France* (GC), Eur. Ct. H.R. 2004-VIII, ¶¶ 75–85.

[63] *Pretty v. the United Kingdom*, Eur. Ct. H.R. 2002-III, ¶ 40. The applicant was a woman suffering from an incurable and degenerative illness who was seeking assurances that her husband would not be prosecuted for murder if he assisted her, according to her wishes, in committing suicide.

could be found not to constitute a breach of Article 2 – but this had no bearing on the case of the applicant, since UK law prohibited such practice.[64]

b. *Protection by Law*

The obligation to protect the right to life goes beyond enshrining such safeguards under domestic law. As the Court has repeatedly observed, it entails further action by States, such as putting in place effective criminal laws to deter the commission of violent offenses against the person, backed up by an efficient law-enforcement machinery for the prevention, suppression, and sanctioning of relevant crimes.[65] Where the State authorities know or should have known that a person's life is at "real and immediate risk," they must take measures that might have been "reasonably" expected to avoid such risk.[66] This duty applies not only with regard to threats to life connected to a person's political or professional activities, or emanating from mentally unstable individuals, fellow prisoners, or from a detainee's suicidal tendencies. The obligation of protection arises also with respect to dangerous industrial activities and other such environmental threats,[67] as well as to the operation of hospitals.[68] It even applies in relation to natural disasters, inasmuch as States must take appropriate preventive measures, such as establishing an early-warning system or putting in place the necessary infrastructure.[69]

c. *Death Penalty*

Article 2(1), drafted in 1950, allows for the imposition of capital punishment in accordance with national law. In 1983, Protocol No. 6 to the Convention abolished the death penalty in peacetime, without allowing any derogations

---

64 *Id.* ¶ 41. The Court went on to examine the refusal of the British authorities to provide assurances of non-prosecution in light of other provisions of the Convention, such as the prohibition of ill-treatment or the right to privacy, but found no violation in the circumstance of the case.

65 *See, e.g., Osman v. the United Kingdom* (GC), Eur. Ct. H.R. 1998-VIII, ¶ 115.

66 *Id.* ¶ 116.

67 In *Öneryıldız v. Turkey* (GC), the Court referred to the duty to have in place regulations governing the licensing, setting up, operation, security and supervision of a dangerous activity. Special emphasis was placed on the public's right to information (Eur. Ct. H.R. 2004-XII, ¶ 90).

68 As stated in Erikson v. Italy (dec.), States must compel hospitals to have regulations for the protection of patients' lives as well as provide an effective judicial system for establishing the cause of a death in a hospital and address possible issues of medical malpractice (App. No. 37900/97 (Eur. Ct. H.R. Oct. 26, 1999)).

69 *Budayeva and Others v. Russia*, App. Nos. 15339/02, 21166/02, 20058/02, 11673/02 and 15343/02 (Eur. Ct. H.R. Mar. 20, 2008), ¶¶ 147–160.

in emergency situations or any reservations. Two decades later, Protocol No. 13 lifted the remaining exception concerning acts committed "in time of war or of imminent threat of war," thus abolishing the death penalty in all circumstances.

The issue of capital punishment is a prime illustration of the Court's evolutive interpretation method. In the 1989 *Soering* judgment, it foreshadowed the possible abrogation of the exception to the right to life in Article 2(1), but considered that this had not yet occurred at the time, since States Parties had chosen to adopt an *optional* instrument (Protocol No. 6) to introduce a new obligation in this respect, then ratified by just over half of them.[70] In the next sixteen years, all States Parties abolished the death penalty *de jure* except Russia (but it had imposed a moratorium) and all but two ratified Protocol No. 6 – commitments on abolition had in fact become pre-requisites for membership in the CoE since the mid-nineties. In light of these developments, the Court held in the 2005 *Öcalan* judgment that capital punishment *in peacetime* had come to be regarded as an unacceptable form of punishment, no longer permissible under Article 2.[71] The next five years saw further evolution: Russia became the only non-Party to Protocol No. 6, while Protocol No. 13 was signed by almost all Members of the CoE (forty-five) and ratified by forty-two. As the Court stated in the *Al-Saadoon and Mufdhi* case, these latest facts, together with consistent State practice, are "strongly indicative" that the exception in Article 2 has been lifted so as to prohibit the death penalty *in all circumstances*.[72]

The Court's interpretation of Article 2(1) has also impacted on its interpretation of the prohibition of inhuman or degrading punishment under Article 3.[73] In *Soering*, it held that the death penalty as such could not be said to be prohibited under Article 3 (since it was still allowed under Article 2(1)), although factors such as the manner in which that penalty was imposed or executed, the personal circumstances of the individual, the lack of proportionality with the gravity of the crime or the conditions of detention could in fact lead to a finding of inhuman or degrading treatment or punishment.[74]

---

[70] *Soering v. United Kingdom*, 161 Eur. Ct. H.R. (ser. A) (1989), ¶¶ 102–103.

[71] *Öcalan v. Turkey* (GC), App. No. 46221/99 (Eur. Ct. H.R. May 12, 2005), ¶ 163.

[72] *Al-Saadoon and Mufdhi*, *supra* note 59, ¶ 120.

[73] *See* section B.2 below. Most cases relating to the death penalty have been brought before the ECtHR in connection with the applicant's (possible) deportation or extradition to a non-abolitionist country, and the Court has pronounced itself on the conformity or otherwise of such transfer with Article 3.

[74] *Soering*, *supra* note 70, ¶¶ 104, 111. In that case, the Court found that the prolonged anguish of being on death row in the particular circumstances amounted to such prohibited treatment.

Its above-mentioned statement on Article 2 in *Al-Saadoon and Mufdhi*, however, led the Court to the conclusion that it is now possible to interpret "inhuman or degrading treatment or punishment" under Article 3 as including the death penalty.[75]

d. *Use of Force by State Agents*
Article 2(2) enumerates specific, carefully circumscribed situations in which the use of lethal force would not be considered a violation of the right to life: protection against *unlawful* violence, *lawful* arrest or prevention of escape of a *lawfully* detained person; and *lawful* action for quelling a riot or insurrection. The Court has clearly stated that this provision should not be understood as defining instances when it is permitted to intentionally kill, but rather when it is permitted to use force, which may have the unintended result of deprivation of life.[76]

In all situations mentioned in Article 2(2), the use of force must have been "no more than absolutely necessary." The circumstances of the case will determine whether this standard was met, but the ECtHR has provided some indication as to the factors to be taken into account. These include the existence of a legislative and administrative framework for the use of force and firearms by law-enforcement officials[77] as well as the requisite care to minimize risk to life in the planning and control of the operation.[78]

In order to hold a State responsible for a violation of Article 2, the applicant must normally satisfy the evidentiary standard of "proof beyond a reasonable doubt." But, as clarified by the Court, in practice, such proof may follow from the "co-existence of sufficiently strong, clear and concordant inferences or of similar unrebutted presumptions of fact."[79] As to the burden of proof, it rests in principle with the applicant, but where the events at issue lie wholly, or in large part, within the exclusive knowledge of State authorities, it is the latter that must provide a "satisfactory and reasonable explanation." This applies in particular as regards the death in custody of persons previously in good health.[80] Similarly, when a State fails to provide a reasonable explanation for the disappearance of a person and there is suf-

75 *Al-Saadoon and Mufdhi*, *supra* note 59, ¶ 120.
76 *McCann and Others v. the United Kingdom* (GC), 324 Eur. Ct. H.R. (ser. A) (1995), ¶ 148.
77 *See, e.g.*, *Makaratzis v. Greece* (GC), Eur. Ct. H.R. 2004-XI, ¶¶ 58–59, 70.
78 *See, e.g.*, *Isayeva v. Russia*, App. No. 57950/00 (Eur. Ct. H.R. Feb. 24, 2005), ¶¶ 175–176.
79 *See, e.g.*, *Ireland v. the United Kingdom*, *supra* note 55, ¶ 161.
80 *See, e.g.*, *Aktaş v. Turkey*, App. No. 24351/94 (Eur. Ct. H.R. Apr. 24, 2003), ¶ 291.

ficient circumstantial evidence from which it can be reasonably presumed that the person died in custody, the Court will find a violation of Article 2.[81]

e. *Procedural Obligation to Undertake an Effective Investigation*

The Court's jurisprudence has established that, aside from the above-mentioned substantive duties, protection of the right to life under article 2 entails a procedural obligation: undertaking an effective investigation into a death resulting from the use of force. Where State agents have been involved, accountability must be ensured.

Although the ECtHR has acknowledged that there is no one model for such investigation, it has indicated a number of pre-requisites for an investigation to be qualified as effective: *proprio motu* initiation by the authorities, independence, promptness and reasonable expedition. It must involve a degree of public scrutiny and be capable of leading to a determination of whether the force used was justified as well as to the identification and punishment of those responsible.[82]

In addition to situations involving the use of force, the Court has applied the procedural obligation to undertake an official investigation in the context of dangerous industrial activities as well as natural disasters, when loss of life occurred as a result of events engaging the State's responsibility for not taking appropriate preventive action.[83]

2. *Prohibition of Torture, Inhuman or Degrading Treatment or Punishment*

Article 3[84] is another provision of the Convention which, as emphasized by the ECtHR, enshrines one of the basic values of the democratic societies making up the CoE.[85] It is non-derogable under any circumstance. It embodies an absolute prohibition, allowing for no exceptions whatsoever. The Court has repeatedly stressed that the conduct of a person or the nature of his or her alleged offense is irrelevant in that regard. In particular, the "scale of the

---

81 *See, e.g., Timurtaş v. Turkey*, Eur. Ct. H.R. 2000-VI, ¶¶ 82–86.

82 *See, e.g., Kelly and Others v. the United Kingdom*, App. No. 30054/96 (Eur. Ct. H.R. May 4, 2001), ¶¶ 94–98.

83 *Öneryıldız, supra* note 67, ¶¶ 93–94; *Budayeva, supra* note 69, ¶ 142.

84 For a comprehensive analysis of relevant ECtHR case-law, *see, e.g.*, A. Reidy, *The Prohibition of Torture: A Guide to the Implementation of Article 3 of the European Convention on Human Rights* (Strasbourg: CoE Pub., Human Rights Handbooks Series No. 6, 2003); *INTERIGHTS Manual for Lawyers – Prohibition of Torture, Inhuman or Degrading Treatment or Punishment under the European Convention on Human Rights (Article 3)* (London: Interights, 2009).

85 *See, e.g.*, Al-Saadoon and Mufdhi, *supra* note 59, ¶ 118.

danger of terrorism today and the threat it presents to the community" cannot have the effect of calling into question the absolute nature of Article 3.[86]

a. *Scope*

In order to fall within the scope of Article 3, ill-treatment must attain "a minimum level of severity." But this is a relative standard, depending on the circumstances of the case. Relevant factors include the duration of the ill-treatment and its physical and mental effects, as well as personal characteristics of the victim such as gender, age, and state of health.[87]

b. *Torture*

Unlike the UN Convention Against Torture and Other Cruel, Inhuman or Degrading Treatment or Punishment,[88] Article 3 does not define the term "torture." The ECtHR has not attempted to provide its own definition, but has clarified the term in Article 3 in a number of ways – clearly also inspired by the UN Convention.

As pointed out in *Ireland v. the United Kingdom*, torture carries a "special stigma" and in that sense is distinct from other forms of ill-treatment.[89] Elements specific to torture are the intensity of the suffering inflicted, but also its deliberate and purposive character.[90] The classification of an act as "inhuman or degrading treatment" rather than "torture" may evolve with time. As noted by the Court in the 1999 *Selmouni* judgment, "the increasingly high standard being required in the area of the protection of human rights and fundamental liberties correspondingly and inevitably requires greater firmness in assessing breaches of the fundamental values of democratic societies."[91] It is telling in this regard that, already over a decade ago, the ECtHR recognized in the *Aydin* case that rape of a detainee by a State official could amount to torture.[92]

c. *Inhuman or Degrading Treatment or Punishment*

In *Ireland v. the United Kingdom*, the Court also clarified what constitutes other forms of ill-treatment under Article 3. Thus, treatment is characterized as "inhuman" when, *inter alia*, it was premeditated, was applied for hours at a stretch and caused either actual bodily injury or intense physical and

86 *Saadi v. Italy* (GC), App. No. 37201/06 (Eur. Ct. H.R., Feb. 28, 2008), ¶¶ 137–138.

87 *See, e.g., Ireland v. the United Kingdom, supra* note 55, ¶ 162.

88 Dec. 10, 1984, 1465 U.N.T.S. 85.

89 *Ireland v. the United Kingdom, supra* note 55, ¶ 167.

90 *See, e.g., Salman v. Turkey* (GC), Eur. Ct. H.R. 2000-VII, ¶ 114.

91 *Selmouni v. France* (GC), Eur. Ct. H.R. 1999-V, ¶ 101.

92 *Aydin v. Turkey* (GC), Eur. Ct. H.R. 1997-VI, ¶ 86.

mental suffering. "Degrading" treatment is such as to arouse in the victims feelings of fear, anguish and inferiority capable of humiliating and debasing them.[93]

To a large extent, cases examined by the Court have concerned persons in detention. It has found a violation of the prohibition of "inhuman or degrading treatment" on the grounds of conduct of State officials, lack of appropriate medical care, but also conditions of detention in themselves.[94] The ECtHR has further established that, in the case of disappearances, family members may, under certain circumstances, qualify as victims of inhuman treatment as a result of the anguish they have endured over a long period of time in the absence of any official information.[95] Other examples of treatment contrary to Article 3 include the destruction of villages and homes by security forces.[96]

Concerning punishment, the Court found in one case that judicial corporal punishment constituted "degrading punishment." But not all instances of corporal punishment have been found to be "degrading" under Article 3.[97] As to the issue whether the death penalty constitutes "inhuman or degrading punishment," it has been examined, as mentioned above, in connection with the interpretation of Article 2(1).

d. *Non-Refoulement*

The above-mentioned *Soering* case established that extradition of persons to a country where they may be subjected to treatment in violation of Article 3 engages the responsibility of the extraditing State under the Convention.[98] Subsequent and consistent case law has applied this principle also to deportation and any other forms of removal.

The standard of proof is that there be "substantial grounds for believing that the person faces a real risk"[99] of treatment contrary to Article 3 in the receiving country. In making the relevant assessment, the Court takes into

---

93 *Ireland v. the United Kingdom, supra* note 55, ¶ 167.

94 In assessing whether the conditions of detention in a particular case amount to a violation of Article 3, the Court often takes into account, in particular, the standards developed by the European Committee for the Prevention of Torture and Inhuman or Degrading Treatment or Punishment (CPT) as well as its reports on country visits.

95 *Kurt v. Turkey*, Eur. Ct. H.R. 1998-III, ¶¶ 133–134. For an elaboration of the factors relevant to characterizing a family member as a victim of a violation of article 3, *see Orhan v. Turkey*, App. No. 25656/94 (Eur. Ct. H.R. June 18, 2002), ¶ 358.

96 *See, e.g., Hasan İlhan v. Turkey*, App. No. 22494/93 (Eur. Ct. H.R. Nov. 9, 2004), ¶ 108.

97 *See, e.g., Costello-Roberts v. the United Kingdom*, a case involving corporal punishment in school (247-C Eur. Ct. H.R. (ser. A) (1993), ¶¶ 31–32).

98 *Soering, supra* note 70, ¶¶ 88–91.

99 *Id.* ¶ 91.

account not only the general situation in the country in question, but also the personal circumstances of the person.[100] It has refuted the argument that, in the case of persons presenting a threat to national security, the standard of proof should be higher ("more likely than not"), stressing the absolute character of the prohibition in Article 3 even in the context of the fight against terrorism.[101]

e. *Positive and Procedural Obligations*

Taken together with Article 1, which requires States Parties to secure to every person within their jurisdiction the rights and freedoms defined in Convention, Article 3 – although framed as a prohibition – also entails positive obligations. As emphasized by the Court, States must take appropriate measures to ensure that such persons are not subjected to treatment envisaged in the latter provision. This applies to ill-treatment by acts of private individuals as well. Children and other vulnerable individuals are entitled to particular protection in this respect.[102]

As with Article 2, there is also a procedural aspect to Article 3: according to well-established ECtHR case-law, States must conduct effective investigations into arguable or credible allegations of torture and ill-treatment. The Court has found a violation in this respect even where it did not find the claim of ill-treatment as such to be sufficiently substantiated.[103]

3. *Right to Liberty and Security of Person*

The ECtHR has found a violation of Article 5 in almost eleven percent of judgments involving breaches of the Convention.[104] In other words, there is abundant case law[105] interpreting in detail the various aspects of a right that is fundamental to a "democratic society."[106] A few illustrative elements are reviewed below.

---

[100] *See, e.g., Saadi v. Italy, supra* note 86, ¶ 130.

[101] *Id.* ¶ 140.

[102] *See, e.g., A. v. the United Kingdom*, Eur. Ct. H.R. 1998-VI, ¶ 22.

[103] *See, e.g., Martinez Sala and Others v. Spain*, App. No. 58438/00 (Eur. Ct. H.R. Nov. 2, 2004), ¶¶ 156–160.

[104] Figure for the period 1959–2009 (*50 Years of Activity, supra* note 5, p. 6).

[105] For an extensive survey, *see, e.g.*, M. Macovei, *The Right to Liberty and Security of the Person: A Guide to the Implementation of Article 5 of the European Convention on Human Rights* (Strasbourg: CoE Pub., Human Rights Handbooks Series No. 5, 2002); *INTERIGHTS Manual for Lawyers – Right to Liberty and Security under the European Convention on Human Rights (Article 5)* (London: Interights, 2007).

[106] *See, e.g., De Wilde, Ooms and Versyp v. Belgium*, 12 Eur. Ct. H.R. (ser. A) (1971), ¶ 65.

a. *Scope*
The "right to liberty and security of person" is a single concept (i.e. the notion of security of person is not an independent one). Thus, as explained by the Court, the primary concern of Article 5 is protection from an arbitrary deprivation of liberty.[107] In *Guzzardi*, it clarified that "the difference between deprivation of and restriction upon liberty is merely one of degree or intensity, and not one of nature or substance." Whether the threshold has been reached will naturally depend on the circumstances of the case. Relevant criteria include the type, duration, effects and manner of implementation of the restrictive measure in question. In that particular case, the ECtHR found a violation of article 5, on the basis of a combination of factors: compulsory residence on a small island subject to strict police supervision, strict limitations on free movement, little contact with the outside world, 16-month duration.[108]

b. *Concept of Arbitrary Deprivation of Liberty*
Article 5(1) list a series of grounds on which deprivation of liberty is permissible, as long as the measures in question are "lawful" and carried out "in accordance with a procedure prescribed by law."[109] According to the ECtHR, this entails also certain requirements as regards the "quality of the law": it must be compatible with the rule of law, that is, accessible, precise and foreseeable as to its effects, in order to avoid all risk of arbitrariness.[110]

As the Court has established, compliance with the substantive and procedural rules of national law is not sufficient. It reaffirmed in *Saadi v. the United Kingdom* that Article 5(1) "requires in addition that any deprivation of liberty should be in keeping with the purpose of protecting the individual

---

[107] *See, e.g., Altun v. Turkey*, App. No. 24561/94 (Eur. Ct. H.R. June 1, 2004), ¶ 57.

[108] *Guzzardi v. Italy*, 39 Eur. Ct. H.R. (ser. A) (1980), ¶¶ 92–95.

[109] These are: (a) detention of a person after conviction by a competent court; (b) arrest or detention of a person for non-compliance with the lawful order of a court or in order to secure the fulfillment of any obligation prescribed by law; (c) arrest or detention of a person effected for the purpose of bringing him before the competent legal authority on reasonable suspicion of having committed an offense or when it is reasonably considered necessary to prevent his committing an offense or fleeing after having done so; (d) detention of a minor by lawful order for the purpose of educational supervision or his detention for the purpose of bringing him before the competent legal authority; (e) detention of persons for the prevention of the spreading of infectious diseases, of persons of unsound mind, alcoholics or drug addicts or vagrants; (f) arrest or detention of a person to prevent his effecting an unauthorized entry into the country or of a person against whom action is being taken with a view to deportation or extradition.

[110] *See, e.g., Varbanov v. Bulgaria*, Eur. Ct. H.R. 2000-V, ¶ 51, and *Gusinskiy v. Russia*, Eur. Ct. H.R. 2004-IV, ¶ 62.

from arbitrariness." Drawing on its case law, the ECtHR recalled a number of general principles for determining whether a detention is "arbitrary" in that sense. Thus, the deprivation of liberty will be in conformity with the Convention when: it has been carried out in good faith; both the order to detain and the execution of the detention genuinely conform with the purpose of the relevant provision in Article 5; and there is some correlation between the ground of permitted deprivation of liberty and the place and conditions of detention. Additional criteria may apply depending on the type of detention involved.[111]

c. *Duty of Prompt Information of Reasons for Arrest and of Any Charge*

As clarified by the Court, this procedural safeguard under Article 5(2) does not only apply in the obvious context of criminal proceedings, but to any ground of detention (including, for instance, detention in a psychiatric hospital).[112] The ECtHR has repeatedly stressed that the purpose of informing persons, in simple, non-technical language that they understand, of the essential legal and factual grounds for the arrest, is to enable them, if they wish, to challenge the lawfulness of their detention before a court. Whether the content and promptness of the information conveyed are sufficient will depend on the circumstances of the case.[113]

d. *Right to be Brought Promptly Before a Judge and to Trial Within a Reasonable Time or Release*

As emphasized by the ECtHR, the purpose of the safeguard in Article 5(3) is to protect an individual from arbitrary detention by ensuring that the act of deprivation of liberty is subject to independent judicial scrutiny. It is therefore automatic and does not depend on an application by the detainee.[114]

There is, according to the case law, a clear presumption in favor of release: "[c]ontinued detention may be justified in a given case only if there are clear indications of a genuine public interest which, notwithstanding the presumption of innocence, outweighs the right to liberty."[115]

No set period of time satisfies the criterion of "promptness" – the Court makes the relevant assessment in the particular circumstances of a case. Similarly, what constitutes a "reasonable" period of pre-trial detention may vary,

---

[111] *Saadi v. the United Kingdom* (GC), App. No. 13229/03 (Eur. Ct. H.R. Jan. 29, 2008), ¶¶ 67–73.

[112] *See Van de Leer v. the Netherlands*, 170-A Eur. Ct. H.R. (ser. A) (1990), ¶¶ 27–28.

[113] See, e.g., *Fox, Campbell and Hartley v. the United Kingdom*, 182 Eur. Ct. H.R. (ser. A) (1990), ¶ 40.

[114] *See, e.g., Niedbala v. Poland*, App. No. 27915/95 (Eur. Ct. H.R, July 4, 2000), ¶ 50.

[115] *See, e.g., Punzelt v. the Czech Republic*, App. No. 31315/96 (Eur. Ct. H.R. Apr. 25, 2000), ¶ 73.

but in any event the national authorities must display "special diligence" in the conduct of the investigations.[116]

e. *Right to Challenge the Legality of the Detention*
In *Reinprecht*, the ECtHR reviewed some of the principles emerging from its case law on the right enshrined in Article 5(4): an arrested or detained person is entitled to a review bearing on both the procedural requirements of the national law and substantive conditions under Article 5 on the lawfulness of the deprivation of liberty; such procedure must have a judicial character and provide guarantees appropriate to the kind of deprivation of liberty in question; proceedings must be adversarial and must always ensure "equality of arms" between the parties (including right of access to the file or to the assistance of a lawyer); in the case of a person detained on criminal charges, a hearing is required (although not necessarily public); a person detained on remand must be able to take proceedings at reasonable intervals to challenge the lawfulness of his or her detention.[117]

f. *Derogations Under Article 15 of the Convention*
The Court has sometimes been called upon to consider, in relation to applications alleging violations of Article 5, derogations by States under Article 15 in situations of "public emergency threatening the life of the nation" - especially in the context of the fight against terrorism. Generally, the ECtHR allows the State a wide margin of appreciation as regards the nature and scope of the derogating measures necessary to avert the emergency. But it is for the Court to determine whether the measures were "strictly required by the exigencies of the situation," as provided in Article 15. "In particular, where a derogating measure encroaches upon a fundamental Convention right, such as the right to liberty, the Court must be satisfied that it was a genuine response to the emergency situation, that it was fully justified by the special circumstances of the emergency and that adequate safeguards were provided against abuse."[118]

---

[116] *Id.*

[117] *Reinprecht v. Austria*, Eur. Ct. H.R. 2005-XII, ¶¶ 31–41.

[118] *See A. and Others v. the United Kingdom* (GC), App. No. 3455/05 (Eur. Ct. H.R. Feb. 19, 2009), ¶ 184. In that case, the Court considered the derogation regarding preventive detention of foreign nationals incompatible with Article 5, as it discriminated unjustifiably between nationals and non-nationals (¶ 190). In *Brannigan and Mc Bride v. the United Kingdom*, in contrast, it had upheld a derogation whereby there was no judicial control over extended detention, having regard to the nature of the terrorist threat, the limited scope of the derogation and the reasons advanced in support of it, as well as the existence of basic safeguards against abuse (258-B Eur. Ct. H.R. (ser.A) (1993), ¶ 66).

4. *Right to a Fair Trial*

A violation of Article 6 is by far the most frequent finding by the Court.[119] Just about every concept in this long provision has been interpreted in some detail. In the words of a former Registrar, "[o]ne could almost draft a code of criminal procedure on the basis of the [ECtHR] case-law."[120] The Court has also expounded on the right to fair trial in civil proceedings in its numerous judgments on the issue.

As it has done with other rights under the Convention, the ECtHR has adopted an extensive approach to the safeguards in Article 6, given the "prominent place" held by the right to a fair administration of justice in a democratic society.[121] As a result, additional guarantees not expressly mentioned in the text of the provision have emerged through the case law, such as the right of access to a court or the principle of equality of arms.

In considering alleged violations of Article 6, the ECtHR applies the "fourth instance" doctrine. In other words, its role does not entail re-opening of domestic proceedings or substituting its own findings of facts or law for those of the domestic courts. The Court's task is to examine whether the proceedings, taken as a whole, were fair.[122]

a. *Scope*

The right to a fair hearing in Article 6 applies to proceedings regarding either the "determination of civil rights and obligations" or the "determination of any criminal charge" (in relation to which additional guarantees are expressly provided). For the Court, both concepts have an autonomous meaning under the Convention and cannot be determined solely in relation to classifications under national law.[123] Thus, in deciding whether to characterize proceedings as criminal for the purposes of Article 6, the Court

---

[119] *50 Years of Activity, supra note* 5, p. 6. For an extensive survey of the relevant case-law, *see, e.g.*, N. Mole & C. Harby, *The Right to a Fair Trial: A Guide to the Implementation of Article 6 of the European Convention on Human Rights* (Strasbourg: CoE Pub., Human Rights Handbooks Series No. 3, 2d. ed, 2006); *INTERIGHTS Manual for Lawyers – Right to a Fair Trial under the European Convention on Human Rights (Article 6)* (London: Interights, 2009).

[120] P. Mahoney, "Right to a Fair Trial in Criminal Matters under Article 6 E.C.H.R.," 4 *Jud. Studies Inst. J.* 107 (2004), pp. 107–129.

[121] *See, e.g., Delcourt v. Belgium*, 11 Eur. Ct. H.R. (ser. A) (1970), ¶ 25.

[122] *See, e.g., Bernard v. France*, Eur. Ct. H.R. 1998-II, ¶ 37.

[123] *See, e.g., König v. Germany*, 27 Eur. Ct. H.R. (ser. A) (1978), ¶ 88. For instance, a State cannot escape the obligation to provide the full guarantees that attach to criminal proceedings by characterizing an offense as "disciplinary" rather than "criminal" (*Engel and Others v. the Netherlands*, 22 Eur. Ct. H.R. (ser. A) (1976), ¶ 81).

may take into account two additional criteria: the nature of the proceedings and the nature and degree of severity of the penalty.[124] Similarly, the Court has recognized that, in addition to disputes between private persons, certain disputes between individuals and the State may also fall under the concept of "civil rights and obligations" for the purposes of the Convention, even if under national law they are a matter for "administrative" or "public" law. An important criterion is whether the result of the proceedings in question is "decisive for private rights and obligations."[125] This was found to be the case, inter alia, for proceedings involving property,[126] the right to practice a profession,[127] the right to engage in a commercial activity,[128] or certain social security entitlements.[129] The case law on the applicability of Article 6 is evolving – for instance in 2008, the Court recognized for the first time that the right of access to higher education was a right of a civil nature.[130] But there remain areas outside the scope of that provision, such as tax[131] or immigration[132] matters.

b. *Right of Access to a Court*

In *Golder*, the ECtHR established that the right of access to a court is inherent in the right to a fair trial under the Convention: "It would be inconceivable, in the opinion of the Court, that [Article 6 (1)] should describe in detail the procedural guarantees afforded to parties in a pending lawsuit and should not first protect that which alone makes it in fact possible to benefit from such guarantees, that is, access to a court."[133] In subsequent cases, the Court clarified that the right of access to a court includes not only the right to institute proceedings but also the right to obtain a "determination" of the dispute by a final judicial decision.[134]

The right of access to a court, however, is not absolute. It can be regulated under national law, as long as the limitations applied are not so restrictive as to impair its very essence. They must further pursue a legitimate aim,

---

[124] *See, e.g., Benham v. the United Kingdom* (GC), Eur. Ct. H.R. 1996-III, ¶ 56.

[125] *See, e.g., Ringeisen v. Austria*, 13 Eur. Ct. H.R. (ser. A) (1971), ¶ 94.

[126] *Id.*

[127] *See, e.g., Le Compte, Van Leuven and De Meyere v. Belgium*, 43 Eur. Ct. H.R. (ser. A) (1981), ¶¶ 47–48.

[128] *See, e.g., Tre Traktörer Aktiebolag v. Sweden*, 159 Eur. Ct. H.R. (ser. A) (1989), ¶ 43.

[129] *See, e.g., Salesi v. Italy*, 257-E Eur. Ct. H.R. (ser. A) (1993), ¶ 19.

[130] *Emine Araç v. Turkey*, App. No. 9907/02 (Eur. Ct. H.R. Sep. 23, 2008), ¶ 24.

[131] *See, e.g., Ferrazzini v. Italy* (GC), Eur. Ct. H.R. 2001-VII, ¶¶ 29–30.

[132] *See, e.g., Maaouia v. France* (GC), Eur. Ct. H.R. 2000-X, ¶ 38.

[133] *Golder v. the United Kingdom*, 18 Eur. Ct. H.R. (ser. A) (1975), ¶ 35.

[134] *See, e.g., Dubinskaya v. Russia*, App. No. 4856/03 (Eur. Ct. H.R. July 13, 2006), ¶ 41.

and there must be "a reasonable relationship of proportionality between the means employed and the aim sought to be achieved."[135]

c. *Equality of Arms*

The Court has repeatedly stressed that the right to a fair trial encompasses the principle of equality of arms: each party must be afforded a reasonable opportunity to present his or her case, including evidence, under conditions that do not place that party at a substantial disadvantage vis-à-vis the opponent. This principle applies to both criminal and civil cases.[136]

The case law addresses "typical" issues in this context, such as examination of witnesses, presentation of evidence and disclosure. But the Court has also found a violation of the principle where the Parliament of the State concerned adopted legislation aimed at ensuring the defeat of the applicant's claim while it was proceeding through the national courts.[137]

d. *Reasonable Time Guarantee*

A violation of the requirement of adjudication within a reasonable time is the single most common finding by the Court.[138] Judicial delay is the quintessential systemic problem causing massive backlog in its work.

The period to be taken into consideration normally begins to run with the institution of proceedings in civil cases and with the charge in criminal cases. It ends at the date of the final determination of the issue at stake.[139] The Court has established in its particularly rich case law on the matter that the following factors should be taken into account when assessing whether the length of the proceedings was reasonable (together with the specific circumstances): the complexity of the case, the conduct of both the applicant and the competent State authorities, and what is at stake for the applicant.[140]

5. *Right to Respect for Private and Family Life*

As is the case with other provisions, the interests protected under Article 8,[141] i.e. private life, family life, home, and correspondence, have, for the ECtHR,

---

[135] *See Ashingdane v. the United Kingdom*, 93 Eur. Ct. H.R. (ser. A) (1985), ¶ 57.

[136] *See, e.g., Dombo Beheer B.V. v. the Netherlands*, 274 Eur. Ct. H.R. (ser. A) (1993), ¶ 33.

[137] *Stran Greek Refineries and Stratis Andreadis v. Greece*, 301-B Eur. Ct. H.R. (ser. A) (1994), ¶¶ 49–50.

[138] *50 Years of Activity, supra note* 5, p. 6.

[139] *See, e.g., Scopelliti v. Italy*, 278 Eur. Ct. H.R. (ser. A) (1993), ¶ 18, and *Deweer v. Belgium*, 35 Eur. Ct. H.R. (ser. A) (1980), ¶ 42.

[140] *Buchholz v. Germany*, 42 Eur. Ct. H.R. (ser. A) (1981), ¶ 49.

[141] For a review of the case-law, see, for example, U. Kilkelly, *The Right to Respect for Private and Family Life: A Guide to the Implementation of Article 8 of the European Convention on Human Rights* (Strasbourg: CoE Pub., Human Rights Handbooks Series No. 1, 2001).

an autonomous meaning under the Convention. But while it has laid down certain guiding principles, the Court has generally approached these concepts on a case-by-case basis. On certain issues, there has been an evolution in the Court's interpretation, reflecting changing perceptions in European societies as well as technological developments.[142]

a. *Private Life*

The Court recognized in *Niemietz* that it is neither possible nor necessary to attempt an exhaustive definition of the notion of "private life." At the same time, it considered it "too restrictive to limit the notion to an 'inner circle' in which the individual may live his own personal life as he chooses and to exclude therefrom entirely the outside world not encompassed within that circle. Respect for private life must also comprise to a certain degree the right to establish and develop relationships with other human beings."[143] In the above-mentioned *Pretty* case, the Court reviewed some of its case law up to that point on what is encompassed in the concept of "private life:" the physical and psychological integrity of a person; aspects of an individual's physical and social identity; elements such as name, gender identification, sexual orientation and sexual life; the right to personal development. It stressed that the underlying principle is the notion of "personal autonomy."[144] More recently, the ECtHR recognized that "reputation" also falls within the scope of "private life."[145]

b. *Family Life*

The Court's understanding of what constitutes "family life" has evolved over the years, as it has been confronted with situations other than the more traditional married couple with children. The ECtHR has thus established that the concept of family life under Article 8 applies, inter alia, to unmarried couples with children;[146] the relationship between a parent and his or her child regardless of marital status[147] and, in principle, even in the absence of cohabitation;[148] or the relationship between adoptive parents and their

[142] For instance, in the 2007 judgment in *Copland v. the United Kingdom*, the Court found that the collection and storage of personal information relating to a person's e-mail and internet usage, without his or her knowledge, amounted to an interference with the right to respect for private life and correspondence within the meaning of Article 8 (App. No. 62617/00 (Eur. Ct. H.R. Apr. 3, 2007), ¶ 44).

[143] *Niemietz v. Germany*, 251-B Eur. Ct. H.R. (ser. A) (1992), ¶ 29.

[144] *Pretty, supra* note 63, ¶ 61.

[145] *Pfeifer v. Austria*, App. No. 12556/03 (Eur. Ct. H.R. Nov. 15, 2007), ¶ 35.

[146] *See Johnston and Others v. Ireland*, 112 Eur. Ct. H.R. (ser. A) (1986), ¶ 56.

[147] *See Marckx v. Belgium*, 31 Eur. Ct. H.R. (ser. A) (1979), ¶ 45.

[148] *See Boughanemi v. France*, Eur. Ct. H.R. 1996-II, ¶ 35.

children.[149] In the recent *Schalk and Kopf* case, the Court, overturning previous decisions, recognized that same-sex couples living in a stable *de facto* partnership are covered by the concept of "family life" within the meaning of Article 8. In arriving at this determination, it took into account the rapid evolution of social attitudes towards same-sex couples in many CoE Member States, a considerable number of which have granted them legal recognition.[150]

c. *Permissible Interference*

Article 8(2) permits interferences with the right to private and family life under three conditions: the measures must be "in accordance with the law," "necessary in a democratic society" and pursue one of the following legitimate aims: national security, public safety, economic well-being of the country, prevention of disorder or crime, protection of health or morals or protection of the rights and freedoms of others.

The first criterion has been interpreted by the Court as including the requirement that the law be sufficiently precise and foreseeable as to its consequences and that it afford a measure of protection against arbitrariness.[151] Regarding the question of whether an interference is in pursuance of one of the public interests under Article 8(2), the ECtHR has generally allowed States a margin of appreciation, given the wide variety of approaches to these concepts in the national legal and social orders.

In examining whether an interference was "necessary in a democratic society," the Court seeks to determine "whether there existed a pressing social need for the measure in question and, in particular, whether the interference was proportionate to the legitimate aim pursued, regard being had to the fair balance which has to be struck between the relevant competing interests in respect of which the State enjoys a margin of appreciation." Thus, the breadth of such margin of appreciation is a crucial element in making the above assessment. As established in the case law, where a particularly important facet of an individual's existence or identity is at stake, the margin allowed to the State will normally be restricted; where, however, there is no consensus at European level either as to the relative importance of the inter-

---

149 *See, e.g.*, *Pini and Others v. Romania*, Eur. Ct. H.R. 2004-V, ¶ 140.

150 *Schalk and Kopf v. Austria*, App. No. 30141/04 (Eur. Ct. H.R., June 24, 2010), ¶¶ 92–94. However, the Court did not find that, at present, the Convention guaranteed same-sex couples a right to marry (¶¶ 108–110).

151 *See, e.g.*, *Olsson v. Sweden (no. 1)*, 130 Eur. Ct. H.R. (ser. A) (1988), ¶ 61.

est at stake or as to the best means of protecting it, particularly where the case raises sensitive moral or ethical issues, the margin will be wider.[152]

d. *Positive Obligations*

According to the ECtHR, in addition to the obligation of non-interference with the right to private and family life, Article 8 establishes positive obligations to ensure effective respect for such right. This applies also as regards the sphere of relations between private individuals.[153] In this area as well States enjoy a margin of appreciation. As the Court has repeatedly recognized, the "notion of 'respect' is not clear cut especially as far as positive obligations are concerned: having regard to the diversity of the practices followed and the situations obtaining in the contracting States, the notion's requirements will vary considerably from case to case." Once again, it is a matter of balancing the competing interests of the individual and those of the community as a whole (in light also of the specific legitimate purposes under Article 8(2)).[154]

6. *Freedom of Thought, Conscience, and Religion*

The case law on Article 9 of the Convention (and Article 2 of Protocol No. 1 on the right of parents to ensure that their children's education conforms to their own religious and philosophical convictions) is less voluminous than on the previously examined provisions and has developed more recently.[155] But it is no less authoritative - albeit, judging from the turmoil created by the *Lautsi* case on the use of religious symbols in public schools (see below), particularly controversial at times.

a. *Freedom to Manifest Religion or Beliefs in a "Democratic Society"*

Much of the Court's jurisprudence on freedom of thought, conscience, and religion concerns State interferences with the freedom to manifest one's religion or beliefs.[156] As with other rights under the Convention, Article 9(2)

---

[152] *See* the Court's review of its case law on the matter in the recent judgment *A, B and C. v. Ireland* (GC), App. No. 25579/05 (Eur. Ct. H.R. Dec. 16, 2010), ¶¶ 229–232. *See* also *supra* note 58.

[153] *See, e.g., X and Y v. the Netherlands*, 91 Eur. Ct. H.R (ser. A) (1985), ¶ 23.

[154] *See, e.g., A, B and C. v. Ireland, supra* note 152, ¶¶ 247–249.

[155] For a review, see, e.g., J. Murdoch, *Freedom of Thought, Conscience and Religion: A Guide to the Implementation of Article 9 of the European Convention on Human Rights* (Strasbourg: CoE Pub., Human Rights Handbooks Series No. 9, 2007).

[156] It must be noted that cases raising issues under Article 9 are often addressed in terms of other freedoms guaranteed by the Convention, in particular freedom of expression or freedom of association.

permits such restrictions if they are "prescribed by law" and "necessary in a democratic society" for certain legitimate aims – in this case, public safety, protection of pubic order, health or morals, or protection of the rights and freedoms of others. Generally, the Court's determination has centered on the criterion of the necessity of the particular measure in a "democratic society."

In *Kokkinakis*, the first significant judgment on Article 9, the Court established the basic principle that

> freedom of thought, conscience and religion is one of the foundations of a 'democratic society' within the meaning of the Convention. It is, in its religious dimension, one of the most vital elements that go to make up the identity of believers and their conception of life, but it is also a precious asset for atheists, agnostics, skeptics and the unconcerned. The pluralism indissociable from a democratic society, which has been dearly won over the centuries, depends on it.[157]

It is thus from the perspective of a "democratic society" characterized by pluralism, as well as tolerance and broadmindedness,[158] that the Court approaches the test of necessity. But it has recognized that, since several religions coexist in democratic societies, it may be necessary to place restrictions on the freedom of manifestation of religion in order to reconcile the interests of the various groups and ensure that everyone's beliefs are respected.[159]

In this context, the ECtHR has generally allowed States a wide margin of appreciation – which is not to say that it has not exercised its supervisory function and has not found violations of Article 9, *Kokkinakis* being a prime example. Deferring to State authorities is justified, in the Court's view, by the lack of a uniform European conception of the requirements of "the protection of the rights of others" in relation to attacks on their religious convictions. Thus, "[w]hat is likely to cause substantial offense to persons of a particular religious persuasion will vary significantly from time to time and from place to place, especially in an era characterized by an ever growing array of faiths and denominations."[160]

b. *Dress Codes as a Manifestation of Religious Beliefs*

Among other interferences with manifestations of religious beliefs, the Court has been called upon to consider restrictions on the wearing of the Islamic headscarf. It considered the measure compatible with the Convention with

157 *Kokkinakis v. Greece*, 260-A Eur. Ct. H.R. (ser. A) (1993), ¶ 31.
158 *See Handyside, supra* note 58, ¶ 49.
159 *Kokkinakis, supra* note 157, ¶ 33.
160 *Wingrove v. the United Kingdom*, Eur. Ct. H.R. 1996-V, ¶ 58.

respect to a teacher at a primary public school, stressing, in particular, that it was "difficult to reconcile the wearing of an Islamic headscarf with the message of tolerance, respect for others and, above all, equality and non-discrimination that all teachers in a democratic society must convey to their pupils."[161] Similarly, it upheld the ban in a case concerning a public university student in Turkey, in light of the fact that secularism, a fundamental principle of the Turkish State, was consistent with the values of the Convention and could be considered necessary to protect the democratic system in that country.[162] Drawing on both precedents, it also did not take issue with the prohibition on the wearing of the headscarf applied to a university professor in Turkey – a public servant.[163]

On the contrary, in a case involving the wearing of religious garments by private individuals in open public spaces, in contravention of a law banning such practice except for religious ceremonies, the Court considered that the interference by the State constituted a violation of article 9.[164]

c. *Use of Religious Symbols in Public Schools*

In the November 2009 *Lautsi* judgment, the Court held that the compulsory display of a symbol of a particular faith – in this case a crucifix – "in the exercise of public authority in relation to specific situations subject to governmental supervision, particularly in classrooms," restricted the right of parents to educate their children in conformity with their convictions and the right of schoolchildren to believe or not believe. It found such restrictions to be incompatible with the State's duty to respect neutrality in the exercise of public authority, especially in the field of education.[165]

The case was referred to the Grand Chamber at the request of the Respondent State, Italy. An unprecedented number of States, NGOs, and groups of persons intervened as third parties, with the "Crucifix case" adding fuel to the ongoing debates in Europe on issues such as the place of religious heritage in the definition of collective identity. The Grand Chamber delivered its judgment in March 2011, reversing the Chamber's finding – which is only likely to generate more discussion. The Grand Chamber held that the decision whether crucifixes should be present in State-school classrooms fell within States' margin of appreciation, all the more so as European consensus is lacking on the presence of religious symbols in public schools. It further

---

161 *Dahlab v. Switzerland* (dec.), Eur. Ct. H.R. 2001-V.

162 *Leyla Şahin v. Turkey* (GC), Eur. Ct. H.R. 2005-XI, ¶¶ 114–122.

163 *Kurtulmuş v. Turkey* (dec.), Eur. Ct. H.R. 2006-II.

164 *Ahmet Arslan and Others v. Turkey*, App. No. 41135/98 (Eur. Ct. H.R. Feb. 23, 2010), ¶¶ 48–52.

165 *Lautsi v. Italy*, App. No. 30814/06 (Eur. Ct. H.R. Nov. 3, 2009), ¶ 57.

considered a crucifix on a wall to be an "essentially passive symbol," which "cannot be deemed to have an influence on pupils comparable to that of didactic speech or participation in religious activities."[166]

7. *Freedom of Opinion and Expression*

In its landmark *Handyside* judgment, the ECtHR set out its approach to freedom of expression: it is one of the essential foundations of a democratic society, one of the basic conditions for its progress and for the development of every man. Subject to the permissible restrictions under Article 10(2) of the Convention,[167] freedom of expression "is applicable not only to 'information' or 'ideas' that are favorably received or regarded as inoffensive or as a matter of indifference, but also to those that offend, shock or disturb the State or any sector of the population."[168]

Thus the Court has generally interpreted in a broad manner the forms of expression falling under the protection of Article 10, irrespective of content or means of dissemination (subject to the exceptions in section a. below). It has also taken a narrow approach to the requirements for legitimate interferences, applying in particular a strict test of proportionality on any penalties imposed, although it has allowed States a margin of appreciation on certain issues, such as the concept of "morals."[169]

a. *Limits to Article 10 Protection*

While, in the view of the Court, the use of strong and provocative terms is generally encompassed within the notion of freedom of expression,[170] incite-

---

[166] *Lautsi and Others v. Italy* (GC), App. No. 30814/06 (Eur. Ct. H.R. Mar. 18, 2011), ¶¶ 63–76.

[167] Article 10(2) provides that, since the exercise of the freedom of expression carries with it "duties and responsibilities," it "may be subject to such formalities, conditions, restrictions or penalties as are prescribed by law and are necessary in a democratic society, in the interests of national security, territorial integrity or public safety, for the prevention of disorder or crime, for the protection of health or morals, for the protection of the reputation or rights of others, for preventing the disclosure of information received in confidence, or for maintaining the authority and impartiality of the judiciary."

[168] *Handyside, supra* note 58, ¶ 49. For a survey of the relevant case law, *see, e.g.*, M. Macovei, *Freedom of Expression: A Guide to the Implementation of Article 10 of the European Convention on Human Rights* (Strasbourg: CoE Pub., Human Rights Handbooks Series No. 2, 2d ed., 2004); *INTERIGHTS Manual for Lawyers – Freedom of Expression under the European Convention on Human Rights (Article 10)* (London: Interights, 2007).

[169] *See, e.g., Müller and Others v. Switzerland,* 133 Eur. Ct. H.R. (ser. A) (1988), ¶ 35.

[170] *Lopes Gomes da Silva v. Portugal,* Eur. Ct. H.R. 2000-X, ¶¶ 14, 34–35.

ment to violence[171] and hate-speech are not protected under the Convention. Holocaust denial falls within this exception as well, since "[d]enying crimes against humanity is...one of the most serious forms of racial defamation of Jews and of incitement to hatred of them."[172]

The case of Mr. Le Pen, the former Chairman of the French "Front National" Party, who has found himself on both ends of the prohibition of hate-speech, is very telling. In *Lindon and Others*, the Court held that comments made about him in a book, given that their content was such as to stir up violence and hatred, went "beyond what is tolerable in political debate, even in respect of a figure who occupies an extremist position in the political spectrum."[173] But it also rejected as inadmissible a complaint he brought concerning a fine imposed on him for comments made about the Muslim community in France, which he depicted in a negative, and even disturbing, light.[174]

b. *Special Protection of the Press and of Political Expression*

In its case law, the Court has afforded the press a special status in relation to the rights under Article 10, given its "vital role of 'public watchdog.'"[175] It has repeatedly emphasized that the press has the task to impart information and ideas on political issues and any other areas of public interest, while the public has a right to receive them. Press freedom is one of the best means for the public to become aware of and form opinions on ideas and attitudes of political leaders. This, as established in *Lingens*, also means that politicians must tolerate a higher degree of scrutiny of words and deeds and wider limits of acceptable criticism than private individuals.[176]

If journalistic sources are deterred from assisting the press, the latter's vital public-watchdog role would be undermined and its ability to provide accurate and reliable information might be adversely affected. On that basis, the ECtHR held in *Goodwin* that, in the absence of an overriding requirement in the public interest, an order of source disclosure was not compatible with

[171] *See, e.g., Sürek v. Turkey (no. 3)* (GC), App. No. 24735/94 (Eur. Ct. H.R. July 8, 1999), ¶¶ 40–41.

[172] *See Garaudy v. France* (dec.), Eur. Ct. H.R. 2003-IX.

[173] *Lindon, Otchakovsky-Laurens and July v. France* (GC), App. Nos. 21279/02 and 36448/02 (Eur. Ct. H.R. Oct. 22, 2007), ¶ 57.

[174] *Le Pen v. France* (dec.), App. No. 18788/09 (Eur. Ct. H.R. Apr. 20, 2010).

[175] *See, e.g., The Sunday Times v. the United Kingdom (no. 2)*, 217 Eur. Ct. H.R. (ser. A) (1991), ¶ 50.

[176] *Lingens v. Austria*, 103 Eur. Ct. H.R. (ser. A) (1986), ¶¶ 41–42.

Article 10.[177] In a recent case, the Court further elaborated on the need for procedural safeguards in this context, including *ex ante* review by a judge or other independent and impartial decision-making body.[178]

Not long ago, the Court extended the special protection enjoyed by the press in relation to the freedom of expression to a civil society organization (a human rights association), characterizing it as a "social watchdog."[179]

c. *Disclosure of Confidential Information*

Interestingly, the ECtHR has already addressed one of the topical questions raised by the WikiLeaks disclosures, namely whether freedom of expression extends to the publication of leaked diplomatic communications. At issue in *Stoll* was the fining of a journalist who published excerpts of a leaked confidential strategy paper by the Swiss Ambassador in the United States addressed to other Swiss diplomats regarding the request by the World Jewish Congress to Swiss banks for unclaimed assets of Holocaust victims. The Court took a number of factors into account in balancing the various interests at stake and eventually found no violation. Inter alia, it considered that the disclosure of parts of the document in question "was capable of undermining the climate of discretion necessary to the successful conduct of diplomatic relations in general and of having negative repercussions on the negotiations being conducted by Switzerland in particular. Hence, given that they were published at a particularly delicate juncture, the articles written by the applicant were liable to cause considerable damage to the interests of the Respondent party in the present case."[180]

8. *Prohibition of Discrimination*

Article 14 of the Convention prohibits discrimination in the "enjoyment of the rights and freedoms set forth in [the] Convention." It is not a self-standing anti-discrimination provision, and this has naturally impacted on the development of the principle through the case law of the ECtHR. There has been some criticism of what has been considered as a limited perspective on discrimination, especially in earlier years, but also acknowledgement of the

177 *Goodwin v. the United Kingdom*, Eur. Ct. H.R. 1996-II, ¶ 39.

178 *Sanoma Uitgevers B.V. v. The Netherlands* (GC), App. No. 38224/03 (Eur. Ct. H.R. Sep. 14, 2010), ¶¶ 88–92. This judgment of the Grand Chamber reversed a finding of no-violation by a Chamber.

179 *Társaság A Szabadságjogokért v. Hungary*, App. No. 37374/05 (Eur. Ct. H.R. July 14, 2009), ¶ 27.

180 *Stoll v. Switzerland* (GC), App. No. 69698/01 (Eur. Ct. H.R. Dec. 10, 2007), ¶ 136.

broader approach adopted by the Court over the last decade.[181] This trend is bound to continue as the latter has begun to examine cases invoking also Protocol No. 12, which contains a general non-discrimination clause extending the scope of protection to "any right set forth by law."[182]

a. *Applicability of Article 14*

The Court has declined to apply Article 14 when no other substantive provision of the Convention is applicable to a case, i.e. where no right or freedom under the Convention is at issue.[183] But where a complaint falls within the scope of any such provision, the Court examines claims under Article 14, even if it has found no violation of the substantive article. It has thus recognized a certain degree of autonomy to Article 14. For instance, in *Abdulaziz* – a case involving immigration rules allowing wives to join husbands resident in the UK, but not husbands to join wives – the ECtHR considered that Article 8 on family life was applicable, but had not been breached, *taken alone*, in the particular circumstances of the applicants. It held, however, that the latter had been victims of discrimination on the ground of gender, and thus Article 14, *taken together with Article 8*, had been violated.[184]

Another way in which the Court has broadened the scope of application of Article 14 is through a wide interpretation of what issues fall under the rights and freedoms protected under the Convention. For example, by determining that an entitlement to welfare benefits based on contributions was covered by the right to property, it could proceed to examine a claim of discrimination based on nationality in the payment of such benefits.[185]

b. *Direct, Indirect, and Positive Discrimination*

Most of the case law concerns direct discrimination, which for the Court means "treating differently, without an objective and reasonable justification, persons in similar situations." The applicable test is whether the distinction at issue pursues a "legitimate aim" and there is a "reasonable relationship

[181] R. O'Connell, "Cinderella Comes to the Ball: Article 14 and the Right to Non-Discrimination in the ECHR," *Leg. Studies* 211 (2009), pp. 211–229, *available at* http://ssrn.com/abstract=1328531. For another survey of the jurisprudence, *see, e.g.*, M.W. Janis, R.S. Kay & A.W. Bradley, *European Human Rights Law – Text and Materials* (Oxford: Oxford University Press, 3rd ed., 2008), pp. 457–516.

[182] The first judgment finding a violation of its Article 1 was delivered on Dec. 22, 2009 (*Sejdić and Finci v. Bosnia and Herzegovina* (GC), App. Nos. 27996/06 and 34836/06).

[183] *See, e.g., Botta v. Italy*, Eur. Ct. H.R. 1998-I, ¶ 39.

[184] *Abdulaziz and Others v. the United Kingdom*, 94 Eur. Ct. H.R. (ser. A) (1985), ¶¶ 62–63, 69, 71, 83.

[185] *Gaygusuz v. Austria*, Eur. Ct. H.R. 1996-IV, ¶¶ 41–52.

of proportionality between the means employed and the aim sought to be realized."[186] Depending on the ground for the difference in treatment, the ECtHR takes a strict approach to the test or allows States a margin of appreciation. Distinctions based on race or ethnicity, among others, fall into the former category – in fact, for the Court, "no difference in treatment which is based exclusively or to a decisive extent on a person's ethnic origin is capable of being objectively justified in a contemporary democratic society built on the principles of pluralism and respect for different cultures."[187] On the contrary, States have a wide margin of appreciation with respect to general measures of economic or social strategy, such as welfare or pension systems.[188]

In 2000, the Court upheld for the first time in the *Thlimmenos* case a claim of indirect discrimination – an apparently neutral treatment which has the effect of perpetuating disadvantage or exclusion. The ECtHR thus recognized another facet of discrimination prohibited under Article 14: "when States without an objective and reasonable justification fail to treat differently persons whose situations are significantly different."[189]

It is also well-established case law that, in certain situations, measures of "positive discrimination" (affirmative action) may be necessary to correct "factual inequalities." Actually, the ECtHR has recognized that sometimes States may have a positive *duty* under Article 14 to attempt to correct inequality through different treatment.[190]

9. *Right to Property*

A violation of the right to property is the second most frequent finding by the Court after breaches of Article 6 on the right to a fair trial.[191] The case law[192] covers a vast array of economic interests and assets, in the diverse historical, social and political contexts of CoE member States – ranging from restitutions of property nationalized by communist regimes in Eastern

[186] *See, e.g., Sejdić and Finci, supra* note 182, ¶ 42.

[187] *Id.* ¶ 44.

[188] *Carson and Others v. the United Kingdom* (GC), App. No. 42184/05 (Eur. Ct. H.R. Mar. 16, 2010), ¶ 61.

[189] *Thlimmenos v. Greece* (GC), Eur. Ct. H.R. 2000-IV, ¶ 44.

[190] *See, e.g., Stec and Others v. the United Kingdom* (GC), Eur. Ct. H.R. 2006-VI, ¶ 51.

[191] *50 Years of Activity, supra note* 5, p. 6.

[192] For an analysis, *see, e.g.*, A. Grgić, Z. Mataga, M. Longar & A. Vilfan, *The Right to Property under the European Convention on Human Rights: A Guide to the Implementation of the European Convention on Human Rights and its Protocols* (Strasbourg: CoE Pub., Human Rights Handbooks Series No. 10, 2007); C.B. Schutte, *The European Fundamental Right of Property* (Deventer: Kluwer, 2004).

Europe[193] to property located in the area of northern Cyprus occupied by Turkish armed forces.[194]

a. *Scope*
Article 1 of Protocol No. 1 enshrines the right of both natural and legal persons to the peaceful enjoyment of their "possessions." The latter term has been interpreted very broadly by the ECtHR, thus encompassing not only immovable and movable property, but also non-physical assets. Examples of such "possessions" include a security right *in rem*,[195] an entitlement under an arbitral award,[196] intellectual property[197] or an entitlement to welfare benefits.[198] A relevant criterion is whether the legal position in question gave rise to financial rights and interests and thus had an economic value.[199]

The concept of "possessions" covers existing possessions or assets, including claims, "in respect of which the applicant can argue that he or she has at least a 'legitimate expectation' of obtaining effective enjoyment of a property right"– 'hope' of recognition of a property right which it has been impossible to exercise effectively for a long time does not qualify.[200] Moreover, a claim in this context must be sufficiently established to be enforceable.[201]

b. *Approach to Allegations of Violations*
In the landmark *Sporrong and Lönnroth* case, the ECtHR analyzed the text of Protocol No. 1, Article 1, and the three distinct but connected rules it contains: first, the principle of peaceful enjoyment of property, which is of a general nature; second, the conditions to be fulfilled in case of deprivation of property;[202] third, the recognition that States are entitled, amongst other

---

193 *See, e.g., Jantner v. Slovakia*, App. No. 39050/97 (Eur. Ct. H.R. Mar. 4, 2003).

194 *See, e.g., Loizidou, supra* note 29.

195 *See Gasus Dosier- und Fördertechnik GmbH v. the Netherlands*, 306-B Eur. Ct. H.R. (ser. A) (1995), ¶ 53.

196 *See Kin-Stib and Majkić v. Serbia*, App. No. 12312/05 (Eur. Ct. H.R. Apr. 20, 2010), ¶ 84.

197 *See Melnychuk v. Ukraine* (dec.), Eur. Ct. H.R. 2005-IX.

198 *See, e.g., Gaygusuz, supra* note 185.

199 *See Paeffgen GmbH v. Germany* (dec.), App. Nos., 25379/04, 21688/05, 21722/05 and 21770/05 (Eur. Ct. H.R. Sep. 18, 2007).

200 *See, e.g., Prince Hans-Adam II of Liechtenstein v. Germany* (GC), Eur. Ct. H.R. 2001-VIII, ¶ 83.

201 *See, e.g., Kin-Stib and Majkić, supra* note 196, ¶ 83.

202 The second sentence of the Article reads: "No one shall be deprived of his possessions except in the public interest and subject to the conditions provided for by law and by the general principles of international law."

things, to control the use of property in accordance with the general interest, by enforcing such laws as they deem necessary for the purpose.[203]

The Court thus establishes which rule is applicable in the particular circumstances of a case. In that light, it examines whether the interference meets the criteria of lawfulness (including as regards the quality of the law),[204] of being "in the public/general interest" and of proportionality. States are in principle allowed a wide margin of appreciation to determine what is in the public interest, since social and economic policies are at stake.[205]

c. *The Proportionality Test*

When assessing if the interference struck a fair balance "between the demands of the general interest of the community and the requirements of the protection of the individual's fundamental rights,"[206] two factors take on special importance. One is the degree of protection from arbitrariness that is afforded by the relevant domestic proceedings.[207] The other is financial compensation. In this connection, the Court has emphasized that the taking of property without payment of an amount reasonably related to its value will normally constitute a disproportionate interference. Sometimes, however, legitimate objectives of "public interest" may call for less than reimbursement of the full market value. But only in exceptional cases can a total lack of compensation be considered justifiable.[208]

C. *Conclusion*

Even such a sketchy overview of the case law of the ECtHR can leave no doubt as to its significance. Through its dynamic interpretation of the Convention and the Protocols, the Court has been leading the way to higher standards of human rights protection. Hundreds of victims of human rights violations have been vindicated by the Court's findings. Other regional and international judicial and quasi-judicial bodies have been influenced by its decisions.[209] Reforms have been undertaken in CoE member States either

---

203 *Sporrong and Lönnroth v. Sweden*, 52 Eur. Ct. H.R. (ser. A) (1982), ¶ 61. *See also James and Others v. the United Kingdom*, 98 Eur. Ct. H.R. (ser. A) (1986), ¶ 37.

204 *See, e.g., Beyeler v. Italy* (GC), Eur. Ct. H.R. 2000-I, ¶ 109.

205 *See, e.g., James and Others, supra* note 203, ¶ 46.

206 *See, e.g., Sporrong and Lönnroth, supra* note 203, ¶ 69.

207 *See, e.g., Hentrich v. France*, 296-A Eur. Ct. H.R. (ser. A) (1994), ¶ 45.

208 *See, e.g., The Holy Monasteries v. Greece*, 301-A Eur. Ct. H.R. (ser. A) (1994), ¶ 71.

209 *See* J.G. Merrills, *The Development of International Law by the European Court of Human Rights* (Manchester: Manchester University Press, 2nd ed., 1993); *see also* the papers pre-

in implementation of a particular judgment, but also indirectly, through the more general influence of its jurisprudence on legislators, governments and national judges. This effect is not easy to measure,[210] but as a recent study regarding eighteen States concludes, "national systems are increasingly porous to the influence of the [Convention] and the case law of its Court"[211] – to varying degrees, of course, depending on the country or the issue. Nevertheless, "[n]ational officials are, gradually but inexorably, being socialized into a Europe of rights, a unique transnational legal space now seeking to develop its own logic of political and juridical legitimacy."[212]

This path is not without hurdles. If anything, the ongoing stormy debates in the United Kingdom regarding the Court's decisions on prisoners' voting rights[213] serve as a reminder that some do not always take kindly to what they perceive as a "dictate" from Strasbourg on issues best dealt with at the domestic level – even in countries that are original signatories of the Convention and "old acquaintances" of the Court. The fact that the overall level of human rights protection in some CoE members presents particular challenges turns the above-described convergence into a more distant goal. And one must accept that, by definition, it will take time to overcome certain deep-rooted structural problems indentified by the Court.

While States may find that the ECtHR is overstepping its boundaries, the latter is also not immune from the criticism of human rights defenders and commentators for not taking a more progressive stand on certain issues or not restricting the margin of appreciation it allows the national authorities.[214]

---

sented at the Seminar held at the opening of the judicial year 2009 on the topic: "50 years of the Court viewed by its fellow international Courts" *available at* http://www.echr.coe.int/ECHR/EN/Header/The+Court/Events+at+the+Court/Opening+of+the+judicial+year.

[210] For an in-depth discussion of this issue, *see* S. Greer, *The European Convention on Human Rights: Achievements, Problems and Prospects* (Cambridge: Cambridge University Press, 2006), pp. 60 *et seq.*

[211] A. Stone Sweet & H. Keller, "Assessing the Impact of the ECHR on National Legal Systems," *Faculty Scholarship Series*, Paper 88 (Yale Law School, 2008), p. 677, *available at* http://digitalcommons.law.yale.edu/fss_papers/88. The country reports are included in H. Keller & A. Stone Sweet, eds., *A Europe of Rights: The Impact of the ECHR on National Legal Systems* (Oxford: Oxford University Press, 2008).

[212] *Id.* p. 710.

[213] *See, e.g.*, "MPs urged to defy Europe over prisoner voting ban," http://news.bbc.co.uk/democracylive/hi/house_of_commons/newsid_9390000/9390987.stm. In the unimplemented *Hirst v. the United Kingdom (no. 2)* (GC) (Eur. Ct. H.R. 2005-IX), the Court found a violation of Article 3 of Protocol No. 1 regarding the right to free elections. On Nov. 23, 2010, it delivered a pilot judgment on the same issue arising from two other applications (*Greens and M.T. v. the United Kingdom*, App. Nos. 60041/08 and 60054/08).

[214] *See, e.g.*, J.A. Brauch, "The Margin of Appreciation and the Jurisprudence of the European Court of Human Rights: Threat to the Rule of Law," 11 *Colum. J. Eur. L.* 113 (2004).

But the greatest challenge facing the Court is undoubtedly its caseload. As mentioned at the beginning, a number of measures have already been taken in that regard and the reflection on further reform is ongoing. The underlying debate[215] as to whether the Court should provide "individual" justice for victims of human rights violations or "constitutional" justice focusing on issues of principle of general and Europe-wide interest - or both - is not likely to subside very soon.

[215] For a survey of the various points of view, *see* Bowring, *op. cit., supra* note 7, pp. 600–605.

[11]

The European Court of Human Rights after 50 Years

*Anthony Lester**

It is a privilege to contribute to this distinguished book, marking the fiftieth anniversary of the European Court of Human Rights. There is much to celebrate about the Court's work. As its Deputy Registrar, Michael O'Boyle, observes:[1]

> There seems to be unanimous agreement in Europe today that the European Convention on Human Rights . . . is one of the major developments in European legal history and the crowning achievement of the Council of Europe. The emergence of the authority of the European Court of Human Rights has been described as one of the most remarkable phenomena in the history of international law, perhaps in the history of all law.

However, it is important to think imaginatively and boldly about practical ways of alleviating the profound crisis which threatens the Court's achievements during its next half century, ways which go beyond useful but insufficient procedural changes, or increasing funding without tackling fundamental institutional problems. These are hard times across Europe as we face a deep economic crisis, but hard times might help to concentrate the minds of our European political and judicial leaders to tackle the worsening crisis of the Convention system. As O'Boyle has noted,[2] there is no or little public or media discussion about the Court's problems, and the arduous process of securing ratification of Protocol No 14, for example, took place 'under the radar' and was 'confined to the corridors in Strasbourg'.

In his speech on the occasion of the opening of the judicial year, on 30 January 2009, Mr Jean-Paul Costa, President of the Court, proposed a major conference in the first half of 2010, to articulate a new commitment, a reaffirmed legitimacy, and a clarified mandate for the Court. Coming only weeks after the Russian ratification of Protocol No 14, the Interlaken Conference held on 18 and 19 February 2010 was the first important step in the strategic response to the ongoing issues facing the

* The author is grateful to the staff at the Odysseus Trust for their help in preparing this chapter. His views have been informed by practical experience and discussion with many within the system to whom he is also grateful.

[1] M. O'Boyle, 'On Reforming the Operation of the European Court of Human Rights', 1 *European Human Rights Law Review* (2008), 1.

[2] Ibid at 11.

Court to be taken during the Swiss presidency. In reaffirming the commitment of States Parties to the role played by the Court in the protection of human rights in Europe, the Interlaken Declaration proposed a number of key reforms to the operation of the Court in the form of an 'Action Plan'. The swift implementation of these new reforms is essential to ensure the ongoing operational success of the Court. There is no doubt about the urgency of what is at stake—nothing less than the survival of a viable Convention system in which those it was designed to protect have confidence. And it is essential that the issues are openly discussed by the media and the public across Europe.

I. The Court's Past Life

> When to the sessions of sweet silent thought
> I summon up remembrance of things past,
> I sigh the lack of many a thing I sought,
> And with old woes new wail my dear time's waste.[3]

That was Shakespeare's melancholic recollection. But for me, remembrance of things past in using the Convention system as a human rights advocate brings happy memories and not 'old woes'. More recent and new woes are a different matter!

The master builders of the European Convention on Human Rights were determined, in the aftermath of a second terrible war in half a century, never again to permit State sovereignty to shield from international liability the perpetrators of crimes against humanity; never again to allow governments to shelter behind the argument that what a State does to its own citizens or to the stateless is within its exclusive jurisdiction, and beyond the reach of the international community. So they resolved to create a binding international code of human rights, with safeguards against abuses of power and effective remedies for victims of violations by Contracting States.

The birth pangs of the Convention were not easy. The European Movement approved a 'Declaration of Principles of the European Union'. It stated that:

> No State should be admitted to the European Union which does not accept the fundamental principles of a Charter of Human Rights and which does not declare itself willing and bound to ensure their application.

The Consultative Assembly carried that proposal forward, seeking enforcement via an independent European Commission and Court. The proposal for a Commission, in addition to a Court, was made to protect the Court from being inundated with frivolous litigation and being exploited for political ends. The Commission was envisaged as a filter of admissible applications, as the fact-finding body, and as the body whose authorization was necessary for an individual to initiate proceedings before the Court.

[3] William Shakespeare, Sonnet 30.

The Committee of Ministers of the Council of Europe attempted to block the proposal for a Court, but, after a political struggle, the Consultative Assembly overcame opposition from governments, and the Convention and its institutions were born. What is now striking is the speed with which the Convention was drafted and adopted. It was prepared within the Assembly and not by diplomats meeting in secret. And, above all, there was a political will to create a new international human rights instrument and a supranational court without precedent.

It is more than 40 years since I argued my first case in Strasbourg. It was in the European Commission of Human Rights. It was also the very first case brought against the UK, soon after the British government had accepted the right of individual petition in January 1966.[4] At that time, when the Court was ten years old, it had dealt with only one case, *Lawless v Ireland*,[5] and acceptance of the right of petition was precarious. Several governments, including my own, used to accept the right only for limited periods of a few years at a time, playing a game of cat and mouse with the Commission, with the implied threat of non-renewal.

The Commission drew on the considerable diplomatic skills of Anthony McNulty and Hans-Christian Krüger, within the Secretariat, to win the confidence of governments, whose commitment to the system was precarious because of their concern to preserve national sovereignty and State power. The Commission was brilliantly led by its Presidents, each a fine jurist—including Max Sørensen and Carl Aage Nørgaard from Denmark, and Sir James Fawcett from the UK.

The right of individual petition was especially important to those in the UK because, 40 years ago, there was no developed British system of public law and judicial review. We had no framework of positive rights to match the Convention rights and freedoms; and, without a written constitution or human rights legislation, our common law system was in many respects ethically aimless. There was no recognition of fundamental human rights. Habeas corpus was easily overridden by positive law. The courts did not even recognize that racial discrimination was contrary to legal public policy.[6]

So British advocates like me began to use the Convention system to challenge administrative action, judicial decisions, and the laws made by our sovereign Parliament. We were used to developing legal principles in our common law system, and, in my case, I had the advantage of having studied American constitutional law before being called to the English Bar. It was a great advantage that the government's advocates—including Lord Slynn and Judge Sir Nicolas Bratza, as they later became as judges of the two European Courts—shared a common determination to make the system work fairly and effectively.

The idea of fundamental human rights was anathema to Jeremy Bentham and his Utilitarian ideology, as it was to the philosophy of the Scandinavian legal realism of Alf Ross and Axel Hägerström. British ministers and civil servants did not

[4] *Alam and Khan v United Kingdom* Appl no 2991/66 (1967) 24 CD 116.
[5] *Lawless v Ireland (No 3)* Series A no 3 (1961).
[6] A. Lester and G. Bindman, *Race and Law* (Harmondsworth: Penguin, 1972), ch 1.

welcome the prospect of European judges looking over their shoulders. As Sir James Fawcett, President of the Commission, once told me, the British pathology of human rights violations sprang from a tradition of uncontrolled administrative discretion. The benevolent paternalism of administrators was seen as preferable to judicial review. To put it only slightly unfairly, for many ministers and civil servants power was delightful, and absolute power was absolutely delightful.

I have told elsewhere[7] the story of the British experience in gradually coming to terms with the Convention system. I shall not repeat that story now. Just as it took the Nordic countries many years to make the Convention rights part of their legal systems, so it took some 30 years after acceptance of the right of petition for the UK to give domestic effect to the Convention rights in the Human Rights Act 1998.[8]

During the 1960s and 70s, the main business of the developing Convention system was carried out by the Commission, in fact-finding and giving opinions. Their work was of a very high standard, and the fact-finding, for example, in the interstate case between Ireland and the UK[9] was impressive by any standard.

The Court gave a handful of important judgments, for example, in *Wemhoff*,[10] *Neumeister*,[11] and the *Belgian Linguistics case*,[12] but at that stage the Commission referred cases to the Court infrequently. There was a feeling within the Commission that the Court was too remote and that the Commission was better able to interpret and apply Convention standards. That was gradually replaced by a reluctant recognition that the Court needed to develop the jurisprudence authoritatively. As more cases began to reach the Court, it won public confidence through a series of landmark cases—*Golder*,[13] *Kjeldsen, Busk Madsen and Pedersen*,[14] *Tyrer*,[15] *König*,[16] *Klass*,[17] *Marckx*,[18] *Sunday Times*,[19] *Winterwerp*,[20] *Dudgeon*,[21] *Sporrong and Lönroth*,[22] and *Lingens*,[23] to name just a few of the vintage judgments.

[7] See A. Lester, D. Pannick, and J. Herberg, *Human Rights Law and Practice* (3rd edn, London: LexisNexis Butterworth, 2009), ch 1. See also A. W. B. Simpson, *Human Rights and the End of Empire: Britain and the Genesis of the European Convention* (Oxford: Oxford University Press, 2001).

[8] The Coalition Government has announced plans to set up a Commission to examine the Human Rights Act 1998 and whether or not it should be replaced by a British Bill of Rights. HM Government, 'The Coalition: Our Programme for Government', May 2010. Available at: <http://www.cabinetoffice.gov.uk/media/409088/pfg_coalition.pdf>.

[9] *Ireland v United Kingdom*, 15 *Yearbook of the European Convention* (1972), 76.

[10] *Wemhoff v Germany* Series A no 7 (1968).

[11] *Neumeister v Austria* Series A no 8 (1968).

[12] *Belgian Linguistics case (No 2)* Series A no 6 (1968).

[13] *Golder v United Kingdom* Series A no 18 (1975).

[14] *Kjeldsen, Busk Madsen and Pedersen v Denmark* Series A no 23 (1976).

[15] *Tyrer v United Kingdom* Series A no 26 (1978).

[16] *König v Germany* Series A no 27 (1978).

[17] *Klass v Germany* Series A no 28 (1978).

[18] *Marckx v Belgium* Series A no 31 (1979).

[19] *Sunday Times v United Kingdom (No 1)* Series A no 3 (1979).

[20] *Winterwerp v Netherlands* Series A no 33 (1979).

[21] *Dudgeon v United Kingdom* Series A no 45 (1981).

[22] *Sporrong and Lönroth v Sweden* Series A no 52 (1982).

[23] *Lingens v Austria* Series A no 103 (1986).

The Court's case law makes[24] 'a continuing contribution to the evolving public law of Europe as the norms it contains are received into the national law and practice of 47 states', and has developed constitutional principles, including the judicial review of legislation, the principle of proportionality, the importance of freedom of political speech, and the full recognition of the dignity of the human person as a constitutional imperative.

For the first 30 years of the Court's life, Central and Eastern Europe were divided from the West by Winston Churchill's 'Iron Curtain'. The number of States Parties to the Convention was relatively small and most of them were well-established democracies which adhered to the rule of law. The Strasbourg machine coped well enough, with the Commission controlling the admissibility of applications and doing the fact-finding, and the Court deciding important issues of legal principle when cases were referred by the Commission or the respondent government for final adjudication.

The system was more user-friendly than was the English judicial system at that time. Today I feel nostalgic when I walk along the Allée de la Robertsau, past the unpretentious user-friendly building which housed the Commission and the Court, on my way to the modernist and functionalist palace of justice which now houses the Court and its staff.

In the early life of the Convention system, when the caseload was small, cases were argued for hours, occasionally even for days, in a friendly atmosphere. During coffee breaks we chatted with the Commissioners and judges and their staff. Admissibility decisions in important cases were fully reasoned and were usually reasonable too. The Commission acquired great expertise both in fact-finding[25] and in achieving friendly settlements compatible with human rights. The Commission was far better than the present Court in identifying urgent and important cases, a skill acquired over many years which appears to have been lost in the transition to the present system.

But, for all that, the old regime was imperfect. The judges and Commissioners were part-timers and included former agents of the governments which secured their appointment. The Secretariat and Registry staff had to do their best to uphold the integrity of the system. I remember a senior judge and former government legal adviser telling me that he saw it as his duty to uphold national interests! Of necessity the dedicated Commission staff came to assume a dominant role, seeing themselves as Platonic guardians of the Court's integrity and the European rule of law.

The procedures were cumbersome, repetitive, and inefficient. The right to effective national remedies under Art 13 was narrowly interpreted,[26] and not much attention was paid in individual cases to the need for systemic remedies for systemic violations.[27] The Committee of Ministers did not perform a useful role in independently

[24] O'Boyle, n 1 above, at 2.

[25] See eg in *Ireland v United Kingdom* Series A no 25 (1978).

[26] See Lester, Pannick, and Herberg, n 7 above, para 4.13.2.

[27] See Lord Lester of Herne Hill QC, 'The European Convention in the New Architecture of Europe', 5 *Public Law* (1996), 6.

supervising the execution of the Court's judgments or giving effect to the Commission's opinions. There was no equality of arms in access to the Court because, unlike governments, the applicants had no right of access and depended on the Commission to make a referral. That flaw was addressed in 1990 when Protocol No 9 enabled individual applicants to bring their cases to the Court after lodging their complaints with the Commission.

II. The Loss of Balance in the Reform of the System

In March 1985, the Swiss delegation to a European Ministerial Conference on Human Rights in Vienna proposed that the Commission and the Court should be merged into a single Court. The proposal was controversial, but I supported the creation of a single Court in the hope that it would promote speedy justice and enhance the Court's authority. A minority of governments, led by the UK, initially argued for a Court of First Instance to replace the Commission but their view did not prevail.

With hindsight it was a mistake to abolish the Commission. There will be considerable reluctance now, as Professor Caflisch observes,[28] to revert, in any form, to the two-tier system of the Commission and Court. Caflisch suggests[29] that 'in the long run, such a return may prove unavoidable'. But as the great economic reformer, John Maynard Keynes, reminds us from his grave[30] 'long run is a misleading guide to current affairs. In the long run we are all dead.' That is especially true when the patient is at risk of terminal decline and all that is available is palliative care. The need for a new streamlined two-tier system must be recognized as a high priority if we are to preserve both the right of individual petition and a Court able to command public confidence.

It took 13 years for the single Court system to be created by Protocol No 11, which came into force on 1 November 1998.[31] Europe had changed dramatically during those years, but unfortunately it was too late to argue that it would be better to retain the Commission to screen out inadmissible applications and do the fact-finding, working together with the Court to cope with the far-reaching effects of the enlargement of the Council of Europe.

Protocol No 11 dissolved the Commission, made the Court permanent and full time, and gave it compulsory jurisdiction for all individual applications. But it failed to provide a sufficient length of tenure to guarantee judicial independence, and it created further problems of overload from which the Court cannot recover without urgent and radical reforms.

[28] L. Caflisch, 'The Reform of the European Court of Human Rights: Protocol No 14 and Beyond', 6(2) *Human Rights Law Review* (2006), 414.

[29] Ibid.

[30] *A Tract on Monetary Reform* (1923), ch 3.

[31] See *Protocol No 11 to the Convention for the Protection of Human Rights and Fundamental Freedoms, restructuring the control machinery, established thereby ETS No 155, Explanatory Report.*

David Maxwell Fyfe, rapporteur of the drafting committee and one of its main architects, described the Convention in a speech made to the Parliamentary Assembly in 1950 as 'a beacon to the peoples behind the Iron Curtain and a passport for their return to the midst of the free countries'.[32] But when the proposal to create a single Court was first put forward, no one foresaw that the Soviet system was soon to collapse, resulting in a vast enlargement of the Council of Europe to its present membership of 47 States.

Everyone knows of the massive burdens the Court carries in attempting to deal with the backlog of applications and new complaints which have increased exponentially during the decade since Protocol No 11 came into force. Like Sisyphus, the Court is cursed to roll a huge boulder up a hill, only to watch it roll down again, and, in the absence of further reform, to repeat this throughout eternity! In 2008 alone, there were 50,000 new applications, 20 per cent more than in 2007. Fifty seven per cent of applications were lodged against just four States—the Russian Federation, Turkey, Romania, and Ukraine. They and Poland are the countries giving rise to the greatest number of judgments. In 2009, 57,200 applications were allocated to a judicial formation, while the backlog of cases reached 119,300 applicants.[33]

The Russian Federation is the worst offender.[34] Since it was admitted to the Council of Europe 13 years ago, it has failed to comply with its obligations under the Convention, including providing effective domestic remedies and abiding by the Court's judgments. Some 3,300 cases with similar factual background were lodged with the Court between August 2008 and January 2009 against Georgia concerning hostilities in South Ossetia.[35] It is reasonable to suppose that this has been done with encouragement from the Russian authorities.[36] Under the present Russian regime, there is seemingly little commitment to the European rule of law

[32] *Political Adventure: The Memoirs of the Earl of Kilmuir* (London: Weidenfeld & Nicolson, 1964), 183, quoting from his speech made in August 1950. The Earl of Kilmuir, formerly David Maxwell Fyfe, was a British Conservative MP who became Solicitor General, Attorney General, Home Secretary, and Lord Chancellor. He was Britain's chief prosecutor in the Nuremberg trials and conducted a brilliant and effective cross-examination of Hermann Göring.

[33] ECtHR Factsheet, 'Protocol 14: The Reform of the European Court of Human Rights'. See: <http://www.echr.coe.int/NR/rdonlyres/57211BCC-C88A-43C6-B540-AF0642E81D2C/0/CPProtocole14EN.pdf>.

[34] At the end of September 2010 there were 38,850 cases pending cases against the Russian Federation, constituting 27.8 per cent of all pending applications. See European Court of Human Rights Statistics, 2010 Pending cases pie chart at: <http://www.echr.coe.int/NR/rdonlyres/99F89D38-902E-4725-9D3D-4A8BB74A7401/0/Pending_applications_chart.pdf>.

[35] Press release issued by the Registrar, 14 January 2009.

[36] One may speculate that it was the interstate application brought by Georgia against the Russian Federation in respect of the events in South Ossetia in the summer of 2008 which caused the Russian Federation to retaliate by supporting the bringing of large numbers of individual applications against Georgia. Indeed, the Russian Prosecutor's Office has assisted South Ossetia residents in preparing complaints against Georgia to international and regional courts. On 12 August 2008, the prosecutor general of the Russian Federation, Yury Chaika, announced that he had created 'a special brigade of prosecutors that would provide legal assistance in preparing appeals and complaints to the European Court of Human Rights and the Hague International Criminal Court'. See Human Rights Watch, 'Up in Flames: Humanitarian Law Violations and Civilian Victims in the *Conflict over South Ossetia*', 23 January 2009, available at: <http://www.hrw.org/en/node/79681/section/31>.

and no sense of solidarity or collective responsibility with the other States Parties. And across Europe, ***realpolitik*** abounds. The Parliamentary Assembly and the Committee of Ministers have no appetite to apply dissuasive sanctions, for example by suspending voting rights in the Council of Europe, as was done for nine months in 2000 for alleged gross violations of human rights in Chechnya. And it is improbable that interstate proceedings will be taken against the Russian Federation (or other States) whose systemic and persistent violations place heavy and unacceptable burdens upon the Court and the Convention system. And I doubt whether the peoples of that long-suffering nation would benefit if the Russian Federation were expelled from the Council of Europe.

Alone among the 47 Member States, Russia's long-standing resistance thwarted the implementation of Protocol No 14, which had been devised as a means of improving the efficiency of the Convention system and reducing the Court's backlog.[37] Adopted by the Committee of Ministers in May 2004, Russia's long-awaited ratification in January 2010 paved the way for its adoption in June 2010. This may indicate a new willingness on the part of Russia to engage in a commitment to the Convention regime, but it remains to be seen to what extent the ratification amounts to a change of heart. Protocol No 14 contains a number of key institutional reforms. It:

(a) permits single judges to declare cases inadmissible where they are clearly without merit;
(b) permits committees of three judges (instead of Chambers of seven judges) to give judgments in repetitive cases where the Court's case law is already well established (for example, the many cases on length of proceedings);
(c) introduces a new admissibility requirement concerning cases where the applicant has not suffered a significant disadvantage, provided that the case has already been considered by the domestic courts, and provided that there are no general human rights reasons why the application should be examined on its merits;
(d) provides for a single term of office of nine years for the judges of the Court;
(e) gives the Committee of Ministers new powers to bring proceedings before the Court against a party that refused to abide by one of the Court's judgments, and to request the Court to give an interpretation of a judgment;
(f) allows the Commissioner for Human Rights to submit written observations and take part in proceedings before the Court; and
(g) provides that the European Union may accede to the Convention.

Under current circumstances, the Court's caseload is likely to increase at an annual rate of about 14 per cent. Regardless of the accession to Protocol No 14 the load will probably only increase, as it will as more States ratify Protocol No 12, enabling cases to be brought under a free-standing guarantee of equal treatment without

[37] Protocol No 14 was adopted by the Committee of Ministers on 13 May 2004.

discrimination.[38] However, while Protocol No 14 is not a panacea, its provisions need to be translated into short-term practical measures while longer term solutions are discussed and developed.

The Court's expenditure is borne by the Council of Europe.[39] Its expenditure accounts for a quarter of the Council's total budget, but it needs more money to function properly. It does not have its own ring-fenced budget.[40] Its budget is part of the general budget of the Council of Europe. The contributions of Member States to the Council of Europe are fixed according to scales taking into account population and gross national product. The Court's budget for 2010 amounted to €58,588,600. Since 2000, the Council of Europe's budget has been prepared on the basis of zero real growth (that is, the same amount as the previous year to take into account inflation, salary adjustments, etc). Since 2006, the principle of zero growth has been extended to Member States' contributions. In 2009, the Court received an extra €1,542,300 for its enhancement programme (for the creation of seven additional posts in the Department of Execution of Judgments and 47 additional posts in the Court). A group of leading human rights NGOs have rightly observed that[41] the Court 'has been hampered by a lack of sufficient human and financial resources'. The Ministers' Deputies have made it clear to the Secretary General of the Council of Europe[42] that 'they would not accept proposals departing from the principle of zero real growth in member states' contributions'. Within the confines of the total Council of Europe budget, it has been treated generously, but the underlying problem is that the Court should not have to compete for resources within the overall budget. It needs its own budget calculated according to its needs in delivering what the Convention requires, without being constrained by the requirement of zero growth for the rest of Council of Europe expenditure.

The resources at the Court's disposal are meagre compared with those of the European Court of Justice (ECJ). To give one example, the ECJ's library budget for acquisitions is about €800,000 per year, while that of the Strasbourg Court is €70,000 and reducing. Of course the European Courts have different functions, but it is difficult to understand why the European Union should fund the Luxembourg

[38] Matching Art 26 of the UN International Covenant on Civil and Political Rights.

[39] Art 50 of the Convention.

[40] Unlike the Inter-American Court of Human Rights which, in accordance with Art 72 of the Inter-American Convention on Human Rights, draws up its own budget and submits it for approval to the General Assembly through the General Secretariat which may not introduce any changes to it. In accordance with Art 26 of its Statute, the Court administers its own budget.

[41] Amnesty International, the European Human Rights Advocacy Centre, INTERIGHTS, JUSTICE, Liberty, the International Commission of Jurists, and the AIRE Centre, 'Comments on Reflection Group Discussions on enhancing the long-term effectiveness of the Convention system', DH-S-GDR (2009) 008, March 2009, para 50. They refer to the Report of the Group of Wise Persons, 15 November 2006, para 37, which noted that 'no other international court is confronted with a workload of such magnitude while having at the same time such a demanding responsibility for setting the standard of conduct required to comply with the Convention.'

[42] 'Budgets of the Council of Europe for the financial year 2009', Report on Economic Affairs and Development (Rapporteur, Mr Paul Wille), Doc 11599, 25 April 2008, Explanatory memorandum, para 14.

Courts so generously while the Council of Europe deprives the Strasbourg Court of the financial and human resources needed to perform its Herculean labours.[43]

It is also essential, as the Group of Wise Persons recommended[44] that, in the interests of enhancing the Court's independence and effectiveness, the Court should be granted 'the greatest possible operational autonomy, as regards in particular the presentation and management of its budget and the appointment, deployment and promotion of its staff'. It is important too, as the Group of Wise Persons also recommended,[45] for the judicial system of the Convention to be made more flexible and for there to be a Statute of the Court.

Since the accession to Protocol No 14 in January 2010, the Court's rules have changed significantly, allowing for greater flexibility and the faster processing and dismissal of cases. Prior to the introduction of Protocol No 14, the Court was forced to spend most of its time striking out inadmissible cases. The new 'Protocol No 14' introduces changes in three areas. It bolsters the Court's ability to strike out clearly inadmissible applications by allowing single judges to do so. The Protocol introduces a new power to refuse to hear cases in which the applicant has not suffered a significant disadvantage, so that the Court can focus on cases which raise important human rights issues. And, it provides the Court with measures for dealing more efficiently with repetitive cases, so that the Court will have significant new powers to punish States that repeatedly fail to comply with its judgments. It can now initiate proceedings of non-compliance in the Grand Chamber of the Court, and these sanctions can potentially include suspension or expulsion from the Council of Europe.[46]

Even though the giving of reasons is an important safeguard encouraging a rational and fair process of decision-making, there is no duty for the Court to give reasons for rejecting an application without communicating it to the government. The applicant is informed of the decision by a peremptory letter reminiscent of the reply to the young narrator in Ring Lardner's novel *The Young Immigrants* who asked her father tenderly whether he was lost on the journey to their new home. '"Shut up," he explained.'

This peremptory procedure is adopted even in cases raising novel issues of interpretation and application of the Convention which are of general importance, and where lawyers have taken great care on behalf of applicants in cases which deserve to be communicated to the respondent governments. The rejection letters inform them that:

> The decision is final and not subject to any appeal . . . You will therefore appreciate that the Registry will be unable to provide any further details about the Committee's deliberations or to conduct further correspondence relating to its decision in this case.

[43] The 2010 budget for the ECJ is €329,300,000, about 5.5 times the budget of the European Court of Human Rights.

[44] Report of the Group of Wise Persons to the Committee of Ministers, CM(2006)203, 15 November 2006, para 124.

[45] Ibid, paras 127–8.

[46] ECtHR Factsheet, n 33 above.

I recognize that the absence of proper reasons does not mean that behind the scenes there has been an absence of detailed reasons to inform the Committee in reaching inadmissibility decisions, but it would enhance public confidence if they or a summary of them could be provided to applicants. There is widespread dissatisfaction among applicants and their advocates about the current practice.

The Court's refusal to provide short but clear reasons for decisions on inadmissibility is unacceptable, given that every proposal to the Committee is accompanied by a report containing the grounds for the proposed rejection of an application. It would not be a significant burden for this analysis to provide the basis for a short, clear set of reasons, and it is wrong to suppose that only the Committee needs to see that analysis. The Court should surely set a good example to national courts and administrators in the way in which it communicates its decisions to applicants.

Several of the senior Registry staff are old personal friends. We grew up together as the system grew and changed. They do a fine job as Platonic guardians of the *acquis*, but I hope they will forgive my observing that they are somewhat inbred. The Section Registrars and Deputy Section Registrars are grown from within the Registry, and their experience is not enriched by adding those from outside with experience of running and reforming overburdened national courts. This old friend may be forgiven for saying that younger advocates representing applicants often complain (privately) that they find access to Registry staff difficult and believe that government agents have much easier access.

III. The Independence of the ECtHR

Seven years ago, INTERIGHTS (the International Centre for the Legal Protection of Human Rights) published a report by a group of eminent jurists[47] describing the current system of appointments to the Court, in light of the principles of judicial independence. It contained a number of recommendations. In particular, the report proposed that the Council of Europe should devise and distribute minimum standards for national nomination procedures, and should set up an independent group of experts in international human rights law to make recommendations to the Parliamentary Assembly after having interviewed the candidates. In the words of INTERIGHTS' report, internal processes are 'often inadequate, politicised and so opaque that they are barely understood.... There is no meaningful review of these procedures at the international level, and no effective safeguards against arbitrariness.'

[47] *Judicial Independence: Law and Practice of Appointments to the European Court of Human Rights*, May 2003. The authors were: Professor Dr Jutta Limbach, former President of the Federal Constitutional Court of Germany (Chair); Professor Dr Pedro Cruz Villalón, former President of the Constitutional Court of Spain; Mr Roger Errera, former member of the Conseil d'Etat and of the Conseil supérieure de la magistrature in France; Professor Dr Tamara Morshchakova, former Vice President of the Constitutional High Court of the Russian Federation; the Rt Hon Lord Justice Stephen Sedley, of the English Court of Appeal; Professor Dr Andrzej Zoll, former President of the Constitutional High Court of Poland; and myself, as Hon President of INTERIGHTS.

The Parliamentary Assembly has recently called for improvements in national and European procedures, building upon the INTERIGHTS report.[48] They recommend new requirements to make the selection process fair and transparent, and to make it possible for judges to retain judicial office in their own countries while serving as members of the Court, thereby strengthening judicial independence. Fortunately, the rigid and inflexible requirements imposed by the Assembly to secure gender balance have been interpreted by the Court in an advisory opinion so as to secure appointment on the basis of personal merit rather than gender.[49]

Strasbourg judges do not manage the cases in any real sense; that key responsibility is left to the Registry staff. It is the staff who manage the cases and make the vital selection as to which cases have priority and which cases are sent to the judges in batches for summary disposal. Lord Woolf noted in his Review[50] that within the 20 divisions in the Registry, arranged primarily according to language and country, 'there is constant pressure to meet targets and increase productivity'. And again, according to Lord Woolf,[51] the lawyers in the Registry 'work to fulfil numerical targets; they have to complete a certain number of cases each year . . . it is often the more important Chamber cases that get left at the bottom of the pile'. It is a factory system, dominated by the Registry, attempting to achieve high productivity in delivering mass production of mainly negative decisions.

Even cases which have been given priority treatment by the Court—urgent cases involving arbitrary arrest and detention, solitary confinement, inhuman and degrading treatment threatening an applicant's health and life, the coerced sterilization of Romani women, and other gross abuses—may be left in abeyance for years. As I know from personal experience, when the lawyers in these cases write to the Registry, they are simply told to wait. The judges remain in ignorance of the way in which priorities are being determined or operated by the Registry. There is a lack of transparency about the relationship between the judges and the Registry, and a lack of a proper system of judicial oversight to ensure that urgent cases are given proper priority. I understand that the Court has been examining this problem and look forward to the publication of the new system for ensuring that urgent cases are dealt with expeditiously. It is really important that the criteria are clear and transparent and widely available.

The Convention envisages[52] that the Court is to be assisted by legal secretaries. It is presumably for the judges, in partnership with the Registry, to decide how that assistance should be provided. Unlike the judges of the ECJ and the International

[48] Report of the Committee on Legal Affairs and Human Rights, 'Nomination of candidates and election of Judges to the European Court of Human Rights' Parliamentary Assembly Doc 11767, 1 December 2008. See also Parliamentary Resolution 1646 (2009).

[49] The Court held that 'in not allowing any exceptions to the rule that the under-represented sex must be represented, the current practice of the Parliamentary Assembly is not compatible with the Convention'. Advisory opinion on certain legal questions concerning the lists of candidates submitted with a view to the election of judges to the European Court of Human Rights, Strasbourg, 12 February 2008.

[50] *Review of the Working Methods of the European Court of Human Rights*, the Rt Hon Lord Woolf et al, December 2005, at 53.

[51] Ibid, 55. [52] Art 25.

Court of Justice, Strasbourg judges are not assisted by their own *référendaires* in analysing the facts, the law, and the case law, and in seeking to improve the reasoning in the decisions and judgments. They depend on lawyers within the Registry who may be assigned to them in particular cases. If judges wish to do independent research they often have to do it themselves.

It is unlikely that extra funds would be made available to pay for additional support for the judges, but it is important to ensure that their working conditions are such as to attract able candidates to become and remain members of the Court, and that the judges are able themselves to decide cases with adequate time for analysis and reflection. It is also essential to involve the judges themselves in case management. This has been done in the UK with great success, after judges have received the necessary training in case management.

It is also essential in the interests of judicial independence for salaries to be sufficient, and for serving judges to have both security of tenure and security when they return to their home countries after their term of office. Protocol No 14 gives them nine years' tenure, but does not provide for judicial retirement benefits. In 1997, the Committee of Ministers adopted a resolution on the status and conditions of service of judges of the Court to be set up under Protocol No 11.[53] It provided that the conditions of service would be governed by provisional regulations which would be reviewed by the Committee of Ministers within 12 months following the entry into force of Protocol No 11. That review did not take place.

The 'provisional' regulations which remain in force require the judges to provide, at their own expense, for their retirement or pension benefits corresponding with the period of their terms of office, as well as arranging, at their own expense, for insurance for temporary or permanent incapacity to work due to illness or accident, costs of health care, and death. Judges of the Court are well paid while they are in office, but it is very important that they should have proper social cover and security for their retirement. Otherwise, they will fear the consequences if they displease the government of their country and are not renewed in office, leaving them with no prospects of earning a living in a worthwhile occupation on their return home or receiving a pension. This has already happened in at least two cases of judges who were not re-elected, and constitutes a serious threat to judicial independence. There is no justification for treating them less favourably than the judges of the International Court of Justice,[54] or the ECJ.[55]

[53] Resolution (97) 9 adopted on 10 September 1997.

[54] The UN General Assembly fixes the conditions for retirement pensions for those judges of the International Court of Justice who have served a full nine-year term at one half the annual salary. There are differing amounts for those serving for shorter or longer periods: Art 32 of the Statute of the Court.

[55] The terms and conditions for judges and advocates-general of the ECJ are set out in European Communities staff regulations. Members of the ECJ belong to the contributory final salary pension scheme paid for from the general EU budget. A contribution of 10.25 per cent is deducted from their monthly basic salary. After ceasing to hold office, members of the ECJ are entitled to a pension for life payable from the age of 65. The amount of pension is calculated on the basis of 4.275 per cent of their final basic salary per year in office. The maximum pension is 70 per cent of the basic salary last received.

Members of the ECJ are entitled to sickness, occupational disease, industrial accident, and birth and death benefits under a social security scheme funded by the Communities, to which they contribute

IV. Serving Justice

Professor Caflisch has asked[56] whether the increase in the Court's output has been at the expense of quality. As a serving judge, he cannot answer that important question. I agree with the group of leading human rights NGOs that:[57]

> The Court has ensured that applicants have obtained redress for violations of human rights when states have failed to provide an appropriate remedy. In doing so it has played a crucial role in holding states accountable for these violations.... The judgments of the Court have provided essential guidance... on the steps necessary to respect and secure fundamental human rights.

Despite the intolerable conditions in which it has to work, the Court has continued to produce landmark judgments of high quality.[58] However, in important areas there is a lack of consistency and coherent principles in Chambers judgments which await clarification by the Grand Chamber.

For example, although the Court's case law includes landmark judgments explaining and applying the fundamental right to free expression, it has often been closely divided, and its reasoning has always suffered from a use of ad hoc balancing under the margin of appreciation doctrine which lacks legal certainty and adherence to clear principles.[59] In recent cases, the Court's case law on free expression has become less consistent and coherent and faithful to legal principle. In the core area of political expression where a speaker seeks to criticize governmental actions, the Court has rightly emphasized that restrictions on speech will be permitted only in the most exceptional circumstances.[60] Because of the role played by politicians in a democratic society, the limits of acceptable criticism of such persons are wider than with respect to private persons.[61]

2 per cent of their basic salary. This scheme reimburses 80 per cent of medical costs. See House of Lords Hansard, cols WA165–6, 18 June 2008.

[56] See n 28 above, 405.

[57] Amnesty International et al, n 41 above, para 2.

[58] Recent important Grand Chamber judgments include *Ilascu v Moldova and Russia* Appl no 48787/99 (2004); *Bosphorus Hava Yollari Turizm Ve Ticaret Anonim Sirketi v Ireland* Appl no 45036 (2005); *DH and others v Czech Republic* Appl no 57325/00 (2007); *Saadi v Italy* Appl no 37201/06 (2008);*Nachova v Bulgaria* Appl no 43577/98 (2005); *Hirst v United Kingdom (No 2)* Appl no 74025/01 (2005); *Sørensen & Rasmussen v Denmark* Appl no 52562/99 (2006); *Jalloh v Germany* Appl no 54810 (2006); *Dickson v United Kingdom* Appl no 44362 (2007); *S and Marper v United Kingdom* Appl no 30562/04 (2008); *A and Others v United Kingdom* Appl no 3455/05 (2009); *Rantsev v Cyprus and Russia* Appl no 25965/04 (2010), 22; *Orsus and Others v Croatia* Appl no 15766/03 (2010), 337; *Konstantin Markin v Russia* Appl no 300078/06 (2010), 1435.

[59] A. Lester, 'Universality Versus Subsidiarity: A Reply', 1 *European Human Rights Law Review* (1998), 73.

[60] See eg *Castells v Spain* Series A no 236, 14 *European Human Rights Review* (1992), 445, para 46. However, in the recent case of *Karako v Hungary* (Appl no 39311/05 (2009)) the Court accepted in principle that defamatory comments made in the course of an election campaign by a political opponent could constitute a breach of the claimant's Art 8 rights, although in that case they were insufficiently serious to do so.

[61] *Lingens v Austria* Series A no 103 (1986); *Worm v Austria* Appl no 22714/93 (1997), para 50; *Colombani v France* Appl no 51279/99 (2002).

Unfortunately, in some of its recent decisions concerning situations of conflict between freedom of expression and the right to protection of one's reputation, the Court has not fairly weighed the various interests against each other in order to ascertain whether a fair balance has been struck between the competing rights and interests. Rather, the decisions display a disproportionate weight being given to reputational rights. The most striking example of this is the case *Lindon, Otchakovsky-Laurens and July v France*,[62] as well as the decisions which show the emergence of a dangerous doctrine pursuant to which court-imposed standards or claimed duties of responsible journalism are being invoked to police the way in which the press reports on matters of clear public interest. It is hoped that the Court will curtail the development of this doctrine and return to applying the established jurisprudence which rightly accorded substantial importance to the role and duties of the press in a democratic society, particularly when commenting on the actions of political actors or other public figures.

The problem with the Court's loose invocation of the margin of appreciation is that it removes the need for the Court to discern and explain the criteria appropriate to particular problems. What is needed is a careful, skilful, and consistent application of the principle of proportionality. That is lacking in some of the Court's recent case law.

On 28 January 2010,[63] the President of the Court, President Costa, cited the entering into force of the Lisbon Treaty, Russia's ratification of Protocol No 14, and the Interlaken Conference as three reasons for optimism regarding the Court's reform. However, he also noted that the ever-increasing caseload of the Court meant that urgent reform is ever more necessary. At a press conference in 2009, President Costa outlined a road map for reform. He said that the main lines of the reform were clear, and that they would involve:

> comprehensive implementation of the Convention standards at domestic level; effective execution of the Court's judgments by member states to ensure that the Court was not overloaded with large numbers of similar cases and a re-structured protection mechanism allowing the Court's efforts to be concentrated as a matter of priority on the important well-founded cases.[64]

[62] *Lindon, Otchakovsky-Laurens and July v France* Appl nos 21279/02, 36447/02 (2007), in which Judge Loucaides said 'The right to reputation should always have been considered as safeguarded by Article 8 of the Convention, as part and parcel of the right to respect for one's private life . . . '. There is some indication of a recent change of direction: in *A v Norway* Appl no 28070/06 (2009) the Court drew attention to the fact that Art 8 does not expressly provide for a right to protection against attacks on personal reputation, unlike Art 12 of the Universal Declaration of Human Rights and Art 17 of the International Covenant on Civil and Political Rights. Further, in *Karako v Hungary* ECHR Appl no 39311/05 (2009) the Court said 'In the Court's case-law, reputation has only been deemed to be an independent right sporadically . . . and mostly when the factual allegations were of such a seriously offensive nature that their publication had an inevitable direct effect on the applicant's private life.'

[63] ECtHR, Press release issued by the Registrar, 'President Costa expresses optimism about prospects for reform', 28 January 2010. See: <http://cmiskp.echr.coe.int/tkp197/view.asp?action=html&documentId=861681&portal=hbkm&source=externalbydocnumber&table=F69A27FD8FB86142BF01C1166DEA398649>.

[64] ECtHR, Press release issued by the Registrar, 'Press conference with the President of the European Court of Human Rights', 29 January 2009. See: <http://cmiskp.echr.coe.int/tkp197/

These praiseworthy aspirations are not likely to be achieved in the current political climate. Comprehensive implementation of the Convention standards at domestic level could happen only if there were the necessary collective will within the Council of Europe and among the governing national authorities to achieve this. That will is at present lacking. And the judicial systems in many European States are not yet genuinely independent and impartial in dealing with human rights cases and other politically sensitive cases. In Professor Caflisch's words, 'A reason for the high number of applications from Eastern Europe is the distrust of individuals vis-à-vis their national judicial systems.'[65]

Effective execution requires speedy and full compliance by the States with their obligation to abide by the Court's judgments and effective monitoring of the obligation of States Parties to abide by the Court's judgments. Many governments are not complying with that obligation, and are not called to account by their Parliaments for failing to do so.[66] At the end of 2009, about 8,600[67] cases were pending before the Committee of Ministers of the Council of Europe in its supervisory capacity. Despite the best efforts of the dedicated staff of the Directorate of Human Rights, the Committee finds it difficult to muster sufficient collective energy to secure speedy and proper execution by recalcitrant governments.

President Costa did not amplify his reference to a 'restructured protection mechanism'. This could mean a judicial filtering system as recommended by the Group of Wise Persons, or a new two-tier system of Commission or Court of First Instance and a Final Court, or further limiting or even abolishing the right of individual petition. I would suppose that President Costa agrees with the Group of

view.asp?action=html&documentId=846335&portal=hbkm&source=externalbydocnumber&table=F69A27FD8FB86142BF01C1166DEA398649>.

[65] See n 28 above, 405. That is why the proposal by Professor Laurence R. Helfer to embed the Convention regime as a 'deep structural principle' in national legal systems lacks practical reality: 'Redesigning the ECHR: Embeddedness as a Deep Structural Principle of the European Human Rights Regime', 19 *European Journal of International Law* (2008), 125. Every Contracting State has already purported to do this, but Helfer's proposals depend on the existence of independent and impartial courts willing to act in partnership with the European Court of Human Rights, eg by asking the Strasbourg Court to review the Convention-compatibility of existing or proposed legislation. Apart from the matter of the capacity of national courts to carry out this task in many Contracting States, this proposal would further burden the Court with the need to give advisory opinions on proposed or actual legislation. It would interrupt and delay the law-making processes of national legislatures, and would tend to violate the separation of the judicial from the other branches of government.

[66] Committee of Ministers, 'Supervision of the execution of judgments of the European Court of Human Rights', 1st annual report, 2007, Council of Europe, March 2008; Recommendation CM/Rec (2008) 2 of the Committee of Ministers to member states on efficient domestic capacity for rapid execution of judgments of the European Court of Human Rights; Parliamentary Assembly Resolution 1516 (2006) on Implementation of judgments of the European Court of Human Rights; Committee on Legal Affairs and Human Rights, AS/Jur (2008) 24, 26 May 2008. In the UK, the Joint Parliamentary Committee on Human Rights monitors the government's response to the judgments of the European Court of Human Rights as well as of the judgments of domestic courts: 'Monitoring the Government's Response to Human Rights Judgments: Annual Report 2008', HL Paper 2173; HC 1078, 7 October 2008.

[67] Enhancing Parliament's role in relation to human rights judgments, Fifteenth Report of the Joint Committee on Human Rights, Session 2009–10, HL 85/HC 455 (para 3).

Wise Persons[68] that to give the Court a discretionary power (analogous to the *certiorari* procedure of the US Supreme Court) to decide whether or not to take up cases would be:

> alien to the philosophy of the European human rights protection system. The right of individual application is a key component of the control mechanism of the Convention and the introduction of a mechanism based on the *certiorari* procedure would call it into question and thus undermine the philosophy underlying the Convention. Furthermore, a greater margin of appreciation would entail a risk of politicising the system as the Court would have to select cases for examination. The choices might lead to inconsistencies and might even be considered arbitrary.

In my view, the problems of the present system should not result in yet further procedural obstacles to the right of individual application. As Michael O'Boyle rightly observes[69] the success of the Convention system is 'undoubtedly linked to the immeasurable value over the years of the right of individual petition' and that right should not be 'trammelled or curtailed in any way'. Instead, there is a pressing need to create a new streamlined two-tier system which would enable the Grand Chamber of the Court to concentrate its efforts, as a matter of priority, on cases involving serious questions of public importance about the interpretation and application of the Convention. At the same time, there needs to be a body—whether a judicial filtering system within the Court, or a Commission or a Court of First Instance—to deal fairly and speedily with admissibility in all cases. In my view, it would be important for the body to be able to establish the facts, as was done by the European Commission of Human Rights.

V. A View to the Future

A new Protocol No 15 will be needed to make these changes, but there are reforms which could now be made without waiting for further amendments to the Convention. The Court is rightly requiring State authorities to provide effective remedies and to eliminate systemic practices which violate Convention rights. The pilot judgment procedure is important in enabling the Court to deal with repetitive complaints that highlight such practices. But the Court needs to develop a fair procedure for dealing with pilot cases so that other parties with a common interest are able to be represented. And the Committee of Ministers must be more vigorous in ensuring that States introduce effective general measures to eliminate systemic and structural problems and provide effective remedies to victims.

In addition, the Court should enable its judges to decide, in cooperation with the Registry, which cases should be given priority, and what procedure should be adopted for those cases. The criteria should be developed and made public.

[68] Report of the Group of Wise Persons to the Committee of Ministers, CM(2006)203, 15 November 2006, para 42.
[69] See n 1 above, 3–4.

The power conferred on the Secretary General of the Council of Europe to obtain explanations from Contracting States on the manner in which their internal laws ensure the effective implementation of the Convention has fallen into disuse. It should be activated. And the Committee of Ministers should be more rigorous in requiring States to abide by judgments of the Court by which they are directly bound, as well as seeking to ensure that judgments of general importance are given effect across Europe—the so-called *erga omnes* principle.

President Costa has rightly called for a Special Conference to consider the future of the Court and Convention system. It should consider what kind of Court we need, and with what level of political and financial support. There is an urgent need to take stock and strengthen the foundations of what has been built up over the past 50 years. One risk in holding such a conference is that it could be used to dismantle, to wreck, and to weaken. The moment of reform of any type is always a dangerous one. There are certainly States whose governments would dearly love to have the opportunity to hobble the Court. But the risks should be faced and overcome.

To adapt the poet's description of the Mosaic Code,[70] the ethical and legal code protected by the Convention system is 'a moon for mutable lampless men'. It is often described as a beacon of hope for the 800 million peoples of Europe. But the lamplighters who lit the beacon more than half a century ago are no more, and the light will fail unless our generation rekindles the flame. Let us hope that those who govern us will take heed.

[70] Isaac Rosenberg, 'The Jew'.

[12]

Rethinking the European Court of Human Rights

*Luzius Wildhaber**

The European Convention on Human Rights (ECHR) originated in 1949/50, the European Commission of Human Rights (ECommHR) began its work in 1954, the European Court of Human Rights (ECtHR) in 1959. There can be little doubt that the edifice and the instruments launched some 50 to 60 years ago had a profound impact on subsequent developments. I shall discuss some of the most important aspects of these developments.

In a first section, I shall point out what I consider to be some signal achievements of the ECHR and the European Court of Human Rights (Section I). In a second section, I distinguish between five functions of the ECtHR: filtering and wailing wall, routine adjudication, borderline fine-tuning, grave human rights breaches, and structural and systemic problems (Section II). In a third section, I address the evolutive interpretation of the ECHR (Section III). The fourth section takes up issues of defective legislation or practice and asks whether and to what extent the ECtHR has ordered general measures and has considered such laws as incompatible with the Convention (Section IV). In a fifth section, on the overload of the ECHR system, I go beyond what I call 'incrementalism and tinkering' and sketch a reformed system, one which in my view would provide for more stability, predictability, transparency, and honesty (Section V). In a last section, I try to define and evaluate issues of individual, constitutional, and administrative justice (Section VI).

I. Some Achievements of the ECHR

Binding judgments of an international human rights court

The ECHR is a product of realistic idealism. It is a direct reaction to the atrocities of the 1930s and 1940s.[1] It is anchored in the belief that democratic regimes,

* Revised and amplified text of a Keynote Address delivered on 21 March 2009 at the University of Copenhagen. Sections V and VI are based on lectures at the University of Bristol (on 6 May 2009) and at Yale Law School (on 24 April 2009).

[1] D. Nicol, 'Original Intent and the ECHR', *Public Law* (2005), 152–72; A. W. Brian Simpson, *Human Rights and the End of Empire* (Oxford: Oxford University Press, 2001).

respectful of fundamental rights, do not go to war with one other, and that it can therefore no longer be an issue of purely domestic jurisdiction whether democracies relapse into dictatorships.

As it has turned out, the ECHR may be said to constitute the most successful attempt to implement the Universal Declaration of Human Rights through binding court decisions to which the Member States undertake to abide, rather than through recommendations, reports, information, exhortations, or lamentations. In putting matters this way, one distinguishes between binding legal obligations and non-binding soft law. One characterizes issues of the implementation of UN-based human rights law as largely soft law and of a political nature, and suggests that the effect of judgments of the ECtHR should go beyond that.

Of course, such a methodological approach might be qualified as somewhat old fashioned and as an oversimplification of issues of considerable complexity.[2] However, the ground on which international human rights are built is slippery enough. The risk that some States might feel tempted to consider all human rights of the ECHR as soft law and as subject to the 'sovereignty veto' of their governments exists. Indeed the Court has repeatedly been reviled for ignoring the boundaries between law and politics. For example, the Russian government called the *Ilaşcu v Moldova and Russia* judgment 'incoherent, controversial, subjective, political and based on double standards', and it further added that the *Ždanoka v Latvia* judgment 'ignored objective historical facts'.[3] While I do not believe that these insults are pertinent (or even proper), I nevertheless tend to think that the Court would be well advised to stay on safe ground.

In the recent case of *Demir and Baykara v Turkey*, the ECtHR departed from its earlier case law and considered the right of trade unions to bargain collectively as an essential element of Art 11 of the ECHR.[4] Relying on the doctrine of the 'living' nature of the Convention,[5] the Court stated that it:

> can and must take into account elements of international law other than the Convention, the interpretation of such elements by competent organs, and the (consensus emerging from) the practice of European States reflecting their common values.[6]

And it added a remark which must come as a big but unwelcome surprise from the perspective of international law, noting:

> that in searching for common ground among the norms of international law it has never distinguished between sources of law according to whether or not they have been signed or ratified by the respondent State.[7]

[2] D. Thürer, 'Soft Law—Norms in the Twilight between Law and Politics' in D. Thürer, *Völkerrecht als Fortschritt und Chance* (Zurich: Nomos, 2009), 159–78.

[3] Press Release no 1569 of 8 July 2004 of the Russian Ministry of Foreign Affairs. Cf *Ilaşcu and others v Moldova and Russia* Appl no 48787/99 (2004), ECHR 2004-VII (n 13 below); *Ždanoka v Latvia* Appl no 58278/00 (2006), ECHR 2006-IV.

[4] *Demir and Baykara v Turkey* Appl no 34503/97 (2008), paras 153–4 and concurring opinion of Judge Zagrebelsky.

[5] Ibid, para 68. [6] Ibid, para 85. [7] Ibid, para 78.

Jean-François Flauss has pointedly criticized the methodology of this judgment, remarking that the Court, by extending its 'consensual' method in all directions, adhered to a system of 'pick and choose'. He has qualified this system as shattering, alarming, presumptuous, and iconoclastic.[8]

Extension of the Convention to the whole of Europe

The second achievement I wish to emphasize is that the Convention was conceived in 1949/50 as an instrument to prevent democracies from relapsing into dictatorships, but was then extended to the whole continent of Europe. In a first step, it was gradually accepted by the whole of Western Europe. Not only was the Convention as such ratified, but over time the States also acceded to the optional clauses (individual applications to the ECommHR and compulsory jurisdiction of the ECtHR).[9]

In a second step, the Convention was extended, after the fall of the Iron Curtain, to practically all countries of Central and Eastern Europe, democratic or not so democratic, willing or not so willing, as one of the most visible signs of an attempted change in their systems of government. Future historians may well write that one of the main merits of the Convention and the Court's case law was simply to be there after the fall of the Iron Curtain, at the right time and the right place, as a credible model for those States which intended to demonstrate their commitment to democracy, the rule of law, and human rights. The changes which the ECHR brought about or supported in Central Europe have been praiseworthy and have not only benefitted individuals, but also the national courts and ultimately the separation of powers.

As a result, the ECHR is the only regional human rights catalogue which is binding on practically a whole continent.

An instrument of European public order

In a few important cases, the ECtHR has emphasized 'the Convention's special character as a human rights treaty'[10] and as an 'instrument of European public order (ordre public) for the protection of individual human beings',[11] as well as the 'objective obligations' and the 'collective enforcement' of the ECHR guarantees.[12]

[8] J.-F. Flauss, 'Actualité de la Convention européenne des droits de l'homme', *Actualité juridique droit administratif* (2009), 872–84. See also the less lofty, but nevertheless cautious comments by R. Nordeide in 103 *American Journal of International Law* (2009), 567–74.

[9] L. Wildhaber, 'Changing Ideas about the Tasks of the ECtHR' in L. Wildhaber, *The ECtHR 1998–2006: History, Achievements, Reform* (Strasbourg, Kehl: N. P. Engel, 2006), 138–43.

[10] *Al-Adsani v United Kingdom* Appl no 35763/97 (2001), ECHR 2001-XI, para 55.

[11] *Loizidou v Turkey* (Preliminary Objections) Series A no 310 (1995), ECHR A/310, paras 75 and 93; *Banković v Belgium et al* Appl no 52207/99 (2001), ECHR 2001-XII, para 80; *Bosphorus Hava Yollari Turizm ve Tikaret Anonim Şirketi v Ireland* Appl no 45036/98 (2005), ECHR 2005-VI, para 156.

[12] *Ireland v United Kingdom* Series A no 25 (1978), para 239; *Loizidou* (Preliminary Objections), n 11 above, para 70; *Mamatkulov and Askarov v Turkey* Appl nos 46827/99, 46951/99 (2005), ECHR 2005-I, para 100.

These formulations could be interpreted in different ways as claims:

(a) to achieve effective application of the ECHR in all territories of all Member States (this view would explain why the ECtHR decided it had jurisdiction in the *Loizidou* and the *Ilaşcu* cases, but not in the *Banković* case);[13] or

(b) to a special, constitutional character of the ECHR, which should be given primacy over national law, being an instrument of both international law and the municipal legal systems of the Member States (either in all its aspects or with respect solely to its core principles); or

(c) to a special, constitutional character of each specific judgment or decision of the ECtHR (since according to Art 46(1) the States 'undertake to abide by the final judgment of the Court in any case to which they are parties', judgments to which other States are parties will ordinarily be observed as precedents).[14] There is in my view no specific need to regard every judgment as an instrument of a pan-European public order.[15]

Without analysing these claims in more detail, it could at any rate be maintained that the core content of the triad of democracy, rule of law, and human rights has become indispensable for any contemporaneous, value-oriented understanding of a European Constitution.[16] In the same vein, the European Court of Justice in its early leading cases emphasized that human rights constituted general principles of Community law and were inspired by constitutional traditions common to the Member States, so that they could 'supply guidelines which should be followed'.[17]

Confirmation of the right of individual application

As a fourth achievement I would stress that the Convention has become a living illustration and confirmation of the right of individual application. Along with this has come an enormous workload and backlog.[18]

The ECHR was launched in the 1950s with an optional right to bring individual applications before the ECommHR, whose reports were authoritative but not binding. Proposals to give the Court the power to declare null and void national legislation and court decisions which violated the Convention were rejected. Only in 1994 did the 9th Additional Protocol give individuals direct access to the Court, and even that access was subject to leave given by the Court. The 11th Additional

[13] *Loizidou* (Preliminary Objections), n 11 above, *Loizidou v Turkey* (Merits) Appl no 15318/89 (1996), ECHR 1996-VI; *Ilaşcu* et al *v Moldova and Russia* Appl no 48787/99 (2004), ECHR 2004-VII; *Banković*, n 11 above.

[14] See n 81 below.

[15] If such a need were asserted, it would be indispensable to define what elements of a judgment would be binding, on the basis of what facts. It would also be necessary to agree whether only Grand Chamber judgments would be binding or also Chamber judgments (and, if so, under what conditions).

[16] By European Constitution I obviously refer to a wider notion than that of a constitution of the European Union.

[17] Case 4/73 *Nold* (1974) ECR 491; and see Case 29/69 *Stauder* (1969) ECR 419; Case 11/70 *Internationale Handelsgesellschaft* (1970) ECR 1125.

[18] I shall address this point under Section V.

Protocol then merged the ECommHR and the ECtHR in 1998, rendered the optional clauses obligatory, and thus fully institutionalized the right of individual application to the Court.

Only a few words are needed to emphasize the imposing significance of individual applications in the edifice of the ECHR. Article 34 ECHR does not provide for an *actio popularis,* but the Court may receive applications from any person, NGO, or group of individuals claiming to be the victim of a Convention violation. Individual applications are the Court's daily bread. Interstate cases are few and far between. Only 22 interstate applications have reached the Court, the most recent ones being the two pending cases of *Georgia v Russia.* Not all conflicts between States are submitted to the Court in the form of an interstate application. For instance, there have been no interstate cases concerning the dissolution of the former Yugoslavia or the conflicts and secession or autonomy claims of Chechnya or Nagorno-Karabach. Over time most conflicts reach the Court anyway by means of individual applications. Advisory opinions play a very negligible role before the Court. And as is well known, the ECHR does not provide for national filter systems or for preliminary rulings, or for writs of certiorari or leave-to-appeal systems.

For someone reflecting over the merits of different human rights protections systems,[19] the delivery of individual justice might seem the obvious answer. Quantitatively, such a system will soon attract applicants, at least if governments do not hinder the effective exercise of the right of petition. From the standpoint of autonomy, individuals choose themselves whether they want to complain, and no State or third party will be given this choice instead. Difficult cases and issues embarrassing for a government can readily be brought by individuals, whereas report systems are in the hands of the States and therefore reveal an amount of shadow-boxing and endeavours to gloss over real problems. Even a system of preliminary rulings initiated by national tribunals as it exists in the European Court of Justice may in some Council of Europe States be exposed to governmental pressures or excessive self-restraint on the part of the national tribunals. Last but not least, recourse to an international court seems to hold out the promise of a remedy to victims of human rights violations, although admittedly the Convention itself guarantees only declaratory, pecuniary, and procedural (and no substantive) remedies.

To sum up, if you want to launch an effective human rights protection procedure, a system of individual applications leading to binding judgments of an independent international court looks pretty good. This is, of course, what the human rights advocacy groups have emphasized all along, irrespective of the Court's overload, procedural delay, and loss of credibility, which constitute the main drawbacks of an individual application.[20]

[19] As Steven Greer has remarked aptly, a full and coherent argument that the systematic delivery of individual justice should be the key objective, has yet to be articulated: S. Greer, *The ECHR: Achievements, Problems and Prospects* (Cambridge: Cambridge University Press, 2006), 167.

[20] A typical illustration would be the article of P. Leach, 'Access to the ECtHR—From a Legal Entitlement to a Lottery?', 27 *Human Rights Law Journal* (2006), 11–25, who sees the right of applicants to an individualized adjudication as almost unconditional, but has no helpful proposals for the Court's overload problem.

II. Functions of the ECtHR

Premises

Courts should decide analogous facts according to the same rules. They should therefore normally follow precedent, unless significant changes of societal values and ideas or of living conditions require an overruling of prior judgments.[21] This follows from the core principles of predictability of the law, avoidance of arbitrariness, and equality before the law. Moreover, it is particularly important, but at the same time difficult, for international courts to avoid double standards, given the wide, sometimes obvious divergences between the Member States. In homogeneous national societies it may well be easier for courts to achieve a higher degree of coherence in their case law.

Let us inquire in the light of these premises which tasks and functions the ECtHR has to fulfil. Five categories may be distinguished.

Filtering and wailing wall

Individual applications must first be ruled admissible; in fact some 96 per cent of all applications do not reach that stage. Once they are declared admissible, however, the Court will find one or more violations in more than 90 per cent of all cases. To formulate matters somewhat differently, in practice the right of individual application is a right of access to the ECtHR, but cannot guarantee a specific treatment. Different categories of cases call for judicial treatment of varying scope. Taking into account the massive overload of the Court, it is just not possible to have a generalized guarantee for every applicant to have his or her case declared admissible or to have it debated at a public hearing or to have it submitted to the Grand Chamber.

Routine adjudication

Among the admissible applications, I classify some as falling into special categories: some concern grave breaches of human rights, some result from structural or systemic problems, some may be qualified as 'borderline fine-tuning'.

The ECtHR's database classifies cases by level. In early 2009, there were 1,361 (13 per cent) Level 1 ('most significant') cases, 1,725 (16 per cent) Level 2 ('significant contribution'), and 7,656 (71 per cent) Level 3 ('little legal interest') cases.[22] A sizeable number of the 'not so significant' cases are more or less routine judgments, whether or not the Court finds violations.

[21] See the authors quoted n 81 below.

[22] R. C. A. White and I. Boussiakou, 'Voices from the ECtHR', 27 *Netherlands Quarterly of Human Rights* (2009), 168–9.

Borderline fine-tuning

The ECtHR takes pride in its evolutive interpretation of the ECHR in light of changing societal values or changing needs of individuals. I leave aside for the moment the possibility that societal values might change in the sense that more restrictive approaches are advocated (for example with respect to terrorism or sexual abusers).[23] Undoubtedly, however, a good many judges of the Court see themselves more or less at the forefront of those courts that are active in further developing, evolving, and fine-tuning human rights.[24]

Grave breaches of human rights

The ECHR does not operate with the notions of core guarantees or kernels of fundamental freedoms. Even the Court's case law only rarely uses such terms. Nevertheless, unfortunately, clear cases of grave and massive human rights breaches have reached the ECtHR: random killings and torture, disappearances of persons, mass rapes, but also prolonged illegal detention, thoroughly unfair or arbitrary proceedings, or systematic elimination of effective political opposition would fall into this category. There is little doubt that it is an obvious task of a human rights court to sanction such grave breaches, even though the respective governments will resent the Court's judgments and will try to qualify them as political rather than legal.[25]

Structural or systemic problems

One of the biggest problems facing the Convention system is how to deal with large numbers of well-founded applications deriving from structural or systemic problems existing in the Contracting States, the so-called repetitive cases or mass claims. The best-known examples are the excessive length of court proceedings and the failure to execute final court judgments, problems which have existed or continue to exist in about half the Member States.[26]

I have been told that no matter how many cases concerning these problems arrive in the ECtHR, each applicant is equally aggrieved. This implicitly suggests that the Court should look at each case with equal care. If this is to be the task of a European Court with over 100,000 pending cases, one must be forgiven for questioning how

[23] In essence this possibility raises two fundamental problems, whether human rights necessarily prevail over democratic decision-making, and whether there is a human rights *acquis* that is irreversible. See Section III below.

[24] Very tentatively, with some trepidation and keeping in mind linguistic limits, the following courts outside Europe (but including the European Union) might deserve mention: Inter-American Court of Human Rights, European Court of Justice, Supreme Courts of Canada, USA, Israel, and India, Constitutional Court of South Africa.

[25] See text at n 3 above.

[26] For these and other illustrations, see Wildhaber, n 9 above, 121; L. Wildhaber, 'Europäischer Grundrechtsschutz aus der Sicht des Europäischen Gerichtshofs für Menschenrechte', 32 *Europäische Grundrechte Zeitschrift* (2005), 689–92.

this should happen. I grant that the lobby of NGOs, professors, and even judges who warn against what they consider to be restrictions on the right of individual application has been noisy and effective, and that there is virtually no lobby advocating effective reform. Before we look at the excessive workload of the ECtHR, I first take up the question of whether the differing functions of the Court can be reconciled.

On harmonizing the differing functions

The ECtHR has, first, the inevitable wailing wall-filter function for sifting out the large majority of applications which will not be decided on their merits.[27] An important part of all complaints will fail on formal grounds (for example, non-exhaustion of domestic remedies); others on mixed grounds (for example, being incompatible with the Convention); still others on substantive grounds (for example, being 'manifestly ill-founded'). There may be a 'spectrum of standards' concerning the notion of a 'manifestly ill-founded' application, 'ranging from totally unmeritorious to no *prima facie* breach'.[28] Indeed, given the impossible workload situation, it would be in the interest of honesty and transparency to concede that the Court cannot handle all applications; to continue to insist on admissibility conditions; however (going beyond these conditions), also to acknowledge that many applications cannot be examined, whether or not they are admissible (for example when the applicants have suffered no substantial disadvantage or when a case has no 'general repercussion in society').[29]

The ECtHR will, secondly, have to handle claims alleging grave breaches of human rights, since human rights courts cannot elude this task. If they tried to elude it, they would lose not only their credibility, but also their soul and their right to exist.

Thirdly, the Court must decide what should be the guiding principles with respect to structural or systemic problems. The details of the execution of the guiding principles should in my view be entrusted to the national authorities, but the ECtHR should have ways and means of controlling the national execution periodically in individual cases. Given the overload of the ECtHR, it is in my view simply not feasible to rely throughout on a case-by-case control by the Court. It is,

[27] Under Art 35 ECHR, applications are admissible:

(a) after exhaustion of all domestic remedies, provided they are adequate and effective;
(b) within a period of six months from the date of the final domestic decision;
(c) if they are not anonymous;
(d) if the complaint is not substantially the same as a matter already examined by the Court or another procedure of international investigation or settlement;
(e) if they are not abusive, a condition which the Court interprets quite restrictively;
(f) if they are not 'manifestly ill-founded', a condition which the Court handles with more discretion, all the way endeavouring not to make this criterion appear too intimately linked to issues of policy or management; and finally
(g) if they are not incompatible with the Convention.

[28] D. J. Harris, M. O'Boyle, E. P. Bates, and C. M. Buckley, *Law of the ECHR* (2nd edn, Oxford: Oxford University Press, 2009), 785.

[29] This criterion was introduced in Brazil's Supreme Federal Tribunal, which was so overburdened that it was 'overstretched to the point of mutiny', *The Economist*, 23 May 2009, p 53.

furthermore, open to doubt whether a European Court can on its own discipline national systems which simply do not have the will to play by the rules of the game.

As to routine adjudication and fine-tuning in an open society, attitudes will necessarily oscillate between more activist and more self-restrained approaches.[30] Why is it that such a large number of controversial Grand Chamber judgments are accompanied by dissenting and separate opinions? Because agendas and perceptions differ, and because there are various ways of safeguarding human rights. There is on the whole nothing wrong with such divergences. Open and pluralistic societies must try to tolerate them. My own preference is for an ECtHR which develops an acute sense for effectivity and priorities and a realistic sense for what should be secondary, which takes the principle of subsidiarity seriously and which can accept that in many respects the reality of human rights is and will continue to be decentralized.

It is almost self-evident that the ECtHR will work hard to harmonize and reconcile the various functions assigned to it. Yet, objectively, such harmonization is delicate and dependent on the standpoints and agendas of the various players. 'Judicial activists' and 'perfectionists' will consider the Court's agenda to be, first, the steady expansion of human rights on a widening front; secondly, the abandonment of notions such as subsidiarity and margin of appreciation in favour of ambitious standard-setting; and consequently, thirdly, the lack of the distinctions advocated here such as 'routine adjudication', 'fine-tuning', and 'grave breaches', which would presumably be replaced by the simple concept of 'human rights violations writ large'. Advocates of 'judicial self-restraint', 'realism', and 'minimalism' might differ, but all would go less far; they would accept the ECHR's ineluctable and inexorable dependence on, and interconnectedness with, the various national courts, parliaments, and governments;[31] and they would insist on priorities and a sense of proportion in European human rights protection, so that the ECtHR would provide above all for inspiration, guidelines, minimal standards, and a programme of realistic idealism and idealistic realism.

This discussion leads us directly to issues of the evolutive interpretation and the overload and reform of the ECtHR.

[30] See F. J. Bruinsma and M. de Blois, 'Rules of Law from Westport to Wladiwostok: Separate Opinions in the ECtHR', 15 *Netherlands Quarterly of Human Rights* (1997), 175–86; P. Mahoney, 'Judicial Activism and Judicial Self-Restraint in the ECtHR: Two Sides of the Same Coin', 11 *Human Rights Law Journal* (1990), 60–88; F. Rivière, Les Opinions Séparées des Juges à la Cour européenne des droits de l'homme (2004), 366–427; E. Voeten, 'The Politics of International Judicial Appointments: Evidence from the ECtHR', 61 *International Organization* (2007), 699–701; R. C. A. White and I. Boussiakou, n 22 above.

[31] Cf. H. Keller and A. Stone Sweet (eds), *A Europe of Rights: The Impact of the ECHR on National Legal Systems* (Oxford: Oxford University Press, 2008); L. Garlicki, 'Some Observations on Relations between the ECtHR and the Domestic Jurisdictions' in J. Iliopoulos-Strangas (ed), Cours suprêmes nationales et cours européennes: concurrence ou collaboration, In Memoriam of Louis Favoreu (Brussels: Bruylant, 2007), 305–25; N. Krisch, 'The Open Architecture of European Human Rights Law', 71 *Modern Law Review* (2008), 183–216; S. Oeter, 'Rechtsprechungskonkurrenz zwischen nationalen Verfassungsgerichten, Europäischem Gerichtshof und Europäischem Gerichtshof für Menschenrechte', 66 *Vereinigung deutscher Staatsrechtslehrer* (2006), 361–91; C. Vedder, 'Integrierter Grundrechtsschutz in Europa—Görgülü und Bosphorus' in H. Bauer, D. Czybulka, W. Kahl, and A. Vosskuhle (eds), *Wirtschaft im offenen Verfassungsstaat, Festschrift Reiner Schmidt* (Munich: C. H. Beck, 2006), 179–203.

III. A Few Words on the Evolutive Interpretation of the ECHR

Where does evolutive interpretation lead?

The ECHR guarantees classical civil and political rights. As is the case with national catalogues of human rights, such guarantees cannot be interpreted like a Code of civil or criminal procedure or of taxation. The guarantees are more programmatic than normative formulations, open in time and into the future, to be unfolded and developed in light of changing conditions and societal values, a deteriorating environment, increasing global mobility, migration streams, rapid technological progress, and financial crises. Moreover, in my view, it is often hardly possible to demonstrate conclusively that a specific decision is uniquely correct. Tribunals can render their judgments acceptable if these appear as the reasoned product of informed impartial choice. The task of a judge, and in particular of a judge at an international human rights court, is doing justice and fairness through a vision of reasonableness.[32]

The ECtHR's hallmark has been the idea of a continuing development and the evolutive interpretation of the ECHR.[33] The notion of such an evolution may be evocative. But it is neither precise nor free of subjectivity. To a certain degree an evolution of human rights in the course of time is almost unavoidable.[34] Suffice it to invoke the irresistible expansion and generalization of the right to vote in the course of the past 220 years, the wide-ranging change of ideas and values concerning private and family life, the stigmatization of discrimination, and the profound changes in the underlying civil and criminal law in Europe in order to establish that an evolutive interpretation of human rights may often be rather self-evident, simply reflecting the course of history and modified philosophies, behaviour patterns, and beliefs.

So it will hardly come as a surprise that neither the Court as an institution nor I personally can really believe in historical interpretation and originalism. Far less than half the present 47 Member States of the ECHR had a say when the Convention was drafted. From a democratic standpoint it is not very satisfactory to

[32] J. Christoffersen, *Fair Balance: Proportionality, Subsidiarity and Primarity in the ECHR* (Leiden: Martinus Nijhoff, 2009), 198–204, 566–77.

[33] See Christoffersen, ibid, 44–68; Harris, O'Boyle, Bates, and Buckley, n 28 above, 5–18; O. Jacot-Guillarmod, 'Règles, méthodes et principes d'interprétation dans la jurisprudence de la Cour européenne des droits de l'homme' in L. E. Pettiti, E. Decaux, and P. H. Imbert (eds), *La Convention européenne des droits de l'homme* (2nd edn, Paris: PUF, 1999), 41–63; G. Letsas, *A Theory of Interpretation of the ECHR* (Oxford: Oxford University Press, 2007); S. C. Prebensen, 'Evolutive Interpretation of the ECHR' in P. Mahoney, F. Matscher, H. Petzold, and L. Wildhaber (eds), *Protecting Human Rights: The European Perspective, Mélanges Rolv Ryssdal* (Cologne: Carl Heymanns Verlag, 2000), 1123–37; Rivière, n 30 above, 323–421; C. Tomuschat, 'Das Europa der Richter' in J. Bröhmer, R. Bieber, C. Calliess, C. Langenfeld, S. Weber, and J. Wolf (eds), *Festschrift Georg Ress* (Cologne: Carl Heymanns Verlag, 2005), 867–8.

[34] In the same sense R. Bernhardt, 'Rechtsfortbildung durch den Europäischen Gerichtshof für Menschenrechte' in S. Breitenmoser, B. Ehrenzeller, M. Sassòli, W. Stoffel, and B. Wagner Pfeifer (eds), *Human Rights, Democracy and the Rule of Law, Liber amicorum Luzius Wildhaber* (Zurich: Dike, 2007), 91–101.

consider all newcomers bound to rules which they did not shape. This is why the 1969 Vienna Convention on the Law of Treaties (which expresses customary law in this respect) considers historical interpretation as only a 'supplementary means of interpretation'.[35] We must therefore never forget that it is a Convention we are expounding.[36]

Undoubtedly the autonomous and evolutive interpretation of ECHR concepts, and the desire to regard the Convention guarantees as something more than illusory and empty rhetoric and make them effective and tangible, aspire to establish more than minimal standards of protection.[37] In terms of the functions of the ECtHR, the ambition would seem to be to reach beyond 'routine adjudication' into the realm of 'borderline fine-tuning'. For some, evolutive interpretation would seem to encourage judicial activism to the detriment of judicial self-restraint.[38] The notion of evolutive interpretation certainly does not offer an easy recipe. It rather leads into the thicket of controversies.

A few illustrations may be helpful. Although Art 6 ECHR, the due-process guarantee of the Convention, does not expressly mention a right of access to a court, the ECtHR recognized such a right in the *Golder* case, saying that the 'fair, public and expeditious characteristics of judicial proceedings are of no value at all if there are no judicial proceedings'.[39] Along the same lines, the ECtHR noted in the *Hornsby v Greece* case that the right of access to a court 'would be illusory if a Contracting State's domestic legal system allowed a final, binding judicial decision to remain inoperative to the detriment of one party'.[40] The obligation to protect the right to life and the prohibition of torture require, in the ECtHR's view, by implication that there should be an effective official investigation when individuals have been killed as a result of the use of force or have disappeared or credibly assert that they have been tortured.[41] The discrimination of homosexuals and transsexuals

[35] Arts 32 and 31(1) and (3).

[36] Borrowed and paraphrased from Chief Justice Marshall in *McCulloch v State of Maryland* 17 US (4 Wheaton) 306 at 405–7, 415 (1819).

[37] See the authors quoted n 33 above; and see *Tyrer v United Kingdom* Series A no 26 (1978), para 31; *Marckx v Belgium* Series A no 31 (1979), para 41; *Selmouni v France* Appl no 25803/94 (1999), ECHR 1999-V, para 101; *Stafford v United Kingdom* Appl no 46295 (2002), ECHR 2002-IV, para 68; *Christine Goodwin v United Kingdom* Appl no 28957/95 (2002), ECHR 2002-VI, para 74; *Mamatkulov and Askarov v Turkey* Appl nos 46827/99, 46951/99 (2005), ECHR 2005-I, paras 101 and 121.

[38] Lord Hoffmann, 'The Universality of Human Rights, 125 *Law Quarterly Review* (2009), 428: 'The proposition that the Convention is a "living instrument" is the banner under which the Strasbourg Court has assumed power to legislate what they consider to be required by European public order'. And see at 431: 'The problem is the Court; and the right of individual petition, which enables it to intervene in the details and nuances of the domestic laws of Member States'. Similar expressions have emerged in France, see B. Edelmann, 'La Cour européenne des droits de l'homme: Une juridiction tyrannique?', *Recueil Dalloz* (2008), 1946; Flauss (text at nn 7–8 above); L. Gannagé, 'A propos de l' "absolutisme" des droits fondamentaux' in *Vers de nouveaux équilibres entre ordres juridiques: Liber amicorum Hélène Gaudemet-Tallon* (Paris: Dalloz, 2008), 265–84; Y. Lequette, 'Des juges littéralement irresponsables' in L. Cadiet, P. Callé, T. le Bars, and P. Mayer (eds), *Mélanges dédiés à la mémoire du doyen Jacques Héron* (Paris: LGDJ, 2008), 309–30.

[39] *Golder v United Kingdom* Series A no 18 (1975), para 35.

[40] *Hornsby v Greece* Appl no 18357/91 (1997), Reports 1997-II, para 40.

[41] *McCann v United Kingdom* Series A no 324 (1975), para 161; *Kaya v Turkey* Appl no 22729/93 (1998), Reports 1998-I, para 105; *Assenov v Bulgaria* Appl no 24760/94 (1998), Reports 1998-VIII,

was treated by the ECtHR as an issue of disproportionate interference with private life under Art 8 ECHR;[42] in the last analysis, I believe, these are issues of each person's freedom to choose himself or herself the aim, the sense, and the direction of his or her life. In the case of *Marckx v Belgium*, the discrimination of illegitimate children was found to constitute violations of Arts 8 and 14 ECHR and of Art 1 of Protocol No 1 and to lack objective and reasonable justification.[43] In the case of *MC v Bulgaria*, the Court considered that 'States have a positive obligation inherent in Arts 3 and 8 of the Convention to enact criminal-law provisions effectively punishing rape and to apply them in practice through effective investigation and prosecution'.[44] And since the Court found a clear and steady trend in Europe towards no longer requiring physical resistance as an element of the offence of rape,[45] Bulgaria's legislation which failed to reflect this trend was found to be in violation of Arts 3 and 8 ECHR. Similarly in the case of *Opuz v Turkey*, the lacking protection of Turkish women from domestic violence led to the finding of violations of Arts 2, 3, and 14 ECHR.[46]

I admit that these are some of my favourite examples of an evolutive interpretation. Other persons prefer other cases. Some would like to see even more of such cases, some less.

The one-way-street theory

In his partly dissenting opinion in the recent case of *Gorou v Greece (No 2)*, Judge Casadevall advocated a theory which he called the 'standstill' or 'cogwheel' technique and which I would propose to call the 'one-way-street theory'. This is how he put it:

> Once the Court 'has decided to extend individuals' rights in a particular aspect of the right to a fair hearing, it should not—unless there has been a manifest mistake—reverse its decision. Acquired rights in the cause of human rights are at least as precious as acquired rights in other branches of the law and therefore the principle of non-regression must prevail.[47]

para 102; *Tanrikulu v Turkey* Appl no 23763/94 (1999), ECHR 1999-IV, para 101; *Nachova v Bulgaria* Appl no 42577/98 (2005), ECHR 2005-VII, paras 110–13; *Isayeva v Russia* Appl no 57950/00 (2005), EuGRZ 2006 32, 37–8, paras 208–13.

[42] *Dudgeon v United Kingdom* Series A no 45 (1981), paras 60–1; *Norris v Ireland* Series A no 142 (1988), para 46; *Modinos v Cyprus* Series A no 259 (1993), para 25; *Christine Goodwin v United Kingdom*, n 37 above; *Karner v Austria* Appl no 40016/98 (2003), ECHR 2003-IX, para 26; *EB v France* Appl no 43546/02 (2008).

[43] *Marckx*, n 37 above, paras 31–4.

[44] *MC v Bulgaria* Appl no 39272/98 (2003), ECHR 2003-XII, para 153.

[45] Ibid, paras 156–66.

[46] *Opuz v Turkey* Appl no 33401/02 (2009).

[47] *Gorou v Greece (No 2)* Appl no 12686/03 (2009), partly dissenting opinion of Judge Casadevall, para 8. Similar ideas can be found in an early contribution by (Judge) W. Ganshoff van der Meersch, 'Le caractère "autonome" des termes et la "marge d'appréciation" des gouvernements dans l'interprétation de la Convention européenne des droits de l'homme' in F. Matscher and H. Petzold (eds), *Protecting Human Rights: The European Dimension—Studies in Honour of Gerard Wiarda* (The Hague: Kluwer Law International, 1988), 201–2. And see P. Mahoney, n 30 above, 62–6.

This theory is in my view flawed in several ways. First of all, since human wisdom has its limits, courts may be wrong and should be allowed to make amends.[48] Secondly, the world of human rights not only takes place in the relationship between State and applicants, but in a comprehensive context with many actors who may have very different interests, all of which deserve consideration: victims and witnesses in criminal proceedings, spouses and children in family quarrels, media and the persons about whom they report, terrorists and the persons they threaten, to mention just a few examples. Thirdly, democratic societies may change their values and laws. Their views, if expressed in democratic decisions, deserve respect, even deference.[49] This is the more so because it is clearly more difficult to amend the substantive guarantees of the ECHR than municipal rights guarantees. Fourthly, the weighing and balancing of all sorts of public and private interests is at the centre of the ECtHR's activities. A truncated, lopsided, and ultimately formalistic version of such balancing would serve neither the cause of the Court nor that of human rights. As the Court has stated as early as in the *Belgian Linguistic* case, the Convention 'implies a just balance between the protection of the general interest of the community and the respect due to fundamental human rights, while attaching particular importance to the latter'.[50] And as Jonas Christoffersen expressed it:

> The Court's use of the fair balance-test in widely different areas of case-law reflects the inherent and unavoidable resolution of conflicting interests flowing from the complex nature of the cases put before the Court as well as the flexibility of the norms of the ECHR.[51]

Fifthly, and finally, in the *Gorou (No 2)* case the judges of the Grand Chamber did not agree about the extent to which the Chamber had established a clear practice. As a matter of the Court's internal decision-making, it is not judicious to impose one Section's tentative practice on all other Sections in the name of an alleged 'human rights *acquis*'.

IV. Defective Legislation or Practice

Judgments on the facts of individual cases

As a rule the ECtHR refrains from attacking domestic statutes as such, both out of respect for democratic decision-making and because the ECHR does not give it that power, at least not expressly. A sort of a corollary of the right of individual petition

[48] A. Guiterman, *Poet's Proverbs* (1924), 38 quoted by E. H. Wilson, 'Stare Decisis, Quo Vadis? The Orphaned Doctrine in the Supreme Court', 33 *Georgetown Law Journal* (1945), 251 at 254: 'You're sure that you are Right? How fine and strong! But were you never just as sure—and Wrong?'

[49] Cf L. Wildhaber, 'Glossen zum Verhältnis von Demokratie und Europäischer Menschenrechtskonvention' in A. Fischer-Lescano, H. P. Gasser, T. Marauhn, and N. Ronzitti (eds), *Frieden in Freiheit: Festschrift Michael Bothe zum 70. Geburtstag* (Baden-Baden: Nomos, 2008), 1243–51.

[50] *Belgian Linguistic* case, Series A no 6 (1968), 32, para 5. See also *Klass v Germany* Series A no 28 (1978), para 59; *Sporrong and Lönnroth v Sweden* Series A no 52 (1982), para 69.

[51] Christoffersen, n 32 above, 203.

is therefore the Court's constant jurisprudence that it decides individual cases on the facts of each case. However, this has never been as clear as it appeared to be. In the 1978 judgment in the interstate case of *Ireland v United Kingdom*, the Court stated that its 'judgments in fact serve not only to decide those cases brought before the Court but, more generally, to elucidate, safeguard and develop the rules instituted by the Convention, thereby contributing to the observance by the States of the engagements undertaken by them as Contracting Parties'.[52] In varying shades and formulations, this idea was taken up later on and manifested itself also when the possibilities of issuing so-called 'judgments of principle' or of an '*erga omnes* effect' of the Court's judgments or of new ways of handling mass claims were discussed. In the *Karner v Austria* case of 2003, the Court affirmed that while

> the primary purpose of the Convention system is to provide individual relief, its mission is also to determine issues on public-policy grounds in the common interest, thereby raising the general standards of protection of human rights and extending human rights jurisprudence throughout the community of Convention States.[53]

Can the Court state general rules irrespective of the facts of each case?

Three recent cases of the Court's Grand Chamber demonstrate striking disagreements among the judges as to what the role of the Court should be.

In the well-known *Hirst* case,[54] the ECtHR was confronted with a domestic legislation which provided for a general and automatic disenfranchisement of convicted prisoners from voting in parliamentary and local elections. Hirst was serving a sentence of discretionary life imprisonment for manslaughter. He complained of a disproportionate interference with his right to vote under Art 3 of Protocol No 1. The Court found a violation, although it reaffirmed that under its case law States enjoyed a wide margin of appreciation.[55] It did not give the UK government detailed guidance, beyond commenting that individuals who had 'seriously abused a public position or whose conduct threatened to undermine the rule of law or democratic foundations' could be deprived of their electoral rights.[56]

Judges Tulkens and Zagrebelsky wrote in their concurring opinion that the 'fact that by law a convicted person's imprisonment is the ground for his or her disenfranchisement [was] . . . conclusive'.[57] Apparently in their view any statute providing for a general disenfranchisement of prisoners is incompatible with the ECHR; restrictions of the right to vote must respect the 'principle of universal suffrage'.[58]

52 *Ireland v United Kingdom*, n 12 above, para 154.
53 *Karner v Austria*, n 42 above, para 26.
54 *Hirst v United Kingdom (No 2)* Appl no 74025/01 (2005), ECHR 2005-IX.
55 Ibid, paras 60–2 and 82.
56 Ibid, para 71.
57 Ibid, p 226.
58 Ibid, para 62 (in the wording of the Court's majority).

This sort of creative law-making led to the protest in the joint dissenting opinion of Judges Wildhaber, Costa, Lorenzen, Kovler, and Jebens 'that the Court is not a legislator and should be careful not to assume legislative functions'.[59] They further added that in the instant case it was hard to see how the UK legislation was incompatible with the ECHR: 'Since restrictions on the right to vote continue to be compatible, it would seem obvious that the deprivation of the right to vote for the most serious offences such as murder or manslaughter, is not excluded in the future'.[60]

In the case of *DH v Czech Republic*[61] the Court found a violation of Art 14 ECHR in conjunction with the right of education under Art 2 of Protocol No 1, on account of the disproportionately high number of Roma children in Czech special schools. The majority of the Grand Chamber summarized its approach as follows:

> since it has been established that the relevant legislation as applied in practice at the material time had a disproportionately prejudicial effect on the Roma community, the Court considers that the applicants as members of that community necessarily suffered the same discriminatory treatment. Accordingly, it does not need to examine their individual cases.[62]

As was pointed out by one of the dissenters, the question of consent by the parents and other factors would have necessitated a more thorough inquiry into the facts of each individual case.[63]

In the case of *EB v France*,[64] the French authorities and courts refused the request of a lesbian to adopt a child on two grounds: the lack of a paternal referent and the ambivalence of the applicant's partner's commitment to her adoption plans. The majority of the Grand Chamber considered that the reference to the lack of a paternal referent was tantamount to a reference to the applicant's homosexuality, which was 'if not explicit, at least implicit'.[65] They concluded that 'the illegitimacy of one of the grounds [had] the effect of contaminating the entire decision'.[66] Most of the dissenting judges accepted that refusals to adopt a child 'could not be based on homosexuality without violating Art. 14 and 8',[67] and would have been willing to state that much, in the abstract. Yet in their view, the contamination theory was wrong in the instant case because it was not the applicant's homosexuality, but rather the grounds indicated by the French courts (and specifically the ambivalence of the applicant's partner), that had prevented her from obtaining the authorization.

One could perhaps sum up by saying that the majority in all three cases wanted to formulate a general principle and took the liberty of considering the facts of the individual cases as of secondary importance. Put differently, it is not always so that

[59] Ibid, para 6 at 230. [60] Ibid, para 8 at 231.
[61] *DH v Czech Republic* Appl no 57325/00 (2007).
[62] Ibid, para 209.
[63] Ibid, dissenting opinion of Judge Borrego Borrego.
[64] *EB v France*, n 42 above.
[65] Ibid, para 89.
[66] Ibid, para 80.
[67] Ibid, dissenting opinion of Judge Costa, joined by Judges Türmen, Ugrekhelidze, and Jočienė.

the Court decides individual cases exclusively on the facts of each case. Especially in recent years, it would seem that a majority insists on formulating general jurisprudential rules underlying the judgments, some rather abstract, some more narrow. While I think that this is quite understandable, in my view the facts of individual cases should always square with the jurisprudential rules, because, if they do not, either the jurisprudential rules should have been drafted differently, or the individual case should have been decided differently.

The Committee of Ministers as supervisory organ in charge of executing the Court's judgments has repeatedly tried to induce the States concerned to change their legislation and practices.[68] The ECtHR has imposed on States a duty to take remedial measures, which went beyond granting reparation for past prejudice.[69] In pilot judgments, it has furthermore indicated legislative measures in order to overcome structural problems. However, as the following discussion will show, the Court still does not declare national laws per se null and void. It finds violations in respect of certain applicants and, by following its (new) case law, hopes to achieve legislative changes over time.

The question of general rules in the *Marckx* and the *Vermeire* cases

Cases insisting on the principle of non-discrimination in a general way (for example the cases concerning illegitimate children such as *Marckx*, *Vermeire*, or *Mazurek*,[70] or transsexuals such as *Christine Goodwin*,[71] or homosexuals such as *Dudgeon*, *Norris*, *Modinos*, *Smith and Grady*, or *Karner*)[72] are usually meant to be extended to all Member States. In the famous *Marckx* case of 1979, the Belgian government defended its legislation containing discriminatory provisions against children born out of wedlock, claiming that it was 'not the Court's function to rule *in abstracto* on the compatibility with the Convention of certain legal rules'.[73] The Court flatly

[68] R. Bernhardt, 'Judgments of International Human Rights Courts and Their Effects in the Internal Legal Order of States' in *Studi di diritto internazionale in onore di Gaetano Arangio-Ruiz* (Naples: Editoriale Scientifica, 2004), 435; Garlicki, n 31 above, 319–24; P. Mahoney, 'Judgments of International and Supranational Courts: Effect, Non-Compliance and Enforcement. The ECtHR as a Case Study', Manuscript of a conference at the University of St Gallen, 2–3 October 2008, 6–11.

[69] *Papamichalopoulos v Greece* (Just Satisfaction), Series A no 330-B (1995), para 34; *Scozzari and Giunta v Italy* Appl no 39221/98 (2000), ECHR 2000-VIII, para 249; *Maestri v Italy* Appl no 39748/98 (2004), ECHR 2004-I, para 47; *Assanidze v Georgia* Appl no 71503/01 (2004), ECHR 2004-II, paras 198, 202–3; *Ilaşcu v Moldova and Russia* Appl no 48787/99 (2004), ECHR 2004-VII, paras 487 and 490; *Öcalan v Turkey* Appl no 46221/99 (2005), ECHR 2005-IV, para 210. And see L. Caflisch, 'La mise en œuvre des arrêts de la Cour: nouvelles tendances' in F. Salerno (ed), *La nouvelle procédure devant la Cour européenne des droits de l'homme après le Protocole no 14* (actes du Colloque de Ferrara) (Brussels: Bruylant, 2007), 157–74; L. Wildhaber, 'The Execution of Judgments of the ECtHR: Recent Developments' in P.-M. Dupuy, B. Fassbender, M. N. Shaw, and K. P. Sommermann (eds), *Essays in Honour of Christian Tomuschat* (Kehl: N. P. Engel, 2006), 671–80.

[70] *Marckx v Belgium*, n 37 above; *Vermeire v Belgium* Series A no 214-C (1991); *Mazurek v France* Appl no 34406/97 (2000), ECHR 2000-II.

[71] *Christine Goodwin v United Kingdom*, n 37 above.

[72] *Dudgeon v United Kingdom*, n 42 above; *Norris v Ireland*, n 42 above; *Modinos v Cyprus* Series A no 259 (1993); *Smith and Grady v United Kingdom* Appl no 33985/96 (1999), ECHR 1999-VI; *Karner v Austria*, n 42 above.

[73] *Marckx*, n 37 above, para 26.

rejected this argument, however, stating that 'Article 25 of the Convention entitles individuals to contend that a law violates their rights by itself, in the absence of an individual measure of implementation, if they run the risk of being directly affected by it'.[74]

It is of course correct to explain these passages of the *Marckx* judgment as extensions of the victim status, allowing certain victims of violations of Convention guarantees—in rather exceptional situations—to attack national legislation directly.[75] But one could also broaden the scope of inquiry (as Wojciech Sadurski and Lech Garlicki have done recently)[76] and ask how one should analyse the powers of the ECtHR where a widespread practice or a law or statute fails to match the Convention standards. As I have explained, traditionally the Court's role was restricted to the consideration of fact-specific, concrete acts and decisions rather than to the law underlying the concrete acts. As a consequence, the Court's finding of a Convention violation was expressed in the operative part of the judgment as a finding that the impugned concrete act was incompatible with Convention standards, 'with respect to the applicants', as the Court put it in the *Marckx* judgment of 1979.[77] Certainly, the reasoning of the *Marckx* judgment made it clear that the challenged acts or decisions were taken on the basis of a law, and the Court's scrutiny inevitably involved a critical analysis of the flawed law itself.[78] The finding of Convention violations in the *Marckx* judgment in reality resulted from the discriminatory content of the Belgian legislation and not from an allegedly incorrect application of that legislation by municipal courts or administrative agencies. In effect, the Court left the problem of the execution of its judgments largely to the Committee of Ministers,[79] which had to decide whether a judgment of the Court called for a change of legislation. Sadurski calls this approach inadequate and hypocritical.[80] This would seem a somewhat harsh criticism. Since the ECtHR normally follows its own precedents, it will become clear over time anyway that in each case of reliance on flawed legislation the Court will find a Convention violation.[81]

74 Ibid, para 27.

75 Cf L. Wildhaber,'Internationaler Kommentar zur Europäischen Menschenrechtskonvention, Art 8' in H. Golsong, W. Karl, H. Miehsler, E. Riedel, K. Rogge, T. Vogler, L. Wildhaber, and S. Breitenmoser (eds), *Internationaler Kommentar zur Europäischen Menschenrechtskonvention* (Cologne: Carl Heymanns Verlag, 1992), 28–9, nos 47–50.

76 W. Sadurski, 'Partnering with Strasbourg: Constitutionalisation of the ECtHR, the Accession of Central and East European States to the Council of Europe, and the Idea of Pilot Judgments', 9 *Human Rights Law Review* (2009), 397–453; L. Garlicki, 'Broniowski and After: On the Dual Nature of "Pilot Judgments"' in L. Caflisch, J. Callewaert, R. Liddell, P. Mahoney, and M. Villiger (eds), *Human Rights—Strasbourg Views: Liber Amicorum Luzius Wildhaber* (Kehl: N. P. Engel, 2007), 182–3.

77 *Marckx*, n 37 above, paras 29–30.

78 Characteristically, the sharp criticism of the *Marckx* judgment by François Rigaux carries the title 'La loi condamnée', 94 *Journal des Tribunaux* (1979), 513–24. Rigaux did not doubt that the ECtHR had undermined the Belgian legislation as such.

79 Under Art 46 (2) ECHR.

80 Sadurski, n 76 above, 413–14.

81 See generally R. Post (ed), 'Global Constitutionalism' (Yale Law School Seminar, 2009), V-1-85; with respect to the ECtHR: K. Lucas-Alberni, *Le revirement de jurisprudence de la Cour européenne des droits de l'homme* (Brussels: Bruylant, 2008); A. Mowbray, 'An Examination of the ECtHR's Approach

And this is precisely what happened. In the *Vermeire* case of 1991,[82] the Court followed the *Marckx* judgment of 1979. It had taken Belgium until 1987, that is to say eight years, to modify its legislation to take into account the *Marckx* judgment. The Court in *Vermeire* did not accept this delay and commented ungraciously that there had been 'nothing imprecise or incomplete about the rule which prohibited discrimination' against illegitimate children.[83] And it added:

> The freedom of choice allowed to a State as to the means of fulfilling its obligation under Article 53 cannot allow it to suspend the application of the Convention while waiting for such a reform to be completed, to the extent of compelling the Court to reject in 1991, with respect to a succession which took effect [in] 1980, complaints identical to those which it upheld [in] 1979.[84]

This sequence from the *Marckx* to the *Vermeire* judgments anticipates to a certain extent the modern pilot judgment procedure, introduced in the *Broniowski* and *Hutten-Czapska* cases of 2004 and 2005.[85] Already in the early Belgian cases, not much was left of fact-specificity, except for the operative part of the judgments. Apart from that, the Court's insistence on a modification of the Belgian legislation became quite clear.

Pilot judgment procedures

The boldest attempt to tackle the problem of defective national legislation or practice has undoubtedly been the development of the so-called pilot judgment procedure.[86] The Committee of Ministers of the Council of Europe invited the Court in 2004

> to identify, in its judgments finding a violation of the Convention, what it considers to be an underlying system problem and the source of this problem, in particular when it is likely to give rise to numerous applications, so as to assist States in finding the appropriate solution and the Committee of Ministers in supervising the execution of judgments.[87]

to Overruling its Previous Case Law', 9 *Human Rights Law Review* (2009), 179–201; G. Ress, 'Aspekte der Stabilität der Rechtsprechung des Europäischen Gerichtshofs für Menschenrechte' in A. Epiney, M. Haag, and A. Heinemann (eds), *Die Herausforderung von Grenzen, Festschrift Roland Bieber* (2006); L. Wildhaber, 'Precedent in the ECtHR' in P. Mahoney, F. Matscher, H. Petzold, and L. Wildhaber (eds), Protecting Human Rights: The European Perspective, Studies in Memory of Rolv Ryssdal (Cologne: Carl Heymanns Verlag, 2000), 1529–45, reproduced in L. Wildhaber, 'Changing Ideas about the Tasks of the ECtHR' in L. Wildhaber, n 9 above, 154–73.

[82] *Vermeire v Belgium*, n 70 above.

[83] Ibid, para 25.

[84] Ibid, para 26.

[85] See W. Sadurski, 'Partnering with Strasbourg: Constitutionalisation of the ECtHR, the Accession of Central and East European States to the Council of Europe, and the Idea of Pilot Judgments', 9 *Human Rights Law Review* (2009), 412–26.

[86] See L. Garlicki, 'Some Observations on Relations between the ECtHR and the Domestic Jurisdictions' in J. Iliopoulos-Strangas (ed), n 31 above; V. Zagrebelsky, 'Questions autour de Broniowski' in *Human Rights*, n 76 above, 521–35; L. Wildhaber, 'Pilot Judgments in Cases of Structural or Systemic Problems on the National Level' in R. Wolfrum and U. Deutsch (eds), *The ECtHR Overwhelmed by Applications: Problems and Possible Solutions* (Berlin: Springer, 2009), 69–75 and the discussion at 77–92.

[87] Res (2004) 3.

Ever since, the Court has been feeling its way as regards recourse to the pilot judgment procedure. There appear to be several variants, and this may recognize the flexibility needed to accommodate the range of different situations with which the Court is confronted. In what we might call the classical or the enriched version of pilot judgments of the *Broniowski* and the *Hutten-Czapska* type,[88] the Court will specify the type of general measures required to bring the domestic law within the Convention, will include its recommendation as to general measures in the operative part of the judgment, and will adjourn consideration of all similar applications. The *Broniowski* and the *Hutten-Czapska* judgments were based on judgments of the Polish Constitutional Court and amounted to a sort of a dialogue with the national judiciary. They served less to reduce the number of pending applications, but rather helped to deflect future potential applications from the Court.

It remains to be seen whether pilot judgments can be similarly successful if they go against the national judiciary and encounter a recalcitrant government. The pending case of *Burdov v Russia (No 2)* will constitute an important landmark in that respect.[89] This is a case of a rescue worker who had been exposed, in the nuclear reactor incident at Chernobyl in 1986, to massive radioactivity. Several Russian court judgments concerning his pension and insurance benefits were left unexecuted; one for three years, one for two years and only half of the sum allotted to him in the third judgment was paid promptly. The Court found violations of the guarantee of fair procedure (Art 6), of an effective national remedy (Art 13), and of the right to property (Art 1, Protocol No 1).

But given the fact that it had found in more than 200 cases that final Russian court judgments had been left unexecuted for too long, it decided to launch a pilot judgment procedure. It did not indicate specific general measures which Russia should take, apart from the fact that an effective national remedy should be introduced within six months. In addition, it suspended the handling of all new applications until one year after the final judgment in the *Burdov* procedure. With respect to cases already pending, Russia was told that it must pay adequate compensation to all applicants within one year after the final judgment in the *Burdov* procedure. It should be clear that the introduction of a new national remedy is based on the understanding that the new remedy must be effective and non-arbitrary in practice. Since the ECtHR has encountered at least as much defective practice as defective legislation in Russian cases, neither the *Burdov (No 2)* judgment nor the new Russian remedy may constitute the last word on the problem.

[88] *Broniowski v Poland* Appl no 31443/96 (2004), ECHR 2004-V (GC); (2005) ECHR 2005-IX (friendly settlement); *Hutten-Czapska v Poland* Appl no 35014/97 (2006) (GC), (2008) (friendly settlement).

[89] *Burdov v Russia (No 2)* Appl no 33509/04 (2009).

V. Overload and Reform of the ECtHR

Some essential figures

Whereas in the 1960s, the ECtHR proclaimed one or two cases per year, since the entry into force of Protocol No 11 on 1 November 1998, the Court has handed down some 188,000 inadmissibility decisions and some 10,000 judgments on the merits.[90] In 1999 8,400 new applications were submitted, in 2008 some 50,000.[91] More than 100,000 cases are pending before the Court.[92]

Incrementalism and tinkering

The Court has responded to this avalanche of applications by constantly simplifying, accelerating, re-evaluating, and modernizing its procedures. It has vastly improved its case management and statistics, extended its research facilities, has more and more decided on admissibility and merits together, created a Fifth Section, admitted unilateral declarations on ECHR violations, introduced pilot judgment procedures, simplified the drafting of judgments, and endeavoured to clarify the order in which cases are handled. It has almost continuously tried to improve a very difficult workload situation.[93]

One feels tempted to call the past decade a period of 'tinkering' and of 'muddling through'. Owing to the Court's will to renovate and reappraise ceaselessly, the overall picture is less gloomy than it would otherwise be. Nevertheless, and despite the Court's efforts, in all these years the number of new applications reaching the Court has mercilessly surpassed the number of decisions rendered by the Court.[94]

The tinkering system (or lack of a system) is minimalist and consensual in the sense that it has helped the Court to stay together. It has expressed the political reality that the lobby of those resisting change (which often consisted of groups otherwise supporting the ECHR) has been more effective than those advocating reform. But, over time, delays and tinkering are bound to undermine the credibility of the ECtHR. Paul Mahoney, the former Registrar of the Court, has termed the caseload 'unmanageable';[95] Steven Greer and Andrew Williams have called the systematic delivery of individual justice a 'doomed quest';[96] Jonas Christoffersen

[90] 'Mémorandum du Président de la Cour européenne des droits de l'homme aux Etats en vue de la Conférence d'Interlaken du 3 juillet 2009', section I, available at: <http://www.echr.coe.int/NR/rdonlyres/D61B67EF-07E6-49E5-BD26-ED8588E01C10/2791/03072009_Memo_Interlaken_fran%C3%A7ais.pdf>.

[91] Ibid, II, para 1.

[92] Ibid.

[93] Ibid, II, para 2.

[94] Wildhaber, n 9 above, 138–45.

[95] P. Mahoney, 'Thinking a Small Unthinkable: Repatriating Reparation from the ECtHR to the National Legal Order' in *Human Rights*, n 76 above, p 266.

[96] S. Greer and A. Williams, 'Human Rights in the Council of Europe and the EU: Towards "Individual," "Constitutional" or "Institutional" Justice?' 15 *European Law Journal* (2009), 469–70.

speaks of the 'Court's increasingly restricted capacity';[97] and I have said that 'the inexorable accumulation of... both inadmissible and substantial cases will increasingly asphyxiate the system so as to deprive the great majority of... cases... of any practical effect'.[98]

The ECtHR's responsibilities

Much has been said, written, and done about the reform of the ECHR system, which I need not repeat here. If all constructive proposals were lumped together, if some of the ideas contained in the Management Report of Lord Woolf of Barnes were added, if class actions were handled collectively, and if repetitive matters were sent directly to the Committee of Ministers and/or the States (as President Costa suggests in his Memorandum of 3 July 2009[99]), matters would definitely look more hopeful. However, the problem of the Court's overload would only move closer to a permanent solution, if (and that is a big 'if') the judges of the ECtHR could be persuaded that it is their responsibility not only to render the Convention guarantees effective and real, but also and just as much to make the ECHR system effective and real, too. The priorities and the management of the ECHR system should be reappraised and insofar as necessary re-ordered; the inevitable conclusion that the ECtHR cannot cope with its workload should lead to a more restrictive practice with respect to both admissibility and merits; and a new modesty should allow the recognition that the ECHR can continue to make effective and real, rather than illusory, progress, but only provided it functions properly.

For the benefit of those who might believe that these arguments shift all the blame to the Court, I wish to add that this is not how I would look at matters. To the contrary, most political actors—in the understandable, though heady, optimism of the period after the fall of the Iron Curtain—have underestimated the difficulties and overestimated the real possibilities of the ECtHR to change national judicial and political systems. And they have failed to evaluate the changed situation comprehensively and to draw consequences from it.

A realistic Court system at last

Since incrementalism and tinkering could not resolve the ECtHR's workload problem in the long run, the access of individuals to the Court is today in fact restricted. Once this is recognized, it would be worthwhile to look beyond, even if this requires an amendment of the ECHR. Without discussing alternatives or indulging in wishful thinking, I would propose a threefold approach which should at least be pondered seriously:

97 Christoffersen, n 32 above, 577.
98 Wildhaber, n 9 above, 50 (speech at the Opening of the Judicial Year, 22.1.2004).
99 'Mémorandum', n 90 above, IIIB.2, para 3.

1. On the level of sifting out cases, we should probably give up thinking in terms of 'admissible' applications. Instead we should distinguish between cases which the Court should handle and those which it cannot handle. Time and again judges will encounter national judgments which they would have decided differently. The issue is not, however, what are the judges' predilections, but what will promote the reality of human rights in the whole of Europe. Applications which are manifestly ill-founded, incompatible with the Convention, trivial, or in which applicants suffered no significant disadvantage should not be handled.

2. Certain categories of cases should automatically be decided on the merits, provided they are admissible.[100] These could include:

(a) right to life, prohibition of torture, prohibition of slavery;
(b) long periods of illegal detention;
(c) wholly arbitrary and unfair procedures;
(d) overruling of well-established ECtHR precedents;
(e) issues gravely affecting national constitutions;
(f) issues vital to the survival of a democracy and a democracy's right to defend itself against its enemies;
(g) guidelines for structural and systemic problems;[101]
(h) pilot judgments;
(i) interstate applications.

3. The ECtHR is overloaded with both admissible and inadmissible applications. Lamentably, at present 29 per cent of the cases which will be decided in Chambers constitute backlog, that is to say, they have been pending for more than three years,[102] a duration which the ECtHR would consider as a Convention violation if it occurred in national courts. We should therefore abandon the idea of an unrestricted individual petition in favour of a system with manageable priorities, in which the Court would decide itself, within the framework of a leave-to-appeal system, which cases it should handle. Since the Court can hardly adjudicate more than 2,000 applications per year, and since there is a sizeable number of cases which the Court must handle automatically, a good solution would be to let the Court select a number of some 1,000 cases per year which would be adjudicated, whereas the other cases would not be handled.

These proposals look radical. However, the end result would be surprisingly similar to the system presently in force. In 2008, the ECtHR handed down 1,543 judgments, that is, approximately the same number it would decide under the system which I have sketched.[103] Instead of disposing of thousands of cases administratively, losing

[100] In this category, cases would be decided in the traditional way, first being examined with respect to admissibility, then being decided on the merits.

[101] Structural problems should first be scrutinized in this category of cases. They should in other words be handled automatically. The follow-up cases should be assigned to the domestic level, but some cases should be re-appraised periodically by the ECtHR in the leave-to-appeal procedure.

[102] ECtHR, 'Analysis of Statistics 2008' (2009), 11.

[103] ECtHR, *Some Facts and Figures 1959–2009* (2009), 5.

thousands of applicants who realize that years will pass by before their turn has come, declaring cases manifestly ill-founded which may not be manifestly ill-founded, the new system would bring more predictability, transparency, and honesty, would concentrate on real priorities, and would therefore serve the overall effectiveness of human rights better. I realize that these proposals will be harshly criticized. I myself see some factors which are left without answers. If I nevertheless formulated these proposals, it is because I feel that the cause of human rights would be much better served if the period of tinkering came to an end and clear and more honest priorities became visible again.

Paul Mahoney and Jonathan Sharpe have taken up the ideas of Judge Carlo Russo and Frédéric Sudre and have submitted a proposal to create a new Supreme European Court of Human Rights.[104] This Court would be permanent, be composed of 15 judges and would more or less take the place of the Grand Chamber of the present Court. Instead of creating a purely filtering body below the present ECtHR, the two authors would create a Supreme Court above the present Court, endeavouring to concentrate and focus the case law and improve its quality. Such a two-tier system is obviously reminiscent of the pre-Protocol No 11 system with Commission and Court. Since, however, not all Member States would be represented in the Supreme Court, it is easy to foresee opposition to this proposal. Nonetheless my ideas about Court reform would also necessitate an amendment to the ECHR, and the proposal for a Supreme European Court of Human Rights might well be considered in such a context.

VI. Individual, Constitutional, and Administrative Justice

Recent years have witnessed a discussion about the so-called 'constitutional justice' of the ECtHR. Such a discussion may be an attempt to save the Court from its chronic overload, but also an attempt to redefine the role and the priorities of the Court. I shall submit various interpretations of what could be meant by 'constitutional justice'.

Although the intention of the founders of the Convention to avert totalitarianism and to preserve democracy is still a very legitimate aim of the ECHR, this is hardly how the system looks 60 years later. While there have been many important cases, only a few have been so exceptional as to influence, per se, the fate of a European democracy. The *Greek military junta* case may qualify,[105] perhaps also the cases which recognized the existence of a democracy's right to defend itself against its enemies, such as *Rekvényi*, *Refah Partisi*, or *Ždanoka*.[106] The founders of

[104] P. Mahoney and J. Sharpe, 'The Legacy of Carlo Russo: Creation of a Supreme European Court of Human Rights' in M. Romeris (ed), *Liber amicorum Pranas Kūris* (Vilnius: University Vilnius Press, 2008), 281–94.

[105] G. Nolte and S. Oeter in R. Bernhardt (ed), *Encyclopaedia of Public International Law* (2nd edn, Amsterdam: North Holland, 1995), 146–8.

[106] *Rekvényi v Hungary* Appl no 25390/94 (1999), ECHR 1999-III; *Refah Partisi* Appl nos 41340/98, 41342/98, ECHR 2003-II; *Ždanoka v Latvia*, n 3 above.

the Convention had intended to contribute to the prevention of war in Western and perhaps even in the whole of Europe. The 50 years of the ECtHR's existence have, however, witnessed much more normalcy than exeptionalism. To a large extent, the ECtHR has decided the same kind of issues as a domestic Supreme or Constitutional Court, according to similar principles, exploring whether the aims invoked to restrict human rights are legitimate, whether the restrictions are grounded in a sufficient legal basis, and whether they are proportionate and necessary in a democratic society.[107] Because of that similarity the ECtHR has been qualified as a quasi-Constitutional Court *sui generis*.[108] Despite the similarity, the ECtHR remains of course an international tribunal. This is why it operates in the fragmented and less-developed context of the international legal order,[109] with doctrines such as subsidiarity and margin of appreciation, and why its judgments are only declaratory and are not directly executory in municipal law, unlike those of the European Court of Justice.

I realize that those who take up the discussion among international law scholars about the so-called constitutionalization of international law might be warned (as Anne Peters puts it graphically) that the 'danger of blowing up an academic paper tiger is very real'.[110] Without wishing to speculate about the pleasures of 'a ride on a tiger', in my view democracy and human rights should be counted among the formative principles of contemporary international law. Also in that (second) sense the ECtHR could be classified as a 'quasi-Constitutional Court', and the ECHR is an important part of the constitution of Europe.

There are authors like Steven Greer who have still another (third) approach.[111] They speak of the constitutionalization of the ECtHR, meaning that only the most essential and grave issues should be submitted to it. This could be understood as a device to respond to the insoluble workload problem, which in turn leads to an insidious undermining of the credibility of the Court. It could also be understood as an attempt to distinguish between more or less absolute Convention guarantees, irrespective of workload issues, in an attempt to prevent the Court from encroaching on too many aspects of local concern only.

To complicate matters even more, complaints alleging administrative and governmental partiality and arbitrariness have led to a steady increase of right to

[107] Alec Stone Sweet and Jud Matthews speak in that context of 'Proportionality Balancing and Global Constitutionalism', 47 *Columbia Journal of Transnational Law* (2008), 27.

[108] Wildhaber, n 9 above, 113. And see S. Greer, n 19 above, 7: the ECtHR 'is already "the Constitutional Court for Europe," in the sense that it is the final authoritative judicial tribunal in the only pan-European constitutional system there is'.

[109] See for a general discussion, P. Mahoney, 'The International Judiciary—Independence and Accountability', 7 *Law and Practice of International Courts and Tribunals* (2008), 313–49; for a discussion which is more focused on the ECtHR, P. Mahoney, 'Separation of Powers in the Council of Europe: The Status of the ECtHR vis-à-vis the Authorities of the Council of Europe', 24 *Human Rights Law Journal* (2003), 152–61; Wildhaber, n 9 above, 113–35, 196–211, and passim. And see Judge Ziemele's dissenting opinion in *Andrejeva v Latvia*, 18.2.2009, no 55707/00.

[110] J. Klabbers, A. Peters, and G. Ulfstein, *The Constitutionalization of International Law* (Oxford: Oxford University Press, 2009), 343 (quoted from Anne Peters' Conclusions).

[111] S. Greer, 'Constitutionalizing Adjudication under the ECHR', 23 *Oxford Journal of Legal Studies* (2003), 405–33.

property cases before the ECtHR. At present 17 per cent of all applications are right to property cases.[112] If the Court were able to cope with its workload of more than 50,000 applications per year, then it would contribute not only to the protection of property, but also to the reduction of arbitrariness. Looking at recent complaints about inadequate compensation for expropriations, or about hidden or de facto expropriations, or about excessively high fines or fees, one should probably ask whether the ECtHR is in the process of becoming not only a quasi-Constitutional Court of Europe, but even (in a fourth sense) a 'quasi-Supreme Administrative Court of Europe', in charge of standing up against arbitrariness and excesses of State authorities.[113] In essence, there seems to be a development to treat the notion of arbitrariness as identical with the violation of human rights guarantees under the ECHR.[114] The described trend would confirm the idea advocated by some human rights lawyers that international human rights law is all-inclusive and therefore leaves no human rights free zones.[115] Indeed it would constitute an enormous success if the ECtHR could tame the arbitrariness of some State administrations and tribunals. There remains the anxious question of what would happen if the workload of the Court further exploded, and since such an explosion seems plausible enough that must of course be a very anxious question indeed, because a further explosion would further undermine the credibility of the Court.[116] In an imperfect world, the Court is flatly incapable of resolving all problems. As I have written elsewhere, 'If it suffices to say—as does the *Mamidakis v. Greece* judgment—that a fine constitutes "an element of property,"[117] then any amount of applications complaining about fines, fees, taxes or the like might reach the Court'.[118]

Elaborating on this last consideration about arbitrariness, a word of warning is needed. The notion of constitutional justice according to my firm conviction does not have a fifth sense and does not mean that all Member States have agreed to unleash a subsidiary international court from its fetters and to let it operate without any subsidiarity, without any margin of appreciation, and at the same time without any accountability.

VII. Conclusion

The ECHR has been qualified as 'the most effective human rights regime in the world'.[119] Of course, this cannot mean that it has not encountered major

[112] ECtHR, *Some Facts and Figures* (January 2008).

[113] Cf L. Wildhaber and I. Wildhaber, 'Recent Case Law on the Protection of Property in the ECHR' in C. Binder, U. Kriebaum, A. Reinisch, and S. Wittich (eds), *International Investment Law for the 21st Century: Essays in Honour of Christoph Schreuer* (Oxford: Oxford University Press, 2009), 674–6.

[114] The question arises whether the production of arbitrary judgments by a national system amounts to a structural problem.

[115] J. Viljanen, The ECtHR as a Developer of the General Doctrines of Human Rights Law (Tampere: Tampere University Press, 2003), 25.

[116] See Section V above.

[117] *Mamidakis v Greece* Appl no 35533/04 (2007).

[118] See n 113 above, 676.

[119] H. Keller, and A. Stone Sweet, n 31 above, 3.

challenges. The overload is the most obvious one. But to find a proper long-term perspective and balance, to identify lasting and new problems, without neglecting the necessary willingness of the national instances and particularly tribunals, remains an ongoing challenge. The ECHR system and especially the right of individual application has many merits. But it should not be understood as untouchable. Otherwise—alluding to the expression that the Court is a victim of its own success—the Court might indeed one day become a victim. And that would surely not help the right of individual petition, which would become a victim, too.

[13]

The European Court of Human Rights: The Past, the Present, the Future*

Luzius Wildhaber**

INTRODUCTION

Today, I wish to introduce you to the European Court of Human Rights. I shall first offer some remarks about the history of the Court, the changing perceptions, the underlying theories, and the way the Court has shaped European reality. Then I shall discuss a few recent cases as specific illustrations of the Court's work. Towards the end, I shall add a few remarks about the difficult relationship between terrorism and human rights.

I. PAST

We began the 20th century with an international law that viewed only sovereign States as actors, unbridled and uncontrolled, entitled to go to war, and also entitled to treat citizens and foreigners alike as

---

* This piece is based on remarks given by President Wildhaber at the American University Washington College of Law on April 21, 2006.

** Mr. Luzius Wildhaber, President of the European Court of Human Rights 1997–2007, Doctor of Law, Basel, 1961; LL.M. Yale, 1965; J.S.D., Yale, 1968; Dres.h.c., LL.D.h.c.

objects, whose legal status and whose human rights were defined solely by national law. We end the 20th and begin the 21st century with individuals who have become subjects of international law and a European Court of Human Rights which is the most spectacular illustration of this change in paradigms.[1] In the same vein, modern sovereignty should be understood as requiring respect for, rather than the breach of human rights, minority rights, democracy, and the rule of law.

One of the founding fathers of the European Convention on Human Rights, the Frenchman Pierre-Henri Teitgen, explained this in 1949 in moving words. He spoke about the time when he was in the Gestapo prisons while one of his brothers was at Dachau and one of his brothers-in-law was dying at Mauthausen.[2] He said: "I think we can now . . . confront 'reasons of State' with the only sovereignty worth dying for, worthy in all circumstances of being defended, respected and safeguarded—the sovereignty of justice and of law."[3]

Let us look even farther back into history. Already in ancient and medieval times, European political theories endeavoured to moderate the power of the rulers and to realise justice. Bracton demanded in 1250 the rule of law and the restriction of the unbridled State and the King. Even the King, he said, was subject to God and the law, because only the law made him King (*quia lex facit regem*). For there was no King, where arbitrariness and not the law ruled.[4]

Let me now bring you back to the year of 1950 and the signing ceremony of the European Convention on Human Rights in Rome.[5] A small group of far-sighted, idealistic lawyers, determined to

---

1. *See* Luzius Wildhaber, *Sovereignty and International Law*, *in* THE STRUCTURE AND PROCESS OF INTERNATIONAL LAW: ESSAYS IN LEGAL PHILOSOPHY DOCTRINE AND THEORY 425, 438 (R. St. J. Macdonald & Douglas M. Johnston eds., 1983) (describing the evolution of international law from that dealing with relations between states to law relating to a wide range of issues, including human rights).

2. 1 COLLECTED EDITION OF THE "TRAVAUX PRÉPARATOIRES" 48–50 (1975).

3. *Id.* at 50.

4. *See* 2 BRACTON (HENRY OF BRATTON), DE LEGIBUS ET CONSUETUDINIBUS ANGLIAE 33 (G.E. Woodbine & S.E. Thorne eds., Cambridge/Massachusetts 1968), *cited by* LUZIUS WILDHABER, MENSCHEN- UND MINDERHEITENRECHTE IN DER MODERNEN DEMOKRATIE 4 (1992).

5. COLLECTED EDITION OF THE "TRAVAUX PRÉPARATOIRES," *supra* note 2, at XXII.

prevent the recurrence of the devastation of war and the attendant horrendous crimes, argued that the best way to achieve that end was to guarantee respect for democracy and the rule of law at the national level. They believed that only by the collective enforcement of fundamental rights was it possible to secure the common minimum standards that form the basis of democratic society. It was Churchill himself who had referred first to a "European Court before which the violation of [human] rights . . . might be brought to the judgment of the civilised world."[6] Lord Layton, a member of the British delegation, saw the Convention as "a means of strengthening the resistance in all our countries against insidious attempts to undermine our democratic way of life, and thus to give to Western Europe as a whole a greater political stability."[7] For the first time individuals could challenge the actions of Governments before an international mechanism under a procedure leading to a binding judicial decision. The mandate which the founders of the Convention intended to entrust to the Court was eminently, even surprisingly, political.[8] The Court was to constitute a collective insurance policy against the relapse of democracies into dictatorships. What is nowadays identified as the hallmark of the Court, i.e. a generalised right of individual application for all sorts of possible victims, does not figure prominently in the original discussions on the Convention.

II. PRESENT

Now we move fifty years ahead, to 1998, when the Convention system underwent a major reform.[9] The original institutions, the European Court and the Commission of Human Rights, were replaced by a single Court functioning on a full-time basis.[10] The optional elements of the earlier system, the right to individual petition and the acceptance of the Court's jurisdiction, were

6. *Id.* at 34.

7. *Id.* at 30.

8. *See id.* (describing the Convention's goal of upholding democracy by preventing the destruction of democracy by dictatorships).

9. *See* EUROPEAN COURT OF HUMAN RIGHTS, HISTORICAL BACKGROUND, http://www.echr.coe.int/ECHR/EN/Header/The+Court/The+Court/History+of+the+Court/ (last visited Jan. 20, 2007).

10. *See id.*

eliminated; so was the Committee of Ministers' adjudicative role.[11] The Convention process, directly accessible to individuals, became fully judicial in character. The two initial bodies, the Commission from 1954 and the Court from 1959, gave life to the Convention, through their pioneering case-law.[12] Their purposive, autonomous, and at times creative interpretation of the Convention enhanced the rights protected to ensure that they had practical effect. Just to take one example, the right of access to a court, a right that lies at the heart of the Convention and a key element of the rule of law, was not expressly mentioned in the due process provision, Article 6, Section 1.[13] The Court's observation was of beautiful simplicity: "[t]he fair, public and expeditious characteristics of judicial proceedings are of no value at all if there are no judicial proceedings."[14] To this the Court later added that the right of access "would be illusory if a Contracting State's domestic legal system allowed a final, binding judicial decision to remain inoperative to the detriment of one party."[15] On the basis of such case-law, the Court established the principle that the Convention is to be interpreted as a living instrument, to be construed in the light of present day conditions.

Let me add a few personal remarks on the doctrine of the Convention as a living instrument. Our Court has of course followed precedent, except where cogent reasons impelled it to adjust the interpretation of the Convention to changes in societal values or in present-day conditions. And it has followed precedent not only with respect to judgments against a respondent State, but it recognises that the same European minimal standards should be observed in all member States. It is indeed in the interests of legal certainty, of a coherent development of the Convention case-law, of equality before

11. *See id.*

12. *See id.* (explaining the respective roles of the Commission, which made initial determinations on the admissibility of applications, and the Court, which could issue binding judgments).

13. European Convention for the Protection of Human Rights and Fundamental Freedoms art. 6, Nov. 4, 1950, Europ. T.S. No. 5 [hereinafter European Convention on Human Rights] (establishing the right to a "fair and public hearing").

14. Golder v. United Kingdom, 18 Eur. Ct. H.R. (ser. A) 1, 17–18 (1975).

15. Hornsby v. Greece, 1997-II Eur. Ct. H.R. 495, 510.

the law, of the rule of law, and of the separation of powers for the Court to follow in principle a moderated doctrine of precedent.[16]

Obviously in describing the Court's tasks in this way, I espouse a certain image of what the role of a European quasi-constitutional Judge should be. Our Court is to a certain extent a law-making body. How could it be otherwise? How is it possible to give shape to Convention guarantees such as the prohibition of torture, equality of arms, freedom of expression or private and family life, if—like Montesquieu—you see in the judge only the mouthpiece of the law? Such guarantees are programmatic formulations, open to the future, to be unfolded and developed in the light of changing conditions. My personal philosophy of the task of judges is that they should find their way gradually, in a way experimentally, inspired by the facts of the cases that reach a court. As you will realise, I do not believe in closed theoretical systems that are presented as sacrosanct on the basis of speculative hypotheses or ideologies. Such mono-causal explanations ignore the complex and often contradictory manner in which societies and international relations (and incidentally also individual human beings) evolve. Conversely, it has to be acknowledged that in developing the law it is difficult to avoid value judgments, whether on domestic or on international law. This applies especially to human rights, which, anchored as they are in the concepts of constitutionalism, democracy and the rule of law, are value judgments *par excellence*.

I might emphasise that I do not plead for a "Gouvernement des Juges."[17] Giving broad answers which are in no way called for by the facts of a case is to confuse a judicial mandate with that of the legislature or of the executive, and cannot and should not be the role of courts. In the famous "Federalist" Papers, Alexander Hamilton, the great theoretician of the American Constitution, wrote that the

16. *See* Luzius Wildhaber, *Precedent in the European Court of Human Rights*, *in* PROTECTING HUMAN RIGHTS: THE EUROPEAN PERSPECTIVE 1529 (Paul Mahoney, Franz Matscher, Herbert Petzold, Luzius Wildhaber eds., 2000).

17. *See* Un gouvernement des juges est-il à craindre?, http://www.oboulo.com/expose/gouvernment-juges-est-il-craindre.html (last visited Jan. 26, 2007) (describing that "Gouvernment des Juges" is a shift of power to the judiciary to make arbitrary decisions at the expense of the balance of powers found in modern day democratic governments; namely the Executive and Legislative branches of government).

government holds the sword, the legislature holds the money box, and the only thing the courts hold for themselves is their independence.[18] It is that independence which places us in a position to watch over fairness and justice within governments.

Let me also add that whereas international human rights judges should do what is fair and fear no one, as the puritans would have put it, they should at the same time have regard for the context in which they live and for the aims they are serving. Human rights are our common responsibility. First and foremost they must be respected by the national parliaments, governments, courts and civil society at large. Only if they fail does our Court come in. The subsidiary aspect I describe and advocate here is more than pragmatic realism; it is also a way of paying respect to democratic processes (always provided they are indeed democratic); and I am firmly convinced that it is the best means of translating the "human rights-law-in-the-books" not only into a "human rights-law-in-the-court", but into a "human rights-law-in-action" and—hopefully—in reality in all of our member States.

The full-time European Court of Human Rights which was set up in 1998 under Protocol No. 11 to the European Convention on Human Rights is the biggest international Court that has ever existed.[19] It is composed of a number of judges equal to that of the Contracting States.[20] With the sole exception of Belarus, all European States are today members of the Council of Europe and have ratified the European Convention on Human Rights, whose protection now stretches from Iceland to Turkey, from Lisbon to Wladúwostok, from Riga to Malta, but also from Chechnya to the

18. THE FEDERALIST NO. 78, at 378 (Alexander Hamilton) (Terence Ball ed., 2003) (asserting that of the three branches, the judiciary poses the least threat to individual liberties).

19. *See* Protocol 11 to the European Convention for the Protection of Human Rights and Fundamental Freedoms, Nov. 4, 1950, Europ. T.S. No. 5 [hereinafter Protocol 11]; *see also* European Court of Human Rights – Description, http://www.worldlii.org/int/other/PICTRes/2003/10.html (last visited Jan. 27, 2007) (recounting that over the years the ECHR has grown into the largest international bench and into one of the biggest and most respected international judicial bodies).

20. *See* Protocol 11, *supra* note 19, art. 20.

Basque region, from Northern Ireland to Cyprus and Nagorno-Karabach.[21]

Whereas the official languages of the Court are English and French, applications may be drafted in any one of the official languages of the Contracting States, and there are at present 41 official languages in these States.

The Court receives around 900 letters per day and some 250 international telephone calls a day. Its internet site was visited by 57 million hits in 2005. From 1998 to 2003, the number of applications has increased by about 15% in comparison with each preceding year.[22] In 2005, there was only an increase of 2%.[23] We now have some 81,000 pending applications before us.[24] In the past two years, we received some 45,000 applications.[25] The highest number of cases have come from Russia, Poland, Turkey and Romania (the so-called "big four"), which account for some 50% of all applications that reach our Court.[26] Some 63% of all cases have in recent years come from the 21 new member states of Central and Eastern Europe (at present about 18% come from Russia), some 11% from Turkey and only some 26% from the traditional Western European States.[27] Future historians might well argue that one of the biggest achievements of the Convention system was to be present and active when the Iron Curtain fell in 1989, so that the new member states had a whole body of case-law of which they could avail themselves.

---

21. *See generally* The Council of Europe's Member States, http://www.coe.int/T/E/Com/About_Coe/Member_states/default.asp (last visited Jan. 21, 2007).

22. *See* EUROPEAN COURT OF HUMAN RIGHTS, SURVEY OF ACTIVITIES 2005, at 33 *available at* http://www.echr.coe.int/NR/rdonlyres/4753F3E8-3AD0-42C5-B294-0F2A68507FC0/0/2005_SURVEY__COURT_.pdf [hereinafter SURVEY OF ACTIVITIES 2005].

23. *See* EUROPEAN COURT OF HUMAN RIGHTS, STATISTICS 2005, *available at* http://www.echr.coe.int/NR/rdonlyres/5211CDBA-8208-47DE-A9CA-AE8B8FD13872/0/stats2005.pdf (noting that 45,000 applications were filed in 2005, compared to 44,100 in 2004) [hereinafter STATISTICS 2005].

24. *See id.* (reporting a 4% increase in pending applications from Jan. 1 through Dec. 31, 2005).

25. *See id.*

26. *See* SURVEY OF ACTIVITIES 2005, *supra* note 22, at 35.

27. *See id.*

All sorts of cases reach our Court. Issues of the Communist nationalizations of property in Czechoslovakia, Slovakia and Eastern Germany and the question of whether the Czech Republic after the fall of the Iron Curtain could restrict the restitution of nationalized goods to Czech nationals only were declared inadmissible.[28] Two applicants elected to the parliament of San Marino refused to take the required oath on the Holy Gospels and were disqualified from sitting in the parliament, which our Court qualified as a violation of the freedom of religion in the *Buscarini* case.[29] A French-Moroccan drug trafficker held in custody was beaten up so severely by the police that medical certificates listed about 40 visible injuries all over his body, for which no plausible explanation was given, so our Court had to decide in the *Selmouni* case that he had been tortured.[30] The Swiss Animal Protection Society wanted to run an ad on TV, showing piglets and encouraging people to "eat less meat"; the TV refused saying this was "political" speech, whereas, if people had been invited to "eat more meat", this would have been "commercial" speech and therefore permissible; our Court saw in this a violation of the freedom of expression in the case of *Vereinigung gegen Tierfabriken*.[31] An imaginative applicant complained that the right to marriage of Article 12 must mean that the State was under an obligation to provide him with a suitable wife; unfortunately for him, the applicant was turned down.[32]

Functionally speaking, the European Court of Human Rights is becoming a European quasi-Constitutional Court. It is less handling the exceptional cases which captivated the attention of the founders of the Convention, but is becoming more and more a broad-based, "normal" institution, although a very symbolic one. Let me now discuss a few recent cases as illustrations.

28. *See generally* Malhous v. Czech Republic, 2000-XII Eur. Ct. H.R. 533; Gratzinger & Gratzingerova v. Czech Republic, 2002-VII Eur. Ct. H.R. 399; Kopecký v. Slovakia, 2004-IX Eur. Ct. H.R. 131.

29. Buscarini v. San Marino, 1999-I Eur. Ct. H.R. 605, 616.

30. Selmouni v. France, 1999-V Eur. Ct. H.R. 149, 183.

31. VgT Verein gegen Tierfabriken v. Switzerland, 2001-VI Eur. Ct. H.R. 243, 266.

32. European Convention on Human Rights, *supra* note 13, art. 12.

III. RECENT CASELAW

In a series of important judgments over the past few years, the Court has sought to explain the implications the Convention has for the political systems of the Contracting States and, in particular, the notion that pluralist democracy is the only political system that is compatible with the Convention. In an earlier judgment in 1998, in the *Turkish Communist Party* case the Court had found that democracy appeared to be the sole political model contemplated by the Convention and, consequently, the only one that was compatible with it.[33] But this raised the question of what that concept meant.

It is here that the Court has a role to play in identifying the constituent elements of democracy and in reminding us of the minimum essential requirements of a political system where human rights are respected. In the *Refah Partisi (Welfare Party) v. Turkey* judgment,[34] it carried out a thorough examination of the relationship between the Convention, democracy, political parties, and religion. The case concerned the dissolution, by the Turkish Constitutional Court, of a political party, the Welfare Party, on the grounds that it wanted to introduce sharia law and a theocratic regime.[35] A Grand Chamber of the Court found unanimously that there had been no violation of Article 11 of the Convention, which protects freedom of association.[36] The judgment provides some elements of an answer to the question which we have raised today concerning the dimensions of the New Europe.

The Court first noted that freedom of thought, religion, expression, and association as guaranteed by the Convention could not deprive the authorities of a State in which an association jeopardized that State's institutions, of the right to protect those institutions.[37] It necessarily followed that a political party whose leaders incited to violence, or put forward a policy which failed to respect democracy, or which was aimed at the destruction of democracy and the flouting

33. United Communist Party of Turkey v. Turkey, 1998-I Eur. Ct. H.R. 1, 22.

34. Refah Partisi v. Turkey, 2003-II Eur. Ct. H.R. 267, 300–03.

35. See *id.* at 269–70.

36. *See id.* at 316 (reasoning that Refah's dissolution, restricting the freedom of assembly and association guaranteed in Article 11, was necessary to protect the rights and freedoms of others).

37. *Id.* at 303.

of the rights and freedoms recognised in a democracy, could not invoke the protection of the Convention.[38] Penalties imposed on those grounds could even, where there was a "sufficiently established and imminent" danger for democracy, take the form of preventive intervention.[39]

The Court noted that the leaders of the Welfare Party had pledged to set up a regime based on sharia law.[40] It found that sharia, as defined by the leaders of the Welfare Party, was incompatible with the fundamental principles of democracy as set forth in the Convention.[41] It considered that "sharia, which faithfully reflects the dogmas and divine rules laid down by religion, is stable and invariable.[42] Principles such as pluralism in the political sphere or the constant evolution of public freedoms have no place in it."[43] According to the Court, it was difficult to declare one's respect for democracy and human rights, while at the same time supporting a regime based on such a sharia.[44] Such a regime clearly diverged from Convention values, particularly with regard to its criminal law and criminal procedure, its rules on the legal status of women, and the way it intervened in all spheres of private and public life in accordance with religious precepts.[45]

Next, let me describe the case of *Ilaşcu, Ivanţoc, Leşco and Petrov-Popa v. Moldova and Russia* which concerned events that occurred in the "Moldavian Republic of Transdniestria" ("MRT"), the region of Moldova to the East of the river Dniester known as Transdniestria.[46] This region declared its independence in 1991, which in turn led to a civil war and to the self-proclamation of a breakaway regime. This regime is not recognized by the international community. The case concerned the unlawful detention of the four applicants, following their arrest in 1992 and their subsequent trial

38. *Id.* at 303–04.

39. *See id.* at 305 (recognizing the possibility of a preventative intervention where "the national courts, after detailed scrutiny subjected to rigorous European supervision," identify an imminent danger).

40. *Id.* at 310–11.

41. *Id.* at 312.

42. *Id.*

43. *Id.*

44. *Id.*

45. *Id.*

46. *See* Ilaşcu v. Moldova & Russia, 2004-VII Eur. Ct. H.R. 179.

by the so-called "Supreme Court of the MRT" and the ill-treatment, inhuman prison conditions and torture inflicted on them during their detention, as well as the death penalty imposed on Mr. Ilaşcu and the mock executions to which he was subjected.[47]

The European Court of Human Rights established the responsibility of both respondent States (that of Moldova for the period after 2001) and found a violation of Articles 3, 5 and 34 of the Convention.[48] The Court ordered the immediate release of the applicants still in detention.[49] It emphasised the urgency of this measure in the following terms: "any continuation of the unlawful and arbitrary detention of the . . . applicants would necessarily entail a serious prolongation of the violation of Article 5 found by the Court and a breach of the respondent States' obligation under Article 46 § 1 of the Convention to abide by the Court's judgment."[50]

Only two of the four applicants have been released to date. Mr. Ilaşcu was released in May 2001 and Mr. Leşco at the expiry of the sentence imposed on him by the "Supreme Court of the MRT" in June 2004.[51] The other two applicants, Mr. Ivanţoc and Mr. Petrov-Popa, are still in custody.[52]

States have to report to the Committee of Ministers of the Council of Europe on the execution of judgments.[53] During the first examination of the case before the Committee of Ministers, the Moldovan authorities considered that, for the time being, their influence on the separatists was minimal or even non-existent.[54] As regards just satisfaction, the Ministry of Finance had ordered its

---

47. *See generally id.* at 232–45 (discussing in depth the arrest, detention, and conviction of the applicants as well as the events occurring after their convictions including actions taken to secure their release).

48. *Id.* at 303–05.

49. *Id.* at 302.

50. *Id.*

51. Press Release, European Court of Human Rights, Forthcoming Judgments (June 25, 2004).

52. *Ilaşcu*, 2004-VII Eur. Ct. H.R. at 302.

53. *See* European Convention on Human Rights, *supra* note 32, art. 46(2) (granting the Committee of Ministers the power to supervise the execution of final judgments of the Court).

54. Meeting of the Comm. of Ministers, 896th Sess., Notes on the Agenda ¶ 9 (2004).

payment.[55] The Representative of the Russian Federation in the Committee of Ministers emphasised the Russian authorities' disagreement with the judgment on both the legal and political levels and their view that since the applicants' lives were not in danger, the Convention was not pertinent.[56] Concerning possible execution measures or measures already taken, the Russian authorities considered that they were not in a position to execute the judgment, since the use of force to release the applicants was out of the question.[57] Furthermore, the Representative informed the Committee that he had been instructed not to participate in its examination of the case until directed otherwise.[58] He said that the Court's judgment was "inconsistent, controversial, subjective, politically and legally wrong and based on double standards."[59] It should therefore be noted that the Court's judgment in the *Ilaşcu* case has yet to be fully complied with.[60] In the meantime, Russia has paid the just satisfaction sums awarded by the Court.[61]

Next I wish to describe the case of *Broniowski v. Poland.*[62] The *Broniowski* case concerned the Polish State's continued failure to implement the applicant's "right to credit" under Polish legislation. This "right to credit" furnished compensation with respect to property abandoned by his family at the end of the Second World War in the territories "beyond the Bug River", as a result of the change of boundary between the former USSR and Poland.[63] The *Broniowski* application was chosen as a "pilot case" since at that time many similar applications were already pending before the

55. *See id.* ¶ 10.
56. *See id.* ¶ 15.
57. *See id.*
58. *See id.*
59. Press Release, European Court of Human Rights, Grand Chamber Judgement in the Case of Ilascu and Others v. Moldova and Russia (Jul. 8, 2004) http://cmiskp.echr.coe.int/tkp197/view.asp?action=html&documentId=800708&portal=hbkm&source=externalbydocnumber&table=F69A27FD8FB86142BF01C1166DEA398649.
60. Council of Europe Adopts New Resolution in Ilascu Case (March 3, 2006), http://politicom.moldova.org/stiri/eng/10221/.
61. See *id.* (noting that the new resolution was an attempt to achieve progress in releasing the prisoners and thereby adhere to the Court's ruling).
62. Broniowski v. Poland, 2004-V Eur. Ct. H.R. 1.
63. *Id.* ¶¶ 11–12.

Court.[64] The Section relinquished jurisdiction in favour of the Grand Chamber and adjourned the remaining applications pending the outcome of the leading case.[65]

By adopting both the 1985 and 1997 Land Administration Acts, the Polish State reaffirmed its obligation to compensate the "Bug River claimants" and to incorporate into domestic law obligations it had taken upon itself by virtue of international treaties concluded in 1944.[66] However, the Polish authorities, by imposing successive limitations on the exercise of the applicant's right to compensation, and by resorting to practices which made it unenforceable in concrete terms, rendered that right illusory, and destroyed its very essence.[67] Moreover, the right was extinguished by legislation of December 2003 under which claimants in the applicant's position who had been awarded partial compensation (2% of the value of the property, in the applicant's case) lost their entitlement to additional compensation, whereas those who had never received any compensation were awarded an amount representing 15% of their entitlement.[68] This obviously raised an issue of discrimination.[69] In the light of these considerations, the European Court concluded that the applicant "had to bear a disproportionate and excessive burden which cannot be justified in terms of the legitimate general community interest pursued by the authorities."[70]

The Court was informed that there were roughly 80,000 potential applicants with analogous claims.[71] It concluded in the operative provisions of the judgment that the violation found had

> originated in a systemic problem connected with the malfunctioning of domestic legislation and practice caused by the failure to set up an effective mechanism to implement the "right to credit" of Bug River claimants; . . . the respondent State must, through appropriate legal measures and administrative practices, secure the implementation of the

64. Id. ¶ 5.
65. *Id.*
66. *Id.* ¶ 162.
67. *Id.* ¶ 173.
68. *Id.* ¶ 186.
69. *Id.* ¶ 110.
70. *Id.* ¶ 187.
71. *Id.* ¶ 193.

> property right in question in respect of the remaining Bug River claimants or provide them with equivalent redress in lieu, in accordance with the principles of protection of property rights under Article 1 of Protocol No. 1.[72]

The Court reiterated that the violation of Article 1 of Protocol No.1 had originated in a widespread problem which resulted from deficiencies in the domestic legal order which affected a large number of people, and which might give rise in future to numerous, subsequent well-founded applications.[73] It decided to indicate the measures that the Polish State should take, under the supervision of the Committee of Ministers, and in accordance with the subsidiary character of the Convention, so as to avoid a large number of additional cases being referred to it.[74] It also decided that all similar applications—including future applications—should be adjourned pending the outcome of the leading case and the adoption of measures at the national level.[75] This is the first time that the Court has ruled in the operative provisions of a judgment on the general measures that a respondent State should take to remedy a systemic defect at the origin of the violation found.[76]

IV. HUMAN RIGHTS AND TERRORISM

Allow me now to briefly address the topical question of human rights and terrorism. Let me say first of all that I hope that it will have been obvious from what I have said that human rights law does not operate in a vacuum, but in a given context. It is an integral part of democratic society and a threat to that society will impact the way in which it is applied. The majority of the rights set out in the Convention are not absolute in that they may be curtailed in the wider interest of the community, to the extent strictly necessary and provided that this does not impose an excessive and disproportionate burden on individuals or a sector of the population. This could be formulated the other way round, that is that the individual exercising his civil liberties cannot be allowed to impose a disproportionate burden on the

72. *Id.* ¶ 200.
73. *Id.* ¶ 189.
74. *Id.* ¶190.
75. *Id.* ¶ 5.
76. *Id.* ¶ 193.

community. So essentially the Convention guarantees are applied in a context defined by the democratic society in which they function. This is just common sense. Human rights cannot be and should not be divorced from the practical day-to-day functioning of society.

The Strasbourg Court has consistently recognised the particular difficulties which combating terrorism creates for democratic societies.[77] It has accepted that the use of confidential information is essential in combating terrorist violence and the threat that organised terrorism poses to the lives of citizens and democratic society.[78] This does not mean however that the investigating authorities should be given *carte blanche* under Article 5 of the Convention to arrest suspects for questioning free from effective control by the domestic courts or by the Convention supervisory mechanism.[79] Again, in the context of Article 5 of the Convention, "the Contracting States cannot be asked to establish the reasonableness of the suspicion grounding the arrest of a suspected terrorist by disclosing the confidential sources of supporting information or even facts which would be susceptible of indicating such sources or their identity".[80] But the exigencies of the situation cannot justify stretching the notion of reasonableness to the point where the essence of the safeguard secured by Article 5, Section 1 (c) (requiring among other things "reasonable suspicion" of having committed an offence) is impaired.[81]

Democratic society acting in full conformity with the Convention is therefore not defenceless in the face of terrorism. It would run counter to the fundamental object and purpose of the Convention, for national authorities to be prevented from making a proportionate response to such threats in the interests of the safety of the community as a whole.

In saying this, one should never forget that the insidious undermining of fundamental rights is one of the dangers of terrorism. Limitations which may be possible within the margin of appreciation granted under the Convention must not be so broad as to impair the

77. Chadhal v. United Kingdom, 1996-V Eur. Ct. H.R. ¶ 79.

78. *Id.* ¶ 131.

79. *See id.*; *see also* Murray v. United Kingdom, 300 Eur. Ct. H.R. (ser. A) 1, 27 (1996).

80. Fox, Campbell & Hartley v. United Kingdom, 182 Eur. Ct. H.R. (ser. A) 1, 17 (1990).

81. *See id.* at 16–18.

very essence of the right in question; they must, in Strasbourg terms, also pursue a legitimate aim and bear a reasonable relationship of proportionality between the means employed and the aims sought to be achieved.[82] One question that needs to be asked in connection with exceptional measures taken to combat terrorism is whether there are techniques that can be employed which both accommodate legitimate security concerns and yet accord the individual a substantial measure of procedural justice.[83] Nor should it be possible for the national authorities to free themselves from effective control by the domestic courts, or ultimately international jurisdiction, simply by asserting that national security and terrorism are involved. At the same time "the Convention should not be applied in such a manner as to put disproportionate difficulties in the way of the police authorities of the Contracting States in taking effective measures to counter organised terrorism."[84]

There are moreover Convention rights which are absolute in nature and in respect of which no derogation is possible under Article 15 of the Convention.[85] Thus Article 3 prohibiting torture and inhuman or degrading treatment enshrines one of the most fundamental values of democratic society.[86] While the Strasbourg Court is well aware of the immense difficulties faced by States in protecting their communities from terrorist violence, even in these circumstances the Convention prohibits torture or inhuman or degrading treatment or punishment. Where substantial grounds have been shown for believing that an individual would face a real risk of being subjected to treatment contrary to Article 3 if removed to a particular receiving State, the responsibility of the Contracting State to safeguard him or her against such treatment may be engaged in the event of expulsion.

Let me turn to two other courts for a moment. In rendering his court's decision of September 1999 that physical interrogation

---

82. *See generally* Chadhal v. United Kingdom, 1996-V Eur. Ct. H.R. ¶¶ 135, 136.

83. *See, e.g.*, *id.* ¶ 131 (illustrating that there are ways to both accommodate concerns about the security of intelligence information and give the individual procedural justice).

84. *Fox, Campbell & Hartley*, 182 Eur. Ct. H.R. (ser A.) at 17.

85. European Convention on Human Rights, *supra* note 13, art. 15.

86. *Id.* art. 3.

techniques were unlawful even in ticking-bomb situations, Justice Aharon Barak, the President of the Israeli Supreme Court, said this:

> We are aware that this decision does not ease dealing with [the harsh] reality. This is the destiny of democracy, as not all means are acceptable to it, and not all practices are open to it. Although a democracy must often fight with one hand tied behind its back, it nonetheless has the upper hand. Preserving the rule of law and recognition of an individual's liberty constitutes an important component in its understanding of security. At the end of the day they strengthen its spirit and strength and allow it to overcome its difficulties.[87]

Given the particular context existing in Israel, at the time and unfortunately still today, his words carry special weight.

In the same vein, Judge Anand, former Chief Justice of the Supreme Court of India, when confronted with the deaths and torture of alleged terrorists in police custody, had this to say:

> [The] challenge of terrorism must be met with innovative ideas and approach. State terrorism is no answer to combat terrorism. State terrorism would only provide legitimacy to 'terrorism'. That would be bad for the State, the community and above all for the rule of law. The State must, therefore, ensure that various agencies deployed by it for combating terrorism act within the bounds of law and not become law unto themselves.[88]

CONCLUSION

So my conclusion is that human rights are not anti-democratic; terrorism is anti-democratic; arbitrary interference with individual rights and freedoms is anti-democratic; democracy without the rule of law is anti-democratic as is, self-evidently, the rule of law without democracy. In their wisdom the authors of the European Convention on Human Rights over fifty-five years ago constructed a framework for the effective operation of democracy and the rule of law based on minimum standards that are now in principle shared throughout

87. HCJ 5100/94 Public Committee Against Torture v. Israel [1999] IsrSC 37, http://www.hamoked.org.il/items/260_eng.pdf.
88. Shri D.K. Basu v. State of West Bengal (1997) 1 S.C.C. 416, 418.

forty-six European States. That framework, evolving as it has done through the Strasbourg case-law, remains as relevant today as it was then. It still represents a more long-term but ultimately more effective means of protecting democracy than short-term, disproportionately repressive measures which may purport to do the same, but which in the end court the risk of undermining the foundations of democratic society. In the *Klass* case in 1978, the Court warned against the danger of undermining or even destroying democracy on the ground of defending it.[89] That is a warning that we would all do well to keep in sight, if we wish to preserve a living democracy, one which is neither under-protected nor over-protected.

89. Klass v. Germany, 28 Eur. Ct. H.R. (ser. A) 1, 23 (1978).

[14]

'Europe as a Common Home'
Address to the Council of Europe, 6 July 1989

by Mikhail Gorbachev

Mr President, ladies and gentlemen, I thank you for the invitation to make an address here – in one of the epicentres of European politics and of the European Idea.

This meeting could, perhaps, be viewed both as evidence of the fact that the pan-European process is a reality and of the fact that it continues to evolve.

Now that the twentieth century is entering a concluding phase and both the post-war period and the cold war are becoming a thing of the past, the Europeans have a truly unique chance – to play a role in building a new world, one that would be worthy of their past, of their economic and spiritual potential.

Now more than ever before, the world community is experiencing profound changes. Many of its components are currently at the turning point of destinies.

The material foundation of life is changing drastically as are its spiritual parameters. There are new, and increasingly more powerful factors of progress emerging.

But alongside these factors and in their wake, there continue to persist and even escalate the treats emanating from this very progress.

There is an inevitable need to do everything within the power of modern intellect so that Man would be able to continue the role assigned to him on this earth, perhaps in the universe at large, so that he would be able to adapt himself to the stress-inducing newness of modern existence and win the fight for the survival of the present and succeeding generations.

This applies to all mankind. But it applies three times as much to Europe – both in the sense of its historic responsibility and in the sense of the urgency and immediacy of problems and tasks at hand, and in the sense of opportunities.

It is also the specific feature of the situation in Europe that it can cope with all this, live up to the expectations of its peoples and do its international duty at the new stage of world history, only by recognising its wholeness and by making the right conclusions.

The 1920s saw the theory of 'a declining Europe' gain wide currency. But that theme seems to be in vogue with some people even today. As far as we are concerned, we do not share the pessimism regarding the future of Europe.

Europe experienced, before everyone else, the consequences of the internationalism first and foremost of economic and subsequently of the whole public life.

The interdependence of countries, as a higher stage of the process of internationalisation, made itself felt here before it did in other parts of the world.

Europe experienced more than once the attempts at unification by force. But it also experienced lofty dreams of a voluntary democratic community of European people.

Victor Hugo said that the day would come when you, France, you, Russia, you, Italy, you, England, you, Germany – all of you, all the nations of the continent – will, without losing your distinguishing features and your splendid distinctiveness, merge inseparably into some high society and form a European brotherhood (...). The day would come when the only battlefield would be markets open for trade and minds open to ideas.

Nowadays it is no longer enough merely to ascertain the commonality of destiny and interdependence of European states.

The idea of European unification should be collectively thought over once again in the process of the co-creation of all nations – large, medium and small.

Is it realistic to raise the question in these terms? I know that many people in the West perceive that the main difficulty lies in the existence of two social systems.

Yet the difficulty lies elsewhere – it lies in the rather widespread belief (or even in the political objective) that what is meant by overcoming the division of Europe is actually overcoming socialism.

But this is a course for confrontation, if not something worse. There will be no European unity along these lines.

The fact that the states of Europe belong in different social systems is a reality. The recognition of this historical fact and respect for the sovereign right of each people to choose their social system at their own discretion are the most important prerequisite for a normal European process.

The social and political order in some particular countries did change in the past, and it can change in the future as well. But this is exclusively a matter for the peoples themselves and of their choice.

Any interference in internal affairs, any attempts to limit the sovereignty of states – whether of friends and allies or anybody else – are inadmissible.

Differences between states cannot be eliminated. In fact, they are even salutary, as we have said on more than one occasion – provided, of course, that the competition between different types of society is aimed at creating better material and spiritual conditions of life for people.

Thanks to perestroika, the Soviet Union will be in a position to take full part in such an honest, equal and constructive competition. For all our present shortcomings and lagging behind, we know full well the strong points of our social system which follow from its essential characteristics.

And, we are confident that we shall be able to make use of them both to the benefit of ourselves and of Europe.

It is time to consign to oblivion the cold war postulates when Europe was viewed as an arena of confrontation divided into 'spheres of influence' and someone else's 'forward-based defences', as an object of military confrontation – namely a theatre of war.

In today's interdependent world the geopolitical notions, brought forth by a different epoch, turn out to be just as helpless in real politics as the laws of classical mechanics in the quantum theory.

In the meantime, it is precisely on the basis of the outmoded stereotypes that the Soviet Union continues – although less than in the past – to be suspected of hegemonistic designs and of the intention to decouple the United States from Europe.

There are even some people who are not unwilling to put the USSR outside of Europe from the Atlantic to the Urals by confining it to the space 'from Brest to Brest'. To them, the Soviet

Union is ostensibly too big for joint living: the others will not feel very comfortable next to it, or so they say.

The realities of today and the prospects for the foreseeable future are obvious: the Soviet Union and the United States are a natural part of the European international and political structure.

Their involvement in its evolution is not only justified, but also historically conditioned. No other approach is acceptable. In fact, it will even be counterproductive.

For centuries Europe has been making an indispensable contribution to world politics, economy, culture and to the development of the entire civilisation.

Its world historic role is recognised and respected everywhere.

Let us not forget, however, that the metastases of colonial slavery spread around the world from Europe. It was here that fascism came into being. It was here that the most destructive wars started.

At the same time Europe, which can take a legitimate pride in its accomplishments, is far from having settled its debts to mankind. It is something that still has to be done.

And it should be done by seeking to transform international relations in the spirit of humanism, equality and justice and by setting an example of democracy and social achievements in its own countries.

The Helsinki process has already commenced this important work of world-wide significance.

Vienna and Stockholm brought it to fundamentally new frontiers. The documents adopted there are today's optimal expression of the political culture and moral traditions of European people.

Now it is up to all of us, all the participants in the European process, to make the best possible use of the groundwork laid down through our common efforts. Our idea of a common European home serves the same purpose too.

It was born out of our realisation of new realities, of our realisation of the fact that the linear continuation of the path, along which inter-European relations have developed until the last quarter of the twentieth century, is no longer consonant with these realities.

The idea is linked with our domestic, economic and political perestroika which called for new relations above all in that part of the world to which we, the Soviet Union, belong, and with which we have been tied most closely over the centuries.

We also realised that the colossal burden of armaments and the atmosphere of confrontation did not just obstruct Europe's normal development, but at the same time prevented our country – economically, politically and psychologically – from being integrated into the European process and had a deforming impact on our own development.

These were the motives which impelled us to decide to pursue much more vigorously our European policy which, incidentally, has always been important to us in and of itself.

In our recent meetings with European leaders questions were raised about the architecture of our 'common home', on how it should be built and even on how it should be 'furnished'.

Our discussion of this subject with President François Mitterrand in Moscow and in Paris were fruitful and fairly significant in scope.

Yet even today, I do not claim to carry a finished blueprint of that home in my pocket. I just wish to tell you what I believe to be most important.

In actual fact, what we have in mind is a restructuring of the international order existing in Europe that would put the European common values in the forefront and make it possible to replace the traditional balance of forces with a balance of interests.

What are the questions that deserve specific mention in this context?

First and foremost, these are security issues.

As part of the new thinking, we began with a critical reassessment of our perceptions of the military confrontation in Europe, of the dimensions of the external threat and of the factor of force in strengthening security.

This did not come easy, sometimes it was downright painful. But as a result, decisions were made that have made it possible to break the vicious circle of 'action-reaction' in East–West relations.

No doubt, joint Soviet–US efforts in the area of nuclear disbarment played a major starting role in the process.

The INF Treaty got something more than just approval from the Europeans. Many contributed to its conclusion.

The Vienna talks opened a fundamentally new stage in the arms reduction process.

Twenty-three states, rather than just two powers are participating in it. All the thirty-five participants in the CSCE process continue to work out military confidence-building measures. Although the two negotiating processes are going on in different rooms, they are closely interrelated.

There are no 'bystanders', nor can there be any, in peace-building in Europe; all are equal partners here, and everyone, including neutral and non-aligned countries, bears his share of responsibility to his people and Europe.

The philosophy of the concept of a common European home rules out the probability of an armed clash and the very possibility of the use or threat of force, above all military force, by an alliance against another alliance, inside alliances or wherever it may be.

It suggests a doctrine of restraint to replace the doctrine of deterrence. This is not just a play on notions, but a logic of European development imposed by life itself.

Our objectives at the Vienna talks are well-known. We believe – and the US President has also spoken in favour of it – that substantial reductions within two or three years in the level of armaments in Europe can well be achieved, naturally, given the elimination of all asymmetries and imbalances.

I emphasise, all asymmetries and imbalances. No double standards are admissible there.

We are convinced that it is high time talks on tactical nuclear systems were initiated among all interested countries. The ultimate objective is to completely eliminate those weapons. Only Europeans who have no intention of waging war against one another are threatened by those weapons. What are they for then and who needs them?

Are nuclear arsenals to be eliminated or retained at all costs? Does the strategy of nuclear deterrence enhance or undermine stability?

On all these questions the positions of NATO and the Warsaw Pact appear to be diametrically opposed.

We, however, are not dramatizing our differences. We are looking for solutions and invite our partners to join us in this quest.

After all, we see the elimination of nuclear weapons as a stage-by-stage process. Europeans can travel part of the distance separating us from complete destruction of nuclear weapons together, without backing away from their positions – with the USSR remaining faithful to its non-nuclear ideals, and the West to the concept of 'minimum deterrence'.

However, there is merit in figuring out what lies behind the concept of 'minimum' deterrence and where the limit is, beyond which nuclear retaliation capability is transformed into an attack capability. Here much remains unclear, and ambiguity breeds mistrust.

Why shouldn't experts from the USSR, the United States, the Unites Kingdom and France, as well as from the states who have nuclear weapons on their territories, hold an in-depth discussion of those questions?

If they arrive at some common views, the problem would become simpler at the political level, too.

If it becomes clear that NATO countries are ready to join us in negotiations on tactical nuclear weapons, we could, naturally after consulting our allies, carry out without delay further unilateral reductions in our tactical nuclear missiles in Europe.

The Soviet Union and other Warsaw Pact countries, notwithstanding the Vienna talks, are already unilaterally reducing their armed forces and armaments in Europe.

Their posture and operational structure are changing in line with the defensive doctrine of reasonable sufficiency.

That doctrine – both in terms of quantities of armaments and troops and in terms of their deployment, training and all military activities – makes it physically impossible to launch an attack or to conduct large-scale offensive operations.

In any case, as was declared at the USSR Supreme Soviet, we intend, if the situation permits, to cut sharply – by one and a half to two times – the share of our defence expenditure in national income by 1995.

We have seriously addressed conversion of the military industry. All CSCE participating countries will come to face this problem one way or another. We are ready to exchange views and share experience.

We think that the opportunities offered by the United Nations can also be used and, say, a joint working group can be set up within the Economic Commission for Europe to look into conversion problems.

Facing the European parliamentarians, and consequently the whole of Europe, I should like to say once again a few words about our straightforward and clear-cut positions on disarmament. These positions are the result of the new thinking and they were laid down on behalf of our entire people in the Resolution of the Congress of People's Deputies of the USSR according to which: we are in favour of a nuclear-free world and in favour of eliminating all nuclear weapons by the turn of the century; we are in favour of complete elimination of chemical arms at the earliest possible date, and we favour the destruction, once and for all, of all the production base for the development of such arms; we are in favour of a radical reduction in conventional arms and armed forces down to a level of reasonable defence sufficiency that would rule out the use of military forces against other countries for the purposes of attack; we are in favour of complete withdrawal of all foreign troops from the territories of other countries; we are absolutely opposed to the development of any space weapons; we are in favour of creating an atmosphere of trust that would rule out any surprises; we are in favour of a deep, consistent and effective verification of all treaties and agreements that may be concluded with respect to disarmament issues.

I am convinced that it is high time the Europeans brought their policies and their conduct into line with a new common sense – not to prepare for war, not to intimidate one another, not to compete with one another either in improving weapons, or, especially, in attempts to offset the initiated reductions, but rather to learn to make peace together and to lay jointly a solid basis for it.

If security is the foundation of a common European home, then all-round co-operation is its bearing frame.

What is symbolic about the new situation in Europe and throughout the world in recent years, is an intensive inter-state dialogue, both bilateral and multilateral. The network of agreements, treaties and other accords has become considerably more extensive. Official consultations on various issues have become a rule.

For the first time contacts have been established between NATO and the Warsaw Pact, between the European Community and the Council for Mutual Economic Assistance (CMEA), not to mention many political and public organisations in both parts of Europe.

We are pleased with the decision of the Parliamentary Assembly of the Council of Europe to grant the Soviet Union the status of a special guest state. We are prepared to co-operate. But we think that we can go further than that.

We could accede to some of the international conventions of the Council of Europe that are open to other states – on the environment, culture, education, television broadcasting. We are prepared to co-operate with the specialised agencies of the Council of Europe.

The Parliamentary Assembly, the Council of Europe and the European Parliament are situated in Strasbourg. Should our ties be expanded in the future and be put on a regular basis, we would open here, with the French Government's consent, of course, a Consulate General.

Interparliamentary ties have major significance for making the European process more dynamic. An important step has already been made: late last year a first meeting of the parliamentary leaders of thirty-five countries was held in Warsaw.

We have duly appreciated the visit to the USSR of the delegation of the Parliamentary Assembly of the Council of Europe headed by its President, Mr Björck.

The delegation could, I hope, feel directly the potent and energetic pulse of the Soviet perestroika.

We regard as particularly important the recently initiated contacts with the European Parliament.

Inter alia, we took note of its resolutions on military-political issues which are seen by the Parliament as the core of the Western European consensus in the area of security.

In this connection I cannot but mention the plans for 'the Western European defence'. Of course, any state or any group of states have the right to take care of their security in the forms they consider most appropriate.

It is important, though, that these forms are not in contradiction with the prevailing positive trends, that is, the trend towards a military détente, that they do not lead to the reappearance of confrontational tendencies in European politics and hence to a renewed arms race.

The need to convene within the next eighteen to twenty-four months a second Helsinki-type meeting is coming to the fore with ever increasing urgency. It is time for the present generation of the leaders of the European countries, the USA and Canada to discuss, in addition to the most immediate issues, how they contemplate future stages of progress towards a European Community of the twenty-first century.

As far as the economic content of the common European home is concerned, we regard as a realistic prospect – though not a close one – the emergence of a vast economic space from the Atlantic to the Urals where Eastern and Western parts would be strongly interlocked.

In this sense, the Soviet Union's transition to a more open economy is essential; and not only for ourselves, for a higher economic effectiveness and for meeting consumer demands.

Such a transition will increase East–West economic interdependence and, thus, will tell favourably on the entire spectrum of European relations.

Similarities in the functioning of economic mechanisms, strengthening of ties and economic interest, mutual adaptation, training of experts – these are all long-term factors of co-operation, a guarantee of stability of the European and the international process as a whole.

My contacts with prominent representatives of the business communities of the United Kingdom, the Federal Republic of Germany, France, Italy and the United States during my trips abroad and on numerous occasions in Moscow, testify to an increased interest in doing business with us in the conditions of perestroika.

Many of them do not overdramatise our difficulties, but take into account the specificity of the moment, when the reform is more successful in destroying obsolete mechanisms than in introducing new ones.

I have also noted the resolve of experiences businessmen with a broad political outlook to take justified risks, demonstrate audacity and act with long-term prospects in mind.

And incidentally, not only in the interests of business but also in the interests of progress and peace and in universal human interests.

We also feel aware that focusing on the immediate commercial profit may mean missing out on the chance for broad-scale and much more beneficial long-term economic co-operation with us as an integral part of the European process.

I think that the distinguished audience will agree that in our age segregating economic ties from scientific and technological ties is something less than normal. Yet, East–West relations have of late been bled white by COCOM.

If one could justify such practices at the peak of the cold war, today many restrictions seem utterly ridiculous.

Of course, we, too, are often excessively closed. However, we have begun to straighten this out. We have started to take down our 'domestic COCOM' – the wall separating military and civilian production – in particular, in connection with conversion.

So maybe experts and representatives of the respective governments could get together and break all these cold war log-jams, bring secrecy down to reasonable limits which are indeed required for security, and give the green light to the normal two-way flow of scientific knowledge and technical art?

The following projects, for example, are equally urgent both for the East and West of Europe: a trans-European high-speed railway; a common European programme on new solar-energy technologies and equipment; processing and storing nuclear waste and enhancing the safety of nuclear power stations; additional fibre optic channels for transmitting information; an all-European satellite television system.

Of great interest is the proposed high definition television. The research is under way in several countries and this system has a promising future for us within a European home. Naturally, one would prefer the most advanced and inexpensive system.

In 1985 in Paris, President Mitterrand and I put forward the idea of developing an international experimental thermo-nuclear reactor. It is an inexhaustible source of environmentally clean energy.

Under the aegis of the International Atomic Energy Agency (IAEA), this project – the result of pooling the scientific capabilities of the Soviet Union, West European countries, the United States, Japan and other countries – is moving to the stage of practical research.

Scientists believe that such a reactor could be built by the end of the century. It is a great achievement of academic thought and technological art, which will serve the future of Europe and the entire world.

The model of economic rapprochement between Eastern and Western Europe will to a large extent be determined by the relations between Western regional organisations – the European Community, EFTA, and the CMEA. Each of them has its own dynamics of development and its own problems.

We do not doubt that the integration processes in Western Europe are acquiring a new quality. We are far from underestimating the emergence in the next few years of a single European market.

The Council for Mutual Economic Assistance is also working towards establishing an integrated market though we are lagging far behind in this respect.

The rate of internal change in the CMEA will to a considerable degree determine what will have a priority development in the near future: ties between the CMEA and the European Community as groups or ties between individual socialist countries and the European Community.

It is quite possible that now and then one or the other form will come to the forefront. What is important is that both forms fit into the logic of establishing a common European economic dimension.

As for the Soviet Union, we shall shortly see a trade and economic agreement between our country and the European Community. We attach substantial significance to this act from the standpoint of all-European interests too.

We are, naturally, far from seeing out ties with the EC as opposed to ties with other associations or states. The EFTA countries are our good and old partners.

It might be reasonable to talk also about developing ties between the CMEA and EFTA and use this channel of multilateral co-operation, too, in the construction of a new Europe.

The common European home will have to be environmentally clean as well. Life has taught us bitter lessons. Major ecological problems have long ago transcended national confines. Setting up a regional ecological security system is therefore an urgent task.

It is quite possible that it is in this direction, which is indeed a priority direction, that the all-European process will advance most rapidly.

Elaborating a long-term continental ecological programme could be a first step.

We have proposed setting up a United Nations centre for emergency ecological assistance.

Such a centre or agency with a warning and monitoring system is urgently needed in Europe.

We might also give thought to establishing an all-European institute for ecological research and assessment, and ultimately to the creation of an organ with binding authority.

The Vienna meeting decided that an environmental forum of the thirty-five would be held this autumn in Sofia, Bulgaria. It could also discuss the problems in practical terms.

Humanity is suffering increasingly grave losses as a result of natural and technological disasters. Scores and even hundreds of thousands of lives are lost each year. Huge sums are spent to control the consequences. Scientists are alarmed because the largest cities are increasingly vulnerable in the face of natural disasters.

We are aware of the major projects designed to cope with this growing global threat.

The USSR Academy of Sciences has established an International Institute for the Theory of Earthquake Prediction, and it invites scientists from around the world to take part in developing a scientific basis for the problems of security and safety of larger cities, forecasting of droughts and possible climatic catastrophes.

The Soviet Union is ready to provide for these purposes satellites, oceanic vessels and new technology. It would probably be useful to involve also the military services of various countries, above all medical and engineering units, I the international rescue and restoration efforts.

The humanitarian content of the pan-European process is one of the crucial aspects.

A world where military arsenals would be reduced but where human rights would be violated would not be a safe place.

We have come to this conclusion ourselves once and for all.

The decisions made by the Vienna meeting represent a real breakthrough in this respect. It laid down a programme of joint actions by European countries, made up of all kinds of activities. Understanding was reached on many issues which until very recently had been stumbling blocks in East–West relations.

We are convinced that the all-European process should rest on a solid legal ground. We are thinking of an all-European home as a community rooted in law. And for our part we have begun to move in that direction.

The Resolution adopted by the Congress of People's Deputies of the USSR says, inter alia:

> Guided by international rules and principles, including those in the Universal Declaration of Human Rights, the Helsinki accords and agreements, and bringing its domestic legislation in line with the above, the USSR will seek to contribute to the establishment of a world community of states rooted in law.

Europe could set an example in that respect. Naturally, its international legal integrity includes national and social specific features of states. Each European country, the United States and Canada have their own laws and traditions in the humanitarian sphere, even though there exist some universally recognised rules and principles.

It would, perhaps, be useful to make a comparison of the existing legislation on human rights by setting up to that end an ad hoc working group or a kind of European institute for comparative humanitarian law.

In view of the different social systems we are not likely to achieve a complete identity of views. However, the Vienna meeting and the recent London and Paris conferences have demonstrated that common views and common approaches do exist and can be multiplied.

This makes it possible to speak of the possibility of creating a European legal space.

At the Paris Humanitarian Forum, the Soviet Union and France co-sponsored an initiative to that effect. They were joined by the Federal Republic of Germany, Austria, Hungary, Poland and Czechoslovakia.

What we need is to expand greatly cultural co-operation, increase interaction in the field of humanitarian sciences and to attain a higher level of information exchanges. In a word, the Europeans must step up the process of getting to know each other better. A special role here could be played by television, which brings into contact scores and hundreds of millions, rather than hundreds or thousands, of men and women.

There are also certain dangers inherent in that. They should be seen. Performing stages, screens, exhibition halls, and publishing houses are flooded with commercial pseudo-culture alien to Europe. National languages are treated with disdain. All this calls for our common attention and joint work in the spirit of respect for the true national values of each and every one.

That may involve sharing of experience in the preservation of cultural heritage; actions to familiarise European peoples with the original present-day culture of each other; and collective promotion of language studies.

This may also involve co-operation in the preservation of historical and cultural monuments, and joint production of films for cinema, television and video which promote national cultural achievements and the best examples of artistic creation of the past and of today.

Ladies and gentlemen, Europeans can meet the challenges of the coming century only by pooling their efforts.

We are convinced that what they need is one Europe – peaceful and democratic, a Europe that maintains all it diversity and common humanistic ideas, a prosperous Europe that extends its hand to the rest of the world. A Europe that confidently advances into the future.

It is in such a Europe that we visualise our own future.

Perestroika, which seeks to radically renew Soviet society, determines our policy aimed at the development of Europe precisely in that direction.

Perestroika is changing our country, advancing it to new horizons. That process will continue, extend and transform Soviet society in all dimensions: economic, social, political and spiritual, in all domestic affairs and human relations.

We have firmly and irreversibly embarked on that road. This was confirmed by the resolution passed by the Congress of People's Deputies on the 'Basic guidelines of domestic and foreign policies of the USSR'. That document confirmed in the name of the people our choice, our path of perestroika.

I commend this resolution to your attention. It has a fundamental and revolutionary significance for the destinies of the country to which you yourselves refer as a superpower.

As a result of its implementation, you and your governments, your parliaments and people will soon be dealing with a socialist nation totally different from what it has been up to now.

And this will have and cannot but have a favourable impact on the entire world process.

I thank you.

[15]

Speech delivered at the 'Strasbourg dialogues' public forum, 2 October 2009

by Mikhail Gorbachev

Thank you for inviting me to this forum. On this trip to Strasbourg – 20 years after my first official visit to the Council of Europe as the leader of the Soviet Union – it is very important for me to meet not only representatives of States and parliamentarians but also members of the public.

1989 was a pivotal year in the unfolding of events in Europe and in the world. History suddenly picked up pace, and this acceleration was symbolised by the fall of the Berlin wall. 'Velvet revolutions' took place in the countries of central and eastern Europe. Totalitarian and authoritarian regimes made their exit from the historical scene.

Those events and the peaceful manner in which they took place were possible thanks to the changes embarked upon in the Soviet Union in the mid-eighties. We initiated those changes because the time was ripe for them. They were demanded by the people, who did not want to live shackled and cut off from the outside world.

We began with 'glasnost', or openness, allowing our citizens to openly discuss the country's problems. With freedom of speech came freedom of assembly, freedom of conscience and real, not sham, elections. People were allowed to have their own businesses and private property.

So, after a few years – a very short space of time in history – the fundamental constructs of the totalitarian system were dismantled and conditions created for democratic processes and economic reform. And having done this in our own country, we could not prevent similar things happening in neighbouring countries.

We did not foist changes on them. From the very outset I said to the leaders of the Warsaw Pact countries: We need 'perestroika', we are going to reform our country. How you go about it is for you to decide yourselves. You are answerable to your own people. We will not get involved.

In essence this was a rejection of the so-called 'Brezhnev doctrine', the concept of 'limited sovereignty'. The initial reaction to that statement was scepticism – just another purely formal statement by just another general secretary, they said. But we followed it through. And for that reason, the various processes going on in Europe in the years 1989 to 1990 happened peacefully, without bloodshed. And that included the extremely complex process of reunifying Germany.

That happened by the will of the German people. Not because it was wanted by Gorbachev or Kohl or Bush. In America they often recall President Reagan's challenge: 'Mr Gorbachev, tear down this wall!' But could one person really do that? Especially as others were pushing in a quite different direction: Margaret Thatcher quite openly told us to keep the wall there.

When millions of Germans in east and west clamoured for reunification, we had to act responsibly. And the leaders of the countries of Europe and the USA lived up to that responsibility. As a result, it was possible to overcome the doubts and misgivings – and there were some, naturally enough –, avoid the closing off of borders and preserve mutual trust. And in so doing we definitively drew a line under the Cold War.

The ending of the Cold war opened up unprecedented opportunities – it was a real chance for the new Europe, and that was echoed in the title of the Charter of Paris adopted at the end of 1990. It was the starting point for changes whose benefits are still felt today.

At the same time it has to be admitted that we could not really take full advantage of the opportunities that had opened up. And that was reflected in European development. Consequently, Europe did not become the force in world politics and did not acquire the political strength commensurate with its potential. New dividing lines appeared on the continent, wars broke out and blood was shed.

Instead of creating an all-embracing architecture for Europe's security NATO began to take on a function of Europe's and even the world's policeman. That organisation embarked on enlargement. The promises made when States emerged from the Cold war were forgotten. For ten years no one gave a thought to the Charter of Paris.

After the dissolution of the Soviet Union, the USA and the whole of the West were overcome by a 'victor's mentality'. We are not looking to accuse other people of the collapse of our country. That was caused by internal processes. But when the West started rubbing its hands with glee and people began vaunting 'reforms' that dropped tens of millions of Russians below the poverty line, our people felt very badly let down.

The 'victor's mentality' did a great disservice to the West itself. Both politically and economically. After all, why would a 'winner' change anything? Leave everything as it was – that was the mood prevailing at the beginning of the 1990s.

Europe succumbed to that mood. What is more, an attack was launched on the role of the State in the economy, with the dismantling of its social obligations to citizens and the social protection system for employees. On a global level, the principles of monetarism, corporate social and ecological irresponsibility, excess profits and hyper-consumption began to take hold as all but key driving forces and criteria for the development of the economy and society as a whole.

Because of that, we have been plunged into the crisis that is now shaking the world economy and is far from over. And if we limit ourselves to mere 'fire-fighting' and do not start shifting towards a new model, the next crisis will be even more devastating.

Another problem of our time which people need reminding of over and over again is the persistent militarisation of world policy, the burden of stockpiled arms and the possibility of a new arms race.

Nuclear weapons are an extreme expression of the militarisation of international relations and political thinking. In recent years we have seen a worsening of the problem where the non-proliferation of nuclear weapons is concerned. But that problem must not be considered in isolation, solely in connection with Iran and North Korea.

The essence of the problem lies above all in the failure of the members of the nuclear club to honour the obligation they entered into in article 6 of the treaty on non-proliferation, namely to move towards nuclear disarmament. As long as this situation persists, the danger of new nuclear powers emerging will also persist. Today there are dozens of countries that have the technical capability.

Ultimately, eliminating nuclear danger will be possible only through nuclear disarmament. But is it a realistic prospect that, as a result, there will be one country with an arsenal of conventional arms bigger than that of all the other countries put together and will therefore have total world military supremacy?

I will be frank here: such a situation would be an insurmountable obstacle to saving the world from nuclear arms.

So if we do not tackle the issue of demilitarising world policy, cutting military budgets, curtailing the creation of new types of arms and preventing the militarisation of space, talks on a nuclear-free world will be left hanging in the air.

Europeans must not think that this is basically an issue only for the leading nuclear powers – Russia and the USA. Firstly there are nuclear powers in Europe, including France and Great Britain. They also have to reduce their arsenals. Secondly, up to now US nuclear weapons have been deployed in Europe. And, most importantly, without an active political role for Europe it will be impossible to resolve the issue of demilitarising world policy.

The same applies, by the way, to any other global issue, be it ecology, combating poverty, migration, illness or attenuating the consequences of natural disasters. Only a strong Greater Europe will be able to play a truly decisive role in resolving these problems. And for that reason it is important to consider multilaterally how to build that greater Europe.

At the beginning of the 1990s a course was set for the accelerated enlargement of the European Union. I am not calling the achievements of that process into doubt. They are very tangible. But the results are nevertheless contradictory. Not everything in that process has been carefully thought through.

Every process, every joint-venture has its limits as to what is possible in terms of pace and scale. The scope for 'digesting' the results is not unlimited. Expectations that all the continent's problems would be resolved by building Europe only from the West proved to be exaggerated.

A more measured pace for unification processes in the EU would allow more time to devise a model for relations with Russia and other countries which will not become European Union members in the foreseeable future.

It is self-evident that the model for relations with other European countries based on the fastest possible 'absorption' of the majority of them into the EU while leaving relations with Russia unstable and uncertain has had its day.

But it seems that not everyone in Europe has understood this. We are justified in wondering whether that uncertainty is not perhaps linked to a reluctance to participate in Russia's renaissance. What kind of Russia do you need – a strong, truly independent country or merely a supplier of resources that 'knows its place'?

In Europe, unfortunately, there are a fair few politicians who would like to impose a one-sided model for relations with Russia, such as 'teacher and pupil' or 'prosecutor and accused'. Russia will not accept a model like that. What we want is to be understood. What we favour is mutually beneficial cooperation on an equal footing.

We have many problems. We are only half-way to sustainable democracy, effective state institutions and civil society, and a social market economy. We see what our problems are and talk about them. But Russia will move forward, we have managed to resolve the issue of our survival and integrity and we will resolve the problem of modernisation on all fronts. You can all be sure of that.

Russia is ready to be a reliable, honest partner, not only in the energy sector, which people love to talk about out of context, but above all in the construction of a genuinely unified European area, that common European home I talked about 20 years ago.

And I would like to emphasise: in a climate of increasing unpredictability, which will clearly characterise world development in the 21st century, at a time when there is ever more talk of shifting the centre of gravity of world development to the Asia-Pacific region, it would be irrational not to make use of the resource offered by Russia and even more irrational to try to weaken it.

I very strongly believe that Greater Europe cannot be built on anti-Americanism or on anti-Russianism. We have a common future.

Russia's position on most international issues is close to the position of the European Union and constructively complements it. European politicians should be clear that it is not Russia which is dividing EU members into 'good' and 'bad' and causing divisions in their ranks. In a Greater Europe, our common European home, we will all be stronger.

It would of course be naïve to think that such relations would do away with all the problems or disagreements. These are bound to happen, even between the closest of friends. But in no circumstances must we look at those issues in a spirit of confrontation. We must not squander the immense opportunities created by our history and geography and our common cultures that will enable the future Europe to become a driving force for progress towards global peace.

And it is here that an organisation like the Council of Europe can play an essential, key role. Its 60-year history spans two periods of European development. The values of democracy, human rights and the rule of law laid down as its foundation are genuine, pan-European and, ultimately, universal human values.

But the Council must remain true to those values and traditions in its work. It must not divide States into 'good' and 'bad' ones. It must help all European countries to overcome problems – and there are problems everywhere, in each European country – in the area of human rights, development of democratic institutions, strengthening of the judicial system and humanitarian issues. It must seek its place in efforts to enhance economic cooperation and surmount the ecological crisis. It must become closer to Europe's citizens, many of whom feel alienated from politics. When I spoke yesterday at the Council of Europe, I mentioned the idea of setting up a pan-European security structure. As soon as the Cold war ended and Germany was reunified, the Charter of Paris for a new Europe raised this issue. Eminent political figures proposed creating an operational mechanism along the lines of a Security Council (or Directorate) for Europe.

To sum up, by way of conclusion, we all need the Greater Europe of the 21st century:

- a Europe without old and new dividing lines;
- a Europe effectively realising its moral values and cultural potential;
- a Europe forming a centre of power and influence in the world;
- a Europe capable of taking a lead role in devising responses to the major challenges of our time.

These goals are realistic and achievable. Success in attaining them is a necessity for Europe and the entire world.

[16]

Parliamentary **Assembly**
Assemblée parlementaire

Parliamentary Assembly
Assemblée parlementaire

COUNCIL OF EUROPE CONSEIL DE L'EUROPE

OPINION No. 193 (1996) 1

on Russia's request for membership of the Council of Europe

1. The Russian Federation applied to join the Council of Europe on 7 May 1992. By Resolution (92) 27 of 25 June 1992, the Committee of Ministers asked the Parliamentary Assembly to give an opinion, in accordance with Statutory Resolution (51) 30 A.

2. Special guest status with the Parliamentary Assembly was granted to the Russian Parliament on 14 January 1992.

3. Procedure for an opinion on Russia's request for membership was interrupted on 2 February 1995 because of the conflict in Chechnya. On 27 September 1995, with the adoption of Resolution 1065, procedure was resumed on the grounds that Russia was henceforth committed to finding a political solution and that alleged and documented human rights violations were being investigated.

4. The Assembly has followed the events of December 1995 in Gudermes and the recent events in Pervomayskoye with deep concern. It firmly condemns the taking of hostages as an act of terrorism and a flagrant violation of human rights, which no cause can justify. At the same time, it considers that the Russian authorities did not show sufficient concern for the safety of the hostages. The apparently indiscriminate use of force cost the lives of many innocent people and violated international humanitarian law. The Chechen conflict cannot be resolved by the use of force. There will be no peace in the region, nor an end to terrorist attacks, without a political solution based on negotiation and on European democratic values.

5. The Assembly notes that political, legal and economic reforms have been sustained. The legal system continues to show shortcomings, as noted by Council of Europe legal experts (7 October 1994). Nonetheless, there is progress towards a general awareness of - and respect for - the rule of law.

6. Assurances of continued progress were given to the Council of Europe by the President of the Federation, the Prime Minister, the President of the Duma and the President of the Council of the Federation in their letter of 18 January 1995.

7. On the basis of these assurances and of the following considerations and commitments, the Assembly believes that Russia - in the sense of Article 4 of the Statute - is clearly willing and will be able in the near future to fulfil the provisions for membership of the Council of Europe as set forth in Article 3 ("Every member of the Council of Europe must accept the principles of the rule of law and of the enjoyment by all persons within its jurisdiction of human rights and fundamental freedoms, and collaborate sincerely and effectively in the realisation of the aim of the Council ..."):

i. Russia has been taking part in various activities of the Council of Europe since 1992 - through its participation in intergovernmental "co-operation and assistance" programmes (notably in the fields of legal reform and human rights), and through the participation of its special guest delegation in the work of the Parliamentary Assembly and its committees;

ii. "political dialogue" between Russia and the Committee of Ministers has been established since 7 May 1992;

iii. Russia has acceded to several Council of Europe conventions, including the European Cultural Convention;

iv. the following legislation is being prepared as a matter of priority, with international consultation, on the basis of Council of Europe principles and standards: a new criminal code and a code of criminal procedure; a new civil code and a code of civil procedure; a law on the functioning and administration of the penitentiary system;

v. new laws in line with Council of Europe standards will be introduced: on the role, functioning and administration of the Procurator's Office and of the Office of the Commissioner for Human Rights; for the protection of national minorities; on freedom of assembly and on freedom of religion;

vi. the status of the legal profession will be protected by law: a professional bar association will be established;

vii. those found responsible for human rights violations will be brought to justice - notably in relation to events in Chechnya;

viii. effective exercise will be guaranteed of the rights enshrined in Article 27 of the constitution and in the law on freedom of movement and choice of place of residence;

ix. conditions of detention will be improved in line with Recommendation R (87) 3 on European prison rules: in particular, the practically inhuman conditions in many pre-trial detention centres will be ameliorated without delay;

x. responsibility for the prison administration and the execution of judgments will be transferred to the Ministry of Justice as soon as possible;

xi. the state and progress of legislative reform will permit the signature and ratification, within the indicated timetable, of the European conventions listed hereunder in paragraph 10;

xii. the Russian Federation will assist persons formerly deported from the occupied Baltic states or the descendants of deportees to return home according to special repatriation and compensation programmes which must be worked out.

8. With a view to the fulfilment of these assurances and respect for these commitments, the Assembly resolves to establish - with the close co-operation of Russia's national parliamentary delegation - its own parliamentary "advisory and control" programme under the authority of the committees responsible for the implementation of Order No. 508 (1995) on the honouring of obligations and commitments by member states of the Council of Europe. This programme will complement, and not prejudice, the monitoring procedure under Order No. 508 (1995).

9. As a contribution to long-term assistance and co-operation, the Assembly welcomes the European Union/Council of Europe joint programme for the strengthening of the federal structure and of human rights protection mechanisms and for legal system reform: particular attention should also be paid to support for, and the strengthening of, non-governmental organisations in the field of human rights and to the establishment of a civil society.

10. The Parliamentary Assembly notes that the Russian Federation shares fully its understanding and interpretation of commitments entered into as spelt out in paragraph 7, and intends:

i. to sign the European Convention on Human Rights at the moment of accession; to ratify the Convention and Protocols Nos. 1, 2, 4, 7 and 11 within a year; to recognise, pending the entry into force of Protocol No. 11, the right of individual application to the European Commission and the compulsory jurisdiction of the European Court (Articles 25 and 46 of the Convention);

ii. to sign within one year and ratify within three years from the time of accession Protocol No. 6 to the European Convention on Human Rights on the abolition of the death penalty in time of peace, and to put into place a moratorium on executions with effect from the day of accession;

Council of Europe Parliamentary Assembly

iii. to sign and ratify within a year from the time of accession the European Convention for the Prevention of Torture and Inhuman or Degrading Treatment or Punishment;

iv. to sign and ratify within a year from the time of accession the European Framework Convention for the Protection of National Minorities; to conduct its policy towards minorities on the principles set forth in Assembly Recommendation 1201 (1993), and to incorporate these principles into the legal and administrative system and practice of the country;

v. to sign and ratify within a year from the time of accession the European Charter of Local Self-Government and the European Charter for Regional or Minority Languages; to study, with a view to ratification, the Council of Europe's Social Charter; and meanwhile to conduct its policy in accordance with the principles of these conventions;

vi. to sign and ratify and meanwhile to apply the basic principles of other Council of Europe conventions - notably those on extradition; on mutual assistance in criminal matters; on the transfer of sentenced persons; and on the laundering, search, seizure and confiscation of the proceeds of crime;

vii. to settle international as well as internal disputes by peaceful means (an obligation incumbent upon all member states of the Council of Europe), rejecting resolutely any forms of threats of force against its neighbours;

viii. to settle outstanding international border disputes according to the principles of international law, abiding by the existing international treaties;

ix. to ratify, within six months from the time of accession, the agreement of 21 October 1994 between the Russian and Moldovan Governments, and to continue the withdrawal of the 14th Army and its equipment from the territory of Moldova within a time-limit of three years from the date of signature of the agreement;

x. to fulfil its obligations under the Treaty on Conventional Armed Forces in Europe (CFE);

xi. to denounce as wrong the concept of two different categories of foreign countries, whereby some are treated as a zone of special influence called the "near abroad";

xii. to negotiate claims for the return of cultural property to other European countries on an ad hoc basis that differentiates between types of property (archives, works of art, buildings, etc.) and of ownership (public, private or institutional);

xiii. to return without delay the property of religious institutions;

xiv. to settle rapidly all issues related to the return of property claimed by Council of Europe member states, in particular the archives transferred to Moscow in 1945;

xv. to cease to restrict - with immediate effect - international travel of persons aware of state secrets, with the exception of those restrictions which are generally accepted in Council of Europe member states, and to facilitate the consultation of archives kept in the Russian Federation;

xvi. to ensure that the application of the CIS Convention on Human Rights does not in any way interfere with the procedure and guarantees of the European Convention on Human Rights;

xvii. to revise the law on federal security services in order to bring it into line with Council of Europe principles and standards within one year from the time of accession: in particular, the right of the Federal Security Service (FSB) to possess and run pre-trial detention centres should be withdrawn;

xviii. to adopt a law on alternative military service, as foreseen in Article 59 of the constitution;

xix. to reduce, if not eliminate, incidents of ill-treatment and deaths in the armed forces outside military conflicts;

xx. to pursue legal reform with a view to bringing all legislation in line with Council of Europe principles and standards: in particular, Presidential Decree No. 1226 should be revised without delay;

xxi. to extend its international co-operation to prevent - and eliminate the ecological effects of -

natural and technological disasters;

xxii. to sign and ratify within a year from the time of accession the General Agreement on Privileges and Immunities of the Council of Europe and its additional protocols;

xxiii. to co-operate fully in the implementation of Assembly Order No. 508 (1995) on the honouring of obligations and commitments by member states of the Council of Europe, as well as in monitoring processes established by virtue of the Committee of Ministers' Declaration of 10 November 1994 (95th session);

xxiv. to respect strictly the provisions of international humanitarian law, including in cases of armed conflict on its territory;

xxv. to co-operate in good faith with international humanitarian organisations and to enable them to carry on their activities on its territory in conformity with their mandates.

11. The Assembly recommends that the Committee of Ministers - on the basis of the commitments and understandings indicated above:

i. invite the Russian Federation to become a member of the Council of Europe;

ii. allocate eighteen seats to the Russian Federation in the Parliamentary Assembly;

iii. guarantee that the Organisation's means and capabilities, in particular those of the Assembly and of the human rights institutions, are increased to meet the consequences of these decisions, and refrain from using the Russian Federation's accession to reduce the contributions of states which are already members.

---

1. Assembly debate on 25 January 1996 (6th and 7th Sittings) (see Doc. 7443, report of the Political Affairs Committee, rapporteur: Mr Muehlemann; and Doc. 7463, opinion of the Committee on Legal Affairs and Human Rights, rapporteur: Mr Bindig).

Text adopted by the Assembly on 25 January 1996 (7th Sitting).

[17]

A Human Rights Law of Internal Armed Conflict: The European Court of Human Rights in Chechnya

William Abresch*

Abstract

The cases on Chechnya recently decided by the European Court of Human Rights force us to re-evaluate the relationship between human rights law and humanitarian law. Since the International Court of Justice held that humanitarian law is lex specialis *to human rights law in 1996 – if not since the Tehran Conference of 1968 – it has been widely accepted that 'human rights in armed conflict' refers to humanitarian law. The ECtHR has directly applied human rights law to the conduct of hostilities in internal armed conflicts. The rules it has applied may prove controversial, but humanitarian law's limited substantive scope and poor record of achieving compliance in internal armed conflicts suggest the importance of this new approach.*

1 Introduction

In February 2005, the European Court of Human Rights (ECtHR) issued its first judgments on claims arising out of the armed conflict in Chechnya. Two of the judgments dealt with the conduct of hostilities, an issue that has generally been seen as the exclusive province of humanitarian law.[1] These judgments draw on and further develop the ECtHR's case law on the use of force in law enforcement operations. This jurisprudence has previously been applied to incidents involving the Irish Republican Army (IRA) and the Workers Party of Kurdistan (PKK), and the Chechen cases break no new ground on a narrow, doctrinal level. On the other hand, when we consider

* Director, Project on Extrajudicial Executions, Center for Human Rights and Global Justice at New York University School of Law. JD (New York University School of Law). Email: william.abresch@nyu.edu. I would like to thank Philip Alston, Nehal Bhuta, James Cockayne, Lisa Genn, and Antonios Tzanakopoulos for many helpful comments and conversations.

1 *Isayeva, Yusupova and Bazayeva v Russia*, ECtHR, App Nos 57947–49/00 (24 Feb. 2005) (hereinafter *Isayeva I*); *Isayeva v Russia*, ECtHR, App No 57950/00 (24 Feb. 2005) (hereinafter *Isayeva II*).

their relationship to humanitarian law, they mark a paradigm shift in the approach of international law to regulating internal armed conflicts.

The accepted doctrine has been that, in situations of armed conflict, humanitarian law serves as a *lex specialis* to human rights law. If, for example, a state were to launch artillery into a gathering of its citizens, it has been generally accepted that the legality of the attack under human rights law – was anyone's right to life violated? – would be determined not by interpreting human rights law, as such, but by applying the relevant rules of humanitarian law. This was considered both the proper manner in which to reconcile the two bodies of law and all but necessary given the lack of guidance that human rights treaties provide with respect to the conduct of hostilities. While the ECtHR has not openly relied on humanitarian law in its decisions, it has long been possible to argue that the *lex specialis* approach was being followed. Either the ECtHR was, *sub silentio*, applying the rules and principles of humanitarian law, or the events in Northern Ireland and southeastern Turkey did not actually constitute armed conflicts within the meaning of humanitarian law. These interpretations of the case law have been foreclosed by the Chechen cases.

The Chechen cases force us to re-evaluate both the ECtHR's past jurisprudence on the use of lethal force and the future of the *lex specialis* approach to reconciling human rights law and humanitarian law in internal armed conflicts. It is now clear that the ECtHR will apply the doctrines it has developed on the use of force in law enforcement operations even to large battles involving thousands of insurgents, artillery attacks, and aerial bombardment. It is also clear that it will do so by directly applying human rights law, not only without reference to humanitarian law but also in a manner that is at odds with humanitarian law.

While the humanitarian law treaties governing internal armed conflicts are largely silent on the conduct of hostilities, lawyers have generally borrowed from the humanitarian law of international armed conflict to fill this gap. This borrowing has taken three basic forms. One method has been to interpret the broad rules provided in Common Article 3 and Protocol II in light of the detailed rules provided in the Geneva Conventions of 1949 and Protocol I. Another method has been to argue that internal conflicts are governed by customary international law rules paralleling the treaty law rules governing international conflicts. A third method has been to extend the reach of treaties governing international conflicts to apply to internal conflicts; thus, Protocol I deemed struggles for national liberation to be international conflicts, and the International Criminal Tribunal for the Former Yugoslavia (ICTY) construed foreign support and control over a rebel group to 'internationalize' an otherwise internal armed conflict. While opinions differ as to when the rules of international armed conflict apply to internal armed conflicts as a matter of binding law (*lex lata*), there is little question but that most humanitarian lawyers consider the law of international armed conflicts to be an ideal – the *lex ferenda* – toward which the law of internal armed conflicts should be developed.

The rules regulating the use of lethal force that the ECtHR has derived from the 'right to life' provision of the European Convention on Human Rights (ECHR) break with this internationalizing trajectory. First, the rules espoused by the ECtHR are not limited by any conflict intensity threshold; they form a single body of law that covers everything from confrontations between rioters and police officers to set-piece battles between rebel groups and national armies. Second, while in humanitarian law the independence of the *jus in bello* from the *jus ad bellum* is axiomatic, the ECtHR's approach to evaluating the lawfulness of armed attacks assesses the means used within the terms of the justified grounds for employing lethal force. Third, in contrast to humanitarian law's principle of distinction, the ECHR permits the use of lethal force only where capture is too risky, regardless of whether the target is a 'combatant' or a 'civilian'. These rules are not perfect, but given the resistance that states have shown to applying humanitarian law to internal armed conflicts, the ECtHR's adaptation of human rights law to this end may prove to be the most promising basis for the international community to supervise and respond to violent interactions between the state and its citizens.

2 Bypassing the *lex specialis* Application of Humanitarian Law to Directly Apply Human Rights Law to Internal Armed Conflicts

Two bodies of international law govern internal armed conflicts, such as civil wars and revolutions.[2] Humanitarian law, or 'the law of armed conflict', applies to the parties to a conflict, laying down certain rules for the conduct of hostilities (combat), detaining prisoners, etc. The rules provided by humanitarian law are typically fairly specific, as they are designed to be interpreted and applied by military commanders. Human rights law applies to interactions between a state and its citizens, requiring the government to respect rights to life, liberty, etc. In a typical internal armed conflict, the government is one party to the conflict and some of the citizens, banded together as, say, a revolutionary army, are the other party to the conflict. The rules provided by human rights law are often rather vague, as they are designed to be interpreted and elaborated by courts and diplomatic discussion. Often the rules provided by human rights law and humanitarian law are harmonious or even redundant, but sometimes they appear to conflict. This is especially so with respect to the conduct of hostilities.

The leading theory among publicists[3] and advocates[4] is that humanitarian law is *lex specialis* to human rights law in situations of armed conflict. The most influential

2 This is affirmed in both the preamble to Protocol II and the derogation clause of the ECHR. See Protocol II, Preamble, para. 2 ('Recalling furthermore [in addition to Common Article 3] that international instruments relating to human rights offer a basic protection to the human persons.'); ECHR, Art. 15(1) (providing for derogation '[i]n time of war.').

3 An International Committee of the Red Cross (ICRC) summary of the conclusions reached at a gathering of humanitarian law experts states that '[T]he great majority of participants simply recalled that IHL represented a special law in as much as it has been specifically framed to apply in a period of armed conflict. They noted that, in offering ground rules adapted to this particular context of violence, this body of law makes it possible – in many cases – to specify the precise content of the non-derogable human rights. In this regard, many references were made to the reasoning followed by the International Court of Justice in its advisory opinion [on] the *Legality of the Threat or Use of Nuclear Weapons*.' ICRC, 'International Humanitarian Law and Other Legal Regimes: Interplay in Situations of Violence' (Nov. 2003).

4 Human Rights Watch and Amnesty International have increasingly applied humanitarian law rather than human rights law in reports on armed conflicts. See Bennoune, 'Toward a Human Rights Approach to Armed Conflict: Iraq 2003', 11 *UC Davis J Int'l L & Pol'y* (2004) 171, 216–219.

statement of this doctrine was given by the International Court of Justice (ICJ) in its 1996 Advisory Opinion on the *Legality of the Threat or Use of Nuclear Weapons*:

> The Court observes that the protection of the International Covenant of Civil and Political Rights [ICCPR] does not cease in times of war. . . . In principle, the right not arbitrarily to be deprived of one's life applies also in hostilities. The test of what is an arbitrary deprivation of life, however, then falls to be determined by the applicable *lex specialis*, namely, the law applicable in armed conflict which is designed to regulate the conduct of hostilities. Thus whether a particular loss of life, through the use of a certain weapon in warfare, is to be considered an arbitrary deprivation of life contrary to Article 6 of the Covenant, can only be decided by reference to the law applicable in armed conflict and not deduced from the terms of the Covenant itself.[5]

Confronted with two legal regimes – human rights law and humanitarian law – containing rules on the taking of lives, the ICJ resorted to the principle that *lex specialis derogat lex generali* to reconcile them, holding that the ICCPR provision on the right to life must be construed by making a *renvoi* to humanitarian law. *Lex specialis derogat lex generali*, or, the specific provision overcomes the general provision, is a canon of construction that is widely considered to be a general principle of law, as applicable in the international legal system as it is in national legal systems.[6] Koskenniemi provides the principle's rationale: a 'special rule is more to the point ("approaches more nearly the subject in hand") than a general one and it regulates the matter more effectively ("are ordinarily more effective") than general rules do'.[7] The thinking goes that because many of the same states have negotiated and acceded to the human rights law and humanitarian law treaties, we should presume that these treaties are consistent with one another.[8] We should not think, for example, that it violates the right to liberty under the ICCPR or ECHR to hold a combatant as a prisoner of war until the end of active hostilities when, after all, the same states that negotiated the ICCPR and ECHR also negotiated an entire treaty on prisoners of war that allows exactly that. Because general rules ('No one shall be subjected to arbitrary arrest or detention.'[9]) may be interpreted in more than one way, we should interpret them in light of specific rules ('Prisoners of war shall be released and repatriated without delay after the cessation of hostilities.'[10]) rather than vice versa.

5 ICJ, Advisory Opinion on the Legality of the Threat or Use of Nuclear Weapons (8 July 1996), paras. 24–25; see also ICJ, Advisory Opinion on Legal Consequences of the Construction of a Wall in the Occupied Palestinian Territory (9 July 2004), paras. 102, 105.

6 Koskenniemi, 'Fragmentation of International Law: Topic (a): The function and scope of the lex specialis rule and the question of "self-contained regimes": an outline', prepared for the Study Group on Fragmentation of International Law of the International Law Commission, available at http://www.un.org/law/ilc/sessions/55/fragmentation_outline.pdf, para. 2.2.

7 *Ibid.*, § 2.2 (internal quotations are from Grotius).

8 Jenks surveys the various principles available to resolve conflicts among law-making treaties, helpfully emphasizing their heuristic character and the importance of a pragmatic approach. He concludes that: '[a] solution to a conflict deduced from abstract legal principles is always possible when no alternative is available, but in the interest of developing a coherent body of law fully adjusted to changing practical needs recourse to such a process of abstract reasoning should always be regarded as a last resort': Jenks, 'The Conflict of Law-Making Treaties', 30 *BYBIL* (1953) 401, 450.

9 ICCPR, Art. 9(1).

10 Geneva (III), Art. 118.

The case for the *lex specialis* approach to reconciling the conduct of hostilities with the right to life would appear even stronger under the ECHR than under the ICCPR.[11] This is due to unique characteristics of the ECHR's derogation regime. Most human rights treaties provide that the right to life is non-derogable, leaving the word 'arbitrary' as the only hook for humanitarian law. In contrast, the ECHR permits derogation from Article 2, the right to life, 'in respect of deaths resulting from lawful acts of war', so long as it is '[i]n time of war or other public emergency threatening the life of the nation', the measures leading to such deaths are 'strictly required by the exigencies of the situation', and the state has formally availed itself of this right of derogation. The drafters of the ECHR presumably envisioned that states involved in armed conflicts would derogate to humanitarian law with respect to the right to life, effectively incorporating humanitarian law as a *lex specialis* regulating the conduct of hostilities. However, no derogation from Article 2 'in respect of deaths resulting from lawful acts of war' has ever been made.[12] Russia, Turkey, and the United Kingdom have all defended their conduct in internal armed conflicts within the terms of Article 2(2)(a),

11 The approach outlined here is that taken by Draper, who wrote that 'under article 15 of the European Convention, the whole of the Law of War as to killing has been incorporated by reference.... [A]rticle 15 is here spelling out the new philosophy of the essential relationship between the Law of Armed Conflicts and that of Human Rights. The latter is the normal ordering of civil society. The Law of War, international or internal, is the exceptional situation derogating from the full application of the Human Rights system. The two systems are essentially complementary, and that is an end to the old dichotomy between the Law of War and the Law of Peace into which International Law was traditionally divided': Draper, 'Human Rights and the Law of War', 12 *Va J Int'l L* (1972) 326, 338. See also Bruscoli, 'The Rights of Individuals in Times of Armed Conflict', 6 *Int'l J Human Rights* (2002) 45.

12 All of the ECtHR's jurisprudence on the conduct of hostilities could be dismissed as an anomaly created by states' failure to derogate. This would be a mistake. In *Isayeva II, supra* note 1, at para. 191, the ECtHR explained that the Russian operation had to be 'judged against a normal legal background' because no derogation had been made. If a state did derogate to humanitarian law 'in respect of deaths resulting from lawful acts of war', the ECtHR would presumably take the *renvoi* to humanitarian law, but the legal implications of this should not be overestimated. The ECtHR could simply apply humanitarian law, but it would not be difficult for it to continue to apply essentially the same doctrine it has already developed in *McCann, Ergi, Isayeva*, etc. In her study of the *travaux*, Svensson-McCarthy notes, *inter alia*, that all derogations are subject to the Art. 15(1) requirement that they be limited 'to the extent strictly required by the exigencies of the situation' and concludes that '[i]n interpreting the derogation provisions of human rights treaties in *armed conflicts*, international humanitarian law should not be ignored, because it provides an *absolute minimum level of protection* beyond which no interpretation of the human rights treaties could possibly ever be allowed to go. On the other hand, whilst this absolute minimum level *may perhaps* in certain particularly severe circumstances be allowed to guide the interpretation of the aforementioned derogation provisions, *it is in no way of any conclusive importance for the interpretation of these provisions*, which may in many respects provide a higher and more general level of protection. These derogation provisions do thus have a life of their very own, and they should in all circumstances be interpreted with due respect for the object and purpose of the treaties within which they are contained, so as to preserve to a maximum degree the full enjoyment of the rights and freedoms guaranteed therein': Svensson-McCarthy, *The International Law of Human Rights and States of Exception: With Special Reference to the Travaux Preparatoires and Case-Law of the International Monitoring Organs* (1998), 378. It would also be regrettable were the ECtHR to give broad effect to a derogation from Art. 2 inasmuch as this would allow states to pick and choose among the standards provided in the two legal regimes.

which permits recourse to lethal force when 'absolutely necessary . . . in defence of any person from unlawful violence'.[13]

Despite the decisions of states not to derogate to humanitarian law, has the ECtHR gone ahead and applied humanitarian law as *lex specialis?* Those who believe that it has point to its use of words that are terms of art in humanitarian law – for instance, 'incidental loss of civilian life',[14] 'legitimate military targets',[15] 'disproportionality in the weapons used'.[16] The ECtHR has never stated that it applies humanitarian law, but this vocabulary has been taken as evidence that the ECtHR applies humanitarian law principles and concepts when dealing with cases arising out of armed conflicts, that it applies, *sub silentio*, humanitarian law as a *lex specialis*.[17] This vocabulary is not, however, unique to humanitarian law. Terms like 'civilian' and 'the civilian population' are part of the general discourse on war, and words like 'proportionality' belong as much to human rights law as to humanitarian law. The use of a vocabulary that overlaps with the vocabulary of humanitarian law tells us little. The important question is whether the ECtHR has adopted the legal rules and standards of humanitarian law. Comparison between the ECtHR's holdings and the rules of humanitarian law reveals that if the ECtHR is attempting to apply humanitarian law, it is doing so in a highly imprecise manner.

After the Chechen cases, the better question is whether the ECtHR has made a mistake in disregarding humanitarian law. Construing humanitarian law as a *lex specialis* to human rights law has lent some unity and coherence to the otherwise fragmented standards governing armed conflicts. Does the ECtHR's approach return us to confusion and conflicting legal requirements? The answer would be yes if the ECtHR were to directly apply human rights law to the conduct of hostilities in *international* armed conflicts. The Geneva Conventions of 1949, Protocol I, and the Hague Convention provide detailed rules on distinguishing civilians from combatants and for selecting the targets, weapons, and methods of armed attacks. For the ECtHR to simply invent a new set of rules would be to flout the express intention of states. But if we understand the ECtHR's jurisprudence on the conduct of hostilities to be limited to *internal* armed conflicts, it is much harder to argue that the ECtHR has overreached. The ECtHR has, however, shown great caution in applying the ECHR to a state's actions outside of its territory.[18]

[13] Art. 2(2)(c), 'in action lawfully taken for the purpose of quelling a riot or insurrection', has also been invoked with respect to riots. See *Güleç v Turkey*, ECtHR, App. No. 21593/93 (27 July 1998).

[14] *Ergi v Turkey*, ECtHR, App No 23818/94 (28 July 1998); at para. 79; *Isayeva II, supra* note 1, at para. 176.

[15] *Isayeva I, supra* note 1, at para. 175.

[16] *Ibid.*, at para. 197.

[17] Heintze, 'On the Relationship Between Human Rights Law Protection and International Humanitarian Law', 86 *IRRC* (2004) 789; Heintze, 'The European Court of Human Rights and the Implementation of Human Rights Standards During Armed Conflicts', 45 *German Yearbook Int'l L* (2002) 60; Reidy, 'The Approach of the European Commission and Court of Human Rights to International Humanitarian Law', 80 *IRRC* (1998) 513.

[18] *Bankovic v Belgium*, ECtHR, App. No. 52207/99 (2001).

The rationale that makes resort to humanitarian law as *lex specialis* appealing – that its rules have greater specificity – is missing in internal armed conflicts. While the humanitarian law of international armed conflicts is copious and sometimes painstakingly detailed, the humanitarian law of internal armed conflicts is quite spare and seldom specific. In most internal conflicts, the only applicable treaty law is Common Article 3 of the Geneva Conventions of 1949, a legal regime consisting of 263 words. With respect to the taking of lives, Common Article 3 provides that:

> (1) Persons taking no active part in the hostilities, including members of armed forces who have laid down their arms and those placed *hors de combat* by sickness, wounds, detention, or any other cause, shall in all circumstances be treated humanely, without any adverse distinction founded on race, colour, religion or faith, sex, birth or wealth, or any other similar criteria. To this end, the following acts are and shall remain prohibited at any time and in any place whatsoever with respect to the above-mentioned persons:
> (a) violence to life and person, in particular murder of all kinds, mutilation, cruel treatment and torture; ...
> (d) the passing of sentences and the carrying out of executions without previous judgment pronounced by a regularly constituted court, affording all the judicial guarantees which are recognized as indispensable by civilized peoples. ...

In comparison, Article 2 of the ECHR provides that:

> 1. Everyone's right to life shall be protected by law. No one shall be deprived of his life intentionally save in the execution of a sentence of a court following his conviction of a crime for which this penalty is provided by law.
> 2. Deprivation of life shall not be regarded as inflicted in contravention of this article when it results from the use of force which is no more than absolutely necessary:
> (a) in defence of any person from unlawful violence;
> (b) in order to effect a lawful arrest or to prevent escape of a person lawfully detained;
> (c) in action lawfully taken for the purpose of quelling a riot or insurrection.[19]

When we consider that other human rights law provisions lay out detailed due process guarantees[20] and require that rights be respected 'without discrimination on any ground such as sex, race, colour, language, religion, political or other opinion, national or social origin, association with a national minority, property, birth or other status',[21] it is difficult to see how Common Article 3 is 'more specific', 'more to the point', or 'more effective' than the ECHR or other human rights instruments. While still quite brief, Protocol II is more extensive than Common Article 3. In addition to further developing Common Article 3's guarantees for the humane treatment of persons not taking part in hostilities, it protects medical and relief efforts, and it provides that civilians shall not be targeted and shall 'enjoy general protection

[19] The other principal human rights instruments have provisions similar to that in Art. 6(1) of the ICCPR: '[e]very human being has the inherent right to life. This right shall be protected by law. No one shall be arbitrarily deprived of his life.' See American Convention on Human Rights (hereinafter ACHR), Art. 4(1); African Charter on Human and Peoples' Rights (hereinafter African Charter), Art. 4.

[20] See ECHR, Art. 6; ICCPR, Art. 14; ACHR, Art. 8; African Charter, Art. 7.

[21] ECHR, Art. 14; see also ICCPR, Art. 2(1); ACHR., Art. 1(1); African Charter, Art. 2.

against the dangers arising from military operations'. With respect to the provisions on humane treatment, humanitarian law and human rights law are consistent, often redundant. However, Common Article 3 does not regulate the conduct of hostilities at all,[22] and Protocol II only does so with respect to civilians, and then only in general terms.[23] Neither instrument, for example, provides any guidance on the legality of attacks that are likely to unintentionally kill persons not taking part in hostilities. The innovation of the ECtHR fills this gap in humanitarian law by beginning to develop a human rights law of the conduct of hostilities in internal armed conflicts.[24]

The treaty law of internal armed conflict is not the only possible point of comparison for the ECtHR's jurisprudence. There is a broad consensus that Common Article 3 and Protocol II fail to effectively regulate many aspects of those conflicts, but some lawyers and advocates look to customary international law – unwritten rules that states consider to be legally binding – to fill the gaps. This approach has received a major boost with the publication, in early 2005, of an extensive study by the International Committee of the Red Cross (ICRC) on the current state of customary international humanitarian law.[25] This study identified 161 customary rules, many of which purportedly apply to internal armed conflicts. The authors concluded that 'the gaps in the regulation of the conduct of hostilities in Additional Protocol II have largely

[22] While the text of Common Art. 3 will sustain the interpretation that it prohibits the targeting during combat of persons not taking active part in hostilities, most experts consider its field of application limited to persons within the power of a party to the conflict. In any case, Common Art. 3 clearly does not regulate the conduct of hostilities in any other aspect: ICRC, *Commentary: I Geneva Convention for the Amelioration of the Condition of the Wounded and Sick in Armed Forces in the Field* (hereinafter *ICRC Commentary on Geneva I*), (1952), 52–57; ICRC, *Commentary on the Additional Protocols of 8 June 1977 to the Geneva Conventions of 12 August 1949* (hereinafter *ICRC Commentary on Additional Protocols*) (1987), 1325; M. Bothe *et al.*, *New Rules for Victims of Armed Conflicts: Commentary on the Two 1977 Protocols Additional to the Geneva Conventions of 1949* (1982), 667, note 1.

[23] Protocol II includes the 'principle of distinction' but regulates the conduct of hostilities only in so far as they are implicit in the 'general protection against the dangers arising from military operations' accorded the civilian population in Art. 13(1). Early drafts of Protocol II did regulate the conduct of hostilities, but the negotiating states became uneasy with the draft's scope, and 'the provisions on means of combat were . . . among the first provisions to fall beneath the guillotine': A. Cassese, 'Means of Warfare: The Traditional and the New Law', in Cassese (ed.), *The Humanitarian Law of Armed Conflict* (1979), 191, 195. The exclusion of these provisions from Protocol II has led one scholar to characterize the means and methods of warfare in internal conflict as 'at the "vanishing point" of international humanitarian law': Turns, 'At the "Vanishing Point" of International Humanitarian Law: Methods and Means of Warfare in Non-international Armed Conflicts', 45 *German YIL* (2002) 115, 116. See also discussion *infra* in Part 3(C).

[24] The argument can, of course, be made in the other direction. Gasser notes the substantial overlap between the humane treatment provisions of the ICCPR and Protocol II, but suggests that it is Protocol II that fills the conduct of hostilities gap in the ICCPR: Gasser, 'International Humanitarian Law and Human Rights Law in Non-international Armed Conflict: Joint Venture or Mutual Exclusion', 45 *German YIL* (2002) 149. In the final instance, there is a strategic choice to be made as to whether it is more legitimate for advocates to construe Protocol II broadly or for courts extensively to develop human rights standards.

[25] J.-M. Henckaerts and L. Doswald-Beck (eds.), *Customary International Humanitarian Law, Vol. 1: Rules* (hereinafter *ICRC Customary Humanitarian Law Study*) (2005).

been filled through State practice, which has led to the creation of rules parallel to those in Additional Protocol I, but applicable as customary law to non-international armed conflicts'.[26] It is impossible to evaluate the ECtHR's jurisprudence on the conduct of hostilities without considering its relationship to customary humanitarian law as discerned by the ICRC's study. On the one hand, if there were a substantial body of customary humanitarian law that applied to internal conflicts, the case for applying humanitarian law as *lex specialis* to human rights law would be stronger. On the other hand, if human rights law could effectively regulate such conflicts, the case for promoting the acceptance of customary rules would be weaker. The dilemma could be finessed if the rules provided in the ICRC study and the rules given by the ECtHR were the same, but, as shown in Section 3, they are quite different and by no means parallel those in Protocol I. As a practical matter, 'the customary humanitarian law of internal armed conflicts' and 'the human rights law of internal armed conflicts' are competing projects.

The pressing question regarding the ICRC's study is whether states do, in fact, consider the rules it enumerates to be legally binding. In international armed conflicts, customary law has a long and relatively uncontroversial history, but in internal armed conflicts, it has generally been assumed to play only a minor role. When Protocol II was concluded two and a half decades ago, it was impossible for states to reach consensus even on the *existence* of a customary humanitarian law of internal armed conflicts. This is reflected in Protocol II's truncated rendition of the Martens Clause: '[I]n cases not covered by the law in force, the human person remains under the protection of the principles of humanity and the dictates of public conscience.'[27] In contrast, Protocol I provides that 'In cases not covered by this Protocol or by other international agreements, civilians and combatants remain under the protection and authority of the principles of international law derived from established custom, from the principles of humanity and from the dictates of public conscience.'[28] The contrast is indicative of 'the insistence by states that non-international armed conflicts are, except upon recognition of belligerency, governed by national rather than international law'.[29] In order to arrive at a customary humanitarian law of internal armed conflicts, the ICRC study typically infers that military manuals and declarations by states are (a) intended as statements of international law, rather than domestic law or

26 *Ibid.*, at p. xxix.

27 Protocol II, Preamble, para. 5.

28 Protocol I, Art. 1(2).

29 T. Meron, *Human Rights and Humanitarian Norms as Customary Law* (1989), 73–74. Meron argues that other features of Protocol II 'strengthen the proposition that beyond the express provisions of Protocol II, regulation of internal armed conflicts is relegated to the domestic law of states'. Meron points in particular to the failure of Protocol II, Art. 13(1) to include the reference to 'other applicable rules of international law' in contrast to Protocol I, Art. 51(1), the absence of an obligation for other states to 'ensure respect' for Protocol II in contrast to Protocol I, Art. 1(1)), and the 'especially strong prohibition of intervention in the affairs of the state in whose territory the conflict occurs' in Protocol II, Art. 3. Bothe explains the exclusion of customary law from Protocol II's Martens Clause 'by the fact that the attempt to establish rules for a non-international conflict only goes back to 1949 and that the application of common Art. 3 in the practice of States has not developed in such a way that one could speak of "established

policy, and (b) apply to internal armed conflicts unless explicitly limited to international armed conflicts. These assumptions appear unwarranted. When, as discussed in Section 3A, states are reluctant to acknowledge the applicability of treaty-based humanitarian law, it is difficult to credit that they consider themselves bound under customary humanitarian law.[30]

The same states that refused to acknowledge any customary humanitarian law of internal conflicts expressly recognized in Protocol II that 'international instruments relating to human rights offer a basic protection to the human person'.[31] While they did not anticipate the application of human rights law to the conduct of hostilities, this preambular invocation does indicate that human rights law is broadly accepted as a legitimate basis on which the international community can supervise and respond to interactions between a state and its citizens. In some regions, including much of Europe, a practice of routine compliance with international human rights law has been achieved.[32] This legitimacy and pattern of compliance may be less entrenched with respect to the violent interactions of armed conflict, but states reluctant to acknowledge that more than 'law enforcement' in a 'stable country and healthy society' is underway may be unlikely to affirmatively renounce the binding character of human rights law in times of conflict. There is no place for great optimism regarding what, for example, the ECtHR might achieve in Chechnya, but given that Russia at least accepts that the ECHR is a relevant source of law, its direct application to the conduct of hostilities must be considered a promising strategy.

It is not enough for the direct application of human rights law to internal armed conflicts to be appropriate and desirable; it must also be possible. The challenge is to apply the broad principles of human rights law to the conduct of hostilities in a manner that is persuasive and realistic. Human rights law must be realistic in the sense of not categorically forbidding killing in the context of armed conflict or otherwise making compliance with the law and victory in battle impossible to achieve at once. These realistic rules must be persuasively derived from the legal standards of human rights law. Many have thought these goals unrealistic, maintaining that human rights law is simply inadequate to the task of regulating the conduct of hostilities. In *Abella*, the Inter-American Commission on Human Rights was asked to resolve claims arising out of a pitched battle. An armed group had seized a military base from which it believed a *coup d'état* was to be launched. The base was promptly surrounded by

custom" regarding non-international conflicts': Bothe, *supra* note 22, at 620. The ICRC commentary interprets the omission of customary law as due to a 'cautious point of view' on the development of state practice, and argues that 'the existence of customary norms in internal armed conflicts should not be totally denied. An example that might be given is the respect for and protection of the wounded': *ICRC Commentary on Additional Protocols, supra* note 22, at 1341.

30 See also discussion on deriving custom from military manuals in Turns, *supra* note 23, at 138–143, and T. Meron, *Human Rights and Humanitarian Norms as Customary Law* (1989), 41.

31 Protocol II, Preamble, para. 3.

32 For an attempt to explain the success of the ECtHR and develop strategies for other bodies to become more effective, see Helfin and Slaughter, 'Toward a Theory of Effective Supranational Adjudication', 107 *Yale LJ* (1997) 273.

Argentine armed forces, and a 30-hour battle ensued. After characterizing these events as an armed conflict, the Commission concluded that its

> ability to resolve claimed violations of [the right to life] arising out of an armed conflict may not be possible in many cases by reference to . . . the American Convention alone. This is because the American Convention contains no rules that either define or distinguish civilians from combatants and other military targets, much less,[sic] specify when a civilian can be lawfully attacked or when civilian casualties are a lawful consequence of military operations. Therefore, the Commission must necessarily look to and apply definitional standards and relevant rules of humanitarian law as sources of authoritative guidance in its resolution of this and other kinds of claims alleging violations of the American Convention in combat situations.[33]

The Commission then turned to Common Article 3 and to two United Nations General Assembly Resolutions that it found to reflect customary international law.[34] The ECtHR has now done exactly what the Inter-American Commission avoided, by directly applying human rights law rather than turning to humanitarian law. Its jurisprudence must be judged by whether it provides satisfactory rules to 'specify when a civilian can be lawfully attacked or when civilian casualties are a lawful consequence of military operations' and resolve the other issues routinely confronted in armed conflict.

3 New Rules on the Conduct of Hostilities in Internal Armed Conflicts

Article 2(2) of the ECHR permits no more use of force 'than absolutely necessary' to achieve a permitted aim, such as the 'defence of any person from unlawful violence'. The ECtHR has held that

> the use of the term 'absolutely necessary' in Article 2(2) indicates that a stricter and more compelling test of necessity must be employed from that normally applicable when determining whether State action is 'necessary in a democratic society' under paragraph 2 of Articles 8 to 11 of the Convention. In particular, the force used must be strictly proportionate to the achievement of the aims set out in sub-paragraphs 2(a), (b) and (c) of Article 2. In keeping with the importance of this provision in a democratic society, the Court must, in making its assessment, subject deprivations of life to the most careful scrutiny, particularly where deliberate lethal force is used, taking into consideration not only the actions of the agents of the State who

33 Case of Juan Carlos Abella (Argentina), Inter-Am CtHR, Case 11.137 (1997), para. 161.

34 *Ibid.*, para. 177. The Inter-American Court of Human Rights has thus far rejected the *lex specialis* application of humanitarian law on jurisdictional grounds, but continues to refer to and consider humanitarian law provisions: Las Palmeras (Colombia), Preliminary Objections, Inter-Am CtHR (Ser. C) No. 67, para. 33 (2000); Bámaca Velásquez (Guatemala), Judgment, Inter-Am CtHR (Ser. C) No. 70, para. 209 (2000). The Commission continues to apply humanitarian law as *lex specialis*: see the letter from Juan E. Méndez, President of the Commission, to attorneys for those requesting provisional measures (13 Mar. 2002) (quoting letter notifying the US of the imposition of provisional measures), available at http://www.ccr-ny.org/v2/legal/september_11th/docs/3-13-02%20IACHRAdoptionofPrecautionaryMeasures.pdf. See also Zegveld, 'The Inter-American Commission on Human Rights and International Humanitarian Law: A Comment on the Tablada Case', 80 *IRRC* (1998) 505.

actually administer the force but also all the surrounding circumstances including such matters as the planning and control of the actions under examination.[35]

Most of what follows unpacks this passage and compares its implications to those of the humanitarian law of internal armed conflicts. The latter is discussed both as it is (*de lege lata*) and in the form to which it aspires (*de lege ferenda*).

Four comparisons are drawn. In Section 3A the ECtHR's application of a single set of rules to all uses of lethal force is contrasted with humanitarian law's multiple regimes. In Section 3B the requirement under the ECHR that any use of lethal force be 'absolutely necessary' is contrasted with humanitarian law's acceptance that states may choose to shoot rather than capture combatants, even when the latter would not be especially difficult or dangerous. Section 3C argues that, in effect, the ECtHR's jurisprudence extends the rules requiring military operations to be planned and conducted so as to minimize loss of life incidental to their objective from the humanitarian law of international conflicts to that of internal conflicts. Finally, Section 3D asks whether the ECHR invites the entangling of *jus in bello* and *jus ad bellum*. The differences between the human rights and humanitarian law regimes prove more subtle than the passage suggests. The differences are not a matter of degree – 'strict proportionality' versus 'proportionality' – but of normative architecture. Human rights law is not simply, or even necessarily, more humane, and humanitarian law is not inherently better suited to achieving military victories.

A Replacing Conflict Qualification with Unified Rules for the Use of Lethal Force

Discussing a battle between the Russian armed forces and more than one thousand armed insurgents, the ECtHR described the insurgents as manifesting 'active resistance to . . . law-enforcement bodies'[36] and criticized the armed forces for not showing 'the degree of caution expected from a law-enforcement body in a democratic society'.[37] Euphemism? Or paradigm shift? Regulating 'law enforcement operations' leads to a very different kind of law than regulating 'armed conflicts'. Under humanitarian law, the rules applicable in a given situation depend on the 'characterization' or 'qualification' of the conflict as a whole. In contrast, the rules espoused by the ECtHR have no 'triggers' or 'thresholds' but form a single body of law that covers everything from confrontations between rioters and police officers to pitched battles between rebel groups and national armies. Under humanitarian law, the rules apply to all parties to a conflict – government forces

[35] *McCann and Others v United Kingdom*, ECtHR, App No 18984/91, paras. 149–150 (27 Sept. 1995). The ECtHR has repeated this passage nearly verbatim in subsequent cases concerning armed conflicts: see *Ergi*, *supra* note 140, at para. 79; *Isayeva I*, *supra* note 1, at para. 169; *Isayeva II*, *supra* note 1, at para. 173.

[36] *Isayeva II*, *supra* note 1, at para. 180.

[37] *Ibid.*, at para. 191; see also *McCann*, *supra* note 35, at para. 212.

and dissident armed groups alike. Under human rights law, the rules apply only to the government.[38]

The ECtHR has analysed the conduct of hostilities in three conflicts — those between the UK and IRA, between Turkey and the PKK, and between Russia and the separatists in Chechnya. It has applied the same body of doctrine, grounded in Article 2 of the ECHR, to the use of lethal force in each of these conflicts. A small ambush in a relatively low-intensity conflict (*Ergi*), a major battle in a high-intensity conflict (*Isayeva II*), and a confrontation between a handful of plainclothes special forces officers and several IRA members (*McCann*) were all subjected to the same basic rules. This does not mean that the same conduct was permitted and prohibited in each situation. For example, one basic rule that has been derived by the ECtHR from Article 2 of the ECHR, and which is discussed further in Section 3B, is that the use of lethal force is prohibited unless, *inter alia*, capture would be too risky to bystanders or the forces involved. In form, the rule is invariant; in application, it varies according to the risks of a particular situation. The risk posed by attempting to capture a group of thousands of heavily armed insurgents holed up in a village is clearly different than that posed by attempting to capture three possibly armed terrorists walking on a sidewalk, and what the rule requires varies accordingly.

Rather than human rights law's single regime of flexible rules, humanitarian law has several different regimes of relatively rigid rules. Which set of rules governs a particular armed conflict depends on the conflict's characteristics. If it is a struggle for national liberation against 'alien occupation' or 'colonial domination', it is considered an 'international armed conflict' and thus falls under Protocol I and the Geneva Conventions of 1949.[39] If it is a high-intensity civil war in which the armed groups are 'under responsible command' and 'exercise such control over a part of [the state's] territory as to enable them to carry out sustained and concerted military operations', then it is governed by Protocol II.[40] If it is a civil war of lower intensity, then it is governed by Common Article 3.[41] If it consists only of riots or other internal disturbances

[38] As compared to humanitarian law, the relevance of human rights law to the behaviour of non-state armed groups is quite limited. However, groups that claim to govern a state or aspire soon to govern a state may be responsive to human rights law arguments even if they are not subject to the jurisdiction of any judicial or quasi-judicial human rights body: L. Zegveld, *Accountability of Armed Opposition Groups in International Law* (2002); Matas, 'Armed Opposition Groups', 24 *Manitoba LJ* (1997) 621.

[39] Protocol I, Art. 1(4).

[40] Protocol II, Art. 1(1).

[41] The text of Common Art. 3 refers to 'armed conflict not of an international character' without defining 'armed conflict' as such. Proposals to include a definition of armed conflict within Common Art 3 tended to provide criteria similar to those triggering Protocol II, but ultimately no definition was included: see *ICRC Commentary on Geneva I, supra* note 22, at 49–50. Today, it seems to be widely accepted in principle that Common Art. 3 will be triggered at a much lower threshold of violence, as attested to by Protocol II, Art. 1(2). The International Criminal Tribunal for the Former Yugoslavia has held that 'an armed conflict exists whenever there is a resort to armed force between States or protracted armed violence between governmental authorities and organized armed groups or between such groups within a State': *Tadic*, Case No. IT-94-1-AR72 (Appeals Chamber)(2 Oct. 1995), para. 70.

and strife, then it is not governed by humanitarian law at all,[42] although a number of proposals have been made for a new humanitarian law instrument to be adopted for that purpose.[43] Each of the conflicts analysed by the ECtHR would be governed by a different body of humanitarian law.

The Russian government has refused to recognize the existence of an armed conflict in Chechnya, characterizing the events there as terrorism and banditry.[44] *Isayeva I* and *Isayeva II* concern the siege of Grozny and its immediate aftermath.[45] Most of the insurgents who held Grozny apparently belonged to an organization styled 'the Chechen Republic of Ichkeria', which, somewhat paradoxically, characterized the situation as an internal armed conflict subject to Common Article 3 and Protocol II.[46] The facts amply support a Protocol II characterization. Journalistic accounts strongly suggest that the insurgents were 'under responsible command': while they held Grozny, the insurgents employed a centralized communication system,[47] and they retreated from Grozny through Katyr-Yurt *en masse* under military command and the ultimate leadership of President Aslan Maskhadov.[48] During the siege, the insurgents exercised sufficient territorial control to carry out sustained and concerted military operations: besides holding absolute control over Grozny,[49] they routinely attacked Russian outposts in groups of 15–20.[50]

42 Protocol II, Art. 1(2) states that the Protocol 'shall not apply to situations of internal disturbances and tensions, such as riots, isolated and sporadic acts of violence and other acts of a similar nature, *as not being armed conflicts*' (emphasis added).

43 T. Meron, *Human Rights in Internal Strife: Their International Protection* (1987).

44 Russia acceded to the Geneva Conventions of 1949 on 10 May 1954; Protocols I and II on 29 Sept. 1989. See http://www.icrc.org/ihl. In 2000 the Russian Minister of Justice informed the then UN High Commissioner for Human Rights, Mary Robinson, that Russia regards 'the events in Chechnya not as an armed conflict but as a counter-terrorist operation': 'The Russian Authorities Regard the Events in Chechnya not as an Armed Conflict but as a Counter-Terrorist Operation', *RIA Novosti*, 4 Apr. 2000. And in 2004 Russia succeeded in getting a report of the UN Secretary-General amended to state that Chechnya 'is not an armed conflict within the meaning of the Geneva Conventions' and to refer to 'Chechen illegal armed groups' rather than 'Chechen insurgency groups': Lederer, 'U.N. Seeks to Stop Use of Child Soldiers', *Associated Press*, 23 Apr. 2004. During the First Chechen War, in 1995, the Russian Constitutional Court indicated that the conflict was governed by Protocol II; however, inasmuch as the Court found that it lacked competence to apply Protocol II, the view of the executive is here more important than that of the judiciary. See Gaeta, 'The Armed Conflict in Chechnya before the Russian Constitutional Court', 7 *EJIL* (1996) 563.

45 *Isayeva I, supra* note 1, deals with civilians escaping the city during the siege. *Isayeva II, supra* note 1, deals with the Russian attack on an outlying village as insurgents retreated through it from Grozny. A thorough exploration of the attack on another such village can be found in A. Meier, *Chechnya: To the Heart of a Conflict* (2005).

46 'A Forgotten Conflict' (21 Mar. 2005), available at http://www.chechnya-mfa.info/print_press.php?func=detail&par=12765.

47 Thomas, 'Grozny 2000: Urban Combat Lessons Learned', *Military Review* (July-Aug. 2000); Bagrov, 'Chechen Rebels Put Up Tough Fight', *AP*, 25 Jan. 2000.

48 Thomas, *supra* note 47; Cockburn, 'Chechen Leader Pledges to Retake Grozny', *The Independent* (London), 8 Feb. 2000, Foreign News, 15; Alkhan-Kala, 'Russian Troops Advance as Chechens Flee Capital', *St Louis Post-Dispatch* (Missouri), 4 Feb. 2000, A5.

49 Thomas, *supra* note 47; Bagrov, 'Chechen Rebels Put Up Tough Fight', *AP*, 25 Jan. 2000.

50 Bagrov, 'Russians Encircle Chechen Rebels', *AP*, 27 Feb. 2000.

Even at its peak in the early 1990s, the conflict between Turkey's government and the Workers Party of Kurdistan (PKK) probably would not have qualified as a Protocol II conflict – even had Turkey acceded to Protocol II.[51] There is little question but that the highly centralized PKK was under 'responsible command'. It demonstrated the capacity to declare and hold ceasefires, and when its captured leader, Abdullah Öcalan, instructed his followers to end the insurgency and enter normal politics, this order was largely obeyed.[52] However, the PKK's territorial control was quite limited. It was never capable of holding towns, and its reliance on bases in Syria and northern Iraq suggest the limits of its control over even rural areas.[53] The numerous violent engagements between the Turkish military and the PKK[54] do indicate the existence of an armed conflict, but one subject only to Common Article 3. This characterization was not accepted by either party. Öcalan declared in 1995 that the PKK would adhere to Protocol I and the Geneva Conventions;[55] however, the legal effect of this declaration was undercut by the PKK's failure to formally accede to Protocol I following the procedures of Article 96,[56] and it is doubtful that Turkey was exercising 'colonial domination [or] alien occupation'. The Turkish government, on the other hand, denied the existence of an armed conflict, characterizing its operations instead as domestic counter-terrorism.[57]

The United Kingdom treated the events in Northern Ireland as terrorism to be met with law enforcement operations and, while receptive to its regulation as a state of emergency under the ECHR, denied that it was an armed conflict.[58] While the Irish Republican Army (IRA) at one point expressed the intention of acceding to Protocol I, it never did so. The IRA had insufficient territorial control to warrant the application

51 Turkey acceded to the Geneva Conventions of 1949 on 10 Feb. 1954; it has never acceded to Protocol I or II. See http://www.icrc.org/ihl.

52 Kinzer, 'Rebel Kurds Back Leader In Peace Offer To the Turks', *New York Times*, 3 June 1999, A7.

53 Kocher, 'The Decline of PKK and the Viability of a One-state Solution in Turkey', 4 *International Journal on Multicultural Societies* (2002) 5.

54 Cowell, 'Turks' War With Kurds Reaches a New Ferocity', *New York Times*, 18 Oct. 1993, A3.

55 Veuthey, 'Learning from History: Accession to the Conventions, Special Agreements, and Unilateral Declarations', 27 *Collegium* (2002) 139, at 144.

56 Protocol I, Art. 96(3) provides that a people engaged in a national liberation struggle 'may undertake to apply the Conventions and this Protocol in relation to that conflict by means of a unilateral declaration addressed to the depositary'.

57 Turns, *supra* note 23, at 133: 'The Turkish Foreign Ministry expressly denies the suggestion that the insurgency in south-eastern Turkey can be regarded as an armed conflict, however characterized, within the meaning of the Geneva Conventions, on the following grounds: (1) the PKK does not respect the rules of war; (2) the PKK's unilateral declaration of a "cease-fire" in Sept. 1999 has no effect on the organization's legal status; (3) the PKK does not control territory in the sense of being able to conduct sustained and concerted military operations and to implement humanitarian law; (4) the PKK's attacks occur all over Turkey and also in foreign States, thereby negating the concepts of civil war and armed conflict as such.' The first, second, and fourth points are irrelevant; the third point would go to the applicability of Protocol II were Turkey a party to that treaty.

58 See Meron, 'The Humanization of Humanitarian Law', 94 *AJIL* (2000) 239, at 272. The UK acceded to the Geneva Conventions of 1949 on 23 Sept.1957 and to Protocols I and II on 28 Jan. 1998 (but with a reservation undercutting Protocol I's application to national liberation movements). See http://www.icrc.org/ihl.

of Protocol II: while exercising considerable power in some neighbourhoods, it never succeeded in ousting the government's authority.[59] The guerrilla warfare between the IRA and government forces that continued at the time of the *McCann* case[60] points toward the application of Common Article 3. On the other hand, the IRA then numbered in the hundreds and the conflict remained of a relatively low intensity,[61] suggesting that the official position that Common Article 3 did not apply was at least tenable.

Russia, Turkey and the United Kingdom all denied that they faced internal armed conflicts and, consequently, all denied that international humanitarian law applied. At one level, this should not be surprising: states routinely reject the application of the humanitarian law instruments to violence within their borders. In situations that objectively constitute armed conflicts, the application of Common Article 3 is frequently rejected, the application of Protocol II has been accepted by only a handful of states, and the application of Protocol I to a conflict against a national liberation movement has never been acknowledged by the state involved.

States refuse to apply humanitarian law to internal armed conflicts for reasons that are more political than legal. Humanitarian law's substantive requirements are, after all, far less onerous in internal conflicts than in international conflicts. The problem is that to apply humanitarian law is to tacitly concede that there is another 'party' wielding power in the putatively sovereign state.[62] The political consequences of acknowledging that Common Article 3 applies include conceding the inability of the government to stop large-scale violence, facilitating rebel claims that they have the requisite international personality to carry on diplomacy and participate in 'peace conferences', and allowing rebels to insist that, pursuant to Common Article 3's injunction that '[t]he Parties to the conflict should further endeavour to bring into force, by means of special agreements, all or part of the other provisions of the present Convention', the rebels merit prisoner-of-war status and immunity from criminal prosecution. Conceding the applicability of Protocol II further entails acknowledging that a group other than the government exercises control over portions of the state's territory. Applying Protocol I to an internal conflict constitutes the government's admission that it is exercising alien occupation or colonial domination against the will of the people. States deciding whether to apply humanitarian law often find the

[59] See, e.g., Pogatchnik, 'Harsh Brand of Justice in Belfast: IRA Gun Squads Mete Out Punishment for "Anti-Social Behavior" ', *San Francisco Chronicle*, 5 Dec. 1990, A6.

[60] See, e.g., Lohr, 'I.R.A. Shifts Tactics, and the Results Are Deadly', *New York Times*, 23 Aug. 1988, A3.

[61] *Ibid.*

[62] While Common Art. 3 specifies that its application 'shall not affect the legal status of the Parties to the conflict' – see also Protocol II, Art. 3 (affirming the sovereignty of the state) – it does in fact carry both legal and political implications for the status of the rebels. As Abi-Saab notes, 'common article 3 does confer a certain *objective legal status* on "rebels" ': T. Meron, *Human Rights in Internal Strife: Their International Protection* (1987) 38 (quoting Abi-Saab, 'Wars of National Liberation and the Laws of War', 3 *Annals Int'l L Studies* (1972) 93, at 96, emphasis added). Meron points out that, while Common Art. 3 does not make rebels 'privileged combatants' and impede their prosecution under criminal law, 'the reluctance of States to acknowledge the applicability of Article 3 demonstrates the cogency of Abi-Saab's analysis'.

benefits of legal compliance outweighed by the political costs of these implied admissions of weakness.

While states should be encouraged to deal candidly with their internal conflicts, the ECtHR's jurisprudence on the conduct of hostilities is so interesting and important precisely because it has unfolded in the context of officially unacknowledged armed conflicts. The ECtHR's approach has the potential to induce greater compliance, because it applies the same rules to fights with common criminals, bandits, and terrorists as to fights with rebels, insurgents and liberation movements. To apply human rights law does not entail admitting that the situation is 'out of control' or even out of the ordinary.

B Recognizing the Right to Life of Civilians . . . and Combatants

The 'principle of distinction' is fundamental to humanitarian law, but its precise content varies according to the kind of conflict. In national liberation struggles – and international armed conflicts – the distinction is between 'civilians' and 'combatants'. Combatants have no right to life under humanitarian law. Every individual is classified as either a combatant or as a kind of protected person, such as a prisoner of war (a captured combatant) or a civilian. An individual's rights change when his classification changes. A civilian has the right not to be targeted for attack and the right to receive some protection from attack. If the civilian joins the armed forces, he *exchanges* the rights of a civilian for the rights of a combatant. A combatant has the right to take part in hostilities. On the one hand, this means that if he is captured a combatant may not be prosecuted as a murderer for killing enemy combatants; instead, he becomes a prisoner of war, held only until the end of active hostilities. On the other hand, as a combatant, the individual also loses any right not to be attacked. As W. Hays Parks notes, while surrender must be accepted and those who are *hors de combat* may not be executed, 'neither proscription precludes the attack of enemy combatants with the intent to kill rather than capture'.[63] Loosely, the combatant trades his right to life for the right to kill.

Neither Common Article 3 nor Protocol II recognizes the status of 'combatant'. This omission is due to the great reluctance of states to accept that domestic insurgents ever have any *right* to attack government forces.[64] Instead, states have generally

[63] Parks, 'Memorandum of Law: Executive Order 12333 and Assassination', *Army Lawyer*, Dec. 1989, 4, at 5.

[64] Solf, who was a member of the US delegation to the 1974–1977 Diplomatic Conference that produced Protocols I and II, has attempted to convey 'the concrete objections' that the delegations from 'newer third world states' had with extending international armed conflict concepts of 'combatant status' and 'distinction between combatants and civilians' to internal armed conflicts: Solf, 'Problems with the Application of Norms Governing Interstate Armed Conflict to Non-International Armed Conflict', 13 *Ga J Int'l & Comp L* (1983) 291. 'Do you really think', such a delegate asks, 'that we would concur in any treaty that would grant immunity from our treason laws to our domestic enemies, and by doing so grant them a license to attack the government's security personnel and property, subject only to honorable internment as prisoners of war for the duration of the conflict?': *ibid.*, at 292. In a state already 'plagued with ideological and ethnic rivalries, aided and abetted by external states', this would only 'encourage[] rebellion by reducing the personal risk of "the rebels" ': *ibid.* Under Common Art. 3 and Protocol II, it is absolutely

treated insurgents as criminals. A combatant who kills a soldier is guilty of nothing; an insurgent who kills a soldier is guilty of murder. Even with respect to targeting in combat, the principle of distinction has been moderately controversial. This is because states have feared that, for example, prohibiting attacks on civilians under international law lends 'an aura of legitimacy for acts of violence against the military personnel . . . of the *de jure* Government', despite the fact that such acts could still be criminalized under national law.[65] These concerns have not, however, prevented the principle of distinction from being incorporated into the humanitarian law of internal armed conflict.

In the humanitarian law of internal armed conflicts, the distinction is between 'civilians' and persons who are 'taking a direct part in hostilities'.[66] The latter may be targeted; the former may not. If Common Article 3 is understood to regulate only the treatment of persons who are within the power of party to the conflict, then its protection of '[p]ersons taking no active part in the hostilities' does not speak to the principle of distinction in the conduct of hostilities.[67] Nevertheless, the applicability of the principle of distinction to low-intensity internal conflicts is widely acknowledged.[68] The consensus that there is a principle of distinction in internal conflicts may be due partly to its ambiguity. While the conditions for receiving combatant status are relatively well defined in Protocol I and the Third Geneva Convention of 1949, debate continues over what it means to take a direct part in hostilities.[69] For purposes of comparison with the doctrine of the ECtHR, however, the important point is that taking a direct part in hostilities subjects an individual to armed attack even if he could be captured instead.

Even with respect to persons taking an active part in hostilities, the ECHR only permits the use of lethal force when capture is too risky.[70] For killing a person to be 'absolutely necessary' under Article 2(2) means that attempting to capture him would be too dangerous for the government officers involved or for other citizens. In *McCann*, the ECtHR found that the United Kingdom had violated the right to life of three members

permissible to treat an insurgent as a criminal: *ICRC Commentary on Geneva I*, *supra* note 22, at 39. By unabashedly treating rebels as criminals – who, like other criminals, have rights – the ECtHR's approach avoids implying that rebels have any status above – or below – that of other citizens.

65 Bothe, *supra* note 22, at 669. With respect to the principle of distinction in the conduct of hostilities, Solf's delegate says, 'My government knows that needlessly attacking *innocent* civilians tends to strengthen dissident movements and we will take strong measures against such misbehavior by our armed forces. But to prescribe an international norm prohibiting attacks against civilians and civilian objects implicitly suggests that it is permitted to attack security personnel and objects': Solf, *supra* note 64, at 292. These objections were overcome, but the attitudes remain. By affirming everyone's right to life, the ECtHR's approach avoids any implication that attacks on government forces are permitted.

66 Protocol II, Art. 13(3): 'Civilians shall enjoy the protection afforded by this Part [not to be an object of attack], unless and for such time as they take a direct part in hostilities'.

67 See *supra* note 22.

68 Kretzmer, 'Targeted Killing of Suspected Terrorists: Extra-Judicial Executions or Legitimate Means of Defence?', 16 *EJIL* (2005) 171, at 197–200.

69 *Ibid.*, at 189–201.

70 See also *ibid.*, at 177–183; Watkin, 'Controlling the Use of Force: A Role for Human Rights Norms in Contemporary Armed Conflicts', 98 *AJIL* (2004) 1, at 32–33.

of the IRA who were on a terrorist mission in Gibraltar. The ECtHR held that the decision of the soldiers to shoot the suspects when they made sudden movements complied with the ECHR, because the soldiers had been informed that at least one of the IRA members possessed a push-button remote control detonator that would set off a car bomb. Killing the suspects had appeared 'absolutely necessary in order to safeguard innocent lives'.[71] However, the plot had yet to reach that stage – no car bomb had been put in place – and the ECtHR held that the actions of the officials running the operation had breached the ECHR. Given the consequences of communicating to the soldiers that a car bomb had been deployed and that one of the IRA members had a push-button remote control detonator, 'the authorities were bound by their *obligation to respect the right to life of the suspects* to exercise the greatest care in evaluating the information at their disposal before transmitting it to the soldiers whose use of firearms automatically involved shooting to kill'.[72] By hastily – in the view of the ECtHR – jumping to the conclusion that a parked car contained a bomb, the officials had failed to exercise adequate care, thus violating the suspects' rights to life.

McCann dealt with an attempted arrest involving a small number of soldiers – acting essentially as plain-clothes police officers – and three terrorism suspects. In the higher-intensity engagements presented by the Chechen cases, the ECtHR *has* sometimes singled out the right to life of 'civilians'.[73] Does this imply that the existence of an armed conflict or presence in a combat zone triggers a categorically different body of doctrine? At this point, the ECtHR does not appear to be using the word 'civilian' as a term of art. Even in the Chechen cases, the ECtHR cited to *McCann* for the applicable law.[74] The case law is best interpreted as providing the same rule for battles as for arrests, and for civil wars as for riots. This does not mean that the intensity of conflict is legally immaterial. Resort to lethal force is more likely to be lawful if the insurgent is actively participating in battle, because then he poses an actual or imminent threat to others and capturing him would more likely unreasonably endanger government soldiers. But there is no *per se* rule that insurgents may be targeted with lethal force.[75]

71 *McCann, supra* note 35, at para. 200.

72 *Ibid.*, at para. 211 (emphasis added).

73 See *Ergi, supra* note 14, at para. 79 ('[state responsibility] may also be engaged where [agents of the state] fail to take all reasonable precautions in the choice of means and methods of a security operation mounted against an opposing group with a view to avoiding and, in any event, to minimising, incidental loss of civilian life.'); *Isayeva II, supra* note 1, at para. 183 (inquiring 'whether the operation was planned and conducted in such a way as to avoid or minimise, to the greatest extent possible, harm to civilians, as is required by Article 2 of the [ECHR].'); *Isayeva I, supra* note 1, at paras. 177, 199.

74 *Isayeva I, supra* note 1, at para. 171; *Isayeva II, supra* note 1, at para. 175; see also *Ergi, supra* note 14, at para. 79.

75 See also the position of the *amici* in *Isayeva I*: *Isayeva I, supra* note 1, at para. 167: 'The submission argued that the law of non-international armed conflicts as construed by international human rights law established a three-part test. First, armed attacks on mixed combatant/civilian targets were lawful only if there was no alternative to using force for obtaining a lawful objective. Second, if such use of force was absolutely necessary, the means or method of force employed could only cause the least amount of foreseeable physical and mental suffering. Armed forces should be used for the neutralization or deterrence

Does recognizing the right to life of insurgents endanger the lives of civilians? The debates over Protocol I and the principle of distinction in international armed conflicts have often focused on this very issue, but the arguments in those debates do not transfer well to the non-international context. In the law of international armed conflict, the principle of distinction is twinned with an incentive – immunity from prosecution – for persons taking part in hostilities to play the role of 'combatants' by, most notably, wearing uniforms. It unquestionably helps protect civilians when people who are legitimate military targets make themselves easy to identify. However, in the law of internal armed conflict, the principle of distinction is not accompanied by any incentive for persons taking part in hostilities to wear uniforms. The customary rules advanced in the ICRC study do not, in this respect, go any further than Protocol II and Common Article 3. The ECtHR's rule should not, then, make targeting mistakes more likely, but there is also a danger that the fact-specific nature of the ECtHR's rule will make it easier for states to justify the intentional targeting of people who are not playing a direct part in hostilities. Governments conducting counter-insurgency campaigns often target 'sympathizers' as well as insurgents. This is understood to violate the humanitarian law of internal armed conflict, but could it be rationalized in the ECtHR's framework? That danger and others like it inhere in the ECtHR's approach, but these can be overcome if the case law is developed with care. In the course of continuing to resolve cases arising out of armed conflicts, the ECtHR will presumably refine its balancing test and even derive some *per se* rules. There is the potential for the ECtHR to actually improve on the protection of civilians, as well as combatants, in internal conflicts. We should not, however, assume that the ECtHR will – or should – mimic the combatant–civilian distinction of the humanitarian law of international armed conflict.

C *Rigorous Scrutiny of Operational Planning and Proportionality in Attack*

While humanitarian law prohibits the intentional targeting of civilians in internal as well as international armed conflicts, the danger posed to civilians by attacks on military targets are adequately accounted for only in international conflicts. Protocol I prohibits attacks that 'strike military objectives and civilians or civilian objects without distinction' (indiscriminate attacks),[76] prohibits attacks that may be expected to lead to an excessive loss of civilian life in relation to the value of the military target

---

of hostile force, which could take place by surrender, arrest, withdrawal, or isolation of enemy combatants – not only by killing and wounding. This rule required that states make available non-lethal weapons technologies to their military personnel. Furthermore, the authorities should refrain from attacking until other non-lethal alternatives could be implemented. Third, if such means or method of using force did not achieve any of its lawful objectives, then force could be incrementally escalated to achieve them.'

[76] Protocol I, Art. 51(4) ('Indiscriminate attacks are prohibited. Indiscriminate attacks are: [list] and consequently, in each such case, are of a nature to strike military objectives and civilians or civilian objects without distinction.').

(proportionality),[77] and requires that attacks be planned and executed so as to minimize civilian casualties (precautionary measures).[78] The precautionary measures required are elaborated in some detail. At the planning stage, Protocol I requires 'all feasible precautions' in vetting targets[79] and choosing the means and methods of attack.[80] At the operational stage, Protocol I 'reasonable precautions' against civilian losses,[81] cancellation of attack if the planning assumptions prove faulty,[82] and advance warning to the civilian population if circumstances permit.[83]

Humanitarian law leaves the planning and execution of attacks essentially unregulated in internal conflicts. Protocol II provides only that '[t]he civilian population and individual civilians shall enjoy general protection against the dangers arising from military operations'.[84] It does not include any provisions on indiscriminate attacks, proportionality in attack, and precautionary measures. Unfortunately, these omissions were not inadvertent, nor was their scope primarily one of simplifying the text. A ban on indiscriminate attacks had been included in an early draft of Protocol II but was deleted. The Canadian delegation claimed that indiscriminate methods were both inevitable (on the rebel side) and necessary (on the government side).[85] With respect to precautionary measures and the principle of proportionality, the ICRC proposed a short provision and Finland proposed a provision based on that of Protocol I.[86] Both of these proposals were rejected.[87] Bothe, *et al.*, observe that this 'virtually invites' the argument that much conduct prohibited in international conflicts is permitted in internal conflicts.[88] To rescue the text, they argue that the 'principles of humanity' mentioned in the preamble include the principle of proportionality[89] and that the 'general protection' accorded the civilian population in Protocol II may be

[77] Protocol I, Art. 57(2)(a) ('[T]hose who plan or decide upon an attack shall: . . . refrain from deciding to launch any attack which may be expected to cause incidental loss of civilian life, injury to civilians, damage to civilian objects, or a combination thereof, which would be excessive in relation to the concrete and direct military advantage anticipated.').

[78] Protocol I, Art. 57(2)(a) ('[T]hose who plan or decide upon an attack shall: . . . take all feasible precautions in the choice of means and methods of attack with a view to avoiding, and in any event minimizing, incidental loss of civilian life, injury to civilians and damage to civilian objects.'); Protocol I, Art. 57(2)(c) ('[E]ffective advance warning shall be given of attacks which may affect the civilian population, unless circumstances do not permit.').

[79] Protocol I, Art. 57(2)(a)(i).

[80] Protocol I, Art. 57(2)(a)(ii).

[81] Protocol I, Art. 57(4).

[82] Protocol I, Art. 57(2)(b).

[83] Protocol I, Art. 57(2)(c).

[84] Protocol II, Art. 13(1).

[85] See Cassese, *supra* note 23, at 194–195; but see Bothe, *supra* note 22, at 677 ('It is certainly arguable that attacks against densely populated places which are not directed at military objectives, those which cannot be so directed, and the area bombardments prohibited by para. 5(a) of Art. 51 [of Protocol I] are inferentially included within the prohibition against making the civilian population the object of attack. Their deletion may be said to be part of the simplification of the text.').

[86] *Ibid.*, at 670.

[87] *Ibid.*, at 671.

[88] *Ibid.*

[89] *Ibid.*, at 677–678.

interpreted to proscribe some indiscriminate attacks,[90] but they conclude that there is no textual basis for requiring precautionary measures in attack.[91] The ICRC's commentary sounds a more optimistic note by construing Article 13 to codify in general terms customary law requiring the protection of civilians against attacks.[92] Of course, Protocol II's text itself reflects a lack of consensus regarding any customary law on the conduct of hostilities in internal conflicts, and the value of law that is not accepted as such by states is limited. The *travaux préparatoire* inflict a heavy burden on anyone arguing for strong customary protections for civilians against the incidental effects of hostilities.[93]

The ECtHR has developed a vigorous jurisprudence on the planning and execution of military operations in internal conflicts. Here the rules it has promulgated largely track those that humanitarian law provides for international conflicts. While the ECtHR refers to 'strict proportionality' rather than 'proportionality', the most significant difference lies in the protection accorded non-civilians rather than in the calculus of proportionality itself. Similarly, while the idea of an 'indiscriminate attack' loses some of its precision when even persons taking part in hostilities are not categorically subject to attack, the ECtHR shares humanitarian law's attention to careful targeting and the avoidance of incidental losses.

The ECtHR's approach to precautionary measures in attacks is grounded in Article 2 read in conjunction with Article 1.[94] While Article 2 defines the right to life and specifies the legitimate grounds for its deprivation, Article 1 provides that states 'shall *secure* to everyone within their jurisdiction the rights and freedoms defined [in the ECHR]'. This affirmative obligation of states to protect the lives of their residents extends to the planning and execution of military operations. This textual foundation has given the ECtHR a broad mandate to scrutinize military practices.

90 *Ibid.*, at 677.

91 *Ibid.*, at 670–671, 677 (arguing that because Protocol II, Art. 13(1) tracks the language of Protocol I, Art. 51(1) except to exclude the clause specifying that the rules given 'are additional to other applicable rules of international law', it is difficult to argue that precautionary measures or proportionality are implicit in the phrase 'general protection'); but see *ICRC Commentary on Additional Protocols*, *supra* note 22, at 1450–1451 ('The question may well be asked whether the reference to international law was intentionally omitted in order to suggest that customary law is deemed not to apply to situations of non-international armed conflict. It would seem that this is not the case. The discussions in Conference do not indicate that any doubt was cast on the applicability of customary law. The reference to other rules of international law was probably omitted because it was not considered necessary, given that the only rule explicitly laid down for non-international armed conflicts is common Article 3 of the 1949 Conventions, which does not contain provisions relating to the protection of the civilian population as such.').

92 *Ibid.*, at 1448–1450.

93 Protocol II's unusual drafting history does, however, leave at least some room for disagreement regarding the state of customary law even as of 1977. As negotiations came to a close, a text elaborated in private, mainly by the Canadian and Pakistani delegations, supplanted the text negotiated in committee and was adopted without extensive discussion or modification: Eide, 'The New Humanitarian Law in Non-International Armed Conflict', in A. Cassese (ed), *The New Humanitarian Law of Armed Conflict* (1979), at 277, 277–278. The resulting record casts less light on the legal views of each state than would otherwise be the case.

94 *Ergi*, *supra* note 14, at para. 79.

The ECtHR's case law on proportionality, indiscriminate attacks, and precautionary measures is highly fact-specific.

- In *Isayeva I*, the ECtHR found that the use of 12 missiles with impact radii exceeding 300 metres was disproportionate to the destruction of two insurgent vehicles, given that they – assuming they existed at all – were part of a civilian convoy.[95] In *Isayeva II*, it found the use of 'free-falling high-explosion aviation bombs... with a damage radius exceeding 1,000 metres' on targets within a village to be disproportionate.[96]
- In *Isayeva I*, the ECtHR indicated that operations should be conducted pursuant to planning that includes 'assessment of the perceived threats and constraints' and of the available weapons and tactics.[97] The large convoy of civilians was present because a 'humanitarian corridor' had been arranged, apparently by the Russian government, to allow people to leave Grozny.[98] Moreover, Russian soldiers were manning the roadblock that controlled the administrative border through which safe passage was being assured.[99] The ECtHR noted the failure of any organ of the Russian government to communicate this 'safe passage' to persons planning military operations in the area.[100] The ECtHR also noted the absence of 'forward air controllers' to evaluate the pilots' targeting choices.[101] These factors led the ECtHR to conclude that civilians had been put 'at a very high risk of being perceived as suitable targets by the military pilots'.[102]
- In *Ergi*, the ECtHR found that Turkey had failed to secure the right to life because its forces had organized an ambush 'without the distance between the village and the ambush being known'[103] and with the Turkish forces positioned such that 'the villagers had been placed at considerable risk of being caught in the cross-fire between security forces and... PKK terrorists'.[104] The ECtHR noted that '[e]ven if it might be assumed that the security forces would have responded with due care for the civilian population in returning fire against terrorists caught in the approaches to the village, it could not be assumed that the terrorists would have responded with such restraint'.[105]
- The ECtHR found a similar violation in *Isayeva II*, where the Russian military had devised a ruse by which to entice rebels to leave Grozny through what they were led to believe would be a 'safe passage'.[106] Given that the route of the corridor

95 *Isayeva I, supra* note 1, at paras. 195–197.
96 *Isayeva II, supra* note 1, at para. 190.
97 *Isayeva I, supra* note 1, at para. 175.
98 *Ibid.*, at para. 183.
99 *Ibid.*, at para. 187.
100 *Ibid.*, at para. 186.
101 *Ibid.*, at para. 188.
102 *Ibid.*, at para. 189.
103 *Ergi, supra* note 14, at para. 80.
104 *Ibid.*, at para. 80.
105 *Ibid.*, at para. 80.
106 *Isayeva II, supra* note 1, at paras. 13, 185, 187.

opened to the rebels, the military should have expected a large number of rebels to enter the village of Katyr-Yurt and should have foreseen the danger this posed to the village's residents.[107] Despite this knowledge, there was 'no evidence that at the planning stage of the operation any serious calculations were made about the evacuation of civilians, such as ensuring that they were informed of the attack beforehand, how long such an evacuation would take, what routes evacuees were supposed to take, what kind of precautions were in place to ensure safety, what steps were to be taken to assist the vulnerable and infirm etc.'.[108] The ECtHR found the absence of any attempt to consider the risks the plan posed to civilians a violation of Article 2.

As the ECtHR's jurisprudence in this area begins to crystallize into more definite rules, it has the potential to drive military reform and improvement at an institutional level.

D *Beyond Military Necessity? Evaluating Tactics in Light of the Permitted Aims of Law Enforcement in a Democratic Society*

The ECtHR's approach to the proportionality of attacks is generally quite similar to that of humanitarian law – *de lege ferenda* if not always *de lege lata* – but there are points in which the two regimes are in tension. With respect to the principle of distinction, this tension has already ripened into contradiction. With respect to humanitarian law's axiomatic separation of the *jus in bello* from the *jus ad bellum* – of humanitarian law from the law on going to war – the tension thus far remains latent.

Two steps in the ECtHR's analysis of an attack's proportionality may be distinguished. First, the means must be proportionate to the ends. Second, the ends must be justified by the collective defence of society and its laws. These steps are derived directly from Article 2(2) of the ECHR, which requires the use of potentially lethal force to be '[First] no more than absolutely necessary [Second] in defence of any person from unlawful violence [or to make an arrest or quell a riot or insurrection].' In other words, unless the force employed is 'strictly proportionate *to the achievement of the permitted aims*', an attack violates the right to life.[109]

This two-step analysis is most fully displayed in *Isayeva II*, in which Russia defended its bombardment of a town under Article 2(2)(a) of the ECHR. The Court agreed that '[t]he presence of a very large group of armed fighters in Katyr-Yurt, and

[107] *Ibid.*, at para. 187.

[108] *Ibid.*, at para. 189.

[109] *McKerr v United Kingdom*, ECtHR, App No 28883/95, 4 May 2001, para. 22 (emphasis added); see also *Isayeva II*, *supra* note 1, at para. 181 ('Accepting that the use of force may have been justified in the present case, it goes without saying that a balance must be achieved between the aim pursued and the means employed to achieve it. The Court will now consider whether the actions in the present case were no more than absolutely necessary for achieving the declared purpose.'); *Güleç*, *supra* note 13, at para. 16 ('The Court, like the Commission, accepts that the use of force may be justified in the present case under paragraph 2 (c) of Article 2, but it goes without saying that a balance must be struck between the aim pursued and the means employed to achieve it.').

their active resistance to the law enforcement bodies . . . may have justified use of lethal force by the agents of the state'.[110] The Court found a violation of the right to life, however, in part because the operation's planning was inconsistent with its putative Article 2(2)(a) justification: 'Even when faced with a situation where, as the Government submits, the population of the village had been held hostage by a large group of well-equipped and well-trained fighters, the primary aim of the operation should be to protect lives from unlawful violence.'[111] The operation's design prioritized killing the insurgents over protecting the town's residents, evincing an aim that was inconsistent with the justification pleaded by Russia.

The humanitarian law analysis includes only the first step of the human rights law analysis. Protocol I applies the principle of 'military necessity', requiring that acts of war be 'useful and proportionate to the victory being sought'.[112] This principle is invoked, for example, in the Protocol I rule that attacks 'shall be limited to military objectives [which are] objects . . . whose total or partial destruction, capture or neutralization . . . *offers a definite military advantage*'.[113] It is invoked again in the rule that attacks on military objectives are prohibited when they 'may be expected to cause incidental loss of civilian life which would be *excessive in relation to the concrete and direct military advantage anticipated*'.[114] To assess the magnitude of the military advantage that an attack will confer requires reference to the strategic aims of the attacking party, but humanitarian law is agnostic regarding the legality of the aims themselves.[115] While 'aims' are relevant to its application, humanitarian law has no concept of 'permitted aims' precisely because it has no concept of illegitimate aims. To take the second step of the ECtHR's analysis would be to trespass on the *jus ad bellum*.

Does the ECtHR's inquiry into whether attacks are proportionate to a 'permitted aim' threaten to erode the separation of the *jus in bello* from the *jus ad bellum*? With respect to international conflicts, the *jus ad bellum* is identified mainly with the United Nations Charter. Whether there is really any such body of law as the '*jus ad bellum* of internal conflict' may be doubted. Nevertheless, concepts of self-determination, the right of rebellion, secession, constitutional succession, etc., play an analogous role. The danger of conflating issues like these with humanitarian law is that the ends will be used to justify the means. The permitted aims enumerated in Article 2(2) may be too limited and banal for the ECtHR's approach to go beyond the analysis in *Isayeva II*, which was indistinguishable in its result from an analysis of indiscriminate attacks

110 *Isayeva II, supra* note 1, at para. 180.

111 *Ibid.*, at para. 191.

112 M. Walzer, *Just and Unjust Wars: A Moral Argument with Historical Illustrations* (3rd edn., 2000), at 132–133.

113 Protocol I, Art. 52(2) (emphasis added).

114 Protocol I, Art. 51(5)(b) (emphasis added).

115 See Eide, 'The Laws of War and Human Rights – Differences and Convergences', in C. Swinarski (ed.), *Studies and Essays on International Humanitarian Law and Red Cross Principles in Honour of Jean Pictet* (1984), at 675, 681: 'It is beyond the laws of war to determine whether it is necessary, or legitimate, for a State to bend another's will, or to conquer. Thus, the question of what is necessary is left completely to each State concerned. Their own, subjective discretion in determining what is necessary, is a key factor in this law.'

and precautionary measures. However, the potential for the doctrine's further development is worth exploring.

Eide has persuasively identified the idea of limitation necessary in a democratic society as the human rights law correlate of the humanitarian law concept of military necessity.[116] All of the principal human rights instruments – and, more generally, the *jus commune* of the human rights regime – allow the enjoyment of individual rights to be limited only in the general interest of society. This principle originates in the Universal Declaration of Human Rights, which declared that the free exercise of rights may be limited only to meet 'the just requirements of morality, public order and the general welfare in a democratic society'.[117] With shifts of emphasis and wording, the idea that state interests must meet stringent requirements when they limit or endanger human rights has been incorporated into the limitation clauses and derogation regimes of subsequent human rights conventions. The effect is to permit only the general interest of society, rather than the interests of the state *per se*, to weigh against the individual's unfettered enjoyment of his or her rights, including the right to life.

The permitted aims clause, Article 2(2) of the ECHR, should be understood in light of the limitation clauses used in other human rights instruments and in other provisions of the ECHR. This approach is suggested by the ECtHR's conclusion that 'the use of the term "absolutely necessary" in Article 2(2) indicates that a stricter and more compelling test of necessity must be employed from that normally applicable when determining whether State action is "necessary in a democratic society" under paragraph 2 [the limitation clause] of Articles 8 to 11 of the Convention'.[118] Articles 8 (privacy), 9 (religion), 10 (expression), and 11 (assembly) all contain a generally-worded limitation clause similar to that provided for the right to privacy:

> There shall be no interference by a public authority with the exercise of this right except such as is in accordance with the law and is necessary in a democratic society in the interests of national security, public safety or the economic well-being of the country, for the prevention of disorder or crime, for the protection of health or morals, or for the protection of the rights and freedoms of others.

In the midst of a civil war, insurrection, or terrorist campaign, it would be very tempting for a state to justify summary executions and lax rules of engagement as 'necessary in a democratic society in the interests of national security, public safety, [or] for the prevention of disorder and crime'. Given the singular importance of the right to life, the drafters of the ECHR apparently elected to cabin states' powers of appreciation with respect to the social interests justifying deprivations of life by providing an exhaustive list.

This may not, however, push the limitation clause origin of Article 2(2) from the ECtHR's view. Situations in which it might be tempting to construe Article 2(2) in light of the interests of a democratic society, more broadly construed, are easy to

[116] *Ibid.*, at 681–682.

[117] Universal Declaration of Human Rights, Art. 29(2).

[118] *McCann*, *supra* note 35, at para. 149.

imagine.[119] If a state were to plead that an attack was taken 'for the purpose of quelling a riot or insurrection', the ECtHR could inquire as to whether the 'insurrection' was an attempt to restore constitutional government. If a state were to plead that force was used 'in order to effect a lawful arrest', the ECtHR could inquire as to the democratic provenance of the 'law' underpinning the arrest. Given the wide variety of events that might be termed internal conflict and the broad subject matter regulated by the ECHR, this kind of analysis cannot be rejected in absolute terms, but its drawbacks are similar to those of mixing *jus ad bellum* with *jus in bello*.

4 Conclusion

The case law of the ECtHR on Chechnya and, in retrospect, on southeastern Turkey and Northern Ireland is likely to be received by specialists in humanitarian law with some disquiet. The ECtHR's disregard for the principle of distinction, its attention to military aims as well as methods, and its failure to distinguish between riots and full-blown civil wars may all appear as grave errors or amateur blunders. But the ECtHR has taken a new approach, and one that shows great promise. It is providing rules for the conduct of hostilities where, as it applies to internal armed conflicts, humanitarian law that is accepted as legally binding is inadequate and seldom obeyed. Moreover, with rules that treat armed conflicts as law enforcement operations against terrorists, the ECtHR has begun to develop an approach that may prove both more protective of victims and more politically viable than that of humanitarian law.

[119] See also Haßenpflug, 'Comment' (on paper by Heintze), 45 *German YIL* (2002) 78, at 80–81: 'The proportionality test as enshrined in many IHL provisions . . . seeks to maintain a careful balance between standards of humanitarian law and objectives of military necessity, whereas the proportionality test to be applied in human rights cases envisages restrictions of individual rights for the necessary safeguard of public interests. The concept of public interest may in some situations prove to be broader than that of military necessity, e.g., the use of certain weapons may fail the proportionality test of Article 35 Additional Protocol I but still meet the proportionality requirement of Article 2 para. 2 lit. c ECHR. On the other hand, situations are thinkable where the military necessity would justify the infringement of humanitarian standards although the public interest justifying the violation of those standards is rather low. Additionally, it could be argued that in armed conflict situations where the right to life has been violated (Article 2 para. 2 lit. c ECHR), the IHL proportionality test should prevail because of the "lex specialis" character of IHL. At least, it should be taken into consideration that the proportionality tests as applied in human rights and IHL are based on different criteria (i.e., notions of public interest and military necessity).'

[18]

'GENTLEMEN AT HOME, HOODLUMS ELSEWHERE'? THE EXTRA-TERRITORIAL EXERCISE OF POWER BY BRITISH FORCES IN IRAQ AND THE EUROPEAN CONVENTION ON HUMAN RIGHTS

FRANCESCO MESSINEO

HOW far do obligations to respect human rights travel? Do British troops using military force outside Europe need to comply with the European Convention on Human Rights? And if so, do these obligations persist even when British troops are using force alongside non-European countries during military operations authorized by the United Nations? Two ground-breaking judgments by the Grand Chamber of the European Court of Human Rights addressed these questions in July 2011: *Al-Skeini v United Kingdom* (Application no. 55721/07) (2011) 53 E.H.R.R. 18 and *Al-Jedda v United Kingdom* (Application no. 27021/08) (2011) 53 E.H.R.R. 23. The applicants in *Al-Skeini* were relatives of Iraqi citizens killed by British soldiers during the post-2003 occupation of Iraq: three were shot at by British soldiers, one died during a cross-fire between British soldiers and "insurgents", another was allegedly drowned in a river after being arrested, and the sixth died of torture while in detention. They claimed that the UK had breached its obligation to carry out an independent investigation on their relatives' death under Article 2 ECHR. The applicant in *Al-Jedda* was detained by British forces in Basrah for unspecified "imperative reasons of security" between October 2004 and December 2007. He was not charged with any crime, and he claimed a violation of his Article 5 ECHR right not to be arbitrarily imprisoned.

Did any of these events constitute an internationally wrongful act? To answer this question affirmatively, the ECtHR needed to establish two things: first, that the acts or omissions considered had indeed been carried out by the UK; second, that such conduct was in breach of the obligations owed by the UK under the ECHR.

The first question was one of attribution of conduct. Its solution should have been straightforward. British troops are State "organs" under Article 4 of the International Law Commission's Articles on the Responsibility of States for Internationally Wrongful Acts of 2001, UN Doc. A/RES/56/83 (ARSIWA). All British soldiers' on-duty acts or omissions are thus attributable to the United Kingdom, even if they act *ultra vires*. If a British soldier shoots, detains or tortures someone, the United Kingdom is also deemed to be shooting, detaining or torturing someone. The point is so obvious that it was taken for granted in all domestic stages of the proceedings in *Al-Skeini* (see *R. (Al-Skeini) v Secretary of State for Defence* [2007] UKHL 26, [2008] 1 A.C. 153). Indeed, the question only arose when the *Al-Jedda* case reached the House of Lords (*R. (Al-Jedda) v Secretary of State for Defence* [2007] UKHL 58, [2008] 1 A.C. 332) because the British government sought to rely on the notorious ECtHR Grand Chamber admissibility decision in *Behrami and Saramati v France, Germany and Norway* (Application number 71412/01 and 78166/01) (2007) 45 E.H.R.R. SE10. In *Behrami*, the ECtHR had found that it had no jurisdiction *ratione personae* to adjudicate upon the conduct of European soldiers belonging to K-FOR – the Kosovo peace enforcement operation authorized by UNSCR 1244 (1999) – because K-FOR's conduct should be attributed exclusively to the UN by virtue of the "ultimate authority and control" of the UN Security Council over the operation. The British Government claimed that the same reasoning would apply to British soldiers acting as members of the Multinational Force in Iraq (MNF-I), an operation authorized by UNSCR 1511 (2003). Therefore, the ECtHR would lack jurisdiction *ratione personae* in *Al-Jedda* too: the conduct of British soldiers would be attributed exclusively to the UN, not the UK. However, most legal commentators and the UN Secretariat strongly criticised *Behrami* because the "ultimate authority and control" test was wrong and led to absurd results. Attributing K-FOR (or MNF-I) conduct exclusively to the UN ran counter to the over sixty years of UN practice accepting responsibility only for UN-run peacekeeping, not for UN-authorized (but member-states-run) peace enforcement (see UN Doc. A/64/10, 67). When the question was decided upon by the House of Lords, the late Lord Bingham's majority opinion succeeded in setting *Behrami* aside by (unpersuasively) distinguishing it on the facts rather than openly criticizing it. In July 2011, the ECtHR in *Al-Jedda* was grateful for this rhetorical accomplishment and happily endorsed it, by concluding that whatever the correct test of "control", the UN in fact exercised no meaningful control over the MNF-I, so the detention of Al-Jedda was indeed only attributable to the UK (*Al-Jedda*, at [84]). Likewise, when the British Government tried to advance the same *Behrami* argument in *Al-Skeini*, the ECtHR declared that it was estopped from doing so (*Al-Skeini*, at [97]–[100]). In sum, in both *Al-Jedda* and *Al-Skeini* the ECtHR found that the conduct under consideration was attributable to the United Kingdom.

This led to the second question: what was the territorial and hierarchical scope of ECHR obligations? Could Articles 2 and 5 ECHR apply in Iraq? And, as to *Al-Jedda*, did Article 5 ECHR continue to apply even if the MNF-I was authorized by the UN Security Council to intern people? Let us address the question of extra-territoriality first. How far do ECHR obligations travel? Article 1 ECHR defines the scope of Convention obligations by affirming that "the High Contracting Parties shall secure to *everyone within their jurisdiction* the rights and freedoms" of the Convention (including Articles 2 and 5). According to Judge Bonello's concurring opinion in *Al-Skeini*, the case law on Article 1 had so far "enshrined everything and the opposite of everything". Indeed, *Al-Skeini* is a landmark judgment because it sought to clarify the Court's approach on extra-territoriality previously expounded upon in *Banković v Belgium* (Application no. 52207/99) (2007) 44 E.H.R.R. SE5 and many other cases conflicting therewith. In the Court's view, the term "jurisdiction" must be interpreted as a "primarily territorial" concept. States are generally presumed to exercise jurisdiction "throughout [their] territory", while extra-territorial exercises of power or authority are "exceptional" (*Al-Skeini*, at [131]). Among such exceptions, the Court first identified two uncontroversial cases: the acts of diplomatic and consular agents and the acts of foreign State organs invited by a host State to exercise some of its public powers (at [134]–[135]). The Court then moved on to consider two more complex strands of extra-territorial exercises of jurisdiction: control over persons and control over foreign territory. First, whenever there is an "exercise of physical power and control over [a] person" (at [136]), i.e. "control and authority" over him or her, a State is under an obligation to respect all those ECHR rights "that are relevant to the situation of that individual" (*Al-Skeini*, at [137], explicitly overruling *Banković*, at [75]). Second, whenever a State exercises "effective control" over foreign territory "as a consequence of lawful or unlawful military action", it is bound by the "obligation to secure, in such an area, the rights and freedoms set out in the Convention" irrespective of whether such control is "exercised directly, through the Contracting state's own armed forces, or through a subordinate local administration" *Al-Skeini*, at [138]; see also *Loizidou v Turkey* (Application no. 15318/89) (1997) 23 E.H.R.R. 513, at [52]. In sum, and contrary to some interpretations of *Banković*, ECHR obligations *do* travel outside the "legal space" of Europe (*Al-Skeini*, at [141]–[142]). Applying these principles to the facts in *Al-Skeini*, the ECtHR found that a "jurisdictional link" under Article 1 ECHR existed between the six victims and the UK, because of the "authority and control" exercised over them (at [149]–[150]). This was basically the end of the matter: the Court then found that the UK had violated some of the obligations arising from Article 2 ECHR with respect to five of the six applicants (at [168]–[177]).

In *Al-Jedda*, the question of jurisdiction was similarly resolved on the basis of such personal "authority and control" (*Al-Jedda*, at [85]), but a further complicating element arose. The Security Council had authorized the MNF-I to operate in Iraq and detain people for imperative reasons of security. According to the British Government, this was an "obligation" to detain, not a discretionary power, and as such it displaced Article 5 ECHR by virtue of Articles 103 and 25 of the UN Charter, which establish the hierarchic superiority of Charter obligations (and Security Council resolutions) over other rules of international law (*Al-Jedda*, at [87]–[92]). However, according to the ECtHR, and contrary to what the majority of the House of Lords had held in 2007, there was no such conflict of norms: internment was indeed one of the available options, but "in the absence of clear provision to the contrary, the presumption must be that the Security Council intended states within the [MNF-I] to contribute towards the maintenance of security in Iraq while complying with their obligations under international human rights law" (at [105]). These obligations included Article 5 ECHR, which the UK had thus violated.

In his concurring opinion in *Al-Skeini*, Judge Bonello stigmatized the British Government's approach to extra-territorial human rights obligations: "In substance the United Kingdom is arguing, sadly, I believe, that it ratified the Convention with the deliberate intent of regulating the conduct of its armed forces according to latitude: gentlemen at home, hoodlums elsewhere." In July 2011, the contrary message from Strasbourg appeared clear: European States must comply with their human rights obligations everywhere they actually exercise power over persons or territory.

[19]

Assessing the Impact of the ECHR on National Legal Systems

Helen Keller and Alec Stone Sweet

This book tracks and evaluates the impact of the ECHR on eighteen national legal orders. As the reports demonstrate, national systems are increasingly porous to the influence of the ECHR and the case law of its Court. European States no longer embody insular, autonomous, self-defined legal systems, if ever they did. At the constitutional level, the systems of every country surveyed in this volume have experienced significant structural change. To take two dramatic examples, judges once prohibited from engaging in judicial review of statute now do so routinely, with reference to European rights; and the dualist features of many legal systems have given way to a sophisticated monism, when it comes to the Convention. Further, how the different branches of Government interact with one another has been changed, radically in some States, to the extent that the regime's evolution has served to undermine traditional separation of powers dogmas. This volume also examines the impact of the Strasbourg Court's jurisprudence on legislators, executives, and judges. Thousands of discreet legal and policy outcomes have been altered as a result of the influence of Convention rights. It is also clear that legal education and scholarship are also changing in ways that will help to consolidate the regime's domestic presence and legitimacy.

The impact of the ECHR is organized by a complex social process that we call *reception*.[1] The reports identify a diverse range of *mechanisms* of reception: those stable procedures that national officials construct and use in order to adapt the national legal order to the ECHR, as it develops over time. The reports show that no State can fully insulate itself from the regime's reach and influence. The best States can do is to build and maintain their own system of strong national rights protection, and to develop effective mechanisms of reception. The reports also show that the intensity of the influence of the jurisprudence of the Strasbourg Court on domestic systems varies widely across States; and the Court's impact has increased over time, in some legal domains more than others, within each

[1] Reception is defined and discussed at length in chapter 1 of this book, Section B.1.

State. Although we will venture a number of general propositions about reception processes in this chapter, such statements should be carefully considered in light of the cross-national and temporal diversity documented and evaluated in the national reports.

A. Reception as Process

Viewed as a cross-national phenomenon, the reception of the ECHR into domestic law and practice can neither be easily summarized, nor neatly encapsulated in overarching generalizations. Indeed, it would seem to be all but impossible to model the Court's impact on States in any scientifically parsimonious way. The reasons are clear enough. First, although we can identify the most important factors that condition, or impinge upon, the reception process, not all of these factors are present or carry the same weight across all jurisdictions. When they are present, they typically combine in diverse ways to affect States differently. Second, the ECHR regime – considered sociologically as a continuous set of interactions between individual applicants, national political and legal systems, and the Strasbourg Court – does not possess a stable social structure. Convention rights, for example, have evolved in ways that have been virtually impossible to predict, not least by national officials, from any specific *ex ante* moment. States have been put under pressure to adapt national law to the Convention, but the manner in which they have done so has never been fixed or pre-determined. Instead, the relationship between the ECHR and domestic legal orders has been an open-ended product of interactive social processes. In this section, the most important factors that have impinged upon the reception process will be briefly analyzed.

1. Accession and Expansion

Most of the original Contracting States (including the UK, Ireland, Italy, Germany, Belgium, the Netherlands, Austria, Norway and Sweden in this volume) seriously underestimated the degree to which the ECHR would impact on their domestic legal systems. The *travaux préparatoires* provide scant evidence to the contrary. When the ECHR entered into force, none of these States (with the important exception of Ireland) possessed effective systems of rights protection in the contemporary sense. The fact that the Convention system developed during the same period that many national systems of rights protection emerged and matured no doubt facilitated the Court's efforts to build its own political legitimacy. During this formative period, the absence of sceptical States, such as France (which was hostile to supranational authority in general) was a benefit: the Court avoided the kinds of head-on collisions that had paralyzed the EC in the 60's and 70's. Both France and Switzerland (which was concerned with issues of neutrality) ratified relatively late, after several failed tries. For other late-ratifying States (Spain, Slovakia, Poland and the re-ratification of Greece after military rule), the political legitimacy of the Convention and the Court was largely taken for granted. Each of these States were then in the throes of democratization, following long years under repressive, authoritarian rule. Democracy and rights protection were strongly equated. It is testimony to the remarkable success of the ECHR that, for these States, the Convention offered an established, "external", and therefore legitimate, normative standard for the transition to constitutional democracy. Accession would serve, in effect, to certify their membership in the circle of good European countries, otherwise dominated by Western Europe. These States ratified the Convention enthusiastically without lodging important reservations. Russia, Turkey, and Ukraine also took advantage of certification, if perhaps with less commitment to common values.

The use of declarations and reservations also varies across States and time. Some countries (France, Switzerland) once made extensive use of reservations and declarations; others have done so sparingly or not at all (Poland). Some States (Turkey) did not seriously examine the compatibility of national law with the ECHR at the time of ratification. Over time, the use of reservations and declarations has declined, and many States have allowed those they had lodged to elapse. One reason for this is that, as it has evolved, the Convention system has gained the trust and goodwill of its members; consider the ratification of Protocol no. 11, and the broad incorporation of the ECHR into national law. At the same time, most countries have made considerable progress in redressing incompatibilities between the domestic law and the Convention guarantees. Reservations made it possible for many States to join the regime, given quite specific concerns, but these concerns have been relaxed with changing circumstances and socialization into the regime. For its part, the ECtHR interprets reservations narrowly, to ensure that the Contracting Parties do not undermine the Convention's purposes.[2]

The Council of Europe, too, has played an important role in developing Convention rights. It is a well-established practice of international law for States to amend treaties to which they belong through supplementary instruments, like protocols. Since 1952, the Council of Europe has adopted fourteen Protocols to the ECHR. Most importantly, Protocol no. 11 reformed the institutional structure, and made obligatory State acceptance of the individual complaint procedure and of the Court's compulsory jurisdiction. Today, acceptance of Protocol no. 11 is a pre-condition for the ratification of the ECHR.[3] In hindsight, we observe that the ratification of Protocols nos 2, 3, 5 and 8 proved to be relatively unproblematic, and all Contracting States would eventually ratify them. It is important, therefore, to recognize that the Contracting States have themselves fully participated in expanding the Court's competences, as well as the ECHR's rights

[2] *Belilos v. Switzerland* (appl. no. 10328/83), Judgement (Plenary), 29 April 1988, Series A, Vol. 132. See *in extenso* Thurnherr, this volume, Section A.2.b.

[3] Protocol no. 9 has been repealed as from 1 November 1998, the date of entry into force of Protocol no. 11. Since then, Protocol no. 10 has lost its purpose.

catalogue, including rights to peaceful enjoyment of property, to education, and to free elections by secret ballot, and the abolition of the death penalty.

These reforms have fundamentally altered the ECHR, compared with the *status quo ex ante* of the 50's. When the ECHR was negotiated, States failed to agree on the inclusion of the right to property. In the end, Article 6(1) ECHR provided for procedural guarantees for "civil rights", which the Court interpreted broadly, but not so broadly as to include property rights *per se*. The right to property in Protocol no. 1,[4] which entered into force in 1954, proved to be tremendously important in the 90's, as statistics on the Court's activities demonstrate. In the post-Protocol no. 11 era, the Court has been flooded with applications claiming violations of the right to property, which have in turn revealed systemic failures (Greece, Italy, and Turkey's administration of Cyprus). Having received literally hundreds of clone applications from Poland, the Court began to experiment with pilot judgments to help States resolve such failures.[5]

On the other hand, Protocol no. 4 generated reluctance, with Greece, Turkey, Italy, Spain, Switzerland and the United Kingdom, among the States covered in this book, withholding ratification. That Protocol established human rights in a politically sensitive domain (*inter alia* prohibiting expulsion of nationals and collective expulsion of aliens); States that ratified it may now regret having done so.[6] In another once sensitive area – the death penalty – the Council of Europe has had more success, banning its use through Protocols no. 6 and no. 13. Russia alone has not ratified these Protocols. Russia is also the only country that blocks the entry into force of Protocol no. 14, which the Court, the Council of Europe, and we see as an essential reform, given the regime's present burdens.[7] Russia's general reluctance to enhance the discretionary authority of the Court should be understood in the context of the conflict-filled relationship it has with both the ECHR and the Council of Europe.[8]

Finally, the fate of Protocol no. 12 (non-discrimination) remains an open question. Among the States covered in our survey, only the Netherlands, Spain,[9] and Ukraine have ratified it. The others resist transitioning from the limited non-discrimination guarantee provided by the Convention (Article 14 ECHR) to a general, stand-alone right on various grounds. Failure to ratify Protocol no. 12 (only 16 of the 46 States have done so[10]) may well be a blessing in disguise for the

[4] Among the countries in our survey, Switzerland is now the only country that has not yet ratified. See, this volume, Thurnherr, Section A.2.a.

[5] *Broniowski v. Poland* (appl. no. 31443/96), Judgement (Grand Chamber), 22 June 2004, Reports 2004-V, 1. See Krzyżanowska-Mierzewska, this volume, Section H.1.a.

[6] For the situation in Spain, see Candela Soriano, this volume, Section III.A.1.a.

[7] See also *infra* Section E.3.

[8] See Nußberger, this volume, Section A.1.a.

[9] Spain ratified Protocol no. 12 on 13 February 2008, after this book went into production.

[10] Information on ratification presented by the Council of Europe on its website: http://conventions.coe.int/Treaty/Commun/ChercheSig.asp?NT=177&CM=8&DF=3/2/2008&CL=ENG (Unless indicated otherwise, all websites were visited last at end of March 2008).

system. The Court is already overloaded; and non-discrimination claims would require it to intrude even more deeply into policy areas that are, by their very nature, politically controversial. It may be that some national Governments have reached a saturation point, feeling that the time is not ripe to develop new human rights standards, given the density of problems that have yet to be resolved.

2. European Integration and Reception

European integration – the evolution of the EU's legal system, in particular – has shaped reception in a number of crucial ways. First, the ECJ's commitment to the doctrines of the supremacy and direct effect of Community law provoked processes that, ultimately, transformed national law and practice. Supremacy required national courts to review the legality of statutes with respect to EC law, and to give primacy to EC norms in any conflict with national norms. For judges in many EU States, the reception of supremacy meant overcoming a host of constitutional orthodoxies, including the prohibition of judicial review of statute, the *lex posteriori derogat legi priori*, and separation of powers notions. These same structural issues arose anew under the Convention. Second, as the EU's legal system evolved, national judges were required to develop new remedies, including in the sensitive area of State liability for damages to individuals. Further, as the ECJ embraced the proportionality principle in one area after another (e.g., the four freedoms, sex discrimination, administrative and competition law), it pressured national courts to replace deference postures (under manifest error, reasonableness and *ultra vires* doctrines, for example) with much more intrusive forms of judicial review (requirements of necessity and proper balancing of rights against the public good). Although one can describe these innovations in formal doctrinal language, it is indisputable that these changes served to enhance judicial authority – across the Community – relative to political authority. Further, national courts also learned to interact closely, and to enter into a dialogue with a supranational court, giving to, as well as receiving from, the ECJ. The ECJ's move to embrace rights as general principles of EU law, citing the ECHR and the constitutional traditions of the Member States as sources, is a striking example. Thus, in a myriad ways, European legal integration under the Treaty of Rome helped to prepare national legal systems for the kinds of major challenges that were to come under the ECHR.

With the disintegration of the Soviet bloc, the EU worked to reinforce the authority of the ECHR in a more direct way. In the 90's, the EU (whose Members also belonged to the Council of Europe) made ratifying the ECHR a prerequisite for EU membership,[11] which entailed a great deal of preparatory work in the human rights field for candidate countries in Central Europe.[12] In two States covered in this volume, Poland and Slovakia, the EU demanded specific reforms

[11] Pinelli (2004).

[12] In Greece and Turkey, the implementation of EU law and the accession process has served as a

(countering anti-corruption, enhancing judicial independence and efficiency, re-organizing the penitentiary system, etc.) to safeguard the rule of law and the effective guarantee of Convention's rights.

3. Mechanisms of Reception and Coordination

The national reports make it possible to evaluate mechanisms of reception in terms of their relative capacity to enhance the ECHR's status in domestic law. The ECHR can be said to be effective, domestically, to the extent that national officials recognize, enforce, and give full effect to Convention rights and the interpretive authority of the Court, in their decisions. The most important mechanisms operate at the constitutional level and are associated with the monist-dualist distinction and how States incorporate the ECHR. They serve to coordinate the national legal order, as a whole, on an ongoing basis, with the Convention. Other mechanisms operate in discrete institutional settings, including those procedures that require legislative and judicial officials to take account of the ECHR in their decision-making. A third set of practices – related to knowledge and its production – also impinge on the reception process and, arguably, ought to be considered to be informal mechanisms of coordination, in their own right.

a. Doctrinal Factors

A formal, doctrinal understanding of the reception process is an indispensable first step in any attempt to explain the impact of the ECHR on national legal systems. The reports focus on four interrelated questions. First, does a given constitutional order adopt a monist or dualist posture with respect to international treaty law? Second, what rank does the legal system assign to the Convention in the national hierarchy of norms? Third, are the Convention's guarantees directly binding on public authority, can they be pleaded before national courts, and can judges directly enforce them against conflicting national norms, including statute? And, fourth, have the answers to these questions changed over time, and through what procedures? The national reports address these questions, and they trace the impact of these formal elements on the decision-making of national officials.

The domestification of the ECHR constitutes the most important, overarching narrative of this volume. Convention rights are domesticated through their incorporation into national legal orders. As Polakiewicz has emphasized,[13] the ECHR does not require any specific mode of incorporation and, for many decades, some States refused to incorporate it. Until the 80's, for example, the French position was that the Convention had virtually no legal status in the internal order. In that State's view, a High Contracting Party, faced with a violation of the Conven-

more direct catalyst for changes in the domestic law than the reception of the ECHR, see Kaboğlu and Koutnatzis, this volume, Section D.3.

[13] Polakiewicz (2001), 31–33.

tion, entirely discharged its responsibilities merely by compensating the affected applicant. It incurred no obligation to change its internal law even when the Court had ruled that law to be in breach of the Convention. Today, every State covered by this book has incorporated the Convention, albeit in different ways, and no States argue in favour of the former French position.

Other things being equal, the ECHR is most effective where Convention rights, *de jure* and *de facto*: (1) bind all national officials in the exercise of public authority; (2) possess at least supra-legislative status (they occupy a rank superior to that of statutory law in the hierarchy of legal norms), and (3) can be pleaded directly by individuals before judges who may directly enforce, while disapplying conflicting norms. In such States, the Convention is not subject to the principle of *lex posteriori derogat legi priori*, but takes precedence over all conflicting infra-constitutional norms. From the point of view of the international lawyer, the status of these systems toward the ECHR can be characterized as strongly monist. Among West European States covered in this book, Austria, Belgium, the Netherlands, Spain, and Switzerland have reached this position, through different routes. Of course, the fact that national officials, including judges, are well positioned to enforce the ECHR does not mean that they will always choose to do so.

b. Incorporation and the Hierarchy of Norms

One of our core comparative findings is that formal distinctions between systemic monism and systemic dualism *ex ante* do not, in and of themselves, determine the status of the ECHR in national law *ex post*. What ultimately matters is if and how the Convention is incorporated. France, for example, is a monist country, under Article 55 of its Constitution. However, for decades, Article 55 was simply overridden by the prohibition of judicial review of statutes (a corollary of separation of powers).[14] Belgium is formally dualist, but that State's courts – on their own and without constitutional authorization – embraced a sophisticated monism with respect to the ECHR (and EU law).[15] As the national reports show, over the past three decades, the ECHR has had far more impact in Belgium than in France, precisely because Belgian judges chose to confer supra-legislative status on Convention rights and to directly apply them, while French judges declined to do so. The French position began to change only in the late 80's; today, the Convention overrides conflicting law, including statutes adopted later in time. Consequently, complex reception processes are now underway in France, and the gap between the Convention's *de jure* and *de facto* status is bound to narrow.

The Spanish and Dutch Constitutions are both monist but, again, it is the position of the courts that makes the difference. The Spanish Constitutional Court has consistently worked to enforce the ECHR as a quasi-constitutional body of law. The Tribunal will strike down any statutes that violate the Convention as un-

[14] For the reasons, see Lambert-Abdelgawad and Weber, this volume, Section B.1.a.

[15] De Wet, this volume, Section B.2.a.

constitutional; it interprets Spanish constitutional rights in light of the ECHR; and it has ordered the ordinary courts to abide by the Strasbourg Court's case law, as a matter of constitutional obligation. If the judiciary ignores the dictates of the Convention, individuals can use the *amparo* procedure to appeal the issue directly to the Constitutional Tribunal. In Spain, then, the capacity of the legal system to guarantee the effectiveness of the ECHR is virtually perfect. Indeed, by every measure, Spain is one of the great success stories of post-authoritarian, rights-based democratization, and the ECHR is an important part of that story. The Netherlands, arguably, is the world's most monist State. The Dutch Constitution provides for the supremacy of treaty law over the Constitution itself, but it does not provide for the judicial review of Statutes. The Supreme Court, however, has chosen to directly enforce the ECHR, in effect, incorporating it as a *de facto* Bill of Rights. In her report, Erika de Wet notes that, generally, the Dutch Court has thus far used its judicial review powers cautiously.[16] However, she also stresses that the relationship between the courts and the legislature is changing as a result, and that the Court is developing some of the features of a constitutional jurisdiction with respect to rights enforcement.

Norway and Sweden are formally dualist States, but each has moved to monist positions with respect to the Convention, embracing the effectiveness criteria listed above, at least formally. Austria blends both dualist and monist features, but it too has moved to a strong monist posture. The Austrian Constitution provides for a Constitutional Court and review, but it contains only a short list of rights in comparison with the Convention. The Constitutional Court's initial position, which the administrative and civil courts followed, was that the ECHR neither possessed supra-legislative status nor was directly enforceable in the domestic legal order. In 1964, the political parties revised the Constitution, to confer upon the Convention constitutional status and direct effect. Today, conflicts between the Austrian Constitution and the ECHR are governed by the *lex posteriori derogat legi priori* rule, an apparently unique situation. Norway and Sweden also possessed, at the time of ratification, a short list of basic rights, and judicial review was known but virtually never used. In the 90's, four decades later, both countries adopted comprehensive Bills of Rights modeled on the Convention. In Norway, the charter is entrenched, requiring two successive votes of Parliament, the second after an intervening election. The Charter overrides conflicting statutes. The Swedish Charter has only the rank of a statute, and Sweden maintains certain dualist orthodoxies, including the application of the *lex posteriori* rule to resolve conflicts between norms of statutory rank. However, the Constitution states that all Swedish laws shall be interpreted and applied in light of international treaties.

A State may be formally monist but nonetheless treat the Convention as alien, foreign law, leaving it without much force in the domestic order. Such has

[16] De Wet, this volume, Section B.1.b.bb.

been the case, for different reasons, in pre-Protocol no. 11 France, and – today – in Russia, Slovakia, Turkey (at least until 2004), and the Ukraine. In these latter States, a surface, systemic monism is belied by a lack of commitment to the ECHR among political officials, and by massive structural problems in the functioning of judicial institutions. In Poland, a nominally monist State, the Constitutional Court has worked hard to enhance the status of the Convention before the courts.

Finally, most dualist systems have incorporated the Convention either through statute or the decisions of Constitutional or Supreme Courts, the details and consequences of which vary widely. In the UK, under the 2000 Human Rights Act (HRA) litigants may plead Convention rights against any public authority, and courts may enforce the ECHR against all but conflicting Parliamentary statutes, while certain appellate judges have the authority to declare such statutes incompatible with Convention rights (but not to annul them). As Besson's report emphasizes, the HRA is in the process of transforming the UK's legal system, not least, because it carves out important exceptions to doctrines of parliamentary sovereignty.[17] For the first time, UK judges have jurisdiction over what is, in effect, a Bill of Rights. In Ireland, which incorporated the ECHR in 2003, Convention rights function only as a supplement to its own highly effective domestic Charter and system of rights protection. Parties may not plead the Convention in Irish courts against judges or the legislature, and the *lex posteriori* rule holds sway, but this situation has yet to expose Ireland to the scrutiny and censure of the Strasbourg Court in any systematic way.

In Germany and Italy, both dualist States with complete systems of domestic rights protection, the incorporation has proceeded through rulings of the constitutional courts. In Germany, the ECHR was initially treated according to dualist orthodoxy: treaty law occupied the same rank as statute (*lex posteriori* taking primacy in case of conflict). Gradually, however, the Federal Constitutional Court began to treat the ECHR as *lex specialis* and, in 2004, it threw its weight behind the ECHR. It now requires the judiciary to enforce Convention rights even against statutes passed later in time, an activity that can be monitored through the individual constitutional complaint. In Italy, the courts' attitude towards the Convention has been marked by longstanding reluctance to recognize the Convention's primacy over statutes. In this context, a 2007 ruling of the Italian Constitutional Court declaring the unconstitutionality of a statute found to contravene Article 1 of Protocol no. 1, may well be a landmark change.[18] It remains to be seen whether this new approach will be followed consistently by the Italian Constitutional Court and other high courts.

In summary, there is no necessary causal linkage between *ex ante* monism or dualism, on the one hand, and the reception of the ECHR on the other.

17 See Besson, this volume, Section III.B.1.b.

18 See Candela Soriano, this volume, Section III.B.2.b.

Put differently, the manner in which the ECHR is incorporated is an outcome of the reception process which will, in turn, impinge on reception *ex post*. The assumption that dualistic States have, *a priori*, an unfriendly attitude towards international law, and will, therefore, generate a relatively poorer rights record, is untenable. That point accepted, some States – including Ireland, Norway, Italy, Sweden, and the UK – have found it difficult to confer supra-legislative rank on the Convention, precisely because of their dualist natures, though there is a great deal of variation even among this small group.[19] Other dualist States (notably Belgium) have done so relatively quickly and easily. Dualistic countries tend to incorporate through statute, whereas monist States tend to do so through judicial decisions. Clearly, a monistic constitutional structure can provide the judiciary with more leeway in the reception process, as in the Netherlands, helping courts overcome certain obstacles when they are motivated to do so. Finally, in dualistic countries where a powerful Constitutional or Supreme Court defends national human rights, we observe reticence among judges to base their rulings on the Convention as an independent source of rights. This is the case with Germany, Italy, and Ireland. Paradoxically, perhaps, a pre-existing human rights judicial tradition in a particular country can sometimes hamper reception of the Convention or, at least, the jurisprudence of the ECtHR.

c. The Convention as a Shadow Constitution

Today, in Belgium, France, the Netherlands, Switzerland, and the UK, we can say that the ECHR constitutes a kind of surrogate, or shadow, Constitution. These are States that, while not possessing their own judicially enforceable Bills of Rights have incorporated the Convention in ways that make Convention rights directly effective, supra-legislative norms in the domestic system. In the Scandinavian countries in our survey, new Bills of Rights have been modeled on the ECHR, but the latter text tends to be more important than the former. This type of reception is deeply structural and is, or will be, momentous in its significance. In States where Constitutions provide both an entrenched Bill of Rights and an effective system of constitutional justice, the ECHR tends to function as a supplement to the Constitution. We find this situation in Germany, Ireland, Spain and, arguably, in some Central European States.

d. Legislative Coordination Mechanisms

As the ECHR has evolved, national officials have developed procedures designed to provide legislative authorities with information and counsel on the relevance of the ECHR to their agenda. In many States (including Austria, Belgium, France, Italy, the Netherlands, Slovakia, Spain, and Switzerland), one of the tasks of the Government's legal advisor is to provide an opinion on the conformity of pro-

[19] With regard to the differences between the UK and Ireland, see Besson, this volume, Recapitulative comparative table.

posed Bills with the Convention, or on reforms that ought to be undertaken in order to bring the national legal order into conformity. The Government is free to disregard this advice. In most States (an important exception is Russia), one or more Parliamentary Committees also routinely examine the conventionality of Bills. In some (including France, Greece, Ireland, and Italy), lawmakers are now advised by independent Human Rights Committees. In Poland and Spain, an Ombudsman may advise executive and legislative bodies, and she or he possesses the power to challenge laws before the Constitutional Court. In Scandinavia, *ex ante* review of a legislative Bill is undertaken by judges, but these decisions (of the Swedish Law Council and the Norwegian Supreme Court) are non-binding. By contrast, in Ukraine, a 2006 reform made *ex ante* Ministerial review of the conventionality of proposed legislation obligatory. If a Bill is found to be contrary to the ECtHR, it will be declared void.

Although the national reports identify and discuss these mechanisms, much more research would be needed to evaluate their effects on policy outcomes. Their impact on the overall reception process, we suspect, depends heavily on the general commitment of political officials to improving rights protection and compliance with the ECHR. Many Russian national officials regularly expressed scorn for the Court's judgements. In Turkey, the Chairman of the Human Rights Advisory Board was prosecuted in 2004 for authoring a report criticising the Government's lack of commitment to rights, and the Board was then dissolved. Some States have no such mechanisms *per se*, but we know that German legislators take very seriously their responsibility to assess the conventionality of Bills before them, both in the Cabinet and the Bundestag, whereas Russian lawmakers do not.

e. Judicial and Other *Ex Post* Mechanisms of Coordination

Judges play a special role in the reception process. Due to the requirement that local remedies be exhausted, it is normally the courts that have the last word on the compatibility of national law with the ECHR, prior to an applicant going to Strasbourg. In addition, the Convention establishes standards that govern the operation of national systems of justice (notably through Articles 5, 6, and 13 ECHR). Of all national officials, judges are the most systematically exposed to the direct supervision of the ECtHR. It is hardly surprising that, in many States, the courts have taken the lead in incorporating the Convention, and in strengthening other quasi-constitutional mechanisms of reception. Today, all national high courts have a powerful interest in closely monitoring the ECtHR's activities, and in staying one step ahead of the latter when it comes to developing standards of rights protection. Such may be easier said than done, of course.

The national reports provide a rich trove of detail on specific interactions between the ECtHR and national courts. At the risk of some over-generalization, three overlapping points deserve emphasis. First, in most States, the incorporation of the ECHR has enhanced the overall authority of the ordinary courts *vis-à-vis* all other non-judicial officials. As judges have consolidated their jurisdiction over the ECHR, they have increased their capacities to control policy outcomes; the move to proportionality review is a strong example.[20] In Europe today, judicial authority includes the competence to review the legal validity of all Government acts under the Convention. Second, the authority of national Constitutional Courts has been weakened: their final word (if not monopoly) on rights interpretation can no longer be presumed. It is to the credit of the constitutional courts on the continent (in Spain, Poland, Slovakia; and, more recently, in Germany and Italy) that they have chosen to require the judiciary – as a matter of constitutional duty – to enforce the ECHR and to follow the Strasbourg Court's jurisprudence. At the same time, all constitutional courts have taken pains to stress that it is the national Constitution that ultimately regulates the relationship between the domestic legal order and the Convention system. Third, rights protection in Europe is characterized by an important jurisdictional pluralism, an "open architecture"[21] whose tensions and contradictions will not be worked out easily, if at all. With the accession of the EU to the Convention, this architecture will become even more complex and its future development even less predictable.

The courts also manage the most important reception mechanisms following a finding of violation by the ECtHR, to the extent that they harmonize the substance of their jurisprudence to relevant judgments of the Court. Courts in most States do so routinely (though Russian, Ukrainian, and Turkish courts are exceptions). The national reports also identify a number of non-judicial *ex post* mechanisms of coordination. The fast-track procedure in the UK is a prominent example[22]; and it will be fascinating to monitor the Ukrainian experiment, just underway, to build a host of innovative mechanisms of reception, in order to improve its future record.[23] Some States have also adopted major legislative reforms in order to deal with failures of a systemic nature identified by the Court. Italian lawmakers, for instance, fashioned the *Azzolini* law with the hope of improving its capacity – notoriously infirm – to implement the Court's rulings.[24]

f. Informal Mechanisms: Knowledge and Practice

The state of knowledge about the ECHR and the Court's jurisprudence in national legal systems conditions the reception process in obvious ways. The more ignorant of the Convention are national officials, the less likely it is that they will be able to perform their duties properly. In all States, teaching and scholarly research about the ECHR and the Court's case law have steadily increased since the entry into force of Protocol no. 11 in 1998, but problems remain. Among

[20] See *infra* C.4
[21] Krisch (2008).
[22] See Besson, this volume, Section III.E.1.b.
[23] See Nußberger, this volume, Section E.2.a.
[24] See Candela Soriano, this volume, Section III.E.2.

lawyers and lower court judges in many States, knowledge of the Court's case law and access to translations of judgments involving applications from other States remains poor, a situation that weakens the judiciary's overall capacity to guarantee the ECHR's effectiveness.[25]

One negative finding concerning practice deserves comment. As the importance of the ECHR to domestic law increased, we expected networks of human rights litigators and Non Governmental Organizations (NGOs) to grow at both the national and transnational levels. We also expected that these networks would steadily develop capacity to influence the reception process. While human rights NGOs have at least some relevance in most States, none of the reports shows that they regularly exercise decisive influence on important outcomes.[26] Further, law firms seem to have little incentive to invest in the domain. Compared with litigating EU law in national courts, which typically has a heavy commercial content, the sums at stake in litigating the ECHR are relatively small. If a case does make it through the admissibility stage in Strasbourg, it will be subject to long delay and little hope of a large financial payout. Despite these initial findings, more systematic research on the organization and impact of human rights litigating in Europe is clearly needed.

B. The Court's Docket

In this section, we examine, from the point of view of the reception process, inputs into the ECHR legal system (applications) and the most important outputs (judgements of the Court and other decisions).

1. Applications to the ECtHR

The entry into force of Protocol no. 11 on November 1, 1998 removed any formal obstacle to access to the Court for individuals, beyond the requirement that petitioners exhaust available domestic remedies. In addition, the Court makes applying to it simple and virtually cost-free: the required forms and easy-to-follow instructions are posted online, and applicants do not need legal counsel, at least not initially. The data on Post-Protocol no. 11 applications are, therefore, a fairly direct measure of the social demand for rights protection under the Convention. Table 1 reports these data, broken down by State and per annum.

[25] See also the Committee of Ministers Recommendation Rec (2004)4 on the ECHR in universities and professional training, 12 May 2004.

[26] For a prominent exception concerning the Warsaw Helsinki Foundation of Human Rights, see Krzyżanowska-Mierzewska, this volume, Section J.1.g.

Table 1: Individual Applications to the ECtHR (November 1, 1998–December 31 2006)

	Received	Per Year	Per Cap.*	Admissible	Per Cap.**	Rank p/c*
Average per state	12,631	1,546	41.29	332.4 (4.7%)	1.64	
Spain	5,367	656.9	15.13	38 (1%)	0.108	2
Ireland	522	63.9	15.21	12 (2%)	0.357	4
Norway	603	73.8	16.04	17 (3%)	0.456	6
Germany	16,005	1,958	23.73	69 (0.4%)	0.101	1
Belgium	2,095	256.4	24.41	89 (4%)	1.038	11
UK	12.072	1,477.6	24.54	303 (3%)	0.616	9
Netherlands	3,641	445.6	27.33	57 (2%)	0.429	5
Greece	2,935	359.2	32.36	295 (10%)	3.252	17
Turkey	20,141	2,465.2	33.81	1,500 (7%)	2.518	15
Russia	48,791	5,972	41.93	353 (0.7%)	0.303	3
Switzerland	2,542	311.1	42.04	31 (1%)	0.513	8
France	23,582	2,886.4	47.39	590 (3%)	1.185	12
Sweden	3,590	439.4	48.82	37 (1%)	0.500	7
Ukraine	18,860	2,308.4	49.53	310 (2%)	0.813	10
Italy	24,141	2,954.8	50.42	1,617 (7%)	3.377	18
Austria	3,427	419.5	51.15	156 (5%)	2.329	14
Slovakia	3,823	467.9	86.64	133 (3%)	3.018	16
Poland	35,225	4,311.5	112.86	377 (1%)	1.206	13

* Calculated as the number of applications per State divided by population.

** Calculated as the number of admissible applications per State divided by population. Rank p/c refers to the ordinal ranking of States, from lowest to highest, on the basis of admissible applications generated, *per capita*.

The source for the raw data on applications is the annual *Survey of Activities*, the European Court of Human Rights, 1998–2006. The source for the population data is Eurostat (2006).

Applicants activate the ECHR's legal system in order to achieve outcomes – justice, a change in national law and practice, and so on – that have been denied to them in the domestic system. Although any given application may be unique in important respects, it is reasonable to assume that the aggregate data can tell us something of general significance about the relationship between the ECHR and national legal orders. Consider, for example, the following simple proposition, in effect, a "pathology hypothesis": the more a State violates the Convention rights of individuals, the more it will generate applications to Strasbourg. In this view of the regime, the ECHR functions to reveal problems in domestic orders which the Court helps States to resolve. The cross-national data will, therefore, chart the relative extent to which rights are protected in national legal orders or, much the same thing, the degree to which States are in non-compliance with the Convention. This view has much to recommend it, but it does not provide a complete picture, as the case studies demonstrate.

A second view, which may partly overlap with the first, emphasizes a different function. The ECHR will be important to the extent that it fills important gaps in national legal orders. In those States that do not possess a comprehensive, entrenched Bill of Rights, for example, the ECHR may be used to perform that role, as a shadow Bill of Rights. If and how it does so depends heavily on how the Convention is incorporated into the national legal order. In addition, a State's constitutional rights provisions may not accord precisely with the Convention, or national judges may give a narrower reading to a right than the Strasbourg Court, situations that will attract applicants to Strasbourg. In this account, the data will reflect, at least in part, gaps between domestic rights protection and the ECHR, as the latter evolves.

In contrast to the "pathology hypothesis", we would not assume, under the "gap-filling hypothesis", that levels of petitions only measure the extent of pathology. The numbers may also chart a healthy social demand for perfecting rights protection in States whose basic commitment to protecting rights is already relatively robust. In many contexts, national law is likely to be more ossified and path dependent than the more malleable Convention. In so far as it is, Strasbourg will attract applicants.

A third logic rests on a still more complex view of how individual applicants, national officials, and the Strasbourg Court interact with one another. This view takes seriously the capacity of the Court's case law to "feedback" on petitioners and national officials. Applications from each country tend to be clustered in specific areas, due to pathology (including systemic failures), national gaps in protection, or for other reasons. Nonetheless, the extent to which applications in these domains increase over time will be partly a function of how the Court constructs its jurisprudence. If the Court responds positively to the demand for the expansion in the scope and application of a specific right, it will tend to attract more applications in that area. A feedback loop is thereby constituted. Theoretically, the inverse might be true. It is possible that applications will decline or stop altogether, in a given domain, if a State successfully adapts its law to the relevant case law. However, such instances may be rare in important areas of litigation in which relatively large or coherent classes of applicants are concerned. Petitions may actually increase even after a State adequately complies with a specific ruling, as individuals seek to extend the scope of a new interpretation of rights.

At the heart of this dynamic lies a tension (which inheres in rights adjudication more generally) between two functions of the Court. The Court constructs Convention rights as general norms, which it treats as having prospective legal consequences for States. At the same time, its powers are largely limited to the rendering of individual (retrospective and particular) justice to victims of specific abuse. The Court may move to recognize a new right, or it may clarify the nature and scope of an existing right in an innovative way, while narrowly tailoring its ruling to the facts of the case. Indeed, this is a standard technique of judicial prudence in rights adjudication. Yet this type of ruling invites future applications, whose purpose will be to extend the coverage of the right even further, given remaining restrictions of national law. In this view, then, numbers of applications will also reflect the Court's own engagement in rights innovation, in the context of the social demand for such innovation (which varies cross-nationally).

Such propositions, and the data presented in Table 1, should be assessed in conjunction with the case studies presented in this volume. In the left-hand column, States are listed, lowest to highest, in terms of the average annual number of applications generated per one million inhabitants. States are ranked ordinally, in the right-hand column, with reference to the annual number of applications that are judged to be admissible by the Court, on a *per capita* basis. These numbers comprise a direct measure of the extent to which each State contributes to establishing the Court's agenda.

Not surprisingly, the States with the largest, most intractable, problems supply the Court with the bulk of its case load. The average number of applications judged admissible by the Court per year, among our 18 States, is 40.6. Only five States – Russia, Poland, France, Turkey, and Italy, in that order – exceed this average. States that have relatively high levels of admissible applications *per capita*[27] also include Greece and Slovakia which, like France, Italy, Russia and the Ukraine, have not succeeded in rectifying various structural failures, particularly as regards the functioning of the judiciary. In its 2006 Report,[28] the Court presented data on the 89,900 cases pending before it on 1 January 2007. Eight of the regime's forty-seven States generated 70% of all pending cases: Russia (21.5%), Romania (12.1%), Turkey (10%), Ukraine (7.6%), Poland (5.7%), France (4.8%), Germany (3.9%), and Italy (3.8%);[29] and applications from the first five comprise a majority of pending cases. For the foreseeable future, then, the Court will expend the bulk of its time and resources dealing with pathology: massive structural problems in sometimes intransigent States.

The countries that generate the least number of admissible petitions *per capita*[30] are Germany, Ireland, and Spain, States that possess the most effective domestic

[27] Austria (14th) is also ranked in the bottom third of admissible applications per year, *per capita*. In Austria, a small State with a legalistic culture, the ECHR possesses directly effective, constitutional status, but its courts remain hesitant to apply the Convention aggressively.

[28] European Court of Human Rights, Annual Report 2006, Registry of the European Court of Human Rights, Strasbourg, 2007.

[29] Ibid., p. 114.

[30] Third on that list is Russia (with by far the largest population). Arguably (see Nußberger's report, this volume, Section D.2.e.), Russia has the worst record of rights protection among ECHR Contracting States (even blocking the mailing of applications to the Court). Petitions from Russia are now flooding the Court.

systems of rights protection in Europe, as well as Norway, which possesses little experience with rights review. Although Belgium, Germany, Norway, Spain, and Switzerland, among other countries, interact with the ECHR less systematically or only sporadically than most of the States covered in this volume, the influence of the ECHR on their respective legal systems should not be underestimated. Considered on their own, each is experiencing significant legal change as a result of membership in the regime. As the respective national reports show, we find some of the dynamics of gap filling and feedback discussed above. The ECHR is an important structural backdrop, and the Court is a powerful agent, for steady progress in the direction of stronger rights protection.

2. *Findings of Violations*

Cross-national data on rulings of violation against States are relatively direct measures of the pressure that the ECHR regime places on national officials to adapt national legal orders to the Convention. Table 2 reports this information for the 18 States examined in this volume. States are listed, from lowest to highest, with respect to the number of violations declared annually by the Court, since 1 January 1998. States with the best records (under 6 violations found per year) include, in order, Ireland, Norway, Sweden, Spain, the Netherlands, Switzerland, Belgium, and Germany. At the bottom of the table, with more than 50 violations found per year, we find France, Turkey, and Italy. If we control for population – ranking countries with respect to the number of violations per annum and *per capita* – the order changes dramatically. Spain and Germany have far better records than all other States in our survey; whereas Slovakia, Italy, and Greece (in that order) have the worst records.

Table 2: Rulings on the Merits and Friendly Settlements: 1998-2006

	Judgements / Per Yr		Violations / Per Yr / Per Cap*			Non-Viol.	FS**
Average	260.7	29	246.3	27.4	0.926	14.9	40.2
Ireland	11	1.2	7	0.8	0.190 (6)	4	0
Norway	10	1.1	8	0.8	0.173 (4)	2	0
Sweden	21	2.3	14	1.6	0.177 (5)	7	13
Spain	34	3.8	26	2.9	0.066 (1)	8	1
Netherlands	52	5.8	39	4.3	0.263 (7)	13	8
Switzerland	60	6.7	41	4.6	0.621 (11)	29	2
Belgium	57	6.3	51	5.7	0.542 (9)	6	7
Germany	67	7.4	53	5.9	0.071 (2)	14	4
Slovakia	112	12.4	107	11.9	2.203 (16)	5	17
Austria	120	13.3	111	12.3	1.500 (14)	9	17

	Judgements	/ Per Yr	Violations	/ Per Yr	/ Per Cap*	Non-Viol.	FS**
UK	175	19.4	146	16.2	0.269 (8)	29	15
Russia	206	22.9	199	22.1	0.155 (3)	7	0
Ukraine	260	28.9	258	28.7	0.615 (10)	2	0
Greece	271	30.1	265	29.4	2.648 (18)	6	18
Poland	340	37.8	321	35.7	0.934 (13)	19	32
France	500	55.6	447	49.6	0.814 (12)	53	84
Turkey	1111	123.4	1080	120	1.646 (15)	31	182
Italy	1285	142.8	1260	140	2.389 (17)	25	324

* Ordinal rank in parentheses: Ireland is ranked sixth in terms of violations found per annum and per 1 million inhabitants; Spain is ranked first, and Greece last.

** Friendly settlements.

Source: Appendix, this volume.

Although our project was not designed to explain the cross-national variation depicted in Table 2, at least some of that variation is a product of the reception process. Those States with stable, robust systems of national rights protection (Germany, Ireland, Spain) are less vulnerable to censure from Strasbourg, all the more so once constitutional courts decided to require the judiciary to enforce both the Convention and the Court's case law directly and with fidelity, even against Parliamentary statutes. The majority of States in our survey, however, did not possess strong domestic systems of constitutional justice when they began to confront a more expansive ECHR and a more aggressive Court. These States can best reduce their exposure to censure in Strasbourg by developing effective reception mechanisms: stable rules and procedures that serve to coordinate the national legal order and the ECHR, on an ongoing basis. As the national reports demonstrate, developing such mechanisms is rarely an easy, simple, or smooth process, to the extent that it requires significant structural change. Such change will usually be slow and incremental, at least at first. New mechanisms are typically grafted onto older, institutionally embedded, ways of doing things, and some officials may seek to resist change. The evidence presented in this book, however, shows that national officials are being steadily socialized into a Europe whose Convention not only binds the State, as a matter of international law, but also binds domestic officials, as a matter of enforceable national law. Those States for which the Convention now functions as a *de facto* or shadow Constitution (Austria, Belgium, the Netherlands, Switzerland, the UK, and, increasingly, Norway, Sweden, and France) provide significant examples of these dynamics.

In some countries (including Italy, Poland), the commitment to protecting rights (of both Constitutional and Conventional origin) may be relatively high but insufficient, in itself, to counter certain structural deficiencies or specific legal pathologies. In other countries (Austria, France), long-standing judicial resistance to the Court and its case law has undoubtedly exposed the national system to more applications and findings of violations than would have been the case had courts been more open to enforcing the ECHR. Finally, there are States whose commitment to rights has not always been strong, though gradually improving (Greece, Slovakia, and perhaps Ukraine); and there are States whose attitude toward the ECHR and its Court has been generally hostile (Russia, Turkey, and until recently Ukraine). In any event, as the data in Table 1 show,[31] it is applications from States with the poorest records that dominate the Court's docket.

C. The Court's Impact on National Legal Systems

The Court protects Convention rights in multiple, highly differentiated ways. While we recognize that the Court operates under unified jurisdictional rules and procedures, the role it performs, in fact, varies across Convention norms and State contexts. The Court functions (1) as a kind of High Cassation Court when it comes to procedure, (2) as an international watchdog when it comes to grave human rights violations and massive breakdowns in rule of law, and (3) as an oracle of constitutional rights interpretation when it comes to fine-tuning the qualified rights of Articles 8–11 and 14 ECHR.

1. Procedural Law

The Court has played its most prominent role in the field of civil and criminal procedure, for three main reasons. First, simplifying what is in fact a fiercely complex topic, Civil Law States on the continent base their procedural law on the so-called accusatorial model, rather than on the adversarial practices of the Anglo-Saxon Common Law. The Court, in its case law on Articles 5 and 6 ECHR, has pointedly criticized civil law systems (including Austria, Belgium, France, Germany, Italy, the Netherlands, and Switzerland) for their general lack of impartiality, insufficient transparency during the pre-merits phase, and the accumulation of functions by the same officials during different phases of the trial, which are values commonly associated with the adversarial system. As John Jackson has cogently argued, the Court is actively constructing a new "participatory model" that lies between the classic forms.[32] In any event, its case law on procedure has not been easy to digest by many States. Since implementation typically requires fundamental changes in judicial organization,[33] the Court's impact in this domain has transformative potential. Second, as the Convention itself does not protect the right to peaceful enjoyment of property, the Court adopted

[31] See Stone Sweet and Keller, this volume, Section A.2.b.
[32] Jackson (2005).
[33] In particular for France, see Lambert Abdelgawad and Weber, this volume, Section D.1.c.

a broad interpretation of the procedural guarantee in Article 6(1) ECHR, thereby filling the gap. This move, and others like it, gave an extremely wide scope to civil rights that in turn generated strong resistance in countries like Austria, Switzerland and Germany.[34] Third, the Court's emphasis on procedural guarantees for defendants has to be seen as part of a more general trend toward juridification in international law. After a first phase in which substantive human rights have been developed, the international community is now focused on procedural aspects, and on how domestic institutions enforce rights. Since the 70's, scholars and judges have worked to upgrade procedural rights. It is today a mega-trend of international human rights law, and with it comes an associated expansion of judicial authority. Among international courts, the ECtHR has been the most important progenitor of this trend.[35] In response, several countries have made important legislative efforts to reduce the length of proceedings (Austria, France, Germany, Italy, Poland, Slovakia).[36] Nonetheless, it remains an open question whether these reforms will, in fact, give results that meet the high requirements formulated by the Court.[37]

For every State in our survey, the majority of violations of the ECHR found by the Court concern Article 6 ECHR guarantees. Most alarming are broad failures across Europe to ensure trial within a reasonable time period. As the duration of court proceedings before the ECtHR has stretched to indefensible lengths,[38] the Court's demand for timely proceedings in the Contracting States may lose

[34] See Thurnherr, this volume, Section E.1.a.

[35] Aromaa and Viljanen (2006).

[36] For the famous *Pinto* law see Candela Soriano, this volume, Section III.D.2.a.bb.

[37] *Scordino v. Italy* (appl. no. 36813/97), Judgment (Grand Chamber), 29 March 2006, (not yet reported), para. 183.

[38] For the time period since the date of allocation for pending Committee and Chamber cases in 2006 (all data were provided by the Court), http://www.echr.coe.int/NR/rdonlyres/C8F656AA-94C4-4A3F-A69D-0E4C6D510CA8/0/Analysis_of_statistics_2007.pdf.

Time period	Chamber cases	Committee cases
one year or less	8817 or 32%	27107 or 55%
one to two years	5530 or 20%	15717 or 32%
two to three years	4844 or 17%	5029 or 10%
three to four years	4064 or 15%	999 or 2%
tour to five years	2537 or 9%	
more than five years	1917 or 7%	
Total of cases	27709	48852

It is difficult to say what the final average time period per case is. The large figure of 55% of Committee cases are mainly due to inadmissibility decisions on the grounds of Article 35 ECHR. For nearly one third (31%) of the Chamber cases, the average length of proceedings is between three and more than five years.

much of its persuasive and authoritative force.[39] Lord Woolf has formulated it poignantly: "If 'justice delayed is justice denied', then a large proportion of the ECtHR's applicants – even those who are the victims of serous violations – are effectively denied the justice they seek."[40] In view of the notorious human rights records of countries like Russia, Ukraine and Turkey, the assumption that the Court no longer has the necessary capacity to deal with grave human rights situations due to its own excessive caseload and delays cannot be easily dismissed.

2. *Articles 2 and 3 ECHR*

Violations of the right to life (Article 2 ECHR) and the right to be free from torture, and inhuman and degrading treatment (Article 3 ECHR) are justifiably understood to be the most serious types of violations of the Convention. For every State in our survey, the Court has ruled on at least one claim based on either Article 2 or 3 ECHR. Ireland, Norway, and Slovakia have never been found in violation of either provision. To date, the Court has found a single violation of at least one of these provisions by Austria, German, Italy, Spain, and Switzerland, and it has found only two violations by Belgium, Italy, Poland, and Sweden. Without downplaying the seriousness of any of these cases, it is clear that compliance with Articles 2 and 3 ECHR is not a systemic problem in any of these States. Indeed, one might argue that part of the Court's case law in these areas is a type of fine-tuning (conditions of prisons, food and body searches in detention, and so on). Other countries have had a more difficult time complying with these norms. Greece (5 violations), the Netherlands (8), France (10) make up an intermediate group, followed by Ukraine (16) the UK (21), and Russia (34). Turkey, with 230 findings of violation and 91 friendly settlements, constitutes an unfortunate class by itself.

In its jurisprudence on Article 3 ECHR, the Court has exposed deplorable conditions in detention centres and prisons across Europe, including in France, Greece, Italy, Turkey, Russia, and Ukraine, situations otherwise tolerated by national politicians and judges. In response, the Council of Europe has committed itself to observing these situations closely, and in articulating higher standards for the regime as a whole. Another area of serious concern is the conduct of police authorities. In several countries, including Greece and Italy in our survey, the disproportionate number of immigrants of Roma origin among victims of violations of Articles 2 and 3 ECHR is disquieting.[41] Across Europe, the trend towards an increasingly multicultural composition of society has taken its toll on

[39] In a similar vein, see Paraskeva, 189 et seq.

[40] The Right Honourable the Lord Woolf, Review of the Working Methods of the European Court of Human Rights, December 2005, http://www.echr.coe.int/Eng/Press/2005/Dec/LORDWOOLFSREVIEWONWORKINGMETHODS.pdf, 8.

[41] See Kaboğlu and Koutnatzis, this volume, Section C.1.e. The Council of Europe sees discrimination against the Roma population as a general human rights problem in Europe, see http://www.coe.int/t/dg3/romatravellers/.

standards of protection. In this area, too, the Convention (and Protocol no. 4) will continue to play a vital role, backed up by Council of Europe initiatives.

In countries in which the most serious human rights violations are observed, such as Russia and Turkey, the Court confronts delicate political conflicts (as it had before with respect to the UK's problems in Northern Ireland). Turkey faces long-standing problems with the Greek population on Cyprus, with organized Kurdish separatists in the southeast provinces, and the still fragile control of the military by civilian authorities. In Russia, national officials have justified State-sponsored assassination, torture, and measures resulting in massive dislocation and suffering as necessary responses to rebellion in Chechnya. Moreover, Russia, Turkey, and Ukraine have yet to establish firm foundations for the development of stable pluralist democracy and rule of law. Often enough to matter a great deal, officials in these States express hostility to human rights as alien (West European) norms and values that are imposed upon them. Clearly, the Court is not well equipped to deal with deep-rooted problems such as these; indeed, they test the limits of the supervisory system in dramatic fashion. Moreover, these States (today the biggest drain on the Court's resources) routinely choose not to comply with the Court's rulings, thus undermining the credibility of the system as a whole. On the other hand, these cases reflect the Court's strong commitment to closing gaps in domestic accountability where officials refuse to investigate or choose to ignore credible claims of serious human violations.[42]

3. *Articles 5 and 6 ECHR: Anti-Terrorism*

In Western European countries, anti-terrorism measures have generated serious complaints, most prominently against the UK[43] and Spain.[44] The Court's role in this area has been pivotal. Experience has shown that, in many cases, fundamental rights were not sufficiently guaranteed in the absence of supranational control. National courts, being close to the events, proved unable to accord sufficient weight to fundamental rights when balanced against security imperatives. The Court's caseload in relation to Articles 5 and 6 ECHR will undoubtedly become more politically sensitive in the coming years, as new anti-terrorist measures are implemented in these countries and in France and Italy.[45]

4. *Article 8–11 and 14: Fine-Tuning and Proportionality*

The Strasbourg Court plays an important role as an oracle of rights in Europe to the extent that it helps to define the scope and content of substantive rights, in particular, those provided by Articles 8–11 and 14 ECHR. Because these rights overlap with national rights provisions, or fill a constitutional gap in those States

[42] Helfer (2008), 144.
[43] See Besson, this volume, Section III.C.1.b.
[44] See Candela Soriano, this volume, Section III.C.1.b.aa.
[45] See also Wildhaber (2007), 534 et seq.

without Bills of Rights, the Court's jurisprudence tends to take on a transnational-constitutional character. Through this jurisprudence, the Convention commands the obedience of national legal systems in the way that national constitutional rights do, without being constitutional in any formal sense. Further, the Court has adopted proportionality as the framework for adjudicating qualified rights under the Convention. Proportionality analysis, it can be argued, is an inherently constitutional mode of adjudication.[46] It is also deeply intrusive in that it gives judges the final word on how non-judicial policy makers have already balanced conflicting interests and values. In the ECHR context, the move to proportionality means that it is often the Strasbourg Court that will have the final say on how all national officials, including judges, balance competing interests.

The Court adopted proportionality as a means of ensuring that States would take qualified rights seriously, notwithstanding the principles of subsidiarity and margin of appreciation. The necessity phase of the procedure – a least restrictive means test – narrows the scope of permissible derogations to Convention rights to those measures that are necessary to achieve some important public interest. The Court's move not only empowered ordinary judges across Convention States by making them *de facto* constitutional judges, it also gave life to Articles 8–11 and 14 ECHR.

Of these provisions, Article 8 ECHR has generated the greatest number of applications and findings of violation. Here we find a combination of the gap-filling and feedback effects discussed above.[47] The Court has used proportionality analysis to fashion an innovative and expansive jurisprudence on privacy and family life in ever-expanding zones of protection. The Court developed the right to family reunification as a core value of Article 8 ECHR, and that guarantee now plays a major role in national immigration law throughout Europe. The Court also invoked Article 8 ECHR to exercise control over telephone tapping, now extended to other forms of private communication. Since national legal regimes lagged behind the technological capacity of the State to eavesdrop on its citizens, a flood of complaints gave the Court the opportunity to define the basic standard of rights protection. Perhaps most spectacularly, the Court used Article 8 ECHR to recognize the rights of transsexuals and homosexuals, furthering *inter alia* the decriminalization of homosexuality in Europe and, in conjunction with Article 14 ECHR, the construction of a general right to non-discrimination on grounds of gender and sexual preference.

The Court's caseload concerning Article 10 ECHR (freedom of expression) is also striking, given that these are not new, or boutique, rights. The older States of the Council of Europe, Austria (28 violations), France (11), the UK (9), and Switzerland (7) have generated the highest number of rulings of violation, with

[46] Stone Sweet (2008).

[47] See *supra* Section B.1.

the exception of Turkey (120). In its balancing of freedom of the press and other media against other values, the Strasbourg Court has tended to downplay rights to personality, personal honor, and other values that national systems may accord more weight. The Court appears anxious to accord a vital role to the press in democratic society, as a watchdog of Government, and therefore interprets the scope of possible restrictions narrowly (through the necessity phase of proportionality). In some States, including Russia, Ukraine and Turkey, the Government openly seeks to control the press and visual media for its own, often illiberal, purposes.[48] Given the Court's conception of Article 10 ECHR, it will confront very serious challenges from these and other States in the years to come.

The Court's role in protecting Articles 8–11 and 14 ECHR deserves to be evaluated in light of its overloaded caseload and in light of the principle of subsidiarity. In post-Protocol no. 11 Europe, the Court can expect to receive a steady stream of applications asking it, in effect, to supervise how national officials have balanced, that is, how they have made and applied law with reference to qualified rights. When the Court reviews how national officials have balanced competing interests under this part of the Convention, it rarely if ever guarantees the core essence of a right; neither does it represent an external control on allegations that a State grossly violates the most basic human rights, such as those under Articles 2 and 3 ECHR. It is instead fine-tuning outcomes that would normally be subject to national decision-making. Proportionality is an instrument *par excellence* of judicial fine-tuning, and of helping policy makers achieve the right balance between competing interests and values. There is, however, no fixed limit to its reach: on the contrary, proportionality fixes the boundaries of the margin of appreciation.

This situation poses a delicate problem for the Court. From the standpoint of reception, the Court often ends up with the last word on how rights are to be defined and applied in general measures, and used in concrete situations. From the point of view of its caseload, the Court's position means that it attracts an ever-increasing number of demands for fine-tuning. It is obvious that the ECtHR cannot abandon proportionality as a general approach to the qualified rights; to do so at this point would undermine the Convention and the national judiciary's capacities to enforce it. The Court could, however, take a more permissive posture with respect to how national judges enforce the proportionality principle. The Court could, for example, reiterate that Article 13 ECHR requires national judges to employ proportionality analysis; and it could announce that it will ensure, as a matter of procedure, that judges in fact have done so. At the same time, it could choose to limit the scope of its substantive review on the merits to how national judges have used proportionality analysis in important or extreme cases.

[48] See Nußberger, this volume, Section D.3.c. For the infamous Article 301 of the Turkish Criminal Code, see also Kaboğlu and Koutnatzis, this volume, Section D.2.b.

Such a move would reduce the exposure of the Court, enable it to counter charges of usurping national autonomy and the margin of appreciation, and help to forge a better partnership with national judges. It would also give the Court a tool to manage its docket more flexibly. On the downside, some would accuse the Court of abandoning its true mission, which consists in providing justice in individual cases. Skeptics of proportionality,[49] those who consider the framework to be inherently unprincipled, will renew their attacks, though this cost is already being paid.

D. The ECHR and National Legal Systems

In this Section, we focus on how the evolution of certain structural features of the Convention has complicated the reception process at the domestic level.

1. *Exhaustion of Local Remedies*

The principle of subsidiarity is a cornerstone, a *ratio conventionis*, of the European system of human rights protection. It is a duty of national officials to protect human rights within their domestic legal systems and to ensure respect for the rights safeguarded by the Convention. For its part, the ECtHR may accept an application only after domestic remedies have been exhausted, and within a period of six months from the date on which the final decision was taken (Article 35 ECHR). At first glance, these elements would seem to comprise a framework under which there would be a simple and smooth transition from the national system to the ECHR. Yet as the reports on Switzerland, Poland, Russia, and Italy, among others, make apparent, determining when national remedies have been exhausted may be a difficult and time-consuming task, introducing a great deal of inter-systemic friction. The three factors that matter most – the organization of the national judiciary, the competences of constitutional and high courts, and the effectiveness of ordinary (and the availability of extraordinary) remedies – vary considerably across Europe. When the Court does not pay close attention to these differences, it produces incoherent case law.[50]

The Court also uses Article 35 ECHR strategically, for its own purposes: a restrictive interpretation of the exhaustion of local remedies rule will tend to close the door to applicants, whereas a broader construction will invite more applications. In practice, the Court seems to choose between progressive and narrow approaches, for different reasons. If an applicant can show that there would be no point in exhausting national remedies, and if the problem at hand seems important, the Court may simply ignore the requirement and dismiss the

[49] Bruach (2005) is a good example.

[50] *Sürmeli v. Germany* (appl. no. 75529/01), Judgement (Grand Chamber), 8 June 2006 (not yet reported); *Szott-Medyńska and Others v. Poland* (appl. no. 47414/99), Decision, 9 October 2003 (not reported).

Government's preliminary objections.[51] In doing so, the Court sends a powerful signal about the inadequacy of national rights protection and invites reform. The Court needs to be able to restrict access in order to cope with its overloaded docket, although the result will be denial of justice in some individual cases.

Thus, despite its *prima facie* intelligibility, applying the local remedies rule on the ground is fraught with both factual and political complexity. As this book shows, the Court's decisions on admissibility deserve to be evaluated more closely, both by scholars and States. States should consider translating and distributing such decisions: they are crucial to a proper understanding of the interaction between the national and European systems. In some countries, scholarly commentary on Article 35 ECHR is both abundant and highly technical whereas, in others, the topic is just being noticed. What is clear is that, at the interface of the national legal order and the ECHR, there exists considerable friction, with all the attendant inefficiencies (of time, money, and intellectual effort) that add to the system's burdens.

2. *Convention Rights as Minimal Standards*

As discussed in the introduction, the traditional view was that the Convention established European standards of rights protection in the form of a floor below which national legal protection may not fall.[52] In this sense, it has always been recognized that the Convention harmonizes rights protection, at least at this minimal level. Moreover, under Article 53 ECHR, the Contracting States may develop higher human rights standards than those entrenched in the Convention. As with Article 35 ECHR, however, this view misses what is arguably most important. The Court treats the Convention as a "living instrument", and understands its role to be an autonomous and authoritative defender of human rights. Further, it has expressly committed itself to raising human rights standards whenever possible, although it typically does so only after asserting that it has identified an emerging consensus among the Contracting States. What this means for laggard States – that is, those national legal systems that are not part of the identification of a new consensus – is that the Convention does not constitute the minimal, but rather the sole, obligatory, higher standard. Thus, one important meta-narrative of reception is that States are always playing catch-up to the Court, if some more than others.

[51] See, e.g., *Isayeva, Yusipova, Bazaeva v. Russia* (appl. no. 57947/00; 57948/00; 57949/00), Judgement (First Section), 24 February 2005 (not yet reported); *Isayeva v. Russia*, (appl. no. 57950/00), Judgement (First Section), 24 February 2005, (not yet reported); *Akdivar v. Turkey* (appl. no. 21893/93), Judgement (Grand Chamber), 16 September 1996, Reports 1996-IV (no. 15), 1192, para. 67; *Bosphorus Hava Yollari Turizm Ve Ticares AS v. Ireland* (appl. no. 45036/98), Decision (Fourth Section), 13 September 2001 (not reported); *Selçuk and Asker v. Turkey* (appl. nos 23184/94;23185/94), Judgement (Chamber), 24 April 1998, Reports 1998-II (no. 71), 891, paras 70–71; *McCann and Others v. United Kingdom* (appl. no. 18984/91), 27 September 1995, Series A, Vol. 324, para. 161.

[52] See Stone Sweet and Keller, this volume, Section A.1.

The national reports show clearly that these dynamics have influenced how national judges perform their tasks, and how they justify new, more active, roles in rights protection. Some national courts directly equate national human rights with European standards. Switzerland is a telling example,[53] but one finds variation on this theme wherever the Convention functions as a surrogate Bill of Rights. It is striking that most national courts have learned to follow the Court, and to widen the scope and standards of the rights that they enforce, with few difficulties. There are, arguably, a few notable exceptions. Irish judges, for example, consider the ECHR to state minimal standards in comparison to the higher standards offered under their own Constitution; and German and Italian judges sometimes state, or imply, as much as well. In the UK, where the courts cannot adopt an interpretation of the Convention that goes beyond benchmark standards set by the ECtHR, the Convention constitutes both a minimal and a maximal standard.[54]

This dynamic puts strains on the reception process in obvious ways, not least, since a State in compliance at one moment in time will be put out of compliance at a later point, every time the Court decides to raise levels of protection. In practice, Convention rights do not comprise minimal common-denominator standards, but rather obligatory, relatively free-standing standards above which national judges have an interest in developing, if they are to stay in compliance with the regime.

3. *Beyond Individual Justice*

To read the Convention literally (Articles 41 and 46 ECHR, for example), one might conclude that the regime's legal system is primarily geared to delivering individual justice. States bear a duty to give just satisfaction to any individual who has been a victim of a violation of the ECHR for which they are responsible. However, as this book emphasizes, the Court is increasingly engaged in delivering what the former President of the Court, Luzius Wildhaber, Stephen Greer, and others characterize as "constitutional justice".[55] Today, the Court often behaves more as a general and prospective lawmaker than as a judge whose reach is primarily particular and retrospective. In the post-Protocol no. 11 world, the Court functions as an authoritative oracle of rights jurisprudence for all of Europe; it supervises State compliance with the ECHR, whose standards are continuously rising; and it seeks general solutions to general problems with which it is confronted. This shift in emphasis has enormous consequences for the reception processes. States are routinely required to reform their internal law and practices in response to findings of violation by the Court, not simply to provide compensation to individual victims. Still more problematic, the Court finds itself in the

[53] See Thurnherr, this volume, Sections B.2.b. and B.2.c.
[54] See Besson, this volume, Section III.D.1.b.
[55] Wildhaber (2000); Greer (2006), 173.

role of a socio-political engineer when it seeks to solve systemic failures through pilot judgements and other types of rulings.

4. Reopening of Proceedings

It is now commonplace for States to allow the reopening of national criminal proceedings after a non-favourable judgement from Strasbourg (the only exceptions in our survey are Italy, Spain and Ukraine).[56] This quiet revolution in European procedural law is remarkable for several reasons. Formally, the States enjoy a degree of discretion as to the means by which to comply with a final ECtHR judgement in accordance with Article 46 ECHR, while the Court refers to the well-known principle of *restitutio in integrum* in international law. Thus, whenever the Court concludes that there has been a breach of the Convention, the respondent State is under a legal obligation to put an end to the breach and make reparation for its consequences in such a way as to restore, as far as possible, the situation existing prior to the violation.[57] The idea that proceedings must be reopened after a negative judgement is not required.[58] On the contrary, the idea is clearly borrowed from a hierarchical system with a super-ordinate court structure.

This particular *acquis conventionnel* developed in a domain traditionally reserved to national law. The diversity and complexity of national legal systems concerning procedural requirements (juridical time limits and formal requirements) and jurisdictional competences (e.g., *ratione personae, rationae materiae* and *ratione temporis*) have thus far impeded international harmonization in this area (prominent exceptions like the Lugano Convention[59] and the Brussels Convention[60] only prove the rule). Although national procedural law remains a pretext for national parochialism, the ECHR has provoked a first important

[56] The coordination in civil law and administrative law has not substantially evolved. Only some countries provide –under certain conditions – for the reopening in civil or administrative proceedings (such as Germany, United Kingdom, Ireland, Norway, Russia, Sweden, Switzerland, Ukraine, Turkey).

[57] See, for instance, *Carbonara and Ventura v. Italy* (appl. no. 24638/1994), Judgement (Second Section), 30 May 2000, Reports 2000-VI, 91; *Scordino v. Italy* (No. 1) (appl. no. 36813/97), Judgement (First Section), 29 July 2004, (not reported).

[58] That said, the Committee of Ministers recognized the very importance of the possibility of reopening national proceedings for the reception of the ECHR and recommended the adoption of national remedies to the Member States. Recommendation Rec. (2000)2 of the Committee of Ministers to member States on the re-examination or reopening of certain cases at domestic level following judgements of the European Court of Human Rights, 19 January 2000.

[59] Lugano Convention of 16 September 1988 on jurisdiction and the enforcement of judgments in civil and commercial matters, 28 I.L.M. 620 (1989) (among EC and EFTA Member States).

[60] Brussels Convention on Jurisdiction and the Enforcement of Judgments in Civil and Commercial Matters, 27 September 1968, 8 I.L.M. 229, reprinted as amended in 29 I.L.M. 1413 (1990), substantially replaced by the Council Regulation (EC) No. 44/2001 of December 22, 2000, on jurisdiction and the recognition and enforcement of judgements in civil and commercial matters, OJ 2011 L 12/1 (among EC Member States).

breakthrough in this sensitive area of national procedure. No other international treaty has triggered the same effect.

5. *Inter-Judicial Cooperation and Conflict*

The ECHR does not provide a blueprint for an integrated system of human rights protection for Europe, nor does it establish how the Court should interact with its national counterparts. Nonetheless, the Convention, once incorporated into domestic law, has had an enormous impact on the judiciary across Europe. As discussed above, incorporation has enhanced judicial authority *vis-à-vis* the legislative and executive branches in virtually every country in our survey. The book also documents the extent to which the ECtHR's case law has provoked changes in how national courts operate and, in countries such as France, Italy, and the UK, it has been a decisive factor in judicial reorganization.[61]

The absence of formal rules governing inter-judicial interaction in the regime has meant that national courts have had to choose how to define their relationship with Strasbourg, and these choices have evolved over time. Some national courts initially opted for a strong emphasis on national autonomy, leading to a competitive relationship, or even conflict, open or disguised. Examples include the German Constitutional Court, the Austrian Constitutional Court in its early case-law, the Italian Constitutional Court, the Irish and British courts, and the French high courts until the 90's, although judges on each of these courts have laboured to reduce tensions in recent years. Other courts have chosen to defer to the Convention and to its Court, for their own reasons, as the Spanish Constitutional Tribunal did in its early jurisprudence, and as the Dutch and Belgian judges do. One might identify a mid-point, between conflict and deference, wherein courts seek to forge a cooperative relationship with the Strasbourg Court through dialogue and comity. The Swiss Federal Supreme Court, the Polish Constitutional Court, and, more recently, the House of Lords and the French Supreme Court and Council of State are good examples; and this position may well become the norm. Finally, through negligence or ignorance, some courts have failed to negotiate much of a relationship at all (typical for the Greek courts until the 90's, for the Turkish courts at least until 2004 and for the Russian courts until today).

The reports address why national judges made the choices they did, with what consequences for reception, and why they may have changed their attitudes over time. Although more research on these issues needs to be undertaken, it is clear that no single factor, or simple combination of factors, can explain the choices judges have made. In some important cases (notably France and the UK), high courts became more open to the Strasbourg Court's jurisprudence in order to re-

[61] See this volume, Lambert Abdelgawad and Weber, Section B.1.c. and D.1.c.; Besson, Section III.D.1.b.; Candela Soriano, Section III.D.2.b.

duce their vulnerability to findings of violation. Non-legal factors also influence judicial attitudes to the ECHR regime. Independently of the formal structure and legal constraints (a system's monist or dualist nature, the formal rank of the Convention within the legal order, the existence and extent of judicial review of Government acts, etc.), those national judges who desired to enforce Convention rights directly, as supra-legislative norms, found ways to do so. The reports also show that judicial reception of the ECHR is conditioned by the judges' expertise, access to the Court's case law, trust in the ECtHR to perform its tasks in good faith, and self-understanding as regulators of Government action and rights protectors. The fact that judges interact with non-judicial national officials (who are often pursuing quite different goals) complicates matters. Indeed, the more national judges seek to increase the effectiveness of Convention rights in the domestic order, the more likely it is that they will face resistance on the part of other government actors.

The ECHR has thus evolved in ways that generate politics – between courts, and between courts and non-judicial officials – that will always be, in our view, significantly open-ended and difficult to model.

E. The Future of the Court

The Court faces two dramatic challenges: an exploding case load, and a steady stream of applications that raise very serious human rights abuses from a handful of problematic States. Fears that the Court has reached its extreme capacity are both widespread and justified. It is difficult to see how the individual complaint system can survive without fundamental changes in how the Court processes applications. The Court does not possess the necessary power and resources for it to oversee the kinds of deep structural domestic reform required for some countries to bring domestic rights standards up to bare minimal levels. In this Section, we briefly examine, from the perspective adopted in this book, how the ECHR regime might best meet its challenges in the future.[62]

1. Reception and Burden Sharing

One of the general claims of this volume is that the ECHR and domestic legal systems are significantly enmeshed in one another. If the protection of human rights in Europe is carried out at different levels and through various mechanisms, the question is how one can best distribute the overall charge of protecting human rights. In the Council of Europe system, other bodies such as the European Committee for the Prevention of Torture, the European Commission against Racism and Intolerance, the Advisory Committee on the Framework Conven-

[62] We do not survey all of the reform proposals here, but see Helfer (2008). Helfer reviews the growing literature on ECHR reform, and develops an interesting approach that emphasizes "embeddedness" and burden sharing.

tion for the Protection of National Minorities and the European Committee on Social Rights, also have rights-based remits.[63] The Council of Europe also maintains Information Offices in some States (including Poland and Slovakia in our survey[64]), providing not only potential applicants with information on admissibility issues, but also giving counsel on existing domestic remedies. These offices save potential applicants from initiating proceedings unnecessarily or prematurely. The functions of such offices could be expanded and strengthened, in particular in Contracting States that have a strong share in the Court's docket.

As this volume shows, national officials have a crucial role to play in monitoring and enforcing Convention rights. Most important, they can incorporate the ECHR in ways that make it directly effective in the legal order, and they can develop and use mechanisms of reception. The book also demonstrates a strong correlation between relatively higher domestic human rights standards and relatively lower numbers of applications to Strasbourg. One obvious way to reduce the ECtHR's caseload is, therefore, to enhance rights protection domestically.

As the data show, a small handful of countries, with massive, systemic problems, generate a large proportion of total applications. Such problems include judicial dysfunction (underpaid judges, poor infrastructure, and lack of impartiality), the failure on the part of politicians to commit themselves to values associated with the rule of law, corruption, and deep-rooted political problems, including the oppression of minorities and secessionist movements. Among the countries covered in this volume, Russia, Turkey and Ukraine fit this description. In these contexts, a judgment of the Court may have little effect beyond the individual applicant. The Court, in pilot rulings, may seek to persuade or cajole such States to take comprehensive measures to correct problems at the root, but it can ill afford to allow dealing with the worst pathologies to preempt its other important roles. Since the advent of Protocol no. 11, the number of applications to the ECtHR has also steadily increased in Contracting States with fairly good human rights records (such as Austria, Ireland, Norway, Poland, Slovakia, Spain, Sweden, and Switzerland). We have to accept that in a Europe of Rights, "going to Strasbourg" will be attractive to those who wish to see new rights recognized, or to raise standards of protection for established rights. It is an important function of the Court to respond to these demands and to participate fully in the progressive development of rights in Europe, in meaningful partnership with national judges and other officials.

[63] In addition, it is important to mention the Commissioner for Human Rights established under the auspices of the Council of Europe. See Resolution (99)50 on the Council of Europe Commissioner for Human Rights, adopted by the Committee of Ministers on 7 May 1999 at its 104th Session and Article 13 of Protocol no. 14 amending Article 36(3) ECHR.

[64] See Krzyżanowska-Mierzewska, this volume, Sections J.1.c. and J.2.c.

2. *Remedies*

Reform of the remedial requirements under the Convention could provide another means of burden-sharing between the Strasbourg and the national courts. The Court continuously emphasizes the States' obligation to vest the domestic courts with the necessary competencies and resources to enable them to give full effect to Convention rights.[65] National judges normally constitute the final phase of national remedial systems, and thus act as the gatekeepers between domestic legal orders and the Court. Although Article 13 ECHR was for many years a "dormant effective remedy clause",[66] the Court now stresses the importance of that Article,[67] not least in order to urge a more proactive stance on the part of the national courts. As this volume shows, States will not be able to manage the variegated demands of the ECHR regime without enabling strong judicial enforcement of rights.

Entrusting the determination of "reparation" and "just satisfaction" to the national courts (reform of Article 41 ECHR) has also been proposed,[68] not least since national authorities are normally better acquainted with the relevant criteria for assessing damages. Any delegation of tasks under the ECHR will run the risk of producing too much variation across the States, and the same would be true in the area of compensation. The ECHR makes awards in accordance with its own criteria, autonomously, rather than on the basis of national concepts. Conferring such authority on national courts would entail divergence, and such variation could, if too great, offend the very principles of fairness and justice that the ECHR is designed to protect. There would, therefore, need to be clear safeguards to protect individuals against States that might not live up to expectations, and this control function could only be performed by the Court.

[65] See *Kudła v. Poland* (appl. no. 30210/96), Judgement (Grand Chamber), 26 October 2000, Reports 2000-XI, 197, para. 152: "(...) Article 13, giving direct expression to the States' obligation to protect human rights first and foremost within their own legal system, establishes an additional guarantee for an individual in order to ensure that he or she effectively enjoys those rights. The object of Article 13, as emerges from the travaux préparatoires (...), is to provide a means whereby individuals can obtain relief at national level for violations of their Convention rights before having to set in motion the international machinery of complaint before the Court. From this perspective, the right of an individual to trial within a reasonable time will be less effective if there exists no opportunity to submit the Convention claim first to a national authority; and the requirements of Article 13 are to be seen as reinforcing those of Article 6 § 1, rather than being absorbed by the general obligation imposed by that Article not to subject individuals to inordinate delays in legal proceedings."

[66] Malinverni (1998), 647–650.

[67] See, e.g., *Kudła v. Poland* (*supra* note 65), paras 146–160; *Sürmeli v. Germany* (appl. no. 75529/01), Judgement (Grand Chamber), 8 June 2006 (not yet reported), paras 97–117; *Aksoy v. Turkey* (appl. no. 21987/93), Judgement, 18 December 1996, Reports 1996-IV, 2260, paras. 51–57.

[68] Mahoney (2007).

3. *Reforming the Regime*

Over the past twenty years, the ECHR has been amended by a series of Protocols,[69] ultimately leading to the transformation of the legal system occasioned by Protocol no. 11. This strategy – of building the regime progressively through protocols – may have reached its limits. Most important, with the accession of the Eastern European States, the Council of Europe now comprises a much less homogeneous family of Contracting States. Because each additional Protocol requires ratification by all Contracting States (each State possesses a veto over proposed changes), it may be difficult or impossible to reform the regime through protocols in the future. If so, the ECHR regime may itself become mired in systemic problems for which no systemic solutions will be forthcoming. The Court might be allowed to propose changes to its jurisdiction to the Council of Europe, which would approve them by majority or a qualified majority of States. Yet such a reform would itself require unanimity, which may not be forthcoming.

Protocol no. 14 – which is strongly supported by the Court – illustrates the problem.[70] Protocol no. 14 aims at giving the Court the necessary procedural means and flexibility to process applications within a reasonable time, while enabling it to concentrate on those it finds most important. Under Protocol no. 14, the Court could declare a case inadmissible unless the applicant has not suffered a "significant disadvantage".[71] These and other provisions would reduce the time spent by the Court on manifestly inadmissible and repetitive cases. Although these reforms are no doubt necessary, it is already clear that they would not be sufficient to overcome the Court's overload.[72] Yet, alone among High Contracting Parties, Russia refuses to ratify Protocol no. 14, blocking its adoption.

One possible solution might be to allow the Court to undertake significant systemic reform on its own. The Council of Europe could authorize the Court to use Rule 103 (of the Rules of the Court) to amend its procedures as the Court sees fit, while reserving its own authority (under unanimity) to quash such changes. The Convention (Article 32 ECHR) also confers jurisdiction on the Court over all matters concerning the interpretation and application of the Convention and the Protocols. The Court might use these plenary powers to decide, in an appropriately explicit manner, to delegate some types of cases (of minor importance and without systemic implications) to national judges. As we argued above,[73] the Court could also choose to reduce its level of scrutiny when it comes to how national judges fine-tune the protection of qualified rights through pro-

[69] See *supra* Section A.1.

[70] For an overview of Protocol no. 14, see Caflisch and Keller; Greer (2005). For the ECtHR's view on Protocol No. 14 and other proposed reforms, see *Opinion of the Court on the Wise Persons' Report*, adopted by the Plenary Court, 2 April 2007.

[71] Article 12(3)(b) of Protocol no. 14 amending Article 35 ECHR.

[72] For a discussion of a range of reform proposals, see the *Report of the Group of Wise Persons to the Committee of Ministers*, CM(2006)203, 15 November 2006.

[73] See *supra* Section C.4.

portionality balancing. Such changes would enable the Court to concentrate on cases involving more serious human rights violations, and on defining the content and scope of rights, which national judges would then help to fine-tune.

F. A Europe of Rights

In post-Protocol no. 11 Europe, it makes little sense to conceptualize the ECHR as an international regime, external to the Contracting States. The Convention has a significant presence within national legal orders, even where this presence is resisted and opposed. Today, national officials routinely participate in a transnational judicial process whose reach into domestic law and politics is limited only by the ever-widening scope of the Convention itself, as determined by a transnational court. In virtually every State examined in this book, the Convention has provoked some measure of significant structural and procedural innovation, including the development of mechanisms for coordinating national law and the Convention, as the latter evolves. Reception processes have, in turn, provoked deep changes in European Government, through the accumulation of incremental, step-by-step adjustments to the demands of the Strasbourg Court. National officials are, gradually but inexorably, being socialized into a Europe of rights, a unique transnational legal space now seeking to develop its own logic of political and juridical legitimacy. The success of this endeavor will depend partly on the Council of Europe's ability to reform the ECHR legal system, and partly on the extent to which national officials sustain reception processes as means of further incorporating the Convention into national legal orders.

Bibliography[74]

Aromaa, K. and Viljanen, T. (eds.), International Key Issues in Crime Prevention and Criminal Justice (Helsinki, 2006).
Bárd, K., 'The Role of the ECHR in Shaping the European Model of the Criminal Process', in Aromaa, K. and Viljanen, T. (eds.), International Key Issues in Crime Prevention and Criminal Justice (Helsinki, 2006), 34.
Bruach, J.A., 'The Margin of Appreciation and the Jurisprudence of the European Court of Human Rights: Threat to the Rule of Law', *Columbia Journal of European Law* 11 (2005), 113.
Caflisch, L. and Keller, M., 'Le Protocole additionnel no. 15 à la Convention européenne des droits de l'homme', in Caflisch, L., Callewaert, J., Liddell, R., Mahoney, P., and Villiger, M. (eds.), Liber amicorum Luzius Wildhaber: Human Rights - Strasbourg Views/Droits de l'homme - Regards de Strasbourg (Kehl, 2007), 91.
Greer, S., The European Convention on Human Rights: Achievements, Problems and Prospects (Cambridge, 2006).
Greer, S., 'Protocol 14 and the Future of the European Court of Human Rights', *Public law* (Spring 2005), 83.
Helfer, L.R., 'Redesigning the European Court of Human Rights: Embeddedness as a Deep Structural Principle of the European Human Rights Regime', *European Journal of International Law* 19 (2008), 125.
Jackson, J.D., 'The Effect of Human Rights on Criminal Evidentiary Processes: Towards Convergence, Divergence or Realignment?', *Modern Law Review* 68/5 (2005), 737.
Krisch, N., 'The Open Architecture of European Human Rights Law', forthcoming in *Modern Law Review* 71 (2008), 183.
Mahoney, P., 'Thinking a Small Unthinkable: Repatriating Reparation from the European Court of Human Rights to the National Legal Order', in Caflisch, L., Callewaert, J., Liddell, R., Mahoney, P., and Villiger, M. (eds.), Liber amicorum Luzius Wildhaber: Human Rights - Strasbourg Views/Droits de l'homme - Regards de Strasbourg (Kehl, 2007), 263.
Malinverni, G., 'Observations –Variations sur un thème encore méconnu: l'article 13 de la Convention européenne des droits de l'homme', *Revue trimestrielle des droits de l'homme* 33/9 (1998), 647.
Paraskeva, C., 'Reforming the European Court of Human Rights. An Ongoing Challenge', *Nordic Journal of International Law* 76/2–3 (2007), 185.
Polakiewicz, J., 'The Status of the Convention in National Law', in Blackburn, R. and Polakiewicz, J. (eds.), Fundamental Rights in Europe (Oxford, 2001), 31.
Pinelli, C., 'Conditionality and Enlargement in Light of EU Constitutional Developments', *European Law Journal*, 10/3 (May 2004), 354.
Stone Sweet, 'Proportionality Balancing and Global Constitutionalism,' *Columbia Journal of Transnational Law* 47 (forthcoming 2008).

[74] See also the bibliography of the Introduction.

Wildhaber, L., 'A Constitutional Future for the European Court of Human Rights?', *Human Rights Law Journal* 23 (2000), 161.

Wildhaber, L. 'The European Court of Human Rights: The Past, the Present, the Future', *American University International Law Review* 22 (2007), 521.

Part IV
The African System

[20]

African Court on Human and Peoples' Rights – Response to the Situation in Libya

By Anna Dolidze

Introduction

On March 25, 2011, for the first time in its history, the African Court on Human and Peoples' Rights ("African Human Rights Court") ordered provisional measures against Libya in the case *African Commission on Human and Peoples' Rights v. Great Socialist People's Libyan Arab Jamahiriya*. The provisional measures require that Libya "immediately refrain from any action that would result in loss of life or violation of physical integrity of persons, which could be a breach of the provisions of the African Charter on Human and Peoples' Rights or of other international human rights instruments to which it is a party."[1] In addition, the African Human Rights Court ordered Libya to report to the Court within fifteen days on the steps taken in response to the Order. The Libyan government has ignored the Order.

The African Human Rights Court's action paralleled that of the International Criminal Court ("ICC"). On February 26, 2011, the United Nations Security Council decided to refer the conflict in Libya to the ICC Prosecutor. A few days later, on March 3, 2011, the ICC Prosecutor announced that he would open an investigation.[2] On May 16, 2011, he requested arrest warrants for Muammar Qadhafi, his son Seif al-Islam, and Abdullah Sanussi for crimes against humanity.[3] On June 26, 2011, Pre-Trial Chamber I granted the Prosecutor's request and issued the arrest warrants for the three persons.[4]

This *Insight* highlights the relationships, dynamics, and cooperation that led to the African Human Rights Court's Order. In particular, it emphasizes the complex relationship between the African Union, the African Commission on Human and People's Rights ("African Human Rights Commission"), the African Human Rights Court, and non-governmental organizations ("NGOs").

Background to the African Union, Commission, and Human Rights Court

The African Union's predecessor, the Organization of African Unity ("OAU"), was founded in Addis Ababa in 1963 in the wake of decolonization. On September 9, 1999, the Heads of State and Government of the OAU adopted the Sirte Declaration calling for the establishment of the African Union ("AU"),[5] with increased emphasis on democratic governance and human rights.

The AU's chief organs include the Assembly of the Union, the Executive Council, the African

Human Rights Commission, and the African Human Rights Court. The African Human Rights Commission had been created by the African Charter on Human and People's Rights, adopted in 1981 by the Assembly of Heads of State and Government of the OAU. The Charter, known as the "Banjul Charter," came into force on October 21, 1986, and enjoys universal participation by all fifty-three AU members.

The African Human Rights Commission is an autonomous, quasi-judicial treaty body within the AU, which focuses on promotion and protection of human rights in Africa[6] and on the interpretation of the provisions of the Charter.[7] The AU exercises important leverage in relation to the Commission. First, the African Human Rights Commission's eleven members are elected by the AU's Assembly of Heads of State and Government.[8] Second, the AU exercises the "power of the purse" over the African Human Rights Commission: the finances and the budget of the African Commission are apportioned by the African Union in consultation with the Commission.[9] Moreover, the Commission must inform the AU of funds from other donors.[10] Third, the Commission does not have an independent power to implement its decisions.[11] In accordance with the Article 54 of the African Charter, the Commission must ask the Assembly of States Parties of the AU to take specific and necessary measures for the implementation of its decisions.[12]

The African Court on Human and Peoples' Rights was established by a protocol to the African Charter "to complement the protective mandate" of the African Human Rights Commission.[13] The Protocol was adopted by the OAU in Ouagadougou, Burkina Faso, on June 10, 1998; it came into force on January 25, 2004. The Court became operational about two years after its first judges were sworn in.[14] Its permanent seat is in Arusha, Tanzania.[15] As of March 11, 2011, twenty six of the fifty-three members of the AU have ratified the Protocol. The Court was ready to receive cases after it finalized its rules of procedure with the African Commission,[16] and rendered its first judgment in the case of *Michelot Yogogombaye v. Republic of Senegal* on December 15, 2009.[17]

The relationship between the African Human Rights Commission and the Court is governed by the principle of complementarity, requiring general ongoing cooperation and consultation between the two bodies. In particular, according to Articles 5 and 34 (6) of the Protocol, the Commission has standing to bring cases before the Court.

The relationship between the African Court and the AU is similar to the relationship between the African Human Rights Commission and the AU. First, the judges of the African Court are elected from among the nationals of member states to the Protocol by the Assembly of the AU.[18] Second, as with the African Commission, it is the AU that determines the budget and bears the expenses of the Court in accordance with the criteria previously laid down in consultation with the Court.[19] Third, the Court does not have independent enforcement power of its own orders or judgments. The Court reports annually to the Assembly, specifying the states that did not comply with its judgments.[20] The AU Executive Council monitors the enforcement of the African Court's judgments on behalf of the Assembly.[21]

Ultimately, the African Union can impose sanctions on a member state for its failure to comply with its decisions and policies. Sanctions may be of a political or economic nature, including the denial of transport and communication links with other Member States.[22]

The entities that can make submissions of cases before the Court are: the African Commission, any state party (either as Applicant or Respondent), any state party whose citizen is a victim of a human rights violation, African intergovernmental organizations, and, with the Court's permission, non-governmental organizations with observer status and individuals.[23] It should be noted that the Court does not provide for the direct right of individual petition, a hallmark of the European system of human rights protection. Individuals and organizations that have observer status before the African Human Rights Commission acquire standing before the Court only after a state party delivers a specific declaration recognizing their capacity to do so.[24] The Protocol to the Charter specifically prohibits the

Court from receiving petitions in the absence of such a declaration.[25] So far, only five countries—Ghana, Burkina Faso, Malawi, Mali, and Tanzania—have made such declarations.[26]

Parties to a case, the African Human Rights Commission, or the Court *proprio motu* can order interim measures "in the interest of the parties or of justice."[27] The Court may ask the parties to provide it with information on issues relating to the implementation of the requested measure.[28] In the event of noncompliance with the measure, the Court may put forward specific recommendations in the annual report that it presents to the AU Assembly.[29]

Libyan Conflict and Non-Governmental Organizations

Libya is signatory to the Banjul Charter and a party to the Protocol establishing the Court. However, as Libya has not made a declaration under Article 34 (6) of the latter, NGOs and individuals cannot file petitions against Libya. Consequently, NGOs acting in response to the Libyan crisis turned to the African Human Rights Commission.

On February 24, 2011, three non-governmental organizations—the Egyptian Initiative for Personal Rights ("EIPR"), Human Rights Watch, and INTERIGHTS—submitted a joint request for provisional measures to the African Human Rights Commission. EIPR is an organization active in Egypt, while the latter two are international human rights organizations based in New York and London, respectively. In the request, the applicants asked the Commission to order Libya to undertake a number of actions, including stopping and preventing "the use of unjustified lethal force against protesters, whether by the security forces, mercenaries or other bodies or individuals acting on behalf of the State."[30]

On February 25, 2011, the African Commission made a statement on the human rights situation in North Africa, urging the government of Libya to "immediately end the violence against civilians."[31] Three days later, the organizations also submitted a joint complaint against Libya to the Commission, urging it to "respond to the grave and urgent situation" in Libya.[32] Both the request for provisional measures and the complaint chronicled the violent repression of civilian protestors from February 17, 2011.

Subsequently, on March 1, 2011, the Commission condemned the actions of the Libyan government,[33] and on March 3, 2011, the Commission instituted proceedings against Libya in the Court for "serious and massive violations of human rights guaranteed under the African Charter on Human and Peoples' Rights."[34] In the application, the Commission specifically referred to the complaints of human rights violations received during its preceding session.[35]

Although the African Commission did not request indication of provisional measures, the Court decided to order provisional measures *proprio motu*. Article 27(2) of the Protocol allows the Court to order provisional measures on its own volition in case of "extreme gravity and urgency" and "when necessary to avoid irreparable harm to persons."[36] As the Court ascertained the presence of all three criteria in the case of Libya, it ordered Libya to refrain from activities that would result in violation of rights under the Charter or other international instruments. Moreover, the Court ordered Libya to report to it within fifteen days on its progress in implementing the order.[37]

The NGOs initially involved in triggering the litigation issued a subsequent press release, hailing the Order by the Court and urging Libya to enforce it.[38]

Nevertheless, the Libyan government ignored the Order. As its Order was not complied with, in accordance with the Rules, the Court should report the lack of compliance to the Assembly of the AU and to the Council of Ministers. It will be up to the Council and/or the Assembly of the Union, both political bodies, to adopt measures in response to Libya's non-compliance.

Conclusion

The case suggests a number of preliminary observations. First, evidenced by the language of the Order, the situation of "extreme gravity and urgency" as well as the risk of "irreparable harm to persons" prompted the Court to order provisional measures of its own volition without a request by the Commission.[39] Second, the Court emphasized the consensus formed among international organizations on the gravity of the human rights situation in Libya. For this purpose the Court referenced the acts by the Peace and Security Council of the African Union, the Secretary-General of the Arab League, and the United Nations Security Council.[40] Third, the Court stated that it relied heavily on the evidence of human rights violations gathered and submitted by international NGOs initially to the African Commission.[41] This indicates that in the urgency of armed conflict, which does not allow for extensive periods for collecting evidence, the experience and resources of NGOs in quickly gathering relevant evidence proved to be highly important and valuable.

Fourth, it should be noted that the African Charter contains a provision prohibiting forum shopping by states parties. A complaint cannot be submitted to any other procedure of international investigation or settlement.[42] Founding documents of other international human rights bodies, where the individual complaints mentioned in the Commission's application could potentially end up (for instance, the UN Human Rights Committee) contain the same limitation.[43] It is possible therefore that adjudication of these human rights claims on the international level has been halted until a political outcome is found to the situation through the organs of the AU. The Court's involvement in the matter cannot bring the desired outcome of halting human rights violations in Libya without adequate backing from the political organs of the AU.

Last but not least, the degree of effectiveness of the ICC in the prosecution of Libyan leaders will provide an indication of the compatibility and conflict between international criminal law and international human rights mechanisms. The influence and positive change that involvement of the International Criminal Court will bring to the Libyan situation will certainly be subject to further examination and debate.

About the Author:

Anna Dolidze, an ASIL member, is a Candidate for Doctor of the Science of Law at Cornell Law School. Dolidze worked for a number of international organizations, including Save the Children, the Russian Justice Initiative, and Human Rights Watch.

Endnotes:

[1] Press Release, Af. Ct. Human & Peoples' Rights, Order for Provisional Measures Against Libya (Mar. 30, 2011), *available at* http://www.african-court.org/en/news/record/datum/2011/03/30/communique-de-presse-ordonnance-prescrivant-des-mesures-provisoires-a-lencontre-de-la-libye/.

[2] The International Criminal Court, Situations and Cases, http://www.icc-cpi.int/Menus/ICC/Situations+and+Cases/.

[3] Press Release, Int'l Crim. Ct., ICC Prosecutor: Qaddafi Used His Absolute Authority to Commit Crimes in Libya (May 16, 2011), *available at* http://www.icc-cpi.int/NR/exeres/1365E3B7-8152-4456-942C-A5CD5A51E829.htm.

[4] Press Release, Int'l Crim. Ct., Pre-Trial Chamber I Issues Three Warrants of Arrest for Muammar Gaddafi, Saif Al-Islam Gaddafi and Abdualla Al-Senussi (June 27, 2011), *available at* http://www.icc-cpi.int/NR/exeres/D07229DE-4E3D-45BC-8CB1-F5DAF8370218.htm.

[5] Constitutive Act of the African Union, July 11, 2000 (adopted July 11, 2011), *available at* http://www.au2002.gov.za/docs/key_oau/au_act.htm.

[6] Rules of Procedure of the African Commission on Human and People's Rights rule 3, *available at* http://www.achpr.org/english/ROP/Rules%20of%20Procedure.pdf [hereinafter Rules of Procedure].

[7] African Charter on Human and People's Rights art. 45, *available at* http://www.achpr.org/english /_info/charter_en.html [hereafter African Charter].

[8] *Id.* arts. 31, 33. African Commission members serve for six years and are eligible for reelection. *See* Rules of Procedure, *supra* note 6, rule 5.

[9] Rules of Procedure, *supra* note 6, rule 19.

[10] *Id.* rule 66.

[11] *See* African Charter, *supra* note 7, art. 54.

[12] Rules of Procedure, *supra* note 6, rule 125.

[13] Protocol to the African Charter on Human and Peoples' Rights on the Establishment of an African Court on Human and Peoples' Rights art. 2, *available at* http://www.achpr.org/english/_info /court_en.html [hereinafter Protocol to the African Charter]. On July 1, 2008, the AU adopted a protocol to the African Charter merging the African Human Rights Court with the Court of Justice of the African Union into one Court, "The African Court of Justice and Human Rights." The change will become effective when fifteen states deposit their instruments of ratification.

[14] *See* Scott Lyons, *The African Court on Human and Peoples' Rights*, 10 ASIL Insights 24 (Sept. 19, 2006), *available at* http://www.asil.org/insights060919.cfm.

[15] *See* African Court on Human and Peoples' Rights, History, http://www.african-court.org /en/court/history/.

[16] *Id.*

[17] David J. Bederman & Charles Chernor Jalloh, *International Decisions: Michelot Yogogombaye v. Republic of Senegal*, 104 Am. J. Int'l L. 620, 620-28 (2010).

[18] Protocol to the African Charter, *supra* note 13, arts. 13, 14.

[19] *Id.* art. 23.

[20] *Id.* art. 31.

[21] *Id.* art. 29.

[22] *Id.* art. 23.

[23] *Id.* arts. 5, 34.

[24] *Id.* arts. 5, 34 (6).

[25] *Id.* art. 34 (6).

[26] List of Countries Which Have Signed, Acceded to, Ratified the Protocol, http://www.au.int /en/sites/default/files/992achpr.pdf.

[27] African Court of Human and Peoples' Rights, Rules of the Court rule 51, *available at* http://www.african-court.org/fileadmin/documents/Court/Interim%20Rules%20of%20Court /Final_Rules_of_Court_for_Publication_after_Harmonization_-_Final__English_7_sept_1_.pdf [hereinafter Rules of the Court]. Protocol to the African Charter, *supra* note 13, art. 27 (2).

[28] Rules of the Court, *supra* note 27, rule 51 (5).

[29] *Id.* 51(4).

[30] Int'l Ctr. for the Legal Protection of Human Rights, *Request for Provisional Measures to the African Commission on Human and Peoples' Rights*, http://www.interights.org/view-document /index.htm?id=614.

[31] African Union, African Commission, Press Statement on the Human Rights Situation in North Africa (Feb. 25, 2011), http://www.achpr.org/english/Press%20Release /Statement_north%20africa.pdf.

[32] *Id.*

[33] Resolution on the Human Rights Situation in the Great Socialist Peoples' Libyan Arab Jamahiriya, ACHPR/RES.181(EXT.OS/IX)201, *available at* http://www.achpr.org/english/resolutions /9eos_resolution%20%20Libya.pdf.

[34] In the Matter of African Commission on Human and People's Rights v. Great Socialist People's Libyan Arab Jamahiriya, Order for Provisional Measures, 2, App. No. 004/2011 (Mar. 25, 2011), *available at* http://www.african-court.org/fileadmin/documents/Court/Cases /Order_for_Provisinal_Measures_against_Libya.PDF [hereinafter Order for Provisional Measures].

[35] *Id.* ¶¶ 1, 2.

[36] Article 27(2), Protocol to the African Charter on Human and People's Rights on the Establishment of an African Court on Human and People's Rights.

[37] Order for Provisional Matters, *supra* note 34, ¶ 25.

[38] Int'l Ctr. for the Legal Protection of Human Rights, INTERIGHTS, HRW and EIPR Press Release 31 March 2011 (Mar. 31, 2011), http://www.interights.org/view-document/index.htm?id=623

[39] Order for Provisional Matters, *supra* note 34, ¶ 20.

[40] *Id.* ¶ 21.

[41] *Id.* ¶ 2.

[42] African Charter, *supra* note 7, art. 56 (7).

[43] Optional Protocol International Covenant on Civil and Political Rights art. 5(2a), 999 U.N.T.S. 302, (entered into force Mar. 23, 1976).

RELATED ASIL INSIGHTS

Recognition of the Libyan National Transitional Council

Lawfulness of Kosovo's Declaration of Independence

French Court Proceedings against Muammar Qadhafi

A Preview of the Lockerbie Case

Ten Years After the War in Kosovo: International Law, Kosovo and the International Criminal Tribunal for the Former Yugoslavia

Kosovo's Declaration of Independence: Self-Determination, Secession and Recognition

The Kosovo Situation and NATO Military Action

The Right to Participate in the Debates of the Security Council

The Legal Status of Foreign Economic Interests in Occupied Iraq

UN Commission's Report on Violations of International Humanitarian Law in Darfur

The U.N. Responds to the Crisis in Darfur: Security Council Resolution 1556

The Situation in Darfur: Prosecutor's Application under Article 58(7) of the Rome Statute

Acts of Non-State Armed Groups and the Law Governing Armed Conflict

Abyei Arbitration – Final Award

Insights Archive>>

DOCUMENTS OF NOTE

Order for Provisional Measures

Constitutive Act of the African Union

Rules of Procedure of the African Commission on Human and People's Rights

African Charter on Human and People's Rights

Protocol to the African Charter on Human and Peoples' Rights on the Establishment of an African Court on Human and Peoples'

Rights

African Court of Human and Peoples' Rights, Rules of the Court

Resolution on the Human Rights Situation in the Great Socialist Peoples' Libyan Arab Jamahiriya

Security Council Resolutions on Libya

Declaration on Principles of International Law concerning Friendly Relations and Co-operation among States in Accordance with the Charter of the United Nations

Vienna Convention on Diplomatic Relations

ASIL EISIL>>

ORGANIZATIONS OF NOTE

African Court on Human and Peoples' Rights

International Criminal Court

African Commission on Human and People's Rights

African Union

The Libyan Interim National Council

Libya Foreign Affairs

United Nations

Egyptian Initiative for Personal Rights

Human Rights Watch

INTERIGHTS

[21]

STATE COMPLIANCE WITH THE RECOMMENDATIONS OF THE AFRICAN COMMISSION ON HUMAN AND PEOPLES' RIGHTS, 1994–2004

*By Frans Viljoen and Lirette Louw**

Current discourse on international human rights leaves little room for self-satisfaction about near-universal acceptance of wide-ranging normative frameworks with a global and regional scope. Recent times have witnessed growing academic concern with the "impact" or "effect" of international human rights treaties on the *de jure* and *de facto* legal position in state parties.[1] These concerns are embedded in bigger and more enduring questions about the nature of state obligations under international law (including those derived from "nonbinding norms") and compliance with them.[2] However, general questions about obedience to international law have been replaced by attempts to answer the question whether human rights treaties in fact "make a difference."[3]

Those engaged in this debate do not always keep in mind the crucial distinction between the direct and indirect effect of human rights treaties (or human rights law, more generally). The major difference between the two is that direct impact is more or less immediately demonstrable, while indirect effect is incremental and less immediate. If the European Court of Human Rights, for example, finds that a country must compensate a national whose rights have been violated, it may be determined with relative ease whether the state complied. This form of compliance would illustrate the "direct effect" of the European Convention on Human Rights. Quantifying the gravitational pull of international human rights law, exemplified by the role of international human rights law in the adoption of new legislation and its use as a persuasive interpretive source—constituting indirect impact—is much more subtle and complex.

* Frans Viljoen is Professor of Law at the University of Pretoria, South Africa. Lirette Louw has an LLD (Pretoria). For the full results of this study, see Lirette Louw, An Analysis of State Compliance with the Recommendations of the African Commission on Human and Peoples' Rights (Jan. 28, 2005) (unpublished LLD dissertation, University of Pretoria) (on file with Centre for Human Rights and O. R. Tambo Library, University of Pretoria).

[1] *See, e.g.*, L'APPLICATION NATIONALE DE LA CHARTE AFRICAINE DES DROITS DE L'HOMME ET DES PEUPLES (Jean-François Flauss & Elisabeth Lambert-Abdelgawad eds., 2004); Christof Heyns & Frans Viljoen, *The Impact of the United Nations Human Rights Treaties on the Domestic Level*, 23 HUM. RTS. Q. 483 (2001).

[2] *See, e.g.*, ABRAM CHAYES & ANTONIA HANDLER CHAYES, THE NEW SOVEREIGNTY: COMPLIANCE WITH INTERNATIONAL REGULATORY AGREEMENTS (1995); COMMITMENT AND COMPLIANCE: THE ROLE OF NON-BINDING NORMS IN THE INTERNATIONAL LEGAL SYSTEM (Dinah Shelton ed., 2000); Laurence R. Helfer & Anne-Marie Slaughter, *Toward a Theory of Effective Supranational Adjudication*, 107 YALE L.J. 273 (1997); Harold Hongju Koh, *Why Do Nations Obey International Law?* 106 YALE L.J. 2599 (1997); Colter Paulson, *Compliance with Final Judgments of the International Court of Justice Since 1987*, 98 AJIL 434 (2004).

[3] *See, e.g.*, Douglass Cassel, *International Human Rights Law in Practice: Does International Human Rights Law Make a Difference?* 2 CHI. J. INT'L L. 121 (2001); Oona A. Hathaway, *Do Human Rights Treaties Make a Difference?* 111 YALE L.J. 1935 (2002); Linda Camp Keith, *The United Nations International Covenant on Civil and Political Rights: Does It Make a Difference in Human Rights Behaviour?* 36 J. PEACE RES. 95 (1999).

This article focuses on the direct effect of the most recent of the three regional human rights systems, which was established when the African Charter on Human and Peoples' Rights (African Charter) entered into force in 1986.[4] The African Charter called for the establishment of the African Commission on Human and Peoples' Rights (African Commission) to ensure compliance with the Charter's norms.[5] As the drafters considered that Africa not ready for a supranational judicial institution at that time, the African Commission was established as a quasi-judicial supervisory body.[6] Under the African Charter, the findings of the African Commission are not legally binding as such, and the Commission issues "recommendations" to state parties, rather than "orders." In fulfilling its protective mandate, the African Commission has developed a well-established practice of receiving and considering individual complaints alleging violations by state parties of the African Charter. When it has found such a violation, the Commission has further developed a practice not only of listing the articles violated by the state party concerned, but also of recommending remedial measures to be adopted by that state. The Commission's practice in this regard is well documented.[7]

From the time it started functioning in 1987 until mid-2003, the African Commission completed some 122 communications.[8] Of these, 63 were declared inadmissible; another 5 were settled amicably; and 8 were withdrawn. The Commission found violations by state parties in 44 of the remaining 46 admissible communications (that is, in 96 percent of the admissible cases).

In contrast to the individual complaints procedure, what follows once the Commission has made its findings is not well documented. Very little is known about the status of state

[4] African Charter on Human and Peoples' Rights, June 27, 1981, 21 ILM 58 (1982) [hereinafter African Charter]. The Universal Declaration of Human Rights was adopted in 1948 but was actually preceded by the establishment in the same year of the inter-American system with the adoption of the American Declaration of the Rights and Duties of Man. The European system followed shortly thereafter, with the entry into force of the European Convention on Human Rights and Fundamental Freedoms in 1953. All fifty-three member states of the Organization of African Unity (OAU) (now the African Union (AU)), have ratified the African Charter. See the list of parties to the Charter at the AU Web site, <http://www.africa-union.org>.

[5] The mandate of the African Commission on Human and Peoples' Rights (ACHPR) is to promote and protect the rights guaranteed in the African Charter. African Charter, *supra* note 4, Art. 30. The African Commission held its first session in Addis Ababa, Ethiopia, in November 1987. With the transformation of the OAU into the AU in July 2002, the African Commission was retained and the AU Assembly took over the tasks previously performed by the OAU Assembly.

[6] See the introductory comments to the M'Baye draft, which formed the basis of the African Charter's *travaux préparatoires*, highlighting this omission of a judicial institution but explaining that it was "thought premature to [establish one] at this stage." Introduction to M'Baye draft, 4th para., OAU Doc. CAB/LEG/67/1 (1979), *reprinted in* HUMAN RIGHTS LAW IN AFRICA 1999, at 65, 65 (Christof Heyns ed., 2002).

[7] *See, e.g.*, THE AFRICAN CHARTER ON HUMAN AND PEOPLES' RIGHTS: THE SYSTEM IN PRACTICE, 1986–2000 (Malcolm D. Evans & Rachel Murray eds., 2002) [hereinafter Evans & Murray]; EVELYN A. ANKUMAH, THE AFRICAN COMMISSION ON HUMAN AND PEOPLES' RIGHTS—PRACTICE AND PROCEDURES (1996); RACHEL MURRAY, THE AFRICAN COMMISSION ON HUMAN AND PEOPLES' RIGHTS AND INTERNATIONAL LAW (2000); INGER ÖSTERDAHL, IMPLEMENTING HUMAN RIGHTS IN AFRICA—THE AFRICAN COMMISSION ON HUMAN AND PEOPLES' RIGHTS AND INDIVIDUAL COMMUNICATIONS (2002); NASILA S. REMBE, THE SYSTEM OF PROTECTION OF HUMAN RIGHTS UNDER THE AFRICAN CHARTER ON HUMAN AND PEOPLES' RIGHTS: PROBLEMS AND PROSPECTS (1991); U. OJI UMOZURIKE, THE AFRICAN CHARTER ON HUMAN AND PEOPLES' RIGHTS (1997).

[8] Frans Viljoen, *Introduction to the African Commission and the Regional Human Rights System, in* 1 HUMAN RIGHTS LAW IN AFRICA 385, 438–39 (Christof Heyns ed., 2004); Fifteenth Annual Activity Report of the African Commission on Human and Peoples' Rights, 2001–2002; Sixteenth Annual Activity Report of the African Commission on Human and Peoples' Rights, 2002–2003. These reports will be referred to hereinafter as Activity Report, with the corresponding number. The 10th through 16th reports are available at the Commission's Web site, <http://www.achpr.org>.

compliance with the African Commission's recommendations.[9] The African Charter and the Rules of Procedure of the African Commission do not deal with the fate of communications once a finding has been made. The Commission also does not have any follow-up mechanism or policy in place to monitor state compliance with its recommendations.[10] In the past the Commission has made some attempts at follow-up, but these efforts were few and far apart.[11]

Commentators on the African regional human rights system have often cited its absence of "teeth" when it comes to the enforcement mechanisms provided for in the African Charter.[12] The African Commission, in reflecting on its activities, has indicated that the lack of state compliance with its recommendations was "one of the major factors of the erosion of the Commission's credibility."[13] However, in the absence of accumulated data and any policy on follow-up, the commissioners' critical observations about a lack of compliance with their findings remain speculative.[14]

[9] This is not a phenomenon peculiar to the African system. Paulson, in analyzing compliance with the final judgments of the International Court of Justice (ICJ), quoted Judge Robert Y. Jennings of the ICJ, who stated that "[i]t is ironic that the Court's business up to the delivery of judgment is published in lavish detail, but it is not at all easy to find out what happened afterwards." Paulson, *supra* note 2, at 434.

[10] According to Robert Eno:

> Unlike other regional and global human rights bodies, the Commission has not developed any follow-up mechanism to ensure implementation of its recommendations. . . . This has been very frustrating especially for the victims who have to pursue the execution of the decisions on their own. Because there is no pressure from the Commission, states have tended to turn a blind eye to the recommendations and a deaf ear to the victims' pleas for compliance.

Robert Eno, *The Place of the African Commission in the New African Dispensation*, 11 AFR. SECURITY REV. 63, 67 (2002); *see also* MURRAY, *supra* note 7, at 21; E. V. O. Dankwa, The African System for the Protection of Human Rights: The Tasks Ahead 4 (Oct. 1998) (prepared for the National Human Rights Commission of Nigeria, African Human Rights Day Celebration, Nigeria Institute of International Affairs, Lagos, Nigeria) (on file with authors).

[11] *See infra* text at notes 65–68.

[12] *See, e.g.*, CLAUDE E. WELCH, PROTECTING HUMAN RIGHTS IN AFRICA—ROLES AND STRATEGIES OF NON-GOVERNMENTAL ORGANIZATIONS 151–53 (1995).

[13] See the discussion document entitled Non-Compliance of State Parties to Adopted Recommendations of the African Commission: A Legal Approach, DOC/OS/50b (XXIV), para. 2 (1998) [hereinafter Non-Compliance: A Legal Approach], *reprinted in* DOCUMENTS OF THE AFRICAN COMMISSION ON HUMAN AND PEOPLES' RIGHTS 758, 758 (Rachel Murray & Malcolm Evans eds., 2001) [hereinafter ACHPR DOCUMENTS]. In this discussion document, the secretariat highlighted the absence of compliance, save for one case, Pagnoulle (on Behalf of Mazou) v. Cameroon, Communication [Comm.] No. 39/90, 2000 Afr. Hum. Rts. L. Rep. [AHRLR] 55 (ACHPR 1995). The first time the Commission noted that state parties were not complying with its recommendations had been at its twenty-second ordinary session in November 1997, where the secretariat also raised the issue. In the Eleventh Annual Activity Report, covering the November 1997 session, the Commission observed not only that noncompliance affected its credibility, but also that it could probably be to blame for the reduction in the number of communications submitted to it. *See* Section VIII, Protective Activities, 11th Activity Report, 1997–1998, *supra* note 8. Later, in September 2003, during a retreat organized by the Office of the UN High Commissioner for Human Rights in Addis Ababa to evaluate the functioning of the African Commission, problems of noncompliance by state parties were highlighted once more. The retreat also identified the lack of a follow-up system to ensure that decisions and recommendations of the Commission are complied with as one of the challenges facing the Commission. Report of the Retreat of Members of the African Commission on Human and Peoples' Rights (ACHPR) at 4 (Sept. 24–26, 2003), *available at* <http://www.nhri.net/>. Volumes of the *African Human Rights Law Reports* cited herein are available online at <http://www.chr.up.ac.za>.

[14] During the twenty-second session of the Commission, the chairman stated "that none of the decisions on individual communications taken by the Commission and adopted by the Assembly had ever been implemented." Rachel Murray, *Report on the 1997 Sessions of the African Commission on Human and Peoples' Rights—21st and 22nd Sessions: 15–25 April and 2–11 November 1997*, 19 HUM. RTS. L.J. 169, 170 (1998). On another occasion, the Commission stated that "the attitude of State Parties . . . with the exception of Cameroon has been to generally ignore its recommendations." Non-Compliance: A Legal Approach, *supra* note 13, at 758, para. 5 (footnote omitted).

It is against this background that a study was undertaken to determine the status of state compliance with the recommendations of the African Commission. The empirical findings of this study formed the background against which factors were identified that have affected state compliance. This article aims at summarizing the main findings of this study in such a way as to highlight the direct impact of the African Charter, while also suggesting how the main factors that have affected state compliance in the past should be addressed if compliance is to be improved.

I. STATUS AND CATEGORIES OF COMPLIANCE

Since the African Commission has no follow-up policy to monitor the steps taken by state parties to implement its recommendations, the secretariat of the Commission has never compiled data on state compliance. Therefore, to undertake an analysis of the status of state compliance in the African system, information had first to be gathered about the steps taken by state parties to implement the Commission's recommendations.[15] Our study attempted to assess the level of compliance by states regarding all the communications where the Commission found a state party in violation of the Charter.[16] The cases (or "communications") under review start in 1994, when the first activity report of the Commission containing its findings was published,[17] and run to mid-2003, with the publication of the Sixteenth Annual Activity Report. Over this period, the African Commission found violations of the provisions of the African Charter in forty-four communications, involving seventeen of the fifty-three states that are party to the African Charter.[18] Data were collected about the steps states had taken to implement the Commission's recommendations, setting out the degree of state compliance as of

[15] Information about implementation was gathered over a three-year period from January 2002 to December 2004, using a series of interviews with the relevant players such as the commissioners, members of the secretariat, and representatives of state parties, national human rights institutions, and nongovernmental organizations (NGOs). Information on state compliance was also gathered from the records of the African Commission in the few instances where it did attempt to establish follow-up or where state parties offered information about follow-up. The main sources of such information were the reports of the Commission on its missions for promotional or protective reasons and state reports submitted in accordance with Article 62 of the African Charter. Where scholarly works on the African Commission's jurisprudence contained information on state compliance, it was also noted. Finally, information on follow-up was gathered from or verified by media reports.

[16] Cases that the Commission ruled inadmissible were not included, nor were those in which the Commission reported that an amicable settlement had been reached. An attempt was initially made to determine the particulars of these amicable settlements and their implementation, but it was abandoned for lack of access to the relevant files of the Commission and the inability of commissioners to provide pertinent details. Another limitation of this study is that it does not cover the implementation of "interim" or "precautionary" measures, as such, because the African Commission does not adopt separate decisions dealing with these measures. However, insofar as compliance with interim measures can be derived from the implementation efforts of state parties, this aspect was included in the study. In one of the cases categorized as "situational compliance" below, the Commission held that the failure of Nigeria to suspend the execution of Ken Saro-Wiwa and other members of the Movement for the Survival of the Ogoni People amounted to a violation of Article 1 of the Charter. Int'l PEN (on Behalf of Saro-Wiwa) v. Nigeria, Comm. Nos. 137/94, 139/94, 154/96, 161/97 (joined), 2000 AHRLR 212, paras. 113, 114, 116, 122 (ACHPR 1998). Compare the later decision in Interights (on Behalf of Bosch) v. Botswana, Comm. No. 240/2001, 2003 AHRLR 55, para. 51 (ACHPR 2003).

[17] Although the African Commission held its first ordinary session in 1987, it was only in 1994, when it issued its Seventh Annual Activity Report, that the Commission first published its findings on communications decided under the individual complaints procedure. An overly strict interpretation of Article 59 of the African Charter, the confidentiality clause, initially kept the Commission from publishing those findings. Since the Seventh Annual Activity Report, all subsequent activity reports have included a separate annex dealing with communications.

[18] The following state parties have been found to have violated the African Charter: Angola, Botswana, Burkina Faso, Burundi, Cameroon, Chad, The Gambia, Ghana, Kenya, Malawi, Mauritania, Nigeria, Rwanda, Sierra Leone, Sudan, Zaire (now Democratic Republic of the Congo), and Zambia.

December 31, 2004.[19] An effort was then made to categorize state implementation, and to identify the factors giving rise to compliance.[20]

State compliance with the recommendations of the African Commission is divided into five broad categories: "full compliance," "noncompliance," "partial compliance," *sui generis* cases of compliance or partial compliance after a change of government (also termed "situational compliance"), and "unclear" cases.

A state party is deemed to have "fully complied" with the recommendations of the Commission if it has implemented them all or has unequivocally expressed the political will to comply with their substance and has already taken significant steps in this process. However, to make an accurate assessment whether a state has expressed the necessary political will to implement a communication fully is difficult. For this and other reasons, this category is open to revision. The survey shows that in only six of the forty-four communications (or 14 percent) did state parties comply fully and in timely fashion with the recommendations of the African Commission.[21]

The second category, termed "noncompliance," refers to cases in which state parties did not implement any of the Commission's recommendations.[22] The category also includes situations where state parties did not accept the findings of the Commission, challenging it on factual or legal grounds while indicating that they would not implement the Commission's recommendations for those reasons. Among these cases are relatively recent decisions contained in the Sixteenth Annual Activity Report of the African Commission (made public in July 2003). Although these communications were decided fairly near the cutoff mark of the study (the end of 2004), a year and a half later, at the thirty-fifth ordinary session of the Commission, the authors of these communications—all against Sudan—made clear that no steps had been taken by the respective Sudanese governments.[23] According to our study results, state parties clearly did not comply with the Commission's recommendations in thirteen cases (or 30 percent of the total).

[19] Compliance is not a static process. By its very nature, this study provides a snapshot of implementation at a particular time. As indicated above, the category into which a particular communication falls may (and is bound to) change. In that sense, the study (and any similar study) remains a work in progress.

[20] *See infra* part III.

[21] *See infra* part II.

[22] These cases are Lawyers Comm. for Hum. Rts. v. Zaire, Comm. No. 47/90, 2000 AHRLR 71 (ACHPR 1994) [*Zairian Torture* case]; Free Legal Assistance Group v. Zaire, Comm. Nos. 25/89, 47/90, 56/91, 100/93 (joined), 2000 AHRLR 74 (ACHPR 1995) [*Zairian Mass Violations* case]; Mekongo v. Cameroon, Comm. No. 59/91, 2000 AHRLR 56 (ACHPR 1995); Union interafricaine des droits de l'homme v. Angola, Comm. No. 159/96, 2000 AHRLR 18 (ACHPR 1997) [*Angolan Expulsion* case]; Malawi Afr. Ass'n v. Mauritania, Comm. Nos. 54/91, 61/91, 98/93, 164/97–196/97, 210/98 (joined), 2000 AHRLR 149 (ACHPR 2000) [*Mauritanian Widows* case]; Rights Int'l v. Nigeria, Comm. No. 215/98, 2000 AHRLR 254 (ACHPR 1999) [*Nigerian Torture* case]; Avocats sans frontières (on Behalf of Bwampamye) v. Burundi, Comm. No. 231/99, 2000 AHRLR 48 (ACHPR 2000) [*Bwampamye* case]; Ouko v. Kenya, Comm. No. 232/99, 2000 AHRLR 135 (ACHPR 2000); Civil Liberties Org. v. Nigeria, Comm. No. 218/98, 2001 AHRLR 75 (ACHPR 2001) [*Nigerian Military Tribunals* case]; Law Offices of Suleiman (I) v. Sudan, Comm. Nos. 222/98, 229/99 (joined), 2003 AHRLR 134 (ACHPR 2003) [*Sudanese Military Court* case]; Law Offices of Suleiman (II) v. Sudan, Comm. No. 228/99, 2003 AHRLR 144 (ACHPR 2003) [*Suleiman* case]; Doebbler v. Sudan, Comm. No. 236/2000, 2003 AHRLR 153 (ACHPR 2003) [*Sudanese Picnic* case]; Purohit v. Gambia, Comm. No. 241/2001, 2003 AHRLR 96 (ACHPR 2003) [*Gambian Mental Health* case].

[23] Curtis Doebbler, the author of Communication No. 236/2000, distributed an information sheet entitled "Information Relevant to the Consideration of Sudan's State Report to the African Commission on Human and Peoples' Rights" (May 22, 2004) (on file with authors). This document not only pointed out that Sudan had not implemented any of the recommendations forwarded in the three Sudanese cases, *supra* note 22, but also requested that the Commission "keep the item of the implementation of these decisions on its agenda and . . . request the government of Sudan to report to the Commission about the action it has taken to implement these decisions until they have been fully implemented in accordance with the African Commission's decision."

The third category, "partial compliance," refers to communications where the state party implemented some, but not all, of the elements of the Commission's recommendations. It may also represent instances where a state party has not given complete effect to the recommendations. Categorizing state responses as "partial compliance" is even more problematic than it is for "full compliance," primarily because a finding of "partial compliance" most often indicates that the process of implementation is still ongoing. According to the survey, fourteen of the cases (or 32 percent) show partial compliance with the Commission's recommendations. In most of these instances, state parties had made some attempts to implement the recommendations without committing themselves unequivocally to walk the whole distance. Instances where the Commission issued a vaguely formulated or open-ended remedy, and some action by the state was noted, were also designated as "partial compliance."

In another seven cases, partial or full compliance may be derived from the transition from an undemocratic and repressive to a more stable and democratic system of government.[24] These cases do not amount to "compliance," as earlier defined, since the resulting changes occurred because of a change in the circumstances (or "situation") rather than governmental responses to recommendations of the African Commission. A single factor, a relatively dramatic change of government, explains the changes that occurred. Under the principle of state responsibility, compliance is the responsibility of the state, not of transient governments. In these seven cases (all involving Nigeria and Rwanda), the role of the government (and changes of government) takes priority. After the dramatic regime change in Nigeria, in 1998, and in the context of the replacement of a military government with a civilian government, some of the Commission's recommendations were complied with.[25] These recommendations were not implemented during the period of the Abacha dictatorship. In our view, to categorize all these cases as "clear compliance" would present a distorted picture. Nevertheless, if the temporal scope for measuring compliance is extended beyond 1998 or 1999 (when Abacha died and the civilian government was installed, respectively), Nigeria can be said to have complied at least partially in some cases. Compliance mostly took the form of repealing decrees, which could be viewed as a factor directly related to the change from a military to a democratic government. Thus, the obligation on the state to comply is in line with its political policies and is not equivalent to, say, the obligation to make compensation, which has not been paid to any of the victims detained unlawfully during the Abacha regime. Similarly, the fundamental change of government and gradual return to civilian governance in Rwanda after 1994 is of overriding

[24] These cases are Org. mondiale contre la torture v. Rwanda, Comm. Nos. 27/89, 46/91, 49/91, 99/93 (joined), 2000 AHRLR 282 (ACHPR 1996) [*Rwandan Mass Violations* case]; Civil Liberties Org. (*re* Nigerian Bar Ass'n) v. Nigeria, Comm. No. 101/93, 2000 AHRLR 186 (ACHPR 1995) [*Body of Benchers* case]; Constitutional Rights Project v. Nigeria, Comm. No. 102/93, 2000 AHRLR 191 (ACHPR 1998) [*Nigerian Election Annulment* case]; Media Rights Agenda v. Nigeria, Comm. Nos. 105/93, 128/94, 130/94, 152/96 (joined), 2000 AHRLR 200 (ACHPR 1998) [*Nigerian Media* case]; *Saro-Wiwa* case, *supra* note 16; Constitutional Rights Project v. Nigeria, Comm. Nos. 143/95, 150/96 (joined), 2000 AHRLR 235 (ACHPR 1999); Huri-Laws v. Nigeria, Comm. No. 225/98, 2000 AHRLR 273 (ACHPR 2000).

[25] This does not mean that the new government immediately implemented the Commission's recommendations. For example, the *Nigerian Election Annulment* case, *supra* note 24, which was initiated in 1993, was only decided on the merits in October 1998, after the Commission, at the twenty-fourth ordinary session that month, was furnished by the complainants with "a 'supplementary submission on pending communications on Nigeria', basically urging the Commission to continue consideration of communications against Nigeria including the instant one because the violations had not abated, and the change in government following the death of General Sani Abacha has not changed any state responsibility of Nigeria." *Id.*, para. 38.

importance when considering the joint communication against Rwanda, submitted in 1989 and 1992, and decided in 1996.

To the extent that these changes coincided with some form of compliance, these cases are categorized as instances of "situational compliance." This category includes instances of both wholesale changes (approximating "full compliance") and limited adjustments (approximating "partial compliance").

In the remaining four cases (or 9 percent), insufficient information forecloses any pronouncement about state compliance, making them instances of "unclear" compliance.[26]

The various difficulties encountered in undertaking an exhaustive study of this nature rule out the claim that the recorded research findings are a complete or fully accurate account of implementation. The following hindrances constricted the empirical inquiry: communication difficulties, insufficient records, difficulties in tracing victims and authors of communications, lack of quality and continuity of state representatives attending the Commission's sessions, opposing views about compliance by those involved, and lack of media coverage.[27] It comes as no surprise that the Human Rights Committee, after more than ten years of monitoring the implementation of its views, remarked that "[a]ttempts to categorize follow-up replies are necessarily imprecise."[28]

Even if the factual position could be established with some accuracy, categorization remains contentious, because implementation is not a static, but a dynamic process. Different conclusions on the correct category for a particular communication could possibly have been reached. Some of the difficulties encountered in classifying the implementation efforts of states relate to the problematic causal connection between the Commission's findings and the government's action, and the lack of a clear remedy. These two factors are now discussed briefly.

The general problem of determination of causality can be illustrated by cases in which intensive publicity caused significant international pressure to be exerted on a state party. In classifying the state party's efforts as "full compliance," it remains unclear whether the relief sought by the victim came about as a result of the Commission's recommendations or the international pressure. Questions of causality also come into play in situations where, for instance, a civil war was being waged or a military dictator held power when the complaint was submitted, but by the time the Commission's recommendations were made known, these situations had changed considerably.

Another difficulty in categorization arose in situations where the Commission found a state in violation of the Charter but did not specify any recommendations. This procedure

[26] These cases are Achutan (on Behalf of Banda et al.) v. Malawi, Comm. Nos. 64/92, 68/92, 78/92 (joined), 2000 AHRLR 144 (ACHPR 1995); Aminu v. Nigeria, Comm. No. 205/97, 2000 AHRLR 248 (ACHPR 2000); Civil Liberties Org. v. Nigeria, Comm. No. 129/94, 2000 AHRLR 188 (ACHPR 1995); Comm'n nationale des droits de l'homme et des libertés v. Chad, Comm. No. 74/92, 2000 AHRLR 66 (ACHPR 1995).

[27] It was difficult to establish facts when the state party representatives and NGOs held opposite views. In such circumstances, the varying responses were considered carefully, and the benefit of the doubt given to the NGOs' version in instances where doubt persisted.

[28] Report of the Human Rights Committee, UN GAOR, 54th Sess., Supp. No. 40, vol. 1 at 90, para. 459, UN Doc. A/54/40 (1999). In July 1990, during the Committee's thirty-ninth session, it had established a follow-up procedure to its views under Article 5(4) of the Optional Protocol to the International Covenant on Civil and Political Rights and created the mandate of special rapporteur on follow-up. Report of the Human Rights Committee, UN GAOR, 45th Sess., Supp. No. 40, Annex XI, vol. 2 at 205, UN Doc. A/45/40 (1990). With reference to the difficulties in categorizing follow-up replies, see the Committee's 1999 Report, *supra*, para. 459.

left it entirely up to the state party to decide which steps would give effect to the Commission's finding, and, in turn, made it difficult to determine if all the necessary steps had been taken. In many of these instances, the state's response is categorized as "partial" compliance.

Although there is clearly an overall lack of state compliance with the recommendations of the African Commission, full compliance was nevertheless recorded in six cases. The factors that influenced states to comply fully in these six cases, and those that resulted in noncompliance in thirteen cases decided by the Commission, form the focus of the remainder of this article.

The implementation of the recommendations or views of treaty bodies in national law is one of the indicators of the possible direct impact of treaties on national law and on the state practice of parties to these treaties. Therefore, any efforts undertaken to explain state compliance or noncompliance with the recommendations of the African Commission should be viewed as only one part of the bigger question of compliance by states with international treaties.

II. CASES OF FULL COMPLIANCE

The six cases where full compliance with the Commission's recommendations was recorded are briefly summarized here, to form the background against which to identify factors that have influenced states to comply. The cases are discussed in chronological order, according to the time frame of the activity report in which each of them was published.

In *Pagnoulle (on Behalf of Mazou) v. Cameroon,*[29] Abdoulaye Mazou asked Amnesty International to pursue action on his behalf against the government of Cameroon. Mazou had been imprisoned in 1984 by a military tribunal without trial, witnesses, or the right to defense, for hiding his brother who was later sentenced to death for an attempted coup d'état. After serving his five-year sentence and being placed under subsequent house arrest, the accused was not reinstated as a magistrate under the Amnesty Law of April 23, 1992, although others who had been condemned under similar conditions were reinstated. The African Commission found Cameroon in violation of Articles 6, 7(1)(b) and (d), and 15 of the African Charter.[30] The Commission recommended that "the government of Cameroon draw all the necessary legal conclusions to reinstate the victim in his rights."[31] During the delivery of its initial state report in 2002, in accordance with Article 62 of the African Charter, the government of Cameroon reported that it had reinstated Mazou in the judiciary.[32] It further alleged that compensation had been offered to Mazou, but that he had declined it, and the state therefore viewed the case

[29] Pagnoulle (on Behalf of Mazou) v. Cameroon, Comm. No. 39/90, 2000 AHRLR 57 (ACHPR 1997) [hereinafter *Mazou* case]; *see also id., supra* note 13.

[30] Article 6 of the African Charter, *supra* note 4, prohibits arbitrary arrest or detention. According to Article 7(1)(b), every individual has the right to be presumed innocent until proven guilty by a competent court or tribunal, and under paragraph (1)(d), such a trial should take place within a reasonable time. Article 15 of the Charter deals with the rights of every individual to work under equitable and satisfactory conditions and to receive equal pay for equal work.

[31] *Mazou, supra* note 29, at 61, para. [31].

[32] Personal notes taken during the Commission's thirty-first ordinary session, Pretoria, South Africa (May 6, 2002) [hereinafter 31st Session Notes] (on file with authors).

as having been settled. The Commission did not make any additional recommendations to Cameroon.[33]

In *Amnesty International (on Behalf of Banda and Chinula) v. Zambia*,[34] it was alleged that the deportation from Zambia to Malawi, of William Steven Banda and John Luson Chinula, based on their political convictions, violated the African Charter. Both Banda and Chinula were prominent political figures in Zambia and belonged to the party that had been in power since independence in 1964, but was defeated in 1991. They therefore formed part of the opposition to the new incumbent government.[35] Both complainants were deported to Malawi in 1994 on the basis of allegations that they were a threat to peace and stability in Zambia, but only Banda was given an opportunity to contest his deportation order through the Zambian courts. The African Commission concluded that Zambia had violated Articles 2, 7(1)(a), 8, 9(2), 10, and 18(1) and (2) of the African Charter.[36] The African Commission made the following recommendations:

> Zambia must be required to allow the return of William Steven Banda with a view to making application for citizenship by naturalisation. No evidence was led before the Commission for compensation. The evidence is that Banda had lost his job as Governor after the 1991 elections. No award for compensation is called for.
>
> . . . John Lyson Chinula died in Malawi. He was a prominent businessman. His deportation must have caused prejudice to his business interests. His family is requesting the return of his body for burial in Zambia. The government of Zambia should be required to grant that wish.[37]

Three years after the Commission's decision, the Zambian government announced the reversal of Banda's and Chinula's deportation orders.[38] Acknowledging that the deportation orders were not justified, the president authorized the repatriation of Chinula's remains to Zambia for reburial and invited Banda to return to Zambia unconditionally.[39]

[33] The earlier proceeding concerning Mazou is the only case that the secretariat of the Commission had previously cited as an instance of a state's full compliance with the Commission's recommendations. *See supra* note 13.

[34] Amnesty Int'l (on Behalf of Banda & Chinula) v. Zambia, Comm. No. 212/98, 2000 AHRLR 325 (ACHPR 1999) [*Zambian Deportation* case].

[35] They were leading members of the United National Independence Party (UNIP), which was defeated by the Movement for Multiparty Democracy (MMD) in the first multiparty elections in 1991.

[36] Article 2 of the African Charter, *supra* note 4, grants every individual enjoyment of the rights and freedoms recognized in the Charter irrespective of his or her political opinion. Article 7(1)(a) deals with the right of every individual to have his or her cause heard, which includes the right to an appeal to competent national organs. Article 8 guarantees an individual's right to freedom of conscience. Article 9(2) reads as follows: "Every individual shall have the right to express and disseminate his opinions within the law." Article 10 guarantees the right to free association, and paragraphs (1) and (2) of Article 18 deal with the state's duties toward the family as the natural unit and basis of society.

[37] Zambian Deportation case, *supra* note 34, paras. 39, 40.

[38] From September 9 to13, 2002, the African Commission undertook a promotional visit to Zambia. Commissioner Chigovera, who led the visit, engaged the Ministry of Justice in a discussion of the implementation of the findings of the Commission in the case of Banda and Chinula. The ministry confirmed that the president had revoked the deportation order and that the government had authorized the repatriation to Zambia for reburial of the remains of Chinula, who had died in exile. *See* ACHPR, Rapport de la Mission de Promotion en République de Zambie, 9–13 septembre 2002, at 10 (2002).

[39] *Id.*

In *Constitutional Rights Project v. Nigeria*,[40] the five complainants were arrested in June 1995 and detained without being charged or tried for more than two years before a complaint was lodged with the African Commission. This situation had not changed by the time the Commission finally decided the case in November 1999. The Commission found Nigeria in violation of Articles 6, and 7(1)(a) and (d) of the African Charter.[41] The Commission appealed to the government of Nigeria to charge the detainees or release them.[42] Nigeria complied and charged the detainees.[43]

The fourth case of full compliance also involved Nigeria. In *Centre for Free Speech v. Nigeria*,[44] four journalists were tried in secret by a military tribunal and not allowed access to counsel of their choice. Under military decrees the jurisdiction of regular courts to hear appeals from military tribunals was ousted, leaving the journalists without any right to appeal their sentences. The Commission found that Nigeria had violated Articles 6, 7(1)(a) and (c), and 26 of the African Charter.[45] The Commission also urged the Nigerian government to release the four journalists. The journalists were eventually released.[46]

In *Modise v. Botswana*,[47] the complainant John K. Modise alleged that he had been unjustly deprived of his real nationality. He asked the government of Botswana to concede him citizenship by descent (birth). He alleged that owing to his political activities as one of the founders and leaders of an opposition party in Botswana, he had been declared an "undesirable immigrant." He further alleged that on several occasions he had been deported without trial from Botswana to South Africa; as a result, he had suffered financial losses since Botswana had confiscated his belongings and property, and he could not work without the relevant permit. The Commission found that the government of Botswana had violated Articles 3(2), 5, 12(1) and (2), 13(1) and (2), 14, and 18(1) of the African Charter.[48] The Commission urged Botswana to recognize the complainant as a Botswanan citizen by descent and also to compensate him adequately for the violations of his rights. The attorney general of Botswana agreed during the thirty-first ordinary session of the Commission to implement its recommendations upon

[40] Constitutional Rights Project v. Nigeria, Comm. No. 153/96, 2000 AHRLR 248 (ACHPR 1999) [*Nigerian Detention* case].

[41] Article 6 of the African Charter, *supra* note 4, guarantees the right not to be arbitrarily arrested or detained. For Article 7(1)(a), see note 36 *supra*. Article 7(1)(d) guarantees the right to be tried within a reasonable time.

[42] Nigerian Detention case, *supra* note 40, final para.

[43] Interview with Agnes Olowu, legal officer at Constitutional Rights Project, in Lagos, Nigeria (Oct. 28, 2002).

[44] Centre for Free Speech v. Nigeria, Comm. No. 206/97, 2000 AHRLR 250 (ACHPR 1999) [*Nigerian Journalists* case].

[45] The jurisdiction of the courts was revoked by the Treason and Other Offences (Special Military Tribunal) Act, which the Commission found to violate Article 26 of the African Charter. Article 26 reads as follows: "State Parties to the present Charter shall have the duty to guarantee the independence of the Courts and shall allow the establishment and improvement of appropriate national institutions entrusted with the promotion and protection of the rights and freedoms guaranteed by the present Charter."

[46] Interview with Kolawole Olaniyan, then a legal officer at Constitutional Rights Project, during the thirty-third ordinary session of the African Commission in Niamey, Niger (May 20, 2005).

[47] Modise v. Botswana, Comm. No. 97/93, 2000 AHRLR 30 (ACHPR 2000); *see also id.*, 2000 AHRLR 25 (ACHPR 1994), 2000 AHRLR 25 (ACHPR 1997).

[48] Article 3(2) guarantees the right of every individual to equal protection of the law. Article 5 guarantees the right to dignity. Article 12(1) and (2) deals with the rights of freedom of movement and the right of an individual to return to his country. Article 13(1) and (2) deals with the rights of citizens to participate freely in the government of his country. Article 14 guarantees the right to property, which may only be encroached upon in the interest of public need or the general interest of the community. Finally, Article 18(1) provides that the family is the natural unit and basis of society and that it "shall be protected by the State which shall take care of its physical health and moral."

receiving a written request from the Commission in this regard, together with specifications on implementation.[49] The government of Botswana has since agreed in principle to award Modise citizenship by birth, which will also then apply to his children.[50]

Finally, in *Forum of Conscience v. Sierra Leone*,[51] the complaint was lodged on behalf of twenty-four soldiers allegedly tried by a court-martial in contravention of the due process rights guaranteed in the Charter. The soldiers were subsequently sentenced to death without the right to appeal to a higher tribunal. The Commission found Sierra Leone in violation of Articles 4 and 7(1)(a) of the African Charter. The Commission did not make any recommendations but stated that "[a]lthough this process cannot bring the victims back to life, it does not exonerate the government of Sierra Leone from its obligations under the Charter."[52] The Commission sent a delegation to Freetown on a promotional mission between February 14 and 19, 2000, and the subject of the complaint was taken up with relevant government officials, including the attorney general.[53] Legislation was passed granting soldiers the right of appeal to the Court of Appeal or subsequently to the Supreme Court.[54]

[49] 31st Session Notes, *supra* note 32 (May 2–16, 2002).

[50] This agreement by Botswana is the result of follow-up efforts by Interights, a London-based NGO that represented Modise. These follow-up efforts are summarized here to explain why the government has agreed only on the issue of citizenship and not on compensation. While appearing as respondent in the hearings before the Commission, Botswana conceded that the African Charter formed part of its constitutional dispensation and undertook during the public session of the thirty-first ordinary session to implement the Commission's findings. Chidi Odinkalu, a legal officer for Interights, therefore approached the attorney-general of Botswana during that session to discuss implementation, resulting in a formal invitation to Interights to meet in Gaborone with the attorney-general and the permanent secretary for political affairs in the Office of the President. It was agreed there that Interights would draft a memorandum of agreement providing for (1) granting Modise citizenship by birth, and (2) compensating him for all damages suffered in the different phases of the communication, which was first lodged in 1993. But before the memorandum of agreement could be submitted to the attorney-general, the latter left his position for a career in politics. During the same period, however, Modise's children decided to take the matter into their own hands and approached the media to force the government to address compensation, as well as citizenship. The government responded by indicating that it had never agreed in writing to compensate Modise. In a meeting in December 2003 between Interights and the permanent secretary for political affairs in the Office of the President, it was resolved that if Modise sent the Office of the President a formal request, the president would "find a way" to implement the Commission's recommendations. Yet after the media intervention by Modise's children, the government was reluctant to pay compensation to a person they described as a "political opponent." Nevertheless, Modise does have a passport and it is only a matter of administration to accord him citizenship by birth as agreed to in principle by the government, which would then grant his children an equal status. Interviews with Ibrahima Kane and Chidi Odinkalu, senior legal officers of Interights, held during the thirty-second, thirty-third, thirty-fourth, and thirty-fifth ordinary sessions of the African Commission (Oct. 2002–June 2004). Commissioner Dankwa reported that on a promotional visit to Botswana, the "assurance given to me that the President of Botswana had granted citizenship to Modise turned out to be true." He noted, however, that the communication had "lingered before the Commission thereafter for years because the complainant was not satisfied with the type of citizenship granted to him. Counsel for Modise persuasively argued later that he was entitled to citizenship by birth, which placed no limitation on his civil and political rights." E. V. O. Dankwa, *The Promotional Role of the African Commission on Human and Peoples' Rights, in* Evans & Murray, *supra* note 7, at 335, 345. Commissioner Dankwa's follow-up efforts concerned the *Modise* case as adopted in 1997, *see* note 47 *supra*, before Modise returned to the Commission to ask for recognition of his right to citizenship by birth.

[51] Forum of Conscience v. Sierra Leone, Comm. No. 223/98, 2000 AHRLR 293 (ACHPR 2000) [*Sierra Leone Coup* case].

[52] *Id.*, para. 19.

[53] *Id.*, para. 10 (setting out the procedure followed by the Commission).

[54] The Commission "noted with satisfaction that the law has been amended, subsequent to the mission to Sierra Leone, to bring it into conformity with the Charter." *Id.*, para. 20. According to Thomas MacLean, member of the NGO Forum of Conscience, the Commission helped significantly in speeding up the passing of the new law by sensitizing and pressuring the government. He commented that Sierra Leone responds to outside pressure. He also attributed the government's compliance to the mobilization of civil society within Sierra Leone. Thomas MacLean,

III. Factors Indicative of Compliance or Noncompliance

Thus far, the discussion has focused on the status of state compliance with the recommendations adopted by the African Commission until mid-2003 and has established that there was an overall lack of state compliance. This state of affairs raises the question whether certain factors that were present in the six cases of "full compliance" may be identified as factors predictive of compliance, and whether factors that were present in the thirteen cases of noncompliance could be identified as factors predictive of noncompliance.

A distinction should be drawn between factors that are inherent in the institutions that make up and affect the African human rights system, on the one hand, and those that fluctuate from case to case, on the other hand. Arguably, the permanent features of the African human rights system explain the *general trend* toward noncompliance. These factors include the quasi-judicial nature of the African Commission, the recommendatory and nonbinding nature of its decisions, its legitimacy deficit, and the lack of commitment to human rights of the political umbrella body, the Organization of African Unity (OAU, now the African Union (AU)). Important as they are in understanding noncompliance in general, these factors do not account for the variations in compliance by *particular states* and with regard to specific cases. To do so, one must investigate the role of "variable" factors, such as those relating to the treaty body's handling of each case, the issues involved in a specific communication, the nature of the remedial action required in a particular case, the complainant or complainants involved, the conditions prevailing in the state party concerned, the involvement of civil society actors, and the international pressure applied in a given case.

To make this analysis, the six cases where full and timely compliance was recorded are contrasted with the thirteen cases of "noncompliance." Because of the small number of cases, Fisher's Exact Test was used to determine the statistical significance of each factor listed in tables 1 to 4 below as a predictor of compliance or noncompliance by states.[55]

Factors Related to the Treaty Body (African Commission)

The first set of factors relates to the treaty body, the African Commission. Especially since it is generally accepted that the findings under the African Charter are not legally binding on

Comments, Workshop on Human Rights Litigation in Africa, held in Pretoria under the auspices of the Institute for Human Rights and Development in Africa and the Kenyan and Swedish Sections of the International Commission of Jurists (Apr. 29–May 1, 2002) (authors' notes, on file with authors).

[55] Owing to the small number of total cases (19), the Chi-square Test proved to be unreliable and was not used. *See, e.g.*, R. MARK SIRKIN, STATISTICS FOR THE SOCIAL SCIENCES 364 (1995). The small number of cases available for analysis ($n = 19$) also necessitates that these results be interpreted with caution; assessment of the cumulative impact of some factors and the cross-correlation between factors are problematic. It is considered statistically significant if the relationship between (non)compliance and a particular factor is on the 5 percent level of significance (that is, where $p \leq 0.05$), although a relationship on the 10 percent level of significance (that is, where $p \leq 0.1$) may also be statistically appreciable. The probability (in terms of p) for the factors in the tables below that permitted measurement are table 1: period, $p = 0.2554$; state involvement, $p > 0.9999$; reasoning, $p > 0.9999$; formulation of remedy, $p = 0.7892$; Commission follow-up, $p = 0.3498$; table 2: nature of state obligation, $p = 0.5439$; scale of violation, $p = 0.2776$; table 3: type of government, $p = 0.0029$; change of government, $p = 0.5573$; level of stability, $p = 0.0880$; table 4: NGO involvement in case, $p = 0.1093$; NGO involvement in follow-up, $p = 0.0116$. (Where more than one variable featured simultaneously, as with "nature of right," and when data were missing or unclear, as in table 5, the test was not applied.) We acknowledge with appreciation the assistance of Rina Owen, Department of Statistics, University of Pretoria, who applied Fisher's Exact Test.

parties to a dispute, the *way* that the Commission executes its mandate to a great extent determines the moral force of its findings. The implementation of treaty body findings depends on the will of state parties. Instead of coercing states into compliance through sanctions, which is a difficult exercise under international law, the persuasive force of the treaty body's findings is assumed to increase and hence improve compliance.[56] Six aspects are considered here, as set out in table 1 (p. 14): (1) the period in the life of the Commission when the finding was made, premised on improvement in compliance as the system matured; (2) the length of time it took the Commission to decide on the final communication (measured from the time the Commission was "seized" of the matter, until a decision on the merits was taken); (3) the extent of state involvement in the processing and completion of the communication; (4) the degree to which a particular finding was reasoned and substantiated; (5) the extent to which a clear and specific remedy was formulated in the particular case; and (6) the absence or presence of initiatives taken by the Commission to follow up on the implementation of its findings or remedies.

Maturity of the African regional human rights system. Can it be said that compliance has increased as the African regional human rights system has "matured"? In other words, has there been a gradual improvement in compliance over time? In table 1, the communications are divided into two periods: those decided in the early to mid-1990s (1990–1996), and those decided in the late 1990s to early 2000s (1997–2003). All six cases of full compliance were decided in the second (later) period. This factor could be indicative of better compliance as the system matured, especially if it is taken into account that all the cases in the sample decided in the earlier period fall in the category of "noncompliance." However, nine of the thirteen cases of noncompliance were also decided in the second period, a factor that returns us to the difficulty of classifying cases. Arguably, these cases should not have been classified as "noncompliant," because they were decided too recently to have given the state parties an adequate opportunity to implement the findings. Still, these cases were specifically classified as "noncompliant" on the basis that the complainants had made it clear that no steps had been taken by the state parties notwithstanding repeated efforts to secure compliance. Even though the origin of all the cases of compliance in the later life of the Commission is also a noteworthy factor, it is too early to conclude that the maturity of the African regional human rights system has played a decisive role in ensuring the improved implementation of the Commission's recommendations.

Length of time to complete the communication. The African Commission convenes two ordinary sessions per year and during these sessions time is allocated for the consideration of individual communications in hearings closed to the public. The second factor considered in relation to the treaty body, the length of time it took to complete each case, is premised on the notion that a shorter time lapse may lead to better compliance, as the immediacy of the events may stimulate domestic compulsion to implement, and as states may perceive that the procedure met the requirements of due process. This period was measured by counting the number of ordinary sessions between the Commission's seizing of a communication and the decision on the merits. Unfortunately, no clear conclusions can be drawn from the sample under review.

[56] "A preoccupation with outcomes places factors enhancing persuasion in the foreground." Frans Viljoen & Lirette Louw, *The Status of the Findings of the African Commission: From Moral Persuasion to Legal Obligation*, J. AFR. L., Apr. 2004, at 1, 19.

TABLE 1. STATE COMPLIANCE: FACTORS RELATED TO TREATY BODY

Case	Period[a]		Time Lapse[b]	State Involvement[c]	Reasoning			Formulation of Remedy			Follow-up		
	1990–1996	1997–2003			Brief	Limited	Substantial	None	Vague	Specific	None	State Reporting	Other
Full Compliance													
Mazou		X	?	Yes		X				X		X	
Zambian Deportation		X	2	Yes			X			X			X
Nigerian Detention		X	5	No	X					X	X		
Nigerian Journalists		X	4	No	X					X	X		
Modise		X	15	Yes			X			X			X
Sierra Leone Coup		X	3	No	X			X					X
Noncompliance													
Zairian Torture	X		6	No	X			X			X		
Zairian Mass Violations	X		10	No	X			X			X		
Mekongo	X		6	No	X				X			X	
Angolan Expulsion		X	2	No	X				X		X		
Mauritanian Widows		X	20	Yes			X			X		X	X
Nigerian Torture		X	2	No	X			X			X		
Bwampamye		X	3	Yes		X				X	X		
Ouko		X	2	No		X				X	X		
Nigerian Military Tribunals		X	5	Yes			X			X	X		
Sudanese Military Court		X	8	Yes			X			X			X
Suleiman		X	8	Yes			X			X			X
Sudanese Picnic		X	6	Yes			X			X			X
Gambian Mental Health		X	4	Yes			X			X		X	

Sources: For the cases of full compliance, see notes 29, 34, 40, 44, 47, and 51, respectively. For the cases of noncompliance, see note 22.

[a] This column relates to the date when the decision was taken.

[b] The African Commission holds two ordinary sessions per year. This column indicates the number of ordinary sessions from the moment the Commission was seized of a specific communication until the matter was finally decided on the merits.

[c] State involvement is measured in terms of a yes or no response. Yes means that the procedure as stipulated in the decisions of the Commission clearly indicated that the state party was actively involved in the proceedings, in submitting both written and oral replies in response to the Commission's requests in a particular case. A no response means that the state party did not respond to any of the notifications sent out by the secretariat of the Commission, which in turn signifies that the Commission decided the case on the facts provided by the complainant and that the Commission had treated those facts as a given.

On average, it seems to take five ordinary sessions (roughly two and a half years) to complete a case; on that basis, four of the cases of full compliance took five or fewer sessions to complete, while two took significantly longer. These figures might have indicated that faster processing leads to improved implementation, until one looks at the cases of noncompliance. Seven of the thirteen "noncompliant" cases took five or fewer sessions to complete. On average, the cases of full compliance took 5.8 sessions, and those of noncompliance 6.3 sessions.

State involvement in the communication procedures. The third factor in regarding the treaty body is closely related to the above discussion, in that it also concerns the question whether state parties view the Commission's manner of deciding communications against them as in accordance with the rules of due process and procedural regularity. Cases were encoded as yes and no in response to the question "Do the decisions of the Commission indicate that the state party was actively involved in the proceedings?" A yes response means that the state replied to the Commission's queries and was involved in the written and oral proceedings.

When the state made no submission contesting the allegations set out in the complaint, the Commission developed the practice of deciding the case on the facts supplied by the complainant. In the *Zairian Mass Violations* case, the Commission explained this position as follows:

> In the present case, there has been no substantive response from the government of Zaire, despite the numerous notifications of the communications sent by the African Commission. The African Commission, in several previous decisions, has set out the principle that where allegations of human rights abuse go uncontested by the government concerned, even after repeated notifications, the Commission must decide on the facts provided by the complainant and treat those facts as given. This principle conforms with the practice of other international human rights adjudicatory bodies and the Commission's duty to protect human rights. Since the government of Zaire does not wish to participate in a dialogue, the Commission must, regrettably, continue its consideration of the case on the basis of facts and opinions submitted by the complainants alone.[57]

Departing from the assumption that a "participating" state would be more inclined to comply with the Commission's decisions, we compared state involvement in the cases of full compliance with that in the cases of no compliance. Analysis of the data (in table 1) does not provide conclusive evidence that participating states are more likely to implement decisions.[58] However, the level of state involvement and participation has improved over the years. Even if this development cannot be linked to compliance, it nevertheless indicates that state parties have become less likely to ignore the Commission's correspondence and requests pertaining to communications against them.

Reasoning in a particular finding. At first very brief and tersely argued, the Commission's decisions have evolved over the years into more well-reasoned and substantiated judgments. Yet the practice has not been formalized and remains ad hoc.[59] On the assumption that well-reasoned findings are more likely to be implemented, the Commission's findings are divided,

[57] Zairian Mass Violations case, *supra* note 22, para. 40.

[58] According to Fisher's Exact Test (with a p value of >0.999), *supra* note 55, there is no correlation between this factor and (non)compliance.

[59] The decisions of the African Commission that were published in its Seventh Annual Activity Report were very short and merely indicated the facts of the complaint and the Commission's findings, without necessarily indicating any remedial actions for implementation by the state party. This practice has changed significantly and the Commission now issues detailed decisions several pages long stating the facts, the procedures adopted, admissibility grounds, the reasoning on the merits, and a finding on the violation of specific articles of the African Charter followed by (sometimes detailed) recommendations.

for the purpose of our study, into three categories: brief reasoning, limited reasoning, and substantial reasoning.[60] When this analysis is applied to the six cases where full compliance was recorded (in table 1), well-reasoned judgments do not seem to be a prerequisite for compliance. In only two of the six cases does the Commission's decision reflect substantial reasoning; in one case the Commission's reasoning is limited, and in three the Commission's reasoning is brief.

The same conclusion is arrived at as regards cases of clear noncompliance. The majority of the findings in these cases are well reasoned, while some of the Commission's most elaborate decisions are the least implemented.[61] It therefore seems that the depth and width of the reasoning is not decisive in ensuring or predicting compliance.[62]

Formulation of the remedy or order. Linked to the fourth factor is the further hypothesis that the formulation of an exact and detailed remedy may also be predictive of compliance. In this respect, too, the practice has evolved from the total absence of remedies to the inconsistent prescription of remedies with varying precision.[63] Three categories are distinguished: no remedy whatsoever, a vague remedy, and a specific remedy. The six cases analyzed in table 1 demonstrate that in the majority of the cases (five out of six) where full compliance was reported, the Commission articulated specific remedies. This result suggests support for the contention that the formulation of a precise and targeted remedy improves compliance. However, a specific remedy was also spelled out in the majority of cases (eight of the thirteen) that ended in noncompliance. This position undermines the contention that the specificity and targeted nature of a remedy is more likely to lead to state compliance with a finding.[64]

The precision with which a remedy was formulated may not be a factor that predicts compliance, but it is central to the assessment of compliance. A proper analysis of compliance depends on a clearly delineated remedy. If there is no specific remedy, there is no criterion for

[60] Helfer and Slaughter refer to the "quality of legal reasoning" as a factor affecting state compliance and state that "the giving-reasons requirement is the prerequisite for the exercise of persuasive rather than coercive authority, the assurance that," quoting Ost, " 'the authority of a judgment derives from its intrinsic rationality rather than from an "argument" of authority.'" Helfer & Slaughter, *supra* note 2, at 320–21 (quoting François Ost, *The Original Canons of Interpretation of the European Court of Human Rights, in* THE EUROPEAN CONVENTION FOR THE PROTECTION OF HUMAN RIGHTS: INTERNATIONAL PROTECTION VERSUS NATIONAL RESTRICTIONS 283, 283–84 (Mireille Delmas-Marty & Christine Chodkiewicz eds., 1992)). Byrnes, listing factors that influence states to give effect to a decision of the UN Human Rights Committee, includes "whether the decision . . . is persuasively reasoned." Andrew Byrnes, *An Effective Complaints Procedure in the Context of International Human Rights Law, in* THE UN HUMAN RIGHTS TREATY SYSTEM IN THE 21ST CENTURY 139, 151 (Anne F. Bayefsky ed., 2000). Another aspect of delivering a well-reasoned decision that would contribute to the authority of a treaty body's decision and thus exert a greater compliance pull on state parties is judicial cross-referencing to and reliance on the findings of other treaty bodies. The African Commission, in its more recent decisions, has referred to the treaty body output (decisions as well as general comments) of the Human Rights Committee, the Inter-American Commission on Human Rights, and the European Court on Human Rights. *See, e.g.*, Legal Res. Found. v. Zambia, Comm. No. 211/98, 2001 AHRLR 84 (ACHPR 2001); *Suleiman* case, *supra* note 22.

[61] *See, e.g.*, Mauritanian Widows case, *supra* note 22.

[62] This impression is borne out by Fisher's Exact Test, *supra* note 55, where the predictability of this factor was measured as >0.9999.

[63] The Commission has not been consistent in its approach to the formulation of remedies. It has sometimes awarded no remedies to the victims of human rights abuses (for a recent example, see *Huri-Laws* case, *supra* note 24). On occasion it has formulated vague recommendations stating merely that "a state party should bring its laws into conformity with the African Charter." *See, e.g.*, Nigerian Media case, *supra* note 24. Vague recommendations not only leave the victims without any recourse, but also make it difficult to determine whether a state party actually complied with the Commission's recommendations.

[64] There is no statistical correlation between this factor and (non)compliance (with $p = 0.7892$).

measuring compliance, which makes the categorization of factual information on compliance ("full," "partial," and so on) problematic.

Follow-up by the treaty body. The sixth factor analyzed with reference to the treaty body is follow-up by the treaty body itself. Despite not having been explicitly mandated to undertake follow-up measures to ensure state compliance with its findings, the Commission has taken the initiative in several ways. First, it has sent letters to state parties calling on them to implement its decisions.[65] On occasion it has made use of promotional visits or visits for protective reasons to follow up on the status of state compliance.[66] At times the Commission has incorporated follow-up measures as part of its findings in deciding individual communications by calling on state parties to enumerate in their next periodic report under Article 62 of the African Charter the measures taken with a view to complying with the Commission's recommendations.[67] During the examination of state reports, members of the Commission have also directed questions to government delegates about the implementation of its decisions on communications.[68] However, these efforts have been few and far apart and have not developed into an established practice.

Our survey of the factors that influenced state compliance in the six cases of full compliance indicates that in four of these cases the African Commission made some attempt at following up on the steps taken by state parties to implement its recommendations.[69] As the Commission did not undertake any similar actions in the majority of "noncompliant" cases, this factor seems relevant to compliance. The lack of a follow-up provision in the Charter, which led to the ad hoc practice of exceptional follow-up, can therefore be described as a factor that has inhibited state compliance with the Commission's recommendations.

Factors Related to the Communication

The nature of a case presumably also plays a significant part in influencing state compliance. This statement should be understood with reference to the following four questions: (1) Is the

[65] African Commission [ACHPR], Communication Procedure, Information Sheet No. 3, at 17 (n.d.), *available at* <http://www.achpr.org/english/information_sheets/ACHPR%20inf.%20sheet%20no.3.doc>.

[66] *See* Report of the African Commission's Promotional Mission to Burkina Faso, Objectives, Sept. 22–Oct. 2, 2001, DOC/OS/(XXXIII)/324b/i (available on request from the Secretariat of the African Commission, achpr@achpr.org).

[67] *See* Legal Res. Found. v. Zambia, *supra* note 60. Although decided outside the temporal scope of this study, see also Lawyers for Hum. Rts. v. Swaziland, Comm. No. 251/2002, 18th Activity Report, AU Doc. EX.CL/199(VII) at 12, 22, last (unnumbered) para. (2005), where the Commission recommended that "the Kingdom of Swaziland should inform the African Commission in writing within six months on the measures it has taken to implement the above recommendations."

[68] Questions about compliance with decisions were posed, for example, to the government delegates of Cameroon and Mauritania during the examination of their initial reports, at the Commission's thirty-first session in May 2001. 31st Session Notes, *supra* note 32.

[69] In the communications decided against Botswana, Sierra Leone, Cameroon, and Zambia, the Commission did make some attempts at follow-up. In the Botswana case, the Commission inquired about the status of implementation during the public session at its thirty-first ordinary session. It sent a delegation to Sierra Leone on a promotional mission during which it made such an inquiry. In the cases decided against Cameroon and Zambia, implementation was already completed, so that the follow-up efforts should be seen as intended to establish the status of compliance, rather than as encouraging compliance through follow-up, as in the other two cases cited above. In one of the cases where partial compliance was recorded by Burkina Faso, follow-up also played a role. The Commission sent a promotional mission to Burkina Faso, which made inquiries about implementation, and in its state report under Charter Article 62 Burkina Faso indicated the relevant steps taken. Mouvement burkinabé des droits de l'homme et des peuples v. Burkina Faso, Comm. No. 204/97, 2001 AHRLR 51 (ACHPR 2001).

subject matter of violations "civil and political" or "socioeconomic" in nature? (2) Does the right that is invoked imply a duty on the government to "respect," "protect," or to "fulfill"? (3) What is the scale of the violations? That is, does the case reveal violations of the rights of individuals, or have the violations occurred on a wider scale and are they of an institutional nature, linked to the system of governance of a state party? (4) Does the type of remedy required to redress the violations have a bearing on compliance? The role that the answers to these questions (as set out in table 2, p. 19) play in state compliance is assessed briefly in this section with reference to the cases where states fully complied with the Commission's recommendations, as well as those of noncompliance.

Nature of the right most prominent in the decision. A distinction based on subject matter may be drawn between three categories of human rights, namely, "civil and political rights," "economic, social, and cultural rights," and "collective or solidarity rights" such as the right to development and environmental rights.[70] Although this "content-driven" division has lost much of its currency, it is adopted here for two reasons peculiar to the African Charter. First, the African Charter was the first international human rights treaty to include socioeconomic rights as justiciable equals to other rights. Second, the African Charter includes an elaborate list of collective rights ("peoples' rights"). In any event, this analysis is supplemented by the discussion that deals with the duty imposed by these rights, which immediately follows this one. An analysis of the violations found in the six cases of compliance with the Commission's recommendations shows that they mostly concerned civil and political rights, and fair-trial rights in particular.[71] The data suggest that when compliance occurs, it is likely to pertain to the violation of civil and political rights, especially Article 7 of the African Charter (fair-trial rights). Any conclusion based on these data is problematic, though, since by far the majority of *all* the cases decided by the Commission deals with civil and political rights, often involving rights related to a fair trial. It is therefore not surprising that cases of noncompliance also deal almost exclusively with violations of civil and political rights.

However, the three instances in which socioeconomic rights were invoked—albeit in conjunction with civil and political rights—all fall in the category of full noncompliance,[72] suggesting that states may still deem these rights less justiciable.

Nature of the obligation imposed on the state by the most prominent right in the decision. Another system for classifying human rights, as first articulated by Henry Shue, is according to the obligations they impose on state parties.[73] This system of classification is best illustrated by the *SERAC* case.[74] The obligation to respect (the obligation to refrain from taking any action that would result in the violation of a right) is exemplified by the Commission's recommendation

[70] For a detailed discussion on the categorization of human rights, see Allan Rosas & Martin Scheinin, *Categories and Beneficiaries of Human Rights*, *in* AN INTRODUCTION TO THE INTERNATIONAL PROTECTION OF HUMAN RIGHTS: A TEXTBOOK 49, 54–55 (Raija Hanski & Markku Suksi eds., 2d rev. ed. 1999).

[71] The right to a fair trial (Article 7 of the Charter) was actually the subject of violations in five of the six cases (Cameroon, Zambia, Nigeria (two cases), and Sierra Leone).

[72] These are the *Zairian Mass Violations* case, *supra* note 22, the *Mauritanian Widows* case, *supra* note 22, and the *Gambian Mental Health* case, *supra* note 22.

[73] HENRY SHUE, BASIC RIGHTS/SUBSISTENCE, AFFLUENCE, AND U.S. FOREIGN POLICY (1980). The tripartite division of governmental obligations has since been echoed by many authors and also by the UN Committee on Economic, Social and Cultural Rights, General Comment No. 14: The Right to the Highest Attainable Standard of Health, UN Doc. E/C.12/2000/4, para. 33.

[74] Soc. & Econ. Rts. Action Centre (SERAC) v. Nigeria, Comm. No. 155/96, 2001 AHRLR 60 (ACHPR 2001). Partial compliance was recorded in this case.

TABLE 2. STATE COMPLIANCE: FACTORS RELATED TO THE COMMUNICATION

Case	Nature of Right			Nature of State Obligation			Scale of Violation			Remedial Action Required		
	Civil/ Political	Socio/ Economic	Collective/ Solidarity	Respect	Protect	Fulfill	Single	Multiple	Massive	Compensation	Legislation	Administrative Action
Full Compliance												
Mazou	X			X				X				X
Zambian Deportation	X			X				X				X
Nigerian Detention	X			X			X					X
Nigerian Journalists	X			X			X					X
Modise	X			X				X		X		X
Sierra Leone Coup	X				X		X				X	
Noncompliance												
Zairian Torture	X			X					X			X
Zairian Mass Violations	X	X		X					X			X
Mekongo	X			X			X			X		
Angolan Expulsion	X			X					X	X	X	X
Mauritanian Widows	X	X		X					X	X	X	X
Nigerian Torture	X			X				X		X		X
Bwampamye	X			X			X				X	X
Ouko	X			X			X					X
Nigerian Military Tribunals	X			X				X		X	X	
Sudanese Military Court	X			X				X		X	X	
Suleiman	X			X			X			X	X	
Sudanese Picnic	X			X				X		X	X	
Gambian Mental Health	X	X		X		X			X		X	X

that Nigeria stop all attacks on Ogoni communities.[75] The obligation to protect (the duty to ensure that a state takes action to protect individuals from third parties) is typified by the Commission's recommendation to the state to investigate the human rights violations by private parties identified in the case and to prosecute those who were responsible.[76] Last, the state's obligation to fulfill (the duty of the state to effectuate a specific outcome) is embodied in the Commission's recommendation that the government undertake a comprehensive cleanup of lands and rivers damaged by oil operations.[77]

In terms of compliance, state parties seem to find it easier to respect rights,[78] than to protect[79] or fulfill rights.[80] An analysis of the six cases of full compliance reveals that in none of these cases were the state parties under an obligation to fulfill. In other words, the subject matter of the cases analyzed dealt mostly with obligations to respect and protect, with which states seemingly find it easier to comply.[81] The obligation to respect requires states to refrain from action, or to change a law that is violating rights. The duty to respect, though less burdensome than the duty to fulfill, is not only a negative obligation, but may entail scrapping existing laws or enacting new ones.[82]

Cases of noncompliance also mostly involve the duty of governments to respect. Just because the only case where the Commission found a violation of the government's duty to fulfill figures among the instances of noncompliance is an inconclusive ground for supporting the contention that the nature of a state's obligations determines compliance.[83]

Scale of the violation found. To assess whether the scale of violations influences compliance, the cases were categorized into those involving a single complainant, those involving multiple complaints, and those that occurred on a massive scale. Of the six cases of full compliance, three dealt with violations of the rights of an individual, three with multiple complainants, and none with massive violations. Conversely, the majority of the cases of clear noncompliance (five cases) concerned violations on a massive scale,[84] and three each involved an individual scale and multiple complainants, respectively.

[75] *Id.*, para. [71].

[76] *Id.*

[77] *Id.*

[78] Even in cases of only partial compliance, it is usually where the state was prepared to meet its obligations to respect by, for example, releasing victims from prison. *See* Constitutional Rights Project v. Nigeria, Comm. No. 148/96, 2000 AHRLR 241 (ACHPR 1999) (the state was prepared to release the prisoners to stop the violation of their rights, but not to compensate them).

[79] In the *Sierra Leone Coup* case, discussed in text at notes 51–54 *supra*, the state amended its legislation to guarantee fair-trial rights in future for cases appearing in front of the Court Martial in Sierra Leone. This is an example of a state's fulfilling its obligation to protect, which is clearly linked to civil and political rights.

[80] The obligation to fulfill is linked to socioeconomic rights.

[81] Put differently, states find it easier to implement obligations arising from a violation of civil and political rights than of socioeconomic rights.

[82] See, in this regard, the distinction between freedom in a negative and in a positive sense, where the former relates to "the area within which the subject . . . should be left to do . . . what he is able to do . . . , without interference by other persons"; and the latter to the "source of control" that "can determine someone to do . . . this rather than that." Isaiah Berlin, *Two Concepts of Liberty, in* FOUR ESSAYS ON LIBERTY 118, 121–22 (1969).

[83] This case is the *Gambian Mental Health* case, *supra* note 22.

[84] After a finding of serious and massive violations that was never complied with, the following communications were referred to the OAU Assembly of Heads of State and Government (AHSG), but it took no action: (1) *Achutan v. Malawi, supra* note 26; (2) *Zairian Torture* case, *supra* note 22; (3) *Zairian Mass Violations* case, *supra* note 22.

One of the reasons for this form of noncompliance lies at the macrolevel, and relates to the lack of action by the OAU Assembly of Heads of State and Government under Article 58 of the African Charter. According to this provision, findings of massive or serious violations must be referred to the Assembly. In all the cases where noncompliance was recorded following a finding of serious and massive violations of the Charter, the Commission reported that it had submitted such referrals to the Assembly. The Assembly, however, never took any steps regarding these cases. As a result, the Commission stopped referring cases revealing serious or massive violations to the Assembly.[85] In the absence of any further action by the Assembly or the Commission when states were found to have committed serious or massive violations of the Charter, it comes as no surprise that noncompliance was recorded in all these cases.[86]

Violations on an expansive scale are mostly linked to the system of governance or factors such as political instability due to an ongoing civil war and would require deep, substantial reform to achieve compliance. Even in Nigeria, where the cases were brought during the military dictatorship of General Abacha, the implementation of the recommendations that were complied with did not affect the system of governance in place, as they did not deal, for example, with the amendment of decrees but, rather, with the release of a few individuals.[87] Most of the remedies that were not implemented by Nigeria addressed problems that could be implemented only after a regime change—problems that were inherent in the system of governance.[88]

Nature of the remedial action required. The nature of the remedies required by the Commission is closely linked to the nature of the violations it had found. Some of the above comments about the nature of the violations therefore also hold true for the remedies. In Communication Nos. 48/90, 50/91, 52/91, and 89/93 (joined) against Sudan, the Commission concluded its decision by stating that "[t]o change so many laws, policies and practices will of course not be a simple matter," while also noting "that the situation has improved significantly."[89] It follows that recommendations involving the amendment of laws are usually associated with a more extended domestic procedure involving the state's legislature. In Communication No. 211/98 against Zambia, the Commission urged the state to bring "its laws and Constitution into conformity with the African Charter."[90] This decision was adopted in the Fourteenth Annual Activity Report and is one of the cases where "partial" compliance was recorded, since a process to amend the Zambian Constitution began in 2003 but is yet to be completed. Recommendations seeking amendments to the Constitution of a country would clearly involve more

[85] Commissioner E. V. O. Dankwa, Comments, during a lecture at the University of Pretoria (May 14, 2002) (authors' notes, on file with authors). According to Commissioner Dankwa, the AHSG never conducted in-depth studies under Article 59 of the African Charter.

[86] The following communications also revealed serious and massive violations, but the Commission had stopped referring such cases to the AHSG: *Comm'n nationale des droits de l'homme et des libertés v. Chad, supra* note 26; *Rwandan Mass Violations* case, *supra* note 24.

[87] *See, e.g.*, Body of Benchers case, *supra* note 24. The Commission recommended that the decree that violated the provisions of the Charter should be annulled. Nigeria did not comply, and the decree remained in force until the military dictatorship came to an end.

[88] For example, it was reported in the follow-up to the *Nigerian Election Annulment* case, *supra* note 24, that persons detained for protesting against the annulment of the elections of June 12, 1993, and whom the Commission had ordered to be released, were released only after the death of General Abacha.

[89] Amnesty Int'l v. Sudan, Comm. Nos. 48/90, 50/91, 52/91, 89/93 (joined), 2000 AHRLR 297, para. 83 (ACHPR 1999).

[90] Legal Res. Found. v. Zambia, *supra* note 60, para. [75].

stakeholders than amendments to other domestic legislation, and as such would take place over a longer period of time.

The experience of the inter-American regional human rights system indicates that states are sometimes more willing to pay compensation than to implement remedies of a political nature or remedies involving the amendment of domestic legislation.[91] In the inter-American system, there is a procedure in place to determine the amount of compensation to be awarded to a victim.[92] In the African system, there is no such procedure. As Commissioner E. V. O. Dankwa observed in connection with the *Mekongo* case: "[T]he Commission took the view that the complainant deserved to be paid compensation. It did not, however, have the means to assess the quantum of damages which should be offered to Louis Emgba Mekongo."[93] In the absence of a system to determine the quantum of damages, the Commission referred the victim back to the domestic system, where he had already waited for his appeal to be heard for twelve years, to determine the quantum "under the law of Cameroon."[94] Not surprisingly, the state did not comply with the Commission's recommendation. The state argued that it had had trouble locating Mekongo so as to compensate him.[95] Dankwa criticized the Commission for lacking a policy to determine compensation and wondered whether the Commission expected the victim to return to it if he had difficulty securing compensation under domestic law.[96]

The lack of a policy to determine the quantum of damages in awarding compensation to victims is definitely a factor that has negatively influenced state compliance in the African system. An attempt was made to follow up on six cases where the Commission had recommended the payment of compensation to victims but without stipulating the amount.[97] In none of these cases has compensation been paid. The Botswana *Modise* case is listed as an example of full compliance because, as explained above, negotiations are in the final stage and compensation will most probably be paid to the victim and his family.[98] However, since the Commission did not stipulate the amount of compensation, the determination was wholly dependent

[91] In listing factors that could affect state compliance with international agreements, Gutto referred to a "[l]ack of capacity in the political, legal/technical or economic sense on the part of a State, thus leading to impossibility to comply." Shadrack B. O. Gutto, The Rule of Law, Human and Peoples' Rights and Compliance/Non-compliance with Regional and International Agreements and Standards by African States 5, a paper prepared for presentation at the African Forum for Envisioning Africa, Nairobi, Kenya (Apr. 26–29, 2002), *available at* <http://www.worldsummit2002.org/texts/ShadrackGutto2.pdf>. David Padilla has also referred to states' inability to comply with the findings of treaty bodies due to a lack of resources. David Padilla, Comments during address to NGOs at the thirty-second ordinary session of the African Commission in Banjul, The Gambia (Oct. 17–23, 2002) (authors' notes, on file with authors).

[92] With the entry into force of the 1997 version of the Rules of Procedure of the Inter-American Court of Human Rights, provision was made for the first time in Article 23 for the representatives of the victims or their next of kin independently to submit their own arguments and evidence during the reparations stage of the Court's proceedings. The Court therefore holds separate hearings to determine the quantum of damages.

[93] Dankwa, *supra* note 10, at 5.

[94] *Mekongo* case, *supra* note 22, para. [2].

[95] Comments by the state party in presenting its state report at the ACHPR's thirty-first ordinary session, *in* 31st Session Notes, *supra* note 32.

[96] " 'Come and do what before the Commission for a second time?,' is not an unreasonable question for Louis Emgba Mekongo to ask." Dankwa, *supra* note 10, at 5.

[97] (1) Mauritanian Widows case, *supra* note 22; (2) Modise v. Botswana, *supra* note 47; (3) Nigerian Military Tribunals case, *supra* note 22; (4) SERAC v. Nigeria, *supra* note 74; (5) Sudanese Military Court case, *supra* note 22; (6) Sudanese Picnic case, *supra* note 22.

[98] *See supra* note 50.

on negotiations between the state party and nongovernmental organizations (NGOs) acting on behalf of the victim, which greatly delayed the process.[99]

Table 2 suggests that states are more likely to comply with remedies that require them to take some administrative action than with those that press them to amend legislation or compensate victims. However, no such trend can be discerned regarding the instances of clear noncompliance, as the thirteen cases are divided almost evenly among the three categories of required remedies. It would therefore be risky to conclude, on the basis of the available data, that the nature of the required remedy is an unequivocal ground for predicting state compliance.

Factors Related to the Complainant

Complainants and victims themselves have played an insignificant role in securing follow-up to the findings in their cases.[100] This is probably understandable given that most of the cases in our study took several years to complete.[101] By the time the Commission made its findings known, the victims often could no longer be traced.[102]

Factors Related to the Respondent State

The role of the situation prevailing in the state party during the period of potential compliance should also be assessed. Aspects included here are the type of government, whether a change of government occurred subsequent to the finding, the level of stability, and the level of corruption.[103] (Table 3, p. 24, relates to the discussion of these factors below.)

A recurring theme of the communications where noncompliance was recorded relates to two interrelated aspects, namely, the type of political regime in power and the existence of civil conflict.[104] However, where these factors were present, the Commission often found serious or

[99] Interights, a London-based NGO, negotiated with the government on behalf of the victim. *See id.*

[100] Follow-up could not be established with any of the victims of human rights violations, except where communications were filed by NGOs on behalf of other NGOs. Moreover, it could not be established through any other sources that victims have played a significant role in influencing states to comply with the Commission's findings. Victims such as the widows in the communication decided against Mauritania did work closely with the NGOs, such as the Institute for Human Rights and Development in Africa (IHRDA), that filed the communications on their behalf in support of their efforts to ensure state compliance. Mauritanian Widows case, *supra* note 22. One of the authors was present at meetings held in Banjul, The Gambia, in November 2002, between some of the victims in this case and IHRDA and other Mauritanian NGOs to strategize on lobbying the government to implement the Commission's recommendations. To date, they have not been implemented.

[101] A survey of the forty-four communications indicates that communications never took less than two years to complete, and averaged much longer, even as long as eight years (the *Modise* case).

[102] See, for example, the follow-up established in the *Mekongo* case, *supra* note 22, where the government reported that it could not locate the victim to compensate him. *See* note 95 *supra* and corresponding text.

[103] Many other aspects of governance could be included here, such as the ideology of the government, size of the population, and the influence of various colonial traditions in Africa. See, for example, the inclusion of these factors in Keith's study, note 3 *supra*. However, these factors were deemed less relevant on an impressionistic analysis of the data.

[104] These factors also fall within the ambit of the discussions on factors influencing state compliance in relation to state parties. Factors relating to the system of governance and political stability of a state are discussed here in reference to the role of the OAU. Of the nineteen communications decided against Nigeria, noncompliance was recorded in thirteen. These cases were almost all filed with the Commission during the military dictatorship of General Sani Abacha. Another example of lack of implementation due to the political order of the day is the cases against Malawi. Noncompliance with the Commission's recommendations against Chad and Rwanda could be explained in terms of the civil conflict within these countries at the time the communications were filed and decided.

TABLE 3. STATE COMPLIANCE: FACTORS RELATED TO RESPONDENT STATE

Case	Corruption[a]	Type of Government			Change of Government After Finding		Level of Stability		
		Free	Partly Free	Not Free	Yes	No	Civil War	Relatively Stable	Stable
				Full Compliance					
Mazou	1.4 (1998)			X		X			X
Zambian Deportation	3.5 (1999)		X			X			X
Nigerian Detention	1.6 (1999)		X		X			X	
Nigerian Journalists	1.6 (1999)		X		X			X	
Modise	3.4 (2000)	X				X			X
Sierra Leone Coup	2.2 (2003)		X			X		X	
				Noncompliance					
Zairian Torture	2.2 (2003)			X		X	X		
Zairian Mass Violations	2.2 (2003)			X		X	X		
Mekongo	2.46 (1996)			X		X			X
Angolan Expulsion	1.7 (2000)			X		X	X		
Mauritanian Widows	3.1 (2006)			X		X			X
Nigerian Torture	1.6 (1999)		X		X			X	
Bwampamye	2.4 (2006)			X		X	X		
Ouko	2.1 (2000)			X		X			X
Nigerian Military Tribunals	1 (2001)			X	X			X	
Sudanese Military Court	2.3 (2003)			X		X	X		
Suleiman	2.3 (2003)			X		X	X		
Sudanese Picnic	2.3 (2003)			X		X	X		
Gambian Mental Health	2.5 (2003)			X		X			X

[a] This column makes use of the statistics gathered by Transparency International, as reflected in its Corruption Perceptions Indexes, which draw on multiple expert opinion surveys that poll perceptions of public sector corruption. *See* text at note 122. If a specific country was not scored in the year when the Commission gave its decision, the score of the next closest year is used.

massive violations of the African Charter. Thus, compliance is often influenced by a combination of factors, rather than a single factor. The OAU Charter did not provide for sanctions against state parties under any circumstances.[105] As a result, perpetrators of military coups and authoritarian governments could continue their OAU membership and participate in the meetings of the Assembly without fear of exclusion or confrontation based on their human rights records, even in the face of the African Commission's findings. The OAU's Central Organ of the Mechanism for Conflict Prevention, Management and Resolution existed only on paper.[106]

System of governance. The findings on the status of state compliance with the Commission's recommendations indicate that the system of governance and the level of political stability within a state influence its compliance.[107] A democratic system of governance is characterized by principles such as a functional multiparty electoral system, an independent judiciary, the rule of law, constitutionally guaranteed rights, an active civil society, and a freely functioning NGO community.[108] If present, all these factors will pressure the state to bring its international policies in line with its domestic system of governance.[109]

Nine countries were involved in the thirteen cases of clear noncompliance. Of these, none were categorized as "free," according to the Freedom House Index.[110] Two of them (Cameroon and Nigeria) appear among both these noncompliant states and the fully compliant states. Leaving them aside for the purpose of our analysis, it emerges that six of the seven consistently noncompliant states at some stage during the relevant period were categorized as "not free"; and five of them were categorized as "not free" for most of the period (Angola, Burundi, Mauritania, Sudan, and Zaire (DRC)).[111] The two others (The Gambia and Kenya) were categorized as "partly free" for most of the period. The average rating of 3.875 over the period of the three remaining compliant states (Botswana, Sierra Leone, and Zambia) places them in the lower range of "partly free."[112] One of these countries, Botswana, was consistently categorized

[105] Gutto identifies "[t]he lack of existence and/or efficacy of external enforcement mechanisms and effective sanctions" as a factor that has affected state compliance with international agreements, and he further characterizes the "deliberate breach" of such agreements as often being "informed by a calculated risk of not being 'caught' or 'punished.'" Gutto, *supra* note 91, at 5–6.

[106] This mechanism was later replaced with the AU Peace and Security Council. For the purpose of the period covered in this study, the mechanism is the relevant institution.

[107] Hathaway, for example, found that "ratification of human rights treaties by fully democratic nations is associated with better human rights practices." Hathaway, *supra* note 3, at 1940.

[108] Byrnes, *supra* note 60, at 151–52.

[109] In analyzing state compliance with the final judgments of the International Court of Justice, Paulson came to a different conclusion. He found that "[a]utocratic states were no more likely to disregard a judgment than democracies." Paulson, *supra* note 2, at 460.

[110] Freedom House has rated each of these countries on a scale according to which they are listed as "free," "partly free," or "not free." The lower the rating accorded to a state, the higher the freedoms in that state. "Free" is between 1 and 2.5; "partly free" between 3 and 5.5; and "not free" between 5.5 and 7. A score is given for political rights and one for civil liberties. Freedom House, Freedom in the World, Country Ratings 1972–2004 (Aug. 19, 2005). In this article, we use the average of these two ratings. The time frame used to calculate the state of "freedom" in a country is the period between the publication of the particular decision (in the Annual Activity Report) and the cut-off mark of the study, 2004.

[111] Between 1998 and 2004, Angola scored 6 through 2003, and 5.5 in 2004. Burundi scored 6 in 2001, 5.5 in 2002, and 5 over the next two years. The Gambia was awarded a 4 in 2003 and 2004. Mauritania's rating fluctuated between 5 and 6.5; Sudan was consistently given the worst possible rating (7); and Zaire (DRC) scored between 6.5 and 6 over the period 1994 to 2004.

[112] From 2001 to 2004, Botswana was awarded 2 every year; Sierra Leone was awarded average scores of 4.5, 4, 3.5, and 3.5; and Zambia scored between 4 and 4.5. *See* Freedom House, *supra* note 110.

as "free." These data indicate a strong correlation between the "state of freedom" (that is, the standards of openness and democracy) in a particular state and the likelihood of compliance.

As for Nigeria, our study noted full compliance in two cases, and noncompliance in thirteen cases.[113] This record highlights "system of governance" and "political instability" as recurring predictors of noncompliance. This factor, as mentioned, is usually associated with serious or massive violations of human rights.[114] Civil wars within state parties affect political stability not only within their own borders, but also in neighboring countries.[115] In the face of a series of serious and massive human rights violations, the impact of a treaty body such as the African Commission is negligible if measured in terms of state compliance.[116] However, NGOs do not necessarily file communications with the Commission against an autocratic government or during a time of civil war only to seek specific remedies from the Commission. Interviews with Nigerian NGOs that frequently filed against the dictatorial regime in the 1990s revealed that they used the Commission as a forum to apply pressure on the state party internationally and to publicize the government's human rights violations as widely as possible.

The statistical analysis also supports the conclusion that a stable, open, free, and democratic system of government is conducive to compliance under the African regional human rights system.[117]

Change of government. As seen, noncompliance in cases of serious or massive violations was usually due to the system of governance in place or factors related to the country's political stability. Thus, large-scale violations require large-scale remedies. Under these circumstances, the most significant factor that might influence state compliance for the better is the opportunity to improve a country's human rights record offered by a change in government after years of military dictatorship or civil war.[118] In the African system, the change of government that took

[113] *See supra* note 104. From the high rate of noncompliance, the conclusion can be drawn that in the presence of a military dictatorship there will be no or limited state compliance with regional human rights treaty obligations. Further examples can be found in reference to Zaire; in the *Zairian Torture* and *Mass Violations* cases, the Commission's findings were never implemented. In *Jawara v. The Gambia*, joint Communication Nos. 147/95, 149/96, which related to the coup d'état of 1994, the Commission observed that "the military *coup d'état* was therefore a grave violation of the right of Gambian people to freely choose their government." 2000 AHRLR 107, para. 73 (ACHPR 2000).

[114] Examples where the Commission found that the communications revealed the existence of serious or massive violations as a result of political instability were those decided against Chad, Zaire, and Malawi. The Commission did not formulate any recommendations apart from making its finding, as it probably presumed that only regime changes would bring an end to the violations.

[115] Noncompliance with the recommendations of the African Commission was recorded in the cases decided against Angola, Burundi, and Rwanda. A factor that most probably influenced state compliance with respect to these state parties is the ongoing civil wars, which were closely related to the subject matter of the complaints filed with the Commission. Even though the situation has now changed in both Angola and Rwanda, the Commission's recommendations have not been implemented.

[116] It is not only the African Commission that is "powerless" in cases of serious or massive human rights violations. Helfer and Slaughter reported that "[b]oth the [European Commission of Human Rights] and the [European Court of Human Rights], for example, were relatively powerless in the face of systematic human rights violations in Greece during the military dictatorship in the early 1970s; indeed, Greece ultimately withdrew from the Convention." Helfer & Slaughter, *supra* note 2, at 330.

[117] The *p* value for this factor was 0.0029, indicating a high degree of correlation between compliance and type of government.

[118] Hathaway has summarized it as follows: "Major shocks to the system—such as a change in government—provide limited windows of opportunity for effecting large changes in the system. Indeed, when major changes in human rights practices occur, it is often because of such an event." Hathaway, *supra* note 3, at 2002–03. Evidence that regime changes could lead to the implementation of the findings of treaty bodies, even years after the decisions

place in Nigeria, with the death of General Abacha in 1999, ended the military dictatorship and initiated a period of democratic governance. Although some recommendations still await implementation by Nigeria,[119] the change of government brought about the repeal of the decrees that formed the substance of most of the communications against that country and the release of most of the political prisoners. Moreover, whereas most of the forty-four communications examined in this study were filed against Nigeria, very few cases were filed after the new government took office.[120]

Stability of government. A stable government is more likely to implement the Commission's findings against it than a government that finds itself in the midst of civil war or subject to other forms of instability. If the political situation of states is characterized as "stable," "relatively stable," or "civil war," compliant states are more likely to fall in the categories of "stable" or "relatively stable." Cases of clear noncompliance, such as those involving Angola, Burundi, the DRC, and Sudan, are more likely in contexts of civil war and relative instability.[121]

Corruption as a predictive factor. As mentioned above, most of the factors analyzed in table 3 are interrelated. The final factor, the level of perceived corruption in a country, is analyzed to determine if aspects of society other than, for instance, the type of government might be predictive of compliance. Transparency International's "Corruption Perceptions Index," published annually since 1995, is the source of our data. The "Corruption Perceptions Index" scores countries on a scale from zero to ten; zero indicates the highest possible level of perceived corruption, and ten the lowest. Transparency International interprets a score of three and below as indicative of "rampant" perceived corruption in a country. Our study attempted to allocate scores to the state parties according to the year of the Commission's decision against them. Basically, all the state parties in the survey scored three or below, and the majority's scores were closer to, or even below, two. In its 2006 index, Transparency International found a "strong correlation between corruption and poverty";[122] almost three-quarters of the countries scored below five (including all low-income countries and all but two African states), indicating that the index sees most countries in the world as facing serious perceived levels of domestic

were originally taken, has been recorded in reference to both the Human Rights Committee and the Inter-American Commission on Human Rights. Helfer and Slaughter reported that the Human Rights Committee "must contend with systematic repression and grave abuses anywhere in the world." But they conclude that "persistence may pay off. For example, after many years of nonaction, the Committee received a statement from Uruguay indicating that, after a change of government, it had released from imprisonment or offered amnesty to several individuals whom the Committee had determined were victims of serious human rights abuses." Helfer & Slaughter, *supra* note 2, at 362–63. Dr. David Padilla, a specialist on the inter-American human rights system, highlighted the importance of a change of regime as a "good hook" to get previous decisions of a treaty body implemented. He referred to Ecuador as a case in point: the attorney general of the new regime implemented all the findings of the Inter-American Commission on Human Rights that had never been implemented under the previous regime. Interview with David Padilla at the Centre for Human Rights, University of Pretoria (Apr. 2002).

[119] Although partial compliance was recorded for *SERAC v. Nigeria, supra* note 74, a great many of the recommendations forwarded in this case are still outstanding.

[120] Members of Huri-Laws, a Nigerian-based NGO, commented that cases are now taken to domestic courts, as the jurisdiction of the courts to decide human rights issues is no longer ousted by military decrees. Interview at the Huri-Laws offices in Lagos, Nigeria (Nov. 2002).

[121] The statistical analysis also lends support to this trend, with a p value of 0.0880, placing the predictability of this factor in the 10 percent level of significance.

[122] Transparency International, CPI 2006 Press Conference (Nov. 1, 2006), *at* <http://www.transparencyinternational.org/layout/set/print/news_room/in_focus/cpi_2006/>.

TABLE 4. STATE COMPLIANCE: FACTORS RELATED TO CIVIL SOCIETY ACTORS

Case	NGO Involvement in Submission & Proceedings		NGO Involvement in Follow-Up		Media Involvement	
	Yes	No	Yes	No	Yes	No
			Full Compliance			
Mazou	X			X		X
Zambian Deportation	X		X		X	
Nigerian Detention	X					
Nigerian Journalists	X					
Modise	X		X		X	
Sierra Leone Coup	X		X		X	
			Noncompliance			
Zairian Torture	X			X		X
Zairian Mass Violations	X			X		X
Mekongo		X		X		X
Angolan Expulsion	X		X			X
Mauritanian Widows	X		X		X	
Nigerian Torture	X			X		X
Bwampamye	X		X			X
Ouko		X		X		X
Nigerian Military Tribunals	X			X		X
Sudanese Military Court		X		X		X
Suleiman		X		X		X
Sudanese Picnic		X		X		X
Gambian Mental Health		X		X		X

corruption.[123] For our purposes, since compliant states proved only slightly less corrupt than noncompliant states (with an average score on the index of 2.28 against 2.17), it cannot be concluded that levels of perceived corruption and their correlation to poverty levels in a specific state party are predictive of compliance.

Factors Related to Civil Society Actors

Table 4 above sets out the involvement of NGOs in the submission of cases and follow-up actions, and gives an indication of media involvement.

Involvement of NGOs. NGOs submitted communications on behalf of the victims in five of the six cases of full compliance. In *Modise*, the remaining case, an NGO (Interights) became involved during the proceedings before the Commission. The instances of clear noncompliance are more or less evenly divided between cases where NGOs were involved in both submitting the communications and assisting or appearing on behalf of the complainants, on the one hand, and those where NGOs were not involved, on the other hand. The prospects for compliance seem to be enhanced when communications are framed as communal rather than

[123] CPI Table (2006), *available at* <http://www.tranparency.org/layout/set/print/news_room/in_focus/cpi_2006/cpi_table>.

individualized claims, and when they are invoked as part of a broader social movement rather than an insular interest.[124] By availing themselves of the "usual means of lobbying and public opinion campaigns" at their disposal, NGOs contribute significantly to contextualizing complaints in this way, increasing the prospects for compliance and living up to their role as "'guardians' of compliance by states with certain international obligations."[125]

NGOs, more than other potential players, have assumed a significant role in follow-up efforts. The absence of any follow-up policy meant that NGOs that had filed communications also had to take on the role of follow-up. NGOs have been instrumental in applying pressure on and lobbying states at the domestic and international levels, so as to influence them to comply.[126] State compliance was secured in the *Modise* case mainly as a result of the follow-up efforts of the NGO Interights. In the *Lekwot* case,[127] where partial compliance was recorded, the role of NGOs in pressing the state to comply through a widespread advocacy campaign was noted as a deciding factor in Nigeria's commutation of the victims' sentences from death by hanging to life imprisonment.[128]

It can therefore be concluded that NGO involvement in following up on the Commission's recommendations, occasioning both international and internal pressure, has played an important role in influencing state compliance.[129]

Involvement of the press. In the instances of state compliance noted in table 4, the press involvement did not result from any action by the African Commission, but from the efforts of NGOs. Publication of the findings of treaty bodies plays a major part in influencing state compliance.[130] In the absence of coercive measures, the mobilization of shame is one of the only tools available to a treaty body to apply pressure against state parties on the international level. Most state parties attach importance to their reputation in the international community.

[124] See also the result of Fisher's Exact test, which measures NGO involvement in cases at a p of 0.1093.

[125] Tullio Treves, *Introduction* to CIVIL SOCIETY, INTERNATIONAL COURTS AND COMPLIANCE BODIES 1, 5 (Tullio Treves et al. eds., 2005).

[126] For example, in the communication in the *Zambian Deportation* case, *supra* note 34, filed by Amnesty International, it was reported that the political nature of the case brought a lot of international pressure to bear on the government to comply. The *Sierra Leone Coup* case, *supra* note 51, was one of those instances where the Commission did make an attempt at follow-up through a promotional mission to the state. But implementation of the Commission's recommendations could also be attributed to the mobilization of Sierra Leonean civil society. *See* note 54 *supra*.

[127] Constitutional Rights Project (in Respect of Lekwot and Six Others) v. Nigeria, Comm. No. 87/93, 2000 AHRLR 183 (ACHPR 1995).

[128] The Constitutional Rights Project (CRP) attributed the partial compliance secured in this case to the communication of the Commission, as well as the widespread advocacy campaign run by the CRP. According to the CRP, there was a lot of pressure on the government to comply with the Commission's findings. Interviews with Agnes Olowu, *supra* note 43, and Kolawole Olaniyan, *supra* note 46.

[129] Paulson recorded a similar finding in reference to state compliance with the final judgments of the ICJ, as follows: "International pressure to comply played a prominent role in many states' decisions to implement the judgments, as did internal political pressure . . . ." Paulson, *supra* note 2, at 457. See also the result of Fisher's Exact Test, *supra* note 55, which attached a p of 0.0116 to this factor, making it a primary predictor of compliance.

[130] Proof that state parties do react to "international shaming" to protect their reputations in the international sphere is given by Schmidt, who reported that France and Ecuador "promptly reacted" and "forwarded follow-up replies and provided victims with remedies" upon publication of the 1995 and 1998 annual reports of the Human Rights Committee, listing the uncooperative states under the Committee's follow-up mandate. Markus G. Schmidt, *Follow-up Mechanisms Before UN Human Rights Treaty Bodies and the UN Mechanisms Beyond*, *in* THE UN HUMAN RIGHTS TREATY SYSTEM IN THE 21ST CENTURY, *supra* note 60, at 233, 238; *see also* Byrnes, *supra* note 60, at 151–52; Hathaway, *supra* note 3, at 2008.

Those that have ceased to care about their reputation are not likely to be influenced by any of the factors listed in this article.

In March 1994, the UN Human Rights Committee decided that "publicity for follow-up activities would not only be in the interest of victims of violations of the Covenant's provisions, but could also serve to enhance the authority of the Committee's views and provide an incentive for States parties to implement them."[131] The African Commission initially interpreted Article 59 of the African Charter in an overly strict manner and did not publish any information about individual communications.[132] Now the Commission regularly issues its findings as an annex to its Annual Activity Reports. These reports, however, are published only after their adoption by the AU Assembly, which means that the Commission's findings appear in print once a year. At the third session of the AU Assembly, a decision was adopted to change the schedule of its sessions from once a year to every six months.[133] The Commission's "annual" report should thus become a semiannual report.[134] This step eliminates one of the many delays in deciding communications and should increase the publicity of the Commission's findings by enabling more regular media coverage.

The Annual Activity Reports of the African Commission are not widely disseminated. Even though the Commission's decisions can be accessed on its official Web site,[135] the Commission has not made use of the media to publish its findings on decisions other than in its activity reports. The Commission has also not made use of the media to publicize instances of governmental compliance with its recommendations, not to mention the cases of noncompliance.[136] By publishing examples of state compliance, the Commission might encourage other states to implement its findings. Despite the importance of international and domestic pressure on states in influencing compliance, the African Commission has yet to take this approach. Up to now it has been adopted mainly by NGOs.

International Pressure

As noted above, it has fallen mostly to NGOs to mount international pressure against noncompliant state parties. In the three cases of full compliance cited in table 5 (p. 31) where international pressure played a role in persuading the relevant states to implement the Commission's recommendations, that result can largely be attributed to the efforts of national and international NGOs. Although establishing the existence of international pressure has proved

[131] Report of the Human Rights Committee, UN GAOR, 51st Sess., Supp. No. 40, vol. 1 at 70, para. 436, UN Doc. A/51/40 (1997). Before 1994, the Human Rights Committee considered follow-up information on a confidential basis. The Committee came to the conclusion, however, that "publicity for follow-up activities would be the most appropriate means for making the procedure more effective." *Id.*

[132] Article 59(1) of the African Charter reads as follows: "All measures taken within the provisions of the present Chapter shall remain confidential until the Assembly of Heads of State and Government shall otherwise decide."

[133] Decision on the Periodicity of the Ordinary Sessions of the Assembly, AU Doc. Assembly/AU/Dec.53 (III) (2004).

[134] Article 54 of the Charter, *supra* note 4, provides that the Commission "shall submit" a report to "each Ordinary Session of the Assembly."

[135] *See* note 8 *supra.*

[136] Through its promotional missions, the Commission has been aware of some instances where state parties did implement its recommendations. In the *Zambia Deportation* case, *supra* note 34, for example, where full compliance was recorded, the Commission noted in its Report of the Promotional Visit to the Republic of Zambia, *supra* note 39, at 10, that the state had complied with the recommendations. The Commission did not, however, use this information to praise the state concerned through the media in an effort to encourage other states to follow suit.

TABLE 5. STATE COMPLIANCE: INTERNATIONAL PRESSURE

Case	International Pressure		
	Yes	No	Unclear
Full Compliance			
Mazou			X
Zambian Deportation	X		
Nigerian Detention			X
Nigerian Journalists			X
Modise	X		
Sierra Leone Coup	X		
Noncompliance			
Zairian Torture		X	
Zairian Mass Violations		X	
Mekongo		X	
Angolan Expulsion			X
Mauritanian Widows	X		
Nigerian Torture		X	
Bwampamye	X		
Ouko		X	
Nigerian Military Tribunals		X	
Sudanese Military Court		X	
Suleiman		X	
Sudanese Picnic		X	
Gambian Mental Health		X	

difficult in many instances, and these results are not statistically significant, it may be cautiously stated that an absence of international pressure seems to characterize the overwhelming majority of cases of noncompliance.

IV. CONCLUSION

Improved state compliance with findings by the Commission (or the African Court of Human and Peoples' Rights)[137] is both an indicator and a goal of greater commitment to human rights by African states and the African Union. This article attempts to shift attention

[137] The Protocol to the African Charter on Human and Peoples' Rights on the Establishment of an African Court on Human and Peoples' Rights, June 10, 1998, OAU Doc. OAU/LEG/EXP/AFCHPR/PROT (III) (entered into force Jan. 25, 2004) [hereinafter Court Protocol], established the African Court on Human and Peoples' Rights (African Human Rights Court) to complement the protective mandate of the African Commission. Although the eleven judges, elected by the AU Assembly of Heads of State and Government, were inaugurated on June 2, 2006, and the seat of the Court (Arusha, Tanzania) has been assigned, the Court has not started functioning. Rules of Procedure are in the process of being elaborated. Because of apprehension about duplication and limited financial resources, a process was set in motion to "merge" the African Human Rights Court and the Court of Justice of the African Union into a single judicial body. AU Doc. Assembly/AU/Dec.45 (III), para. 4 (July 2004). According to the version of the draft Protocol on the Statute of the African Court of Justice and Human Rights, adopted in June 2006, the merged institution will be called the "African Court of Justice and Human Rights," will have an increased number of judges, and will consist of two "Chambers" (a "General Affairs Section" and a "Human Rights Section"). AU Doc. EX.CL/235 (IX), Annex II (June 2006).

from the substantive features of the African Charter to questions about the implementation (in the form of "direct effect") of this normative framework.

(Non)compliance with the recommendations of the African Commission is one aspect of a state's compliance with its obligations under the African Charter. The mere fact that a state has complied with some findings does not translate into overall adherence to the normative framework of the Charter; nor does noncompliance with findings mean that in all respects the state is falling short of its obligation to give effect to the African Charter. Nevertheless, timely and full implementation of Commission recommendations may be indicative of a tendency to regard other obligations under the African Charter with seriousness.

This article shows that the attempt to chart compliance empirically and analytically is fraught with methodological difficulties. The most important of these is the Commission's failure to enunciate clear and specific remedies, leaving an unreliable yardstick for measuring compliance. Even when the yardstick is clearer, linking the steps toward compliance to the required remedial action often remains a matter of causal conjecture.

Our analysis of cases of full and clear noncompliance suggests that the most important factors predictive of compliance are political, rather than legal. The only factor relating to the treaty body itself that shows a significant link to improved compliance is its follow-up activities. This finding lends support to arguments for a fully developed and effectively functional follow-up mechanism in the secretariat of the Commission, the consistent integration of follow-up activities into the Commission's mandate, and the appointment of a special rapporteur on follow-up. This observation again points up the importance of an unambiguous normative statement by the Commission calling for the establishment of a coherent and consistent follow-up procedure.

In an encouraging and significant development subsequent to the completion of our study, the Commission in November 2006 adopted a resolution in which it unequivocally called on state parties to the African Charter to "respect without delay the recommendations of the Commission," and to report on compliance within ninety days of being notified of decisions against them.[138] The Commission further decided to include a report on "the compliance with its recommendations" in future activity reports.[139]

Our findings also place in doubt optimistic views that the advent of the African Court will bring about an improvement in state compliance. Cassel concludes, for example, that "Court-ordered hard law seems to generate better compliance than Commission-recommended soft law."[140] In addition, the change of the institutional setting in which the African Charter is

[138] Resolution on the Importance of the Implementation of the Recommendations of the African Commission on Human and Peoples' Rights by States Parties, adopted at the Commission's fortieth session, Doc. ACHPR/Res.97(XXXX)06, paras. 2, 4 (Nov. 29, 2006), *available at* <http://www.achpr.org/english/resolutions/resolution102_en.html>. This resolution reflects almost verbatim the draft recommendation contained in Non-Compliance: A Legal Approach, *supra* note 13, prepared by the secretariat in 1998. This draft resolution calls on all state parties to the Charter to comply with the Commission's recommendations, to "implement them within a maximum period of ninety (90) days," and to "indicate the measures taken for their execution." Draft Resolution on the Implementation of the Recommendations of the African Commission on Human and Peoples' Rights (ACHPR), para. 4, *in* ACHPR DOCUMENTS, *supra* note 13, at 760, 761.

[139] ACHPR Res. 97(XXXX)06, *supra* note 138, para. 3.

[140] Douglass Cassel, *Inter-American Human Rights Law, Soft and Hard, in* COMMITMENT AND COMPLIANCE, *supra* note 2, at 393, 417.

interpreted from a quasi-judicial to a judicial body was designed to promote closer correspondence between the nature of the normative commitment under the Charter and the institutional conclusions and findings.[141] However, our study suggests that the mere fact that the Court will provide legally binding and specific remedies and better formulated judgments will not in itself guarantee improved state compliance. The advent of the Court may coincide with a gradual hardening of human rights commitments and lead to improved human rights adherence, but it would then be on the strength of a stronger domestic and regional political commitment, increased publicity, and greater involvement of civil society.

Inadequate political commitment at the regional level is an important factor underlying the lack of state compliance with the recommendations of the Commission at the macrolevel. To some extent, the goal of strengthening the regional political system was reached by means of the reforms of the OAU, which culminated in the establishment of the African Union.

The OAU Charter was adopted on May 25, 1963, at a stage when state sovereignty stood high on the agenda of member states, while human and peoples' rights did not. Even after the African Charter was subsequently drafted and adopted under the auspices of the OAU, human rights issues continued to be accorded a backseat on the OAU's agenda. This state of affairs is evidenced by the OAU's lack of interaction with the African Commission even where the African Charter specifically calls for such interaction. The OAU did not provide a platform for discussing the findings of the African Commission on individual communications. Under the African Charter, the Assembly of Heads of State and Government was charged with adopting the Annual Activity Reports of the African Commission,[142] to which its decisions on individual communications were attached, but this process never resulted in any significant debate among member states. Under Article 59(1) of the Charter, all "measures" taken within chapter III, dealing with interstate and individual communications, and protective missions, remain "confidential" until the Assembly decides that they may be made public. However, the OAU Assembly never withheld authorization for publication of decisions or protective mission reports. The absence of debate or the imposition of sanctions on states found in violation of the Charter translated into a lack of political pressure within the regional system to comply with the Commission's recommendations.

When the AU Constitutive Act was adopted in July 2000, the African Union replaced the OAU as the regional political body. The Union held its first session in July 2002. However, most of the communications for which follow-up was established in this article were decided while the OAU was the regional political body.[143]

The new institution addressed some of the weaknesses that had marked the OAU. First, the AU Constitutive Act includes the protection of human and peoples' rights among its objectives and founding principles.[144] The African Union therefore seems to be more dedicated to the protection of human rights than its predecessor. Second, in contrast to the OAU, the AU Assembly opted to allow for the possibility of more exhaustive debate on the Annual Activity

[141] See, for example, Article 29(2) of the Court Protocol, *supra* note 137, according to which the AU Executive Council will monitor the execution of the Court's decisions on behalf of the AU Assembly; and Article 30, in whose terms states "undertake to comply" with the Court's judgments.

[142] African Charter, *supra* note 4, Arts. 54, 59.

[143] For this article, we followed up on all communications published until the Sixteenth Annual Activity Report. Only the fifteenth and sixteenth reports were adopted by the African Union.

[144] Constitutive Act of the African Union, Arts. 3(e) & (h), 4(m), July 11, 2000, OAU Doc. CAB/LEG/23.15, *available at* <http://africa-union.org>.

Reports of the Commission by delegating this task to the Executive Council,[145] which indeed resulted in more thorough deliberations on the Commission's report and work during the discussion of the Seventeenth Annual Activity Report.[146] Although this innovation also resulted in the decision not to adopt the activity report, it should be seen in light of its having been the first debate on the activities of the Commission in this forum. Also for the first time the regional political body called upon member states to implement the decisions of the African Commission.[147]

Although Executive Council deliberations allowed for much-needed debate about the Commission's activity reports at the AU level, states have used this opportunity to invoke Article 59(1) of the Charter to delay the publication of an investigative mission report on and a decision against Zimbabwe.[148] They have also withheld authorization for the publication of "resolutions,"[149] contrary to the provisions of the Charter.

The AU Constitutive Act further provides that "[g]overnments which shall come to power through unconstitutional means shall not be allowed to participate in the activities of the Union."[150] The possibility therefore exists for denying participation of states where the leadership seized power through military coups. In future, the AU Peace and Security Council (previously, the Central Organ of the Mechanism for Conflict Prevention, Management and Resolution)[151] may take up cases involving a state party when the Commission's recommendations could not be implemented because of civil conflict.

It therefore seems that some of the problems associated with the weak regional political platform of the OAU have been addressed by its transformation into the African Union. However, some instances of noncompliance have been registered since 2000, after the Union was established. Whether the African Union will develop a practice of taking action on the basis of the theoretical possibilities mentioned above will have to be seen.

[145] Decision on the 16th Annual Activity Report of the African Commission on Human and Peoples' Rights, Doc. Assembly/AU/7 (II)–Assembly/AU/Dec.11 (II), para. 5 (2003).

[146] *See* Frans Viljoen, *Recent Developments in the African Regional Human Rights System*, 2 AFR. HUM. RTS. L.J. 347 (2004).

[147] See Decision on the 17th Annual Activity Report of the African Commission on Human and Peoples' Rights, AU Doc. EX.CL/109 (V)–Assembly/AU/Dec.49 (III), para. 3 (2004), which states that the Assembly "[u]rges all Member States to cooperate with the ACHPR, and the various mechanisms it has put in place, and implement its decisions in compliance with the provisions of the African Charter on Human and Peoples' Rights."

[148] See the Executive Council decision not to "authorize" publication of the Seventeenth Annual Activity Report due to inclusion of the investigative mission report on Zimbabwe. AU Doc. EX.CL/Dec.155(V) (2004). The report was subsequently approved by the Decision on 17th Annual Activity Report of the African Commission on Human and Peoples' Rights (ACHPR), AU Doc. Assembly/AU/Dec.56(IV) (2005), together with a comment by the Zimbabwean government. See also Decision on the Activity Report of the African Commission on Human and Peoples' Rights, AU Doc. EX.CL/Dec.310(IX) (2006), in which the Executive Council approved the 20th Activity Report, with the exception of Communication No. 245/2002 against Zimbabwe, to give the government a further opportunity to respond, even though it had participated in the proceedings before the Commission and the case had been completed.

[149] See Decision on the 19th Activity Report of the African Commission on Human and Peoples' Rights, AU Doc. Assembly/AU/Dec.101 (VI), para. 1 (2006), in which the Assembly—on recommendation by the Executive Council—decided to authorize publication of everything contained in the activity report, with the exception of the (promotional) resolutions on Eritrea, Ethiopia, Sudan, Uganda, and Zimbabwe. Except for the Eritrean resolution, these were all included together with the governments' comments and approved as part of the 20th Activity Report. AU Doc. EX.CL/Dec.310(IX) (2006), *supra* note 148.

[150] Constitutive Act of the African Union, *supra* note 144, Art. 30.

[151] *See* note 106 *supra* and corresponding text.

[22]

The African Regional Human Rights System*

Christof Heyns and Magnus Killander

1. **Introduction**

While the term "human rights" is of relative recent currency on the continent, people have been struggling for freedom, dignity, equality and social justice for centuries in Africa. In Africa, as is the case elsewhere, that which is now called human rights finds its foundations in the struggle to assert these core values of human existence.[1]

Today, the term human rights is used widely in the African context. The written constitutions of every country in Africa recognise the concept; the inter-governmental organisation of African states, the African Union, regards the realisation of human rights as one of its objectives and principles; and the record of ratification of the human rights treaties of the United Nations by African countries is on a par with practices around the world.[2] There is wide acceptance that the security and development of Africa —as in the world at large— will have to be based on human rights.

---

* This article is based on an article by Christof Heyns published in (2004) 108 *Penn State Law Review* 679, also published in Spanish in F. Gomez Isa (Dir.): *La protección internacional de los derechos humanos en los albores del siglo xxi*, Universidad de Deusto, Bilbao, 2003, pp. 595-620.

[1] For an exposition of the approach that human rights and legitimate struggle are two sides of the same coin, see C. Heyns: "A 'struggle approach' to human rights" in A. Soeteman (ed.): *Pluralism and Law*, 2001, p. 171.

[2] For a collection of the primary material dealing with human rights law in Africa on the United Nations, regional, sub-regional and domestic levels of all the countries of Africa, see C. Heyns (ed.): *Human Rights Law in Africa*, 2004. See also C. Heyns (ed.): *Compendium of key human rights documents of the African Union,* 2005.

Not surprisingly, given the history of exploitation of Africa, the struggle roots of the concept of human rights are clearly visible in the human rights documents of the continent. The African Charter on Human and Peoples' Rights also reflects in many ways a reaction to the continental experience of slavery and colonialism, for example by recognising a "peoples" right to self-determination. The excesses of some post-independence leaders are reflected in the fact that a significant number of African constitutions explicitly recognise a direct right, located in the people, to protect constitutional and human rights norms, if need be through political struggle, should they be violated.[3] The Constitutive Act of the African Union uniquely provides for a right of humanitarian intervention in member states by the Union, in cases of grave human rights violations.[4]

As is well known, the struggle for human rights on the African continent is far from over or complete. The continent is plagued by widespread violations of human rights, often on a massive scale. The process to establish effective institutional structures, that will help to consolidate and protect the hard earned gains of the freedom struggles of the past, has become a struggle in its own right. No doubt, the most important task in this regard is to establish legal systems on the national level that protect human rights. At the same time regional and global attempts to change the human rights practices of the continent, and to create safety nets for those cases not effectively dealt with on the national level, are assuming increased importance.

This contribution first introduces the main legal instruments relevant to the continental protection of human rights in Africa, then discusses the norms recognised (individual and peoples' rights and duties, etc) and thereafter turns to the regional institutional structures set up to achieve the implementation of the norms. This institutional overview focuses primarily on four important pillars of the African human rights system: the organs of the African Union, the African Commission on Human and Peoples' Rights, the yet to be established African Court on Human and Peoples' Rights and the newly established African Peer Review Mechanism.

2. **The African Union and Human Rights**

2.1. *Background*

The African regional system has been developed under the auspices of the Organization of African Unity ("OAU"),[5] established in 1963, which was transformed

---

[3] The explicit recognition of a right of resistance to protect constitutional and human rights norms is present in the Constitutions of Benin (1990) (Art. 66); Burkina Faso (1997) (Art. 167); Cape Verde (1992) (Art. 19); Chad (1996) (Preamble); Congo (2001) (Art. 13); The Gambia (1996) (Art. 6); Ghana (1992) (Art. 3); Mozambique (Art. 80); and Togo (1992) (Art. 150).

[4] Article 4(h) of the Constitutive Act.

[5] The Charter of the OAU is reprinted in *Human Rights Law in Africa* 111. The Preamble stated adherence to the principles of the Universal Declaration of Human Rights. See also Art. II(1)(e). The Charter of the OAU was nevertheless a human rights document in the sense that it was aimed at the abolition of colonialism and apartheid. On the OAU see G.J. Naldi: *The Organization of African Unity: An Analysis of its Role*, 1999, p. 109.

in 2001 into the African Union ("AU").[6] All the states of Africa are members of the AU, except Morocco which withdrew in 1984 when the OAU recognised Western Sahara bringing the membership to 53. While the Charter of the OAU of 1963 made only passing reference to the concept of human rights, the Constitutive Act of the AU of 2000 (entered into force 2001) has now placed human rights squarely on the agenda of the new regional body.[7]

2.2. *The Constitutive Act*

The Constitutive Act of the AU, in its Preamble, refers to the African struggles for independence and human dignity "by our peoples" and the determination of the Heads of State and Government "to promote and protect human and peoples' rights". Article 3 sets out the "Objectives" of the AU as follows: "the objectives of the Union shall be to ... (e) encourage international cooperation, taking due account of the Charter of the United Nations and the Universal Declaration of Human Rights;" and to "... (h) promote and protect human and peoples' rights in accordance with the African Charter on Human and Peoples' Rights and other relevant human rights instruments ...".

Article 4 deals with "Principles", and provides that:

> The Union shall function in accordance with the following principles: ... (g) non-interference by any Member State in the internal affairs of another; (h) the right of the Union to intervene in a Member State pursuant to a decision of the Assembly in respect of grave circumstances, namely war crimes, genocide and crimes against humanity; (i) peaceful co-existence of member states and their right to live in peace and security; (j) the right of member states to request intervention from the Union in order to restore peace and security, (l) promotion of gender equality; (m) respect for democratic principles, human rights, the rule of law and good governance; (n) promotion of social justice to ensure balanced economic development; (o) respect for the sanctity of human life, condemnation and rejection of impunity and political assassination, acts of terrorism and subversive activities; (p) condemnation and rejection of unconstitutional changes of governments.

There are no entry requirements in terms of their human rights records and practices for states to join the African Union (as is the case for example with the Council of Europe), and all the members of the OAU became members of the AU without scrutiny of their human rights records. There is, however, at least a theo-

[6] Constitutive Act of the African Union CAB/LEG/23.15, entered into force 26 May 2001. For an overview of the AU see C. Heyns, E. Baimu & M. Killander: "The African Union" 46 *German Yearbook of International Law*, 2003, p. 252. On the transformation from OAU to AU from a human rights perspective see R. Murray: *Human Rights in Africa,* 2004.

[7] For a discussion, see E. Baimu: "The African Union: Hope for better protection of human rights in Africa?" 1 *African Human Rights Law Journal*, 2001, p. 299. The Constitutive Act is reprinted on p. 315 of the same volume. See also B. Manby: "The African Union, NEPAD, and Human Rights: The Missing Agenda", 26 *Human Rights Quarterly*, 2004, p. 983.

retical chance that violations of AU human rights standards may lead to suspension from the AU; certainly lesser forms of sanctions are possible.

According to Art. 23(2)

> ... any Member State that fails to comply with the decisions and policies of the Union may be subjected to ... sanctions, such as the denial of transport and communications links with other Member States, and other measures of a political and economic nature to be determined by the Assembly.

Art. 30 provides: "Governments which shall come to power through unconstitutional means shall not be allowed to participate in the activities of the Union."

The African Union has seen the establishment of a number of new institutions, many with relevance for the implementation of human rights, which will be discussed below.

2.3. *African human rights instruments*

The central document of the African regional human rights system, the African Charter on Human and Peoples' Rights ("African Charter"),[8] was opened for signature in 1981 and entered into force in 1986. It has been ratified by all 53 member states of the OAU/AU.[9] The sole supervisory body of the African Charter currently in existence is the African Commission on Human and Peoples' Rights ("African Commission"). The African Commission was constituted and met for the first time in 1987. The Commission has adopted its own Rules of Procedure (amended in 1995).[10] The work of the African Commission will be discussed later in this article.

The Protocol to the African Charter on Human and Peoples' Rights on the Establishment of the African Court on Human and Peoples' Rights ("African Human Rights Court Protocol")[11] was adopted in 1998 and entered into force in January 2004, but as of February 2006 the Court had not yet been established. The African Charter has further been supplemented by the Protocol to the African Charter on Human and Peoples' Rights on the Rights of Women in Africa, adopted in 2003, which entered into force in November 2005.[12]

In addition to these instruments the African regional human rights system is comprised of the OAU Convention Governing the Specific Aspects of Refugee Problems in Africa of 1969[13] which entered into force in 1974 (45 ratifications); and the

---

[8] OAU Doc OAU/CAB/LEG/67/3/Rev.5. Reprinted in *Human Rights Law in Africa* 134.

[9] See status of ratification of AU treaties, available on www.africa-union.org. Ratification status given for the treaties mentioned in this article is as of February 2006. For the three reservations to the African Charter, see *Human Rights Law in Africa* 108. The last state to ratify was Eritrea, in 1999.

[10] ACHPR/RP/XIX. Reprinted in *Human Rights Law in Africa* 540.

[11] OAU/LEG/MIN/AFCHPR/PROT (I) Rev. 2. Reprinted in *Human Rights Law in Africa* 170.

[12] The Protocol is discussed further below. As of February 2006 the Protocol had been ratified by 17 states.

[13] OAU Doc CAB/LEG/24.3. Reprinted in *Human Rights Law in Africa* 122. See G. OKOTH-OBBO: "Thirty years on: A legal review of the 1969 OAU Refugee Convention" *African Yearbook of International Law* 8, 2000, p. 3.

African Charter on the Rights and Welfare of the Child ("African Children's Charter") of 1990,[14] which came into force in 1999 (38 ratifications). A special monitoring body for the African Children's Charter, the African Committee on the Rights and Welfare of the Child, discussed further below, held its first meeting in 2002.[15]

The relatively unknown Cultural Charter for Africa of 1976 came into force in 1990.[16] Another treaty with relevance for human rights is the Convention on Preventing and Combating Corruption adopted in 2003.[17] This convention has as of February 2006 not entered into force. The Convention for the Elimination of Mercenarism in Africa was adopted in 1977 and entered into force in 1985.[18] The OAU Convention on the Prevention and Combating of Terrorism of 1999 entered into force in 2002.[19] There are also two African regional treaties dealing with the environment.[20]

3. The norms recognised in the African Charter on Human and Peoples' Rights

As alluded to earlier, the 1963 OAU Charter did not recognise the realisation of human rights as such as one of the objectives of that body. It would only be in 1979 that a meeting of experts was gathered by the OAU in Dakar, Senegal, to prepare a preliminary draft of an African human rights charter.[21] This culminated in the Draft African Charter on Human and Peoples' Rights, finalised in Banjul, The Gambia, in 1981 (resulting in the name "Banjul Charter", which is sometimes used for the African Charter). The African Charter was formally adopted by the OAU in Kenya later that year.[22]

---

[14] OAU Doc CAB/LEG/153/Rev 2. Reprinted in *Human Rights Law in Africa* 143.

[15] See A. Lloyd: "The first meeting of the African Committee of Experts on the Rights and Welfare of the Child" 2 *African Human Rights Law Journal*, 2002, p. 320. See also A. Lloyd: "Report of the second ordinary session of the African Committee of Experts on the Rights and Welfare of the Child" 3 *African Human Rights Law Journal*, 2003, p. 329; A. Lloyd: "The Third Ordinary Session of the African Committee of Experts on the Rights and Welfare of the Child", 4 *African Human Rights Law Journal*, 2004, p. 139.

[16] Reprinted in *Human Rights Law in Africa* 125.

[17] See K. Olaniyan: "The African Union Convention on Preventing and Combating Corruption: A critical appraisal", 4 *African Human Rights Law Journal*, 2004, p. 74.

[18] Reprinted in *Human Rights Law in Africa* 132.

[19] Reprinted in *Human Rights Law in Africa* 175. A Protocol to this Convention was adopted in 2004.

[20] The African Convention on the Conservation of Nature and Natural Resources (1968/69), reprinted in *Human Rights Law in Africa* 116, revised version adopted 2003, not yet in force, reprinted in C. Heyns (ed.): *Compendium of key human rights documents of the African Union*, 2005, and the [Bamako] Convention on the Ban of the Import into Africa and the Control of Transboundary Movement and Management of Hazardous Wastes within Africa (1991/98), reprinted in *Human Rights Law in Africa* 153. See M. van der Linde: "A review of the African Convention on Nature and Natural Resources", 2 *African Human Rights Law Journal*, 2002, p. 33.

[21] The meeting was convened in terms of a decision of the Assembly of Heads of State and Government of the OAU, AHG/Dec 115 (XVI) Rev 1 1979, reprinted in C Heyns (ed) *Human Rights Law in Africa 1999*, 2002, p. 127.

[22] For the documents leading up to the adoption of the African Charter, see *Human Rights Law in Africa 1999*, pp. 65-105.

A number of reasons have been advanced why the OAU changed its approach and gave the concept of human rights the prominence offered by the Charter during the late 1970s and the early 1980s. These include the increased emphasis on human rights internationally at the time (as in the foreign policy of President Carter of the United States of America), the use to which the concept of human rights was put in international bodies such as the UN and the OAU to condemn the apartheid practices in South Africa, and abhorrence at the human rights violations that had taken part in some member state in particular Uganda, Central Africa and Equatorial Guinea.[23]

The African Charter recognises a wide range of internationally accepted human rights norms, but also has some unique features.[24] The Charter recognises not only civil and political rights, but also economic, social and cultural rights, not only individual but also peoples' rights, not only rights but also duties, and it has a singular system for the restrictions on rights. The Charter also contains provisions concerning interpretation which are very generous towards international law.

3.1. *Civil and political rights*

The civil and political rights recognised in the African Charter are in many ways similar to those recognised in other international instruments, and these rights have in practical terms received most of the attention of the African Commission.[25]

The Charter recognises the following civil and political rights: The prohibition of discrimination (Art. 2); equality (Art. 3); bodily integrity and the right to life (Art. 4); dignity and prohibition of torture and inhuman treatment (Art. 5); liberty and security (Art. 6); fair trial (Art. 7); freedom of conscience (Art. 8); information and freedom of expression (Art. 9); freedom of association (Art. 10); assembly (Art. 11); freedom of movement (Art. 12); political participation (Art. 13); property (Art. 14); and independence of the courts (Art. 26).

A number of possible shortcomings in respect of civil and political rights in the African Charter could be noted. There is for example no explicit reference in the Charter to a right to privacy; the right against forced labour is not mentioned by name; and the fair trial rights[26] and the right of political participation[27] are given scant

---

[23] See U.O. UMOZURIKE: *The African Charter on Human and Peoples' Rights,* 1997, pp. 27-28.

[24] In his welcoming address in 1979 to the Meeting of African Experts preparing the Draft African Charter in Dakar, Senegal, Leopold Senghor, President of Senegal, referred to the example set by international human rights instruments, and said: "As Africans, we shall neither copy, nor strive for originality, for the sake of originality ... [Y]ou must keep constantly in mind our values of civilisation and the real needs of Africa." Reprinted in *Human Rights Law in Africa 1999,* 78 at 79.

[25] For a full discussion, see C. HEYNS: "Civil and political rights in the African Charter" in M. EVANS & R. MURRAY (eds.): *The African Charter on Human and Peoples' Rights*, 2002, p. 137.

[26] There is, for example, no explicit reference to the right to a public hearing, the right to interpretation, the right against self-incrimination and the right against double jeopardy. However, the Commission has interpreted the Charter protection to encompass some of these rights.

[27] While Art. 13(1) the Charter recognises the right "of every citizen to participate freely in the government of his country", it does not stipulate that this should be done through regular, free and fair elections, based on universal suffrage.

protection when measured against international standards. However, the Commission has in resolutions and in cases before it interpreted the Charter protection to encompass some of the rights or aspects of rights not explicitly included in the Charter.

An overview of some Commission decisions in respect of individual communications provides a sample of the Commission's approach:

— In a number of cases the Commission has held that there is a positive duty on state parties to protect those in their jurisdictions against violations by non-state actors. In a case concerning Mauritania, the Commission found that, although slavery had officially been abolished in that country, this was not effectively enforced by the government.[28] In a case involving Chad, the Commission likewise held that the state's failure to protect people under its jurisdiction during a civil war against attacks by unidentified militants, not proven to be government agents, constituted a violation of the right to life.[29]
— The imposition of *Shari'a* law on non-Muslims in Sudan has been held to violate freedom of religion.[30]
— In *Media Rights Agenda and Others v Nigeria*[31] the Commission ruled against the Abacha government's clampdown on freedom of expression, and determined that politicians should be provided less protection from free expression than other people. As with many of the seemingly more bold decisions of the Commission, this decision was unfortunately handed down only after the Abacha regime had fallen. Nevertheless, a positive precedent was set.
— The suspension of national elections was held to violate the right to political participation in *Constitutional Rights Project and Another v Nigeria*.[32]
— The Commission has held that decrees ousting the jurisdiction of courts to examine the validity of such decrees, violate the fair trial provision of the Charter,[33] and also that the creation of special tribunals, dominated by members of the executive, violated the same right.[34]
— The Commission has held that an execution after an unfair trial is a violation of the right to life,[35] but that the death penalty in itself does not violate the African Charter.[36]

---

28 *Malawi African Association and Others v Mauritania* (2000) AHRLR 149 (ACHPR 2000).

29 *Commission Nationale des Droit de l'Homme et des Libertés v Chad* (2000) AHRLR 66 (ACHPR 1995). See also *Social and Economic Rights Action Centre (SERAC) and Another v Nigeria* (2001) AHRLR 60 (ACHPR 2001).

30 *Amnesty International and Others v Sudan* (2000) AHRLR 297 (ACHPR 1999).

31 (2000) AHRLR 200 (ACHPR 1998).

32 (2000) AHRLR 191 (ACHPR 1998).

33 *Civil Liberties Organisation v Nigeria* (2000) AHRLR 188 (ACHPR 1995).

34 *Constitutional Rights Project (in respect of Akamu and Others) v Nigeria* (2000) AHRLR 180 (ACHPR 1995). The appearance of impartiality is enough to constitute a violation (para 12).

35 *Forum of Conscience v Sierra Leone* (2000) AHRLR 293 (ACHPR 2000).

36 *Interights and Others (on behalf of Bosch) v Botswana*, communication 240/2001, 17th Annual Activity Report.

— A constitutional amendment providing that anyone who wanted to stand for office in the presidential election in Zambia would have to prove that both parents were Zambians by birth or descent was found to be in violation of the Charter in *Legal Resources Foundation v Zambia*.[37]

3.2. *Socio-economic rights*

A unique feature of the Charter is the inclusion of socio-economic rights in a regional human rights treaty, alongside the civil and political rights mentioned above.[38] The inclusion of socio-economic rights in the Charter is significant, in that it emphasises the indivisibility of human rights and the importance of developmental issues, which are obviously important matters in the African context.

At the same time, the fact that only a modest number of socio-economic rights are explicitly included in the Charter, should be noted. The Charter only recognises "a right to work under equitable and satisfactory conditions" (Art. 15), a right to health (Art. 16) and a right to education (Art. 17). Some prominent socio-economic rights are not mentioned by name, such as the right to food, water, social security and housing.[39]

The socio-economic rights in the Charter have received scant attention from the Commission, but in one case the Commission has dealt extensively with the issue, and has in effect held that some internationally recognised socio-economic rights which are not explicitly recognised in the Charter should be regarded as being implicitly included.

The so-called *SERAC v Nigeria*[40] decision dealt with the destruction of part of Ogoniland by Shell, acting in collaboration with the government of Nigeria. The Commission held that the presence of an implicit right to "housing or shelter" in the Charter has to be deduced from the explicit provisions on health, property and family life in the Charter.[41] Similarly, a right to food has to be read into the right to dignity and other rights.[42] It was accepted, without argument or reasoning, that the Ogoni's constituted a "people".

---

[37] (2001) AHRLR 84 (ACHPR 2001).

[38] For a discussion, see C. Odinkalu: "Implementing economic, social and cultural rights under the African Charter on Human and Peoples' Rights" in Evans & Murray (n 23 above) 178.

[39] It is also somewhat surprising that the socio-economic rights that are recognised, are not explicitly made subject to the usual internal qualifiers that apply in respect of such rights in most international instruments —such as the provision that the state is only required to ensure progressive realisation, subject to available resources, etc. This is made more problematic by the absence of a general limitation clause in the Charter, as discussed below. A selected few socio-economic rights, stated in near absolute terms, are recognised, while other obvious candidates for inclusion are not present. The Protocol on the Rights of Women, adopted in 2003 and discussed further below, qualifies the provision of socio-economic rights by providing that the government should take appropriate measures with regard to most socio-economic rights. However, it provides for an unqualified right to adequate housing (article 16).

[40] *Social and Economic Rights Action Centre (SERAC) and Another v Nigeria*, n 29 above.

[41] Para 60.

[42] Para 65.

The approach of the Commission of filling in the gaps in the Charter as was done in the *SERAC* case could be seen as a creative and bold move on the part of the Commission, but it could also be argued that a too wide divergence between the Commission's interpretation of the Charter and the Charter itself could compromise legal certainty.[43]

3.3. *Women's rights*

The way in which the Charter deals with gender issues has been a bone of contention. Article 18(3) provides as follows:

> The state shall ensure the elimination of every discrimination against women and also ensure the protection of the rights of the woman and the child as stipulated in international declarations and conventions.

This lumping together of women and children, in an article which deals primarily with the family, re-enforces outdated stereotypes about the proper place and role of women in society and has been partially responsible for the drive to adopt the Protocol to the African Charter on the Rights of Women in Africa.[44] The Protocol was adopted by the AU Assembly in 2003 and received the required 15 ratifications on 26 October 2005 thereby entering into force on 25 November 2005.

The Protocol on the Rights of Women is detailed with 24 substantive articles, some dealing with specific issues affecting women, while other deal with rights that should apply equally to men and women, some of which are not included in the African Charter. The rights in the Protocol include elimination of discrimination against women (Art. 2); right to dignity (Art. 3); right to life, integrity and security of person (Art. 4); elimination of harmful practices (Art. 5); marriage (Art. 6); separation, divorce and annulment of marriage (Art. 7); access to justice and equal protection of the law (Art. 8); political participation (Art. 9); peace (Art. 10); protection of women in armed conflict (Art. 11); education (Art. 12); economic and social welfare rights (Art. 13); health and reproductive rights (Art. 14); food security (Art. 15); adequate housing (Art. 16); positive cultural context (Art. 17); healthy and sustainable environment (Art. 18); right to sustainable development (Art. 19); widow's rights (Art. 20); inheritance (Art. 21); special protection of elderly women (Art. 22); women with disabilities (Art. 23); and women in distress (Art. 24).

The African Commission (and after its establishment also the African Court) is responsible for monitoring the implementation of the Charter and as a result also for the Protocol, thereby avoiding the duplication that exists with regard to children's

---

[43] C. HEYNS: "The African regional human rights system: In need of reform?", 1 *African Human Rights Law Journal*, 2001, p. 155.

[44] M. NSIBIRWA: "A brief analysis of the Draft Protocol to the African Charter on Human and Peoples' Rights on the Rights of Women", 1 *African Human Rights Law Journal*, 2001, p. 40. See also J. ODER: "Reclaiming women's social and economic rights in Africa - The Protocol to the African Charter on Human and Peoples' Rights on the Rights of Women in Africa" *ESR Review* vol 5 no 4. A further important development for women's rights was the adoption by the AU Heads of State and Government of a "Solemn Declaration on Gender Equality in Africa" in July 2004.

issues, where as mentioned above a separate Committee on the Rights and Welfare of the Child has been established.

3.4. *Peoples' rights*

In its protection of peoples' rights the Charter goes further than any other international instrument.[45]

All "peoples", according to the Charter, have a right to be equal (Art. 19); to existence and self-determination (Art. 20); to freely dispose of their wealth and natural resources (Art. 21); to economic, social and cultural development (Art. 22); to peace and security (Art. 23); and to a satisfactory environment (Art. 24). Clearly part of the motivation for the recognition of "peoples' rights" lies in the fact that entire "peoples' have been colonised and otherwise exploited in the history of Africa.

The concept of "peoples" has been referred to in some of the cases before the Commission, including the following:

- In a case concerning Katangese secessionists in the former Zaire,[46] a complaint was brought on the basis that the Katangese people had a right, as a people, to self-determination in the form of independence. The Commission ruled that there was no evidence that a Charter provision had been violated, because widespread human rights violations or a lack of political participation by the Katangese people had not been proven. This could be understood to suggest that if these conditions were met, secession by such a "people" could be a permissible option. On the other hand the Commission was careful to emphasize that self-determination can also take forms other than secession, such as self-government, local government, federalism, or confederalism.[47]
- In a case concerning the 1994 *coup d'état* against the democratically elected government of The Gambia, the Commission held that this violated the right to self-determination of the people of The Gambia as a whole.[48] The same conclusion was reached when the Abacha government in Nigeria annulled internationally recognised free and fair elections.[49]
- In the abovementioned *SERAC* case the Commission held that the right to a satisfactory environment in Article 24 requires the state "to take reasonable ... measures to prevent pollution and ecological degradation, to promote conservation, and to secure an ecologically sustainable development and use of natural resources."[50] Significantly, here the rights of peoples are also used outside the context of self-determination.

---

[45] See R. Murray and S. Wheatley: "Groups and the African Charter on Human and Peoples' Rights", 25 *Human Rights Quarterly*, 2003, p. 213.

[46] *Katangese Peoples' Congress v Zaire* (2000) AHRLR 71 (ACHPR 1995).

[47] As above, para 4.

[48] *Jawara v The Gambia* (2000) AHRLR 107 (ACHPR 2000).

[49] *Constitutional Rights Project and Another v Nigeria* (2000) AHRLR 191 (ACHPR 1998) para 52.

[50] N 40 above, para 52.

3.5. *Limitations, derogation and duties*

The way in which the African Charter deals with restrictions on all rights, including civil and political rights, presents a significant obstacle. The African Charter does not contain a general limitation clause (although, as is noted below, Article 27(2) is starting to play this role). This means that there are no general guidelines spelled out in the Charter on how its rights should be limited —no clear "limits on the limitations", so to speak—. A well-defined system of limitations is important. A society in which rights cannot be limited will be ungovernable, but it is essential that appropriate human rights norms be set for the limitations.

A number of the articles of the Charter setting out specific civil and political rights do contain limiting provisions applicable to those particular rights. Some of these internal limitations clearly spell out the procedural and substantive norms with which limitations should comply,[51] while others only describe the substantive requirements which limitations must meet.[52]

A last category of these internal limitation clauses merely poses the apparently procedural requirement that limitations should be done "within the law". An example of this category of internal limitations is Article 9(2), which provides as follows: "Every individual shall have the right to express and disseminate his opinions within the law." This kind of limitation is generally known as a "claw-back clause". They seem to recognise the right in question only to the extent that such a right is not infringed upon by national law.

If that was the correct interpretation, the claw-back clauses would obviously undermine the whole idea of international supervision of domestic law and practices and render the Charter meaningless in respect of the rights involved. Domestic law will in those cases have to be measured according to domestic standards; a senseless exercise. What is given with the one hand is seemingly taken away with the other.

As has been noted above, however, the Charter has a very expansive approach in respect of interpretation. In terms of Articles 60 and 61, the Commission has to draw inspiration from international human rights law in interpreting the provisions of the Charter. The Commission has used these provisions very liberally in a number of instances to bring the Charter in line with international practices, and the claw-back clauses are no exception.

In the context of the claw-back clauses, the African Commission has held that provisions in articles that allow rights to be limited "in accordance with law", should be understood to require such limitations to be done in terms of domestic legal provisions, which comply with international human rights standards.[53]

---

[51] For example, Art. 11 recognises the right of freedom of assembly, subject to the following proviso: "The exercise of this right shall be subject only to necessary restrictions provided for by law, in particular those enacted in the interests of national security, the safety, health, ethics and rights and freedoms of others."

[52] Art. 8 provides that the freedom of conscience and religion may only be limited in the interest of "law and order".

[53] The Commission has held, eg, in *Media Rights Agenda and Others v Nigeria*, n 31 above, para 66: "To allow national law to have precedent over the international law of the Charter would defeat the purpose of the rights and freedoms enshrined in the Charter. International human rights standards must always prevail over contradicting national law."

Through this interpretation, the Commission has gone a long way towards curing one of the most troublesome inherent deficiencies in the Charter. However, it remains unfortunate that the Charter, to those who have not had the benefit of exposure to the approach of the Commission, will continue to appear to condone infringements of human rights norms as long as it is done through domestic law.

The African Charter does not contain a provision either allowing or disallowing derogation from its provisions during a state of emergency. This has led the Commission to the conclusion that derogation is not possible.[54] This could mean that in real emergencies the Charter will be ignored, and will not exercise a restraining influence.

The Charter recognises, in addition to rights, also duties.[55] For example, individuals have duties towards their family and society,[56] and state parties have the duty to promote the Charter.[57]

Perhaps the most significant provision under the heading "Duties" is Article 27(2), which reads as follows: "The rights and freedoms of each individual shall be exercised with due regard to the rights of others, collective security, morality and common interest." This provision has now in effect been given the status by the African Commission of a general limitation clause. According to the Commission: "The only legitimate reasons for limitations of the rights and freedoms of the African Charter are found in Article 27(2) ...".[58]

The Commission's use of Article 27(2) as a general limitation clause seems to confirm the view that the concept of "duties" should not be understood as a sinister way of saying rights should first be earned, or that meeting certain obligations is a precondition for enjoying human rights. Rather, it implies that the exercise of human rights, which people have simply because they are human beings[59] may be limited by the duties which they also have. Rights precede duties, and the recognition of certain duties is merely another way of signifying the kind of limitations that may be placed on rights.

4. **Norms recognised in other treaties**

4.1. *OAU Convention Governing Specific Aspects of Refugee Problems in Africa*

The definition of refugee in Article 1 of the OAU Refugee Convention is broader than in the UN Refugee Convention. In addition to "well founded fear of being

[54] *Commission Nationale des Droits de l'Homme et des Libertés v Chad*, n 29 above, para 21.

[55] See M. Mutua: "The Banjul Charter and the African cultural fingerprint", 35 *Virginia Journal of International Law,* 1995, p. 339.

[56] Arts. 27, 28 & 29.

[57] Art. 25. See also Art. 26.

[58] See *Media Rights Agenda and Others v Nigeria*, n 31 above, para 68. See also *Constitutional Rights Project and Others v Nigeria* (2000) AHRLR 227 (ACHPR 1999), para 41.

[59] "[I]nherent in a human being", in the words of Art. 5 of the Charter, in respect of dignity.

persecuted for reasons of race, religion, nationality, membership of a particular group or political opinion"[60] the OAU Convention also stipulates that anyone who is compelled to leave his country because of "external aggression, occupation, foreign domination or events seriously disturbing public order" shall be considered a refugee. The OAU Convention does not provide for any supervisory system but the African Commission has considered a number of communications dealing with refugees.[61]

4.2. *African Charter on the Rights and Welfare of the Child*

The African Children's Charter, adopted in 1990, in many respects has similar provisions to the UN Convention on the Rights of the Child (CRC), adopted less than a year prior to the African instrument. In some respects the African Children's Charter goes further than the CRC. No person under 18 years should be recruited or take part in direct hostilities.[62] The CRC sets the age-limit at 15 years, though a Protocol adopted in 2000 raises it to 18 years. The African Children's Charter goes further than the CRC also in other aspects, for example in prohibiting child marriages.[63] The implementation of the African Children's Charter lies with the African Committee of Experts on the Rights and Welfare of the Child, discussed further below.

4.3. *AU Convention on Preventing and Combating Corruption*

Corruption depletes the resources necessary for a state to be able to fulfil its human rights obligations. This is recognised in the AU Convention on Preventing and Combating Corruption which provides as one of the objectives of the Convention to "[p]romote socio-economic development by removing obstacles to the enjoyment of economic, social and cultural rights as well as civil and political rights."[64] The Convention also provides for rights linked to the fight against corruption such as access to information.[65] The Convention provides for an Advisory Board on Corruption as a follow up mechanism.[66]

---

60 OAU Convention Art. 1(1), UN Refugee Convention Art. 1(a)(2) read with the Protocol relating to the status of refugees (1967) Art. 1(2). For a discussion see Lawyers for Human Rights *African exodus,* 1995.

61 See eg *Organisation Mondiale Contre la Torture and Others v Rwanda* (2000) AHRLR 282 (ACHPR 1996) and Rencontre Africaine pour la Défense des Droits de l'Homme v Zambia (2000) AHRLR 321 (ACHPR 1996).

62 Art. 22(2).

63 Art. 21(2). See F. Viljoen: "Introduction to the African Commission" in *Human Rights Law in Africa* 491. See also D.M. Chirwa: "The merits and demerits of the African Charter on the Rights and Welfare of the Child" 10 *International Journal of Children's Rights,* 2002, p. 157.

64 AU Convention on Preventing and Combating Corruption, Art. 2(4).

65 As above, Art. 9.

66 As above, Art. 22.

5. Organs established for the enforcement of Human Rights

The establishment of the African Union has seen an unprecedented institutional proliferation of bodies with a human rights mandate.[67] Schematically, the continental bodies with a human rights function may be set out as follows:

Organigram: African Union

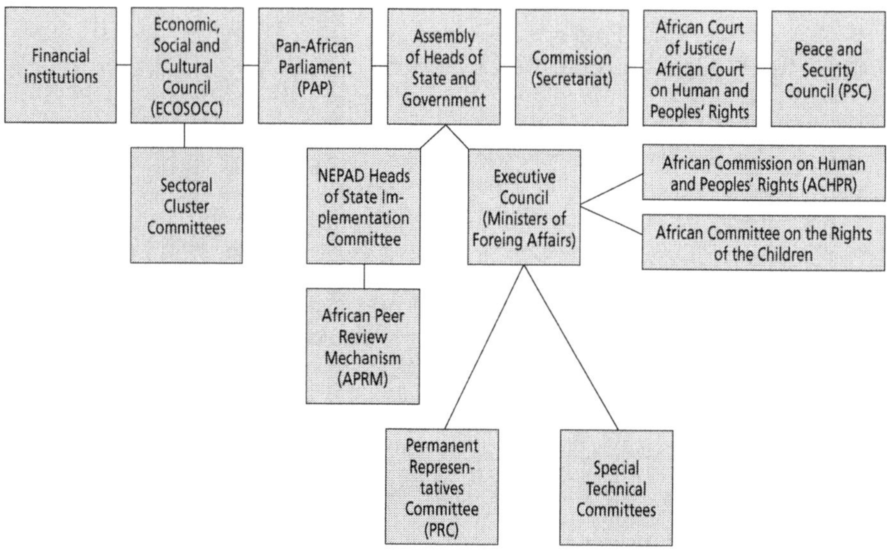

Source: C. HEYNS (ed.): *Compendium of key human rights documents of the African Union,* 2005, p. 92.

5.1. *The role of the main organs of the AU in protecting human rights*

The African Union has the following main organs: the Assembly of Heads of State and Government, the Executive Council, the Permanent Representative Committee, the Pan-African Parliament, the African Court of Justice, the AU Commission, Specialised Technical Committees, the Economic, Social and Cultural Council, financial institutions and the Peace and Security Council.[68]

The Pan-African Parliament shall "ensure the full participation of African peoples in the development and economic integration of the continent."[69] The Parlia-

[67] A. LLOYD & R. MURRAY: "Institutions with responsibility for human rights protection under the African Union", 48 *Journal of African Law,* 2004, p. 165

[68] AU Constitutive Act Art. 5. The PSC is not included as a main organ of the AU in the original Constitutive Act, but will be so under amendments that have not yet entered into force. For a discussion see Heyns and others, n 6 above, 252.

[69] AU Constitutive Act Art. 17(1). The functions of the Parliament is set out in the Protocol to the Treaty Establishing the African Economic Community Relating to the Pan-African Parliament,

ment has as one of its objectives to "promote the principles of human rights and democracy in Africa".[70] The Parliament held its first session in 2004. Each state party to the Protocol establishing the Parliament sends five national parliamentarians to the Parliament that meets twice a year in Midrand, South Africa. Currently its powers are purely consultative and advisory.[71]

The Economic, Social and Cultural Council (ECOSOCC) is "an advisory organ composed of different social and professional groups".[72] Its purpose is to provide a role for civil society in the AU. ECOSOCC has as one of its objectives to "promote and defend a culture of good governance, democratic principles and institutions, popular participation, human rights and freedoms as well as social justice."[73] The statutes of ECOSOCC were adopted by the AU Assembly in July 2004 and the Council held its first meeting in Addis Ababa in March 2005.[74]

The African Court of Justice, one of the main organs of the AU, has not yet been established as the Protocol setting up the court had only received eight of 15 ratifications required to enter into force by November 2005. The Court of Justice will be further discussed below in relation to the African Court on Human and Peoples' Rights.

The attempts to develop mechanisms to deal with conflict in Africa are also of importance in trying to prevent massive human rights violations.[75] The Protocol on the Peace and Security Council (PSC), adopted in 2002, entered into force in 2003. The PSC is composed of 15 members. The criteria for membership include "respect for constitutional governance ... as well as the rule of law and human rights ..."[76].

---

adopted by the OAU Assembly in March 2001 and entered into force in 2003. Reprinted in *Human Rights Law in Africa* 212. See K.D. Magliveras & G.J. Naldi: "The Pan-African Parliament of the African Union: An overview", 3 *African Human Rights Law Journal,* 2003, p. 222 and T. Demeke: "The new Pan-African Parliament: Prospects and challenges in view of the experience of the European Parliament", 4 *African Human Rights Law Journal,* 2004, p. 53.

70 Protocol on the Pan-African Parliament Art. 3(2).

71 It is clear that the Parliament has yet to find its feet, but among the activities with relevance for human rights are its fact-finding mission to Darfur, which produced a report to the April 2005 session of the Parliament and its decision at the same session to send missions to Côte d'Ivoire and the Democratic Republic of Congo. The Parliament will also play a role in the African Peer Review process. See Recommendations on the New Partnership for Africa's Development and the African Peer Review Mechanism, adopted at second ordinary session of the Pan-African Parliament, 16 September - 1 October 2004, PAP-Rec 002/04. http://www.iss.co.za/AF/RegOrg/unity_to_union/pdfs/pap/3rdres.pdf (accessed 26 September 2005).

72 AU Constitutive Act Art. 22(1).

73 ECOSOCC Statutes Art. 2(5).

74 http://www.africa-union.org/organs/ecosocc/home.htm. ECOSOCC has a membership of 150 organisations, constituting the General Assembly, and a 18-member Standing Committee. To facilitate policy input into the other AU organs the Council has ten sectoral cluster committees, roughly corresponding to the departments of the AU Commission (Political affairs; peace and security; infrastructure and energy; social affairs and health; human resources, science and technology; trade and industry; rural economy and agriculture; economic affairs; women and gender; and cross-cutting issues. Human rights are considered under political affairs.)

75 See Declaration on the Establishment of a Mechanism for Conflict Prevention, Management and Resolution, AHG/DECL. 3 (XXIX). The Central Organ of this Mechanism was included as an organ of the AU at the 37th OAU Assembly in 2001, AHG/Dec. 160 (XXXVII). According to Art. 22 of the Protocol Relating to the Establishment of Peace and Security Council of Africa, ASS/AU/Dec. 2(I), this Council will replace the earlier Mechanism.

76 PSC Protocol Art. 5(2)(g).

Article 4 of the PSC Protocol provides that the Council shall be guided by the AU Constitutive Act, the UN Charter and the Universal Declaration of Human Rights. The Protocol further provides as one of the objectives of the Council to

> promote and encourage democratic practices, good governance and the rule of law, protect human rights and fundamental freedoms, respect for the sanctity of human life and international humanitarian law, as part of efforts for preventing conflicts.[77]

Article 19 of the Protocol provides that:

> the Peace and Security Council shall seek close cooperation with the African Commission on Human and Peoples' Rights in all matters relevant to its objectives and mandate. The Commission on Human and Peoples' Rights shall bring to the attention of the Peace and Security Council any information relevant to the objectives and mandates of the Peace and Security Council.

From its Annual Activity Reports it appears that the Commission has not made use of this provision, though it has made reference to PSC resolutions in its own country specific resolutions.[78]

The development programme of the AU, the New Partnership for Africa's Development (NEPAD), links human rights to development and provides for the African Peer Review Mechanism, (APRM), discussed below.

5.2. *The African Commission on Human and Peoples' Rights*

As was mentioned earlier, the African Charter, as adopted in 1981, provided only for the creation of a Commission and not a Court on Human Rights, in contrast with the other two regional systems in the world —in Europe and in the Americas, which, at the time, had both—.[79] The Commission is not formally an organ of the AU, as it was created by a separate treaty.

5.2.1. The Commissioners

The African Commission consists of 11 commissioners, who serve in their individual capacities.[80] The Commission meets twice a year in regular sessions for a period of up to two weeks. They are nominated by state parties to the Charter and elected by the Assembly.[81] The Secretariat of the Commission is based in Banjul, The

[77] PSC Protocol Art. 3(f).

[78] See eg Resolution on Côte d'Ivoire and Resolution on Darfur (2004), 17th Annual Activity Report of the African Commission on Human and Peoples' Rights

[79] With the entry into force of Protocol 11 to the European Convention on Human Rights in November 1998 the European Commission on Human Rights was abolished.

[80] Art. 31.

[81] Art. 33.

Gambia. The Commission alternates its meetings between Banjul and other African capitals. The Commission has a protective as well as a promotional mandate.[82]

Although the Charter provides that the Commissioners should be independent there have been many instances where the independence of individual Commissioners has been questioned. The fact that many Commissioners have been serving civil servants or ambassadors has received criticism. For example, a Commissioner from Mauritania elected in 2003 became a minister in his home country shortly thereafter. An important step was, however, taken when the AU requested nominations to fill the post of four Commissioners in 2005. In a *note verbale* to the member countries in April 2005 the AU Commission provided guidelines that excluded senior civil servants and diplomatic representatives.[83] The four new Commissioners elected at the July 2005 summit all hold positions which are independent from government.[84]

The main mechanisms employed by the Commission to fulfil its task of supervising compliance with Charter norms by state parties are the following:

5.2.2. The complaints procedure

Both states and individuals may bring complaints to the African Commission alleging violations of the African Charter by state parties.

The procedure by which one state brings a complaint about an alleged human rights violation by another state is not often used.[85] Currently one such case is pending before the Commission, between the Democratic Republic of Congo and three neighbouring countries.[86]

The so-called individual communication or complaints procedure is not clearly provided for in the African Charter. One reading of the Charter is that communications could be considered only where "serious or massive violations" are at stake, which then triggers the rather futile Article 58 procedure, described below. However, the African Commission has accepted from the start that it has the power to deal with complaints about any human rights violations under the Charter even if "serious or massive" violations are not at stake, provided the admissibility criteria are met.[87]

---

[82] Art. 45(1) & (2). See V. Dankwa: "The promotional role of the African Commission on Human and Peoples' Rights" in Evans and Murray (n 23 above) 335.

[83] BC/OLC/66/Vol.XVIII

[84] The four members elected were Ms Peine Alapini-Gansou lawyer and NGO activist in Benin; Mr Musa Ngary Bitaye, president of the Bar Association of The Gambia; Ms Faith Pansy Tlakula, Chief Electoral Officer, Independent Electoral Commission of South Africa; and Mr Mumba Malila, chairperson of the Zambian Human Rights Commission.

[85] Provided for in Arts. 47-54.

[86] Communication 227/99, *Democratic Republic of the Congo v Burundi, Rwanda and Uganda.* In a case brought by a Burundian organisation against a number of neighbouring states it was held by the Commission that the complainant was in essence representing the state. However, the communication was considered under the individual communication procedure as the organisation's standing to bring the complaint was not challenged by the responding governments. Communication 157/96, *Association Pour la Sauvegarde de la Paix au Burundi v Tanzania, Kenya, Uganda, Rwanda, Zaire and Zambia*, 17th Annual Activity Report of the African Commission.

[87] Following directly after the provisions on inter-state communications, Art. 55 provides for "other communications". The Commission has proceeded from the assumption that this refers to individual communications. See *Jawara v The Gambia*, n 48 above, para 42.

The Charter is silent on the question who can bring such complaints, but the Commission practice is that complaints from individuals as well as NGOs are accepted. From the case law of the Commission it is clear that the complainant does not need to be a victim or a family member of a victim.[88] The Commission in the *SERAC* case expressed its thanks to

> the two human rights NGOs which brought the matter under its purview ... This a demonstration of the usefulness to the Commission and individuals of *actio popularis*, which is wisely allowed under the African Charter.[89]

The individual complaints procedure is used much more frequently than the inter-state mechanism of the African Charter, although not as frequently as one would have expected on a continent with the kind of human rights problems that Africa has.[90] This could to some extent be attributed to a lack of awareness about the system, but even where there is awareness, there is often not much faith that the system can make a difference.

According to a recent study on the compliance of states with the findings of the Commission there has been full state compliance in six of the 44 cases where the Commission found state parties in violation of the African Charter. The study finds that there has been non-compliance in 13 cases, partial compliance in 14 cases, seven cases of situational compliance (through change of government) and unclear compliance in four cases.[91] Viljoen and Louw finds that

> in the analysis of cases of full and clear non-compliance, it appears that the most important factors are political, rather than legal. The nature of the case, the elaborateness of reasoning or the type of remedy required seems to have little bearing on the likelihood of adherence by states. The only factor of relevance that relates to the treaty body itself is follow-up activities undertaken by the Commission.[92]

As with other complaints systems, the African Charter poses certain admissibility criteria before the Commission may entertain complaints.[93] These criteria include the requirement of exhausting local remedies. The Commission may be approached only once the matter has been pursued in the highest court in the country in question, without success, or a reasonable prospect of success.

The Commission has stated that for a case not to be admissible local remedies must be available, effective, sufficient and not unduly prolonged.[94] In *Purohit and*

---

88 *Malawi African Association and Others v Mauritania*, n 28 above, para 78.

89 N 29 above, para 49.

90 The Commission has received around 300 individual communications since its inception in 1987, many of them submitted by NGOs.

91 F. Viljoen & L. Louw: "An assessment of state compliance with the recommendations issued by the African Commission on Human and Peoples' Rights between 1993 and 2003" (forthcoming, on file with authors).

92 As above.

93 Art. 56. For a discussion, see F. Viljoen: "Admissibility under the African Charter" in Evans & Murray (n 25 above) 61.

94 *Jawara v The Gambia*, n 48 above.

Moore v the Gambia,[95] a case dealing with detention in a mental health institution, the Commission gave a potentially far-reaching decision on the exhaustion of local remedies when it held that:

> the category of people being represented in the present communication are likely to be people picked up from the streets or people from poor backgrounds and as such it cannot be said that the remedies available in terms of the Constitution are realistic remedies for them in the absence of legal aid services.[96]

The Charter also has a requirement that the communications are "not written in disparaging or insulting language directed against the state concerned and its institutions or to the Organization of African Unity".[97]

When a complaint is lodged, the state in question is asked to respond to the allegations against it. If the state does not respond, the Commission proceeds on the basis of the facts as provided by the complainant.[98] If the decision of the Commission is that there has indeed been a violation or violations of the Charter, the Commission sometimes also makes recommendations that continuing violations should stop (eg prisoners be released);[99] or specific laws be changed[100], but often the recommendations are rather vague, and the state party is merely urged to "take all necessary steps to comply with its obligations under the Charter."[101] Sometimes there is no provision at all as to remedies,[102] while in other cases the remedies provided are elaborate.[103] Recently the Commission required some states to report on measures taken to comply with the recommendations in their state reports to the Commission.[104]

Article 58 provides that "special cases which reveal the existence of serious or massive violations of human and peoples' rights" must be referred by the Commission to the Assembly, which "may then request the Commission to undertake an in-depth study of these cases". Where the Commission has followed this route, the

---

[95] *Purohit and Moore v The Gambia*, communication 241/2001, 16th Annual Activity Report of the African Commission on Human and Peoples' Rights.

[96] As above, para 37.

[97] Art. 56(3). The Commission has only used this provision in one case, see *Ligue Camerounaise des Droits de l'Homme v Cameroon* (2000) AHRLR 61 (ACHPR 1997).

[98] See, for example, *Commission Nationale des Droits de l'Homme et des Libertés v Chad*, n 29 above, para 25. See also R. Murray: "Evidence and fact-finding by the African Commission" in Evans and Murray (n 25 above) 100.

[99] See eg *Constitutional Rights Project (in respect of Akamu and Others) v Nigeria*, n 34 above; *Constitutional Rights Project (in respect of Lekwot and Others) v Nigeria* (2000) AHRLR 183 (ACHPR 1995); *Constitutional Rights Project and Another v Nigeria*, n 49 above; *Constitutional Rights Project v Nigeria I* (2000) AHRLR 241 (ACHPR 1999); *Centre for Free Speech v Nigeria* (2000) AHRLR 250 (ACHPR 1999)

[100] See eg *International Pen and Others (on behalf of Saro-Wiwa) v Nigeria* (2000) AHRLR 212 (ACHPR 1998); *Avocats Sans Frontières (on behalf of Bwampamye) v Burundi*; (2000) AHRLR 48 (ACHPR 2000).

[101] *Constitutional Rights Project and Others v Nigeria*, n 58 above.

[102] *Huri-Laws V Nigeria* (2000) AHRLR 273 (ACHPR 2000)

[103] See eg *Malawi African Association and Others v Mauritania*, n 28 above; *Social and Economic Rights Action Centre (SERAC) and Another v Nigeria*, n 29 above.

[104] See eg *Legal Resources Foundation v Zambia*, n 37 above.

Assembly has failed to respond, but the Commission has nevertheless made findings that such massive violations have occurred. Today, the Commission does not seem to refer cases anymore to the Assembly in terms of Article 58.[105]

The Charter does not contain a provision in terms of which the Commission has the power to take provisional or interim measures requesting state parties to abstain from causing irreparable harm.[106] However, the Rules of Procedure of the Commission grants the Commission the power to do so. The Commission has used these provisional or interim measures in a number of cases. One such case concerned Ken Saro-Wiwa and other Ogoni activists, who had been sentenced to death by a special tribunal, set up by the military government in Nigeria.[107] In that particular case, the interim measures requesting the Nigerian government not to execute them were ignored. The execution of Saro-Wiwa and the others caused a worldwide outcry. The Commission said in its decision that it had tried to assist Nigeria to meet its obligations under the Charter by means of the interim measures, and the execution in the face of the interim measures consequently violated Article 1.[108]

5.2.3. Consideration of state reports

Each state party is required to submit a report every two years on its efforts to comply with the African Charter.[109] Although it is not provided for in the African Charter that the reports should be submitted specifically to the African Commission, the Commission recommended to the Assembly that the Commission be given the mandate to consider the reports. The Assembly has endorsed this recommendation.[110] NGOs are allowed to submit shadow or alternative reports, but the impact of this avenue is diminished by the lack of access of NGOs to the state reports to which they are supposed to respond. The reports are considered by the Commission in public sessions. Reporting by state parties should be done in accordance with guidelines adopted by the Commission. Currently there are two sets of guidelines; one, adopted in 1988[111] is long and complex and one, adopted in 1998[112] which is overly brief.[113] The relationship between these guidelines is unclear and it should be

---

[105] It seems that the Commission will be able to refer such cases to the PSC (Art. 19 of the PSC Protocol, see above).

[106] Rule 111. For a discussion, see G.J. Naldi: "Interim measures of protection in the African system for the protection of human and peoples' rights", 2 *African Human Rights Law Journal,* 2002, p. 1.

[107] *International Pen and Others (on behalf of Saro-Wiwa) v Nigeria,* n 102 above.

[108] However, in a recent decision the Commission held that Article 1 could only be violated if "the State does not enact the necessary legislative enactment". *Interights and Others (on behalf of Bosch) v Botswana*, n 36 above, para 51. In that case non-compliance with interim measures was not held to have constituted a violation of Art. 1.

[109] Art. 62. For a discussion, see M. Evans and others "The reporting mechanism of the African Charter on Human and Peoples' Rights" in Evans & Murray (n 25 above) 36 and GW Mugwanya "Examination of state reports by the African Commission: A critical appraisal", 1 *African Human Rights Law Journal,* 2001, p. 268.

[110] See AHG/Res 176 (XXIV) 1988, reprinted in *Human Rights Law in Africa 1999* 128.

[111] Reprinted in *Human Rights Law in Africa* 507.

[112] Reprinted in *Human Rights Law in Africa* 569.

[113] Evans and others, 45.

a priority of the Commission to clarify the situation as regards guidelines on state reporting.[114]

Reporting under the Charter, as in other systems, is aimed at facilitating both introspection and inspection. "Introspection" refers to the process when the state, in writing its report, measures itself against the norms of the Charter. "Inspection" refers to the process when the Commission measures the performance of the state in question against the Charter. The objective is to facilitate a "constructive dialogue" between the Commission and the states.

Reporting has been very tardy, and 18 of the 53 state parties to the African Charter have never submitted any report. In 2001 the Commission started to issue concluding observations in respect of reports considered. Their usefulness is diminished by the fact that neither the state reports nor the concluding observations are published by the Commission.

5.2.4. Special rapporteurs and working groups

The Commission has appointed a number of special rapporteurs, with varying degrees of success. There is no obvious legal basis for the appointment of the special rapporteurs in the Charter; it has been described as another innovation of the Commission.[115] The special rapporteurs are all members of the Commission.

There has been widespread criticism of the lack of effective action on the part of the Special Rapporteur on Summary, Arbitrary and Extrajudicial Executions, while the same is true of at least the first incumbent of the position of Special Rapporteur on the Conditions of Women in Africa. In contrast, the Special Rapporteur on Prisons and Conditions of Detention in Africa has set the standards for years to come.

The Commission has recently appointed special rapporteurs on freedom of expression; refugees and internally displaced persons; and human rights defenders. The Commission has also established a committee to monitor the implementation of the Guidelines and Measures for the Prohibition and Prevention of Torture, Cruel, Inhuman or Degrading Treatment or Punishment in Africa (Robben Island Guidelines). In addition a Working Group on Indigenous People or Communities and a Working Group on Economic, Social and Cultural Rights have been established. Some of the members of these working groups are not members of the Commission.

---

[114] The Commission's Working Group on Economic, Social and Cultural Rights has in its mandate to "elaborate a draft revised guidelines pertaining to economic, social and cultural rights, for State reporting". Resolution On Economic, Social And Cultural Rights In Africa, ACHPR/Res.73(XXXVI)04, adopted by the African Commission on Human and Peoples' Rights, December 2004.

[115] It has been argued that the legal justification is to be found in Article 46, which allows for "any appropriate method of investigation". For a discussion, see J. Harrington: "Special rapporteurs of the African Commission on Human and Peoples' Rights" 1 *African Human Rights Law Journal*, 2001, p. 247 and M. Evans & R. Murray: "The special rapporteurs in the African system" in Evans & Murray (n 25 above) 280. For the mandates of the special rapporteurs, see www.achpr.org.

5.2.5. On-site visits

The Commission has since 1995 conducted a number of on-site visits.[116] These involve a range of activities, from fact finding to good offices and general promotional visits.[117] Many mission reports have never been published.

5.2.6. Resolutions

The Commission has adopted resolutions on a number of human rights issues in Africa. In addition to country-specific and other more *ad hoc* resolutions, they have adopted resolutions on topics such as the following: fair trial; freedom of association; human and peoples' rights education; humanitarian law; contemporary forms of slavery; anti-personnel mines; prisons in Africa; the independence of the judiciary; the electoral process and participatory governance; the International Criminal Court; the death penalty; torture; HIV/AIDS; and freedom of expression.[118]

5.2.7. Relationship with NGOs

NGOs have a special relationship with the Commission.[119] Large numbers have registered for observer status.[120] NGOs are often instrumental in bringing cases to the Commission; they sometimes submit shadow reports; propose agenda items at the outset of Commission sessions; and provide logistical and other support to the Commission, for example by placing interns at the Commission and providing support to the special rapporteurs and missions of the Commission. NGOs often organise special NGO workshops just prior to Commission sessions, and participate actively in the public sessions of the Commission. NGOs also collaborate with the Commission in developing normative resolutions and new protocols to the African Charter.

5.2.8. Interaction with AU political bodies

The Annual Activity Reports of the Commission, which reflect the decisions, resolutions, and other acts of the Commission, are submitted each year for permission to publish to the meetings of the Assembly of Heads of State and Government

---

[116] Countries that members of the Commission has conducted promotional or fact-finding missions to include: Burkina Faso (2001), Chad (2000), Congo (2004), Côte d'Ivoire (2001, 2003), Democratic Republic of Congo (2004), Djibouti (2000, 2002), Libya (2002), Mauritania (1996), Mozambique (2000), Niger (2002), Nigeria (1997, 2005), Senegal (1996, 2002), Seychelles (2001), Sierra Leone (2000, 2004), South Africa (2001), Sudan (1996, 2002), Togo (1995), Zambia (2001) and Zimbabwe (2002).

[117] See R. Murray: "Evidence and fact-finding by the African Commission" in Evans & Murray (n 25 above) 100.

[118] For the text of the resolutions see *Human Rights Law in Africa* and www.achpr.org.

[119] See A. Motala: "Non-governmental organisations in the African system" in Evans & Murray (n 25 above) 246 and CE Welch: *Protecting Human Rights in Africa: Strategies and Roles of Non-governmental Organisations* (1995).

[120] See the resolution reprinted in *Human Rights Law in Africa* 572. National human rights institutions may also register for observer/affiliate status. See the resolution reprinted in *Human Rights Law in Africa* 574.

("Assembly") of the OAU/AU that have traditionally taken place in June or July of the following year. The Assembly has now delegated the authority to discuss the Activity Report to the Executive Council.[121] However, it is still formally adopted by the Assembly as this is required by the Charter.[122] The AU has recently started to have summits twice a year and it remains to be seen whether the African Commission will submit a report to each summit.

In practice the Assembly has served as a rubber stamp for the publication of the report by the Commission containing its decisions, but the principle that the very people in charge of the institutions whose human rights practices are at stake —the Heads of State— should take the final decision on publicity undermines the legitimacy of the system. When the 17th Annual Activity Report was considered by the Executive Council at the AU summit in July 2004, Zimbabwe complained that it had not had the opportunity to respond to allegations contained in the report concerning a fact-finding mission undertaken by the Commission to Zimbabwe. The Council suspended the publication of the report and its publication was only finally authorised at the summit in January 2005.

5.2.9. Information on the Commission

The decisions of the Commission are published in the *African Human Rights Law Reports* (AHRLR).[123] A small but growing number of secondary publications on the work of the Commission have appeared.[124] Information on the work of the Commission is available on a number of websites.[125] It is unclear why the Commission makes little use of its own web site which should be the main resource on information on the work of the Commission. In December 2005 the Commission published the18th Annual Activity Report, adopted by the AU Assembly in July 2005 on its web site. However, the 17th Annual Activity Report, adopted by the AU Assembly in January 2005 had as of February 2006 not been published on the web site.

5.3. *The African Court on Human and Peoples' Rights*

Several reasons have been advanced why only a Commission, and not a Court, was provided for in the African Charter in 1981 as the body responsible for monitoring compliance of state parties with the Charter. On the one hand there is perhaps

---

[121] Decision on the 16th Annual Activity Report of the African Commission on Human and Peoples' Rights, Doc. Assembly/AU/7 (II), July 2003, para 5.

[122] African Charter on Human and Peoples' Rights Art. 59(3).

[123] The first volume, covering the period 1987-2000 was published in 2004.

[124] Among the most prominent are E. Ankumah: *The African Commission on Human and Peoples' Rights: Practice and Procedures*, 1996; U.O. Umozurike: *The African Charter on Human and Peoples' Rights*; Evans & Murray (eds), n 25 above; and F. Ouguergouz: *The African Charter on Human and Peoples' Rights: a comprehensive agenda for human rights*, 2003. For a detailed overview, see F. Viljoen: "Introduction to the African Commission and the regional human rights system" in *Human Rights Law in Africa* 385. Developments in the system are covered on a regular basis in the *African Human Rights Law Journal*, since 2001.

[125] www.achpr.org; www.africa-union.org; www.chr.up.ac.za.

the more idealistic explanation that the traditional way of solving disputes in Africa is through mediation and conciliation, not through the adversarial, "win or lose" mechanism of a court. On the other hand there is the view that the member states of the OAU were jealous of their newly founded sovereignty.[126]

The notion of a human rights court for Africa would be taken up by the OAU 13 years after the adoption of the African Charter when, in 1994, the Assembly adopted a resolution requesting the Secretary-General of the OAU to convene a Meeting of Experts to consider the establishment of an African Court on Human and Peoples' Rights.[127]

Ostensibly, the concept of human rights was accepted widely enough in Africa in the early 1990s for the decision to be taken to give more "teeth" to the African human rights system, in the form of a Court. This came in the wake of the different waves of democratisation on the national level, epitomised by the watershed elections in Benin in 1991, and the advent of democracy in South Africa in 1994. Worldwide, of course, the idea of human rights also gained prominence after the end of the cold war.

The Protocol on the African Court on Human and Peoples' Rights was adopted in Addis Ababa, Ethiopia, in 1998.[128] The Protocol entered into force in January 2004 and by February 2006 had received 22 ratifications.

The AU Assembly decided at its summit in July 2004 that the African Human Rights Court should merge with the African Court of Justice. The protocol establishing the latter court had been adopted by the Assembly in July 2003,[129] without any reference to a merger with the human rights court. The Protocol on the African Court of Justice had as of February 2006 not received the required 15 ratifications to enter into force. A draft merger protocol has been circulated[130] and at the AU summit in July 2005 the Assembly decided that:

> ...
> 2. ... a draft legal instrument relating to the establishment of the merged court comprising the Human Rights Court and the Court of Justice should be completed for consideration by the next ordinary sessions of the Executive Council and the Assembly ...

---

126 J. HARRINGTON: "The African Court on Human and Peoples' Rights" in EVANS & MURRAY (eds.), n 23 above, 306. For commentary on the envisaged Court, see also G.J. NALDI & K. MAGLIVERAS: "Reinforcing the African system of human rights: The Protocol on the Establishment of a Regional Court of Human and Peoples' Rights", 16 *Netherlands Quarterly of Human Rights,* 1998, p. 431; N.J. UDOMBANA: "Towards the African Court on Human and Peoples' Rights: Better late than never" 3 *Yale Human Rights and Development Law Journal,* 2000, p. 45; M. MUTUA: "The African Human Rights Court: A two-legged stool?" 21 *Human Rights Quarterly,* 1999, p. 350; "The African Court on Human and Peoples' Rights" in EVANS & MURRAY (n 23 above) 305; and F. VILJOEN: "A Human Rights Court for Africa, and Africans", 30 *Brooklyn Journal of International Law,* 2004, p. 1.

127 AHG/Res 230 (XXX) 1994. Reprinted in *Human Rights Law in Africa 1999* 139.

128 The documents leading up to the adoption of the African Human Rights Court Protocol are reprinted in *Human Rights Law in Africa 1999* 233-296. The Protocol is reprinted in *Human Rights Law in Africa,* 2004, p. 170.

129 Protocol of the Court of Justice of the African Union, adopted by the AU Assembly of Heads of State and Government, Maputo, July 2003.

130 AMNESTY INTERNATIONAL: "African Union: The establishment of an independent and effective African Court on Human and Peoples' Rights must be a top priority", IOR 30/002/2005, 28 January 2005.

3. ALSO DECIDES that all necessary measures for the functioning of the Human Rights Court be taken, including particularly the election of the judges, the determination of the budget and the operationalization of the Registry;

4. FURTHER DECIDES that the Seat of the merged court shall be at a place to be decided upon by the Member States of the Eastern Region, which shall also serve as the seat of the Human Rights Court pending the merger.[131]

Once the African Human Rights Court is in place, it will "complement" the protective mandate of the Commission under the Charter.[132] Under the 1998 Protocol the Court will consist of 11 judges, serving in their individual capacities, [133] nominated by state parties to the Protocol,[134] and elected by the Assembly. Only the president will be full-time.[135] The judges were elected by the Assembly in January 2006.[136] The seat of the Court is still to be determined,[137] but as is clear from the above resolution it will be in the Eastern Region.

The Protocol provides that the judges will be appointed in their individual capacities,[138] and their independence is guaranteed.[139] Special provision is made that "[t]he position of judge of the Court is incompatible with any activity that might interfere with the independence or impartiality of such a judge ...".[140] Judges will not be allowed to sit in a case if that judge is a national of a state which is a party to the case.[141]

In respect of the Court's findings, the Protocol determines that "[i]f the Court finds that there has been a violation of a human or peoples' right, it shall make appropriate orders to remedy the violation, including the payment of fair compensation or reparation."[142] The Court is explicitly granted the powers to adopt provisional measures.[143]

By ratifying the Protocol, states accept that the Commission and the states involved will be in a position to take a case that has appeared before them to the African Human Rights Court, to obtain a legally binding decision.[144] Individuals and those who act on their behalf will be able to take cases to the Court only in respect of those states that have made an additional declaration specifically authorising them to do so. In such instances the case will have to be taken "directly" to the Court, presumably

131 Decision on the merger of the African Court on Human and Peoples' Rights and the Court of Justice of the African Union, Assembly/AU/dec.83 (v).

132 Art. 2 of the African Human Rights Court Protocol.

133 Art. 11.

134 Art. 12.

135 Art. 15(4).

136 Assembly/AU/Dec.100(VI).

137 Art. 25.

138 Art. 11.

139 Art. 17.

140 Art. 18. This is significant because one of the criticisms against the Commission has been that a number of Commissioners have been closely associated with the Executive in their countries.

141 Art. 22.

142 Art. 27(1).

143 Art. 27(2).

144 Art. 5(1).

bypassing the Commission or, if the Commission was approached first, the case can be taken to the Court without requiring the authorisation of the Commission.[145]

Article 3(1) reads as follows:

> The jurisdiction of the Court shall extend to all cases and disputes submitted to it concerning the interpretation and application of the Charter, this Protocol and any other relevant human rights instrument ratified by the states concerned.

The phrase "any other relevant human rights instrument ratified by the states concerned", according to most commentators, means that adjudication in respect of even UN and sub-regional human rights instruments will fall within the jurisdiction of the African Human Rights Court, provided that such treaties have been ratified by the states concerned.[146]

It is submitted that nothing is wrong with the African Human Rights Court interpreting the Charter in view of international standards.[147] Advisory opinions[148] could also deal with other treaties.[149] However, if contentious cases could be brought to the African Human Rights Court on the ground that for example UN treaties have been violated, with no reference to the African Charter, this could lead to conflicting decisions in the different systems.[150]

The jurisdiction of the African Human Rights Court to give advisory opinions was mentioned above. In addition to member states and AU organs any "African organization recognized by the [AU]" can request an advisory opinion from the Court.[151] Advisory jurisdiction has proved useful in the Inter-American human rights system and could potentially play a similar role in the African system.

---

[145] Art. 5(3), read with Art. 34(6). Only Burkina Faso has so far made such a declaration, and it will be surprising if many states follow soon. Where a state has not made the additional declaration, the access of the individual to the Court will be as it is under the Inter-American system —the individual does not have the power to seize the Court himself or herself—. Where the additional declaration has been made, the situation of the individual resembles the current European system, where there is no Commission and the Court is accessed directly. For criticism, see Heyns, n 41 above.

[146] See Naldi & Magliveras (n 128 above) 435; Udombana (n 128 above) 90; and Mutua (n 128 above) 354.

[147] It should be noted, however, that technically Arts. 60 and 61 of the African Charter only provide that this should be done by the African Commission.

[148] A.P. van der Mei: "The advisory jurisdiction of the African Court on Human and Peoples" Rights', 5 *African Human Rights Law Journal,* 2005, p. 27.

[149] The American Convention on Human Rights provides in Art. 64(1) that the Inter-American Court can give "interpretation of this Convention or of other treaties concerning the protection of human rights in the American states". The Inter-American Court has interpreted "other treaties" to include "[a]ny provision dealing with the protection of human rights set forth in any international treaty applicable in the American States ...". See Advisory Opinion OC-1/82 of 24 September 1982, Series A No 1, para 52, quoted in van der Mei, n 151 above, 38.

[150] At the same time it should be recognised that the potential of conflicting decisions will arise in practice only in cases of "direct"access to the Court, where the Commission is bypassed, because in other cases one of the admissibility criteria before the Commission will be compatibility with the Charter. It is submitted that the word "relevant" in the phrase "relevant human rights instrument" should be understood to restrict the contentious jurisdiction of the Court beyond the Charter and the Protocol only to those instances where the instrument in question has explicitly provided for the jurisdiction of the Court. See Heyns, n 41 above, 166-167.

[151] African Human Rights Court Protocol Art. 4.

5.4. *African Committee on the Rights and Welfare of the Child*

The African Children's Charter adopted in 1990 entered into force in November 1999. The 11 members of the African Committee on the Rights and Welfare of the Child, provided for under the Charter, were elected in July 2001. The Committee held its first meeting in 2002. The Committee has adopted its Rules of Procedures and Guidelines for State Reports. States shall report to the Committee within two years from the entry into force of the convention for the state party concerned and thereafter every three years.[152] Apart from state reporting the African Children's Charter, uniquely among international instruments for the protection of the rights of children, also provides for a communication procedure. The Committee has recently received one communication but it remains unclear how the Committee will handle this.[153]

The Committee does not have its own secretariat, and is serviced by the Department for Social Affairs. The AU is in the process of recruiting a Secretary to the Committee. The Committee suffers from a serious lack of resources and the question could be asked whether the Committee should not be merged with the African Commission.[154]

5.5. *The African Peer Review Mechanism*

In July 2002 in Durban the OAU/AU Assembly of Heads of State and Government adopted the Declaration on Democracy, Political, Economic and Corporate Governance (Governance Declaration).[155] The Governance Declaration provided for the establishment of an African Peer Review Mechanism (APRM) "to promote adherence to and fulfillment of the commitments" in the Declaration.[156] The initiative grew out of the New Partnership for Africa's Development (NEPAD), adopted by the AU in 2001 as the development framework for the Union.

The Governance Declaration in section 10 provides as follows:

> In the light of Africa's recent history, respect for human rights has to be accorded an importance and urgency all of its own. One of the tests by which the quality of a democracy is judged is the protection it provides for each individual citizen and for the vulnerable and disadvantaged groups. Ethnic minorities, women and children have borne the brunt of the conflicts rag-

---

152 Art. 43. It is unclear how many state parties have actually submitted state reports. However, the Committee has adopted its procedures for considering state reports and has indicated that it will start considering state reports at its meetings. Report of the African Committee on the Rights and Welfare of the Child, EX.CL/200 (VII), report presented to the meeting of the AU Executive Council, 28 June - 2 July 2005, 1.

153 As above, 11

154 This would be in line with the current initiative to merge the UN human rights treaty bodies. See Plan of action submitted by the United Nations High Commissioner for Human Rights, A/59/2005/Add.3, para 99.

155 AHG/235(XXXVIII) Annex I.

156 As above, para 28.

> ing on the continent today. We undertake to do more to advance the cause of human rights in Africa generally and, specifically, to end the moral shame exemplified by the plight of women, children, the disabled and ethnic minorities in conflict situations in Africa.

Under the heading "Democracy and Good Political Governance", section 13 provides:

> In support of democracy and the democratic process, We will: ensure that our respective national constitutions reflect the democratic ethos and provide for demonstrably accountable governance; promote political representation, thus providing for all citizens to participate in the political process in a free and fair political environment; enforce strict adherence to the position of the African Union (AU) on unconstitutional changes of government and other decisions of our continental organization aimed at promoting democracy, good governance, peace and security; strengthen and, where necessary, establish an appropriate electoral administration and oversight bodies, in our respective countries and provide the necessary resources and capacity to conduct elections which are free, fair and credible; reassess and where necessary strengthen the AU and sub-regional election monitoring mechanisms and procedures; and heighten public awareness of the African Charter on Human and Peoples' Rights, especially in our educational institutions.

At the Durban summit the Assembly also adopted a document specifically dealing with the APRM process, the so-called APRM Base Document:

> The process will entail periodic reviews of the policies and practices of participating states to ascertain progress being made towards achieving mutual agreed goals and compliance with agreed political, economic and corporate governance values, codes and standards as outlined in the Declaration on Democracy, Political, Economic and Corporate Governance. [157]

The APRM process consists of a self-evaluation by the country that has signed up to being reviewed and a review by an international review team. It is in this respect similar to the state reporting under the African Charter. However, there are also clear differences such as country visits by the APRM review team and the political stage, when the leader of the country discusses the outcome of the review with his peers in other participating countries.

The highest decision making body in the APRM is the APR Forum consisting of the Heads of State and Government of the participating states. A panel of eminent persons with seven members oversees the review process and a member of this panel is chosen to lead the review team on its country mission.

The international review process consists of five stages.[158] First a background study is carried out by the secretariat assisted by consultants. This stage also includes a support mission to the country that will be reviewed. In the second stage a review team led by one of the eminent persons visits the country for discussions with all

---

[157] The New Partnership for Africa's Development (NEPAD): The African Peer Review Mechanism (APRM), AHG/235(XXXVIII) Annex II (APRM base document), para 15.

[158] As above, paras 18-25.

stakeholders, after which the team prepare its report (third stage). A number of partner institutions and independent consultants assist in the process. The fourth stage consists of the submission of the report to the APRM Forum and the discussion among the peers. The last stage is the publication of the report and further discussion in other AU institutions such as the Pan-African Parliament.

The APRM deals with political, economic and corporate governance and socio-economic development. Initially, there was some debate as to the inclusion of political governance aspects, including human rights, but as pointed out by Cilliers: "Without making political governance the core focus of NEPAD, the Partnership is unlikely to make an impact on the continent."[159]

The APRM is voluntary and as of February 2006 26 out of 53 AU member states have signed the Memorandum of Understanding (MOU)[160] that forms the legal basis for the review. In paragraph 24 of the MOU the signatory state agrees to "take such steps as may be necessary for the implementation of the recommendations adopted at the completion of the review process ...". The MOU does not deal with the substantive undertakings of the signatories, but instead refers to the Governance Declaration. The Governance Declaration makes reference to standards that have already been accepted by the participating states in other declarations and treaties, including global and regional human rights instruments. The Governance Declaration comprises of only 28 paragraphs and covers all the areas that are being reviewed, ie political, economic and corporate governance as well as socio-economic development. Further documents have been developed with regard to standards and indicators, including a questionnaire to help participating states complete their self-assessments.

Many observers have emphasised the necessity for civil society to engage the APRM if the mechanism is to make any difference on the ground.[161] The possibilities for such engagement varies greatly between participating countries, as do the approaches to the independence of the national process from government interference.

The APRM integrates the political level of the AU/NEPAD in a way that other parts of the African human rights system have not done.[162] The situation could to some extent be compared to the role, by many perceived as successful, of the Committee of Ministers of the Council of Europe with regard to the European Conven-

---

159 J. Cilliers: "Peace and Security through Good Governance: A guide to the NEPAD African Peer Review Mechanism" *ISS Occasional Paper* 70, April 2003.

160 Memorandum of Understanding on the African Peer Review Mechanism, adopted by the 6th summit of the NEPAD Heads of State and Government Implementation Committee, 9 March 2003, Abuja, Nigeria, NEPAD/HSGIC/03-2003/APRM/MOU. See also Communiqué on the 4th Summit of the Committee of Participating Heads of State and Government of the African Peer Review Mechanism (APR Forum), 22 January 2006, Khartoum, Sudan, http://www.nepad.org/2005/files/aprm/communiqueKhartoum2006.pdf (accessed 3 March 2006).

161 See eg A. Kajee: "NEPAD's APRM: A progress report" in *South African Yearbook of International Affairs* 2003/2004.

162 The main African human rights body, the African Commission on Human and Peoples' Rights submits its Annual Activity Report to the Executive Council of the AU which submits it to the Assembly for adoption. Though the report in 2003 aroused a certain amount of debate, this was not for trying to implement suggestions in the report but rather to shield Zimbabwe from criticism.

tion on Human Rights and the European Social Charter. However, as shown by the activities of the political bodies of the United Nations involved with human rights, the direct involvement of other states in the protection of rights is not without its problems.[163]

As in other parts of the world African leaders have not shown a great interest in criticising their peers. Hence there are reasons to be sceptical about whether "peer pressure" will be employed in the process. However, to solely focus on the pressure exercised at this level would be to underestimate the process as a whole. The APRM Base Document provides for sanctions as a last resort if peer pressure is not enough to convince governments with a lack of political will to rectify identified shortcomings.[164]

There has not been much cooperation between the APRM and the African Commission, which is unfortunate. A look at the composition of the missions to Ghana and Rwanda, the first two states to be subject to the APRM process, also makes it clear that the focus is more on economic than political governance.

6. **Conclusion**

It is not difficult to criticise the African regional human rights system, and many have done so. Some have argued that given the fact that the African Charter was adopted 25 years ago and the African Commission has been in operation for 20 years, the track record of the Commission is less than impressive. The Commission has been poorly managed by its Secretariat for many years. The Commission suffers from a lack of resources, but questions have been asked about the way in which available resources have been managed.

The perceived lack of impartiality of some Commissioners has been a constant bone of contention, as has been the lack of political will in the OAU/AU on a political level to ensure the effectiveness of the Charter system.

The Charter itself has its own internal limitations and thus has required extensive creative interpretation by the Commission. For example, the main mandates of the Commission —receiving individual communications and state reports— are not clearly recognised in the Charter. Some of the internationally accepted rights are recognised only in a cursory form in the Charter.

Moving beyond the Charter system, the need to have established a separate system for the protection of children's rights (complete with a complaints and reporting mechanism) has been questioned. There is a danger of a proliferation of mechanisms, each one depleting the scarce resources even further, instead of establishing one or two truly effective mechanisms before more are created.

---

163 In his address to the UN Commission on Human Rights on 7 April 2005 UN Secretary General Kofi Annan stated that the work of the Commission had "been undermined by the politicization of its sessions and the selectivity of its work". He proposed the adoption of a permanent Human Rights Council which should "have an explicitly defined function as a chamber of peer review, and its main task should be to evaluate all States" fulfilment of all their human rights obligations...". "Secretary General elaborates on reform of human rights structures in address to Commission on Human Rights' United Nations press release, 7 April 2005, www.ohchr.org.

164 APRM base document, n 154 above, para 24.

Some commentators have also focused on the potential weaknesses of the APRM, which relies on Heads of State —who often don't have much interest in promoting a system of finger-pointing about human rights violations— to police each other.

There is undeniably some truth in these criticisms, and much room for improvement. At the same time the merits of the African regional human rights system also need to be recognised.

The fact that Africa has a regional human rights system in the first place —only one of three regions to have that— provides an entry point for international human rights to play a role which would otherwise not have existed. The arguments about a possible "African exception" to the concept of human rights —the idea that human rights is a foreign concept with little applicability to the African situation— are considerably weaker than they would otherwise have been. The regional human rights system provides the possibility of imminent critique through a mechanism created by African states themselves, which cannot be shrugged off as easily as critique expressed by far-away capitals.

The current make-up of the African regional system in terms of the norms recognised and the enforcement mechanisms followed —largely the result of recent changes to the system— are probably well suited to the African environment. The fact that the norms recognised also reflect socio-economic rights, duties and people's rights does not detract from the recognition of civil and political rights, and the rights of individuals, in the system. Their addition ensures that norms that play a strong role on the continent are also reflected. It should be noted in this regard that the jurisprudence of the African Commission so far by and large reflects internationally accepted standards, and constitutes a valuable point of reference also for national courts.

A wider range of enforcement mechanisms than that which is used elsewhere is followed in Africa. While the European regional human rights system places a strong emphasis on the judicial enforcement of individual civil and political rights through the European Court of Human Rights, the African system operates on a number of levels simultaneously. While the African Human Rights Court (under whatever name that may be used) will provide for a component of judicial suspension, the APRM on the other side of the spectrum has a more political character. This is complimented by the quasi-judicial mechanism of the African Commission, which occupies a place somewhere between the other two mechanisms.

On a continent as diverse as Africa, with its multi-layered landscape of human rights issues, employing an enforcement mechanism with such diverse components seems to be a wise approach. Each component of the collective mechanism plays a different and equally important role. Courts can address individual cases in a strong and decisive manner, but they have a more limited role to play in respect of mobilising a political consensus or dealing with widespread human rights violations. A commission on human rights, which can consider state reports and conduct on site visits, can play an important role in identifying human rights issues that need to be addressed in a systematic way and in working towards negotiated solutions which courts cannot always do. To the extent that such a commission functions and is perceived as an independent body, it can to some extent play a role which those placed inside the confines of power politics will have difficulty in playing.

At the same time there is also a role for human rights supervision in the political processes of the continent. A mechanism such as the APRM, although it has limitations because of its political nature, can also precisely for that reason have an impact on aspects of political life which the other mechanisms cannot reach. Standing alone the APRM would probably not have made much of a difference, but as part of a broader network of mechanisms aimed at the protection of human rights the APRM has the potential to play a significant role —and the same probably applies also to the Court and the Commission—.

The issue of political will remains, and it cannot be denied that much remains to be done to turn the potential offered by the available systems and mechanisms into reality. At the same time, the new institutional focus of the African Union on human rights, as reflected in its Constitutive Act, and in the mandates of its organs provides a starting point. Increasingly individuals are encountered within the system in governments and in civil society in Africa who take this orientation seriously. Clearly, it is on their input that the full implementation of an effective African regional human rights system will depend. Much will depend in this regard on the increased realisation of human rights on the domestic level —an international human rights system cannot survive without a critical mass of building-blocks of state parties that take human rights seriously internally at home—.

7. **Postscript: comparative regional Human Rights Systems**

The fairly extensive body of material (primary and secondary) on the African regional system which now exists, allows comparison of the experience in Africa with that in the regional systems of the Americas and Europe, and the development of a new field of study, focusing on the different aspects of the phenomenon of regional human rights systems. Engaging in this task in any detail falls beyond the scope of this study —instead some explanatory remarks will merely be made—.[165]

Some of the issues that will come into play in such a study are how to compare the effectiveness of the different systems and, proceeding from that, to establish why some systems are less or more effective than others. Are regional human rights systems appropriate for all regions? Is it feasible to establish a regional system eg for Asia,[166] or for the Arab-speaking world?[167] Where does regional protection of human rights fit in compared with the global (UN) system on the one hand and the

---

[165] Some of the ideas advanced here draw on L.R. HELFER and A. SLAUGHTER: "Towards a theory of effective supranational adjudication", 107 *Yale Law Journal,* 1997, p. 275. See also H. KOH: "Why do nations obey international law", 106 *Yale Law Journal,* 1997, p. 2599, D. CASSEL: "Does international human rights law make a difference?", 2 *Chicago Journal of International Law,* 2001, p. 121 and E. NEUMAYER: "Do international human rights treaties improve respect for human rights?", 49 *Journal of Conflict Resolution,* 2005, p 1.

[166] V. MUNTARBHORN: "Asia, human rights and the new millennium: Time for a regional human rights charter?", 8 *Transnational Law and Contemporary Problems,* 1998, p. 407, S.R. HARRIS: "Asian human rights: Forming a regional covenant", 17 *Asian-Pacific Law and Policy Journal,* 2000, p. 1

[167] M. RISHMAWI: "The revised Arab Charter on Human Rights: A step forward?", 5 *Human Rights Law Review,* 2005, p. 361.

domestic protection of human rights on the other? What role does civil society have in influencing these systems? What is the relationship between the human rights and the other functions of the parent regional bodies (such as the AU)?

To start answering these questions, a more thorough comparison of the different regional systems in the world today than is currently available would have to be made. To a large extent, existing comparisons take the features of the different regional systems and juxtapose them, seen in isolation and divorced from their context.[168] Such comparisons are quick to point out that the case load of the European system is, for example, much higher than that of the African system, that the facilities of the one system are superior to the other, etc. This is a starting point, but analysis will have to move beyond these superficial comparisons, and also bring into the picture the fact that the challenges faced by the respective systems differ in fundamental respects, and this should in turn affect how they are to be assessed.

For example, it is often said that many of the problems faced by the European system —in particular before the enlargement of the membership after the end of the cold war— were "luxury" problems, compared to the gross and systematic human rights violations often witnessed in Africa and the Americas. In Europe, the finer points of fair trial procedure or freedom of expression are often at stake, involving governments with a strong commitment to human rights. On the other side of the spectrum, human rights violations in Africa have often taken the form of massive violations, in states where the basic mechanisms for the protection of human rights are not in place on the domestic level. A comprehensive assessment of the relative effectiveness of a regional human rights system should take the different contexts into account and ask the question how do the systems compare in terms of meeting the often very different challenges they are confronted with.

Based on an initial overview, it seems that considerations such as the following may play a role in terms of the impact of the different regional systems, and are worth investigating further:

Focusing on the role played by the state parties, the following issues may come into play:

— Are there effective domestic systems for the protection of human rights in place in the countries that form part of the regional human rights system? These seem to be the building blocks of any functioning regional system.

— Do states parties have the political will to be subjected to human rights scrutiny? This is reflected among other things in the extent to which they make acceptance of human rights treaties subject to debilitating reservations, and whether they are willing to comply with formal treaty requirements (eg submitting state reports where required, engaging with individual complaints, and implementation of recommendations). It also impacts on the question whether they are prepared to support the creation of a strong regional human rights system through the role they play in the parent regional body (see below).

---

168 See for example C. HEYNS, D. PADILLA & L. ZWAAK: "A schematic comparison of regional human rights systems: An update", 5 *African Human Rights Law Journal,* 2005, p. 308.

— What is the balance in the region between the countries where there is a strong commitment to human rights, and the countries where there is not? Do the majority of the states have a poor or a good domestic human rights record and at what point is a critical mass reached on either side?

On the regional level, a number of considerations could affect the impact of the system:

— Does the human rights system form part of a range of activities of the regional parent body which, taken as a whole, is to the clear benefit of the states concerned? If human rights protection is one part of a broader mandate which includes for example diplomatic, environmental and trade activities, it may have a stronger chance of success. The more attractive the net benefits of membership of the regional body are, the more likely states may be to accept effective human rights supervision as part of the package. In Europe the human rights criteria for membership of the European Union with all the associated financial benefits have led to reforms in many candidate countries.
— Is the human rights component of the activities of the regional human rights body well resourced, in terms of financial as well as human resources (both the number of people involved but also their ability in this field).
— Do the member states follow an approach of appointing independent and capable experts to be members of supervisory bodies?
— Do the members of the supervisory bodies maintain the highest standards of independence and impartiality, and do they develop a jurisprudence which is compelling and persuasive on principled grounds?
— Is there sufficient correspondence or "norm resonance" between the values of the societies in question, and the values recognised in the regional systems? For example, if the concept of the group is important among the people of the region, some emphasis on peoples' rights and duties could be important in ensuring the legitimacy and as a result the spontaneous acceptance of the systems.
— Is there resonance between the traditional ways of resolving disputes in the region and the methods followed by the supervisory bodies. For example, as was alluded to above in Europe the traditional emphasis on judicial processes could support the central role of the European Court of Human Rights in that system, while the emphasis on non-judicial methods of resolving disputes in Africa could require a more mixed system of supervision, eg not only by a court, but also by a quasi-judicial commission and also by institutions with a strong political component such as the APRM.
— Is there effective publicity for the work of the regional human rights bodies? This appears to be essential in a system based on peer and public pressure.
— Do trade and other links exist between the states involved? Without such links states seem to have little leverage over each other, to implement peer pressure.
— Are the mechanisms in place focused and well coordinated to ensure maximum efficiency in the use of resources? At first glance there seems to be an unnecessary proliferation of systems in the African region.

— Is civil society active in the field of human rights? This applies to NGOs but also other institutions such as universities.
— Is a certain level of homogeneity required for a regional system to be effective?

The issues raised above serve merely to introduce the idea that a comparative study of regional systems in the world today is now a feasible and necessary endeavour, given the availability of information on the African and other regional human rights systems. Comprehensive and ongoing studies of comparative regional human rights systems are bound to open up avenues for the improvement of the existing systems, and will support informed decision-making on the question whether similar systems should be established in other parts of the world.

Regional human rights studies will also serve to integrate into the understanding worldwide of the concept of human rights the experience gained in Africa over the last 20 years in a situation where the concept of human rights is often strongly challenged, but where it arguably also can make its strongest contribution.

[23]

Limited deployment of the African system within African states: further evidence and a general evaluation

Obiora Chinedu Okafor

6.1 Introduction

One of the major tasks accomplished in this chapter is the mapping and analysis of the extent and significance of the more modest impact that the African system has had within some other African states (that is, other than Nigeria and South Africa). This discussion will form the basis for the argument that the available evidence points tentatively to the conclusion that the African system (like other IHIs)[1] can under certain conditions contribute to the production of valuable correspondence, facilitated by activist forces, between some of its norms and the behavior of key domestic governmental institutions within some African states (what I have referred to earlier in this book as the "ACHPR phenomenon"). This discussion will of necessity be shorter than our examination, in chapter 4, of the African system's influence within Nigeria. This is explained by the fact that the bulk of the available evidence regarding the African system's domestic impact tends to lie outside these other countries.

The other major task that will be accomplished in this chapter is to attempt to specify, as broadly and accurately as possible, the conditions for the optimization of the African system's impact within African states. This analytical exercise will be grounded in the evidence adduced in chapter 4 (in respect of in Nigeria), chapter 5 (regarding South Africa), and in the present chapter (in respect of a sample of other African countries). What, it will be asked, are the factors that have combined to facilitate the African system's modest influence within the relevant African states? What factors have combined to militate against that system's influence within those same states? To what extent

[1] See C. Heyns and F. Viljoen, "The Impact of United Nations Human Rights Treaties on the Domestic Level" (2001) 23 *Human Rights Quarterly* 483 at 487.

have activist forces such as civil society actors (CSAs), activist judges, labor activists, student unionists, activist journalists, and activist politicians played a role in generating the domestic impact of the African system? What does an analysis of the operation of these factors suggest about the possibility of maximizing the production of the kind of correspondence that this book is concerned with within African states? What does this analysis also suggest about the ways in which an IHI like the African system can help shape the self-understandings, conceptions of interest, or logics of appropriateness held within key domestic institutions? Under what conditions can the broadly constructivist process via which these changes are fostered be optimized?

In the above connection, it is important at the outset to note that only eight years after the adoption of the African Charter, and just three years after its entry into force, a Nigerian judge, Olusola-Thomas J, had felt able to declare most optimistically in *Gani Fawehinmi* v. *IGP* that:

> The [African] Charter has no doubt exerted and is still exerting unquestionable influence within member states of the Organisation of African Unity and provides public opinion with a yard-stick for judging political behaviour by each member state.[2]

Over a decade later, in 2003, Curtis Doebbler reached a somewhat similar conclusion in respect of the African Commission when he declared that while many criticisms of the Commission are often justified:

> it is wrong to conclude that the Commission has not made a valuable contribution to the protection of human rights. Indeed, the Commission has extended human rights protections to areas where no other international human rights body has dared to tread ... Also in reaction to problems of implementation, the Commission has taken a more proactive role in confronting governments that ignore its decisions by acting either directly or through the Assembly of Heads of States and Government[s].[3]

However, writing almost twenty years after the adoption of the Charter, and over thirteen years after its entry into force, Joe Oloka-Onyango, a very knowledgeable observer of the African human rights

[2] Suit M/324/89 (Lagos High Court, unreported).

[3] See C. F. J. Doebbler, "A Complex Ambiguity: The Relationship between the African Commission on Human and Peoples' Rights and Other African Union Initiatives affecting Respect for Human Rights" (2003) 13 *Transnational Law and Contemporary Problems* 7 at 14–15.

terrain, reached a much more pessimistic conclusion about the level of influence exerted so far by the African Commission (the other major component of the African system). In his view, after more than a decade in existence, the Commission has "hardly made a dent" in the African human rights scene.[4]

An accurate assessment of the African system's continent-wide impact today would lie somewhere between these two positions. Indeed, even relatively harsher critics of the African system, such as Oloka-Onyango himself and Nsongura Udombana, now seem to have shifted to the middle ground. For example, despite his identification of many problems with the Commission's operations and jurisprudence, Oloka-Onyango has recently described the Commission's landmark decision in *Social and Economic Rights Action Centre and Centre for Economic and Social Rights* v. *Nigeria* (the "Ogoni" case)[5] as "a critical turning point both for the Commission and for human rights law on the African continent."[6] And even while suggesting that "there is still a wide gap between the promise in the Charter and the performance of African states," Udombana has made bold to declare that:

> By recognizing *actio popularis* [anyone's ability to petition the Commission regardless of whether or not she is an actual victim of the violation], the African Charter has enabled many individuals, CSAs, and indirectly, states, to test its guarantees. These communications, in turn, have enabled the Commission to develop human rights jurisprudence in Africa and provide guidance to domestic courts.[7]

In an attempt to systematically map the complex terrain of the African system's even more modest impact thus far within other African states, as well as to assess its promise within those states, I have organized the rest of the chapter in the following way. In section 6.2, I discuss the available evidence regarding the very modest impact that

[4] See J. Oloka-Onyango, "Human Rights and Sustainable Development in Contemporary Africa: A New Dawn, or Retreating Horizons?" (2000) 6 *Buffalo Human Rights Law Review* 39 at 72.

[5] See Communication 155/96, available at www1.umn.edu/human rts/africa/comcases/155-96b.html.

[6] See J. Oloka-Onyango, "Reinforcing Marginalized Rights in an Age of Globalization: International Mechanisms, Non-State Actors, and the Struggle for Peoples' Rights in Africa" (2003) 18 *American University International Law Review* 851 at 913.

[7] See N. J. Udombana, "Between Promise and Performance: Revisiting States' Obligations under the African Human Rights Charter" (2004) 40 *Stanford Journal of International Law* 105 at 138.

the African system has had on the executive branches of government within a number of African states. In section 6.3, I detail and analyze the equally modest influence that the African system has exerted on the judiciaries of certain African states. In section 6.4, I focus on the significance of the very modest impact of the African system on legislative action within a number of African states. In section 6.5, I examine the very modest evidence of the modest impact that the system has had on the operations of CSAs within certain African states. It is in section 6.6, however, that I concentrate on specifying the factors that have facilitated or militated against the African system's ability to exert influence within the relevant states. This is a systematic way of focusing my analysis on the specification of the minimum conditions for the optimization of the African system's domestic impact within African states. Section 6.7 concludes the chapter. There, I summarize the arguments presented in this chapter and link them to the analysis that will be conducted in the chapter that follows.

To be clear, two over-arching arguments will be made in this chapter. Though dependent on the first argument, the second argument will be more important. The first is that the African system has had a much more modest impact within other African countries than it has had within Nigeria and South Africa, and that this more modest feat was accomplished in "alliance" with the local activist forces (mainly activist judges, CSAs, and activist lawyers who operate within the relevant countries).[8] It is these activist forces which have, in one way or the other, acted as the intelligent transmission-lines between the African system and various domestic governmental institutions in the relevant states (such as the courts, the executive, and the legislature). In this process of trans-judicial communication, these activist forces played the role of brainy relays that did not merely transmit, but also contributed actively to the development and strengthening of both the relevant domestic socio-legal regime and the African system. The African system and these activist forces were allied in a "virtual partnership," a human rights network. It will be suggested that the constructivist approach to IHIs is strengthened by this argument. The second and more important

[8] On the remarkably close alliance between the African system and CSAs, see G.W. Mugwanya, *Human Rights in Africa: Enhancing Human Rights through the African Regional Human Rights System* (Ardsley, NY, Transnational, 2003), pp. 249–251 (describing the African Commission and CSAs as extraordinarily "close partners" to an extent that surpasses the closeness between CSAs and the United Nations and other regional human rights systems).

over-arching argument which is made in this chapter is dependent on the first. It is that the evidence that is discussed in the chapter suggests that the African system has had, and can have, an appreciable domestic impact within a significant number of African states; and that under certain specified conditions, the African system can optimize that promise.

On a methodological note, it is important at the outset to justify the consideration in this chapter of evidence from some but not all African states. Aside from the fact that space does not allow the consideration in a book such as this of the position in all fifty-four African states, the reality is that the relevant evidence is distributed unevenly on the continent. Indeed, as has already been shown, most of it is concentrated in countries such as Nigeria and South Africa. What is more, the remainder of the evidence is concentrated in a few other states. What has been done here, therefore, is to seek the evidence purposively and to follow it wherever it has led. This is quite appropriate given the fact that one of the underlying aims of the present chapter is to show that other evidence exists which supports the orientation of the key Nigerian and South African case studies. In any case, the present chapter certainly does not pretend to be comprehensive. The objective here is not to show that the African system has had domestic effect *across all of Africa* (in which case a representative sample from South, East, West, North, Francophone Africa, Islamic Africa, and so on, would be required), but that there are a few African countries in which the extant phenomenon is beginning to occur. Thus, the method adopted is purposive. In the purposive method, there is no *a priori* test for including one country but not the other (other than that evidence regarding the identified trend has been found there). This is hardly problematic, since the point of the whole book (including the chapters on Nigeria and South Africa) is to identify, discuss, and analyze evidence that tends to show a *possibility* of domestic correspondence with the African system's norms; rather than to account comprehensively for that system's domestic impact across the continent.

6.2 Impact on executive thought and action

The overall aim of this section is to show that the available evidence supports the proposition that, due in part to the African system and to the efforts of the activist forces that operate as its "virtual network" partners, a significant though still very modest level of "correspondence" between the system's norms and the behavior of executive branches of government within certain African states (other than Nigeria and South Africa) has sometimes been generated. Put differently, the evidence suggests that the ACHPR phenomenon can also occur within certain other African states. A number of examples will suffice to demonstrate this point.

In the now famous decision in *Attorney General of Botswana* v. *Unity Dow*,[9] Ms. Unity Dow, a citizen of Botswana who had married a US citizen, sued the government of Botswana. Her claim was that by in effect denying the citizenship of Botswana to the children of that marriage, the Citizenship Act of Botswana of 1984 was discriminatory and unconstitutional. The relevant Act granted citizenship to the children of male citizens of Botswana who had married foreign women, but not to the children of female citizens of Botswana who had married foreign men. Ms. Dow won at the court below. The government appealed that decision. The Court of Appeal of Botswana struck down a provision of the citizenship law of that country that had in effect discriminated against women. In response to this decision, the government of Botswana eventually moved to amend the citizenship law in issue so as to repeal the offensive provisions. In coming to its decision, the Court of Appeal made very significant references to the African Charter, especially as an interpretive tool.[10] The court felt able to rely in this manner on the Charter despite the fact that that treaty had not been incorporated into Botswana's domestic legal order. The court was of the view that since "Botswana is a signatory" and is "one of the credible prime movers behind the promotion and supervision of the Charter," domestic legislation in Botswana should be interpreted so as not to conflict with that country's obligations under the Charter. The Charter was thus a very important factor that helped to justify, complement, and legitimate this court's assault against the legislation and those prevailing norms of Botswana's society that were patriarchal. The Charter, and Botswana's participation at the forefront in the African system, clearly helped to inspire the progressive orientation and tone of this decision. And since the Court of Appeal's decision was eventually reflected in the impugned law, key as it was to the decision, the African Charter cannot

9 (1992) LRC (Const.) 623. Also cited at (1994) 6 BCLR 1 (Botswana) and (1992) SACLR LEXIS 7. See Oloka-Onyango, *supra* note 4, at 63–64. See also F. Viljoen, "Application of the African Charter on Human and Peoples' Rights by Domestic Courts in Africa" (1999) 43 *Journal of African Law* 1 at 3–4.

10 See, e.g., Aguda J at 135–136 (1992) SACLR LEXIS 7.

but be viewed as having exerted a significant level of influence, albeit indirectly, on both legislative and executive action within Botswana. This indirect influence was exerted on the executive because it was that branch of government that moved to amend the impugned law. This indirect influence was also exerted on the legislature because it agreed to change that law. As such, this decision will be referred to again in sections 6.3 and 6.4. It is important to note that the end result of the *Unity Dow* case may not have been achieved without the facilitative role that was played by the activist lawyers and judges who invoked the relevant international human rights instruments, including the African Charter, as a critical resource that allowed them to reformulate the character of women's civic rights in Botswana, and alter existing beliefs and logics around the state's interest in conferring citizenship rights in a manner that discriminated against women. The elements of this transformational process bear many of the hallmarks of the quasi-constructivist account of IHI impact: the activist lawyer (who is a part of the domestic activist forces) as norm entrepreneur; the detailed ends-means calculations that these activist lawyers made; and the ideational, epistemic, and normative (non-material) power that is transmitted from the given IHI to the local context.

Botswana's eventual reaction to a decision of the African Commission is as instructive. In *John K. Modise* v. *Botswana*,[11] the complainant was the child of a Botswanan father and South African mother. He had been born in South Africa but was raised in Botswana. He later became one of the founders of the opposition Botswana National Front. He claimed that this was the cause of his subsequent declaration by the government as a "prohibited immigrant." In October 1978, he was arrested and deported to South Africa. He was also deported on subsequent returns to Botswana. He later moved to the then Bantustan of Bophuthatswana, but was also deported from there to the "no-person's land" that lay between Bophuthatswana and Botswana. He lived in that space for five weeks before being admitted to Botswana on a humanitarian basis. He subsequently lived in Botswana under temporary three-month resident permits, renewable at the absolute discretion of the minister concerned. He requested to no avail that the government of Botswana recognize him as a citizen of that country by birth. Aided by a CSA, he then filed a petition at the African Commission. The Commission's resilient

[11] Communication 97/93 (1999) 6 International Human Rights Reports 828.

intervention in the matter of Mr. Modise's repeated deportation from 1978–1995, through several letters and communications, led to the concession on the part of the government of a partial remedy for this opposition leader's citizenship problems. The government granted him a form of citizenship (citizenship by registration), which while it was not as ample and beneficial as "citizenship by birth" to which he seemed to be entitled, still left him in a much better situation than he had been for the previous seventeen years. In all those years, he had been forced to live as a stateless person outside Botswana. What is more, in November 2000, the Commission decided that although it had already granted Mr. Modise citizenship by registration, Botswana was in breach of several provisions of the African Charter, and was under a legal duty to recognize him as a citizen by birth.[12] This can only be a bonus. The key point is that even the partial remedy that was conceded by Botswana was a significant indication of the ideational and normative impact that the Commission had exerted on the executive branch of government in this country. Here, the invocation of the African system worked within the domestic context (without direct compliance as such) to produce important changes in the logics of entitlement to and denial of citizenship, as well as in the treatment of political opponents. There was no direct compliance with the Commission's decision that Mr. Modise was entitled as of right to citizenship by birth, just correspondence with that body's general normative inclination. Indeed, the concession from the government was made independently of the Commission's decision, and the correspondence that occurred was brokered to an appreciable extent by the work of the CSA that brought the petition to the African system and kept the matter in the public eye. Many of the key hallmarks of quasi-constructivism that were identified in chapter 2 and mentioned above are also visible in this story.

Evidence of the influence that has been exerted by the African system on executive decision-making and action within other African states is present in the success enjoyed at various times by the African Commission in breaking down and overcoming the resistance of target states (such as Togo, Mauritania, Senegal, and the Sudan) to its conduct

[12] See Institute for Human Rights and Development, *Compilation of Decisions on Communications of the African Commission on Human and Peoples' Rights 1994–2001* (Banjul, The Gambia, Institute for Human Rights and Development, 2002), p. 42 (hereafter "*Compilation of Decisions 1994–2001*").

of on-site investigative missions within their respective territories.[13] In the early days of its existence, the conduct of such missions by the Commission was considered almost too difficult a project to undertake given the historically understandable resistance of almost all of the newly decolonized African states to "international" interference within their borders. In the first six or so years of the Commission's existence, no such missions were conducted at all. Yet the human rights situation in most African states was not more benign during that period than it has been in subsequent years. What has changed is the thaw in the resistance of many African states to the conduct of such missions. Even then, in some of these states, government officials still view such visits as somewhat misguided and hostile. As a one-time Chair of the African Commission has noted, "when consent is given [by states] and visits take place, occasionally the distinct impression is gained that the host country's stance is that it could well have done without the visit."[14] Given such resistance from relevant government officials, and given the Commission's youth and perennial resource-funding challenges, it is remarkable that the Commission and its network partners have been able to sustain the amount of direct and indirect pressure on states needed to ensure that such visits do take place. Here again, the Commission's modest success has been in relation to securing the needed consent from the executive branches of government in those states. In the cases in which its efforts have been successful, local activist forces played a key role in the local campaigns that created the buzz and attention on the particular situation and in pressuring the Commission to undertake the mission that helped shape the government's decision to invite the Commission to investigate its human rights record. Pressure was maintained by CSAs (acting as the brokers) at two main nodal points: on the Commission (which CSAs wanted to undertake the particular investigative mission) and on the relevant government (which CSAs wanted to invite the Commission to conduct the mission). Thus, the various governments' hands were forced more by this domestically-generated pressure than by any formalistic adhesion to or compliance with the African system's norms or decisions by the relevant governments. Although this process is akin to a process of producing

[13] See E. V. O. Dankwah, "The African System for the Protection of Human Rights: The Task Ahead," National Human Rights Commission Lecture Series No. 3, delivered at Abuja, Nigeria in 1998 (on file with the author) at 10.

[14] *Ibid.* at 6.

voluntary state compliance, it is not exactly that and is not easily explained as such. In any case, since the state compliance measure is incorporated in the concept of correspondence, the existence of some overlap between the processes via which correspondence was produced in these cases and those through which state compliance can be attained is not in itself worrisome or fatal to the argument.

In addition, facilitated in like fashion, the Commission has also successfully undertaken promotional missions to states such as Zimbabwe, Malawi, Botswana, Namibia, Ghana, Mozambique, and Lesotho.[15] Even though states are usually not as irritated by such promotional visits as they are by investigative missions that seem to single them out for closer inspection, the arguments made above apply nevertheless. Without the invitation of the executive branches of government in these states no such visits would have been undertaken. In each such case, the promotional visit was undertaken partly in reaction to the extensive work that had been done by local activist forces in highlighting the need for such a visit. In any case, the very fact that such visits were allowed at all by the relevant states indicates a measure of influence on the "thinking" that occurred within the relevant domestic institutions. It seems that the relevant officials reversed decades of "stonewalling" against such visits in part because they had increasingly come to realize that it was in fact more in their self-interest than otherwise to allow such visits to occur. Such visits often helped portray them as more reasonable than they would have appeared had they refused permission for the visits.

As significantly, the African Commission's Special Rapporteur on Prisons in Africa has been able to conduct on-site inspections of the prisons of a number of African countries, such as Zimbabwe, Mali, Mozambique, and Madagascar.[16] The consent of these states to a visit that would expose some of their "dirtiest linen" in public is a significant triumph for the African system. It indicates to some extent that the Commission has had some success in influencing the decision-making processes of the executive branch which usually consents to such visits. Moreover, as Dankwah has noted, in the end, a state like Mali responded quite favorably to the Commission's recommendations on measures that would improve the conditions of its prisons.[17] The arguments made above regarding the activist forces-facilitated alterations in conceptions of interest that precede the grant of permission for visits also

[15] *Ibid.* at 10. [16] *Ibid.* [17] *Ibid.*

apply here with necessary modifications. This evidence also lends added credence to the broadly constructivist approach to IHI impact.

Again, even though his attribution of credit to the African system may have been somewhat excessive, Dankwah has correctly noted that the Commission has exerted a modest but significant amount of influence on the executive branch within Togo and other countries during very difficult periods in the lives of these countries. In his view:

> Violations have abated ... as a result of exchange of correspondence between the Commission and those countries against which complaints had been made.[18]

As in the other cases discussed above, no direct state compliance occurred as such in this process of CSA-brokered communication (exchange of letters) via which some correspondence was produced between the behavior of the government in the country and some norms of the African system.

In Ghana, despite the non-incorporation of the African Charter into its domestic legal order, the chief legal officer of its government, (i.e, the Attorney General of Ghana) has found it useful to rely on certain provisions of the Charter in formulating the arguments that the government made in a case that was heard fairly recently by the Supreme Court of Ghana.[19] While this use of the Charter was not of momentous import, and no activist forces actively mediated this particular communication of the African system's norms, it is still clear evidence of the subtle percolation of the African system's norms into the "thinking" processes of the executive branch in Ghana – the branch of government which is usually the most resistant to IHI influence. Moreover, the ideational/epistemic and normative communication that occurred, and the detailed ends-means calculations that were made by this high official, testify to the power of the broadly constructivist IHI optic.

Evidence that supports the Commission's increasing (although still quite modest) influence on, and its relevance as a factor to be taken seriously by, the executive branches of government in many African states is decipherable from the character of a number of other events and

[18] *Ibid.*

[19] See (1996) *Africa Legal Aid Quarterly* 45 (October–December). See also Viljoen, *supra* note 9, at 6; and E. A. Ankumah, "Introduction to the Conference on the Legal Profession and the Protection of Human Rights in Africa" in E. A. Ankumah and E. K. Kwakwah (eds.), *The Legal Profession and the Protection of Human Rights in Africa* (Accra, Africa Legal Aid, 1999), p. 13.

occurrences. For instance, in response to the Commission's very critical resolution, Algeria took the pains to send (and bore the costs of sending) a high powered delegation to the Seventeenth Session of the Commission in order to point out what it claimed was a false premise on which the resolution was founded.[20] The Commission graciously admitted its fault and withdrew the resolution. Clearly, although we must be careful not to over-estimate the significance of this event, it is fair to say that Algeria was worried enough by the resolution to take this trouble to persuade the Commission to withdraw it. Since the Commission's resolutions are formally non-binding, an obvious explanation is that it was worried by the extent to which such a resolution would damage its reputation. In this way, Algeria's executive decision-making process and actions were affected and influenced by the Commission's work. An account of the seriousness with which Algeria took the Commission's work in this case cannot be complete without mention being made of the mildly facilitative role that was played by CSAs in publicizing the Commission's work, campaigning against states that do not treat seriously with it, and purveying Commission and Charter norms within states. These activities created the overall context – the normative lure – that affected to some extent the thinking processes that led to Algeria's actions.

Again, Mali's invitation to the Commission (in 1992) to send a mission to observe its elections buttresses the point that many African states have come to take the Commission's work more seriously than has hitherto been the case as a (de)legitimating factor which has to be considered in executive decision-making and action.[21] Clearly, Mali's invitation was well calculated. States do not go out of their way to invite an international institution to observe elections within their borders unless the presence of that institution at the elections can somehow inspire confidence. That invitation was, it is reasonable to deduce, aimed at harvesting some of the legitimacy that it viewed the Commission as possessing. The argument that was made above about CSA-facilitated alterations in understandings that preceded such invitations to visit also apply to this context as well.

The growing (although still modest) stature of the African Commission in the eyes of officials of the executive branches of

[20] See E. A. Ankumah, *The African Commission on Human and Peoples' Rights* (The Hague, Martinus Nijhoff, 1996), p. 24.

[21] *Ibid.* at 23.

government within African states is also evident from the number of states that are represented at its sessions, as well as deducible from the high status of such state representatives. Since states parties are not really bound to attend most of these sessions or to send officials of a high status, especially when their state reports are not being considered, their increasing presence at these sessions is in itself remarkable given the time and expense involved. For example, at its Sixteenth Ordinary Session, government officials from eight countries were in attendance. At the time, many observers considered this to be a remarkable upsurge in the level of attention paid by African states to the Commission's work.[22] This trend continued at subsequent sessions.[23] And at its Twenty-seventh Ordinary Session, the representatives of twenty-seven states parties were present.[24] The African Commission explicitly remarked at the exponential increase in the participation of states parties at its sessions, describing the increase in numbers as "massive."[25] Twenty states participated in the Commission's Twenty-eighth Ordinary Session, while thirty-one were present at its Twenty-ninth Ordinary Session.[26] Its Thirtieth Ordinary Session attracted twenty-nine states, and thirty-six states attended its Thirty-first Ordinary Session.[27] A substantial number of states (nineteen and twenty-two respectively) attended the Commission's Thirty-second and Thirty-third Ordinary Sessions.[28] In the same vein, twenty-six countries sent representatives to each of its Thirty-fourth and Thirty-fifth Ordinary Sessions.[29] And as impressively, twenty-nine states attended

[22] See A. Danielsen and G. Oberleitner, "16th Session of the African Commission on Human and Peoples' Rights" (1995) 13 *Netherlands Quarterly on Human Rights* 80 at 82.

[23] See S. Malmstrom and G. Oberleitner, "The 17th Session of the African Commission on Human and Peoples' Rights" (1995) 13 *Netherlands Quarterly on Human Rights* 292 at 293.

[24] See *Thirteenth Annual Activity Report of the African Commission, 1999–2000* (on file with the author) at 2.

[25] See *Final Communique of the 27th Ordinary Session of the African Commission*, para. 17 (on file with the author).

[26] See *Fourteenth Annual Activity Report of the African Commission, 2000–2001* (on file with the author) at 3.

[27] See *Fifteenth Annual Activity Report of the African Commission, 2001–2002* (on file with the author) at 3.

[28] See *Sixteenth Annual Activity Report of the African Commission, 2002–2003* (on file with the author) at 3.

[29] See *Seventeenth Annual Activity Report of the African Commission, 2003–2004* (on file with the author) at 2.

its Thirty-sixth Ordinary Session, while twenty-six countries were present for its Thirty-seventh Ordinary Session.[30]

This type of modest increase in the stature of the Commission is also evidenced by the remarkable seriousness with which the Commission and many of the national human rights commissions which have been established on the continent have treated each other. For one, articles 26 and 45 of the African Charter encourage the creation of national human rights institutions by governments. The articles provide respectively that states parties shall, among other things, "allow the establishment and improvement of appropriate national institutions entrusted with the promotion and protection of the rights and freedoms guaranteed," and that the Commission "encourage national and local institutions concerned with human and peoples' rights." To this end, the Commission has increasingly encouraged member states to create their own national human rights institutions.[31] In its Mauritius Plan of Action, the Commission declared its intent to encourage the establishment of national human rights institutions on the African continent and the development of a program to reinforce such structures.[32] In practice, representatives of national human rights institutions have been allowed to participate in and contribute to the public sessions of the African Commission, sometimes sitting with the delegation of their own state and sometimes with CSA representatives.[33] This highly receptive attitude on the part of the Commission toward these national human rights commissions has been much reciprocated. For instance, in February 1996, the participants at the First African Conference of National Institutions for the Promotion and Protection of Human Rights adopted the "Yaounde Declaration" which affirmed the commitment of member institutions to the principles enshrined in the African Charter.[34] Even more specifically, the Kenyan National Commission

30 See *Eighteenth Annual Activity Report of the African Commission, 2004–2005* (on file with the author) at 2.

31 For example, see the Mauritius Plan of Action of the African Commission, available at www.achpr.org/english/_doc_target/documentation.html?../declarations/declaration_mauritius_en.html; and the Resolution of the African Commission on the Establishment of Committees on Human Rights or other Similar Organs at National, Regional or Sub-Regional Levels (1989) www.achpr.org/english/_doc_target/documentation.html?../resolutions/resolution05_en.html.

32 *Ibid.*

33 See Human Rights Watch, *Protectors or Pretenders? Government Human Rights Commissions in Africa* (New York, Human Rights Watch, 2001).

34 See the Yaounde Declaration, available at www.sahrc.org.za/afr_sec_yaounde_declaration.pdf.

on Human Rights (KNCHR) has explicitly stated that it is obligated to protect the economic and social rights that are guaranteed by the African Charter, but not in the Kenyan Constitution.[35] The KNCHR has also undertaken to "support the African Commission and the African Court on Human and Peoples' Rights."[36] The National Human Rights Commission of Malawi sought observer status with the African Commission during the Twenty-seventh session of the African Commission in Algiers in April 2000.[37] So have its counterparts in Rwanda, Algeria, Libya, Sierra Leone, and Benin.[38] To date, eleven such national commissions have been granted affiliate status at the African Commission.[39] In creating their own national human rights institutions, many states parties were not simply complying with a decision of the African Commission or with the African Charter, but they were influenced to an extent by both the African Charter's norms and the Commission's persistent persuasion. United Nations' efforts at ensuring that states establish such institutions and other factors cannot be ignored, but the African Commission's efforts were an important factor at play.

In this last case, as in the examples before it, activist forces have played important roles in facilitating the desired outcomes. They have done so sometimes by purveying African Charter norms within the body politic and increasing its visibility; at times by deploying that Charter creatively to enable hitherto unavailable arguments to emerge and appear more convincing; and sometimes (as in this last case) by actively encouraging domestic institutions to work with the African system and apply the African Charter. As importantly, the Commission has risen from an early position of being largely ignored by domestic institutions in states parties to a much higher stature in the eyes of these domestic bodies. This is evidence of the alteration that has occurred in the understanding of these institutions as to what attitudes serve their self-interests and what do not; as to logics of appropriate conduct; and thus as to their very identities.

Despite all of this positive evidence of the African system's direct and indirect impact on executive action within a number of African states, it

[35] See the Kenya National Commission on Human Rights, *Strategic Plan of Action: 2003–2008* (on file with the author) at 12.

[36] *Ibid.* at 16. [37] See Human Rights Watch, *supra* note 33, at 69. [38] *Ibid.*

[39] See *African Commission's Directory of National Human Rights Institutions with Affiliated Status*, available at www.achpr.org/english/_info/directory_nhri_en.html.

is important to note that the African Commission can hardly rest on its oars as yet. Clearly it is not yet "uhuru."[40] As the intransigent behavior of the then government of Malawi in *Chirwa* v. *Malawi*[41] shows, the African system is still unable to contribute as much as it could to the production of valuable correspondence with its norms and decisions within states. In that case, Vera and Orton Chirwa, who at one point had been under threat of execution, were held in very harsh detention conditions for many years despite the repeated intervention of the African Commission in their favor and much CSA work in the same direction.[42] Even more importantly, while it is unrealistic to expect that an IHI such as the African system should "solve" these human rights problems, the less than brilliant character of the human rights scenes of many African states (as other states globally) underscores the difficult challenges that the African system must continue to grapple with.

Nevertheless, the grimness of the overall reality does not take away from the fact that the African system, and its virtual network, has *begun* to exert a modest level of influence on executive action within a certain number of African states. In so doing, the system has begun to contribute to an ongoing but slow transformation in the sense of "appropriateness" held by the officials who run the executive branches of government in some African states. Where these officials previously felt that the Commission's request to conduct on-site investigative missions within their respective countries was entirely inappropriate, they now seem to feel less strongly about opposing such missions. This is at the very least a socio-normative alteration. Similarly, the logic of appropriateness underlying certain executive actions, such as the denial of citizenship to the children of Bostwanan women married to foreigners, or the repeated deportation of Mr. Modise by Botswana, has been effectively questioned. The African system has thus helped to foster a process of modest ideational change that seems to be altering

40 I have borrowed this expression from Oginga Odinga. See A. O. Odinga, *Not Yet Uhuru: The Autobiography of Oginga Odinga* (New York, Hill and Wang, 1969). The term "uhuru" has been used to denote the goal of freedom. However, I use it here to mean "the desired goal."

41 (1996) 3 International Human Rights Report 134. See also C. A. Odinkalu, "The Individual Complaints Procedures of the African Commission on Human and Peoples' Rights: A Preliminary Assessment" (1998) *8 Transnational Law and Contemporary Problems* 359 at 385.

42 See *Compilation of Decisions 1994–2001*, *supra* note 12, at 155–158.

the self-understandings and conceptions of interest held by many of these actors. In this way, the system has modestly affected the character of executive action in certain African countries.

6.3 Impact on judicial decision-making and action

The overall objective in this section is to show that the available evidence supports the proposition that due in part to the efforts made by the African system, that system has had a significant (though still very modest) impact on judicial decision-making and action within certain African states. The system has thus helped foster an appreciable and significant level of correspondence between its norms and the behavior of the courts of the relevant states. In other words, the evidence suggests that the ACHPR phenomenon can also be observed (though to a more modest extent) in certain other African countries. This is another pointer to the modest domestic promise of the African system. Here, as before, the key role that has been played by local activist forces – in this case mostly activist lawyers, CSAs, and activist judges – in facilitating such correspondence will be made palpable by the evidence. So will the various ways in which the African system has been invoked within the domestic sphere in order to produce the modest reformulations in logics of appropriateness or conceptions of interest that led to the relevant incidences of correspondence in the first place.

This point is not difficult to demonstrate. As was discussed in section 6.2, in *Attorney General of Botswana* v. *Unity Dow*, the Court of Appeal of Botswana struck down a provision of the citizenship law of that country that had in effect discriminated against women.[43] In coming to its decision that the said provisions were discriminatory, and therefore unconstitutional, the court relied in part on the positive effect that the African Charter must be taken to have had on the meaning of certain provisions of the Constitution of Botswana. The court assimilated the Charter through section 24 of the Interpretation Act of Botswana, which states that as an aid to the construction of an enactment a court may have regard to any relevant international treaty, agreement, or convention.[44] Of note again is that the court felt able to rely on the Charter despite the fact that Botswana had not at the time

[43] See Oloka-Onyango, *supra* note 4, at 63–64.
[44] See (1992) LRC (Const.) 623 at 654, 656 (per Amissah JP); and 673–79 (per Aguda JA).

incorporated the Charter into its domestic legal order.[45] It had merely signed and ratified the Charter. Here, the Charter was one key link in the chain of arguments that enabled the court to reach the progressive pro-women's equality decision that it reached, and that eventually led to the repeal of the offensive portions of the law in question. This is a good example of the generation within states of valuable correspondence with the system's norms and goals without direct state compliance as such. As argued in the preceding section, the invocation in this case of the African Charter by activist lawyers and judges contributed to a process in which previously unavailable arguments regarding women's civic rights were created and rendered more convincing than they would otherwise have been in the circumstances. Here, the key driving force was the panel of activist judges who heard the case.

In the *Developmental Associations* case,[46] a case that Viljoen has reported from the Francophone jurisdiction of the Benin Republic, the Minister of the Interior had made a decree outlawing existing developmental associations whose applications for registration had been refused, and mandating that only one of such organizations were to exist in each administrative region. The Constitutional Court of Benin struck down this decree not merely because it was unconstitutional, but also because it was a violation of the freedom of association provisions in article 10 of the African Charter. As we shall see in section 6.4, the African Charter enjoys constitutional status in Benin, and as a result is superior to any conflicting domestic statute. In the *Madame Bagri* case,[47] another unreported case that Viljoen has brought to our attention, the applicant had sued for wrongful dismissal. She invoked the right to work as guaranteed in the Constitution of Benin, as well as the guarantee of equal access to the public service that is provided for in the African Charter. The Constitutional Court of Benin considered the African Charter even though it reached the conclusion that the dismissal of the aggrieved party was constitutional. As Viljoen has noted,[48] the increasing (though still as yet modest) influence of the African system within Benin's judicial order is also illustrated by the exponential rise in the number of decisions of that country's Constitutional Court which

[45] See C. Beyani, "Toward a More Effective Guarantee of Women's Rights in the African Human Rights System" in R. J. Cook (ed.), *Human Rights of Women: National and International Perspectives* (Philadelphia, University of Pennsylvania Press, 1994), pp. 294–297.

[46] See Viljoen, *supra* note 9, at 2. [47] *Ibid.* [48] *Ibid.* at 3.

refer to the African Charter in order to legitimize their conclusions, as well as by the equally exponential rise in the number of cases in which laws and/or actions were found by this court to be unconstitutional, based in part on the application of the African Charter. Remarkably, of the four cases that were heard by this court in 1993, none applied the Charter,[49] but of the fourteen cases that the same court decided in 1994, seven applied the African Charter, leading to findings of unconstitutionality in all but one of these seven cases.[50] In all these circumstances, the insertion of the African Charter in Benin's corpus of constitutional norms and its imaginative invocation within the courts by activist forces enabled those courts to adopt hitherto unlikely decisions as to the norms of appropriate governmental conduct. Even the insertion of the African Charter in Benin's Constitution was attained as a result of the efforts made by the activist forces who had forced a sovereign national conference to be held in that country and had actively participated in and influenced its direction.[51] As importantly, the judges themselves acted in an activist fashion in receiving and applying the Charter in the way that they did in this case. Nothing less than a broadly constructivist process was at play here.

In *New Patriotic Party* v. *IGP*,[52] the plaintiff, a registered opposition party, sought and was granted a police permit to hold a rally. The police subsequently withdrew the permit. The plaintiff subsequently joined other parties in organizing and conducting a peaceful demonstration against the budget. The police broke up this demonstration. Some of the demonstrators were arrested and brought to court under the Ghana Public Order Decree of 1972. A subsequent permit obtained by the plaintiff was also withdrawn. The plaintiff then sued for a declaration that key sections of the Decree (granting the Minister for the Interior power to prohibit public meetings and processions and making the holding of such activities dependent on the prior grant of police permits) were unconstitutional since they violated the right to freedom of assembly as guaranteed by the 1992 Constitution of Ghana. At least one

49 *Ibid.* 50 *Ibid.*

51 For example, see C. Fomunyoh, "Democratization in Fits and Starts" (2001) 12 *Journal of Democracy* 37; and Democracy Coalition Project, *Defending Democracy: A Global Survey of Foreign Policy Trends 1992–2002*, available at www.demcoalition.org/pdf/Benin.pdf at 1.

52 (1993–94) 2 GLR 459 at 465. For an interesting review of this and similar cases, see J. Stevens, "Colonial Relics I: The Requirement of Permit to hold a Peaceful Assembly" (1997) 41 *Journal of African Law* 118.

judge of the Supreme Court of Ghana relied in part on the African Charter when he agreed with the rest of the court's decision to strike down the relevant legislation. Archer CJ, underscored the important role played by the African system in the court's decision-making process when he stated that:

> Ghana is a signatory of this African Charter and Member States of the Organisation of African Unity and parties to the Charter are expected to recognize the rights, duties, and freedoms enshrined in the Charter and to undertake to adopt legislative and other measures to give effect to the rights and duties. I do not think the fact that Ghana has not passed specific legislation to give effect to the Charter, [means] the Charter cannot be relied upon. On the contrary, article 21 of our Constitution has recognized the right to assembly mentioned in article 11 of the African Charter.
>
> It follows that section 7 of the Public Order Decree, 1972 (NRCD 68) is not only inconsistent with article 21(1)(d) of our Constitution, 1992 but is also in contravention of article 11 of the African Charter on Human and Peoples' Rights adopted by the Assembly of African Heads of State and Government in June 1981 in Nairobi, Kenya.[53]

Here, the African Charter proved invaluable in reinforcing the hand of at least one activist Supreme Court judge in his attempt to formulate an authoritative progressive interpretation of the relevant constitutional provision. Other judges, especially Francois J, did not express any opposition to Archer J's reasoning here. In this way, the African system was relevant to judicial action in this case. In this way also, an alteration in understandings regarding the appropriateness of a particular legislative provision was fostered. This achievement may not have been registered at all without the facilitative role played by the local activist forces which had resisted that law in the courts. But the key "relay" function (in relation to the domestic invocation and utilization of the African Charter) was played in this case by the judges themselves.

In a Namibian case, *Kuesa* v. *Minister of Home Affairs*,[54] the applicant was a serving member of the Namibian police force. He had taken part in a panel discussion that had been broadcast on television in which issues of public concern relating to the administration of the police force were discussed. He had stated, among other things, that white officers in the command structure of the force were determined to undermine the

[53] *Ibid.* at 466.

[54] See *Kuesa* v. *Minister of Home Affairs* (1993) 3 BCLR 1 (Namibian High Court).

government's policy of reconciliation, facilitated corruption, abused their power, and collaborated with "traitors and terrorists" by supplying police weapons to them. Arising from these comments, he faced a departmental hearing on a charge of contravening regulation 58(32) of the Police Regulations made under the Namibian Police Act of 1990. This Act prohibited a member of the Namibian police force from commenting unfavorably in public upon the administration of the force or any other government department, and made such conduct an offence. Even before the departmental hearing, he applied to the High Court of Namibia for an order declaring that regulation unconstitutional. The High Court applied several provisions of the African Charter, noting that since Namibia had formally ratified the Charter, those provisions were binding on Namibia, and had even become a part of its domestic laws. However, the High Court's consideration and application of the African Charter did not in the end lead it to find in favor of the appellant. The key point that is being made here, though, is that the court found the African Charter useful. Given the historical, though waning, tendency among courts in Southern Africa not to refer to the African Charter, it is significant that this court cited the Charter at all. Upon the appellant's appeal to it, the Supreme Court of Namibia set aside the High Court's decision.[55] However, in finding that the challenged regulation did not constitute a permissible derogation from the constitutional guarantee of freedom of expression, the Supreme Court (per Dumbutshena AJA for the court) did not make any reference to the African Charter. This lack of reference to the Charter on appeal does detract from the weight the Charter has had within Namibia's judicial institutions.

However, the weight that was attached to the African Charter in a subsequent decision of the same Supreme Court seems to balance this out. In *Chairperson of the Immigration Selection Board* v. *Frank and another*,[56] the African system proved more or less significant in the reasoning process of the court (albeit in promoting what many will correctly see as a negative outcome). There, a German citizen and long-time lesbian partner of a Namibian citizen who had been denied permanent residence under the Namibian Immigration Control Act 7 of 1993 sued the government. Her claim was that the decision failed to accord her equal status with heterosexuals and violated the rights to

[55] (1995) 11 BCLR 1540 (Namibian Supreme Court). [56] (2001) 3 CHRLD 179.

freedom from discrimination and equality as guaranteed by article 13 of the Constitution of Namibia. More importantly for present purposes, she also claimed that the action of the authorities also violated her right to the protection of her family as guaranteed by article 14 of the same Constitution. She succeeded at the High Court, but failed when the matter was appealed to the Supreme Court of Namibia by the government. For our purposes here, a key aspect of the logic of the Supreme Court was that, unlike under the South African Constitution, there was no provision in the Namibian Constitution for the recognition of homosexual relationships. Consequently, so the court's reasoning went, the lack of specific protection for homosexual relationships in the relevant provisions of the African Charter and the International Covenant on Civil and Political Rights ("both of which influenced article 14 of the Constitution" of Namibia),[57] made their interpretation of the Constitution of Namibia clearer and preferable. In the court's own words, their decision was "*reinforced* by the lack of the specific protection for homosexuals in the relevant provisions of the African Charter."[58] The point here is not, of course, that the Supreme Court was right to interpret the African Charter in this way, but that the highest court in the land explicitly and clearly acknowledged the influence that the Charter had on their decision. In these cases, the formulations of the local norms that were adopted by the relevant courts were explicitly grounded in their own interpretations of the norms of the African system (however misguided these interpretations). Here, an activist judge utilized a provision of the African Charter and drove the process through which he sought to establish correspondence between Namibia's legal system and what he saw as a norm of the African system. As conservative as the outcome of the deployment of the African system was in this particular case, the point is simply that the African Charter played a key role in the judicial reasoning process through which the outcome was produced. Needless to say, the key driver of the process via which the African Charter was utilized was the judiciary itself.

As Frans Viljoen's pioneering work in this context ably shows, and as my own research for this book has since reconfirmed, the African Charter has also performed similar strengthening and legitimization functions in two Tanzanian cases. In *Ephrahim* v. *Pastory*, the High Court relied, in small part, on the Charter's provisions. It felt a need to rely on the Charter in this way in its attempt to justify its decision to

[57] *Ibid.* at 181. [58] *Ibid.*

invalidate a customary law of the Haya people that prohibited a female member of the clan from alienating clan land.[59] The facts of this case were that a male member of the clan of a woman who had inherited land from her father and who now wanted to sell that piece of land filed suit to stop the sale. His suit was premised on the claim that a female clan member could not alienate clan land to a person who did not belong to the clan. In offering an interpretation of the gender equality provisions of the Tanzanian Bill of Rights and Duties which protected the female clan member's right to sell the land, the court still felt a need to seek justification for its position in part in the content of article 18 of the African Charter. This last provision prohibits discrimination on account of sex. In *DPP* v. *Pete*,[60] the Court of Appeal of Tanzania, that country's highest court, supported its decision to invalidate a provision of the Tanzanian Criminal Procedure Act of 1985 by invoking explicitly the spirit and letter of the Charter. That provision had made it extremely difficult for the courts to grant bail in certain kinds of cases. More specifically, one of the relevant provisions directed that "bail had to be denied if the Director of Public Prosecutions issued a certificate to the effect that the release of a detained person would be prejudicial" to national security.[61] Another prohibited the grant of bail to persons charged with offences relating to firearms, etc. The court held that the provisions contravened the intention of the Tanzanian Bill of Rights and Duties as interpreted by the court. And its interpretation was based on the very sound principle that:

> Since our Bill of Rights and Duties was introduced into the Constitution under the Fifth Amendment in February 1985, that is, slightly over three years after Tanzania signed the Charter, and about a year after ratification, account must be taken of the Charter in interpreting our Bill of Rights and Duties.[62]

In these two Tanzanian cases, domestic norms in favour of gender discrimination and restrictions on liberty were altered in part because of the invocation by activist forces within Tanzania of specific norms of the African system. This lends credence to the broadly constructivist account of IHI impact within states.

[59] (1990) 87 ILR 106 (Tanzanian High Court). See also Viljoen, *supra* note 9, at 13.

[60] (1991) LRC (Const.) 553. For an excellent comment on this case, see Viljoen, *supra* note 9, at 14.

[61] See *ibid.* [62] (1991) LRC (Const.) 553 at 565.

In the case of Zimbabwe, at least one case has, to a modest but interesting extent, relied on the African Charter. In *Chinamora v. Angwa Furnishers (Pvt) Ltd.*,[63] the Supreme Court of Zimbabwe dealt with the constitutionality of the law of civil imprisonment in that country. The case involved the applicant's request for an order declaring the procedure of civil imprisonment to be in conflict with guarantees of personal liberty and prohibition of torture or inhuman treatment in the Constitution of Zimbabwe. Having concluded that, divergent as it has been, the relevant foreign case law did not offer adequate guidance to the court as to "the modern trend" in the relevant respect, the court turned to the relevant international human rights instruments in order to strengthen, justify, and/or legitimize its particular interpretation of the Constitution of Zimbabwe. Its view of the relevant aspect of that Constitution was that it, in effect, provided that the short-term imprisonment of a recalcitrant debt-dodger who defiantly refused to pay although able to do so would not amount to degrading treatment. The African Charter was one of the instruments that guided the court in this direction and helped the court answer its questions. In the court's words, the African Charter "contains within its terms no provisions for freedom from civil imprisonment."[64] This was an argumentative move that implied that since the African Charter (and other such instruments) did not prohibit the imprisonment of debtors who are able but unwilling to repay their debts, then the broadly framed provisions of the Constitution of Zimbabwe could not be interpreted in a way that prohibits it. Because local activist forces (activist lawyers and judges) reached out to and invoked the norms of the African system in virtually all of these cases, and because they did so utilizing ends-means calculations that resulted in a subtle process of indirect IHI influence in the shaping of an authoritative logic of appropriate conduct with regard to the right to liberty of recalcitrant civil debtors, quasi-constructivists will recognize this process as supportive of their theoretical orientation. It must be noted, however, that this argument as to the important role played by the Charter in the articulation of the court's reasoning in this case does not imply the author's endorsement of the logic itself.

What is more, as Viljoen has noted, much more marginal references to and interpretive reliance on the African Charter has also

[63] (1997) 2 BCLR 189. [64] *Ibid.* at 13 and para. 34.

characterized a few other judicial decisions in Tanzania, Zambia, and Zimbabwe.[65]

Of relevance here as well is the fact that the application of the African Charter in the decisions of the domestic courts of African states has not been as extensive or deep as it could be. For instance, Viljoen has reported at least one case in which a court in Malawi explicitly declined to apply the Charter on the mere basis that it had not been formally incorporated into the domestic laws of that country.[66] For his part, Mugwanya has noted that Ugandan courts rarely draw upon any international human rights treaties, and that South African courts tend to draw more from global human rights decisions than from the African system.[67] And Adjami has even gone as far as claiming that:

> given the choice of relying upon universalized human rights norms as enshrined in their Western expression in UN treaties and the European Convention or their particularized expression in the African Charter, the *African* Courts have relied more on the universal international treaties than on their regional alternative.[68]

What is more, the influence of the Charter on judicial action within these other African states has definitely not been as pronounced as it has been within Nigeria. Comparison of the evidence adduced here to that provided in chapter 4 makes this point most palpable. Viljoen has captured this wide gap reasonably clearly. In his considered view, with which I am in total agreement:

> It is ironic, but perhaps predictable, that the clearest illustration of the potential effect of the African Charter in domestic law is found in Nigeria under a military regime at a time of severe repression, especially following the nullification of the results of the elections held on 12 June 1993.[69]

[65] See *Munuo Ng'uni* v. *Judge in Charge of High Court, Arusha and another*, Civil Case 3 of 1993 (unreported). See also Viljoen, *supra* note 9, at 15; and G. J. Naldi, "Constitutional Developments in Zimbabwe and their Compatibility with International Human Rights" (1991) 3 *African Journal of International and Comparative Law* 372.

[66] *Ibid.* at 6. [67] See Mugwanya, *supra* note 8, at 267.

[68] See M. E. Adjami, "African Courts, International Law, and Comparative Case Law: Chimera or Emerging Human Rights Jurisprudence?" (2002) 24 *Michigan Journal of International Law* 103 at 152 (emphasis supplied). See also L. Madhuku, "The Impact of the European Court of Human Rights in Africa: the Zimbabwean Experience" (1996) 8 *African Journal of International and Comparative Law* 932.

[69] *Ibid.* at 7.

Nevertheless, the evidence discussed above clearly indicates that to an extent that I consider significant in the light of the particularly harsh historical context in which it has had to function, the African system has so far had a *modest* impact on judicial thought and action within a number of African states. This impact has manifested itself in the incidences of correspondence between domestic judicial action within these states (on the one hand) and the norms of the African system (on the other hand). More importantly, given its increasing domestic visibility, this system promises to be of more judicial utility in many of these states. It is, however, in the penultimate section of this chapter that the conditions for the system's realization of its optimal promise will be specified in as much detail as possible.

6.4 Impact on legislative action

What I want to do in this section is to show that although the African system's impact on legislative debate and/or on the direction and content of legislative action within other African states (other than Nigeria and South Africa) has so far been very modest, it has been significant nevertheless.[70] I want to show as well that in consequence, the system has helped foster an equally modest level of correspondence between its norms and the character of legislative action within those states. Put differently, the evidence suggests that the ACHPR phenomenon can, to a much more modest extent, be observed in the legislative behavior of certain African states. This evidence will also show that a broadly constructivist process has at times been at play in the story of IHI percolation and impact within the legislatures of certain African countries. The hands of local activist forces is in many cases clearly visible in helping produce the desired outcomes. However, it must be noted at the outset that the evidence available in the present respect is not as ample as those discussed either in the preceding sections of this chapter, or in chapter 4; hence the much more modest score awarded.

As has already been noted, in response to the decision of the Court of Appeal of Botswana in the *Unity Dow* case, the offending provisions of

[70] Given the fact that the chief objective here is to show that some significant evidence which grounds the book's arguments exists elsewhere in Africa, the ambition of this chapter is not necessarily to offer a comprehensive survey of all the relevant developments in each and every country. As such, beyond a certain threshold (which I believe is met here) it does not really matter how many pieces of legislation are discussed.

the citizenship law of that country were eventually amended by its Parliament.[71] This is a very clear example of the way in which the African system, albeit in an indirect way, has had an impact on the direction of legislative action within a state party. Here, the court's decision invalidating the offensive provisions relied heavily on the provisions of the African Charter and even invoked the spirit of the African system in an attempt to legitimize its progressive conclusions. Thus, to the extent that its decision had influenced the eventual repeal of the offending parts of the relevant legislation, the system cannot but be credited with some significant (if indirect) influence on the direction of the legislative changes that occurred. Here, as in other parts of this book, the argument that is being made is not at all "causational" in nature. The argument is that the African Charter contributed in a valuable way to this final outcome. The arguments made in section 6.2 and 6.3 regarding the constructivist character of the process of IHI influence in this case also apply here.

Again, as has already been noted above, there is clear and reliable evidence in the Supreme Court of Namibia's decision in *Chairperson of the Immigration Selection Board* v. *Frank and another*[72] that the African Charter was of influence in the drafting and wording of at least one provision of the Namibian Constitution, namely its article 14. In the words of that court, the African Charter "influenced" that provision of the Namibian Constitution.[73] This kind of explicit judicial acknowledgement of the African Charter's legislative influence in Namibia is as rare as it is striking. As has already been shown, the character of the process via which the African system percolated and influenced thinking and action here does bear testimony to the power of the constructivist optic.

In Mozambique, corporal punishment has been illegal for a long time now. And as Langa J noted in *State* v. *Williams*, a decision of the South African Constitutional Court, the abolition of corporal punishment in Mozambique was done so as to allow its laws to "correspond" on this issue with local perceptions of the nature of the country's obligations under the African Charter.[74] According to him "public floggings were abolished [there] in 1989 in accordance with the country's obligations

[71] See Oloka-Onyango, *supra* note 4, at 63.

[72] (2001) 3 CHRLD 179 at 181. [73] *Ibid.*

[74] See *State* v. *Williams* (1995) SACLR LEXIS 249 at para. 46 and n. 58. See also Viljoen, *supra* note 9, at 12.

under the African Charter on Human and Peoples' Rights."[75] Here, this ban was achieved after years of campaigns by local activist forces (especially CSAs). These actors persuaded local actors as to the need for an ideational and normative alteration; purveyed the alternative imagination of punishment contained in the relevant norm of the African system, and made detailed ends-means calculations as to the value of targeting high state officials, public opinion, and the courts for dialogue and "shaming." It was in this broadly constructivist way that the domestic legislation of a state party has been indelibly marked by the content and orientation of the African Charter.

The Charter has also been expressly incorporated into the corpus of Benin's domestic laws.[76] Indeed, the text of the African Charter is specifically annexed to the Constitution of 11 December 1990 (Law 90-32). The Preamble to the Constitution expressly proclaims that the provisions of the African Charter make up an integral part of this present Constitution and of the domestic law of Benin, and have a value superior to the internal law. What is more, in the *High Authority of Audiovisual and Communications* case, the facts of which are not pertinent to the discussion here, the Constitutional Court of Benin affirmed the existing constitutional position and held that the African Charter was clearly an integral part of the 1990 Constitution of Benin.[77] The annexation of the text of the African Charter to the Constitution of Benin and this decision in effect ensure that the very content and character of every other piece of legislation in that country must be affected in one way or the other by the content and orientation of the African Charter. This is a most remarkable situation for any country and any human rights treaty, and underscores the legislative promise of the African system in the context of the Republic of Benin. As has been already argued, even this very act of incorporating the Charter into the Benin Constitution was done at a sovereign national conference that was convoked and so positively oriented in large part as a result of activist forces. It was also these actors which also acted as the norm

[75] See *State* v. *Williams*, *ibid.* at n. 58.

[76] *Final Communiqué of the 16th Ordinary Session of the African Commission on Human and Peoples' Rights* at para. 28 (on file with the author).

[77] (1994) 94-001/HACC (Cour Constitutonelle). Language barriers prevent a direct citation from the text in this case. As such, I am constrained to rely on Viljoen's interpretation. Professor Viljoen is a leading scholar of human rights in Africa. See Viljoen, *supra* note 9, at 3.

entrepreneurs who successfully "sold" the alternative (African system-friendly) formulations of local legislative provisions to the legislature.

In Cape Verde, the African Charter now constitutes a part of its corpus of domestic laws, and more importantly is directly applicable within that country's borders.[78] Article 11 of the 1992 Constitution of Cape Verde creates a general regime that assimilates the African Charter and other such treaties.[79] Moreover, as Cape Verde's recent report to the African Commission categorically states:

> the African Charter has a *superior* position [to Cape Verde's domestic laws]. This is because the Constitution states in article 11 that international conventions or laws override domestic laws.[80]

As such, it is clear that at the very least the African Charter promises to exert some influence on the content of domestic legislation within Cape Verde. The arguments above regarding the ways in which the process of change that occurred bore the hallmarks of a broadly constructivist process also apply here, with necessary adjustments.

In the case of Cameroon, not only has the African Charter been ratified by that country, as a result of the provisions of section 45 of the Constitution of Cameroon, but the Charter's provisions also have the force of law within Cameroon.[81] What is more, section 45 provides that all duly ratified international agreements override domestic legislation in Cameroon.[82] Additionally, as Nelson Enonchong (an authoritative commentator on the legal system of that country) has recently noted, even the Preamble to the Constitution of Cameroon affirms explicitly the formal commitment of that country to the norms enshrined in the African Charter.[83] The arguments made with respect to the annexation of the African Charter to the Constitution of Benin apply here as well, with necessary modifications.

It is also of some very modest interest here that, if the testimony of the representative of Egypt during the consideration of its report to the African Commission is accurate, then the African Charter's norms may have had some influence on the *process* of legislative action within Egypt

[78] See Viljoen, *supra* note 9, at 4.
[79] See Constitutional Law 01/IV/92, cited in *ibid.*
[80] See (1994) 16 African Commission Reports 34 (emphasis added).
[81] See N. Enonchong, "The African Charter on Human and Peoples' Rights: Effective Remedies in Domestic Law?"(2002) 46 *Journal of African Law* 197 at 199.
[82] *Ibid.* [83] *Ibid.*

(at least with regard to the content of the Constitution). According to that report:

> Before Egypt ratified [the Charter] a study had been conducted to determine whether the Charter contradicted any part of the Egyptian Constitution. [The study found that] [i]t did not. If the Charter contradicted lower acts, it would override them. The only confusion that could arise would be if the Charter contradicted some act of equal rank.[84]

While it is not clear what the last sentence of this quotation implies about the status of the Charter within Egypt, the important point is that the Charter inspired a legislative study, commissioned by the government, designed to find out if Egypt could ratify the Charter on the basis that its Constitution did not contradict the Charter. It is also noteworthy, formalistic as it is, that that study found that the Constitution did not in fact contradict the Charter in any way. However, this does not give any definitive information regarding the compatibility of other domestic legislation with Charter norms. As importantly, this domestic invocation of the Charter in the legislative process took place within a socio-legal context that has been shaped by the fierce resistance of Egyptian CSAs to authoritarian rule.

It is also noteworthy that the Initial Report of Ghana to the African Commission claimed that the provisions of the 1992 Constitution of Ghana accords with "all the requirements of the African Charter."[85] To the extent that the report intended to convey the impression that some effort was made to ensure that this level of "correspondence" was achieved, and it is reasonable to deduce that this was so, it becomes apparent that the African system has exerted a measure of influence on the legislative process that produced this constitutional document. Here again, the influence that was achieved by the African system was not mostly as a result of any direct state compliance. It was rather largely as a result of the relentless invocation of the African system within Ghana's domestic institutions; and a measure of engagement between the African system, activist forces, and domestic institutions in that country.

Equally important is the fact that the African Charter now forms a part of the corpus of domestic laws, or is directly applicable within the

[84] See *The African Commission on Human and Peoples' Rights: Examination of State Reports, 11th Session, March 1992* (Oslo, Danish Centre for Human Rights, 1995), p. 11 (on file with the author).

[85] See (1993) 13 African Commission Reports 32.

legal orders of a number of other African states, such as Togo,[86] Algeria,[87] and Senegal.[88] As Viljoen has observed, the available evidence suggests that the extent to which the Charter has been invoked in a particular country correlates, at least in part, with the status that the Charter enjoys in that country's domestic legal order. I agree with this statement for the most part. Given this fact, it is regrettable that certain other states parties such as Zimbabwe[89] and The Gambia[90] have not incorporated the Charter into their corpus of domestic laws.

In the foregoing paragraphs, I have attempted to demonstrate the contextually significant trend toward the domestic impact of the African system on the process of legislative action and on the content of legislation within some African states. In the next section, the extent of the African system's influence on the work of some of the local CSAs which operate within some African states will be discussed. As important as these CSAs have been to the process via which the African system's norms have percolated into the domestic governmental institutions of some states, these activities of groups themselves have in many cases also been influenced by the African system.

6.5 Impact on the activities of civil society actors

The chief objective of this section is to show that the African system has begun to exert a measure of influence on the work of some of the activist forces that operate within certain African states. As these activist forces have as a group been one of the most critical factors in the generation of the kinds of valuable correspondence that has been evident in relation to the African system's relationship with some of these states, this inquiry is quite important. Since the role of local activist forces in the production of correspondence in the relevant states has already been much discussed above, the current discussion of the impact that the African system has had on the work of these activist forces themselves (the intelligent relays of its normative energy) will of necessity be very brief. It will serve only to highlight this role.

[86] See U. O. Umozurike, *The African Charter on Human and Peoples' Rights* (The Hague, Martinus Nijhoff, 1997), p. 110.

[87] See Viljoen, *supra* note 9, at 2. [88] *Ibid.* at 11.

[89] See (1995) 17 African Commission Reports 18.

[90] See (1992) 12 African Commission Reports 7.

As has been argued throughout this book, the relevant activist forces have worked as the "virtual network" partners of the African system, and have been as important as the African system in the generation of "correspondence" between the system's norms and goals, and the content and orientation of executive, judicial, and legislative action within the relevant states. The broadly constructivist process via which modest alterations in logics of appropriateness and/or conceptions of interest have been fostered in the relevant states have in nearly every case been brokered and/or facilitated by these activist forces (be they activist lawyers, CSAs, or activist judges).

Again, it must be noted that the evidence that I rely on here is much sparser than that offered in my discussion (in chapters 4 and 5) of the influence of the African system on the work of activist forces within Nigeria. Regardless of the relative sparseness of the relevant evidence, the modest impact of the African system on the work of these activist forces (these activist lawyers, CSAs, judges, etc.) can be illustrated. Most of the examples offered will be teased out from the discussions in previous sections of this chapter.

For one, in some of these other countries, activist lawyers have brought cases in which they have hinged their arguments either on the African Charter itself, or on a decision of the African Commission.[91] Indeed, as Viljoen has noted, the frequency and innovativeness of the use of the Charter by domestic courts is closely linked to the initiative of local activist lawyers in making Charter-based arguments before such courts.[92] In *Concerned Parents and Teachers Associations* v. *Morning Star Preparatory School and eight others, the Minister for Education and the Attorney General,*[93] a case that was heard before the High Court of Ghana, Accra, the plaintiff was an incorporated "non-profit" group which was concerned by the negative effect that unregulated school fees in private schools in Ghana was having on the accessibility of basic education to the children of ordinary citizens in Ghana. Counsel relied deliberately on the African Charter and on one other international instrument in order to formulate and bring a somewhat novel and creative suit challenging the legality of the arbitrarily imposed and extremely expensive fees charged by private schools in Ghana. Counsel relied in part on the Charter as a way of complementing and

[91] See Viljoen, *supra* note 9, at 17. [92] *Ibid.*

[93] Reported extensively in J. K. M. Premo, "Litigating Educational Rights in Ghana: The Need for Action" (1998) 10 *ASICL Proceedings* 89 at 95–101 (especially at 97).

invigorating the available constitutional and statutory arguments. The facts of the case are sufficient to illustrate the point that is sought to be made here regarding the domestic uses to which local counsel have been able to put the African Charter. The invocation of the Charter allowed activist lawyers to formulate, present as authoritative, and enhance the persuasiveness of, alternative formulations of the "right" domestic norm that ought to guide the decision in the case.

Secondly, CSA cadres have deployed the Charter in similar ways.[94] In the *Modise* case, the petitioner was able to obtain substantial, if partial, relief from the Government of Botswana in part as a result of the efforts of INTERIGHTS and other CSAs. Chidi Odinkalu, then a senior legal officer at this organization, had brought a Communication before the African Commission alleging that Botswana had violated several provisions of the Charter. Due to the direct and persistent intervention of the Commission and the tireless activist work of this CSA, Botswana eventually granted Mr. Modise a substantial part of the remedies that he desired. Indeed, it was as a result of INTERIGHTS' subsequent application that this case was reopened recently by the Commission, and decided in favor of Mr. Modise. The Commission granted his relief in full and urged Botswana to grant him citizenship by descent rather then the partial remedy of naturalized citizenship that Botswana had conceded earlier. While INTERIGHTS is not a Botswanan group, it does from time to time work with local groups in the way shown above.

As importantly, as the discussion in section 6.3 shows, many activist judges (themselves a part of the network of activist forces that help produce the kind of correspondence that is of concern in this book) have relied on these Charter-based arguments to justify and legitimize their constitutional decisions.[95] As the decisions in which judges have done so have been discussed already in section 6.3, they will not be re-iterated here. Suffice it to refer the reader to cases like *Attorney General of Botswana* v. *Unity Dow*; *New Patriotic Party* v. *IGP*; *Kuesa* v. *Minister of Home Affairs*; and *DPP* v. *Pete*.

It is also quite interesting that, as Ankumah has noted, the promotional visit of a member of the African Commission to Ghana was part of the stimuli for the creation of the Ghana Committee on Human and Peoples' Rights, a local human rights CSA.[96]

[94] See, e.g., the *Modise* case, *supra* note 11.
[95] For instance, see the *Unity Dow* case, *supra* note 9.
[96] See Ankumah, *supra* note 20, at 21.

However, the efforts of these activist forces to deploy and mobilize the African Charter within these states have not always been met with success. For instance, a member of the African Commission from Congo (Brazzaville) has lamented that on the occasions when she has, as counsel in cases before the domestic courts, invoked certain provisions of the Charter, the judges have ignored these provisions in reaching their decisions.[97] This parallel trend is disturbing, given the rapidly increasing, (but still relatively low) level of awareness among African judges, lawyers, and general populations, regarding the nature of the norms and processes of the African system.

As the discussion in the previous sections might suggest, and as will be clear from the following section, it is likely that the growing trend toward the deployment of the African system by activist forces within the domestic context of African states will continue. The momentum is certainly in that direction. As will be palpable from our analytical discussion in chapter 7, this trend may present the best chance for the maximization of the potential for the widespread social utility of the African system.[98]

6.6 Specifying the conditions for the optimization of the domestic impact of the African system

Under what broad conditions did the African system modestly help shape and/or reshape the logics of appropriateness, conceptions of interest, and self-understandings held within key domestic institutions within the relevant African states? What factors have combined to facilitate the modest influence of the African system within Nigeria and South Africa; and to produce the kinds of broadly constructivist results that have been suggested above? The broad specification of these factors will be the main focus of this section of the book. But first some introductory points must be made.

First of all, it should be reasonably clear thus far that the African system is better imagined and assessed in the context of its increasing (though still modest) integration with the domestic legal systems of the fifty-three African countries that are party to its work. As such, Odinkalu's recent plea that the African system should no longer be

97 See Viljoen, *supra* note 9, at 5.

98 The proposition that this conclusion can apply to other IHIs is supported by the results of an excellent study of United Nations treaty regimes that was undertaken by Cristof Heyns and Frans Viljoen. See Heyns and Viljoen, *supra* note 1.

imagined as largely separated from these national legal systems is convincing.[99] Consequently, the examination, in this section, of the conditions for the optimization of the domestic impact of the African system (and thus, of the ACHPR phenomenon) will deal as much with domestic factors as it will be concerned with the African system itself. To borrow from Solomon Ukhuegbe, in my own view, the credit for the modest influence that the African system has achieved, as well as the discredit for its failure to achieve much more of such influence, belongs to both "the seed [that is the African system] and the [infertile or] fertile soil [that is the relevant states]."[100]

It is important, at the outset, to underscore the unevenness of the African system's impact within the domestic setting of African states. This should be evident from the discussion in this chapter and the ones before it. For instance, it should be quite clear that the African system's influence within Nigeria has, at least in terms of its profoundness, outpaced its impact within any other African country. It is also important to note, as Viljoen already has, that the courts of Southern African countries have tended to refer more to the European rather than the African system.[101] Mugwanya has reached a similar conclusion with respect to the citation practices of South African and Ugandan courts.[102] This point was also made at length in chapter 5. One reason that this is an interesting puzzle is that the constitutions of a number of Southern African countries such as Namibia and South Africa empower their courts to apply international law.[103] What is more, the courts of this region have been one of the most inclined in Africa towards transjudicialism. Judicial decisions in this region are replete with citations of foreign domestic and international resources.[104] The situation of

[99] See C. A. Odinkalu, "Back to the Future: The Imperative of Prioritizing for the Protection of Human Rights in Africa" (2003) 47 *Journal of African Law* 1 at 22.

[100] See S. Ukhuegbe, *Memo No. 1* (on file with the author) at 4.

[101] See Viljoen, *supra* note 9, at 16. [102] See Mugwanya, *supra* note 8, at 267.

[103] See Ukhuegbe, *supra* note 100, at 5. I must acknowledge the debt I owe to Solomon Ukhuegbe for helping to concentrate my mind on many of the questions raised in the first three paragraphs of this section. I have incorporated some text from his memo to me on these issues into this section of the chapter.

[104] Solomon Ukhuegbe's search of *Butterworths Constitutional Law Reports* (Southern African cases) on the LEXIS database revealed that in Southern African countries, the most frequently cited non-local sources are decisions of the US Supreme Court, the Supreme Court of Canada, and the European Court of Human Rights, in that order. The Canadian Charter of Rights and Freedoms and the European Convention were the most cited instruments. See *ibid.* at 4.

Zimbabwe (another Southern African country) is as interesting. Former Chief Justice Anthony Gubbay was a great enthusiast of trans-judicialism, especially in terms of the use of international law in decision-making. He advocated that all international and regional instruments embodying human rights norms broadly accepted by the international community, even if unratified by Zimbabwe, should be incorporated into domestic jurisprudence by judicial interpretation.[105] Why then has the African Charter not been deployed much more often within Zimbabwe? While the foregoing points do underscore the diversity of attitudes about the African system across African countries, it does not then follow that Mirna Adjami's suggestion that *all* "African courts have relied more on universal international treaties than their regional alternative [the African Charter]" is entirely accurate.[106] That claim is significantly overbroad. While it is an accurate description of the situation in much of Southern and Eastern Africa, there is just no evidence that this is an accurate reflection of the situation in most of Western and Northern Africa. At the very least, it is hardly plausible to make that claim with respect to Nigeria, the country that accounts for nearly 20 percent of the engagement of all African countries with the African system and in which the domestic invocation of the African Charter has become nearly routine in human rights cases. As it turns out, that claim does not also pan out entirely in relation to the behavior of the courts in the Benin Republic.

This section is devoted to the task of shedding as much light as possible on these and related puzzles. Why, it will be asked, have certain African states been more receptive to the influence of the African system than others? Why, for instance, has the influence of the African system been much more appreciable in a Nigeria that has been mostly ruled by military regimes,[107] than in Botswana, a country that is best known for its status as Africa's most stable liberal democracy, and which has had a long tradition of judicial activism?[108] Why do the courts of Southern

[105] See A. R. Gubbay, "The Protection and Enforcement of Fundamental Human Rights: The Zimbabwean Experience" (1997) 19 *Human Rights Quarterly* 227 at 233.

[106] See Adjami, *supra* note 68, at 152.

[107] See A. Olutokun, "Authoritarian State, Crisis of Democratization and the Underground Media in Nigeria" (2002) 101 *African Affairs* 317 at 317–318.

[108] On Botswana's democratic credentials, see K. Good, "Interpreting the Exceptionality of Botswana" (1992) 30 *Journal of Modern African Studies* 69. Indeed, in *Unity Dow*, Aguda JA stated that "I wish to take judicial notice of *that which is known the world over* that Botswana is one of the few countries in Africa where liberal democracy has taken

Africa not deploy the African Charter as frequently as they cite to European and North American sources? Why doesn't the African Charter come within their radar more often?[109] Why do their Nigerian counterparts cite the African Charter with far more frequency? What factors have tended to enable the African system to exert such influence? What factors have tended to militate against its exertion of such influence? How then can the African system's influence within the domestic sphere of most African states be optimized? While not every one of these questions can be answered in a book such as this, most will be addressed in this section.

I shall now attempt to provide as many answers to these questions as are possible by offering an analytical discussion of both the domestic and African system-specific factors that have affected the capacity of the African system to achieve influence within African states. Thereafter, I will attempt to specify as accurately as possible the minimum conditions for optimizing the domestic promise of the African system (and thus for realizing more fully the benefits of the ACHPR phenomenon). Previous analyses in chapters 4 and 5 will shape the discussion here.

6.6.1 Domestic factors

An analysis of the evidence adduced in chapters 4 and 5 reveals that one of the critically important factors that has enabled or impeded the African system's ability to exert influence within the domestic sphere of any African state is the extent to which the local activist forces (especially its CSAs) which operate in a state have been dynamic, creative, courageous, and therefore strong. The less strong the relevant CSA community has been, the less influence the African system has tended to exert within the relevant countries. This is one important reason why the African system has been much more influential within mostly military-ruled Nigeria than in consistently liberal democratic Botswana. Nigeria's CSAs are widely acknowledged to be one of the strongest on the continent,[110] while the CSAs in Botswana have been

root." (1992) LRC (Const.) 623 at 670 (emphasis added). Also reported in 103 ILR 128 at 175. On the age-old activist tradition of the courts of Botswana, see A. J. G. M. Sanders, "Constitutionalism in Botswana: A Valiant Attempt at Judicial Activism" (1983) XVI *CILSA* 350 (Part I) and (1984) XVII *CILSA* 49 (Part II).

109 See Ukhuegbe, *supra* note 100, at 4.

110 See P. O. Agbese, "The State versus Human Rights Advocates in Africa: The Case of Nigeria" in E. McCarthy-Arnolds, D. R. Penna, and D. J. Cruz Sobrepena (eds.), *Africa, Human Rights and the Global System: The Political Economy of Human Rights in a*

much weaker.[111] Almost nowhere else on the continent, except perhaps for South Africa, have local CSAs been as dynamic, creative, and courageous, and therefore as strong as their Nigerian counterparts.[112] Nigerian and South African CSAs are in turn far stronger than any other CSA community on the continent. It follows logically, therefore, that factors that tend to increase the strength of CSAs are important in understanding the factors that can facilitate the domestic influence of the African system. As I have shown in a recent article on the situation of CSAs in Nigeria, these factors relate mostly to the preconditions for those CSAs becoming popularly legitimized, and therefore much more politically powerful, groups.[113] However, it is important to keep in mind that, critical as it is, the strength of the relevant CSAs is not by itself wholly explanatory of the extent to which the African system has exerted influence within a given African country. For one, the relevant CSAs may not have turned their attention enough to the deployment of the African system within the relevant country. For example, South African CSAs have been at least as strong as their Nigerian counterparts, yet the African system has not exerted nearly as much influence in South Africa as it has in Nigeria. This particular counterfactual is explained to a large extent below. What is more, it does not follow that once the relevant CSAs are strong, the relevant domestic institutions will automatically agree with their arguments or act in the ways that the CSAs suggest. Other factors are important as well, however less influential those factors might be. The point here is that, as the evidence provided in chapters 4 and 5 suggest, the presence of strong CSAs (where "CSA strength" is understood in the particular way in which it has been used at the beginning of this paragraph) vastly increases the likelihood that the African system will exert an appreciable degree of influence within an African state. And as we shall see later on in this section, this factor seems

Changing World (Westport, Conn., Greenwood Press, 1994), p. 167. See also O. C. Okafor, *Legitimizing Human Rights NGOs: Lessons from Nigeria* (Trenton, New Jersey, Africa World Press, 2006).

111 See P. Molutsi and J. D. Holm, "Developing Democracy when Civil Society is Weak: The Case of Botswana" (1990) 89 *African Affairs* 323; and P. Takirambudde, "Botswana" in P. Baehr, H. Hey, J. Smith, and T. Swineheart (eds.), *Human Rights in Developing Countries* (The Hague, Kluwer, 1995).

112 See, e.g., T. Shaw, "Africa in the New World Order: Marginal and/or Central?" in A. Adedeji (ed.), *Africa Within the World* (London, Zed Books, 1993), pp. 91–92.

113 See O.C. Okafor, "Modest Harvests: On the Significant (but Limited) Impact of Human Rights NGOs on Legislative and Executive Behaviour in Nigeria" (2004) 48 *Journal of African Law* 23 at 45–48.

to be more important than the political regime-type of the country. However, these last two factors are positively linked to some extent.

A related factor is the extent to which these CSAs have actively engaged with the institutions of the African system. More active engagement with the African system (measured here in terms of cases filed at the African Commission) tends to correlate with the presence of stronger CSAs in the particular country and with the greater incidence of the deployment of the African Charter within the domestic institutions of African states. Strong as they have been, South African CSAs only emerged from the Apartheid era in the mid-1990s, and did not really begin to engage with the African system till the late 1990s and early 2000s. Indeed, as at the end of 2001, the African Commission had not decided a single case from South Africa![114] As has been shown in the last chapter, it was only in late 2005 that the very first such case, the *Garreth Prince* case, was decided. In contrast, Nigerian CSAs have brought almost 20 percent of all the cases that have been decided by that Commission.[115] As such, the relatively much sparser influence of the African system within South Africa, despite the presence there of strong CSAs, is explained in part by the very low level of engagement that most South African CSAs have had with the African system. Part of the explanation for the relative lack of engagement with the African system of South African CSAs may lie in the very long and deep isolation from the rest of the African continent which South Africa suffered during the Apartheid era. What is more, as at 2001, the only case at the African Commission that had originated from Botswana was the *Modise* case. Even then, that case was filed and primarily driven by INTERIGHTS, a London-based CSA. It was not filed by Botswana-based CSAs.[116] Over the same 1987–2001 period, the engagement of other CSAs from other African countries with the African system has almost always been as sparse, ranging from the filing of zero to four cases at the African Commission.[117] This situation has not changed significantly.

Another proxy for "measuring" the extent to which these CSAs have actively engaged with the institutions of the African system is to count the number of local CSAs from a particular country that have been granted observer status at the African Commission. As we saw in chapter 5, in contrast to Nigeria's large and dynamic group of CSAs with observer status at the African Commission (twenty or so in number),

[114] See *Compilation of Decisions 1994–2001*, *supra* note 12, at i–vii.
[115] *Ibid.* at 192–310. [116] *Ibid.* at 17–23. [117] *Ibid.* at i–vii.

as at March 2006 only eleven South African CSAs enjoyed this important access to the inner workings of the African system. What is more, just two years earlier (that is as at 2003) only nine South African CSAs had been granted observer status as compared to Nigeria's eighteen. Thus, at both watermarks, the Nigerian delegation was basically double the size of the South African group. Yet the total number of the local CSAs that operate in Nigeria does not appear to outnumber the total number of their South African counterparts. Similarly, even liberal democratic Botswana does not come close to matching either South Africa or Nigeria in the size and dynamism of its group of CSAs with observer status. The size of their delegations to the African Commission of CSAs with observer status has also *tended* to be relatively small.[118] For example, as at March 2006, there were only eleven Egyptian, nine Senegalese, nine Gambian, seven Beninoise, five Togolese, five Kenyan, four Ivorian, three Ghanaian CSAs which had been granted observer status by the Commission.[119] Less impressively, there was only one Tunisian and one Botswanan CSA among this number![120] Thus, even the largest of these other delegations are about twice as small as the Nigerian group. It could, of course, be argued that Nigeria has a much larger population than any other African country and should as such have a correspondingly much larger delegation of CSA observers. This is a reasonable supposition. However, the size of a country's CSA population often has less to do with the sheer size of its general population, and more to do with other social factors such as a history of resistance to military rule or Apartheid, local culture, the availability of foreign donors, and the existence of sufficient space for socio-political activism within it.[121] As such, it is not necessarily true that the relatively large size of the Nigerian CSA delegation at the African Commission is simply due to that country's disproportionately large share of Africa's population. The main point here is that if these CSAs as a group function as one of the key brainy relays that transmit the African system's normative energy into

[118] See also *List of Organizations Granted Observer Status with the African Commission* (June 2003) (on file with the author); *Directory of NGOs with Observer Status at the African Commission, 2004*, available at www.achpr.org/english/info/directory_ngo_en.html; *Status of Submission of NGO Activist Reports, October 2005* (on file with the author); and *Final Communiqué of the 38th Ordinary Session of the African Commission, Banjul, The Gambia, 21 November–5 December 2005*, available at www.achpr.org/english/communiques/communique38_en.htm at 2.

[119] See *List of Organizations, supra* note 118. [120] *Ibid.*

[121] For some of these factors, see Okafor, *supra* note 113, at 43–45.

the domestic sphere, then Nigeria had many more such brainy relays, hence the much more profound results in its case.

Another related factor has been the extent to which domestic governmental institutions in the given African country have actually established lines of communication (and thus connections) with the African system as a result of the activities of the relevant activist forces (especially activist judges and CSAs). Since activist forces have been the primary intelligent transmission-lines between the African system and domestic institutions in Africa, it follows that the more ably the relevant CSAs have performed this facilitative function, the more considerable the African system's domestic influence has been. As the records of cases filed at the African Commission show, CSAs have performed this function to a far greater extent in Nigeria than in any other African country. This has greatly facilitated the more appreciable influence that the African system has exerted within Nigeria. CSAs have not performed this function nearly as successfully in South Africa, Botswana, Uganda, Zimbabwe, Benin, Tanzania, Namibia, the Congo (Kinshasa), Algeria, Togo, Ghana, Zimbabwe, Cameroon, and virtually any other African country. This fact is confirmed by Oloka-Onyango's observation that "African human rights organizations have only recently woken up to the necessity to deploy the mechanisms of the Banjul Charter to productive domestic use."[122] This situation has contributed greatly to the much more modest extent of the African system's impact within these countries. In the South African and Namibian cases, the long and deep isolation from the rest of Africa which those countries suffered as a result of Apartheid in South Africa and South Africa's harsh colonial rule in Namibia may partly explain the relative (though narrowing) distance between their domestic institutions and the African system. The relative weakness of the CSA sector in most African countries[123] is partly explanatory of the failure of most such CSAs to play the kind of facilitative role discussed here.

Another important factor, one that has been noted above, is the extent to which key domestic constituencies (such as the general public) have been made aware of the existence, character, and relevance of the

[122] See J. Oloka-Onyango, "Beyond the Rhetoric: Reinvigorating the Struggle for Economic and Social Rights in Africa" (1995) 26 *California Western International Law Journal* 1 at 56. See also J. Oloka-Onyango, "Human Rights Activism in Africa: A Frog's Eye View" (1997) *Codesria Bulletin* No 1.

[123] See Shaw, *supra* note 112.

African system (and of each of its components). For instance, four years after the inauguration of the African Commission in 1987, Ellen Sirleaf of Liberia had observed that the system was generally unknown and invisible in that country.[124] There is no evidence that the situation has improved a great deal since then. In the case of Sierra Leone, a survey undertaken by Rhoda Kargbo in December 2003 indicated a similarly low level of awareness of the African system in that country.[125] Similarly, Kairaitu Murungi had observed at the same time that few ordinary people in Kenya had heard about the African Commission,[126] and Patrick Tigere has come to a similar conclusion with respect to Zimbabwe.[127] While some of these assessments are very much dated, they remain somewhat relevant. As recently as 1999, Florence Butegwa had returned a similar and even more worrisome verdict. In her view, the majority of women's grassroots groups did not include the African Charter and Commission in the legal rights awareness programs that they currently implemented. While the basis for such a continent-wide conclusion seems challenged a little bit by the evidence from Nigeria that is adduced in this book, her conclusions are very disturbing nevertheless. To the extent that Butegwa's conclusion is accurate, it reflects a failure on the part of the CSAs (who have been the vanguards of the movement for the actualization of the African system's goals) in helping to disseminate and popularize the African system, and thus to take the African system "home." It also reflects the relatively low literacy levels among the general population in many African states and the relative absence of the Charter, despite efforts in that regard, from the educational curriculum of many such states (including Nigeria and South Africa). However, the growing awareness of the system gives cause for some mild cheer.[128]

Another factor which has affected the level of influence that the African system has exerted within a given African state is the extent to which the local courts (and sometimes, other domestic institutions) have actively identified with the human rights struggles waged by the relevant CSAs as well as with the progressive norms of the African system. In other words, it is dependent on the extent to which the

124 See *Proceedings of the Conference on the African Commission, June 24–26, 1991* (Fund for Peace 3/26/93 MDF) (on file with the author) at 27.

125 See R. Kargbo, *Memo to the author* (on file with the author).

126 *Ibid.*

127 See P. Tigere, "State Reporting to the African Commission: The Case of Zimbabwe" (1994) *Journal of African Law* 64 at 65.

128 See Viljoen, *supra* note 9, at 16.

particular court system has been activist. In countries such as Nigeria, Botswana, South Africa, Benin, and Namibia, with a relatively deep tradition of judicial activism (at least on the part of a significant wing of the judiciary), the African system has tended to have appreciable, although uneven, impact on some key decisions of the relevant courts. Given the fact that it is often the courts that serve as the primary guardians of human rights, the degree to which an activist judiciary that identifies both with the pro-human rights struggles of CSAs and with the norms of the African system is present in a given country seems to be a critical factor that has facilitated or impeded the African system's domestic impact. This is not to say, of course, that the presence in a given African country of an activist judiciary is sufficient on its own to endow the African system with an appreciable level of influence within that domestic context. A number of other factors do matter as well.

A related factor is the level of independence enjoyed by the courts of a given African country. While the continent-wide record of judicial independence is not on balance considered by most observers to be a brilliant one,[129] it is much brighter in some countries than it is in others. Numerous examples of the remarkable judicial courage and independence displayed by Nigerian judges, under harsh political conditions, have been discussed in chapter 4. The courts in South Africa (especially post-Apartheid), Botswana, Namibia, Ghana, and Benin have also displayed such independence and courage. And even in Cameroon, where the record of judicial independence has not been as significant, Enonchong has reported a case that indicates the extent to which, under more or less harsh conditions, judges in countries like Cameroon, Uganda, and Togo have also displayed the courage that was needed to redress many a violation of human rights.[130] Thus, it is an undeniable fact that many judges in many African countries have risked career and even life in the course of deciding against authoritarian regimes, and even in sensitive human rights cases. Such courage and personal independence is often a precondition for judicial activism. And, as has just been noted, such judicial activism is a critical condition for the optimal impact of the African system within virtually every African state.

It also appears that the extent to which the African Charter in itself forms a part of the domestic laws of a given state has been an important factor in the ability of the African system to achieve appreciable impact in at least a few African countries. The domestication of the African Charter in Nigeria, it will be recalled, was a key factor that enabled local

129 See Enonchong, *supra* note 81, at 213 and 214–215. 130 *Ibid.*

courts to apply it in the first place. In Benin, the fact that the African Charter is annexed to and forms a part of the Constitution of that country (what Ukhuegbe refers to as its "super-domestication"),[131] has proven quite material in the increasing reliance of its courts on that document. The Charter also forms a part of the domestic laws of Togo, Algeria, and Senegal, leading in some measure to its application domestically. However, the fact that the African Charter forms a part of the domestic laws of Cameroon does not seem, as Enonchong has noted, to have had a significant impact so far in that country.[132] Also relevant here is the fact that, with the possible exception of the Cameroonian example (where the incorporation of the African Charter into its Constitution does not seem to have led to its increased domestic use), clauses that specifically incorporate the text of the African Charter into domestic law have functioned positively in aid of the African system's domestic impact. Such domestic incorporation is especially important, since local courts primarily apply local law.[133] Regrettably, the kind of general clauses which are contained in the Constitutions of South Africa, Botswana, Kenya, and some other African states, that allow their courts to apply international law as interpretive tools (without formally domesticating these instruments) do not seem to have achieved as much result as they could have with regard to the African Charter. However, as the discussion in chapter 5 of the growing use of the African Charter in South African judicial decisions shows, such clauses can be very useful nevertheless. On the other hand, it does appear that since the African system has had more appreciable impact within South Africa than within most of the countries that have already domesticated the Charter, this factor does not (on its own) determine whether or not the African system will have an appreciable impact in any country. Many factors combine to shape that outcome.

It seems as well that the higher the status of the Charter in the domestic legal order of a given country, the more likely it will be invoked in the domestic context of most African states.[134]

Perhaps the most startling analytical result in the present respect is that the evidence does suggest that the receptiveness of a given African country to the African system's influence (that is, the possibility of the ACHPR phenomenon occurring there) is not necessarily determined by its status as a liberal democracy. Ordinarily, one would expect to find

[131] See Ukhuegbe, *supra* note 100, at 8. [132] See Enonchong, *supra* note 81, at 199.
[133] See Viljoen, *supra* note 9, at 16. [134] *Ibid.* at 2.

that the more established the liberal democratic credentials of a given African country are, the more influence the African system would have had within it. Yet that expectation is not largely borne out by the evidence. If it were, the African system would have exerted its most influence within Botswana (Africa's most established and most deeply formed liberal democracy),[135] rather than within Nigeria (one of the African countries which has been most marked and marred by military rule) or South Africa (which suffered Apartheid and colonial rule for 300 years or so).[136] This is *not* to argue, of course, that domestic democratization has not mattered to the process by which the African system has acquired modest influence within certain African states. For example, in post-Apartheid South Africa, and in Botswana, Benin, Namibia, Ghana, and Mali, the democratic character of domestic institutions clearly facilitated the African system's modest influence within those countries. In the case of South Africa, the African system had virtually no influence there before its current democratic order was established in the mid-1990s. In Benin as well, the impact of the African system dates from about the same time as its democratic reforms. Yet, in the key Nigerian case, such influence was achieved in spite of the absence of liberal democracy for most of the relevant years. It could be argued, of course, that even in the Nigerian case, the presence of democratic institutions may have helped the African system achieve even more influence in that country. That much is conceded in part. Suffice it to point out, nevertheless, that it is in Nigeria that the African system has so far recorded its most profound impact. The point is that the key Nigerian case indicates that given the coincidence of other factors (such as strong CSAs, the active concern of the African Commission, and activist judges) the ACHPR phenomenon is still *achievable* under less-than-democratic conditions. This is a remarkable finding indeed. However, it is important to keep in mind the fact that domestic regime-type (which is not the same as measuring democracy) does matter nevertheless. The more operational space that a particular regime-type affords activist forces (activist lawyers, CSAs, judges, journalists, etc.), the stronger these activist forces are likely to be. And the stronger these

[135] See Good, *supra* note 108.

[136] On the nature of military rule in Nigeria, see A. Olukotun, "Authoritarian State, Crisis of Democratisation and the Underground Media in Nigeria" (2002) 101 *African Affairs* 317. On the nature of the Apartheid regime in South Africa, see the *First Periodic Report of South Africa to the African Commission, 2001*, submitted in November 2005 (on file with the author).

activist forces are, the more likely they will be able to facilitate the African system's influence within the given state. That much is evident from chapters 4 and 5. Here again, the Nigerian case is particularly illustrative. There, for almost all of the relevant years, the coincidence of a long and deep tradition of judicial activism among an important section of the judiciary; relatively strong CSAs; deep and long CSA engagement with the African system; domestic incorporation of the African Charter; and a peculiarly less-than-democratic but constantly negotiated regime-type that afforded some space for a measure of dissent, sufficed to generate the highest level of influence exerted so far by the African system anywhere on the continent. As is generally recognized, repressive as they mostly were, almost all of Nigeria's ruling military juntas adopted a relatively consensual governing format that allowed for a measure of political dissent.[137] They had to adopt this format in order to build alliances, appear people-oriented, garner a measure of popular acceptance, and therefore survive in Nigeria's deeply cleavaged and peculiarly complex ethno-political environment.[138]

6.6.2 *African system-specific factors*

One of the most important factors which has affected the ability of the African system to exert influence within African states is the extent to which it has actively and positively identified with the human rights struggles that rage within African states.[139] The more it has been able to do so, the more it has contributed to whatever impact it has had within the given country. The deep and sustained concern that was shown by the African Commission in the *Modise* case (from Botswana), the *Lekwot, Newspapers Registration*, and *Ogoni* cases (from Nigeria), and in many other such cases, did mostly yield fruit. Yet, even the effect of this factor is dependent to an extent on the facilitative role of activist forces. Oloka-Onyango has put this point so well in relation to the African system's influence in Nigeria that the relevant passage bears reproduction here. According to him:

> On its part, the African Commission had already demonstrated an increasing concern about developments in Nigeria. That concern was spurred by several petitions filed by Nigerian civil society actors challenging the laws passed or

[137] *Ibid.* [138] See Okafor, *supra* note 113, at 45.
[139] See Oloka-Onyango, *supra* note 6, at 5 and 22.

> actions committed by the Nigerian government and highlighting the general deterioration of the human rights situation in the country. The [positive] attitude of the African Commission towards petitions from Nigeria must also have played a part in encouraging more of them to be filed.[140]

Should the evidence in chapters 4 and 5 not suffice to demonstrate this point, the African Commission has itself confirmed its active and positive concern about the human rights situation throughout the African continent. In its recent decision in *Social and Economic Rights Action Centre and Centre for Economic and Social Rights* v. *Nigeria*,[141] the Commission declared that:

> The uniqueness of the African situation and the special qualities of the African Charter on Human and Peoples' Rights impose upon the African Commission an important task ... [the Commission] welcomes the opportunity to make clear that there is no right in the African Charter that cannot be made effective.[142]

Should the Commission continue to think and act in this way, should it continue so positively to identify as a part of the virtual human rights network in Africa that is described elsewhere in this book, it will be more likely to optimize its influence within the domestic spheres of many African states.

Another factor that has affected the ability of the African system to exert influence within African states is the extent to which it has made a really sustained effort to create awareness about its existence, resources, and activities. The more it has done this, the more it has contributed to the effort of activist forces to create or raise awareness as to its usefulness within the relevant states. For instance, as already discussed in this chapter, its intercessional visit to Ghana helped raise awareness there and even led to the establishment of a local CSA. As shown in chapter 4, its mission to Nigeria also generated much discussion there. However, it must be noted that the African system is still far less visible than it could be within the relevant states, especially among the rank and file of the African citizenry. The slowly increasing visibility of the African Commission and the increasing use of the Charter in domestic courts is therefore a most welcome development.[143] Its attempt, in a resolution passed at its Nineteenth Session, to encourage judges and lawyers in

140 *Ibid.* at 5. 141 Communication 155/96, *supra* note 5. 142 *Ibid.* at 71.
143 See Viljoen, *supra* note 9, at 16.

Africa to increase their utilization of its jurisprudence and the provisions of the African Charter in their own decisions and work is similarly commendable.[144] Activists who do not know of the African system's existence or the creative uses to which it could be put are unlikely to use it at all, or to use it effectively. And while the dissemination of information regarding the African Commission's existence and utility has so far been mostly undertaken by CSAs, an increased contribution in that regard by the Commission will be an additional benefit.

Another such important factor relates to how seriously the African Charter and Commission have been taken by the members of key domestic institutions and CSAs. When the relevant domestic actors have taken the African system seriously enough, it has been able to exert more influence within the given state. While its record in this regard has clearly been sub-optimal, the discussions in chapters 4 and 5 show that the system (or one or more of its constituents) has been viewed with some seriousness in many cases and situations. States have definitely cared to some extent about how they are affected by the pronouncements of the Commission and how the Charter is used within their domestic spheres. For example, the Nigerian government cared very much about the series of resolutions passed by the Commission condemning one or more of its actions.[145] It also cared about the many cases that were decided against it at the Commission.[146] And it has also been concerned about the effective uses to which the Charter has been put in its own domestic courts.[147] Botswana has, on occasion, also taken the African system seriously. It did so in the *Modise* case, as well as in *Unity Dow*. These cases have already been discussed elsewhere in this chapter. What is more, the African system has been taken most seriously by a remarkably large number of African CSAs. Although CSA participation in the African Commission's activities is not evenly distributed

[144] See Resolution on the Role of Lawyers and Judges in the Integration of the Charter and the Enhancement of the Commission's Work in National and Sub-Regional Systems, *Ninth Annual Activity Report*, Annex VII at 6; reproduced in African Commission on Human and Peoples' Rights, *Recommendations and Resolutions* (Banjul, The Gambia, African Commission on Human and Peoples' Rights, 1998), p. 44 (hereafter "*Compilation of Resolutions*").

[145] See the discussion in section 4.3.2. See also *Compilation of Resolutions*, *supra* note 144, at 26, 27, and 34.

[146] For example, see the *Zamani Lekwot* case and the *Newspapers Registration Decree* case (discussed in section 4.2).

[147] See the discussion in section 4.4.3 in relation to the Political Parties (Dissolution) Decree 114 of 1999.

across the continent, those which have worked with the Commission have made a tremendous contribution to its work.[148] They have basically functioned as its "close partners."[149] In the end, however, it must be conceded that not every country or CSA has taken the African system as seriously as they could and probably should. Needless to say, this has impeded the African system's ability to optimize its influence within African states.

One obvious reason for the very modest extent to which the African system has been influential on an Africa-wide basis, especially in domestic courts, is its relative youth as an IHI. As we have already seen, although the African Charter was adopted in 1981, both the Charter and the Commission became operative only in 1986/87. What is more, as a result of its youth, many of the provisions of the African Charter have not been as fully interpreted as they could have been.[150] Related to this point is the quality of its jurisprudence.[151] Young as it is, it has only recently begun to issue more extensively reasoned, rather than brief one or two page, decisions. While the quality of most of the latest decisions has been more encouraging, much remains to be done. It cannot expect that its decisions will be sought after at an optimal level by domestic courts if the quality of such decisions is not itself optimal.

Another reason for the African system's failure so far to maximize its impact within African states is the relative elitism of the rights language that it has almost by its very design had to largely favor and the similar elitism of most members of the small group of activist forces that basically drive the system's domestic percolation on the continent. For instance, the powerful language of duties to other individuals that so clearly resonates with the lived experience of most Africans has not received nearly as much attention from the African Commission. The same can be said for almost all other oppositional languages of human dignity. As a number of scholars (the present author included) have shown elsewhere, most African CSAs – especially the self-professed human rights groups – suffer popular legitimacy deficits which arise from the elitism of their modes of struggle.[152] Most are not popular or

148 See Mugwanya, *supra* note 8, at 249–251. 149 *Ibid.*

150 See Adjami, *supra* note 68, at 152.

151 See F. Viljoen and L. Louw, "The Status of the Findings of the African Commission: From Moral Persuasion to Legal Obligation" (2004) 48 *Journal of African Law* 1 at 20.

152 See O. C. Okafor, *Legitimizing Human Rights NGOs: Lessons from Nigeria* (Trenton, NJ, Africa World Press, 2006), pp. 209–237. See also M. Mutua, "A Discussion on the Legitimacy of the Human Rights NGOs in Africa" (1997) *Africa Legal Aid Quarterly*

mass social movements.[153] Most are not fluent in the other oppositional languages that are spoken on the streets of African states.[154] As such, there has been a social and communicative distance between most of these CSAs and the vast majority of subalterns who populate almost all African countries.[155] By speaking the same elite rights language as most of these groups and ignoring the other languages of opposition that are spoken by subaltern Africans, and by being forced by a dearth of resources to remain so physically and socially removed from most ordinary Africans, the African system has also faced the very same popular legitimization problems as most of the CSAs that have helped drive its domestic impact. This has made it much harder for the African system's progressive message to resonate at a sufficient depth among most ordinary Africans, thus increasing the difficulty of popularizing that system. As can be easily imagined, there are inevitable limits to the social impact of the African system vis-à-vis domestic institution correspondence that is driven by a small band of elite activists who deploy the African Charter and the Commission within states. The less popularly validated these activists and the system itself are, the less powerful they are in relation to persuading recalcitrant regimes to alter their character, rules, or conduct. However, it is to the credit of the African system and many of its CSA allies that they have to an extent tried to get away from their elitism, at least in the sense that they have sometimes worked in alliance with more popular movements like trade unions, university student unions, and so on, and have also tried on occasion to reach out to and operate among ordinary Africans.

Similarly, although the African system can only deal with those cases that CSAs, states, and individuals send to it, and despite its many efforts to promote the enjoyment of socio-economic (ESC) rights in Africa, when its ESC rights protection record is evaluated vis-à-vis its civil and political rights (CPR) record, it becomes palpable that it has been relatively inattentive to the protection of ESC rights on the continent. This has impeded its capacity to transform itself from a relatively elitist and far-removed international institution to a much more popular body. While it is no secret that the African Charter does contain a number of ESC rights provisions, as was shown in chapter 5, the

(October–December) 28; C. A. Odinkalu, "Why More Africans Don't Use the Human Rights Language" (2000) *Human Rights Dialogue* 3; and J. Ihonbvere, "Where is the Third Wave? A Critical Evaluation of Africa's Non-Transition to Democracy" (1996) 43 *Africa Today* 343 at 358.

153 *Ibid.* 154 *Ibid.* 155 *Ibid.*

African Commission has since its inception dealt with far fewer ESC rights matters than CPR petitions. In any case, when compared to its CPR sister, there has not been nearly as much ESC rights correspondence to be observed within most African states. The Commission's relative inattentiveness to ESC rights has reflected the historical marginalization of ESC rights activism by both international and African CSAs. Yet, since the vast majority of the populations of most African countries are very poor and tend to experience very serious ESC rights deprivations, any sustained effort to secure the enjoyment of ESC rights will have a particular appeal and potency on the continent. The failure to harness this potential in a fuller way has meant that the African system and its CSA allies have missed a key avenue of getting to their goal of popularizing the system and its work. In the end, the point is that the gap in popular validation of and attention to the African system has definitely helped impede its ability to optimize its domestic impact.

6.6.3 Optimizing the domestic impact of the African system: eight minimum conditions

What, then, are the minimum conditions which must each be present for the African system to successfully shape and/or reshape logics of appropriateness, conceptions of interest, and self-understandings, and thus exert an optimal level of influence within a given African state? What are the minimum conditions for the optimal realization of what I have referred to elsewhere in this book as the ACHPR phenomenon? These minimum conditions are decipherable from the evidence adduced in chapters 4 and 5. The analysis conducted above is particularly important in this regard.

Eight such minimum conditions are evident. These are that: (i) strong (that is, dynamic, creative, and courageous) activist forces (especially CSAs) must function locally; (ii) these CSAs must engage actively and extensively with the African system (especially by participating actively in the work of the African Commission, filing and arguing Communications before the African Commission, and deploying the African Charter within domestic institutions); (iii) a reasonably activist and independent judiciary (or at least a significant activist and independent wing of the judiciary) must exist in the given country; (iv) a reasonably sufficient amount of space for political dissent must exist within the country, whatever the character of its regime-type; (v) the African Charter must form a part of the domestic laws of the given country; (vi) the African Commission, or other institution of the African system, must actively and positively identify with the human rights struggles that rage within that country; (vii) the African Commission should make more effort to speak the other languages of human dignity that bring it much closer to the vast majority of Africans; (viii) that the African system and the activist forces that drive its domestic impact should pay much more attention to ESC rights. In other words, for it to germinate, flower, and yield an optimal harvest, the seed of the African system must find sufficiently fertile soil in the place in which it has been planted. This should not be surprising to a keen observer of IHIs. After all, does the European system not owe much of its success to the fertile Western European soil in which it was sown?

While all eight minimum conditions must co-exist for the African system to *optimize* its impact within almost any African state, it is still possible of course that that system can exert a more modest measure of influence within a given country in the absence of one or more of these conditions. The example of Botswana, where the African system has had significant (though clearly not optimal) influence even in the absence of conditions such as the domestic incorporation of the Charter, strong CSAs, and a sizeable number of CSAs that have engaged actively and extensively with the African system, is particularly instructive in this regard. However, as instructive in this connection (although not necessarily determinative of the question), is the fact that almost all of these conditions (save adequate attention to ESC rights and other oppositional languages) co-existed in the key case of Nigeria (the country in which the African system has been most influential to date). And that is why one would not expect to observe more than minor levels of correspondence in a state like the Democratic Republic of Congo (the former Zaire) which has been characterized for decades by weak civil society, very little space for political dissent, and a much weaker judiciary than in Nigeria.

However, as has been emphasized throughout chapters 4 and 5, it must be noted that, to date, the domestic promise of the African system has only been very modestly realized in almost all of the relevant countries. Its influence has not been hugely felt in any of the countries surveyed. Even its appreciable impact within Nigeria and South Africa has been altogether modest, although it has been much greater than its influence elsewhere on the continent. As such, much work remains, and many changes must first occur, before the African system's domestic impact can be optimized.

6.7 Summary of the arguments

It has been shown in this chapter that the African system has had some impact, however modest, within the executive, legislative, and judicial branches of government in a number of African countries (other than Nigeria and South Africa), and that the manner in which the system achieved such influence tends to support the broad constructivist approach to IHIs. As is obvious from the discussion in this chapter, much of the impact identified here is of a kind that cannot be explained adequately by a focus on identifying state compliance with IHI norms. The lessons for more conventional scholarship on the African system, as well as for much IHI scholarship, are thus obvious. The factors that have facilitated or impeded the ability of the African system to achieve influence within African states were also analyzed and broadly specified. Indeed, in the end, eight minimum conditions for the optimization of the domestic impact of the African system were identified. These are also the minimum conditions that must be present for the African system's capacity to optimally help in shaping the logics of appropriateness, conceptions of interest, or self-understandings held within key domestic institutions in most African states.

Having reached this juncture it is imperative to synthesize existing theory and the emergent data, and consider more fully the need to enlarge (while retaining) the conventional optics with which scholars of the African system (and other IHI scholars) evaluate this type of international institution. In this way can a systematic case be made for centering the study of correspondence – a phenomenon that clearly encompasses state compliance. This will form the subject of the next chapter.

Name Index

For Product Safety Concerns and Information please contact our EU representative GPSR@taylorandfrancis.com Taylor & Francis Verlag GmbH, Kaufingerstraße 24, 80331 München, Germany

Batch number: 10726322

Printed by Printforce, the Netherlands